Handbook of Research on Machine Learning Techniques for Pattern Recognition and Information Security

Mohit Dua
National Institute of Technology, Kurukshetra, India

Ankit Kumar Jain
National Institute of Technology, Kurukshetra, India

A volume in the Advances in Computational Intelligence and Robotics (ACIR) Book Series

Published in the United States of America by
IGI Global
Engineering Science Reference (an imprint of IGI Global)
701 E. Chocolate Avenue
Hershey PA, USA 17033
Tel: 717-533-8845
Fax: 717-533-8661
E-mail: cust@igi-global.com
Web site: http://www.igi-global.com

Library of Congress Cataloging-in-Publication Data

Names: Dua, Mohit, 1982- editor. | Jain, Ankit Kumar, 1986- editor.
Title: Handbook of research on machine learning techniques for pattern recognition and information security / Mohit Dua, Ankit Kumar Jain, editors.
Description: Hershey, PA : Engineering Science Reference, 2020. | Includes bibliographical references and index. | Summary: "This book examines the impact of machine learning techniques on pattern recognition and information security"-- Provided by publisher.
Identifiers: LCCN 2019051101 (print) | LCCN 2019051102 (ebook) | ISBN 9781799832997 (h/c) | ISBN 9781799833017 (eISBN)
Subjects: LCSH: Database security. | Machine learning. | Pattern recognition systems.
Classification: LCC QA76.9.D314 M33 2020 (print) | LCC QA76.9.D314 (ebook) | DDC 005.8--dc23
LC record available at https://lccn.loc.gov/2019051101
LC ebook record available at https://lccn.loc.gov/2019051102

This book is published in the IGI Global book series Advances in Computational Intelligence and Robotics (ACIR) (ISSN: 2327-0411; eISSN: 2327-042X)

British Cataloguing in Publication Data
A Cataloguing in Publication record for this book is available from the British Library.

For electronic access to this publication, please contact: eresources@igi-global.com.

Advances in Computational Intelligence and Robotics (ACIR) Book Series

Ivan Giannoccaro
University of Salento, Italy

ISSN:2327-0411
EISSN:2327-042X

Mission

While intelligence is traditionally a term applied to humans and human cognition, technology has progressed in such a way to allow for the development of intelligent systems able to simulate many human traits. With this new era of simulated and artificial intelligence, much research is needed in order to continue to advance the field and also to evaluate the ethical and societal concerns of the existence of artificial life and machine learning.

The **Advances in Computational Intelligence and Robotics (ACIR) Book Series** encourages scholarly discourse on all topics pertaining to evolutionary computing, artificial life, computational intelligence, machine learning, and robotics. ACIR presents the latest research being conducted on diverse topics in intelligence technologies with the goal of advancing knowledge and applications in this rapidly evolving field.

Coverage

- Synthetic Emotions
- Automated Reasoning
- Robotics
- Artificial Intelligence
- Computational Intelligence
- Artificial Life
- Brain Simulation
- Natural Language Processing
- Machine Learning
- Cyborgs

IGI Global is currently accepting manuscripts for publication within this series. To submit a proposal for a volume in this series, please contact our Acquisition Editors at Acquisitions@igi-global.com or visit: http://www.igi-global.com/publish/.

The Advances in Computational Intelligence and Robotics (ACIR) Book Series (ISSN 2327-0411) is published by IGI Global, 701 E. Chocolate Avenue, Hershey, PA 17033-1240, USA, www.igi-global.com. This series is composed of titles available for purchase individually; each title is edited to be contextually exclusive from any other title within the series. For pricing and ordering information please visit http://www.igi-global.com/book-series/advances-computational-intelligence-robotics/73674. Postmaster: Send all address changes to above address.

Titles in this Series

For a list of additional titles in this series, please visit: http://www.igi-global.com/book-series/advances-computational-intelligence-robotics/73674

Driving Innovation and Productivity Through Sustainable Automation
Ardavan Amini (EsseSystems, UK) Stephen Bushell (Bushell Investment Group, UK) and Arshad Mahmood (Birmingham City University, UK)
Engineering Science Reference • © 2021 • 275pp • H/C (ISBN: 9781799858799) • US $245.00

Examining Optoelectronics in Machine Vision and Applications in Industry 4.0
Oleg Sergiyenko (Autonomous University of Baja California, Mexico) Julio C. Rodriguez-Quiñonez (Autonomous University of Baja California, Mexico) and Wendy Flores-Fuentes (Autonomous University of Baja California, Mexico)
Engineering Science Reference • © 2021 • 346pp • H/C (ISBN: 9781799865223) • US $215.00

Emerging Capabilities and Applications of Artificial Higher Order Neural Networks
Ming Zhang (Christopher Newport University, USA)
Engineering Science Reference • © 2021 • 540pp • H/C (ISBN: 9781799835639) • US $225.00

Machine Learning Applications in Non-Conventional Machining Processes
Goutam Kumar Bose (Haldia Institute of Technology, India) and Pritam Pain (Haldia Institute of Technology, India)
Engineering Science Reference • © 2021 • 313pp • H/C (ISBN: 9781799836247) • US $195.00

Artificial Neural Network Applications in Business and Engineering
Quang Hung Do (University of Transport Technology, Vietnam)
Engineering Science Reference • © 2021 • 275pp • H/C (ISBN: 9781799832386) • US $245.00

Multimedia and Sensory Input for Augmented, Mixed, and Virtual Reality
Amit Kumar Tyagi (Research Division of Advanced Data Science, Vellore Institute of Technolgy, Chennai, India)
Engineering Science Reference • © 2021 • 310pp • H/C (ISBN: 9781799847038) • US $225.00

Cases on Edge Computing and Analytics
Paranthaman Ambika (Impact Analysis, India) A. Cecil Donald (Kristu Jayanti College, India) and A. Dalvin Vinoth Kumar (Kristu Jayanti College, India)
Engineering Science Reference • © 2021 • 310pp • H/C (ISBN: 9781799848738) • US $215.00

701 East Chocolate Avenue, Hershey, PA 17033, USA
Tel: 717-533-8845 x100 • Fax: 717-533-8661
E-Mail: cust@igi-global.com • www.igi-global.com

Editorial Advisory Board

List of Contributors

Table of Contents

Foreword xviii

Preface xx

Chapter 1
Intelligent Vision-Based Systems for Public Safety and Protection via Machine Learning Techniques 1
Rajitha B., Motilal Nehru National Institute of Technology, Allahabad, India

Chapter 2
Comparative Analysis of Various Soft Computing Technique-Based Automatic Licence Plate Recognition Systems 18
Nitin Sharma, Chandigarh University, India
Pawan Kumar Dahiya, Deenbandhu Chhotu Ram University of Science and Technology, India
B. R. Marwah, Independent Researcher, India

Chapter 3
Impact of Syntactical and Statistical Pattern Recognition on Prognostic Reasoning 38
Rithesh Pakkala P., Sahyadri College of Engineering and Management, Mangaluru, India & Visvesvaraya Technological University, Belagavi, India
Prakhyath Rai, Sahyadri College of Engineering and Management, Mangaluru, India & Visvesvaraya Technological University, Belagavi, India
Shamantha Rai Bellipady, Sahyadri College of Engineering and Management, Mangaluru, India & Visvesvaraya Technological University, Belagavi, India

Chapter 4
Challenges and Issues in Plant Disease Detection Using Deep Learning 56
Priyanka Sahu, Guru Gobind Singh Inderprastha University, New Delhi, India
Anuradha Chug, Guru Gobind Singh Inderprastha University, New Delhi, India
Amit Prakash Singh, Guru Gobind Singh Inderprastha University, New Delhi, India
Dinesh Singh, Indian Agricultural Research Institute, New Delhi, India
Ravinder Pal Singh, Indian Agricultural Research Institute, New Delhi, India

Chapter 5
Automatic Animal Detection and Collision Avoidance System (ADCAS) Using Thermal Camera ... 75
Jeyabharathi Duraipandy, Sri Krishna College of Technology, India
Kesavaraja D., Dr. Sivanthi Aditanar College of Engineering, Tiruchendur, India
Sasireka Duraipandy, V. V. College of Engineering, Tisaiyanvillai, India

Chapter 6
Distracted Driver Detection System Using Deep Learning Technique ... 89
Varan Singh Rohila, National Institute of Technology, Hamirpur, India
Vijay Kumar, National Institute of Technology, Hamirpur, India
Karan Kumar Barnwal, National Institute of Technology, Hamirpur, India

Chapter 7
Application of Deep Learning Model Convolution Neural Network for Effective Web Information Retrieval ... 100
Suruchi Chawla, Shaheed Rajguru College, Delhi University, India

Chapter 8
Cosine Transformed Chaos Function and Block Scrambling-Based Image Encryption ... 121
Shelza Dua, National Institute of Technology, Kurukshetra, India
Bharath Nancharla, National Institute of Technology, Kurukshetra, India
Maanak Gupta, Tennessee Technological University, USA

Chapter 9
An Improved Approach for Multiple Image Encryption Using Alternate Multidimensional Chaos and Lorenz Attractor ... 139
Mohit Dua, National Institute of Technology, Kurukshetra, India
Shelza Dua, National Institute of Technology, Kurukshetra, India
Priyanka Jaroli, Banasthali Vidyapith, India
Ankita Bisht, Banasthali Vidyapith, India

Chapter 10
Simple Linear Iterative Clustering (SLIC) and Graph Theory-Based Image Segmentation ... 157
Chiranji Lal Chowdhary, Vellore Institute of Technology, Vellore, India

Chapter 11
COVID-19 Detection Using Chest X-Ray and Transfer Learning ... 171
Aditya Sharma, Jaypee University of Information Technology, India
Arshdeep Singh Chudey, Jaypee University of Information Technology, India
Mrityunjay Singh, Jaypee University of Information Technology, India

Chapter 12
COVID-19-Related Predictions Using NER on News Headlines 187
Bidyut B. Hazarika, Western Michigan University, USA
Urvish Trivedi, University of South Florida, USA
Harshita Dahiya, National Institute of Technology, Kurukshetra, India
Nishtha Nandwani, National Institute of Technology, Kurukshetra, India
Aakriti Gupta, National Institute of Technology, Kurukshetra, India

Chapter 13
Security Issues in Fog Computing and ML-Based Solutions 209
Himanshu Sahu, University of Petroleum and Energy Studies, India
Gaytri, University of Petroleum and Energy Studies, India

Chapter 14
Intrusion Detection Systems: Current Trends and Future Challenges 235
Riya Bilaiya, National Institute of Technology, Kurukshetra, India
Priyanka Ahlawat, National Institute of Technology, Kurukshetra, India
Rohit Bathla, National Institute of Technology, Kurukshetra, India

Chapter 15
Vulnerability Assessment and Malware Analysis of Android Apps Using Machine Learning 255
Pallavi Khatri, ITM University, Gwalior, India
Animesh Kumar Agrawal, ITM University, Gwalior, India
Aman Sharma, Independent Researcher, India
Navpreet Pannu, Independent Researcher, India
Sumitra Ranjan Sinha, Independent Researcher, India

Chapter 16
Locally-Adaptive Naïve Bayes Framework Design via Density-Based Clustering for Large Scale Datasets 278
Faruk Bulut, Istanbul Rumeli University, Turkey

Chapter 17
RFID Security Issues, Defenses, and Security Schemes 293
Atul Kumar, National Institute of Technology, Kurukshetra, India
Ankit Kumar Jain, National Institute of Technology, Kurukshetra, India

Compilation of References 311

About the Contributors 349

Index 353

Detailed Table of Contents

Foreword xviii

Preface xx

Chapter 1
Intelligent Vision-Based Systems for Public Safety and Protection via Machine Learning Techniques 1
Rajitha B., Motilal Nehru National Institute of Technology, Allahabad, India

Abnormal behavior detection from on-line/off-line videos is an emerging field in the area of computer vision. This plays a vital role in video surveillance-based applications to provide safety for humans at public places such as traffic signals, shopping malls, railway stations, etc. Surveillance cameras are meant to act as digital eyes (i.e., watching over activities at public places) and provide security. There are a number of cameras deployed at various public places to provide video surveillance, but in reality, they are used only after some incident has happened. Moreover, a human watch is needed in order to detect the person/cause of the incident. This makes surveillance cameras passive. Thus, there is a huge demand to develop an intelligent video surveillance system that can detect the abnormality/incident dynamically and accordingly raise an alarm to the nearest police stations or hospitals as per requirement. If AI-supported CCTV systems are deployed at commercial and traffic areas, then we can easily detect the incidents/crimes, and they can be traced in minimal time.

Chapter 2
Comparative Analysis of Various Soft Computing Technique-Based Automatic Licence Plate Recognition Systems 18
Nitin Sharma, Chandigarh University, India
Pawan Kumar Dahiya, Deenbandhu Chhotu Ram University of Science and Technology, India
B. R. Marwah, Independent Researcher, India

Traffic on Indian roads is growing day by day leading to accidents. The intelligent transport system is the solution to resolve the traffic problem on roads. One of the components of the intelligent transportation system is the monitoring of traffic by the automatic licence plate recognition system. In this chapter, a automatic licence plate recognition systems based on soft computing techniques is presented. Images of Indian vehicle licence plates are used as the dataset. Firstly, the licence plate region is extracted from the captured image, and thereafter, the characters are segmented. Then features are extracted from the segmented characters which are used for the recognition purpose. Furthermore, artificial neural network, support vector machine, and convolutional neural network are used and compared for the automatic licence plate recognition. The future scope is the hybrid technique solution to the problem.

Chapter 3
Impact of Syntactical and Statistical Pattern Recognition on Prognostic Reasoning 38
Rithesh Pakkala P., Sahyadri College of Engineering and Management, Mangaluru, India & Visvesvaraya Technological University, Belagavi, India
Prakhyath Rai, Sahyadri College of Engineering and Management, Mangaluru, India & Visvesvaraya Technological University, Belagavi, India
Shamantha Rai Bellipady, Sahyadri College of Engineering and Management, Mangaluru, India & Visvesvaraya Technological University, Belagavi, India

This chapter provides insight on pattern recognition by illustrating various approaches and frameworks which aid in the prognostic reasoning facilitated by feature selection and feature extraction. The chapter focuses on analyzing syntactical and statistical approaches of pattern recognition. Typically, a large set of features have an impact on the performance of the predictive model. Hence, there is a need to eliminate redundant and noisy pieces of data before developing any predictive model. The selection of features is independent of any machine learning algorithms. The content-rich information obtained after the elimination of noisy patterns such as stop words and missing values is then used for further prediction. The refinement and extraction of relevant features yields in performance enhancements of future prediction and analysis.

Chapter 4
Challenges and Issues in Plant Disease Detection Using Deep Learning 56
Priyanka Sahu, Guru Gobind Singh Inderprastha University, New Delhi, India
Anuradha Chug, Guru Gobind Singh Inderprastha University, New Delhi, India
Amit Prakash Singh, Guru Gobind Singh Inderprastha University, New Delhi, India
Dinesh Singh, Indian Agricultural Research Institute, New Delhi, India
Ravinder Pal Singh, Indian Agricultural Research Institute, New Delhi, India

Deep learning (DL) has rapidly become an essential tool for image classification tasks. This technique is now being deployed to the tasks of classifying and detecting plant diseases. The encouraging results achieved with this methodology hide many problems that are rarely addressed in related experiments. This study examines the main factors influencing the efficiency of deep neural networks for plant disease detection. The challenges discussed in the study are based on the literature as well as experiments conducted using an image database, which contains approximately 1,296 leaf images of the beans crop. A pre-trained convolutional neural network, EfficientNet B0, is used for training and testing purposes. This study gives and emphasizes on factors and challenges that may potentially affect the use of DL techniques to detect and classify plant diseases. Some solutions are also suggested that may overcome these problems.

Chapter 5
Automatic Animal Detection and Collision Avoidance System (ADCAS) Using Thermal Camera ... 75
Jeyabharathi Duraipandy, Sri Krishna College of Technology, India
Kesavaraja D., Dr. Sivanthi Aditanar College of Engineering, Tiruchendur, India
Sasireka Duraipandy, V. V. College of Engineering, Tisaiyanvillai, India

Animal-vehicle collision is one of the big issues in roadways near forests. Due to road accidents, the injuries and death of wildlife has increased tremendously. This type of collision is occurring mainly during nighttime because the animals are more activate. So, to avoid this type of accident, the chapter

automatically detects animals on highways, preventing animal-vehicle collision by finding the distance between vehicles and animals in the roadway. If the distance between animals and vehicle is short, then automatic horn sound is given, which will alert both drivers as well as animals.

Improvement of public safety and reducing accidents are the intelligent system's critical goals for detecting drivers' fatigue and distracted behavior during the driving project. The essential factors in accidents are driver fatigue and monotony, especially on rural roads. Such distracted behavior of the driver reduces their thinking ability for that particular instant. Because of this loss in decision-making ability, they lose control of their vehicle. Studies tell that usually the driver gets tired after an hour of driving. Driver fatigue and drowsiness happens much more in the afternoon, early hours, after eating lunch, and at midnight. These losses of consciousness could also be because of drinking alcohol, drug addiction, etc. The distracted driver detection system proposed in this chapter takes a multi-faceted approach by monitoring driver actions and fatigue levels. The proposed activity monitor achieves an accuracy of 86.3%. The fatigue monitor has been developed and tuned to work well in real-life scenarios.

Convolution neural network (CNN) is the most popular deep learning method that has been used for various applications like image recognition, computer vision, and natural language processing. In this chapter, application of CNN in web query session mining for effective information retrieval is explained. CNN has been used for document analysis to capture the rich contextual structure in a search query or document content. The document content represented in matrix form using Word2Vec is applied to CNN for convolution as well as maxpooling operations to generate the fixed length document feature vector. This fixed length document feature vector is input to fully connected neural network (FNN) and generates the semantic document vector. These semantic document vectors are clustered to group similar document for effective web information retrieval. An experiment was performed on the data set of web query sessions, and results confirm the effectiveness of CNN in web query session mining for effective information retrieval.

The authors propose an image encryption process based on chaos that uses block scrambling to reduce the correlation among the neighboring pixels and random order substitution for slightly changing the value of the pixel. The chaotic sequence for encrypting the image is generated by using two 3D logistic maps

The novel coronavirus (COVID-19), which started in the Wuhan province of China, prompted a major outbreak that culminated in a worldwide pandemic. Several cases are being recorded across the globe, with deaths being close to 2.5 million. The increased number of cases and the newness of such a pandemic has resulted in the hospitals being under-equipped leading to problems in diagnosis of the disease. From previous studies, radiography has proved to be the fastest testing method. A screening test using the x-ray scan of the chest region has proved to be effective. For this method, a trained radiologist is needed to detect the disease. Automating this process using deep learning models can prove to be effective. Due to the lack of large dataset, pre-trained CNN models are used in this study. Several models have been employed like VGG-16, Resnet-50, InceptionV3, and InceptionResnetV2. Resnet-50 provided the best accuracy of 98.3%. The performance evaluation has been done using metrics like receiver operating curve and confusion matrix.

Today, all the newspapers and online news content are flooded with the news of coronavirus (i.e., COVID-19). The virus has spread across the globe at an alarming rate. Thus, people need to remain updated about news regarding the ongoing pandemic which has taken whole world by storm. Therefore, named entity recognition (NER) is applied to extract important information from these news headlines and articles and further used for more applications related to COVID-19 in India. This chapter uses the SpaCy module to categorize the tokens extracted from the news headlines database into various pre-defined tags. Further, four different machine learning models, namely CRF Model, LSTM Model, LightGBM Model, and AdaBoost Model, are applied for performing tagging. After that, these tags are used to predict different information regarding COVID-19. Some of these applications include finding nearby hospitals and pharmacies, predicting future potential hotspots in India, worst affected states of India, gender-based comparisons, age group-based comparisons, and area-based spreading of the virus.

IoT requires data processing, which is provided by the cloud and fog computing. Fog computing shifts centralized data processing from the cloud data center to the edge, thereby supporting faster response due to reduced communication latencies. Its distributed architecture raises security and privacy issues; some are inherited from the cloud, IoT, and network whereas others are unique. Securing fog computing

naïve Bayes (LANB) learning style, a certain amount of local instances, which are close the test point, construct an adaptive probability estimation. In the empirical studies of over the 53 benchmark UCI datasets, more accurate classification performance has been obtained. A total 8.2% increase in classification accuracy has been gained with LANB when compared to the conventional naïve Bayes model. The presented LANB method has outperformed according to the statistical paired t-test comparisons: 31 wins, 14 ties, and 8 losses of all UCI sets.

Chapter 17
RFID Security Issues, Defenses, and Security Schemes 293
Atul Kumar, National Institute of Technology, Kurukshetra, India
Ankit Kumar Jain, National Institute of Technology, Kurukshetra, India

Radio frequency identification (RFID) consists of a tag and reader. The RFID system is used in various places, such as finding the location of devices and toll payment. In computer security, CIA (confidentiality, integrity, authentication) is the primary concern for RFID security. In existing scenario, there are various threats present in the RFID system such as de-synchronization attack, disclosure attack, tracking attack and so on. There are various threats that RFID systems are vulnerable to such as a de-synchronization attack, disclosure attack, dos attack, and tracking attack. This chapter discusses various attacks on the RFID system in terms of confidentiality, integrity, and availability as these devices contain a limited amount of memory and low power battery. Therefore, these devices need a lightweight solution for the RFID system. Hence, this chapter additionally discusses various authentication schemes such as lightweight scheme and ultra-lightweight scheme for RFID systems.

Compilation of References 311

About the Contributors 349

Index 353

Foreword

It is a matter of great pleasure to record that IGI Global has decided to bring an edited book on the topic of substantial importance: *Handbook of Research on Machine Learning Techniques for Pattern Recognition and Information Security*.

The dominance of machine learning methods for development of accurate and efficient applications in the field of engineering, sciences, statistics, medical etc. can be realized from the number of algorithms or techniques developed during last two decades. The particular interest of researchers to solve challenges that involve huge amount of data has been perfectly catered by the machine learning techniques. These algorithms has enabled them to develop state of the art systems and applications in different as well as important areas. The discussion on challenges and issues faced by the researchers in application of these algorithms in diverse areas is of great importance. The two such areas are Pattern Recognition and Information Security.

This book by Dua and Jain is one of the important efforts to discuss significance of the machine learning techniques in these two areas. While some authors of the chapters in this book have presented theoretical aspects of these techniques by discussing various machine algorithms used in their particular area of research, others have discussed practical aspects of the methods by presenting applications developed by them.

The pattern recognition based systems like video surveillance to detect the abnormality/incident dynamically, automatic license plate recognition systems for Indian vehicle license plates, system to detect foreground, track specified object (animals) in the roadway, and system to detect driver's drowsiness by using machine learning algorithms simultaneously, are some of the perfect examples of the user as well as data centric applications developed by the authors of first four chapters using latest machine learning techniques. In addition, a good analysis of syntactical and statistical approaches of pattern recognition has been presented by one of the chapter author and the next chapter discusses various challenges and issues in plant disease detection using deep learning.

Along with pattern recognition applications, this book provides a good overview of the current trends, issues and future challenges of the machine learning techniques in the area of information security. The authors of different chapters have discussed their applications in a very comprehensive manner. Where, one chapter discusses issues related to RFID security, and multiple image encryption discusses security related applications, the other chapters present, survey and analyze security related issues of Intrusion detection system (IDS) architecture and Fog Computing. Also, two chapters in the book present research related to Covid-19, the latest challenge the whole world is facing nowadays.

I recommend this book as the most readable and concise text material on machine-learning techniques' current issues and future scenario. It is perfectly suited as an important material on the subject and can also be tailored as prototype for some upcoming literature. I hope this book would be of substantial value for the scholars, researchers and industry experts working in the area of developing pattern recognition and information security applications using machine-learning techniques.

R. K. Aggarwal
Department of Computer Engineering, National Institute of Technology, Kurukshetra, India

Preface

It was the year 1959 when Arthur Samuel, an American scientist, first defined the term Machine Learning (Samuel, 1959) and undoubtedly, the last two decades can be denoted as the era of development of various machine learning techniques. Not only, the design of new machine learning techniques has demonstrated significant success in the last two decades, the area of application of these techniques has grown exponentially in last few years and has become increasingly wide than ever. Researchers' acceptance and dependency on these techniques to solve complex engineering problems has resulted in many new, advanced and optimized machine learning algorithms. These algorithms are being extensively used as an instrument for design and implementation of systems that require large as well as diverse data processing. "Supervised learning", "Unsupervised learning", "Reinforcement learning" and "Semi-supervised learning" are the four major categories, when we classify machine learning implementations on the basis of nature of the learning. And, "Classification", "Regression" and "Clustering" are the three defined categories, when we classify machine learning tasks on the basis of the desired output of a machine-learned system.

Pattern recognition and Information security are the two research fields that have been majorly benefited by the machine learning paradigms. The ability of data driven representation learning of machine learning algorithms has raised the interests of scientific community to work in these two research areas. Pattern recognition uses well defined computer paradigms or algorithms to automatic discover data regularities and takes corresponding actions by using these data regularities. Classification of data into various categories is one such example of these actions (Bishop, 2006). The task of looking for the particular patterns in data is very basic and has been taken by the researchers as a challenge in various problems. The machine learning methods surprised the pattern recognition community with its powerful ability to learn complex patterns from data and attaining new state-of-the-art performance in most of the applications.

Also, various machine learning methods are also used to address wide variety of information and data security challenges/problems. The growth of today's network has made it an important and efficient resource for exchange of data services all over the WWW. The design and implementation of these data centric applications is becoming more challenging day by day, as a huge amount of data is required by these applications or services. This exchange of data and services over the networks has also actuated many malicious actions that make efforts to damage and intrude in these data centric applications to serve their own interests. To make our system, applications, networks and services secure from attacks or unauthorized access, we require the set of methods or algorithms. The machine learning techniques trained a classification algorithm with some features that can distinguish a genuine application from the fake one more efficiently than the classical or conventional methods.

Hence, there is a need to discuss current research challenges and future perspective about how machine learning techniques can be applied to improve data security and Pattern recognition applications. The main objective of this book is to provide insights, how the machine learning techniques will impact Pattern Recognition and Information Security Applications, what are their promises, limits and the new challenges. This also provides a publication avenue for researchers working on the recent machine learning approaches to the problems in Pattern Recognition and Information Security. The target audience of this book is academicians, research scholars, industrial expert, scientists, and post graduate students who are willing to work or working in the field of Pattern Recognition and Information Security, and would like to add machine learning to enhance capabilities of their particular work. The core areas covered under the umbrella of this edited book call are:

- Pattern Recognition Principles
- Syntactical and Structural Pattern Recognition
- Statistical Pattern Recognition
- Speaker and Speech Recognition
- Image analysis and security
- Bio metrics
- Cyber Security
- IOT Security
- Cloud Security
- Web Security
- Social Networks Security
- Intrusion Detection and Management
- Anomaly Detection Management System
- Adhoc and Sensor Network Security
- Block chain based Data Security
- Identification and Authentication Mechanism
- Secure Fog/Edge Computing

The following is the detail of the organization of chapter:

In Chapter 1, authors present an intelligent video surveillance system which can detect the abnormality/incident dynamically and accordingly raise an alarm to the nearest police stations, hospitals as per requirement. This surveillance system can play a vital role to provide safety for humans in public places such as traffic signals, shopping malls, railway stations, etc. This chapter has discussed in detail, the some of the machine learning approaches for supervised, semi-supervised and unsupervised based models in-depth for a video surveillance system.

In Chapter 2, authors discuss an automatic licence plate recognition systems based on soft computing techniques. This technique extracts licence plate region from the captured image and thereafter the characters are segmented. Then features are extracted from the segmented characters, which are used for the recognition purpose. The authors have used images of Indian vehicle licence plates as the dataset. Moreover, artificial neural network, support vector machine and convolutional neural network are used and compared for the automatic licence plate recognition.

In Chapter 3, an analyses of syntactical and statistical approaches of pattern recognition has been presented. Authors provide insight on pattern recognition by illustrating various approaches and frameworks, which aid in the prognostic reasoning facilitated by feature selection and feature extraction. Typically, a large set of features have an impact on the performance of the predictive model. Hence, there is a need to eliminate redundant and noisy pieces of data before developing any predictive model. The selection of features is independent of any machine learning algorithms. The content-rich information obtained after the elimination of noisy patterns such as stop words and missing values is then used for further prediction. The refinement and extraction of relevant features yields in performance enhancements of future prediction and analysis.

In Chapter 4, authors have deployed deep learning technique to the tasks of classifying and detecting plant diseases. This study examines the main factors influencing the efficiency of deep neural networks for plant disease detection. The study emphasizes on factors and challenges that may potentially affect the use of deep learning techniques to detect and classify plant diseases.

In Chapter 5, authors have developed an algorithm to detect foreground, track specified object (animals) in the roadway and give the alert to the control room. The algorithm automatically detects animals on highways and prevents animal-vehicle collision by finding the distance between vehicles and animals in the roadway. The algorithm uses deep learning methods. The approach alerts to drivers and animals by giving horn, when the distance between animals and vehicle is very near.

In Chapter 6, authors have proposed a distracted driver detection system that takes a multi-faceted approach by monitoring driver's actions and fatigue levels. The fatigue monitor has been developed and tuned to work well in real-life scenarios. The aim of this work is to present a new approach to detect and guide the driver for a safe drive. The proposed activity monitor achieves good accuracy.

In Chapter 7, authors have implemented an application of CNN in web query session mining for effective information retrieval. CNN has been used for document analysis, to capture the rich contextual structure in a search query or document content. Experiments has been performed on the data set of web query sessions and results confirm the effectiveness of CNN in web query session mining for effective information retrieval.

Chapter 8 proposes an image encryption process based on chaos that uses block scrambling to reduce the correlation among the neighbouring pixels, and random order substitution for a slightly changing the value of the image pixels. The chaotic sequence for encrypting the image are generated by using two 3-dimesnional Logistic maps called Enhanced logistic map and Intertwining logistic map. The proposed method has the capability of encrypting digital colored images into cipher form with high security.

Chapter 9 proposes a multiple image encryption method based on multi-dimensional chaotic equations. Initially, three input images are used in a matrix form, where size of each image is (M×N), and a composite image is derived by combining the one dimensional matrix of the input images. Lorenz Attractor (LA) generates the security key using the composite matrix and then alternate logistic map is applied with one-dimensional and two-dimensional logistic maps to confuse the matrix. In every iteration of logistic maps, XOR operation is used to encrypt the composite image and at last transformation is applied to diffuse the matrix. Finally, the encrypted composite image is obtained in the form of a confused matrix.

A scheme to develop the image over-segmentation task is introduced in the Chapter 10. It considers the pixels of an image with Simple Linear Iterative Clustering and graph theory-based algorithm. In this regard, the main contribution is to provide a method for extracting super pixels with greater adherence to the edges of the regions.

In Chapter 11, authors developed a model to detect Covid 19 using Chest X-ray and Transfer learning. Due to the lack of large dataset pre-trained CNN models are used in this study. Several models have been employed like VGG-16, Resnet-50, InceptionV3 and InceptionResnetV2. The performance evaluation has been done using metrics like Receiver operating curve and confusion matrix.

In Chapter 12, authors have applied Named Entity Recognition (NER) to extract important information from these news headlines and articles, and further used for more applications related to COVID-19 in India. The work uses the SpaCy module to categorize the tokens extracted from the news headlines database, into various pre-defined tags. Further four different machine learning models namely CRF Model, LSTM Model, LightGBM Model and AdaBoost Model are applied for performing tagging.

Chapter 13 discusses the various concept of fog computing and its architecture. Authors identified the various security challenges loopholes in fog computing architecture, which may be exploited by the attackers. Moreover, the authors suggested numerous techniques to solve the vulnerabilities of fog computing. It detailed about all the machine learning algorithm used in the fog layer. The chapter concludes with security challenges and future recommendation to enhance security in fog computing.

Chapter 14 surveys different approaches for intrusion detection systems, compares them and presents a comparative analysis based on their merits and demerits. With the rapid growth of cyberspace for information sharing, attract intruder to perform illegal activity over cyberspace for capturing, tempering or other misuses of private and confidential information available over cyberspace. Therefore, authors aim to presents an exhaustive survey of current trends in intrusion detection systems research along with some future challenges that are likely to be explored.

In Chapter 15, authors present a two-way approach for finding the malicious Android packages (APKs) by using different android applications through static and dynamic analysis. Three cases are considered depending upon the severity level of APK, permission-based protection level and dynamic analysis of APK for creating the dataset for further analysis. Subsequently, supervised machine learning techniques, naive bayes multinomial text, REPtree, voted perceptron and SGD text are applied to the dataset obtained to classify the selected APK's as malicious, benign or suspicious.

In Chapter 16, author presents local conditional probabilities of a query point, which are used in classification rather than consulting to a generalized framework containing a conditional probability. In the proposed Locally Adaptive Naïve Bayes (LANB) Learning style, a certain amount of local instances, which are close the test point, constructs an adaptive probability estimation.

Chapter 17 discusses various attacks on the RFID system in terms of confidentiality, integrity, and availability. As, these devices contain a limited amount of memory, low power battery. Therefore, these devices need a lightweight solution for the RFID system. Hence, this chapter additional discusses various authentication schemes such as lightweight scheme, and ultra-lightweight scheme for RFID system.

Mohit Dua
National Institute of Technology, Kurukshetra, India

Ankit Kumar Jain
National Institute of Technology, Kurukshetra, India

REFERENCES

Bishop, C. M. (2006). *Pattern recognition and machine learning*. Springer.

Samuel, A. L. (1959). Some studies in machine learning using the game of checkers. *IBM Journal of Research and Development*, *3*(3), 210–229.

Chapter 1
Intelligent Vision-Based Systems for Public Safety and Protection via Machine Learning Techniques

Rajitha B.
Motilal Nehru National Institute of Technology, Allahabad, India

ABSTRACT

Abnormal behavior detection from on-line/off-line videos is an emerging field in the area of computer vision. This plays a vital role in video surveillance-based applications to provide safety for humans at public places such as traffic signals, shopping malls, railway stations, etc. Surveillance cameras are meant to act as digital eyes (i.e., watching over activities at public places) and provide security. There are a number of cameras deployed at various public places to provide video surveillance, but in reality, they are used only after some incident has happened. Moreover, a human watch is needed in order to detect the person/cause of the incident. This makes surveillance cameras passive. Thus, there is a huge demand to develop an intelligent video surveillance system that can detect the abnormality/incident dynamically and accordingly raise an alarm to the nearest police stations or hospitals as per requirement. If AI-supported CCTV systems are deployed at commercial and traffic areas, then we can easily detect the incidents/crimes, and they can be traced in minimal time.

INTRODUCTION

Abnormal behavior detection from on-line/offline videos is an emerging field in the area of computer vision. This plays a vital role in video surveillance based applications to provide safety for humans at public places such as traffic signals, shopping malls, railway stations etc. Surveillance cameras are meant to act as digital eyes i.e. watching over activities at public places and provide security. Now a days there are number of cameras deployed at various public places to provide video surveillance, But in reality they are used or analyzed only after some incident happens. Moreover a human watch is needed

DOI: 10.4018/978-1-7998-3299-7.ch001

in-order to detect the person/cause of the incident. This makes the surveillance cameras passive. For example if a theft/murder occurred at some CCTV monitored area, and then the footage is manually checked for crime identification and localization after complaint has been raised. Thus there is huge demand to develop an intelligent video surveillance system which can detect the abnormality/incident dynamically and accordingly raise an alarm to the nearest police stations, hospitals as per requirement. Current developments in computer vision via Artificial Intelligence (AI) have grown vastly by providing high computational video analysis power. Through this high dimension computation power CCTV data analysis tools can be provided intelligence i.e. brains to automatically detect any theft, murder, vehicle accidents etc. If AI supported CCTV systems are deployed at commercial and traffic areas then we can easily detect the incidents/crimes and they can be traced quickly.

AI based video analytics machines include: detecting the humans via face recognition software's, vehicles detection via number-plate/vehicle model (through image processing techniques) and pedestrians detection etc.. They can also be used to detect that a human is waiting at a bus-stop, running from location A to location B, driving a vehicle in some area etc. But they fail to detect that a human has murdered a person at location A and running to location B, a man waiting at some bus-stop is a criminal, a person has just robbed a vehicle, a person had hit a car during his journey etc. These problems occur daily in almost all the cities of our country. But, our efficient policemen are unaware of the incident until any complaint/report (either written or phone-called) has been made manually to them. Thus these problems led us to think and develop systems which can generate an auto-alarm to Police stations, Ambulance services, Fire stations etc. via a secured channel whenever a crime or accident occurs at commercial and traffic areas, and from any CCTV covered locations. Thus this chapter is mainly aimed to focus on these issues and discusses some solutions using AI based computer vision analysis tools and secured network platform generation for incident authentication and transmission of data over web.

Problems Intended in Video Surveillance Systems

In recent years most of the public places and organizations (such as banks, business work stations, universities, hospitals, shopping malls etc) are deploying the cameras i.e. CCTVs (Closed-Circuit Television) for various purposes such as to monitor the public, pedestrian detection, density based traffic signal allocation, crime identification at mass locations, women safety, robbery prevention/identification, murderer identification etc (National Institute of Justice (NIJ) (2003), Gill Martin (2006), and Nieto (1997)). Some of these videos are accessible without any password credentials and some require authorized access. These camera footages could be utilized to develop the intelligent surveillance systems to increase public safety both at personal and public places (Skogan (2004)). It can also help the police in guiding and identifying the other safer routes for common public daily journey without any mishap (after/during any incident). Even the government of U.S, U.K and India etc are deploying surveillance video systems at various cities respectively. They are trying to steam the real-time public networks cameras data for public safety such as abnormal action detection or prevention via central server. These cameras data can be used to identify perpetrator after the crime. Law enforcement agencies in India, United States, Washington and Newyork (Fridell (2004), Braga (2015) and La Vigne (2011)) are embracing the community policies philosophy from past few years in-order to enforce public safety. This might lead to develop and incorporate more efficient and effective strategies to enforce the law. In order to achieve higher accuracy in these applications a vast number of network cameras must be installed to cover all angles of crime/

anomaly detection. A number of new and cost-effective software tools and machines must be deployed. In-order to create such efficient systems some challenges might be encountered such as follows:

Challenges in current video surveillance systems:

- Where exactly to Locate Cameras
- Choosing Best Cameras for public places
- Latest Technology Integration i.e. deep learning with available Software Tools such as Vision Processing Units, OpenCV, Python libraries etc.
- How to Incorporate the Privacy Policies
- How to Incorporate the Active and Dynamic CCTV Monitoring
- How to analyze the Video footage for anomaly detection and prevention
- Dynamic Tracking of perpetrator/vehicle.
- Multi-casting the perpetrator info to nearest police stations in secured channel.

Current Developments in This Area

Police monitored cameras are placed in United States from past few years. They are mostly used after the crime has occurred and to identify the suspects. In U.S and U.K the CCTV's are placed in most of the organizations, schools, commercial areas, railways stations, apartments etc for monitoring the people, prevent/detect the theft suspects, and to identify any misconduct. However, they all are passive (not an auto detecting systems). To develop such high dimensional capable software tools, higher broadband services are required for efficient and faster data transfer over web. Currently U.K stands among top 20 in providing the broadband services. In Indian communities there is lack of high-speed broadband services in the earlier years. But, this has changed drastically from last three to four years. Now India also provides high-speed Internet services at most of the metropolitan cities. Thus implementing intelligent and smart CCTVs in India for law enforcement can improve the technical growth of the country and reduce the crime.

Role of AI in Video Surveillance Systems

Governments of various countries are is now interested in funding the agencies to setup a wireless networks with 4G technology in order to increase the communication among the police stations to respond immediately after an serious incident. Though they are costly the government of U.S, U.K and Canada etc are willing to install high-definition CCTVs in order to reduce the crime rate. Grant Fredericks, a constable and forensic video analysis expert from Columbia, Canada had monitored and evaluated number of the CCTVs located at public transports, city centers, transport locations, apartments, vehicle parking etc.(these analytics was carried-out manually). Simon Goudie, Brandon Welsh and David Farrington, Anne Mellbye, Tanya Kristiansen from Campbell Collaboration and RBUP, Norway had published an article review named as ***"17 Effects of Closed Circuit Television Surveillance on Crime"*** (Zhao (2000)). Their study was conducted in hospitals, residential areas; public transports etc in U.K, USA, Canada, Norway and Sweden and found that ***"CCTVs are not effective until some intelligence is provided, otherwise they are just passive".***

PUBLIC SAFETY AND VIDEO SURVEILLANCE SYSTEMS

The CCTV based network controlled systems are still in development stage in most of the states of India and other countries. Delhi police has installed CCTV networks at various traffic signals to monitor the traffic and crime. The CCTV are also been used by criminals at their respective houses/offices in order to track if any police has entered in to their area, if any such case is found the criminal uses the privacy act of law and accuses the police has harassed/demanded the amount from them. DCP Ishwar Singh, of Delhi has reportedly noticed such cases and observed various such CCTV footages access and a special task force was assigned to track all such gangs. Within 10 days this team has found many cases including liquor illegal supplies, gambling rackets etc. Gurgaon police commissionerate also installed central surveillance systems in urban areas by municipal corporation costing 3.37 crores. Around 61 CCTV cameras are installed and monitored at police headquarters. These areas covered most of the public transport routes. Bangalore traffic police had also installed 170 CCTV cameras later adding another 750 cameras approximately at various public areas and monitored from Bruhat Bengaluru Mahanagara Palike worth 1,500-2,000 crore approximatly. M.N. Anucheth, deputy commissioner of police (administration), said "CCTV can be used as electronic evidence while investigating criminals". "The Journalist Gauri Lankesh murder case has benefitted through this CCTV footage for indentifying the suspects during the absence of an eyewitness".

Offline Crime Prevention

Offline crime identification, here crime related information is gathered once some manual alert (either by phone call/personal complaint) is received to the police. This process is very time consuming and sometimes it might lead to some major loss like deaths, murders, thefts, misleading the case, suspect etc.

Crime Prevention and Identification via Apps

Increasing number of crimes in public places and private places had lead to fear in minds of public. This increasing crime rate had resulted to impose strict rules and regulations on daily routine of common public. People have to fallow these rules wither willingly or unwillingly. So, government is trying to gradually reduce this burden on common public and introduce/develop some new technology based applications which automatically recognizes the crime or incidents and populates the information among the police to enforce the law. There are numerous number of software apps developed for public safety, which needs to be deployed in people's personal mobile phones.

Women safety is one of the major concerns in current public safety aims. In this regard, Eyewatch SOS app was designed to record audio and video of surroundings of the women and automatically transfers them to registered contacts indicating an alert message. iGoSafely app, sends position of the GPS to emergency contact upon activation. Smart 24×7 app, it automatically initiates the phone call to police when a panic button is pressed. bSafe app, it sends multiple information about the location i.e. exact GPS location, video/audio of surroundings to the registered contacts immediately. SpotnSave Feel secure app, it is same as that of bSafe and sends alert for every two minutes. Himmat app, this rated as one of the best apps till date and developed by Delhi police. Here the public must register in the site of Delhi Police through an OTP. It transmits the GPS locations along with audio and video of surrounding to the police control room. Similarly Chennai, Hyderabad, Banglore, etc cities had also developed similar kind of apps for women safety.

Criminal Identification and Localizations is another concerned area of public safety. Police of various states in India, developed separate apps for criminal identification though mobile phones instantly. Here AI-based auto face recognition software systems are developed by expert teams and used by police to verify and authenticate the suspect right from the crime sport locations and trace him. Face recognition, needs many processing stages like: enhance the image, resize the image, locating the face coordinates automatically, matching the query face features with the dataset images, and finally classify that the face in photo/image is a criminal or not. These apps are trained to search the criminal through face as well as textual information. Punjab Police uses PAIS app, which searches based on facial photo/image, text information and etc from 100,000 criminal records approximately. Trinetra, is also one such AI-based app containing more than five lakhs of criminal face features. E-Pragati app, it is also for crime prevention and stores millions of people's information via Aadhaar number linking from the state of Andhra Pradesh alone. Aforementioned apps are passive i.e. they don't act intelligently by themselves. Some external initiative must be taken by the user during the crime or before or after the crime.

Chennai police is also monitoring the traffic and crime through a mobile app designed especially for police cops to communicate among the police team. Similarly in Telangana, Hyderabad police had also designed a mobile app for controlling and tracking the suspects and criminals through the police recorded image sources and surveillance cameras. The app designed by them is COP Connect, Hawk Eye etc. These apps are meant for public safety and women safety. Table 1 and 2 summarizes and compares some of the existing mobile apps developed for public safety and security.

Crime Prevention and Identification via CCTV

Software's apps on smart phones are mainly user initiated processes. So the alternative is to measure and provide public safety via Artificial Intelligence enabled surveillance cameras. Currently, in almost all the major cities huge numbers of CCTV cameras are installed at public and private places. These camera recoding are used for crime identification and tracking the suspect. These CCTV based software's are in developing stage and it can be observed that the suspects or criminals are manually checked in various CCTVs footages after the incident. That is they are used after the incident has occurred and it might take alt-least 1 to 24 hours to trace the suspect after the incident. Hence a highly efficient software system is required to detect the incident immediately from the CCTV footage and track perpetrator in very minimal time, which is lacking in the current available systems.

MACHINE LEARNING FOR PUBLIC SAFETY

The abnormal behavior doesn't happen on daily basis at traffic signals or roots, they occur very often (rare cases). So, detecting such incidents need slots of learning. Thus developing software's must be processed on many video footages inorder to classify the normal and abnormal behavior. These models can be broadly categorized as Semi-Supervised, Supervised and Unsupervised approaches as in Zhu (2009), Niculescu-Mizil (2005) and Coate (2011). If the training dataset is mixture of labeled and unlabelled data then semi-supervised approaches can be used to classify. If the training dataset is completely labeled then supervised approaches can be used to classify. But, If the training dataset of not labeled (none of the relationships are mentioned) at all then unsupervised approaches must be used to identify the class. Each of these approaches has different set of parameters and working strategies. Another special case of learning method is Active Learning given by Beygelzimer (2008); here the system interacts with the user during the process of predicting the class i.e. takes a user input for better class predictions rates. This type of prediction methods are used when there is huge number of unlabelled datasets and cannot be labeled manually with minimal time. All the learning methods first train the system or model by splitting the available dataset into m: n ratio (where m+n is the total number of samples in the dataset). For example, if we have 1000 sample images and ratio is 80: 20 then 800 will be used for training and remaining 200 sample images will be used for testing. That i.e. while training the model no external images can be added. But, in real time the dataset increases or grows dynamically. Thus, researches have proposed another learning mechanism named as Re-inforcement learning like stated in Zoph (2016). This method is built on the concept of self-teaching or self-updating the model as per the new samples. It processes the available data i.e. past data as well as the current generated data and tries to minimize the prediction percentage. This could be taken as resembles to human brain where he/she learns from known facts given by parents and facts from his day to day growth.

Table 1. Comparison of existing software apps

Software/App Name	Users	Purpose
PoliceOne	Police officers	It's an iPhone application for sharing the official news, photos, tactical tips etc among the police officials.
CrimeSceneTracker	Any Individual	This app facilitates the individual who is at the crime scene to take photos, document the scene information in standard format and share with the nearest police station.
Police Field Interview FI Card	Security Officers	Suspects Face can be detected from the records of crime data
US Cop	Street Officers	Helpful for patrolling police.
Police Spanish Guide	Police working and cannot speak Spanish	App converts your speech to Spanish while enquiring with Spanish people
My Police Department	For police officials	Can track the nearest police station and inform the suspects information immediately from the scene.
Karnataka State Police App	Police officials	Users can trace the nearest police stations and lodge complaint directly via app including the Images of suspects
COP Connect by Telangana	Police Officials	Its an group chart app through which the police officials can make groups at different levels like district, zone, sub-division, circle levels etc and share the suspects information like images, audios, videos and documents.
Delhi Police app	Police Officials	Police can notify the people about the helpline numbers in case of emergency, shortcuts to all police official cites, etc.
RAIDS Online	Police officers and public	People can inform about the public safety routes, informs/alerts about the high-crime areas. They can also view details about a crime including crime type, date, time, address, and distance from current location.

Table 2. Comparison of previous approaches

Approach	Limitations	Software Designed	Evaluation-Parameter
Accelerometer and GPS tracking by Zhao (2008)	SPOF	Yes	Accuracy
Smart Phone by Ali Haimd M (2017)	SPOF	Yes	Accuracy
Atmel Micro-controller by Tushara D (2016)	SPOF	Yes	Time
Sensors by Yee (2018)	Informs one mobile no.	Yes	Accuracy
Based on Speed by Dogru, N (2018)	SPOF	GSM and GPS Modem	Time
Smart Phone by Faiz (2015)	SPOF	Yes	Accuracy
Vehicle Features by Fogue (2013)	Delay in the message sending	Prototype	Accuracy
Vector Machine by Liang (2015)	Not a rescue system	Rea-time Traffic	Accuracy
Smart Phone by Bhatti Fizzah (2017)	SPOF	Yes	Accuracy
Camera on Vehicle by Spampinato (2019)	SPOF	Yes	Accuracy

Based on these basic learning methods the machine is trained and tested on test data. The normal learning becomes the deep learning when deep feature are extracted from the training data as well as from test data. Deep features mean the applying more number of filters on the sample images to extract more number of features unlike the manual approaches. For instance, to classify a human and non-human object (like car or animal) manual features or shallow features may be sufficient. But, to classify the a human face from another human face manual features may not give better results, thus require deep features. Thus, machine learning techniques are playing vital role in developing smart and efficient approaches for various vision based applications.

Abnormality Behavior Detection via Deep Learning

Abnormality behavior detection can be broadly categorized in to the following:

- Model-Based approaches: These approaches train the model using a group of parameters. These parameters are learnt via statistical methods. There can be non-parametric and parametric statistical methods. If the structure data pr feature data is created using the probability density function and parametric distribution function then it is called ad parametric based approach. Some of them are regression based methods and Gaussian mixture models specified in Clevelan (2017) and Reynolds (2015). If the structure data pr feature data is created dynamically then it is non-parametric method. Some of them are Bayesian network models given by Maldonado (2019), Dirichlet process mixture models given by Liu (2019) and histogram based models as of Divya Srivastava (2017). Deep neural network models uses weights and biases as parametric to learn the model, hence can be categorized to parametric model i.e. model based approach. Neural network based models use cross entropy to reduce the error between the predicted and actual class outputs, thus comes under the model based approaches.

- Classification-Based approaches: For a given feature dataset space if one can distinguish a line or model (either liner or non-linear separator) then it is said to be a classification. I.e. the line separates the two classes. In general the classification approaches are categorized into two: binary class classification and multiclass classification. Binary class classification approaches train the model to classify the unknown samples to either class 'A' or 'B' (i.e. results as yes or no, true or false etc). Multiclass classifiers also train the model of features extracted similar to the binary class but, classifies the unknown samples to more than one class i.e. class 'A', 'B',...'N'. Rule based classifier used by Gu, Xiaowei (2018) is one such approach where a set of rules are created or formalized on the train data and their attribute relationships and finally classifies the test data on these rules. Decision tress, Bayesian classifiers are also of the similar category. Liu Peng (2017) used Support vector machine which is an advanced and latest approach which classifies both in binary and multiclass data.
- Prediction-Based approaches: Here anomaly detection is achieved by estimating the differences between predicted and actual class characteristics. LSTM (Long Short Term Memory used by Cui Yin (2018) and HMM (Hidden Markov Model) by Guo Qiang (2016) are some of the examples of these categories.
- Reconstruction-Based approaches: This method assumes that the normal image data can be re-represented through a different or lower dimensional representation for differentiating the normal and abnormal behavior image data. For instance, a human visual face image is generally represented including the whole features such as hair, skin, chin, eyes, nose, lips and etc. The same image can be re-represented just as a scaled down feature map (point distribution model). For example, just 2 to 10 points can be uses to represent an eye, 3 to 10 points for nose, 4 to 10 points for lips etc. Thus, instead of visual face image, a set of points can be stored as features map and their mean differences can be used as features (example: Kang (2017) used Principal Component Analysis, Auto-Encoder etc).
- Other variant approaches: Dey Nilanjan (2016), used Clustering here the generated features are grouped into two or multiple sub groups/clusters. The grouping is done on the concept of the data elements within a group has similar properties and data from two different groups has different properties. This applies for the current chapter since the normal data is huge in practical compared to abnormal behavior data. Thus the one cluster will be created for normal data and outliers or smaller clusters belong to abnormal behavior. Heuristic approaches use the spatial location and information of context to classify the abnormality. Fuzzy based clustering is another alternative for grouping. Here the each feature data is assigned a probability to lie in various clusters. That is a feature can belong to cluster A with 80% probability and 20% to another cluster. Thus overcomes the problem of hard thresholding like normal clustering. Similarly there are many hybrid approaches where different approaches are combined to classify the data.

Deep Learning Approaches and Its Variants

Here a computer machine is aimed to take automated decisions. These decisions should not be enabled via any explicit computer programs. They should also include intelligence while processing. If a machine takes an automated decision with intelligence then it is said machine learning based approach. From late 1990's new approaches came into existence based on this methodology both in computer vision and big-data analytics. The advancements in neural networks and artificial intelligence has given rise to new approaches called Convolutional Neural Networks (CNN) as used by LeCun (2010). Hubel and Wiesel has inspired the formation this architecture. First CNN model was designed by LeCun in the year 1989 fro topological data processing (represented in grid-from). Its action is similar to human brain processing unit such as Neocortex. It processes the information through multiple layers in brain and extracts the meaningful information or knowledge automatically. Thus it resembles the human brain visual cortex. The refinotpic visualization locates the visual context and sends the data to visual cortex, here high pass multi-scale filters are applied. Finally the predictions are performed based on the pre-set classes of brain such as v1, v2, v3 and v4. Back propagation is also applied in CNN during the training process by changing the weights with respect to the inputs given. Human brain trains the data on response based learning approach. CNN also tries to learn and minimize the cost function using backpropogation. It can extract high, low and middle level features by varying the filter size and filter type. Thus with all these key features it can learn efficiently from any raw input image (pixels data in 2D matrix form).

CNN is a subclass of neural networks. It has a powerful ability while extracting the features from an image. It includes many hidden layers which automatically learns the inner features of the image. CNN has gained much importance due to vast growing rate of vision data and new developments in processing devices. CNN architecture contains: various activation functions, loss functions, regularization, optimization parameters and processing units etc. This CNN is further enhanced to make it Deep CNN (DCNN). DCNN is constructed by modulating the basic CNN architecture in more depth. CNN uses block based processing units instead of structural layers. Hence gained substantial importance and attention. CNN network architecture has multiple learning layers or stages which combine: Convolutional Layers, Processing units with non-linearity and sampling layer. Every layer transforms the given image data to the next layer using a bank of convolutional filters (kernals). Here the input image is divided into smaller blocks or slices. Local features are extracted on these blocks via a set of filters. The resultant images are forwarded to non-liner processing units. This will help in understanding the semantics of the image. Next, The results are forwarded to sub sampling layer, which combines the results of multiples filters and makes them geometric distortion invariant.

Deep CNN architecture is advantages over shallow architecture or manual approaches for feature extractions and classification. The complex tasks require a rigorous learning of features. The complex learning ability is gained due to multiple non-linear and linear processing units stacking unlike normal CNN. That is DCNN is combination of collection of normal CNN's one after another or in parallel. The hardware advancements like GPU's with high computing capable systems are also the cause of attractions and attention towards its development. Thus it shows high performance over conventional approaches. It also has the ability to learn from unlabelled data, extracting the invariant representation, handle hundreds of categories and etc. DCNN has many variants an short description is given in following:

- **LeNet-5 (1995):** It is designed by LeCun (1995) and et al. in the year 1995. This ia pioneering convolutional neural network with 7 level layers. This is trained to classify the numerals or digits. Several researchers have used this network for recognizing the hand-written numbers, numbers on cheques etc. The input image is resized to 32 X 32 image size in grayscale format. The high resolution image datasets of numbers require high computational layers in designed CNN model where in this model lacks the performance.
- **AlexNet (2012):** This architecture proposed by Krizhevsky (2012) is also similar to LeNet but, it is much deeper and has more number of layers with huge number of convolutional layers stacked. It has won the first rice by resolving almost all the challenges of co competitors and outperformed

the resuts with top-5 error rates to 15.3% on an average. It base model contained 11 X 11 convolutional layers at first stage, 5 X 5 and 3 X 3 convolutional layers in the remaining layers. Each stage has max pooling layers, dropout layers, ReLU activations, data augmentations and SGD momentum. ReLU layer is at every individual convolutional layer and at fully connected layer. It was trained on Nvidia Geforce GPUs for almost six days simultaneous. As it is taking too much time they split the network into two pipelines. Alex Krizhevsky, Ilya Sutskever and Geoffrey Hinton together designed this architecture in SuperVision group.

- **ZFNet(2013):** In the year 2013 another modified variant of CNN was proposed by Zeiler (2014) named ZFNet. It is the winner of ILSVRC in that year. This network has error rate as 14.8% which is lower than the existing approaches till that date.
- **GoogLeNet/Inception(2014):** Szegedy (2015) proposed GoogleNet architecture which is also known as Inception V1 was the winner of ILSVRC in the year 2014 conference competition. The error is further reduced here to just 6.67% in comparison to existing approaches. This was very similar to human brain level thinking. It was hard to beat this error rate challenge during that year. But, after some days an human expert tried hard and achieved 5.1% error rate (Andrej Karpathy) for single model and for ensemble he achived 3.6% error rate. It was inspired by LeNet but had a novel architecture. This architecture had batch normalization, RMS prop and image distortions. Several small level convolutional filter are designed inorder to reduce the parameters. They constructed a 22 layer stacked deep convolutional neural network and reduced the parameters from 60 million to just 4 million as compared to AlextNet.
- **VGGNet (2014):** Simonyan and Zisserman (2014) developed a variant of CNN model called VGGNet. It was the runner up of ILSVRC conference competition in the year 2014. It is very interesting and appealing with uniform architecture and includes 16 convolution layers. Its architecture is similar to AlextNet but has 3 X 3 convolution layers along with more number of filters. They trained the machine for 2 to 3 weeks on four GPU machines. Due to its simple and most profound architecture it gained much importance in DCNN's domain and is the top most preferred model over researchers. It has been widely adopted by many people over web and its architecture and weight configuration is publicly available. One issue with VGGNet is that it has around 138 million number of parameters.
- **ResNet(2015):** Kaiminh He and et al. (2016) has designed an architecture having skip connections and heavy batch normalization for features. These skip connections are known as gated recurrent units or gated units which has similarity to RNN's. They trained this neural network with 152 numbers of layers which is much lesser than the VGGNet. This architecture has even beaten the human expert error rate with 3.57% of GoogleNet. This model has won the completion of ILSVRC in the year 2015 and named the network as ReNet (Residual Neural Network). It has residual connections unlike the two networks for AlexNet and inception for GoogleNet.

Video Analytics Methods for Accident Classification/Detection

As also pointed out by Yun et al., the existing methods for traffic accident detection developed till date can be categorized into three approaches: Modeling of traffic flow patterns: In this category, the typical law-full traffic patterns (namely, go-straight, U-turn, right-turn, etc.) are modeled as baseline, and any deviation from this model is considered as an abnormal traffic event. This approach will work only when the normal traffic pattern appears at a fixed region repeatedly, thus unable to detect collisions which are essential to accident detection.

- Analysis of vehicle activities: The methods in this categories first detect the moving vehicles and then extract motion features such as the distance between two vehicles, acceleration, direction, etc. of a vehicle from moving vehicles' tracks. However, unsatisfactory tracking performance in crowded traffic scenes becomes their bottleneck and limits their usage.

Table 3. Comparison of various DCNNs

CNN Model	Year of Publication	Developed by	Competition Position	Error-Rate of Top-5	Total No.of Parameters
LeNet 5	1998	Y. LeCun, L. Jackel, L. Bottou, A. Brunot, C. Cortes, J. Denker, H. Drucker, I. Guyon, U. Muller, E. Sackinger, P. Simard, and V. Vapnik.			60 thousand
AlexNet	2012	Krizhevsky, Alex, Ilya Sutskever, and Geoffrey E. Hinton	1st Position	15.3%	60 Million
ZFNet	2013	Zeiler, Matthew D., and Rob Fergus	1st Position	14.8%	---
GoogleNet	2014	Szegedy, Christian, Wei Liu, Yangqing Jia, Pierre Sermanet, Scott Reed, Dragomir Anguelov, Dumitru Erhan, Vincent Vanhoucke, and Andrew Rabinovich	1st Position	6.67%	4 Million
VGGNet	2014	Simonyan, Karen, and Andrew Zisserman	2nd Position	7.3%	138 Million
ResNet	2015	He, Kaiming, Xiangyu Zhang, Shaoqing Ren, and Jian Sun.	1st Position	3.6%	----

- Modeling of vehicle interactions: These methods have been inspired by sociological concepts and model the interaction among vehicles and detect accidents. However, a large number of training data and use of speed change information alone limit the performance of these methods.

Challenges and Possibilities Some of the stringent challenges on video-based anomaly detection are: Illumination: Even though a handful of anomaly detection methods have already been proposed, the number methods that can handle illumination variations, are limited. This is due to the incapability's of illuminations agnostic feature extraction from the videos. The criteria or methods used under different illumination conditions can be different for real-life applications. Pose and Perspective: Often camera angles focusing on the surveillance area can have substantial impact on the performance of anomaly detection as the appearance of vehicle may change depending on its distance from the cameras. Though object detection accuracy has increased manifolds using deep neural network based methods, still there are challenges in tracking smaller objects. Humans can detect objects at different poses with ease, while machine learning may face difficulties in detecting and tracking the same object under pose variations. Heterogeneous object handling: Anomaly detection frameworks are largely based on modeling the scene and its entities. However, modeling heterogeneous objects in a scene or learning the movement of heterogeneous objects in a scene can be difficult at times. Sparse vs. Dense: The methods used for detecting anomalies in sparse and dense conditions are different. Though some of the methods are good at locating anomalies in sparse condition, dense scene-based methods can generate many false negatives. Curtailed tracks: Since many anomaly detections are based on vehicle trajectories, underlying tracking algorithms are supposed to perform accurately. Even though tracking accuracies have increased in the last decade, many of the existing tracking algorithms do not work under different scenarios. Tracking under occlusion is also another challenge though humans can easily track them visually. Lack of real-life datasets: There is a need for real-life datasets to see the effectiveness of anomaly detection techniques. There are ample scopes and requirements for anomaly detection research based on the gaps discussed earlier. With the advancements in machine learning techniques and affordable hardware, computer vision-based behavior analysis, anomaly detection and anomaly prediction can leapfrog in the coming years. Deep learning-based hybrid frameworks can handle diverse traffic scenarios. This can also help to build fully automatic traffic analysis frameworks capable of reporting events of interest to the stakeholders.

Feature Selection and Fusion Methods

It is also important to detect good features from these videos so that the incident can be identified automatically and accurately. The uncommon behavior of a suspect can be identified only when the features are extracted correctly and according to the type of incident. The special and frequency transform filter will help in identifying the boundaries via wavelet transforms. The Histogram of Gradients will detect the human very efficiently and vehicles in the desired areas. The following are the list of low level and high level feature models used for video surveillance system incident detection.

- Gaussian process regression
- Gaussian Mixture Model (GMM)
- Dynamic Patch Grouping
- Fuzzy clustering Techniques
- Unsupervised Kernel learning
- SVM classifier
- HOG & SVM
- Hidden Markov Model
- KNN
- Convolution Neural Networks

Table 2 shows the summary of existing approaches for accident detection. The current available trained networks in video surveillance systems are not capable to handle multiple incidents (though they use deep convolution networks). The available models of deep learning in this field are still passive. Hence we need to design a new and novel deep neural network models to address these incidents in real-time. The incidents can be any one from the following but not limited to:

1. Vehicle Accidents at public places.
2. Murder in public places through gunshot and knife.
3. Bomb blasts detection.
4. Gang fights/wars in public places.

However, in visual surveillance, primary data is a video which is a sequence of frames. Hence, it is essential to extract the relevant features from the videos as these features become input to the specific technique used in anomaly detection. The choice of feature plays a key role in the capability of detecting specific anomalies. In some methods, preprocessing essentially involves extracting the foreground information and applying specific techniques for finding objects from the foreground. Also, histograms extracted from the pixel level features can become inputs to anomaly detection methods. Some methods use detected objects or object trajectories as inputs to the anomaly detection methods. Deep neural networks (DNN) extract features automatically and used them for anomaly detection. Features are typically in the form of vectors, corresponding to the data. In DNN-based systems, high level features are automatically extracted. Broadly, the features can be classified as object oriented and non-object oriented. Using object oriented features, anomalies can be detected by extracting the objects or trajectories. Objects or trajectories represented in the form of feature descriptors become the data for anomaly detection. In the latter approach, low-level descriptors for pixel or pixel group features, intensities, optical flows, or resultant features from spatio-temporal cubes (STC) have been used for anomaly detection. Some methods use hybrid features for anomaly detections.

Once the incident is classified, the information must be forwarded to next nearest police stations and sub monitoring systems for tracking the perpetrator immediately after the incident.

SECURING THE CCTV DATA

Image/Video Security Challenges

Recently, dissemination and distribution of digital information over open networks using digital imaging and communication technologies provides an essential and cost effective technique invarious applications. The application includes electronic health, copyright protection; secure information in cloud and distributed environments, fingerprinting, remote education etc. However, transmission, storage and sharing of sensitive information over unsecured communication networks are still a challenging issue and required high degree of security and privacy. Watermarking and encryption methods are providing high degree of confidentiality, integrity, availability and authenticity to sensitive data/information. In addition, ownership identification, avoiding detachment, protection against tampering, access control, non-repudiation, indexing and efficient archiving, reducing memory and bandwidth requirements are some of the extra advantages of potential watermarking techniques. Watermarking techniques are domain specific either in spatial or transform domain. The research concluded that the spatial domain watermarking methods i.e. LSB, patchwork, Correlation-based and Spread-spectrum technique, are less robust than transform based techniques. DWT, SVD, DCT, DFT and KLT are some of the potential examples of transform based techniques.

Block-chain for Image/Video Security

This section discusses a decentralized autonomous application for video content storage and transmission using blockchain technology (Secure and scalable data sharing is essential). In recent years blockchain technology has gained much popularity due to its unique features in providing security. They are highly resistant to data modifications i.e. the data cannot be modified once it is created/secured using blockchain mechanism. Bitcoin is among the most successful blockchain mechanism in digital cryptocurrency applications. That is why it is becoming more and more popular in current research trends. These days all innovative applications where insecurity is a major issue this blockchain is being used widely. Violating the cybersecurity rules might also cause some serious problems in the daily routine of human life (misguiding the public) and in some cases, it might lead to deaths. Thus, there is an urgent need to secure video data over surveillance systems. Inspired by the massive success of blockchain in this aspect, this project focuses on understanding the basics to advanced concepts and critical challenges in the fields of computer vision, video surveillance systems and cybersecurity using the blockchain.

At a broad level, blockchains offer a mechanism for people (or entities) that do not know or trust each other to create a shared record of asset ownership. A blockchain is an "open platform", a distributed system where the processes are open to examination and elaboration. It is a ledger of data, replicated across a plurality of computers organized in a Peer to Peer (P2P) network. Thus, a blockchain records the transactions on a multitude of distributed hosts, given that a replicated, de- centralized database effectively eliminates the possibility of global data corruption (deliberate or accidental). The blockchain is a time-stamped database that retains the complete logged history of transactions on the system; each transaction processor on the network or system retains their own local copy of this database and consensus-formation algorithms allow every copy, no matter where such copy is, to remain synchronized. Specifically, a blockchain consists of *blocks* that hold sets of valid transactions; each blockchain block incorporates the hash of the prior block in the blockchain, juxtaposing the two blocks. The linked blocks form a chain. Members of the network are anonymous entities (processes, individuals, or users) known as *nodes*.

CONCLUSION

This chapter discussed the various methods for abnormal behavior detection from on-line/off-line videos. It is an emerging filed in the area of computer vision. This plays a vital role in video surveillance based applications to provide safety for humans at public places such as traffic signals, shopping malls, railway stations, etc. Surveillance cameras are meant to act as digital eyes i.e. watching over activities at public places and provide security. They are used or analyzed only after some incident has happened. Hence this chapter has detailed some of the learning approaches for supervised, semi supervised and unsupervised based models in depth. Machine Learning is also the important concept which is widely used in computer vision for various applications like: Pattern recognition, classification, optimization etc. Chapter has detailed some of them such as convolutional neural network model in depth followed by its variants: LeNet, AlexNet, GoogleNet, ZFNet, ResNet, VGGNet etc. All these are modified versions of normal CNN model. They all are based on AI-Enabled algorithms so that better and fast detection rate can be achieved. Finally it is concluded that there is a huge demand to develop an intelligent video surveillance system which can detect the abnormality or incident dynamically and accordingly raise an alarm to the nearest police stations, hospitals as per requirement. If AI-supported CCTV systems are deployed at commercial and traffic areas then we can easily detect the incidents/crimes and they can be traced in minimal time.

REFERENCES

Ali, H. M., & Alwan, Z. S. (2017). *Car accident detection and notification system using smartphone.* LAP LAMBERT Academic Publishing.

Beygelzimer, A., Dasgupta, S., & Langford, J. (2008). *Importance weighted active learning.* arXiv preprint arXiv:0812.4952.

Bhatti, F., Shah, M. A., Maple, C., & Islam, S. U. (2019). A novel internet of things-enabled accident detection and reporting system for smart city environments. *Sensors (Basel)*, *19*(9), 2071.

Braga & Weisburd. (2015). *Police innovation and crime pre- vention: Lessons learned from police research over the past 20 years.* Academic Press.

Cleveland, W. S., Grosse, E., & Shyu, W. M. (2017). Local regression models. In *Statistical models in S* (pp. 309–376). Routledge.

Coates, A., Ng, A., & Lee, H. (2011). An analysis of single-layer networks in unsupervised feature learning. *Proceedings of the fourteenth international conference on artificial intelligence and statistics*, 215-223.

Cui, Y., Yang, G., Veit, A., Huang, X., & Belongie, S. (2018). Learning to evaluate image captioning. *Proceedings of the IEEE Conference on Computer Vision and Pattern Recognition*, 5804-5812.

Dey, N., & Ashour, A. (Eds.). (2016). *Classification and clustering in biomedical signal processing.* IGI Global.

Dogru, N., & Subasi, A. (2018). Traffic accident detection using random forest classifier. *Proceedings of the 2018 15th Learning and Technology Conference (LT)*, 40-45.

Faiz, A. B., Imteaj, A., & Chowdhury, M. (2015). Smart vehicle accident detection and alarming system using a smartphone. In *2015 International Conference on Computer and Information Engineering (IC-CIE)*, (pp. 66-69). IEEE.

Fogue, M., Garrido, P., Martinez, F. J., Cano, J.-C., Calafate, C. T., & Manzoni, P. (2013). A system for automatic notification and severity estimation of automotive accidents. *IEEE Transactions on Mobile Computing*, *13*(5), 948–963.

Fridell, L. A., & Wycoff, M. A. (Eds.). (2004). *Community policing: The past, present, and future.* Annie E. Casey Foundation and Police Executive Research Forum.

Gill, M. (2006). *CCTV: Is it effective?* Academic Press.

Gu, X., Angelov, P. P., Zhang, C., & Atkinson, P. M. (2018). A massively parallel deep rule-based ensemble classifier for remote sensing scenes. *IEEE Geoscience and Remote Sensing Letters*, *15*(3), 345–349.

Guo, Q., Wang, F., Lei, J., Tu, D., & Li, G. (2016). Convolutional feature learning and Hybrid CNN-HMM for scene number recognition. *Neurocomputing*, *184*, 78–90.

He, K., Zhang, X., Ren, S., & Sun, J. (2016). Deep residual learning for image recognition. *Proceedings of the IEEE conference on computer vision and pattern recognition*, 770-778.

Kang, X., Xiang, X., Li, S., & Benediktsson, J. A. (2017). PCA-based edge-preserving features for hyperspectral image classification. *IEEE Transactions on Geoscience and Remote Sensing*, *55*(12), 7140–7151.

Krizhevsky, A., Sutskever, I., & Hinton, G. E. (2012). *Imagenet classification with deep convolutional neural networks*. Advances in Neural Information Processing Systems.

La Vigne, N. G., Lowry, S. S., Markman, J. A., & Dwyer, A. M. (2011). *Evaluating the use of public surveillance cameras for crime control and prevention*. US Department of Justice, Office of Community Oriented Policing Services. Urban Institute, Justice Policy Center.

LeCun, Jackel, Bottou, Brunot, Cortes, Denker, & Drucker. (1995). Comparison of learning algorithms for handwritten digit recognition. *International Conference on Artificial Neural Networks*, 60, 53-60.

LeCun, Y., Kavukcuoglu, K., & Farabet, C. (2010). Convolutional networks and applications in vision. *Proceedings of 2010 IEEE International Symposium on Circuits and Systems*, 253-256.

Liang. (2015). Automatic Traffic Accident Detection Based on the Internet of Things and Support Vector Machine. *International Journal of Smart Home*, *9*(4), 97–106.

Liu, C., Li, H.-C., Liao, W., Philips, W., & Emery, W. J. (2019). Variational Textured Dirichlet Process Mixture Model with Pairwise Constraint for Unsupervised Classification of Polarimetric SAR Images. *IEEE Transactions on Image Processing*.

Liu, P., Choo, K.-K. R., Wang, L., & Huang, F. (2017). SVM or deep learning? A comparative study on remote sensing image classification. *Soft Computing*, *21*(23), 7053–7065.

Maldonado, A. D., Uusitalo, L., Tucker, A., & Thorsten Blenckner, P. A. (2019). Aguilera, and A. Salmerón. "Prediction of a complex system with few data: Evaluation of the effect of model structure and amount of data with dynamic bayesian network models. *Environmental Modelling & Software*, *118*, 281–297.

National Institute of Justice (NIJ), US Department of Justice, Office of Justice Programs, & United States of America. (2003). CCTV: Constant cameras track violators. *NIJ Journal*, *249*, 16–23.

Niculescu-Mizil, A., & Caruana, R. (2005). Predicting good probabilities with supervised learning. In *Proceedings of the 22nd international conference on Machine learning*, (pp. 625-632). ACM.

Nieto, M. (1997). *Public video surveillance: is it an effective crime prevention tool?* California Research Bureau, California State Library.

Reynolds, D. (2015). Gaussian mixture models. Encyclopedia of Biometrics, 827-832.

Simonyan, K., & Zisserman, A. (2014). *Very deep convolutional networks for large-scale image recognition.* arXiv preprint arXiv:1409.1556.

Skogan, W. G. (2004). Community Policing: Common Impediments to Success: The Past, Present and Future. In *Community Policing: The Past, Present and Future*. The Annie E. Casey Foundation.

Spampinato, G., & Curti, S. (2019). *Method for advanced and low cost cross traffic alert, related processing system, cross traffic alert system and vehicle*. U.S. Patent Application 10/242,272.

Srivastava, Rajitha, & Agarwal. (2017). An efficient image classification using bag-of-words based on SURF and texture features. In *2017 14th IEEE India Council International Conference (INDICON)*, (pp. 1-6). IEEE.

Szegedy, C., Liu, W., Jia, Y., Sermanet, P., Reed, S., Anguelov, D., Erhan, D., Vanhoucke, V., & Rabinovich, A. (2015). Going deeper with convolutions. *Proceedings of the IEEE conference on computer vision and pattern recognition*, 1-9.

Tushara & Vardhini. (2016). Wireless vehicle alert and collision prevention system design using atmel microcontroller. In *2016 International 22 Conference on Electrical, Electronics, and Optimization Techniques (ICEEOT),* (pp. 2784-2787). IEEE.

Yee, T. H., & Lau, P. Y. (2018). Mobile vehicle crash detection system. In *2018 International Workshop on Advanced Image Technology (IWAIT)*, (pp. 1-4). IEEE.

Zeiler, M. D., & Fergus, R. (2014). Visualizing and understanding convolutional networks. In *European conference on computer vision*, (pp. 818-833). Springer.

Zhao, Y. (2000). Mobile phone location determination and its impact on intelligent transportation systems. *IEEE Transactions on Intelligent Transportation Systems*, *1*(1), 55–64.

Zhu & Goldberg. (2009). Introduction to semi-supervised learning. *Synthesis Lectures on Artificial Intelligence and Machine Learning, 3*(1), 1-130.

Zoph, B., & Le, Q. V. (2016). *Neural architecture search with reinforcement learning.* arXiv preprint arXiv:1611.01578.

Chapter 2
Comparative Analysis of Various Soft Computing Technique-Based Automatic Licence Plate Recognition Systems

Nitin Sharma
Chandigarh University, India

Pawan Kumar Dahiya
https://orcid.org/0000-0002-8513-5355
Deenbandhu Chhotu Ram University of Science and Technology, India

B. R. Marwah
Independent Researcher, India

ABSTRACT

Traffic on Indian roads is growing day by day leading to accidents. The intelligent transport system is the solution to resolve the traffic problem on roads. One of the components of the intelligent transportation system is the monitoring of traffic by the automatic licence plate recognition system. In this chapter, a automatic licence plate recognition systems based on soft computing techniques is presented. Images of Indian vehicle licence plates are used as the dataset. Firstly, the licence plate region is extracted from the captured image, and thereafter, the characters are segmented. Then features are extracted from the segmented characters which are used for the recognition purpose. Furthermore, artificial neural network, support vector machine, and convolutional neural network are used and compared for the automatic licence plate recognition. The future scope is the hybrid technique solution to the problem.

DOI: 10.4018/978-1-7998-3299-7.ch002

INTRODUCTION

Traffic turmoil is the major nuisance in a developing country like India with rapid growth in the vehicles on the road, restricted infrastructure, and roads. An intelligent transportation system (ITS) resolves the mentioned issue. ITS execution results in managed traffic, resolved parking issues, automatic toll collection, safety of mankind, traffic law enforcement, etc. (Du, Ibrahim, Shehata, & Badaway, 2012). A country like India where an accident rate is more than one thousand accidents per day, there is a strong need that people on the road to follow the rules and regulations of Indian laws. Furthermore, the long waiting at toll plazas with on engine results not only the misuse of the resources but also wastage of time. To get rid of it is not only the correct recognition of vehicles but also in a very short span of time. In India, there are 462 toll plazas across India. Vehicles waiting queues at these toll plazas result in the hammering of individual time and money. The process of collection of tolls should be fast so that the time and fuel can be saved at toll plazas. An ALPR system is used to resolve the difficulty stated. Although a number of solutions for the stated problem are available still no full-proof solution is available.

Looking into it there is a need to improve upon the present APLR systems. In an ALPR module, the vehicle is identified with its unique licence plate number which is written on both front and the end face of the vehicle. The image carrying the licence plate of the vehicle is used as an input to the system for vehicle identification. From the licence plate region, the characters are segmented. Tremendous work has been done in this direction for the identification of the vehicle on the basis of its licence plate.

In an ALPR system basically, four steps are involved. The first step is to capture the image of a vehicle using a camera. The image can be a still image or it can be extracted frame out of a video. The considered image quality depends upon the camera used and also upon light conditions, weather conditions, licence plates condition, etc. The second stage is to separate out the licence plate region which is an area of interest, in the captured image. The input image is pre-processed by means of traditional pre-processing methods such as binarisation, filtering, thinning, thresholding, line deletion, bounding box extraction, connected component revealing (Yadav, Purwar, & Mittal, 2018). After pre-processing and licence plate region is identified. This is usually done by considering certain features of the licence plate that is its colour, shape, and the probable area of the licence plate. The third step is to segment the characters from the extracted area of interest. Segmentation of characters is usually done by considering width or height or both of the characters, colour information of characters. The segmented characters are further processed to extract their features, which is used as input to the classifier for the recognition of characters and hence the licence plate number (C. E. Anagnostopoulos, 2014). Some classifiers have been used in the literature, such as an artificial neural network (ANN), convolutional neural network (CNN), random forest, support vector machine (SVM), etc. These classifiers perform extremely well for various applications such as stock exchange predictions (Shastri, Roy, & Mittal, 2019), object detection (Kaur et al., 2018), diabetic diagnosis (Hemanth, Anitha, Son, & Mittal, 2018), handwritten character recognition (Yadav et al., 2018), etc. Lastly, the segmented characters are recognized on the basis of the best match of their features with the help of a classifier (Kulkarni, Khatri, P., & Shah, 2009)(Kranthi, Pranathi, & Srisaila, 2011).

Soft computing techniques have been implemented for the ALPR systems in the past (Kamat & Ganesan, 2002). The techniques proposed in the past are applied to different data set under different conditions. The chapter will provide researchers with a comparative analysis of various soft computing techniques when applied to the same data set under the same conditions and to open a number of issues for upcoming research. Here soft computing techniques are suggested for ALPR systems.

The chapter contributes to the following:

- The basics of ALPR systems along with the ANN, SVM, and CNN are discussed.
- The recognition rate for Indian licence plates of implemented ANN, SVM, and CNN based ALPR systems are compared.

The remaining chapter is structured as follows. In section, 2 a typical ALPR system is discussed. Section 3 discusses different ALPR techniques available in the literature. Section 4 discusses the soft computing techniques implemented for the work. Section 5 discusses, the step by step used the methodology to achieve the research objectives. Section 6 discusses obtained results and their discussions along with their comparison. In section 7, discusses future research directions and Section 8, discusses the conclusion of the chapter.

ALPR SYSTEM

An ALPR System firstly uses a camera to capture an image of the vehicle along with licence plate and after that image is processed through a number of preprocessing steps like binarization, filtering, dilation, labelling, histogram before going for the character segmentation. The segmentation of characters is done on the basis of their dimensions that is their height and width. The characters height is nearly the same since the x coordinates of starting pixels of all the characters will be nearly the same except for the tilt cases. Furthermore, the width of characters is also used to separate out them from the whole image. The segmented characters are further processed to extract their features, which is used as input to the classifier for the recognition of characters and hence the licence plate number using the character recognition module. Now the trained classifier such as ANN, SVM, and CNN can be used to recognize the characters (C. E. Anagnostopoulos, 2014). The various steps involved in the process of the ALPR system are presented in the block diagram form in figure 1.

Figure 1. A typical ALPR system

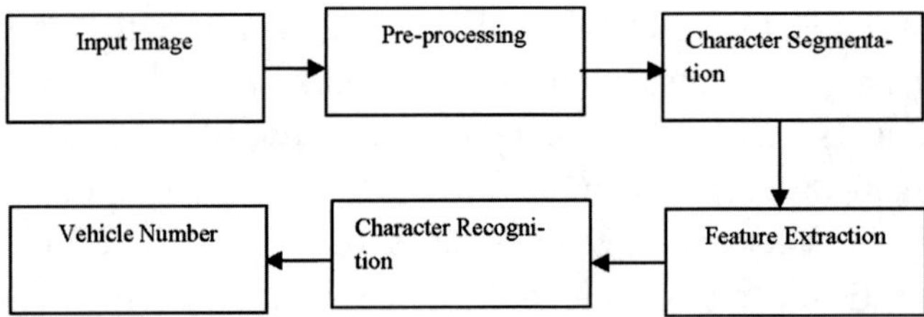

EXISTING ALPR TECHNIQUES

In literature numbers of techniques are presented for the licence plate extraction, character segmentation, and character recognition. The acquired image is searched for the probable region of the licence plate on the basis of certain features such as the colour of licence plate, shape of licence plate or existence of character. These features can be used individually or in a group of two or more for the licence plate region extraction. Adaboosting is a machine learning technique that chooses some of the classifiers out of a set of very large weak classifiers on the basis of their performance and then strong classifier is obtained by combining the individual votes of weak classifier in a weighted way (Zhang, Jia, He, & Wu, 2006) (Louka Dlagnekov, 2004)(L Dlagnekov & Belongie, 2005)(Arth, Limberger, & Bischof, 2007). The various features used as weak classifiers in (Zhang et al., 2006)(L Dlagnekov & Belongie, 2005)(Arth et al., 2007), are Haar-like and gradient density features. After that AdaBoost, a strong classifier is used to detect the licence plate. In (Ho, Lim, & Tay, 2009), two-stage classifiers are used in the first stage classification have the use of Adaboost, while SVM based scale-invariant feature transform descriptor is used as second stage classifier to remove false detection.

In different countries licence plate and characters written on it have a unique colour combination. On the basis of this unique combination, licence plates are extracted. In (Shi, Zhao, & Shen, 2005), pixels are categorized according to illumination in RGB and region of the licence plate is identified and after that region is further verified using width to height ratio. In (F. & H., 2004), the captured image is colour filtered and then binarized by the Niblack technique and finally, licence plate is extracted using blob selection. In (E. R. Lee, Kim, & Kim, 1994), Hue-Lightness-Saturation (HLS) values of the neighbouring pixels are given to ANN to extract the licence plate region. The contour algorithm is useful in finding a close boundary object in an image. In (Megalingam, Krishna, Pillai, & Hakkim, 2010), contour algorithm is used on edging images to detect close boundary objects. In (Parisi, Di Claudio, Lucarelli, & Orlandi, 1998), Discrete Fourier Transform (DFT) analyses the image spectrum to locate the licence plate and characters.

The wavelet transformation technique is used to find the four frequency sub-bands. These sub-bands help in the extraction of licence plate region. In (Hung & Hsieh, 2010), a high-low subband is used for extraction with a 95.33% success rate. Horizontal and vertical gradients from low-high and high-low subbands are used for the licence plate extraction (Y. R. Wang, Lin, & Horng, 2011). Edges are more prominent in the licence plate region. These edges can be found using filtering of images. Sobel operator is used for the detection of the edges (Busch, Domer, Freytag, & Ziegler, 1998)(Sarfraz, Ahmed, & Ghazi, 2003)(Jiang, Mekonnen, Merkebu, & Gebrehiwot, 2012)(Anju & Budhiraja, 2011). Moreover, (Li, Zeng, Zhou, & Dong, 2008) propose texture greyscale jumping and edge density based removal of invalid edges technique. In (Nathan, Ramkumar, & Priya, 2004)(Le & Li, 2006) weight assignment scheme is applied after filtering to locate a probable region. In (Seetharaman, Sathyakhala, Vidhya, & Sunder, 2004) ANN is used after finding edges through filtering. Edge detection, thresholding, binarization, and CCA are carried out in (Thome, Vacavant, Robinault, & Miguet, 2011). The skeleton extraction algorithm is described which is applied after applying Sobel operator in (Jiao, Ye, & Huang, 2009). Another filtering operator canny with the adaptive binary approach is used for the unclear images in (Zhao, Ma, Han, Yang, & Wang, 2012). Gabor filter can be used in unlimited numbers of directions and scales for analysing the texture. In (Kahraman, Kurt, & Gökmen, 2003), the input image is first convolved with 2D Gabor filter and the result is used for the extraction of licence plate.

Fuzzy Logic is used for the extraction of a licence plate by firstly forming fuzzy sets based on the Hue-Saturation-Intensity of the image and then finding the degree of matching. In (Chang, Chen, Chung, Chen, & Member, 2004)(F. Wang et al., 2008), the input RGB image is transformed into the Hue-Saturation-Intensity (HSI). After that fuzzy version of H, S, and I are mapped to find the degree of belonging to the licence plate. Distributed Genetic Algorithm (GA) is used for the licence plate extraction in (Kim, Kim, & Kim, 1996). Firstly image is changed from the RGB to HLS colour space. Then GA is applied which results in improving the processing time. Horizontal lines of the images are scanned to find the contrast changes. The number of times contrast changes in a row is used for histogram analysis of the captured image is used to extract the licence plate region. Edges map is used to find the horizontal and vertical projections in (H. J. Lee, Chen, & Wang, 2004)(Huang, Chen, Chang, & Sandnes, 2009).

Morphological operations are used for extracting boundaries in the image, as these boundaries are helpful in the description and representation of licence plate region (Wu, Chen, Wu, & Shen, 2006) (Mahini, Kasaei, Dorri, & Dorri, 2006). In (Xiong & Huang, 2009), compound mathematical morphology technique is used for the extraction of licence plate. In (Khan & Ali, 2007), edge detection is done after that using morphological operations unwanted edges are removed. Morphological operator dilation is used for the extraction of the licence plate (Wanniarachchi, Sonnadara, & Jayananda, 2007). In the multi-clustering approach, the first image is enhanced by using a fixed filter, minimum filter. Then the image is transformed into blob objects. The clustering technique is applied to identify the cluster of blobs on the basis of their location, height, and width (Abdullah & Khalid, 2006). Sliding Concentric Window (SCW) technique considers two concentric windows of different sizes for the first pixel of the image. After that ratio of statistical measurements of windows is compared with a threshold to find whether the pixel belongs to the region of interest or not. In (Kaushik Deb, Chae, & Jo, 2009) SCW and histogram are used for licence plate detection. Vector Quantization encoding is also useful in finding the contents of image regions that can be used to extract licence plate. In (Zunino & Rovetta, 2000), a vector quantization based method is proposed to extract the region of licence plate.

Character segmentation is complex due to one or many reasons such as stuck characters, noise in an image, frame of the plate, plate rotation, illumination variance, rivet, space mark, and mud-covered plates. Sometimes, before going for segmentation, tilt correction is also required. This improves the rate of segmentation. Numbers of tilt correction methods are reported on the licence plate. In (Pan, Yan, & Xiao, 2008), tilt correction using the least mean square method is proposed. In (Pan, Xiong, & Yan, 2009) a Karhunen-Loeve (KL) transformation based tilt correction method is applied to the image to settle the coordinates of character into two dimensions non-zero mean covariance matrix. In (K. Deb, Vavilin, Kim, Kim, & Jo, 2010), straight-line fitting method along with projection points variation minimization are used for tilt correction. CCA is done to find the pixels having a similar intensity and to group them into different contours. Unwanted contours are removed by prior knowledge like the gap between characters, linearity, and parallelism (Lekhana, G. C. & Srikantaswamy, 2012)(Li et al., 2008)(Thome et al., 2011) (F. Wang et al., 2008). Sometimes characters occupy more than one connected components and in that case, the extended bounding box of the components is prepared to do segmentation of characters as in (Shapiro & Gluhchev, 2004). False alarming is reduced by applying vector quantization before CCA for better results of character segmentation (Nijhuis et al., 1995). Fuzzy logic based on vertical projection is used for the character segmentation of licence plate region (Zhao et al., 2012). In (Jiao et al., 2009), the proposed algorithm is used to quantize the licence plate extracted region into 256 grey levels and then a morphological operator is used for the character segmentation.

Horizontal and vertical histograms are very useful in the process of character segmentation from the extracted licence plate (Shi et al., 2005)(Busch et al., 1998)(Anju & Budhiraja, 2011)(Huang et al., 2009) (Xiong & Huang, 2009)(Chen, Liu, & Chang, 2009). In (Duan, Du, Phuoc, & Hoang, 2005) horizontal histogram is useful to find and segment rows in licence plates having two-rows. Vertical histogram of extracted licence plate image along with prior information is used for the character segmentation (Sarfraz et al., 2003)(Shan B., 2011). The clustering technique, along with a horizontal histogram is used for character segmentation (Abdullah & Khalid, 2006). Hough transformation is a feature extraction technique. This technique is used to detect the lines in an image for segmenting the characters. In (Pan et al., 2008)(Pan et al., 2009) horizontal histogram is used for horizontal segmentation of each block and then Hough Transform is used to remove the incorrect sub-regions. Hough transform based horizontal as well as vertical segmentation is performed in (Vishwanath, Somasundaram, Baburajani, & Nallaperumal, 2012). Binarization is a technique used for segmentation but sometimes dirt presence may cause failure in determining the object size, object connection, and even binarization poor results are obtained. Under such circumstances, the proposed technique in (Guo & Liu, 2008) based on hybrid binarization gives better results. Prior information about the width of the characters is stored in the database which is further used for the character segmentation (H. J. Lee et al., 2004).

The function of sliding concentric windows in the character extraction section, the same can be used for character segmentation. In (C. N. E. Anagnostopoulos, Anagnostopoulos, Loumos, & Kayafas, 2006), the SCW technique is used for the character segmentation. In Window scanning method input image is partitioned into a fixed size. Furthermore mean value of image partition is determine and on the basis of the mean value they determine whether they are part of the character or not(Matas & Zimmermann, 2005).

A number of recognition techniques have been proposed in the literature. The correlation function is used to find the similarity between the vectors of two licence plates. This technique is used to recognize the licence plate for monitoring the traffic (Busch et al., 1998). Numbers of features are associated with each character, which differentiates them from each other. Gabor filter is used to extract the features in (Hu, Zhao, Yang, & Wang, 2002) and the same are used for the recognition of the characters. Other features such as projection, perimeter distance and direction contribution density are used for character recognition (Yan, Hongqing, Jilin, & Langang, 2001). Characters are recognized by having prior knowledge of letters and numbers orientation in (Rahman, Badawy, Tn, Radmanesh, & Tp, 2003). In (Zhao et al., 2012), a fuzzy-based character recognition method is proposed.

OCR is the simplest technique for the recognition of characters (Tran Duc Duan, Duong Anh Duc, & Tran, 2004)(Anju & Budhiraja, 2011)(Zunino & Rovetta, 2000). OCR based on Hidden Markov Model is used for the recognition of characters in (Duan et al., 2005). Characters are categorized into groups using the Euler number. Furthermore, on the basis of similarity or difference in their physical appearance and template matching, groups are divided into subgroups. Finally, the physical characteristics of each character that differentiates it from other characters are used to recognize the character (Choubey & Sinha, 2011). Template matching for character recognition is a simple uncomplicated and trustworthy technique and it is used in (Megalingam et al., 2010)(Sarfraz et al., 2003).

The earlier discussed systems are based on different methodologies but still, it is a really challenging task as some of the factors like high speed of the vehicle, non-uniform vehicle number plate, language of vehicle number and different lighting conditions can affect a lot in the overall recognition rate. Most of the systems work under these limitations. After surveying the above-discussed papers, the following shortcomings are identified:

- Non-Standardized Licence Plates
- Noise Removal in Real-Time Application
- Self Dependency of Features Used in Salient Feature-Based Detection
- Quality of Images in Real-Time Environment.
- Recognition of Plate in Case Colour of Vehicle and Plate is the same.
- Image Blurring and Illumination Variance in Real-Time Environment.
- Multiple Plates in One Image/Frame

The above-mentioned shortcomings are found on the basis of the literature being surveyed.

VARIOUS IMPLEMENTED ALPR TECHNIQUES

The roadside cameras are used to take the image or video of the vehicle with its number plate which is printed on both the front and backside of the vehicles. Here, in the implemented work, the following steps of prepossessing are involved. Firstly, the input image is converted into the black and white one, then with the help of the Sobel filter, the edges are found. After that, the dilation operation is performed on the image with the square as the structuring element. Thereafter, holes in the image are filled and the connected components are found and labelled. The horizontal histogram is used to find out a number of lines and the vertical histogram is used to find the gap between the characters which is used to find the number of characters in the region. After that, same value pixels are analysed to find the connected components which are further used for their segmentation and cropping. The extracted features of the segmented alphabets and numerals are further processed by the recognition module. A number of recognition techniques are used in the literature for this purpose. The three soft computing techniques implemented are explained in the subsections.

NEURAL NETWORK

An ANN is motivated by the human being's brains. Just like the neuron is the basic building block of the human brains, the ANN model is having artificial neurons as its building block. One neuron may have input form many inputs. The inputs are weighted and summed to get the activation value. The activation value act as input to activation function. The activation value of jth neuron is obtained by equation (1):

$$P_j(t) = \sum_i X_i(t) W_{ij} \tag{1}$$

Where,

$P_j(t)$ is the activation value of the j_{th} node.
$X_i(t)$ is the output of the predecessor nodes which is acting as input to the jth node of the network.
W_{ij} is the interconnection branch weight the i_{th} and j_{th} node

The activation value evaluated by equation (1) acts as input to activation function which can be sigmoid, binary step, logistic, etc. The output final output of jth node is given by activation function. The interconnection weights are updated during the training period. Upgradation of weights depends upon the learning rate parameter and the loss function. The loss function depends on the difference between target and actual output.

The pseudo-code for the backpropagation neural network is as follows:

```
Procedure
Initialize
                Number of iterations
Learning rate parameter
Number of layers
         Input layer nodes count
Hidden layers node count
Output layer node count
Initial Weights
While (termination condition do not meet) do Training
                Feedforward ()
                Backpropagation of error ()
                Weight up gradation ()
 end_while
                Validation ()
```

Support Vector Machine

It is a supervised machine learning method that trained the model for the classification or regression purpose using the training data. The labelled training data is used to train the SVM model. After the training is over module can be used to classify a new testing input (Cortes & Vapnik, 1995). An SVM model is an illustration of the data sets as points in space. These points are mapped in such a way that the data set belonging to different categories are apart as much as possible. Once the SVM model is trained and a new input data is given as input then it also mapped into the same space and on the bases of their position in the space, they are categorized into one of the categories.

The SVM classifier separates the data belonging to two different classes by a hyperplane. The feature vector xi and their class labels yi are used as training data. For some dimension d, the $xj \in R^d$, and the $yj = \pm 1$. The equation of a hyperplane is given by equation (2).

$$f\left(x\right) = x'\beta + b = 0 \tag{2}$$

where β□$\in R^d$ and b is a real number.

In the classification problems, there is a need to find the best separating hyperplane which separates out the points in the space and the distance of the hyperplane from either of the two category points in the space is equal. The coefficient b of the hyperplane equation is evaluated such that $||\beta||$ is minimized and all data points (x_j, y_j) satisfy equation (3).

$$yjf\left(xj\right) \geq 1 \tag{3}$$

The x_j which are on the boundaries and satisfy the equation (4) are the support vectors.

$$yjf\left(xj\right) = 1 \tag{4}$$

The classification of a vector z is done using equation (5).

$$class\left(z\right) = sign\left(z'\beta + b\right) = sign\left(f\left(z\right)\right) \tag{5}$$

where f(z) is the classification score and represents the distance z is from the decision boundary. A set of support vectors can also be used to solve multiclass classifications problems. (Hsu & Lin, 2002).

The pseudo-code for SVM is given as under:

```
Procedure
Initialize
         Kernel function
         Learning rate parameter
         Initial Weight Vector
While (termination condition do not meet) do Training
                Classification score ()
                Weight Vector_bias_up gradation ()
   end_while
                Validation ()
```

Convolutional Neural Network

CNN is a multi-layer arrangement. In CNN, first layer is fed by the image to be classified. In the second layer the input image is convolved with the filter masks. The more is the filter mask used the more is the extracted feature of the input image. Due to the discrete convolution is evaluated between the input image and the filters it is called a convolutional layer (Lecun, Bottou, Bengio, & Haffner, 1998). In CNN it is conventional to have Rectified Linear Units Layer (ReLU) after every conventional layer. This is to have nonlinearity in the system (LeCun, Bengio, & Hinton, 2015). The ReLU layer makes all negative values to zero while all positive values are considered as it is (Menotti, Chiachia, Falcão, & Oliveira Neto, 2014), i.e.,

$$f\left(x\right) = \begin{cases} x, x \geq 0 \\ 0, x < 0 \end{cases} \tag{6}$$

The pooling layer is used as the next layer, it is used to do downsampling. Either max pooling or average pooling is used in conventional CNN. The fully connected layer is the fifth layer of the architecture. The sixth layer and seventh layers are softmax and classification layers respectively.

The pseudo-code for CNN is given as under:

```
Procedure
Initialize
Input Layer
                 Convolution2dLayer
                  Relu Layer
                   MaxPooling2dLayer
                   FullyConnected Layer
                   Softmax Layer
                   Classification Layer
Number of Epochs
                 Initial Learning rate
While (termination condition do not meet) do Training
                 Feedforward ()
                 Backpropagation of error ()
                 Weight upgadation ()
end_while
                 Validation ()
```

METHODOLOGY

In India, there is no standard font used for printing the licence plate. On roads one can see a number of fonts used to form the licence plates, such as Times New Roman, Verdana, Lucida console, Cambria, Consolas, Calibri, Lucida bright, Rockwell, Tahoma, Arial, bookman old style, etc. These varieties of fonts result in different features of the character when used with different font. Thus for training the model's datasets with different font types are used. Some samples of the testing dataset are shown in figure 2.

Figure 2. Testing licence plates

Since the licence plate number consists of both alphabets and numerals. So we have used two different modules for alphabets and numerals. Furthermore, the data set used for their training purpose is also separate. We have used 1144 samples of the characters and 440 samples of numerals for training purposes. The samples are processed for extraction of their features. Once the features have been extracted the training of the recognition module is performed. After that trained modules are given Indian licence plates for the recognition. NN, SVM, and CNN soft computing techniques are used for recognition. These modules are discussed below:

NN Module

NN module contains two separate backpropagation neural networks. The extracted feature of the testing image is given as the input to the backpropagation neural networks. One NN is trained for English alphabets and The second NN is trained for numerals. Both networks have input layer and two hidden layers with 35, 200, and 100 neurons each. The number of output nodes is 26 and 10 for the alphabets and numerals NN respectively. The training data of 1144 alphabets and 440 numerals are used for their training. The trained NNs are tested for 80 Indian licence plate recognition and recognition in percentage for alphabets and numerals are 91% and 96.67% respectively, while the overall recognition rate obtained is 94.4%.

SVM Module

The segmented characters are pre-processed and 25 features are extracted for each character. The SVM models are trained using these extracted features. The trained SVM models are tested for 80 Indian licence plate recognition and recognition in percentage for alphabets and numerals are 93% and 97% respectively, while the overall recognition rate obtained is 95.6%.

CNN Module

The segmented image of size 28*28 is given as input to the primary layer of the CNN module. The next layer consists of 20 filters with size 9*9 each. The input image is convolved with each of the filters to extract the features. Next, ReLU layer performs the threshold function which replaces all negative elements by zero to maintain the nonlinearity in the elements. The function of pooling layer is to locate the element having the highest value in the pool of size 2*2. The fifth layer and sixth layer are fully connected and a softmax layer. The seventh layer is used for categorization and is known as the classification layer. The recognition rates obtained are 94% for the alphabets and 97.33% is for the numerals with an overall recognition rate of 96%.

RESULTS AND DISCUSSIONS

A set of Eighty Indian licence plate images was used to run the algorithm . The outputs gained at different step is mentioned below. The picture of the licence plate used as an input is shown in figure 3(a). Then the entered image is converted into a greyscale image as shown in figure 3(b).

Figure 3. Car image with licence plate (a) Input car image, (b) greyscale image

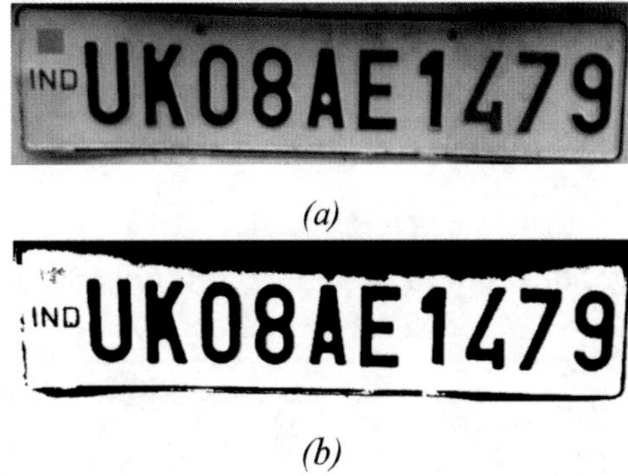

The edges of the input image find out by using Sobel filter. The filtered image is shown in figure 4(a). After that, the filtered image is intensity scaled. Figure 4(b) is the outcome of the intensity scaling pre-processing step. Further horizontal lines are detected in the image as given in figure 4(c). The horizontal line image is subtracted from the intensity scaled image. The resultant image is shown in figure 4(d).

Figure 4. Images of various steps involved in processing (a) BW image with detected edges, (b) Image with scaled intensities, (c) Image with detected horizontal lines detection, (d) Subtracted image

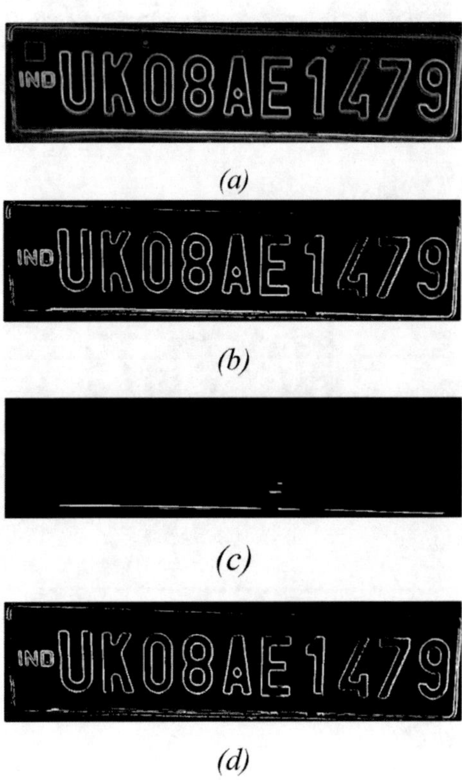

Now the binary image is searched for the holes and the holed are filled. The hole filled image is shown in figure 5(a). The next step to finding the connected components in the image and to label them. To separate the characters more accurately the thinning of the connected components is performed and result of this is shown in figure 5(b). Now all the regions having pixels less more than 300 discarded and the obtained image is shown in figure 5(c).

Figure 5. Images of various steps involved in processing (a) Region filled image, (b) Image of the connected components after thining, (c) Removal of the region

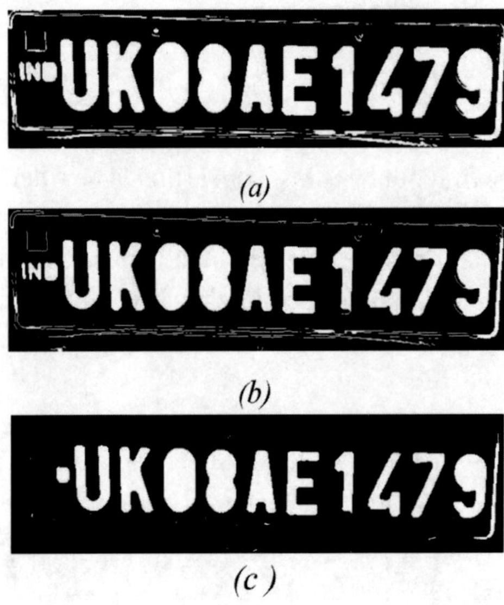

Figure 6. Image of Segmented characters of Licence plate

UK08AE1479

Figure 7. Recognized licence plate

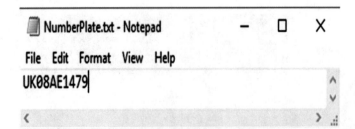

NumberPlate.txt - Notepad

File Edit Format View Help

UK08AE1479

Out of all the connected components are desired characters of licence plate are identified on the basis of the coordinates of their starting pixel, their height, and width. These identified characters are segmented using further processing, the segmented characters obtained are shown in figure 6.

The segmented characters need to be recognized for the recognition of the segmented characters three soft computing techniques are used. The segmented characters are given as the input to the NN, SVM and CNN based classifiers for the recognition of the characters. The recognized licence plate as the output from the ALPR system is as shown in figure 7.

MATLAB 2017a is used for the implementation of soft computing based modules. The 80 Indian licence plates have been tested using the trained network and the obtained results are presented in Table 1.

Table 1. The Recognition rate of implemented techniques

Recognition Based on	Recognition Rate					
	Recognized Alphabets		Recognized Numerals		Overall	
	Out of 320 Alphabets	in %	Out of 480 Numerals	in %	Out of 800 Characters	In %
NN	291	90.93	464	96.67	755	94.37
SVM	299	93.43	466	97.08	765	95.62
CNN	301	94.06	467	97.29	768	96

For NN the recognition rate obtained for alphabets, numerals are 90.93%, and 94.37 respectively. SVM gives recognition rate for alphabets, numerals as 93.43%, and 97.08% respectively. For CNN the recognition rate obtained for alphabets, numerals are 94.06%, and 97.29% respectively. The overall recognition rate is 94.37%, 95.62%, and 96% of the NN, SVM, and CNN based ALPR systems respectively. The overall accuracy of the three developed ALPR systems are compared in the graph as shown in figure 8 given below:

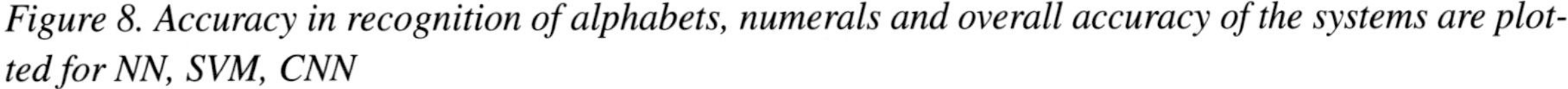

Figure 8. Accuracy in recognition of alphabets, numerals and overall accuracy of the systems are plotted for NN, SVM, CNN

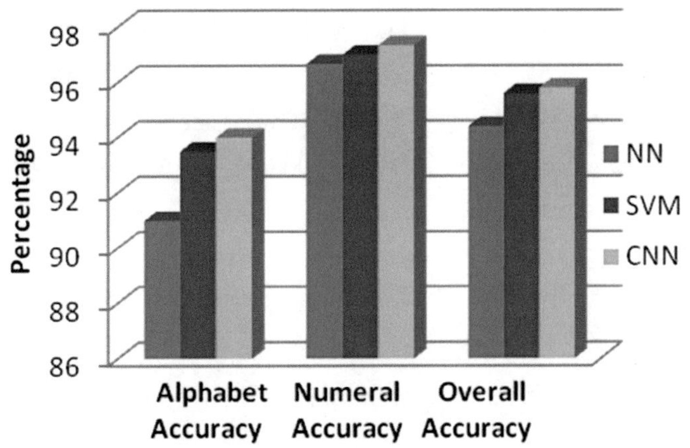

FUTURE RESEARCH DIRECTIONS

In India, the accuracy of recognition is low with reason for the non-standard format of the licence plates. The accuracy obtained by soft computing techniques discussed are good but to achieve 100% accuracy more work to be done. Nature inspiring techniques can also be a good option for the improvement of the recognition rate. Soft computing techniques such as Biogeography Based Optimization (BBO), Bacterial Foraging Optimization (BFO), and Shuffled Frog Leaping (SFL) can be used for ALPR system implementation by researchers in future. A further hybrid of ANN with SVM, CNN with SVM can be tested by researchers in future.

CONCLUSION

In this chapter, ALPR systems are discussed. A review of the existing ALPR system is done. Existing techniques used for the licence plate extraction along with character segmentation and recognition are also disused in detail. Various problems faced and highlighted by different authors are also discussed. Furthermore, NN, SVM, and CNN based ALPR systems are presented. CNN based ALPR system is having edge over other two soft computing techniques. The recognition rate obtained for the CNN based ALPR system is better at 1.63% and 0.38% than the NN and SVM based ALPR system respectively.

REFERENCES

Abdullah, S., Khalid, M., Yusof, R., & Omar, K. (2006). License Plate Recognition Using Multi-Cluster And Multilayer Neural Networks. *Information And Communication Technologies*, *1*(April), 1818–1823. doi:10.1109/ICTTA.2006.1684663

Anagnostopoulos, C. E. (2014). License Plate Recognition : A breif tutorial. *IEEE Transactions on Intelligent Transportation Systems Magazine*, *6*(1), 59–67. doi:10.1109/MITS.2013.2292652

Anagnostopoulos, C. N. E., Anagnostopoulos, I. E., Loumos, V., & Kayafas, E. (2006). A License Plate-Recognition Algorithm for Intelligent Transportation System Applications. *IEEE Transactions on Intelligent Transportation Systems*, *7*(3), 377–392. doi:10.1109/TITS.2006.880641

Anju, & Budhiraja, S. (2011). A Review of License Plate Detection and Recognition Techniques. *National Workshop Cum Conference on Recent Trends in Mathematics and Computing*.

Arth, C., Limberger, F., & Bischof, H. (2007). Real-Time License Plate Recognition on an Embedded DSP-Platform. In *IEEE Conference Computer Vision Pather Recognition* (pp. 1–8). 10.1109/CVPR.2007.383412

Busch, C., Domer, R., Freytag, C., & Ziegler, H. (1998). Feature based recognition of traffic video streams for online route tracing. In *IEEE Vehicular Technology Conference* (pp. 1790–1794). 10.1109/VETEC.1998.686064

Chang, S., Chen, L., Chung, Y., Chen, S., & Member, S. (2004). *Automatic License Plate Recognition*. Academic Press.

Chen, Z., Liu, C., & Chang, F. (2009). *Automatic License-Plate Location and Recognition Based on Feature Salience*. Academic Press.

Choubey, S., & Sinha, G. R. (2011). Pixel Distribution Density based character recognition For Vehicle License Plate. In *IEEE 3rd International Conference on Electronics Computer Technology* (Vol. 5, pp. 26–30). 10.1109/ICECTECH.2011.5941950

Cortes, C., & Vapnik, V. (1995). Support-Vector Networks. *Machine Learning*, *20*(3), 273–297. doi:10.1007/BF00994018

Deb, K., Chae, H.-U., & Jo, K.-H. (2009). Vehicle license plate detection method based on sliding concentric windows and histogram. *Journal of Computers*, *4*(8), 771–777. doi:10.4304/jcp.4.8.771-777

Deb, K., Vavilin, A., Kim, J.-W., Kim, T., & Jo, K.-H. (2010). Projection and least square fitting with perpendicular offsets based vehicle license plate tilt correction. *Proceedings of the SICE Annual Conference*, 3291–3298.

Dlagnekov, L. (2004). *License Plate Detection Using AdaBoost*. Computer Science and Engineering Dept.

Dlagnekov, L., & Belongie, S. (2005). *Recognizing Cars*. Dept. Computer Science Engineering, University. California, San Diego, Tech. Rep. CS2005-0833.

Du, S., Ibrahim, M., Shehata, M., & Badaway, W. (2012). Automatic License Plate Recognition (ALPR): A State-of-the-Art Review. *IEEE Transactions on Circuits and Systems for Video Technology*, *23*(2), 311–325. doi:10.1109/TCSVT.2012.2203741

Duan, T. D., Du, T. L. H., Phuoc, T. V., & Hoang, N. V. (2005). Building an Automatic Vehicle License-Plate Recognition System. *International Conference in Computer Science - RIVF'05,* 59–63.

Duan, T. D., Duc, D. A., & Tran, L. H. D. (2004). Combining Hough Transform and Contour Algorithm for Detecting Vehicles' License-Plates. In *International Symposium on Intelligent Multimedia Video Speech Processing* (pp. 747–750). Academic Press.

F., A., & H., N. (2004). Automatic Licence Plate Recognition System. In *AFRICON Conference Africa* (p. Vol. 1, pp 45–50). Academic Press.

Guo, J. M., & Liu, Y. F. (2008). License plate localization and character segmentation with feedback self-learning and hybrid binarization techniques. *IEEE Transactions on Vehicular Technology*, *57*(3), 1417–1424. doi:10.1109/TVT.2007.909284

Hemanth, D. J., Anitha, J., Son, L. H., & Mittal, M. (2018). Diabetic Retinopathy Diagnosis from Retinal Images Using Modified Hopfield Neural Network. *Journal of Medical Systems*, *42*(12), 247. doi:10.100710916-018-1111-6 PMID:30382410

Ho, W. T., Lim, H. W., & Tay, Y. H. (2009). Two-stage license plate detection using gentle adaboost and SIFT-SVM. In *Proceedings - 2009 1st Asian Conference on Intelligent Information and Database Systems, ACIIDS 2009* (pp. 109–114). 10.1109/ACIIDS.2009.25

Hsu, C. W., & Lin, C. J. (2002). A comparison of methods for multiclass support vector machines. *IEEE Transactions on Neural Networks*, *13*(2), 415–425. doi:10.1109/72.991427 PMID:18244442

Hu, P., Zhao, Y., Yang, Z., & Wang, J. (2002). Recognition of gray character using gabor filters. In *5th International Conference on Information Fusion, FUSION 2002* (*Vol. 1*, pp. 419–424). Academic Press.

Huang, Y. P., Chen, C. H., Chang, Y. T., & Sandnes, F. E. (2009). An intelligent strategy for checking the annual inspection status of motorcycles based on license plate recognition. *Expert Systems with Applications*, *36*(5), 9260–9267. doi:10.1016/j.eswa.2008.12.006

Hung, K., & Hsieh, C. (2010). *A Real-Time Mobile Vehicle License Plate Detection and Recognition.* Academic Press.

Jiang, D., Mekonnen, T. M., Merkebu, T. E., & Gebrehiwot, A. (2012). Car Plate Recognition System. In *IEEE International Conference on Intelligent Networks and Intelligent Systems* (pp. 9–12). IEEE.

Jiao, J., Ye, Q., & Huang, Q. (2009). A configurable method for multi-style license plate recognition. *Pattern Recognition*, *42*(3), 358–369. doi:10.1016/j.patcog.2008.08.016

Kahraman, F., Kurt, B., & Gökmen, M. (2003). License Plate Character Segmentation Based on the Gabor Transform and Vector Quantization. In *International Symposium on Computer and Information Sciences*. (pp. 381–388). Springer. 10.1007/978-3-540-39737-3_48

Kamat, V., & Ganesan, S. (2002). An efficient implementation of the Hough transform for detecting vehicle license plates using DSP'S. In *Real-Time Technology and Applications Symposium* (pp. 58–59). IEEE.

Kaur, B., Sharma, M., Mittal, M., Verma, A., Goyal, L. M., & Hemanth, D. J. (2018). An improved salient object detection algorithm combining background and foreground connectivity for brain image analysis. *Computers & Electrical Engineering*, *71*, 692–703. doi:10.1016/j.compeleceng.2018.08.018

Khan, N. Y., & Ali, N. (2007). *Distance and Color Invariant Automatic License Plate Recognition System*. Academic Press.

Kim, S. K., Kim, D. W., & Kim, H. J. (1996). A Recognition of Vehicle Licence Plate Using A Genetic Algorithm Based Segmentation. In *Proceedings of 3rd IEEE International Conference on Image Processing* (pp. 661–664). IEEE.

Kranthi, S., Pranathi, K., & Srisaila, A. (2011). Automatic Number Plate Recognition. *International Journal of Advance Technology*, *2*(3), 408–422.

Kulkarni, P., Khatri, A. P. B., & Shah, K. (2009). Automatic Number Plate Recognition (ANPR). In *2009 19th International Conference Radioelektronika* (pp. 111–114). IEEE.

Le, W., & Li, S. (2006). A hybrid license plate extraction method for complex scenes. In *Proceedings - International Conference on Pattern Recognition* (Vol. 2, pp. 324–327). Academic Press.

LeCun, Y., Bengio, Y., & Hinton, G. (2015). Deep learning. *Nature*, *521*(7553), 436–444. doi:10.1038/nature14539 PMID:26017442

Lecun, Y., Bottou, L., Bengio, Y., & Haffner, P. (1998). Gradient based learning applied to document recognition. *Proceedings of the IEEE*, *86*(11), 2278–2324. doi:10.1109/5.726791

Lee, E. R., Kim, P. K., & Kim, H. J. (1994). Automatic Recognition of a Car Licence Plate using Colour Image Processing. In *Ist International Conference on Image Processing* (Vol. 2, pp. 301–305). 10.1109/ICIP.1994.413580

Lee, H. J., Chen, S. Y., & Wang, S. Z. (2004). Extraction and recognition of license plates of motorcycles and vehicles on highways. *Proceedings - International Conference on Pattern Recognition, 4*, 356–359.

Lekhana, G. C., & Srikantaswamy, R. (2012). Real Time License Plate Recognition System. *International Journal of Advanced Technology & Engineering Research, 2*(4), 5–9.

Li, B., Zeng, Z., Zhou, J., & Dong, H. (2008). An Algorithm for License Plate Recognition Using Radial Basis Function Neural Network. In *International Symposium on Computer Science and Computational Technology* (pp. 569–572). 10.1109/ISCSCT.2008.272

Mahini, H., Kasaei, S., Dorri, F., & Dorri, F. (2006). An efficient features-based license plate localization method. In *Proceedings - International Conference on Pattern Recognition* (Vol. 2, pp. 841–844). 10.1109/ICPR.2006.239

Matas, J., & Zimmermann, K. (2005). Unconstrained licence plate and text localization and recognition. In *IEEE Conference on Intelligent Transportation Systems, Proceedings, ITSC* (Vol. Sept., pp. 225–230). 10.1109/ITSC.2005.1520111

Megalingam, R. K., Krishna, P., Pillai, V. A., & Hakkim, R. V. I. (2010). Extraction of License Plate Region in Automatic License Plate Recognition. In *International Conference on Mechanical and Electrical Technology (ICMET 2010)* (pp. 496–501). 10.1109/ICMET.2010.5598409

Menotti, D., Chiachia, G., Falcão, A. X., & Oliveira Neto, V. J. (2014). Vehicle license plate recognition with random convolutional networks. In *Vehicle license plate recognition with random convolutional networks. In 2014 27th SIBGRAPI Conference on Graphics, Patterns and Images* (pp. 298–303). 10.1109/SIBGRAPI.2014.52

Nathan, V. S. L., Ramkumar, J., & Priya, S. K. (2004). New Approaches for License Plate Recognition System. In *International Conference on Intelligent Sensing and Information Process* (pp. 149–152). Academic Press.

Nijhuis, J. A. G., Ter Brugge, M. H., Helmholt, K. A., Pluim, J. P. W., Spaanenburg, L., Venema, R. S., & Westenberg, M. A. (1995). Car license plate recognition with neural networks and fuzzy logic. In *Proceedings of ICNN'95-International Conference on Neural Networks* (Vol. 5, pp. 2232–2236). IEEE. 10.1109/ICNN.1995.487708

Parisi, R., Di Claudio, E. D., Lucarelli, G., & Orlandi, G. (1998). Car plate recognition by neural networks and image processing. In *IEEE International Symposium on Circuits System* (Vol. 3, pp. 195–198). 10.1109/ISCAS.1998.703970

Rahman, C. A., Badawy, W., Tn, C., Radmanesh, A., & Tp, C. (2003). *A Real Time Vehicle's License Plate Recognition System*. Academic Press.

Sarfraz, M., Ahmed, M. J., & Ghazi, S. A. (2003). Saudi Arabian License Plate Recognition System. In *IEEE International Conference on Electronic Circuit system* (pp. 898–901). IEEE.

Seetharaman, V., Sathyakhala, A., Vidhya, N. L. S., & Sunder, P. (2004). License plate recognition system using hybrid neural networks. In IEEE Annual Meetig Fuzzy Information (pp. 363–366). doi:10.1109/NAFIPS.2004.1336309

Sen Pan, M., Xiong, Q., & Yan, J. B. (2009). A new method for correcting vehicle license plate tilt. *International Journal of Automation and Computing*, *6*(2), 210–216. doi:10.100711633-009-0210-8

Sen Pan, M., Yan, J. B., & Xiao, Z. H. (2008). Vehicle license plate character segmentation. *International Journal of Automation and Computing*, *5*(4), 425–432. doi:10.100711633-008-0425-0

Shan, B. (2011). Vehicle License Plate Recognition Based on Text-line Construction and Multilevel RBF Neural Network. *Journal of Computers (Taiwan)*, *6*(2), 246–253. doi:10.4304/jcp.6.2.246-253

Shapiro, V., & Gluhchev, G. (2004). Multinational license plate recognition system: Segmentation and classification. In *Proceedings - International Conference on Pattern Recognition* (Vol. 4, pp. 352–355). Academic Press.

Shastri, M., Roy, S., & Mittal, M. (2019). *Stock Price Prediction using Artificial Neural Model: An Application of Big Data*. ICST Transactions on Scalable Information Systems.

Shi, X., Zhao, W., & Shen, Y. (2005). Automatic License Plate Recognition System Based on Color Image Processing. In *International Conference on Computational Science and Its Applications* (pp. 1159–1168). 10.1007/11424925_121

Thome, N., Vacavant, A., Robinault, L., & Miguet, S. (2011). A cognitive and video-based approach for multinational License Plate Recognition. *Machine Vision and Applications*, *22*(2), 389–407. doi:10.100700138-010-0246-3

Vishwanath, N., Somasundaram, S., Baburajani, T. S., & Nallaperumal, N. K. (2012). A Hybrid Indian License Plate Character Segmentation Algorithm for Automatic License Plate Recognition System. In *IEEE International Conference on Computational Intelligence and Computing Research* (pp. 1–4). 10.1109/ICCIC.2012.6510322

Wang, F., Man, L., Wang, B., Xiao, Y., Pan, W., & Lu, X. (2008). Fuzzy-based algorithm for color recognition of license plates. *Pattern Recognition Letters*, *29*(7), 1007–1020. doi:10.1016/j.patrec.2008.01.026

Wang, Y. R., Lin, W. H., & Horng, S. J. (2011). A sliding window technique for efficient license plate localization based on discrete wavelet transform. *Expert Systems with Applications*, *38*(4), 3142–3146. doi:10.1016/j.eswa.2010.08.106

Wanniarachchi, W. K. I. L., Sonnadara, D. U. J., & Jayananda, M. K. (2007). License Plate Identification Based on Image Processing Techniques. In *Second International Conference on Industrial and Information Systems, ICIIS 2007* (pp. 8–11). 10.1109/ICIINFS.2007.4579205

Wu, H. H. P., Chen, H. H., Wu, R. J., & Shen, D. F. (2006). License plate extraction in low resolution video. In *Proceedings - International Conference on Pattern Recognition* (Vol. 1, pp. 824–827). Academic Press.

Xiong, C., & Huang, W. (2009). License Plate Location Based on Compound Mathematical Morphology. In *2009 Third International Conference on Genetic and Evolutionary Computing* (pp. 701–704). IEEE. 10.1109/WGEC.2009.134

Yadav, M., Purwar, R. K., & Mittal, M. (2018). Handwritten Hindi character recognition: A review. *IET Image Processing*, *12*(11), 1919–1933. doi:10.1049/iet-ipr.2017.0184

Yan, D., Hongqing, M., Jilin, L., & Langang, L. (2001). A High Performance License Plate Recognition System Based On The Web Technique. In *IEEE International Conference on Intelligent* (pp. 325–329). IEEE.

Zhang, H., Jia, W., He, X., & Wu, Q. (2006). Learning-Based License Plate Detection Using Global and Local Features. In *International Conference. Pattern Recognition*, *2*, 1102–1105.

Zhao, J., Ma, S., Han, W., Yang, Y., & Wang, X. (2012). Research and Implementation of License Plate Recognition Technology. In *2012 24th Chinese Control and Decision Conference (CCDC)* (pp. 3768–3773). Academic Press.

Zunino, R., & Rovetta, S. (2000). Vector quantization for license-plate location and image coding. *IEEE Transactions on Industrial Electronics*, *47*(1), 159–167. doi:10.1109/41.824138

Chapter 3
Impact of Syntactical and Statistical Pattern Recognition on Prognostic Reasoning

Rithesh Pakkala P.
Sahyadri College of Engineering and Management, Mangaluru, India & Visvesvaraya Technological University, Belagavi, India

Prakhyath Rai
Sahyadri College of Engineering and Management, Mangaluru, India & Visvesvaraya Technological University, Belagavi, India

Shamantha Rai Bellipady
Sahyadri College of Engineering and Management, Mangaluru, India & Visvesvaraya Technological University, Belagavi, India

ABSTRACT

This chapter provides insight on pattern recognition by illustrating various approaches and frameworks which aid in the prognostic reasoning facilitated by feature selection and feature extraction. The chapter focuses on analyzing syntactical and statistical approaches of pattern recognition. Typically, a large set of features have an impact on the performance of the predictive model. Hence, there is a need to eliminate redundant and noisy pieces of data before developing any predictive model. The selection of features is independent of any machine learning algorithms. The content-rich information obtained after the elimination of noisy patterns such as stop words and missing values is then used for further prediction. The refinement and extraction of relevant features yields in performance enhancements of future prediction and analysis.

DOI: 10.4018/978-1-7998-3299-7.ch003

INTRODUCTION

Patterns are the sequence of tokens defined over the set of characters. Characters comprise of alphabets, digits or any other ASCII defined values. Pattern recognition is a process of identifying the predefined sequence of characters stated over a collection of alphabets.

Nowadays due to the rapid growth of digital data, identifying the qualified piece of information over a large quantity of data is a challenging task. Hence there is a need for extracting the useful piece of information, which can be accomplished with the aid of pattern recognition frameworks (Zhong, Li & Grance, 2012).

The pattern recognition plays a pre-phase role in the prognostic reasoning for machine learning applications by constructing a pre-processed trained data set. The refinement of a trained data set relies on the attributes selected based on the objectives of applications chosen. The pattern recognition can also be quoted as identifying the sequence of characters termed as strings in preferred order which is referred to as string mining (Dhaliwal, Puglisi & Turpin, 2012).

The pattern recognition process provides room for the elimination of redundant values and noisy content, identifying missing values based on the attributes of the domain and comparison with known patterns to find a match or mismatch. The study of pattern recognition problems involves the identification of structures in real-time and study of theory and techniques required to represent arrangements in the computer recognized format.

The formal languages and automata theory is one of the computer recognized vertical to analyze the different structures described by central concepts of automata theory. The formal languages enable the machine to interact and the user can define the different structures using formal languages. Formal approaches enable the identification of syntactical structures. The finite state machine is one of the tools to describe the pattern/strings defined over the set of input symbols. The context-free grammars, regular expressions are also used to define the syntactical structures (Brauer, Rieger, Mocan & Barczynski, 2011).

There are various features that make formal grammar an attractive tool. Formal grammars are able to provide a structural and statistical description of the data in a condensed matter. It can also be used as a syntactic source to generate all patterns belonging to a specific class (finite and infinite).

Formal methods are successfully being used in a verity of fields such as natural language processing, bioinformatics, and applied behavior analysis. They proved to be effectual in describing the syntax of a language or the structural relations in patterns or data. Formal Grammars consist of syntax rules that describe the structure of the sentences in the domain. A grammatical parser attempts to parse each input using the inferred grammar. If successful, the input is accepted as part of the domain language. Graphical representation for grammatical parsing is usually done using a parse tree.

Formal grammar is an effective and advanced tool for data association, extraction, and modeling. Formal methods have various qualities that make them an attractive research topic. Formal grammars can deliver a statistical and structural description of the data in a condensed matter. It is also capable of applying highly-integrated data mining with capabilities from data processing to a macro data analysis using a common programming language. When structured data are presented as sequences, formal grammars can overcome location-specific structural characteristics. Using formal grammars can also assist in predicting and associating additional data that belongs to the same class. This makes it suitable to be used for a wide range of structured data classes (Habrard A., Bernard M. & Sebban M., 2003).

The statistical approaches are also playing a major role in defining the finite sequence of symbols. The randomness of the attributes must be tested before applying any of the data mining techniques to improve the performance of the predictive model. The uniformity and independence property determines the randomness of the attributes. The different statistical tests are used to determine the randomness and to choose the relevant attributes from the set of attributes. For example chi-square test, Kolmogorov-Smirnov test, autocorrelation test, etc (Banks, Carson II, Nelson & Nicol, 2010).

The input models provide the driving force to prognostic reasoning. Data collection is one of the major tasks in data modeling. It requires substantial time and resource commitment. In some situations it is not possible to acquire the input, then expert opinion and knowledge of the process must be used to make educated guesses. The faulty data will lead to the uncertain and wrong interpretation of the output thereby resulting in misleading recommendations.

The machine learning algorithms tend to affected by noisy data. Noisy should be reduced as much as possible to avoid unnecessary complexity in the prognostic reasoning. The binning method is used to handle noisy data.

Pattern recognition plays a vital role in analyzing the predictive models derived from large volumes of data such as weather forecasting, medical diagnosis, agriculture, monitoring the data flow over a network, embedded systems, etc.

The chapter mainly focuses on the enforcement of the following objectives:

- Discussion of various feature selection approaches
- Illustration of statistical tests and different pattern matching approaches
- Discussion of solution frameworks

BACKGROUND

Pattern recognition is a process of recognizing relevant pieces of information(patterns) with the aid of machine learning techniques. Machine learning employees extraction of relevant patterns in accomplishing of its supervised techniques.

Pattern recognition has its impact in the domain of text mining from structured data. In this section, various works carried out in the domain of machine learning, pattern recognition and techniques for feature selection have been discussed to provide an insight on syntactical and statistical pattern mining. The main focus of this chapter is to provide an emphasis on various supervised machine learning techniques and provide insight on shortcomings, pitfalls, and constraints encountered in the process of statistical and syntactical pattern recognition.

The following section discusses the various process of pattern recognition that can be deployed in the extraction of useful information which aid in machine learning.

Variable Global Feature Selection Scheme (VGFSS)

VGFSS (Agnihotri, Verma & Tripathi, 2017). facilitates the feature selection process by choosing a variable count of features from each class based on the low threshold value set, as a result of which less number of features are selected from each class. This framework overcomes the limitations of feature selection approaches that adopt fixed length based feature extraction and feature extraction involving a bag of words model. The fixed-length based feature extraction possesses a limitation of missing certain relevant features from the classes of data set. The bag of words model (Zhao & Mao, 2018) though uses all the features from the data set classes, it has a limitation of spending time for matching irrelevant feature patterns, thereby increasing the time taken.

Structure-based Composite Feature Algorithm

Text structure-based algorithm (Wan, Wang, Liu, Jinchao & Feng, 2019) employees a feature extraction technique based on the extraction of composite features from the underlying input document. During the preprocessing phase of the framework, irrelevant patterns such as stop words, punctuation marks, and emojis are eliminated. The elimination takes place with the fact that these irrelevant patterns occur in the length of two to at most three characters. After the elimination of irrelevant patterns, the set containing screened data is further used for text extraction (Mooney & Nahm, 2005). In the extraction phase, the pattern matching and discovery is done based on the relevancy and occurrence composite feature values.

Text Classification Using Term Weighting Scheme

The term weighting scheme (Feng, S Li, Sun, Zhang, 2018) follows a probabilistic approach with a similarity index to uniquely associate each term with appropriate weights. The approach assigns a weigh to discriminative terms with a value nearing to 1 whereas assigns a weigh value as 0 otherwise. The supervised technique is employed in the framework to facilitate better performance in the process of categorizing the text with a matching score. The scheme is found to be more efficient in any variable-length data sets.

Statistical Feature Weighting Scheme

The Statistical Feature Weighting scheme (Saez, Derrac, Luengo & Herrera, 2014) overcomes the problem of performance degradation caused due to factors such as noisy, irrelevant and redundant terms by assigning the weights based on the relevance index. The framework adopts a classification technique that incorporates the estimation of distribution for the given data set and variance between the items in the underlying data set is measured using a suitable statistical test. This approach enhances the performance of the Nearest neighbor classifier by associating relevant values of weights to the extraction terms.

The following section gives insight into different statistical feature selection approaches.

Information Gain

Information Gain (Alhaj, Siraj, Zainal, Elshoush, & Elha, 2016) can be used for feature selection based on the gain value of the attributes. Each attribute's Entropy will be calculated, and using the class entropy and attribute entropy, the gain of that attribute will be computed. These gain values are arranged in decreasing order to rank the attributes. A threshold value will be set and all the attributes gain value that exceeds this threshold value will be selected and those which does not exceed will be discarded. The aim of this feature selection technique is to include additional attributes that contribute to the specified objective. Including these additional attributes increases the accuracy of the prediction. The drawback of this approach is that it cannot handle attributes with a large number of distinct values.

Correlation Coefficient

Correlation describes the relationship between the two attributes. For measuring the correlation, Symmetrical Uncertainty(SU) is used. A graph is constructed between each attribute and the target attribute and a set of attributes is reduced. By measuring the coefficient correlation and considering the highest SU score, the features or attributes are clubbed into clusters. A feature that has large SU value in the cluster is selected and the rest are ignored. When there is insufficient and inconsistent data, the coefficient correlation fails to select the feature (Potharaju & Sreedevi, 2018).

Variance Threshold

In a variance-based feature selection method (Sadeghyan, 2018), the aim is to select the optimum subset of features that helps to attain a specified objective and this method uses the variance of each attribute. Variance is the deviation of a variable from its mean. A threshold value for variance is set for all the attributes and compared with the variance of each attribute. The attribute has a lower variance than the threshold is removed and the remaining are selected. The attribute that don't differ much won't add much information. So the Variance Threshold method removes these attributes. The limitation of this method is that the threshold has to be set manually which may affect the accuracy.

Sequential Selection

Sequential Selection (Ahat & Bankerttt, 1996) is used for feature selection. Sequential selection has two more categories, Forward Sequential Selection, and Backward Sequential Selection. Forward Sequential Selection begins without having any attributes. It evaluates the other entire attribute subsets with specifically one attribute and checks for best performance. It then adds that selected attribute to the subset which yields the best performance for subsets of the next larger size. These steps are repeated until better performance is obtained by extending the current subset. Backward Sequential Selection begins with all features. It will then removes one feature from the subset and evaluates for best performance. These steps are repeated until maximum performance is obtained.

Genetic Algorithm

Genetic Algorithm (Vafaie & Jong, 1997) is an adaptive search technique. It provides improvement for a variety of random search and local search methods. GAs is a domain-independent search technique. So this algorithm can be applied where it is impossible to provide domain knowledge and theories of software applications. The main problem in applying GAs is that it doesn't have proper representation and adequate function. So the simplest way to represent GAs is by using binary form. Each feature is represented as a binary gene and each binary string is of fixed length which represents some subsets of the present feature set.

Recursive Features Elimination

Recursive Features Elimination (RFE) (Khaing, 2010) is used for feature selection techniques when there is a small training set with a large number of features. The advantage of Recursive Features Elimination

(RFE) is that it reduces redundant and recursive features. The attributes are ranked according to their values. This method recursively eliminates a small number of features per loop thus eliminating dependencies. The drawback of this method is that the number of features that are valid will not be known in advance. So for each subset, a score is given and the best scoring subset is chosen by cross-validating with another subset to find the optimal features in Recursive Features Elimination (RFE).

STATISTICAL TESTS AND PATTERN RECOGNITION

Attribute selection is a process of choosing the relevant attributes from data set based on the objectives of the study and then applying any data mining algorithms for the prognostic reasoning which aids in the performance improvement of the model. As the number of irrelevant attributes increases the pre-processing of data takes a large time which impacts the performance of the predictive model. Thus there is a need to state the suitable attribute selection approaches.

In this section, we will be discussing the different statistical tests (Banks, Carson II, Nelson & Nicol, 2010) which enable attribute selection and illustrating different pattern matching algorithms.

Frequency Test

The chi-square test and KS Tests(Banks, Carson II, Nelson & Nicol, 2010) are used to test the uniformity of the attributes. In testing for uniformity, we need to define the hypothesis namely null hypothesis and alternate hypothesis as follows:

Null hypothesis H0: The chosen attributes are uniformly distributed
Alternate hypothesis H1: The chosen attributes are not uniformly distributed

Chi-square Test for Feature Selection

A chi-square test (Banks, Carson II, Nelson & Nicol, 2010) is used for qualitative attributes in a dataset. We determine the Chi-square between each feature and the target and choose the preferred number of features with the best Chi-square scores.

Algorithm:

1. Choose the relevant data set with original features for the study
2. Create feature class and target class
3. Convert the categorical values into integer values
4. Compute the chi-square score for the features using the formula

$$\chi_o^2 = \frac{\left(Observerd\ Frequency - Expected\ Frequency\right)2}{Expected\ Frequency}$$

where the observed frequency is the number of observations in the class interval and the Expected frequency is the number of expected observations in that class interval.

5. Set the number of best features to selected and Select the features with the highest chi-square score
6. Display the reduced features

Illustration of Chi-square Test With Python Implementation

```
import pandas as pd
import numpy as np
from sklearn.feature_selection import SelectKBest
from sklearn.feature_selection import chi2
data = pd.read_csv("PT.csv")
#print (data)
X = data.iloc[:,1:5] #independent columns
y = data.iloc[:,-1] #target column i.e price range
#print (X)
#print (y)
#apply SelectKBest class to extract top 4 best features
bestfeatures = SelectKBest(score_func=chi2, k=4)
#print (bestfeatures)
fit = bestfeatures.fit(X,y)
#print (fit)
dfscores = pd.DataFrame(bestfeatures.scores_)
#print (dfscores)
dfcolumns = pd.DataFrame(X.columns)
#print (dfcolumns)
#concat two dataframes for better visualization
featureScores = pd.concat([dfcolumns,dfscores],axis=1)
featureScores.columns = ['Specs','Score'] #naming the dataframe columns
print(featureScores.nlargest(4,'Score')) #print 4 best features
#graph generator
from sklearn.ensemble import ExtraTreesClassifier
import matplotlib.pyplot as plt
model = ExtraTreesClassifier()
model.fit(X,y)
print(model.feature_importances_) #use inbuilt class feature_importances of tree based classifiers
#plot graph of feature importances for better visualization
feat_importances = pd.Series(model.feature_importances_, index=X.columns)
feat_importances.nlargest(4).plot(kind='barh')
#feat_importances.nlargest(4).plot(kind='pie')
plt.show()
```

Output: See Table 1

Graph Generated: See Figure 1

Data Set: PT.csv: See Figure 2.

Table 1. Resultant Features

	Specs	Score
0	Outlook	1.126749
2	Humidity	0.466667
3	Wind	0.160000
1	Temperature	0.155556

Figure 1. Reduced Feature Set with Chi-Square Score

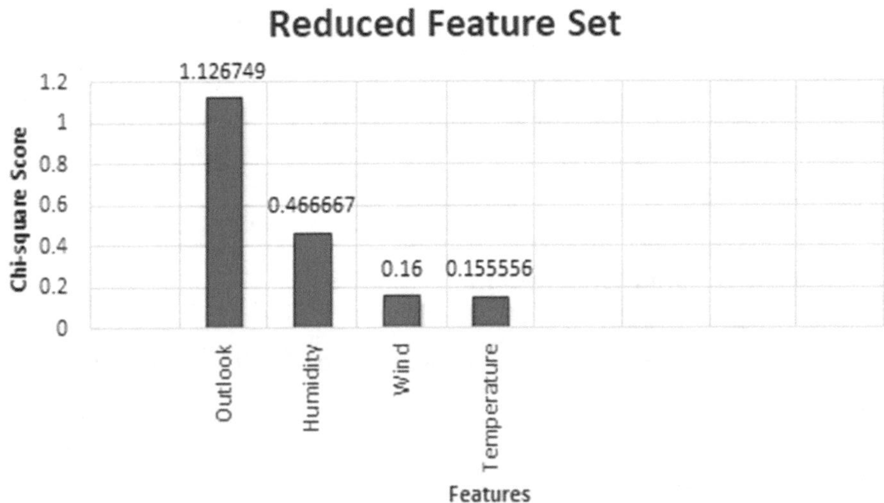

In this Dataset, We have taken 5 attributes. i.e. Sl.No., Outlook, Wind, Humidity, Temperature and PlayTennis, where

- Sl.No. has 0 to 13 numbers.
- Outlook has 3 variety i.e. Sunny, Overcast and Rain those are given as 1,2 and 3 respectively. Totally it has 14 values.
- Wind has 2 variety i.e. weak and strong are given as 1 and 2 respectively. Totally it has 14 values.
- Humidity has 2 variety i.e. high and normal is given as 1 and 2 respectively. Totally it has 14 values.
- Temperature has 3 variety i.e. Hot, Mild and Cool those are given as 1,2 and 3 respectively. Totally it has 14 values.
- PlayTennis has 2 variety i.e. No and Yes are given as 1 and 2 respectively. Totally it has 14 values.

Figure 2. Play Tennis Data Set with Different Attribute Values

Sl. No.	Outlook	Wind	Humidity	Temperature	Play Tennis
0	1	1	1	1	2
1	1	1	1	2	2
2	3	1	1	1	1
3	2	2	1	1	1
4	2	3	2	1	1
5	2	3	2	2	2
6	3	3	2	2	1
7	1	2	1	1	2
8	1	3	2	1	1
9	2	2	2	1	1
10	1	2	2	2	1
11	3	2	1	2	1
12	3	1	2	1	1
13	2	2	1	2	2

Kolmogorov-Smirnov Test (KS Test)

Kolmogorov–Smirnov test (Banks, Carson II, Nelson & Nicol, 2010) is used to measure the uniformity property of the random numbers. It is a very efficient way to find if two samples are significantly different from each other.

Hypothesis is:

Null hypothesis H0: The numbers are uniformly distributed on the interval [0,1].
Alternate hypothesis H1: The numbers are not uniformly distributed on the interval [0,1].

Algorithm:

```
1.        Rank the data from smallest to largest. Let R(i) denote the ith
smallest observation so that R(1) £ R(2) £ … £ R(N)
2.        Compute
                           D+ = max(i/N-Ri) for all i in(1, N)
                           D- = max(Ri-((i-1)/N)) for all i in(1, N)
3.        Compue D = max(D+, D-)
4.        Find the critical value Dα for the specified level of significance α
and the given sample size N
5.        If D > Dα
                             Rejects Uniformity
```

```
        else
                It fails to reject the Null Hypothesis.
```

The chi-square test and KS test ensures that given data samples are uniformly distributed so that it will result in performance enhancement of any prognostic reasoning models.

The strength of text mining relies on underlying pattern recognition algorithms, which have been elaborated with examples as follows:

Boyer-Moore Algorithm

Boyer-Moore tends to yield higher efficiency when employed in applications involving moderately sized characters and relatively lengthier patterns.

```
BOYER_MOORE_MATCHER (T, P)
Input:    Text with n characters and Pattern with m characters
Output: Index of the first substring of T matching P
          Compute function last
          i ¬ m-1
          j ¬ m-1
          Repeat
              If P[j] = T[i] then
                  if j=0 then
                      return i          // we have a match
                  else
                      i ¬ i -1
                       j ¬ j -1
              else
                  i ¬ i + m - Min(j, 1 + last[T[i]])
                  j ¬ m -1
           until i > n -1
           Return "no match"
Text: AABAACAADAABAABA
Pattern: AABA
AABA          AABA
AABAACAADAABAABA
                                    AABA
Output: Pattern found at index 0
                Pattern found at index 9
                Pattern found at index 12
Time Complexity: O(m+n)
```

END INDICES BASED PATTERN MATCHING

The following algorithm illustrates pattern matching. Consider two strings, **string** and **pat**, where **pat** is a pattern to be searched for in **string**. The built-in function **strstr** can be used to perform this operation.

```
char pat[MAX_SIZE], string[MAX_SIZE], *t;
```

The built-in function **strstr** is illustrated as follows,

```
if(t = strstr(string, pat))
                      printf("The string from strstr is: %s\t",t);
else
              printf("The pattern was not found with strstr\n");
```

The call **(t = strstr(string,pat))** returns a null pointer if **pat** is not in **string**. If **pat** is in **string**, **t** holds a pointer to the start of **pat** in **string**. The entire string beginning at position **t** is printed out.

Techniques to improve pattern matching,

- By quitting when strlen(pat) is greater than the number of remaining characters in the string.
- Checking the first and last characters of pat and string before we check the remaining characters.

```
        int nfind(char *string, char *pat)
        {/* match the last character of pattern first, and then match from the
beginning */
                  int i, j,start=0;
                        int ends =strlen(string)-1;
                        int endp=strlen(pat)-1;
                        int endmatch=endp;
                        i=0;
                        while(endmatch<=ends)
                        {
                        if(string[endmatch]==pat[endp])
                        for(j=0,i=start;j<endp && string[i] == pat[j];
i++,j++)

                        ;
                        if(j== endp)
                            return start; /*successful */
                        endmatch++;
                         start++;
                        }
                         return -1;

        }
```

Naive Algorithm

```
1.        Begin
2.        patLen:= pattern Size
3.        strLen:= string size
4.        for i:= 0 to (strLen - patLen), do
5.        for j:= 0 to patLen, do
6.        if text[i+j] ¹ pattern[j], then
a.        break the loop
7.        done
8.        if j == patLen, then
9.        display the position i, as there pattern found
10.        done
11.        End
Time Complexity: O(n-m+1)
```

Knuth Morris Pratt Algorithm

1. Initialize the input variables:

N = Length of the Text
M = Length of the pattern
U = prefix function of pattern (p)
q = Number of characters matched

2. Define the variable: q=0, the beginning of the match.
3. Compare the first character of the pattern with the first character of the text.

If a match is not found, substitute the value of U[q] to q.
If a match is found, then increment the value of q by 1.

4. Check whether all the pattern elements are matched with the text elements. If not, repeat the search process. If yes, print the number of shifts taken by the pattern.
5. Search for the next match.

Time Complexity: O(nm)

Pattern Matching is widely used in text mining applications to identify the correct patterns among larger text such as web documents (Hau, Z Wang, H Wang, Zheng & Zhou, 2017). In the above section, various algorithms such as Boyer Moore, Naive, Knuth Morris Pratt are illustrated and analyzed.

Based on the analysis, it can be inferred that the Naïve algorithm has better efficiency compared to Knuth Morris Pratt and Boyer Moore when the length of the pattern increases. Whereas Knuth morris pratt can be employed in applications involving pattern matching on data with higher character sequence.

SOLUTION FRAMEWORKS

With the aid of above-discussed techniques, the frameworks for prognostic reasoning model and information extraction and knowledge discovery from databases have been proposed:

Framework for Prognostic Reasoning

Figure 3. Proposed Prognostic Reasoning Model

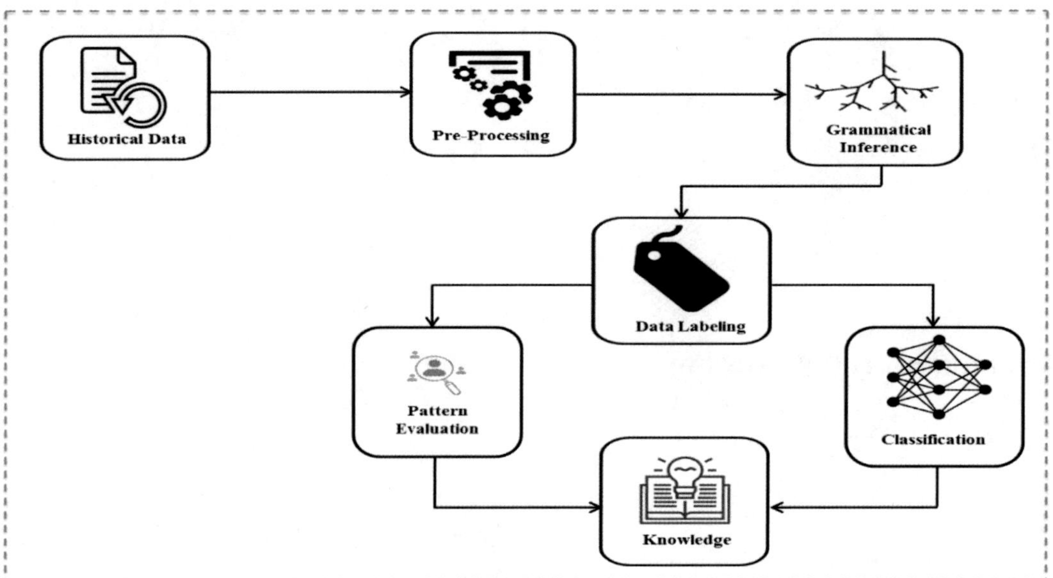

- **Data Preprocessing:** Preprocessing is a procedure that aids in improving the quality of data contents which is then taken as an input for the process of mining. As the quality of data raises, it depicts a useful and interesting piece of information. In the proposed work, incomplete, inconsistent and noisy data is eliminated. After elimination, the formal method namely grammar is used to select the required attributes. The repeated and non-specific attributes are discarded as a result of attribute selection.
- **Grammatical Inference:** Grammars are very useful in analyzing the structural and statistical data. Initially, probabilistic grammar is inferred to build a structural model that describes the data. Given an input sequence, the model parses and generates the probability of the data sequence based on its structural characteristics. The model then accepts or rejects the input by comparing the probability to a pre-set threshold.
- **Data Labeling:** Based on the features selected by grammar, labeling of the acquired preprocessed data will be performed. The labeling can be good, average or bad based on selected attribute values.
- **Classification:** Classification of the data will be done by using a suitable classifier from the data acquired; one part will be used as a training set another part will be used as a validation set. Now based on the performance of the validation set, the necessary modifications or updates can be done

on the classifier before using it to classify the data in the testing data set. The performance of the various classifiers can be evaluated and accuracy can be measured to decide the best one.

- **Pattern Evaluation:** By applying a suitable regression technique on the data acquired, the required prediction can be performed.
- **Knowledge Presentation:** The class generated by the classifier and prediction obtained from pattern evaluation, together will be presented as knowledge which will be the final result of the proposed model. Based on the knowledge obtained, end users can be benefited.

Grammatical Inference Methodologies

The process of learning grammar is called grammatical inference (Habrard A., Bernard M. & Sebban M., 2003). It is defined as learning the set of syntactic rules that governs the structural characteristics of sentences or patterns from a finite set of sample sentences.

The grammatical inference process consists of three steps:

- Identifying and analyzing targeted data using a sample training set. The alphabets that make up a sentence are the terminal symbols. The relationships between these symbols are the production rules. A suitable grammar type is identified based on the structural nature of the sentences in the targeted language.
- Choose an appropriate grammar level and infer a grammar using a sample training set.
- Testing the goodness of the generated grammar using a different testing set. Validating the results using the appropriate fitness measurement. The process may be repeated until testing results are satisfactory. Then, the inferred grammar can be deployed.

Figure 4. Grammatical Inference Process

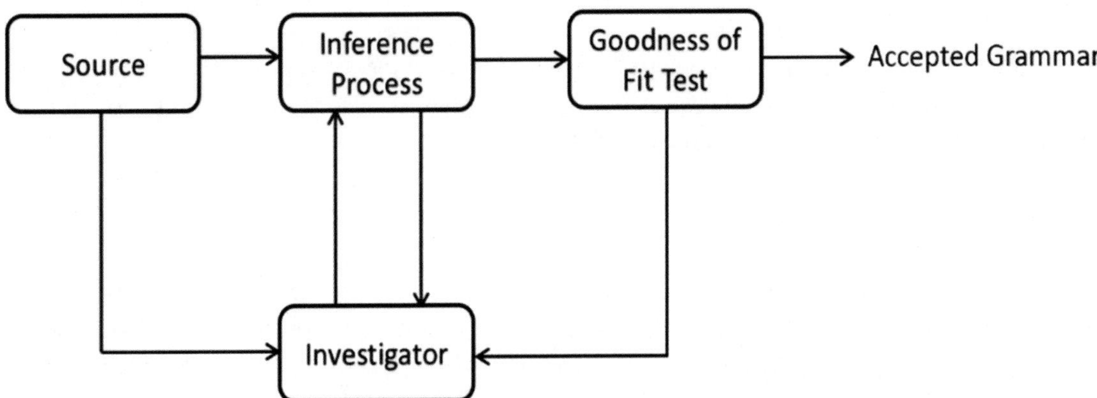

Framework for information extraction and knowledge discovery from databases is shown in Figure 5. The phases are outlined in the following sub-section.

Figure 5. Framework for Information Extraction and Knowledge Discovery

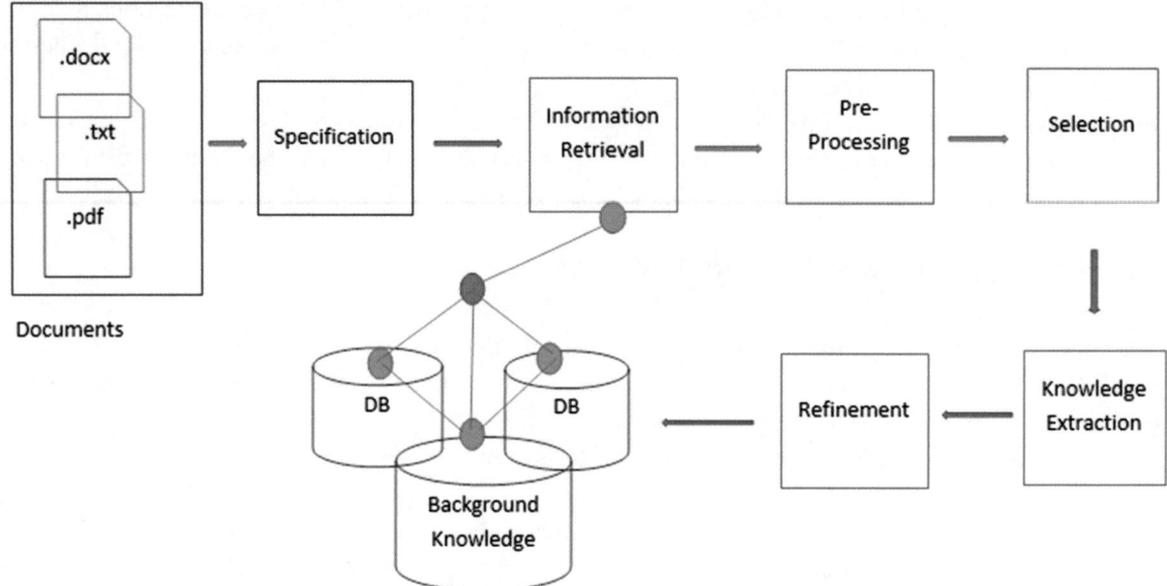

Specification

The specification indicates the cause and workflow of the framework being proposed. The specification helps in describing and illustrating the procedure involved in the process of text refinement adopted by the framework.

Information Retrieval

The information retrieval process relies on the acquisition of documents and files through various modes either online or offline. The documents and files collected are then placed into a specific folder in order to undergo further processing (Yates &Neto,1999).

Pre-Processing

Pre-Processing has mainly two-piece of functionality Screening and Conversion. Screening concentrates on the elimination of non-textual files such as image files, video files or audio files from the folder containing files for processing and places selected textual files such as pdf files, word files, text files or html files in a folder for further processing (Freitag & Kushmerick, 2000). The conversion process translates the textual files which are obtained as a result of the screening process into text documents i.e. into .txt files and places them in the specific folder so as to be used for future procedures in the processing function (Zhang, Niu, Jiang, & Fu, 2012).

Selection

The selection process concentrates on defining protocols or rules to be applied to text documents for the extraction of useful information from text documents (Califf & Mooney, 1999). The selection procedure employees either categorization or clustering technique based on input. The categorization process is a supervised framework that works based on the predefined set of features being matched with input content whereas clustering is an unsupervised technique of placing similar patterns of text in the form of groups termed as clusters (Calvillo1, Padilla1, Muñoz, Ponce1 & Fernandez, 2013).

Knowledge Extraction

The above framework proposes a knowledge extraction procedure which is illustrated in the following example as follows: The preprocessed document is searched to recognize the feature set as described. Consider the pattern to be extracted from a text document is "Microsoft Word". The framework has proposed a technique which not only searches for the occurrence of the pattern "Microsoft Word", but also identifies the synonyms of the pattern "Microsoft Word" such as "MS Word" and "Word Pad" in the underlying text document and returns the success status if found. Thereby improving the accuracy and efficiency of the underlying pattern matching technique (Zhong, Li & Grance, 2012).

Refinement

The process helps in ranking the patterns extracted from the underlying documents based on the rule set being defined. The resultant file is then fine-tuned with the primary word of the synonym rule set. For example consider the sample rule set { "Microsoft Word ": "MS Word", "Word Pad" }.In the above synonym rule set "Microsoft Word" is considered as a primary pattern whereas others were taken as secondary patterns (Spasic, 2018).

Background Knowledge

The background knowledge comprises of data set which serves as a repository comprising of the synonym rule set and other predefined features aiding in the process of knowledge extraction. The framework facilitates dynamic updation of rule set thereby increasing precision, recall and F-measure factors guiding the efficiency of the prototype.

CONCLUSION

The chapter mainly focused on providing an efficient framework for prognostic reasoning and information extraction which can be employed across various machine learning applications. The central aspect of machine learning lies in its trained data set and generation of hypothesis from training data set which can be accomplished by feature selection and extraction. In the background, the various feature selection approaches and information extraction approaches are discussed. Also, different statistical tests and pattern recognition algorithms are illustrated with examples that aid in the process of developing frameworks for prognostic reasoning and information extraction and knowledge discovery which can be deployed in the applications of text mining and information retrieval.

REFERENCES

Agnihotri, Verma, & Tripathi. (2017). *Variable Global Feature Selection Scheme for Automatic Classification of Text Documents*. Elsevier. . doi:10.1016/j.eswa.2017.03.057

Ahat & Bankert. (1996). *A Comparative Evaluation of Sequential Feature Selection Algorithms*. Academic Press.

Alhaj, Siraj, Zainal, Elshoush, & Elha. (2016). *Feature Selection Using Information Gain for Improved Structural-Based Alert Correlation*. Academic Press.

Baeza-Yates, R., & Ribeiro-Neto, B. (1999). *Modern Information Retrieval*. ACM Press.

Banks, J., Carson, J. S. II, Nelson, B. L., & Nicol, D. M. (2010). *Discrete-Event System Simulation* (5th ed.). Pearson Education.

Brauer, F., Rieger, R., Mocan, A., & Barczynski, W. M. (2011, October). Enabling Information Extraction by Inference of Regular Expressions from Sample Entities. *Proceedings of the 20th ACM Conference on Information and Knowledge Management, CIKM 2011*. 10.1145/2063576.2063763

Califf, M. E., & Mooney, R. J. (1999, July). Relational Learning of Pattern-Match Rules for Information Extraction. *Proceedings of the 16th National Conference on Artificial Intelligence (AAAI-99)*, 328-334.

Calvillo, Padilla, Muñoz, Ponce, & Fernandez. (2013). Searching Research Papers Using Clustering and Text Mining. IEEE.

Dhaliwal, J., Puglisi, S. J., & Turpin, A. (2012, April). Practical Efficient String Mining. *IEEE Transactions on Knowledge and Data Engineering*, *24*(4), 735–744. doi:10.1109/TKDE.2010.242

Feng, G., Li, S., Sun, T., & Zhang, B. (2018). A probabilistic model derived term weighting scheme for text classification. *Pattern Recognition Letters*, *110*, 23–29. Advance online publication. doi:10.1016/j.patrec.2018.03.003

Freitag, D., & Kushmerick, N. (2000, July). Boosted Wrapper Induction. *Proceedings of the 17th National Conference on Artificial Intelligence (AAAI-2000)*, 577-583.

Habrard, A., Bernard, M., & Sebban, M. (2003). Improvement of the State Merging Rule on Noisy Data in Probabilistic Grammatical Inference. In N. Lavrač, D. Gamberger, H. Blockeel, & L. Todorovski (Eds.), *Machine Learning: ECML 2003*. doi:10.1007/978-3-540-39857-8_17

Hau, W., Wang, Z., Wang, H., Zheng, K., & Zhou, X. (2017, March). Understand Short Texts by Harvesting and Analyzing Semantic Knowledge. *IEEE Transactions on Knowledge and Data Engineering*, *29*(3), 499–512. doi:10.1109/TKDE.2016.2571687

Khaing. (2010, January). *Enhanced Features Ranking and Selection using Recursive Feature Elimination(RFE) and k-Nearest Neighbor Algorithms in Support Vector Machine for Intrusion Detection System*. Academic Press.

Mooney & Nahm. (2005). Text Mining with Information Extraction. *Proceedings of the 4th International MIDP Colloquium*, 141-160.

Potharaju, S. P., & Sreedevi, M. (2018). Correlation Coefficient Based Feature Selection Framework Using Graph Construction. *Gazi University Journal of Science*, *31*(3), 775–787.

Sadeghyan. (2018). *A New Robust Feature Selection Method using Variance-Based Sensitivity Analysis*. Academic Press.

Saez, J. A., Derrac, J., Luengo, J., & Herrera, F. (2014). Statistical Computation of Feature Weighting Schemes through Data Estimation for Nearest Neighbor Classifiers. *Pattern Recognition*, *47*(12), 3941–3948. Advance online publication. doi:10.1016/j.patcog.2014.06.012

Spasic, I. (2018, February). Acronyms as an Integral Part of Multi-Word Term Recognition – A Token of Appreciation. *IEEE Access: Practical Innovations, Open Solutions*, *6*, 8351–8363. doi:10.1109/ACCESS.2018.2807122

Vafaie & De Jong. (1997, November). *Genetic Algorithms as a Tool for Feature Selection in Machine Learning*. Academic Press.

Wan, C., Wang, Y., Liu, Y., Ji, J., & Feng, G. (2019). *Composite Feature Extraction and Selection for Text Classification*. IEEE. doi:10.1109/ACCESS.2019.2904602

Zhang, C., Niu, Z., Jiang, P., & Fu, H. (2012). Domain-Specific Term Extraction from Free Texts. *Proceedings of 9th IEEE International Conference on Fuzzy System and Knowledge Discovery (FSKD 2012)*, 1290-1293. 10.1109/FSKD.2012.6234350

Zhao, R., & Mao, K. (2018, April). Fuzzy Bag-of-Words Model for Document Representation. *IEEE Transactions on Fuzzy Systems*, *26*(2), 794–804. doi:10.1109/TFUZZ.2017.2690222

Zhong, N., Li, Y., & Grance, T. (2012, January). Effective Pattern Discovery for Text Mining. *IEEE Transactions on Knowledge and Data Engineering*, *24*(1).

Zhong, N., Li, Y., & Grance, T. (2012, January). Effective Pattern Discovery for Text Mining. *IEEE Transactions on Knowledge and Data Engineering*, *24*(1), 30–44. doi:10.1109/TKDE.2010.211

Chapter 4
Challenges and Issues in Plant Disease Detection Using Deep Learning

Priyanka Sahu
Guru Gobind Singh Inderprastha University, New Delhi, India

Anuradha Chug
https://orcid.org/0000-0002-3139-4490
Guru Gobind Singh Inderprastha University, New Delhi, India

Amit Prakash Singh
https://orcid.org/0000-0002-8675-6903
Guru Gobind Singh Inderprastha University, New Delhi, India

Dinesh Singh
Indian Agricultural Research Institute, New Delhi, India

Ravinder Pal Singh
https://orcid.org/0000-0003-0704-1465
Indian Agricultural Research Institute, New Delhi, India

ABSTRACT

Deep learning (DL) has rapidly become an essential tool for image classification tasks. This technique is now being deployed to the tasks of classifying and detecting plant diseases. The encouraging results achieved with this methodology hide many problems that are rarely addressed in related experiments. This study examines the main factors influencing the efficiency of deep neural networks for plant disease detection. The challenges discussed in the study are based on the literature as well as experiments conducted using an image database, which contains approximately 1,296 leaf images of the beans crop. A pre-trained convolutional neural network, EfficientNet B0, is used for training and testing purposes. This study gives and emphasizes on factors and challenges that may potentially affect the use of DL techniques to detect and classify plant diseases. Some solutions are also suggested that may overcome these problems.

DOI: 10.4018/978-1-7998-3299-7.ch004

INTRODUCTION

Plant diseases have always been a significant threat in agriculture, causing a diminution in the crop's quality and consequent yields. Plant diseases' range can vary from mild symptoms to severe damage in entire crop areas, resulting in high financial costs and severe impacts on the agricultural economy (Savary et al., 2012), especially in developing nations that rely on one crop or multiple crops. In order to prevent significant damage, several techniques for the diagnosis of the disease have been developed. Techniques proved in molecular biology deliver accurate identification of pathogenic factors. However, these approaches are not available to many farmers and require a heavy cost and resources to acquire or implement full domain knowledge. Precision farming utilizes state-of-the-art technology to elevate the process of decision-making (Gebbers & Adamchuk, 2010). Several machine learning (ML) approaches are deployed for making optimal decisions that have resulted in cost reduction (Sujatha et al., 2021; Talaviya et al., 2020). Different algorithms and methods can be utilized for the purpose of classification tasks, such as clustering, decision trees (DT), Gaussian models, linear regression, K-nearest neighbors (ANN), logistic regression, random forest, naive Bayesian (NB), and support vector machines (SVM) (Arsenovic et al., 2019). But, approaches based on traditional machine learning algorithms have been moderately effective under constraints and limited setups. With the introduction of Deep Learning (DL) models, further development in artificial intelligence and computer vision may lead to innovative results. These approaches deliver more precise predictions than conventional methods that allow better decision-making. With progress in hardware mechanics, DL techniques are deployed to solve complex problems in a relatively short period of time. In DL frameworks, Convolutional Neural Networks (CNNs) are probably the most common to use (Krizhevsky et al., 2012). This type of neural system involves fewer artificial neurons than traditional feed-forward neural networks and is particularly appropriate for image recognition-related tasks. CNNs typically involve a large number of samples to train the model. In many real-world problems, collecting the necessary training data for the models is expensive or unfeasible (Pan & Yang, 2009).

Therefore, many researchers are using the conception of transfer learning for reusing the pre-trained networks such as AlexNet, Googlenet. In this case, predictions are made based on examples that do not come from the same distribution of training data (Bengio, 2012). CNNs have performed well for plant classification (Chunjing et al., 2017), disease detection (Ferentinos, 2018; B. Liu et al., 2018; Szegedy et al., 2015), yield forecast (Rahnemoonfar & Sheppard, 2017), and general visual vision (Lee & Kwon, 2017). The Alexnet (Krizhevsky et al., 2012) and GoogleNet (Szegedy et al., 2015) frameworks have provided state-of-the-art results in the experimentations (Jayme Garcia Arnal Barbedo, 2019; Ferentinos, 2018; B. Liu et al., 2018; Mohanty et al., 2016; Patr\'\icio & Rieder, 2018). Furthermore, it has been revealed that improved results are obtained if the pre-trained networks are used (Mohanty et al., 2016). With the development of graphics processing units (GPUs) (Ferentinos, 2018), the combination of DL and transfer learning has provided a compelling way to classify and detect diseases present in plants (J. Chen et al., 2020; Gutiérrez et al., 2021). Literature review (Table 1) shows that several researchers use similar kinds of techniques and tools over similar types of datasets. Therefore, it is not surprising that the results reported in the literature do not vary widely. Furthermore, there are numerous aspects that could affect the use of DL-based tools in real-world field conditions, but maximum time these issues are only briefly described. This severely limits the actual use of techniques and tools for automated crop disease detection.

This study provides a detailed analysis of the critical factors that disturb the performance of DL models for identifying plant diseases under realistic environments. The objective is to provide specific guidelines for crop disease detection by making intensive and practical analyses of DL methods. The aim of the study is as follows:

- Implementation of a pre-trained CNN with transfer learning for identifying the diseases present in the leaves of the beans crop.
- A detailed analysis regarding various agricultural factors that could degrade the efficiency of DL models for plant disease detection.
- A detailed analysis regarding various DL challenges that may drop the efficiency of DL models for plant disease detection.

MATERIALS AND METHODS

Dataset

The dataset was selected from GitHub (https://github.com/AI-Lab-Makerere/ibean/). It includes images of beans crop leaves taken with a smartphone from the main field. Figures (4-b), (5-a), and 6 show examples of sample images. Table 2 shows the details of the dataset used. This dataset contains 1296 images, divided into three subsets: training, testing, and validation set. This study used three categories (labels) to identify diseases in crops. Images present in the dataset were collected under a controlled environment with a uniform background.

One of the main advantages of DL approaches is that they generally do not require explicit identification of symptoms in images. However, the related information is primarily focused on the symptom itself and its surroundings. Augmentation techniques were used to raise the size of the database, and for testing the working of CNN with localized information. The original sample is divided into smaller images holding specific lesions and localized symptom areas.

Training of CNN

Transfer Learning was deployed to pre-trained CNN (EfficientNet B0). The training datasets were enhanced by incorporating augmentation (rotation, mirrors, Gaussian noise, adjusting brightness, and adjusting contrast operations). Consequently, the size of the training set has been increased to 12 folds, and thus, overfitting problems have been reduced (B. Liu et al., 2018). Colored and gray-scale images were used for training and testing purposes. The parameters used for network training were as follows:

CNN model was trained using a 100% fine-tuning approach that was pre-trained on the ImageNet dataset. None of the layers has frozen in the pre-trained network. Therefore, the back-propagation algorithm has been capable of changing the bias and the weights in the layers. CNN was trained for twenty epochs using the same hyperparameters as indicated in Table 3.

Table 1. Literature review of recent studies in plant disease detection utilizing DL.

Plant Species Detection	Images Count	Architecture Analysis	Performance Metric	Limitation	Reference
Apple and Orange	5142	Deploying pre-processing techniques (border thickening, contrast increase)	Detection rate (90.8%), F1-score (0.92)	Absence of pre-processing causes light and shadow effects in overlapping leaves.	Kuznetsova et al. (Kuznetsova et al., 2020)
Apple	1200	ResNet Model + FPN + Atrous spatial pyramid pooling applied in the model.	F1- score (0.849)	Recognition fails for overlapping fruits.	Kang et al. (Kang & Chen, 2020)
Branch fruits (apples, apricots, nectarines, peaches, plums, sour cherries)	12443	Three convolutional layers + max-pooling + fully connected + global average pooling.	Accuracy (99.76%), F1- score (0.997)	Activation maps tend to more sensitive towards leaves when fruits and leaves overlapped.	Saiedi et al. (Saedi & Khosravi, 2020)
Cucumber	255	Multipath CNN+ SVM classifier+PCA+ ROI.	Recognition (90%)	Difficulty in fruit extraction from images with busy backgrounds.	Mao et al. (Mao et al., 2020)
Grape	300	Mask R-CNN + ResNet101	F1- score (0.91)	Counting of fruit is very complex, as variation in compactedness, color, shape, and size.	Santos et al. (Santos et al., 2020)
Kiwi	1000	VGG16 model modified to handle, RGB + NIR parameters + fine- tuning	Accuracy (90%)	Unavailability of kiwi fruit dataset, difficulty in comparing the results with some other database.	Liu et al. (Z. Liu et al., 2019)
Rice	5320 images with 4290 frames of videos	DCNN is used with four blocks in which the ReLU layer is placed at a new position that helps to converge better.	Precision (90.0)	Difficulty in lesion identification for videos.	Li et al. (Li et al., 2020)
Tea plants	75222	Ensembled FusionSUM network deployed with three saliency techniques and SPE used to extract the required features.	Identification accuracy (92.43%)	Spectral residual approach fails to highlight all image pixels.	Nanni et al. (Nanni et al., 2020)
Tomato	15000	The modified Yolo-V3 model (with fewer parameters) was deployed over multi-scale images.	Identification accuracy (92.39%)	Time-consuming architecture.	Liu et al. (J. Liu & Wang, 2020)
Tomato	966	YOLO- Tomato architecture based on DenseNet, deployed circular boxes instead of rectangular boxes.	Recognition (94.58%)	Fruit occlusion and overlapping leaves cause false-positive recognition.	Liu et al. (G. Liu et al., 2020)
Vigna Mungo plant	433	Three CNNs; VirLeafNet-1, VirLeafNet-2, and VirLeafNet-3	Accuracy (91.234%) (96.429%) (97.403%)	Operated over limited dataset.	Joshi et al. (Joshi et al., 2021)
14 crop species	55,448	EfficientNet architecture	Accuracy (99.91%), Precision (98.42%)	Accuracy and precision is less when compared with other DL models.	Atila et al. (Atila et al., 2021)

Table 2. Summarization of dataset

Name of Disease	Total Number of Image
Bean Rust	436
Angular Leaf Spot	432
Healthy	428
Total	1296

Experimental Setup

All the experiments were executed using Google Colab (python 3) on a personal computer with GPU specification using DL frameworks running on Windows 10.

1. Python 3.7,
2. 1xTesla K80,
3. 2496 CUDA cores, and
4. 12GB GDDR5 VRAM.

EfficientNet B0 Model

Tan et al. (Tan & Le, 2019) proposed a new model based on the model scaling concept that carefully analyses the resolution, depth, and width of the network. This balancing makes the network perform better. This model is based on a new scaling technique, compound coefficient, that has the ability to scale all the dimensions uniformly. The effectiveness of this model was demonstrated using the scaling of MobileNets and ResNet. EfficientNet achieved the state of the art performance for the ImageNet dataset with a top-1 accuracy of 84.4%. Compound scaling technique utilizes a compound co-efficient factor 'ϕ' to scale the depth, resolution, and width. Figure 1. shows the graphical representation of the EfficientNet model. Depth, width, and resolution of the model can be set as per the approach:

$$\text{depth: } d = \alpha^{\varphi} \quad (1)$$

Table 3. Hyperparameters specification

Hyper-parameters	Value
Optimizer	RMSProp
Learning Rate	0.0001
Decay	1e-6
Momentum	0.9
Parameters	5.3 Million
Batch size	20
Activation function	ReLU
Class mode	Categorical

$$\text{resolution: } r = \gamma^{\varphi} \tag{2}$$

$$\text{width: } w = \beta^{\varphi} \tag{3}$$

$$\text{s.t. } \alpha \cdot \beta^2 \cdot \gamma^2 \approx 2,$$

$$\alpha \geq 1, \beta \geq 1, \gamma \geq 1$$

Where, α, β, γ denotes the scaling multiplier for depth, resolution, and width.

Figure 1. EfficientNet architecture

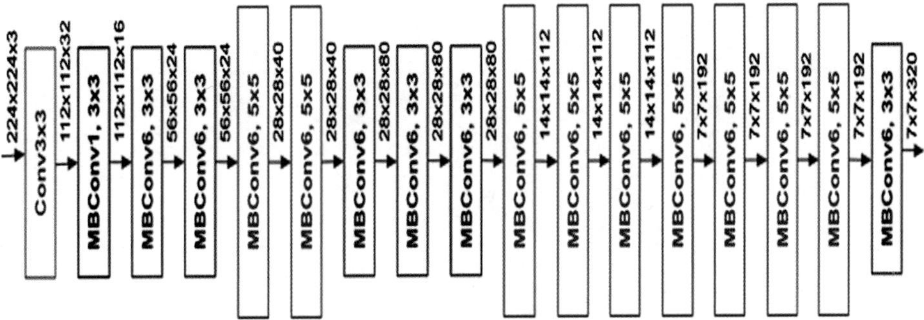

RESULTS

It was observed that when the pre-trained CNN, EfficientNetB0 model, was applied on the colored and gray-scale images, then accuracy was higher for the colored images. The model accuracy and loss were converged by 20 epochs. Accuracy was computed as per the train/test split ratio of 80:20, 60:40, and 50:50 for colored and gray-scaled images. Here, the focus is neither to achieves accuracy nor to compare this implemented approach with the other research work; but to indicate some of the main factors that have a significant impact on the plants' disease detection. The target was to focus on the circumstances which tend to misclassify the trained images. It also reveals the major challenges and factors that may degrade the performance of DL models in the agricultural domain, such as plant disease detection. Table 4 and figure 2 display the accuracy of the deployed CNN model. Augmentation techniques were used to increase the training data samples.

Table 4. Experimental results at the end of 20 epochs

Train/Test Split Ratio	Image Type	Accuracy (approx.)	F1-score (Highest Achieved)
80:20	Color	94%	0.9236
	Gray-scale	89%	0.8814
60:40	Color	92%	0.9045
	Gray-scale	88%	0.8810
50:50	Color	91%	0.9068
	Gray-scale	85%	0.8516

Figure 2. Model performance comparison for colored and gray-scaled images over different train-test splitting ratio

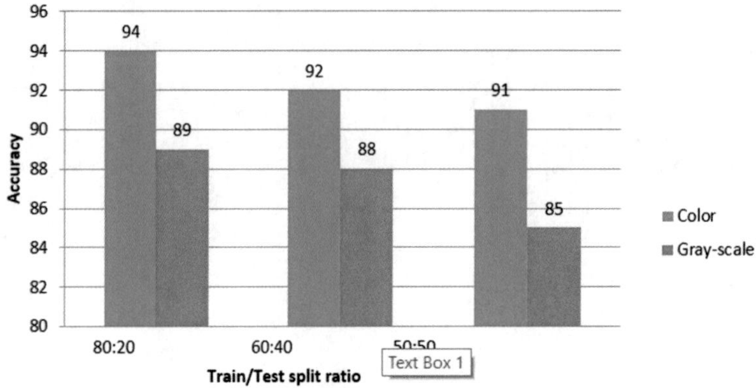

DISCUSSION

Barbedo et al. (Jayme Garcia Arnal Barbedo, 2016) discuss several challenging factors that may affect the automatic detection of plant diseases. These factors are being examined from the perspective of both agriculture and DL. This study retrieves various new aspects from the literature review and practical experience. These issues and challenges are highlighted in (Figures 3 and 8) and discussed in this section. The following agricultural factors were considered as the most important:

- The background image usually contains features that can create difficulty in correct segmentation for the area of interest where symptoms appear.
- Image acquisition surroundings are challenging to control and can lead to images exhibiting characteristics that are hard to predict and making it difficult to identify the disease.
- Many manifestations do not clearly define boundaries and making it challenging to identify healthy and diseased areas.
- The disease can show very diverse characteristics subjected to the stage of development or depend on its location on the plant.

- There may be multiple diseases present at the same time, manifesting either physically separately or in combination in a "hybrid" symptom which may be challenging to recognize.

There is also a need to focus on the DL challenges that could affect the training and testing process for plant diseases. Here is a glimpse of some considerable points:

- The computational time of DL grows explosively with increasing features, feature dependencies, number of data sets, type of features.
- Adding additional neurons to a DL network certainly may also lead to the overfitting problem.
- The DL network could absorb much more training-time due to very small gradients, or training may face deviation because of large gradients.
- Weight variations have a trivial impact on the training of DL models but may take extra time while training the DL model.

AGRICULTURAL CHALLENGES

Insufficient Annotated Dataset (Data Scarcity)

Many of the issues considered in this study are somewhere due to inadequacies in the datasets that are used to train the CNN. Most of the researchers face this kind of situation, but it is not always considered during the analysis of results. Transfer learning allows using some top layers of pre-trained neural networks for adaptation over new data sets. It helps to significantly reduce the requirement for large data sets. In addition, data augmentation techniques and Generative adversarial networks can be used to artificially extend a few training samples by applying augmented techniques (rotation, mirror, segmentation, etc.) and generating artificial or synthetic images, respectively. However, a minimum of hundreds of images are needed (Kamilaris & Prenafeta-Boldú, 2018) and, maybe many more, focusing on the complication of the problem. After collecting image samples, data annotation can be the subsequent task, always needed an expert for image labeling (Kamilaris & Prenafeta-Boldú, 2018). Although, even in some cases, a specialist is not able to provide a specific label without laboratory investigations. If proper care is not taken during the labeling process, it may include a degree of uncertainty associated with the label.

Symptom Representation

Symptoms present on crop leaves can be originated from various sources, including disease, heat and cold damage, nutritional deficiencies, mechanical damage, pests, etc. Therefore, there is a need for a diagnosis system that must be able to cope with multiple classes' classification problems. Even though DL methods have a significant capability to categorize multiple numbers of classes, it is observed that the data available is not sufficient to make such a diagnosis system feasible. In practice, usually, only some of the most common and related diseases are observed. Therefore, when using tools to detect disease symptoms in the real world, it is necessary to find a class that best describes the symptoms from a limited data subset, which often leads to false classification.

Figure 3. Agricultural challenges in plant disease detection

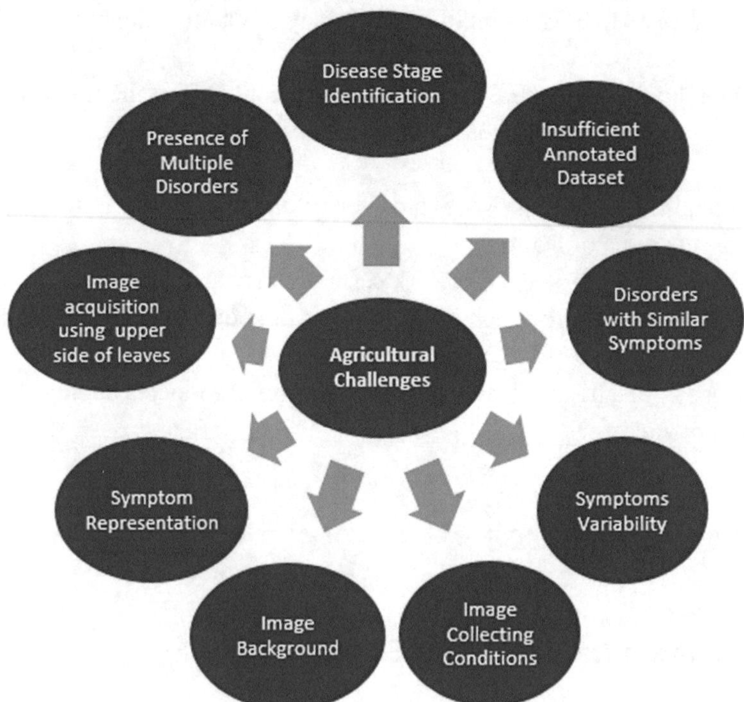

Image Background

Conventional methods of machine learning can be influenced by the background present in the image, such as other leaves, shadows, or soil (Jayme Garcia Arnal Barbedo, 2016). For this reason, leaf segmentation may be a necessary step, and thus, it is a common requirement to place some type of panel behind the leaf during image acquisition. DL techniques are capable of extracting or learn the desired objects of interest even from the busy images (Krizhevsky et al., 2012). Although, the experiments shown by (Mohanty et al., 2016) specified that improved results could be obtained by keeping the background intact. Though, the images were acquired using a regularized procedure which produces images with homogeneous background. Some images contained busy backgrounds (Figure 4), which gave a slightly altered result: the accuracy was approximately 76% and 79% for the original images and images with removed background. There are certain elements present in the background that show the features of certain diseases, and thus, the network might learn these, which leads to error. So, background removal is quite useful when the present elements share the features and characteristics with leaves.

Impact of Image Collecting Conditions

Usually, images are collected under very controlled environments. However, a technology intended for practical use must be prepared to allow different devices and people to process images captured in different backgrounds with different angles and lighting conditions. Figure 5 shows sample images with light reflections and shadows present on leaves. The training database must reflect this reality, regardless of

Figure 4. (a) Bacterial leaf blight diseased rice leaf with busy background, and (b) Angular leaf spot disease in beans crop with busy background

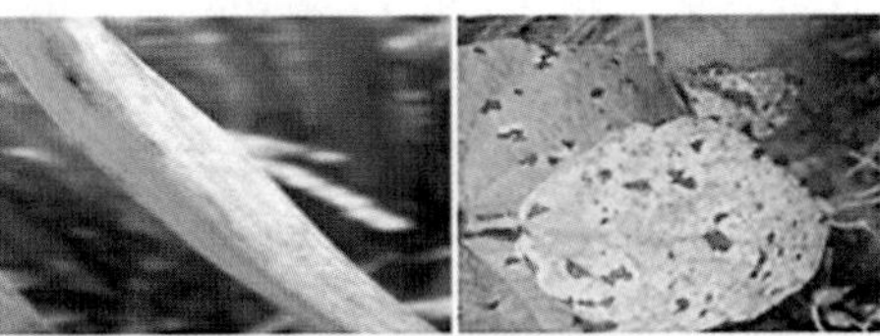

the type of machine learning technique applied. While training a DL model, a large number of labeled images are required to ensure the inclusion of various real-field conditions that are actually expected. Simply said, no image database meets this requirement (Jayme G A Barbedo, 2018). Experiments performed by (Ferentinos, 2018) clearly demonstrated the drawbacks of trained CNNs with an incomplete data set. When the same CNN was deployed with the real field images, the success rate of plant disease detection dropped from 99% to 68%.

Figure 5. Example of (a) Bean rust spot with several light shadows and, (b) healthy apple leaf with shadows

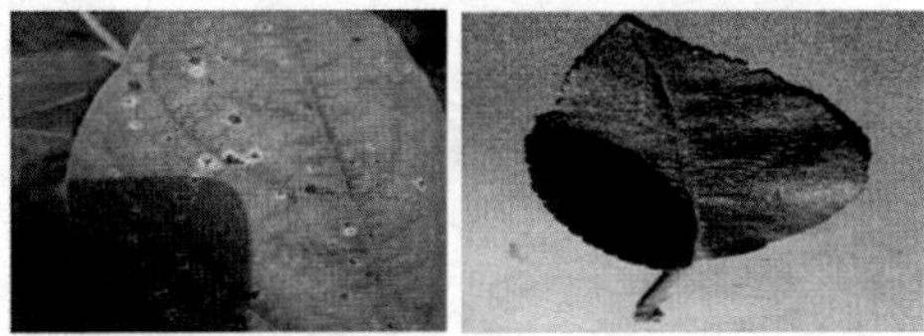

Symptoms Variability

The visual symptoms of many diseases have particular characteristics (features), but there are always several differences in the size, shape, and color of the symptoms. Variation in symptoms might cause problems in image-based diagnosis that use the visible spectrum to depict "healthy" or "infected" pixels (Jayme Garcia Arnal Barbedo, 2016). Disease severity is the major cause of symptom variation. At the early stage of infection, symptoms are very less visible, and as infection spread grows, then severity also grows from mild to severe, respectively. As a result, it can be easy or difficult to distinguish the disease subjected to the stage of infection.

If all the expected variations for a particular symptom are incorporated in the training image dataset, such diversity can pose challenges to deep DL-based tools. Practically, it is difficult to fully predict the symptom variables related to a particular disease and much more difficult to collect a sufficient number of images that represent each of these conditions. Another realistic way is to add samples of new images to the dataset, gradually increasing it to a really large set, thus minimizing the influence of the problem (Jayme Garcia Arnal Barbedo, 2016).

Presence of Multiple Disorders

Usually, images present in the dataset are labeled with a single particular disease. However, there may be multiple diseases present on the fruit or leaves of the crop. Figure 6 shows a sample image with multiple diseases present in it. Along with the bacterial or viral infections, there may be some other elements such as pests, a nutritional deficiency that influence the labeling process. This is because when the infection weakens the plant's immune system, other ailments can move more easily (Jayme Garcia Arnal Barbedo, 2016). A probable way to handle this situation is to generate a mixed class that contains all possible combinations of disorders and diseases. However, it will significantly increase the number of classes and increase the likelihood of misclassification.

Figure 6. Soybeans leaf infected with Cercospora Leaf Blight and Purple Seed Stain

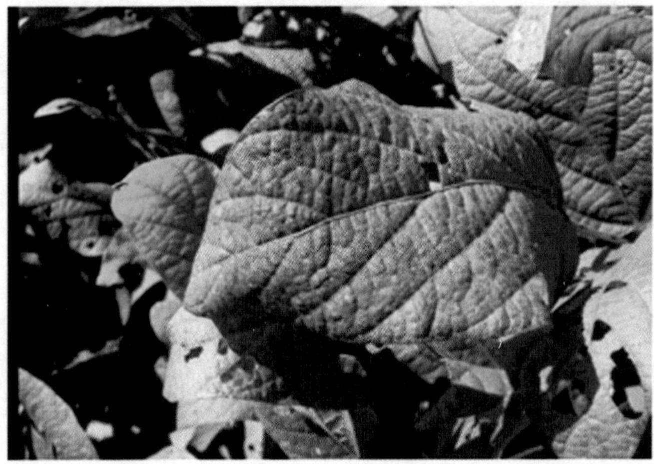

Disorders With Similar Symptoms

There are a number of pathogens or factors (disease, malnutrition, mechanical injuries, pests, etc.) that can cause lesions and other indications in crops. Some of these can generate similar symptoms that cannot be accurately distinguished even by plant pathologists. Therefore, visual cues alone may not be sufficient to settle the classification ambiguities. In order to appeal the precise conclusions, human experts usually look for other signs also, e.g., weather, history of disease data, and general plant growing conditions. Such additional information can be integrated into disease detection systems to increase the classification results (Kamilaris & Prenafeta-Boldú, 2018).

Image Acquisition Using Upper Side Leaves

In literature, most of the systems consider only the upper portion of the leaf surface for image capture (Kamilaris & Prenafeta-Boldú, 2018). Many diseases appear in that area, but these can often improve by symptoms present in other segments of the plant. When the infection in plants spreads through abiotic factors, e.g., rain, wind, etc., there is a higher possibility of starting the disease from the root or any other part of the plant. Figure 7 shows how the infection spread in rainy season. If manifestations are identified at the early stage before reaching in leaves or fruit of the plant, it is relatively easy to control the infection. Thus, it may be useful to handle the images captured from any part of the species even though it constructs a comprehensive, challenging dataset.

Figure 7. Shows how the infection spread in rainy season
(source: internet)

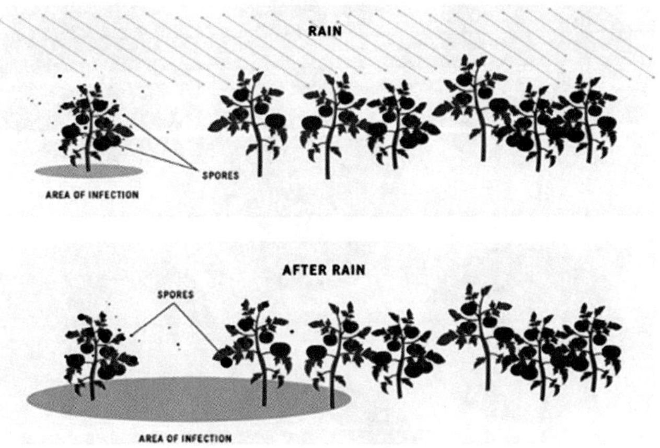

Training and Testing Using the Same Dataset

Many of the systems suggested in the literature were trained and tested on the PlantVillage dataset (Amara et al., 2017; Brahimi et al., 2017; Ferentinos, 2018; Mohanty et al., 2016). It is a publicly available image database that attracts many researchers. Though most of the authors deployed similar types of network frameworks, it creates redundancy in the experiments. In fact, many of the results described in the literature work are identical; only a few of the papers observed diverse aspects of disease detection problems. To advance the research in this field, new tests must be performed with more challenging data sets; otherwise, there will be too many replications without creating additional knowledge.

DEEP LEARNING CHALLENGES

Figure 8. Deep Learning challenges in plant disease detection

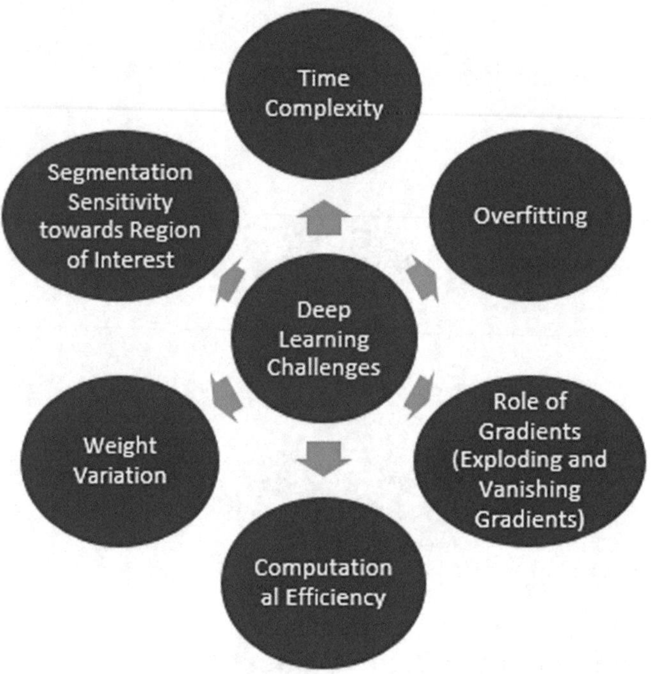

Time Complexity

While deploying DL algorithms in complex datasets, the presence of irrelevant or redundant features can generate computational complexity and latency issues. The computational time of DL grows explosively with increasing features, feature dependencies, number of data sets, type of features, and nested feature ranges that exist in such data sets (Majeed, 2019). Appropriate selection of features during implementing DL is a practical solution to effectively remove the trade-off between computational speed and accuracy when processing large and complex data sets. However, it is very difficult to select the necessary and highly related features to the target concept. So, time complexity may be an issue with unsupervised disease identification models. In (Akhtar et al., 2013), the K-means clustering algorithm still needed more computational time in order to produce high accuracy concerning the index validity term.

Overfitting

A lack of the number of training examples might cause a common issue in DL models known as overfitting. Furthermore, Adding additional neurons to a DL network certainly may also lead to the overfitting problem. Sahu et al. (Sahu et al., 2020) showed the effect of overfitting over trained DL models. In (Y. Chen et al., 2016), hyperspectral image classification was performed using CNN. This research also faces overfitting issues, and thus, dropout and L2 regularization techniques were used to avoid overfitting. In

(Jin et al., 2018), a comprehensive comparison was performed between various DL frameworks, namely, 1D/2D-CNN, LSTM/GRU and, 2D-CNN-LSTM/GRU, where overfitting was observed. Therefore, a novel approach, 2D-CNN-BidLSTM/GRU, was implemented to resolve the issue and perform wheat disease detection. Thus, considering the fact that gathering data is time-consuming and deep classification models can have overfitting in small datasets. It is observed that the use of the augmentation, dropout, regularization techniques, and GAN enhancement method (Hasan et al., 2020) is a powerful tool in such cases.

Computational Efficiency

Computational efficiency can be defined as how to use the minimum amount of resources when gaining the maximum throughput. The existing DL Framework requires a significant amount of computing resources to reach for improved performance. Reservoir computing (Hu et al., 2020), use of incremental approach (Hinton et al., 2012), parallel and scalable DL frameworks (Hong & Kim, 2010), FPGAs (Field-Programmable-Gate-Arrays) (Al-Shamma et al., 2018), GPU (Gao et al., 2020) are some of the techniques and approaches that can overwhelm this computational challenge. GPU is used to speed up the training and testing of DL models. Usually, developers are unknown about the GPU memory consumption requirements before their task executes. Therefore, improper selection of DL architecture or hyper-parameters can get out of limited GPU memory and ultimately fails. Recent studies showed that many DL application failures are due to GPU memory fatigue. These horrific wastes of computing resources and development can lead to significant loss of productivity. Gao et al. (Gao et al., 2020) proposed a GPU memory consumption estimation tool that analytically computes the memory consumption requirements for both the DL framework and run-time computation graph.

Role of Gradients (Exploding and Vanishing Gradients)

Gradients are some important challenges for DL techniques. Each layer present in the DL network computes its gradients (derivatives) in a layered fashion. In every layer, derivatives go exponentially up or down. This technique is responsible for vanishing (exploding) gradients (Hasan et al., 2020). In addition, weights can be adjusted depending on the derivatives and allow decreasing the cost function or error. The DL network could absorb much more training-time due to very small gradients, or training may face deviation because of large gradients. Sigmoid, tanh, etc., are some non-linear activation functions that may worsen the situation. Basodi et al. (Basodi et al., 2020) implemented a gradient amplification technique to train the DL networks (VGG19 and ResNet18, 34 models) and helps to avoid the vanishing gradients. This study also focuses on the effect of amplification parameters on the training time of deep networks.

Weight Variation

Weight variations have a trivial impact on the training of DL models but may take extra time. At the beginning of the training, changes in weight tend to elevate and lead to non-linearity in the network. As training progresses, the number of regions available to gradients (derivatives) becomes smaller and smaller. Thus, the training "gets stuck" in the area of attraction, which is determined by early perturbations of the spatial trajectory of parameters (Erhan et al., 2010). Although, linear activation functions, e.g., ReLU, proper weight normalization, etc., can decrease the consequence of this issue (Hasan et al., 2020).

Segmentation Sensitivity Towards Region of Interest (ROI)

In ROI Segmentation, a specific region is selected in the frame, and objects of specific dimensions are extracted using the rectangle method. Thus, it helps to draw the rectangle-shaped ROI in the frame. Segmented features are characterized in the form of vectors that go through segmentation procedures based on edges, lesions, Otsu, or ROI from the busy background (Hasan et al., 2020). In addition, a fusion process is followed to merge the features in the final vector. Therefore, when an input sample is provided, then, the classifier classifies the infected image area by comparing it to the concluding vector. Alqudah et al. (Alqudah et al., 2020) performed a comparative analysis for different size images: uncropped, cropped, and Segmented Lesions. It was observed that cropped lesions show 98.93% accuracy and 98.18% sensitivity, uncropped lesions have 99% accuracy and 98.52% sensitivity, and segmented lesion images show 97.62% accuracy and 97.40% sensitivity. In (Sharif et al., 2018), a detection method was proposed that combined various processes: Initially, a hybrid Top Hat–Gaussian filter was used to enhance the image; subsequently, the infected regions were emphasized by utilizing threshold skewness to separate them from the background; and lastly, a weighted High-Dimensional Colour Transform (HDCT)-based saliency segmentation was deployed, showing its effectiveness when compared with contour segmentation, Expectation Maximisation (EM), and Otsu.

CONCLUSION AND FUTURE SCOPE

DL applications in the domain of agriculture have grown very rapidly. While observing the DL applications in plant pathology, the reported results are very promising. There are many characteristics that can affect the real-world implementation of such concepts that are not comprehensively explored. Busy backgrounds, lack of symptoms clarity, varying capturing environments, presence of multiple diseases at the same time, Data scarcity, computational efficiency, time complexity, etc. are some of the factors that can degrade the performance of DL models in the agriculture domain and have a major influence on the efficiency of the image analysis practices suggested so far. The aim of this study was to elaborate on those factors and challenges. Several problems focused in this study can be minimized by expanding the available dataset for training and testing. Another future effort can be the contribution of agronomists and plant pathologists in the practice of image acquisition and labeling. Till now, maximum literature reported the use of either leaves or fruits of the crop for detection of the diseases present but using other parts of the plant may be another future direction.

ACKNOWLEDGMENT

Authors are thankful to the Department of Science & Technology, Government of India, Delhi, for funding a project on “Application of IoT in Agriculture Sector” through the ICPS division. This work is a part of the project work.

REFERENCES

Akhtar, A., Khanum, A., Khan, S. A., & Shaukat, A. (2013). Automated plant disease analysis (APDA): performance comparison of machine learning techniques. *2013 11th International Conference on Frontiers of Information Technology*, 60–65.

Al-Shamma, O., Fadhel, M. A., Hameed, R. A., Alzubaidi, L., & Zhang, J. (2018). Boosting convolutional neural networks performance based on FPGA accelerator. *International Conference on Intelligent Systems Design and Applications*, 509–517.

Alqudah, A. M., Alquraan, H., Qasmieh, I. A., Alqudah, A., & Al-Sharu, W. (2020). *Brain Tumor Classification Using Deep Learning Technique—A Comparison between Cropped, Uncropped, and Segmented Lesion Images with Different Sizes.* ArXiv Preprint ArXiv:2001.08844.

Amara, J., Bouaziz, B., Algergawy, A., & others. (2017). A Deep Learning-based Approach for Banana Leaf Diseases Classification. *BTW (Workshops)*, 79–88.

Arsenovic, M., Karanovic, M., Sladojevic, S., Anderla, A., & Stefanovic, D. (2019). Solving current limitations of deep learning based approaches for plant disease detection. *Symmetry*, *11*(7), 939. doi:10.3390ym11070939

Atila, Ü., Uçar, M., Akyol, K., & Uçar, E. (2021). Plant leaf disease classification using EfficientNet deep learning model. *Ecological Informatics*, *61*, 101182. doi:10.1016/j.ecoinf.2020.101182

Barbedo, J. G. A. (2016). A review on the main challenges in automatic plant disease identification based on visible range images. *Biosystems Engineering*, *144*, 52–60. doi:10.1016/j.biosystemseng.2016.01.017

Barbedo, J. G. A. (2019). Plant disease identification from individual lesions and spots using deep learning. *Biosystems Engineering*, *180*, 96–107. doi:10.1016/j.biosystemseng.2019.02.002

Barbedo, J. G. A. (2018). Factors influencing the use of deep learning for plant disease recognition. *Biosystems Engineering*, *172*, 84–91.

Basodi, S., Ji, C., Zhang, H., & Pan, Y. (2020). Gradient amplification: An efficient way to train deep neural networks. *Big Data Mining and Analytics*, *3*(3), 196–207. doi:10.26599/BDMA.2020.9020004

Bengio, Y. (2012). Deep learning of representations for unsupervised and transfer learning. *Proceedings of ICML Workshop on Unsupervised and Transfer Learning*, 17–36.

Brahimi, M., Boukhalfa, K., & Moussaoui, A. (2017). Deep learning for tomato diseases: Classification and symptoms visualization. *Applied Artificial Intelligence*, *31*(4), 299–315. doi:10.1080/08839514.2017.1315516

Chen, J., Chen, J., Zhang, D., Sun, Y., & Nanehkaran, Y. A. (2020). Using deep transfer learning for image-based plant disease identification. *Computers and Electronics in Agriculture*, *173*, 105393. doi:10.1016/j.compag.2020.105393

Chen, Y., Jiang, H., Li, C., Jia, X., & Ghamisi, P. (2016). Deep feature extraction and classification of hyperspectral images based on convolutional neural networks. *IEEE Transactions on Geoscience and Remote Sensing*, *54*(10), 6232–6251. doi:10.1109/TGRS.2016.2584107

Chunjing, Y., Yueyao, Z., Yaxuan, Z., & Liu, H. (2017). Application of convolutional neural network in classification of high resolution agricultural remote sensing images. *The International Archives of the Photogrammetry, Remote Sensing and Spatial Information Sciences*, 42.

Erhan, D., Courville, A., Bengio, Y., & Vincent, P. (2010). Why does unsupervised pre-training help deep learning? *Proceedings of the Thirteenth International Conference on Artificial Intelligence and Statistics*, 201–208.

Ferentinos, K. P. (2018). Deep learning models for plant disease detection and diagnosis. *Computers and Electronics in Agriculture*, *145*, 311–318. doi:10.1016/j.compag.2018.01.009

Gao, Y., Liu, Y., Zhang, H., Li, Z., Zhu, Y., Lin, H., & Yang, M. (2020). Estimating gpu memory consumption of deep learning models. *Proceedings of the 28th ACM Joint Meeting on European Software Engineering Conference and Symposium on the Foundations of Software Engineering*, 1342–1352. 10.1145/3368089.3417050

Gebbers, R., & Adamchuk, V. I. (2010). Precision agriculture and food security. *Science*, *327*(5967), 828–831. doi:10.1126cience.1183899 PMID:20150492

Gutiérrez, S., Hernández, I., Ceballos, S., Barrio, I., Díez-Navajas, A. M., & Tardaguila, J. (2021). Deep learning for the differentiation of downy mildew and spider mite in grapevine under field conditions. *Computers and Electronics in Agriculture*, *182*, 105991. Advance online publication. doi:10.1016/j.compag.2021.105991

Hasan, R. I., Yusuf, S. M., & Alzubaidi, L. (2020). Review of the state of the art of deep learning for plant diseases: A broad analysis and discussion. *Plants*, *9*(10), 1302. doi:10.3390/plants9101302 PMID:33019765

Hinton, G., Deng, L., Yu, D., Dahl, G. E., Mohamed, A., Jaitly, N., Senior, A., Vanhoucke, V., Nguyen, P., Sainath, T. N., & Kingsbury, B. (2012). Deep neural networks for acoustic modeling in speech recognition: The shared views of four research groups. *IEEE Signal Processing Magazine*, *29*(6), 82–97. doi:10.1109/MSP.2012.2205597

Hong, S., & Kim, H. (2010). An integrated GPU power and performance model. *Proceedings of the 37th Annual International Symposium on Computer Architecture*, 280–289. 10.1145/1815961.1815998

Hu, J., Lin, Y., Tang, J., & Zhao, J. (2020). A new wind power interval prediction approach based on reservoir computing and a quality-driven loss function. *Applied Soft Computing*, *92*, 106327. doi:10.1016/j.asoc.2020.106327

Jin, X., Jie, L., Wang, S., Qi, H. J., & Li, S. W. (2018). Classifying wheat hyperspectral pixels of healthy heads and Fusarium head blight disease using a deep neural network in the wild field. *Remote Sensing*, *10*(3), 395. doi:10.3390/rs10030395

Joshi, R. C., Kaushik, M., Dutta, M. K., Srivastava, A., & Choudhary, N. (2021). VirLeafNet: Automatic analysis and viral disease diagnosis using deep-learning in Vigna mungo plant. *Ecological Informatics*, *61*, 101197. doi:10.1016/j.ecoinf.2020.101197

Kamilaris, A., & Prenafeta-Boldú, F. X. (2018). Deep learning in agriculture: A survey. *Computers and Electronics in Agriculture*, *147*, 70–90. doi:10.1016/j.compag.2018.02.016

Kang, H., & Chen, C. (2020). Fast implementation of real-time fruit detection in apple orchards using deep learning. *Computers and Electronics in Agriculture*, *168*, 105108. doi:10.1016/j.compag.2019.105108

Krizhevsky, A., Sutskever, I., & Hinton, G. E. (2012). Imagenet classification with deep convolutional neural networks. *Advances in Neural Information Processing Systems*, 1097–1105.

Kuznetsova, A., Maleva, T., & Soloviev, V. (2020). Using YOLOv3 algorithm with pre-and post-processing for apple detection in fruit-harvesting robot. *Agronomy (Basel)*, *10*(7), 1016. doi:10.3390/agronomy10071016

Lee, H., & Kwon, H. (2017). Going deeper with contextual CNN for hyperspectral image classification. *IEEE Transactions on Image Processing*, *26*(10), 4843–4855. doi:10.1109/TIP.2017.2725580 PMID:28708555

Li, D., Wang, R., Xie, C., Liu, L., Zhang, J., Li, R., Wang, F., Zhou, M., & Liu, W. (2020). A recognition method for rice plant diseases and pests video detection based on deep convolutional neural network. *Sensors (Basel)*, *20*(3), 578. doi:10.339020030578 PMID:31973039

Liu, B., Zhang, Y., He, D., & Li, Y. (2018). Identification of apple leaf diseases based on deep convolutional neural networks. *Symmetry*, *10*(1), 11. doi:10.3390ym10010011

Liu, G., Nouaze, J. C., Touko Mbouembe, P. L., & Kim, J. H. (2020). YOLO-tomato: A robust algorithm for tomato detection based on YOLOv3. *Sensors (Basel)*, *20*(7), 2145. doi:10.339020072145 PMID:32290173

Liu, J., & Wang, X. (2020). Tomato diseases and pests detection based on improved Yolo V3 convolutional neural network. *Frontiers in Plant Science*, *11*, 898. doi:10.3389/fpls.2020.00898 PMID:32612632

Liu, Z., Wu, J., Fu, L., Majeed, Y., Feng, Y., Li, R., & Cui, Y. (2019). Improved kiwifruit detection using pre-trained VGG16 with RGB and NIR information fusion. *IEEE Access: Practical Innovations, Open Solutions*, *8*, 2327–2336. doi:10.1109/ACCESS.2019.2962513

Majeed, A. (2019). Improving time complexity and accuracy of the machine learning algorithms through selection of highly weighted top k features from complex datasets. *Annals of Data Science*, *6*(4), 599–621. doi:10.100740745-019-00217-4

Mao, S., Li, Y., Ma, Y., Zhang, B., Zhou, J., & Wang, K. (2020). Automatic cucumber recognition algorithm for harvesting robots in the natural environment using deep learning and multi-feature fusion. *Computers and Electronics in Agriculture*, *170*, 105254. doi:10.1016/j.compag.2020.105254

Mohanty, S. P., Hughes, D. P., & Salathé, M. (2016). Using deep learning for image-based plant disease detection. *Frontiers in Plant Science*, *7*, 1419. doi:10.3389/fpls.2016.01419 PMID:27713752

Nanni, L., Maguolo, G., & Pancino, F. (2020). Insect pest image detection and recognition based on bio-inspired methods. *Ecological Informatics*, *57*, 101089. doi:10.1016/j.ecoinf.2020.101089

Pan, S. J., & Yang, Q. (2009). A survey on transfer learning. *IEEE Transactions on Knowledge and Data Engineering*, *22*(10), 1345–1359. doi:10.1109/TKDE.2009.191

Patricio, D. I., & Rieder, R. (2018). Computer vision and artificial intelligence in precision agriculture for grain crops: A systematic review. *Computers and Electronics in Agriculture*, *153*, 69–81.

Rahnemoonfar, M., & Sheppard, C. (2017). Deep count: Fruit counting based on deep simulated learning. *Sensors (Basel)*, *17*(4), 905.

Saedi, S. I., & Khosravi, H. (2020). A deep neural network approach towards real-time on-branch fruit recognition for precision horticulture. *Expert Systems with Applications*, *159*, 113594.

Sahu, P., Chug, A., Singh, A. P., Singh, D., & Singh, R. P. (2020). Implementation of CNNs for Crop Diseases Classification: A Comparison of Pre-trained Model and Training from Scratch. *IJCSNS*, *20*(10), 206.

Santos, T. T., de Souza, L. L., dos Santos, A. A., & Avila, S. (2020). Grape detection, segmentation, and tracking using deep neural networks and three-dimensional association. *Computers and Electronics in Agriculture*, *170*, 105247.

Savary, S., Ficke, A., Aubertot, J.-N., & Hollier, C. (2012). *Crop losses due to diseases and their implications for global food production losses and food security*. Springer.

Sharif, M., Khan, M. A., Iqbal, Z., Azam, M. F., Lali, M. I. U., & Javed, M. Y. (2018). Detection and classification of citrus diseases in agriculture based on optimized weighted segmentation and feature selection. *Computers and Electronics in Agriculture*, *150*, 220–234.

Sujatha, R., Chatterjee, J. M., Jhanjhi, N. Z., & Brohi, S. N. (2021). Performance of deep learning vs machine learning in plant leaf disease detection. *Microprocessors and Microsystems*, *80*, 103615. doi:10.1016/j.micpro.2020.103615

Szegedy, C., Liu, W., Jia, Y., Sermanet, P., Reed, S., Anguelov, D., ... Rabinovich, A. (2015). Going deeper with convolutions. *Proceedings of the IEEE Conference on Computer Vision and Pattern Recognition*, 1–9.

Talaviya, T., Shah, D., Patel, N., Yagnik, H., & Shah, M. (2020). Implementation of artificial intelligence in agriculture for optimisation of irrigation and application of pesticides and herbicides. *Artificial Intelligence in Agriculture*, *4*, 58–73. doi:10.1016/j.aiia.2020.04.002

Tan, M., & Le, Q. (2019). Efficientnet: Rethinking model scaling for convolutional neural networks. *International Conference on Machine Learning*, 6105–6114.

Chapter 5
Automatic Animal Detection and Collision Avoidance System (ADCAS) Using Thermal Camera

Jeyabharathi Duraipandy
Sri Krishna College of Technology, India

Kesavaraja D.
https://orcid.org/0000-0002-5036-4238
Dr. Sivanthi Aditanar College of Engineering, Tiruchendur, India

Sasireka Duraipandy
V. V. College of Engineering, Tisaiyanvillai, India

ABSTRACT

Animal-vehicle collision is one of the big issues in roadways near forests. Due to road accidents, the injuries and death of wildlife has increased tremendously. This type of collision is occurring mainly during nighttime because the animals are more activate. So, to avoid this type of accident, the chapter automatically detects animals on highways, preventing animal-vehicle collision by finding the distance between vehicles and animals in the roadway. If the distance between animals and vehicle is short, then automatic horn sound is given, which will alert both drivers as well as animals.

INTRODUCTION

Wild animal surveillance systems installed in the forest and most dangerous intersections in the road side forest, it plays an essential role in accident prevention and monitoring. The proposed system give the novel method for tracking objects in thermal images.

This work attempts to extend technology for the society. Video Surveillance cameras are to be employed to improve the wild animal monitoring in the forest and its safety from roadway accidents.

DOI: 10.4018/978-1-7998-3299-7.ch005

Figure 1. Overall working process of the proposed system

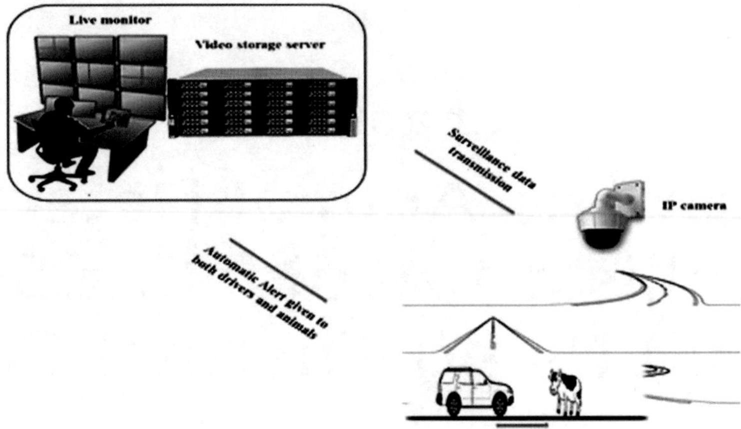

The approach is based on a threshold, dynamically outfitted for every frame, and a novel feature extraction algorithm which is invariant to rotation, scaling and, partly, posture. Detected items are tracked in next images to include temporal statistics inside the reputation a part of the algorithm. The algorithm has been examined in a managed test, the usage of real animals, within the context of natural world-friendly farming.

- The primary objective is to track the animals in the roadway near to forest and alert the Control Room when the animals entering into roadway near to vehicles, to take the remedy such as fixing sound horn, fixing heavy light sources, etc. That is the objective is to save lives and give a peaceful environment to wild animals and people.
- This is to be achieved in this work (Thermal Image) by developing an algorithm that can detect foreground, track specified object (animals) and give the alert to the control room.

The overall structure of the proposed system is shown in Figure 1.

LITERATURE SURVEY

Sharma et al. (2013) have proposed and designed a system supported histogram research including oriented gradients and boosted cascade classifiers for automatic cow detection. the tactic is implemented in Opencv software and tested on various video clips involving cow movements in various scenarios. The proposed system has achieved an overall efficiency of 80% in terms of cow detection. The proposed system could even be a low-cost, highly reliable system which may easily be implemented in automobiles for detection of cow or the other animal after proper training and testing on the highway.

Zahrani et al. (2011) have proposed Camel-Vehicle Accident Avoidance System to avoid the collision between camel and vehicle. this system was designed using global positioning system technology. The CVAAS work took a primary comprehensive step towards a system which can help detect camels on the highway and warn drivers also .The foremost limitation of this approach during this technique the author mainly focused on camel-vehicle accident detection.

Robert et al. (2016) have proposed a camera road sign system of the primary warning, which can help to avoid from vehicle collision with the wild animals. The system consists of camera modules placed down the particularly chosen route and thus the intelligent road signs. The camera module consists of the camera device and thus the computing unit. The video stream is captured from video camera using computing unit. Then the algorithms of object detection are deployed. Afterwards, the machine learning algorithms are getting to be used to classify the moving objects. If the moving object is assessed as animal and this animal are often dangerous for safety of the vehicle, warning are getting to be displayed on the intelligent road sings.

A recent study (Fabre et al. 2001) shown that citizenry got to take the last word call while driving whether or not they will control their car to prevent collision with a response time of 150ms or no. the problem with the above approach is that human eyes get exhausted quickly and need rest, which is why this method isn't that effective. Some scientific researchers (Burghardt et al. 2006) have proposed how that needs the animals to need a pose towards the camera for the trigger, including face detection. the matter with this technique is that face detection requires animals to determine into the camera which is, not necessarily captured by the road travel video. Animals can arrive from a scene from various directions and in several sizes, poses, and color.

Animals are often detected using the knowledge of their motion. the basic assumption here (Walther et al. 2004) is that the default location is static and should simply be subtracted. All blobs, which stay after the operation are measured because the region of interest. Although this technique performs well in controlled areas, e.g. underwater videos, it doesn't work universally, especially road or highway side videos. Researchers (Nascimento et al. 2000) used threshold segmentation approach for getting the targeted animal's details from the background. Recent researches (Kawasaki et al. 1993) also revealed that it's hard to form a choice the sting value because the background changes often. how applicable to moving backgrounds (e.g., because of camera motion) is presented in subsequent studies (Hannuna et al. 2005).The authors also state that other moving objects apart from the thing of interest could even be falsely detected as an animal.

Researchers in (agheb et al. 2008) tried to urge an animal's presence within the scene (image) affecting the power spectrum of the image . This method of animal detection was also considered not appropriate since quicker results with this approach would involve massive amount of image processing during a brief period (Wichmann et al. 2010). Researchers in (Viola et al. 2004) also used the face detector technique initiated by Viola and Jones for a selected animal type. After the animal face is identified, the researchers track it over time. the matter with this technique is that face detection requires animals to determine into the camera not necessarily captured by the road travel video.

- The most important challenge in detecting animals compared to pedestrians or other objects is that animals are available various size, shape, pose, color and their behavior is additionally not entirely predictable. Though the essential shape and size of an individual's being are pretty average and standard, the same isn't true for animals.
- Although various methods and approaches are used and are still ongoing to detect, solve and reduce the quantity of animal-vehicle collisions, the absence of any practical systems related to an animal-vehicle collision on highways has delayed any substantial development within the scenario.
- Animals are appear suddenly when is in bush. that time 100% possibility to satisfy with collision. But within the proposed system uses thermal cameras, which can be used to detect each objects supported temperature difference. therefore the animals are detected albeit it's in bush. For this

reason, the proposed work are often used to avoid the accidents and provides best security to both animals and person in vehicles.

PROPOSED METHOD- TWO LAYERS DEEP LEARNING BASED BACKGROUND SUBTRACTION (TDBS)

The proposed method involves three steps namely: (i) Background Subtraction (ii) Feature Extraction and Multiple Object Tracking (iii) Object Classification and (iv) Animals nearby vehicle determination. Fig 2 shows the proposed two-layer deep learning background subtraction approach.

Figure 2.

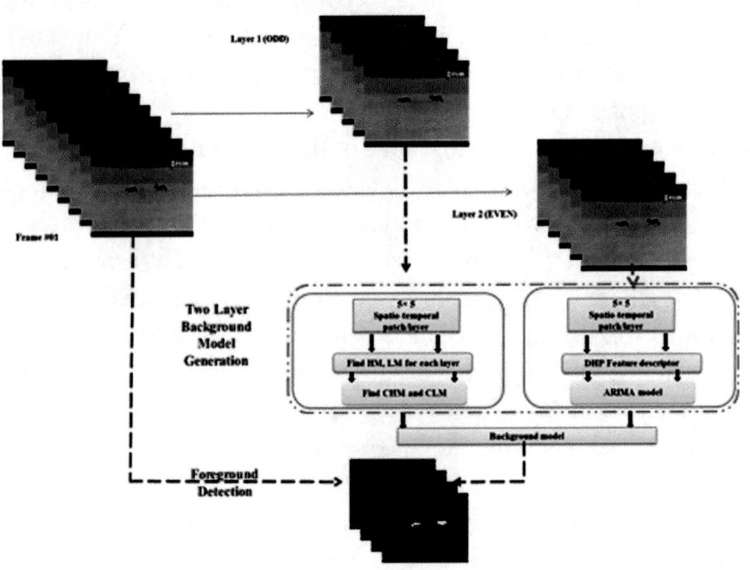

Background Subtraction

The proposed Two layers Deep learning-based Background Subtraction (TDBS) method consist of the following steps

1. First Layer background model is generated using spatio-temporal High Value Matrix (HVM) and spatio-temporal Low Value Matrix (LVM)
2. Second Layer background model is generated using DHP feature descriptors.
3. Apply two background models on the images to get the estimation of foreground regions and background regions.
4. Update background model using temporal relationship between frames.

Figure 3. HVM and LVM spatio-temporal model

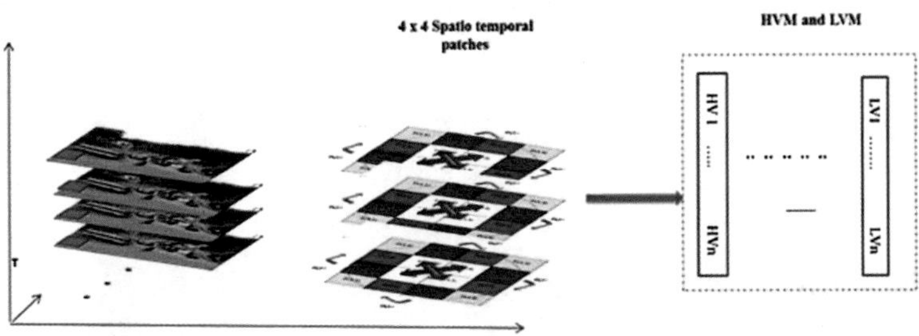

Background Model Generation

Initial background model is generated for the first 10 frames and then the background model is updated using temporal relationship between successive frames. Those 10 frames are splitted into two layers. The first layer includes the odd number of frames and the second layer includes the even number of frames. Each two layers are grouped into 5 × 5 spatio-temporal blocks.

Spatio-Temporal Blocks

A Spatiotemporal is used for managing or dealing with the both space and time information.Spatial and temporal aspects form a first-rate part of the substantial quantity of information generated by cell devices, GIS structures, pc imaginative and prescient programs and plenty of different procedures. The spatial members of the family (distance, direction, form, and so forth.) and temporal members of the family (incidence time, length, incidence before or after different events, and so forth.) must be extracted from the uncooked facts so that useful inferences may be drawn from the facts. Spatial information is different as it consists of complicated gadgets like points, strains polygons and other shapes along with size parameters and elevation etc. additionally, spatial statistics comes inside the form of both raster (e.g. satellite snap shots) or vector facts, which ought to be processed through special techniques. Customers working with spatio-Temporal data are interested in the houses of the facts which makes the translation of records smooth and intuitive. therefore, the statistics can be stored in any form but it is presentation includes visualization and/or manipulation for presentation in human understandable shape. The numerous research troubles associated with the field are powerful visualization of complicated information and the styles taking place in them, scalability of the methods for spatial and temporal information extraction and efficient indexing of spatio-temporal records.

First Layer Background Model

The main aim to find HVM and LVM in spatio temporal block is to reduce the number of observations in the spatio-temporal vicinity of an estimation location to a representative, computationally feasible subset of data. From the subset Covariance between two HVM and LVM are predicted. That value is act as a background

$$CHVM_n = Cov\left[HVM_1, HVM_2 \ldots\ldots\ldots HVM_n\right] \tag{1}$$

$$CLVM_n = Cov\left[LVM_1, LVM_2 \ldots\ldots\ldots LVM_n\right] \tag{2}$$

Foreground Detection

Given a newly appearing spatio temporal block $STB_{i_{(8\times8)}}$, determining whether pixels in $STB_{i_{(8\times8)}}$ belong to the background or not is decided by thresholding its appearance residual and state residual. Appearance residual is the deviation of spatio temporal block from its state. State residual is the deviation from one state of spatio temporal block to another state of spatio temporal block. The state of $STB_{i_{(8\times8)}}$ with appearance consistency A_i (jeyabharathi et al. 2014) is denoted by Z_i.

$$Z_i = A_i * STB_{i_{8\times8}} \tag{3}$$

and further the appearance residual of $STB_{i_{(8\times8)}}$ is W_i, and is given in (4)

$$W_i = \left\|STB_{8\times8} - Z_i\right\| \tag{4}$$

With state Z_i, and the Temporal Coherence T_i, state residual $\in_i$ is estimated as in (5)

$$\in_i = \left\|Z_{i+1} - T_i * Z_i\right\| \tag{5}$$

Challenges in Thermal Images

The main challenges in thermal background subtractions are polarity changes and halo effect.

A) Polarity Changes

The change in polarity is equal to the change in temperature in the scene. So the methods which depend on any prior shape models or motion information are not suitable to handle this situation. HVM and LVM can be used to distinguish the moving object from background effectively.

B) Halo Effect

Halo effect is occurring around very hot or cold objects in thermal domain. The accurate subspace from HVM and LVM can effectively separate the moving object from halo effect.

Experiments

In this section, many experimental results are bestowed which may reveal the feasibleness and effectiveness of the proposed background subtraction technique.

The publicly available thermal databases OTCBVS Database (https://www.cse.ohio-state.edu/otcbvs-bench/) and BU-TIV Database (http://csr.bu.edu/BU-TIV/data/lab1/video/test_seq1_green.mp4), Computer Vision Database (http://wordpress-jodoin.dmi.usherb.ca/dataset2012) and FLIR Scout TS-Series (Animals dataset) are taken for the experiments. The video from YouTube is also taken for experiment.

The proposed work is compared with below methods GMG, IMBS, LOBSTER MultiCue, SuBSENSE, T2FMRF, ViBe.

A) Quantitative Comparison

F-score is a benchmark metric, which measures the segmentation accuracy by considering both the recall and the precision. The F-Score is defined as in (6)

$$FScore = \frac{2 * Precision * Recall}{Precision + Recall} \tag{6}$$

where

$$precision = \frac{TP}{TP + FP} \tag{7}$$

and

$$Recall = \frac{TP}{TP + FN} \tag{8}$$

where TP is True Positive that counts correctly classified foreground pixels, FP is False Positive that counts background pixels incorrectly classified as foreground, FN is False Negative that counts foreground pixels incorrectly classified as background and TN is True Negative that counts correctly classified background pixels. Results are contained in Table 1. Notice that the F-score of the proposed work is relatively higher than those of other methods.

Table 1. Performance analysis based on the metric F-score

Sequences	GMG[Godbehere et al.]	IMBS[Bloisi et al.]	LOBSTER[Godbehere et al.]	MultiCue[Noh et al.]	SuBSENSE[St-Charles et al.]	T2FMRF [Barnich et al.]	ViBe[Barnich et al.]	Proposed Work (TDBS)
OTCBVS Database								
Seq 01	06789	0.7453	0.8809	0.9012	0.9012	0.9012	0.9012	0.9412
Seq 02	0.7090	0.7654	0.8471	0.9123	0.9123	0.9123	0.9123	0.9500
Seq 03	0.7345	0.7400	0.7502	0.5278	0.6324	0.8102	0.9100	0.9102
Seq 04	0.7189	0.7345	0.7623	0.8045	0.8945	0.8012	0.9000	0.9278
Seq 05	0.7345	0.7457	0.7509	0.7546	0.8457	0.8345	0.9412	0.9567
Seq 06	0.6892	0.7789	0.7712	0.7890	0.8290	0.8423	0.9267	0.9300
Seq 07	0.6913	0.7809	0.7829	0.7730	0.8156	0.8322	0.9514	0.9513
BU-TIV Database								
Video_001	0.5278	0.6324	0.8102	0.200	0.8468	0.8102	0.9178	0.920
Video_002	0.5201	0.6423	0.8012	0.8012	0.8134	0.8765	0.9190	0.9312
Video_003	0.5400	0.6674	0.8154	0.8440	0.8546	0.8154	0.9011	09123
Video_004	0.5512	0.6623	0.8423	0.7969	0.7967	0.8423	0.9078	0.9012
Video_005	0.5730	0.6420	0.8322	0.,8014	0.,8014	0.8322	0.9067	0.9134

Figure 4. BU-TIV Database- output for the proposed work

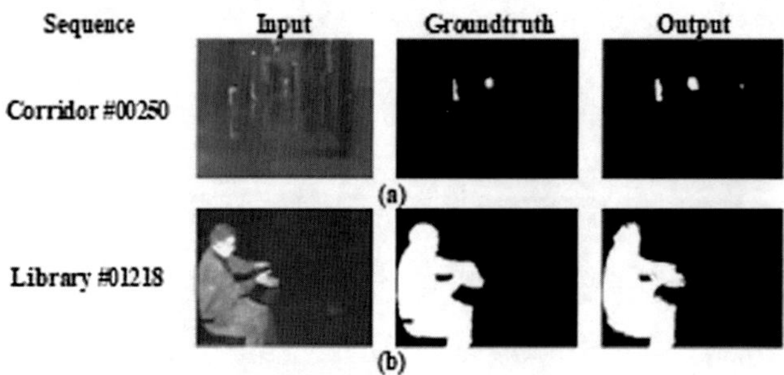

Figure 5. YouTube animal tracking video sequence- output for the proposed work

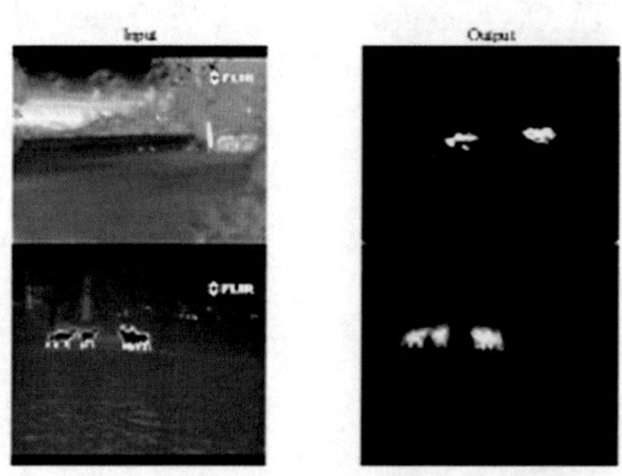

Figure 4 and Figure 5 demonstrates the superiority of the proposed work over all the other combinations. The F-Score values are high for Rotational Symmetry Dynamic Texture (RSDT) when compared with existing methods.

Object Tracking

Object Tracking is an important domain in computer vision. It involves the process of tracking an object which could be a person, ball or a car across a series of frames.

Types of Object Tracking

1. Point tracking
2. Template tracking
3. Kernal tracking
4. Feature based tracking

A) Point Tracking

The point monitoring technique is used when detected objects are represented as points. usually talking, tracking is finished through evaluating their kingdom in terms of position and motion [30].

B) Kernel Monitoring

The kernel monitoring approach is based on computing the motion of an object represented by using a primitive item region. by using the usage of a motion version, i.e. computing the motion of an item from one frame to another, it's far possible to decide its subsequent role.

C) Template Primarily Based

Template based totally look fashions are considered tremendously immediately-ahead to apply and not as complicated as other models. This has made them a famous preference in look model and had been extensively used for long. With the template primarily based technique the methods for monitoring objects vary depending on if it's far a unmarried item or multiple objects being tracked.

Unique identification of target objects is necessary to track the vehicle in a video. Feature vector for every moving object is extracted using the proposed feature descriptor HPTP from the background subtracted video.

D) Feature Based Tracking

Feature based tracking is based on vital data of the object. Based on these data object is tracked frame by frame. The main advantage of feature-based tracking is, more suitable for tracking occluded object. So, the proposed object tracking lies on feature-based object tracking.

Feature Selection

Feature selection is a process of select the informative features that can be used to uniquely identify that particular object. In this chapter Scale Invariant Diagonal Feature (SIDF) is introduced to track the object accurately even in partial as well as full occluation time.

Each object in the first frame is considered as a target object. Target object's location is predicted and its corresponding features are extracted using the proposed SIDF descriptor. That is each object is represented by it SIDF feature. In the subsequent frames, candidates are defined and are represented by their corresponding SIDF features. Tracking procedure starts with the calculation of distance between feature vector of the target objects and candidate objects in the next frame. Based on minimum distance each object is tracked

A) Scale Invariant Diagonal Feature (SIDF) Feature Construction

Scale Invariant Diagonal Feature is mainly based on diagonal elements of each 3×3block in the object. The main reason to choose diagonal matrix is, the most informative and invariant features are in the diagonal portion of the matrix. This information can lead to provide a scale invariant feature that is suitable for track the object accurately. Fig 6 shows the working process of SIFD feature descriptors.

- From 3×3 block, the diagonal element is extracted first and then form 3×3 matrix from first 3 blocks diagonal values, this process is continued until the end of the block.
- Covariance values in between the successive diagonal matrix arecalculated.
- Eigen vectors and Eigen value is calculated, from that larges eigen value from each matrix is formed as a vector, Finally average values is taken as a feature.

Figure 6. Scale Invariant Diagonal Feature (SIDF) working process

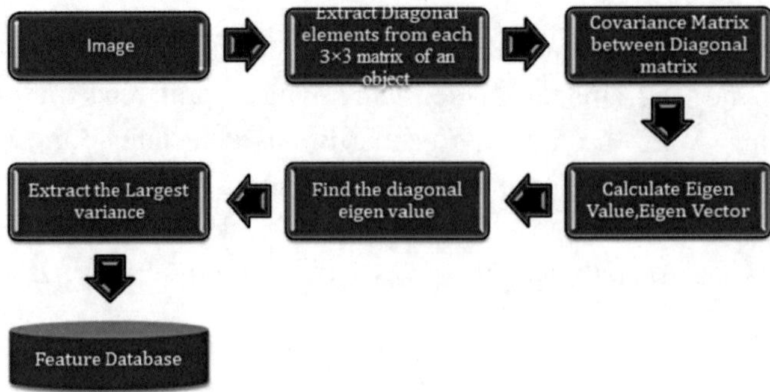

Object Classification

In the proposed system, there is a need for classifying the object. That is find out whether it is an animal or vehicle. Statistics regarding the looks, shape, and motion of moving objects may be classified quickly distinguish individuals, vehicles, carts, animals, doors opening/closing, trees occupancy the breeze, etc.

Proposed system classifies objects into vehicles and animals based on the feature used for tracking. SVM (Support Vector Machine) classifier is for classification purpose.

The below architecture denote the working process of object classification in the proposed system. Figure 7 shows SVM classification process.

Figure 7. SIDF– SVM Classification model

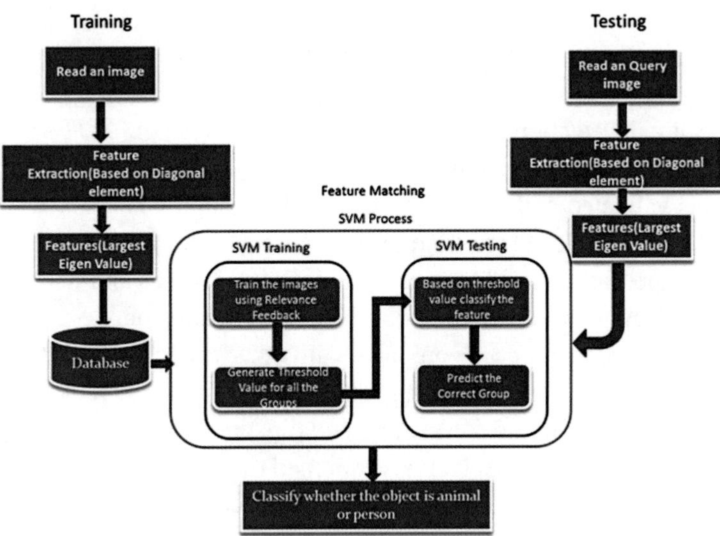

Figure 8. Output of the proposed system (Collision Detection System)

Collision Avoidance System

The occurrence of collision in between animal vehicle is predicted using the position between both animal and vehicles in the inner frame. The corner point of the bounding box in between vehicle and animal is less than threshold then alert is given. YouTube video is taken for experimental setup. The output is given in Fig 8.

CONCLUSION

A novel Automatic Animal Detection and Collision Avoidance System (ADCAS) is proposed. It serves as an effective real time collision detection system. A new background subtraction method is proposed and its effectiveness is validated with extensive testing. The proposed two layers Deep learning based Background Subtraction (TDBS)used to generate the accurate background model using HVM and LVM matrix. This two layer approach is used to overcome polarity changes and halo effect. Proposed SIFD feature descriptor effectively used to track the objects even in occlusion.

The results of the proposed method are compared with other existing methods by using the parameter such as F-score, average running time; Result indicates that the proposed method outperforms other state of the art methods for both background subtraction and object tracking.

In future, GPU based implementation can be developed to process each part of the scene in parallel, and it would probably significantly improve the system's efficiency.

REFERENCES

Babaee, M., Dinh, D. T., & Rigoll, G. (2017). *A deep convolutional neural network for background subtraction.* arXiv preprint arXiv:170201731.

Barnich, O., & Van Droogenbroeck, M. (2009). ViBe: a powerful random technique to estimate the background in video sequences. In *Acoustics, Speech and Signal Processing, 2009. ICASSP 2009. IEEE International Conference on, 2009.* IEEE. 10.1109/ICASSP.2009.4959741

Bloisi, D., & Iocchi, L. (2012). Independent multimodal background subtraction. CompIMAGE, 39-44.

Chai, Y., Ren, J., Zhao, H., Li, Y., Ren, J., & Murray, P. (2016). Hierarchical and multi-featured fusion for effective gait recognition under variable scenarios. *Pattern Analysis & Applications*, *19*(4), 905–917. doi:10.100710044-015-0471-5

Davis, J. W., & Keck, M. A. (2005). A two-stage template approach to person detection in thermal imagery. IEEE. doi:10.1109/ACVMOT.2005.14

Godbehere, A. B., Matsukawa, A., & Goldberg, K. (2012). Visual tracking of human visitors under variable-lighting conditions for a responsive audio art installation. *American Control Conference (ACC)*, 4305-4312. 10.1109/ACC.2012.6315174

Han, J., Zhang, D., Hu, X., Guo, L., Ren, J., & Wu, F. (2015). Background prior-based salient object detection via deep reconstruction residual. *IEEE Transactions on Circuits and Systems for Video Technology, 25*(8), 1309–1321. doi:10.1109/TCSVT.2014.2381471

He, K., Zhang, X., Ren, S., & Sun, J. (2016). Deep residual learning for image recognition. *Proceedings of the IEEE conference on computer vision and pattern recognition*, 770-778.

Hofmann, M., Tiefenbacher, P., & Rigoll, G. (2012). Background segmentation with feedback: The pixel-based adaptive segmenter. In *Computer Vision and Pattern Recognition Workshops (CVPRW), 2012 IEEE Computer Society Conference on, 2012*. IEEE.

Jeyabharathi, D. (2016). Vehicle tracking and speed measurement system (VTSM) based on novel feature descriptor: diagonal hexadecimal pattern (DHP). *J Visual Commun Image Rep, 40*(B), 816–830.

Jeyabharathi, D. (2017). Background subtraction and object tracking via key frame-based rotational symmetry dynamic texture. *Adv Image Process Tech Appl.* . ch013 doi:10.4018/978-1-5225-2053-5

Jeyabharathi, D., & Dejey, D. (2016). A novel rotational symmetry dynamic texture (RSDT) based sub space construction and SCD (similar-congruent-dissimilar) based scoring model for background subtraction in real time videos. *Multimedia Tools and Applications, 75*(24), 17617–17645. doi:10.100711042-016-3772-9

Jeyabharathi, D., & Dejey, D. (2018). *New feature descriptor: extended symmetrical-diagonal hexadecimal pattern for efficient background subtraction and object tracking*. Comput Elect Eng.

Kim, D.-E., & Kwon, D.-S. (2015). Pedestrian detection and tracking in thermal images using shape features. In *Ubiquitous Robots and Ambient Intelligence (URAI), 2015 12th International Conference on, 2015*. IEEE. 10.1109/URAI.2015.7358920

Maddalena, L., & Petrosino, A. (2010). A fuzzy spatial coherence-based approach to background/foreground separation for moving object detection. *Neural Computing & Applications, 19*(2), 179–186. doi:10.100700521-009-0285-8

Nguyen, T.P., Pham, C.C., Ha, S.V-U., & Jeon, J.W. (2018). Change Detection by Training a Triplet Network for Motion Feature Extraction. *IEEE Transactions on Circuits and Systems for Video Technology*.

Noh, S., & Jeon, M. (2012). A new framework for background subtraction using multiple cues. In *Asian Conference on Computer Vision*, 2012. Springer.

Ren, J., Han, J., & Dalla Mura, M. (2016). Special issue on multimodal data fusion for multidimensional signal processing. *Multidimensional Systems and Signal Processing, 27*(4), 801–805. doi:10.100711045-016-0441-0

Ren, J., Jiang, J., Wang, D., & Ipson, S. (2010). Fusion of intensity and inter-component chromatic difference for effective and robust colour edge detection. *IET Image Processing, 4*(4), 294–301. doi:10.1049/iet-ipr.2009.0071

St-Charles, P.-L., & Bilodeau, G.-A. (2014). Improving background subtraction using local binary similarity patterns. In *Applications of Computer Vision (WACV), 2014 IEEE Winter Conference on, 2014*. IEEE. 10.1109/WACV.2014.6836059

St-Charles, P.-L., Bilodeau, G.-A., & Bergevin, R. (2014). Flexible background subtraction with self-balanced local sensitivity. *Proceedings of the IEEE Conference on Computer Vision and Pattern Recognition Workshops*, 408-413. 10.1109/CVPRW.2014.67

Vacavant, A., Chateau, T., Wilhelm, A., & Lequievre, L. (2012). A benchmark dataset for foreground/background extraction. ACCV 2012, Workshop: Background Models Challenge.

Wang, Y., Jodoin, P.-M., Porikli, F., Konrad, J., & Benezeth, Y. (2014). CDnet2014: An expanded change detection benchmark dataset. In *Computer Vision and Pattern Recognition Workshops (CVPRW), 2014 IEEE Conference on, 2014*. IEEE.

Wang, Z., Ren, J., Zhang, D., Sun, M., & Jiang, J. (2018). A deep-learning based feature hybrid framework for spatiotemporal saliency detection inside videos. *Neurocomputing*, *287*, 68–83. doi:10.1016/j.neucom.2018.01.076

Yan, Y., Ren, J., Li, Y., Windmill, J., & Ijomah, W. (2015). Fusion of dominant colour and spatial layout features for effective image retrieval of coloured logos and trademarks. In *Multimedia Big Data (BigMM), 2015 IEEE International Conference on, 2015*. IEEE. 10.1109/BigMM.2015.43

Yan, Y., Ren, J., Li, Y., Windmill, J. F., Ijomah, W., & Chao, K.-M. (2016). Adaptive fusion of color and spatial features for noise-robust retrieval of colored logo and trademark images. *Multidimensional Systems and Signal Processing*, *27*(4), 945–968. doi:10.100711045-016-0382-7

Yan, Y., Ren, J., Sun, G., Zhao, H., Han, J., Li, X., Marshall, S., & Zhan, J. (2018). Unsupervised image saliency detection with Gestalt-laws guided optimization and visual attention based refinement. *Pattern Recognition*, *79*, 65–78. doi:10.1016/j.patcog.2018.02.004

Yan, Y., Ren, J., Zhao, H., Sun, G., Wang, Z., Zheng, J., Marshall, S., & Soraghan, J. (2018). Cognitive fusion of thermal and visible imagery for effective detection and tracking of pedestrians in videos. *Cognitive Computation*, *10*(1), 94–104. doi:10.100712559-017-9529-6

Zabalza, J., Ren, J., Zheng, J., Zhao, H., Qing, C., Yang, Z., Du, P., & Marshall, S. (2016). Novel segmented stacked autoencoder for effective dimensionality reduction and feature extraction in hyperspectral imaging. *Neurocomputing*, *185*, 1–10. doi:10.1016/j.neucom.2015.11.044

Zhao, Z., Bouwmans, T., Zhang, X., & Fang, Y. (2012). A fuzzy background modeling approach for motion detection in dynamic backgrounds. In *Multimedia and signal processing* (pp. 177–185). Springer. doi:10.1007/978-3-642-35286-7_23

Zheng, J., Liu, Y., Ren, J., Zhu, T., Yan, Y., & Yang, H. (2016). Fusion of block and keypoints based approaches for effective copy-move image forgery detection. *Multidimensional Systems and Signal Processing*, *27*(4), 989–1005. doi:10.100711045-016-0416-1

Zhou, X., Yang, C., & Yu, W. (2013). Moving object detection by detecting contiguous outliers in the low-rank representation. *IEEE Transactions on Pattern Analysis and Machine Intelligence*, *35*(3), 597–610. doi:10.1109/TPAMI.2012.132 PMID:22689075

Chapter 6
Distracted Driver Detection System Using Deep Learning Technique

Varan Singh Rohila
National Institute of Technology, Hamirpur, India

Vijay Kumar
National Institute of Technology, Hamirpur, India

Karan Kumar Barnwal
National Institute of Technology, Hamirpur, India

ABSTRACT

Improvement of public safety and reducing accidents are the intelligent system's critical goals for detecting drivers' fatigue and distracted behavior during the driving project. The essential factors in accidents are driver fatigue and monotony, especially on rural roads. Such distracted behavior of the driver reduces their thinking ability for that particular instant. Because of this loss in decision-making ability, they lose control of their vehicle. Studies tell that usually the driver gets tired after an hour of driving. Driver fatigue and drowsiness happens much more in the afternoon, early hours, after eating lunch, and at midnight. These losses of consciousness could also be because of drinking alcohol, drug addiction, etc. The distracted driver detection system proposed in this chapter takes a multi-faceted approach by monitoring driver actions and fatigue levels. The proposed activity monitor achieves an accuracy of 86.3%. The fatigue monitor has been developed and tuned to work well in real-life scenarios.

INTRODUCTION

There are several driver monitoring systems for offices and vehicles available in the market. These are generally based on capturing the image, facial detection, and composite image processing. The work done in eye detection and tracking the face is divided into two categories such as (Wang *et al.* 2007)

DOI: 10.4018/978-1-7998-3299-7.ch006

1. Passive appearance-based methods
2. The active infra-red (IR)-based methods

The basic building block of such systems is facial detection algorithms that is implemented using artificial intelligence or SVMs. The percentage eye closure (PERCLOS) is an eye detection method. PERCLOS method performs well on driving simulators. This method records the total time that the driver's eyes are closed more than 80%. Additional IR methods are used to serve an IR spotlight on the driver's face in case of low light (Abouelnaga *et al.* 2018).

Baheti et al. (Baheti *et al.* 2018) presented a method that utilizes two cameras, an IR spotlight consisting of a twenty-eight IR LED grid, and a computer with computer vision algorithms. In another work, Dinges et al. (Dinges *et al.* 1998) incorporated two different IR sources with distinct wavelengths. Infrared wavelengths of 850nm and 950nm is used to obtain images. Brightness of the pupil in the images is different. Whereas, the rest of images are identical. PERCLOS computes the difference among the photographs that yield eyelids. Fig. 1 demonstrates this conjuncture.

Figure 1. The driver's pupil: (a) first image; (b) second image from another IR sensor; (c) difference image

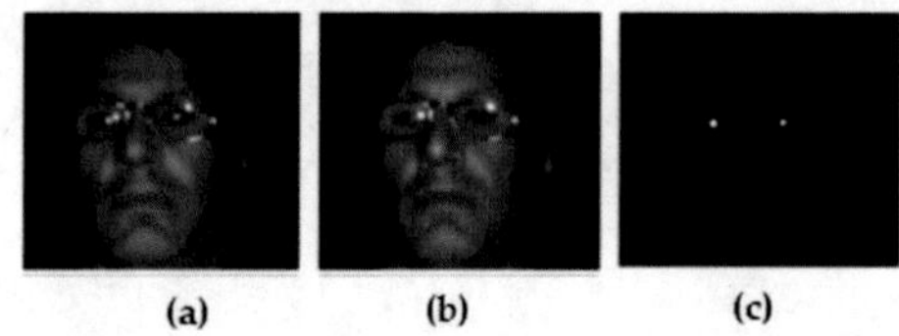

Visual distractions are coined in the following terms: "sleepiness", "drowsiness", "fatigue", and "inattention". And, they usually depend on facial landmarks detection and tracking. Manual distractions are mainly concerned with driver's activities other than safe driving (i.e., reaching behind, adjusting hair and makeup, or eating and drinking). In this kind of distraction, authors often tend to depend heavily on hand tracking and driving posture estimation. In this paper, we focus only on "manual" distractions where a driver is distracted by texting or using cell phone, calling, eating or drinking, reaching behind, fiddling with the radio, adjusting hair and makeup, or talking to a passenger.

Many research projects constitute fatigue detection wherein the camera is pointed directly at driver's gaze. Jiangwei et al. (Jiangwei *et al.* 2004) extracted the mouth shape and its position to determine whether the driver is yawning. In beginning, the seeing machines tool uses two operational cameras, one placed on the left and another on the driver's right. A processing unit finds the similarities between specific point-of-interests from two images that computes the spatial position of every segment. It determines blink rate, eye-opening, and eye gazing, even for driver with glasses. Fatigued drivers usually narrow their field of view and look directly ahead, which reduces their assessment of the mirrors and instruments. This makes monitoring their gaze all the more important. However, the non-commercial systems are costly, which renders them unobtainable for drivers (Horng *et al.* 2004).

Some researchers devised controlled cost schemes using embedded devices and cameras for fatigue detection. Suganya et al. (Suganya *et al.* 2017) utilized a Raspberry Pi and IR-sensitive video camera. In another work, Palani and Kothandaraman (Palani *et al.* 2013) utilized a regular camera and computer in laboratory settings with some constraints. However, it did not work well for drivers with dark skin. This kind of bias is what we aim to reduce. The presented model is generalized and works well irrespective of the characteristics of the driver.

The present work investigates an architecture of distracted driver detection system that uses a Convolutional Neural Networks (CNN). The proposed approach consists of two main parts. The first one detects the activity in which the driver is currently engaging. This process is formally named as Driver Activity Detection System. The latter one detects the driver's fatigue level that is based on facial feature recognition. This process is known as Driver Fatigue Detection System. The distraction of driver is measured independently by both parts. Both parts are working in a complimentary way rather than a supplementary. These provide a driver's 360-degree view and more robust solution as a whole.

DRIVER FATIGUE DETECTION SYSTEM

For this subsystem, a pre-trained facial detection model is used. The facial detection model is used to detect driver's face and his facial landmarks. Landmark points of the eyes are used for eye statistics that determine whether it is safe for the driver or not. If it is not safe, a warning signal is made so that the driver is alerted and can take necessary actions. Necessary actions may include stopping the vehicle to take a quick break, or changing the driver.

Eye Statistics

The eye landmarks are obtained from the pretrained face detection mode. It is a landmark facial detector with pre-trained models, the dlib is used to estimate the location of 68 coordinates (x, y) that map the facial points on a person's face. The model was trained using the ibug 300-W dataset.

- **iBUG 300-W dataset:** The 300-W is a face dataset that consists of 300 Indoor and 300 Outdoor in-the-wild images. It covers a large variation of identity, expression, illumination conditions, pose, occlusion and face size. The images were downloaded from google.com by making queries such as "party", "conference", "protests", "football" and "celebrities". Compared to the rest of in-the-wild datasets, the 300-W database contains a larger percentage of partially-occluded images and covers more expressions than the common "neutral" or "smile", such as "surprise" or "scream". Images were annotated with the 68-point mark-up using a semi-automatic methodology. The images of the database were carefully selected so that they represent a characteristic sample of challenging but natural face instances under totally unconstrained conditions. Thus, methods that achieve accurate performance on the 300-W database can demonstrate the same accuracy in most realistic cases. (C. Sagonas *et al.* 2009).

For our use case, we only use the eye landmarks to detect fatigue out of the 68 landmarks that are given by the pre-trained facial landmark model. The distances *d*1, *d*2, *d*3, *d*4, *d*5, and *d*6 are calculated that are used to compute the safety threshold. All the calculation happens in real time as the face of driver is detected. The distances d1 to d6 are illustrated in Fig. 2.

Figure 2. Distances of Eye Landmarks

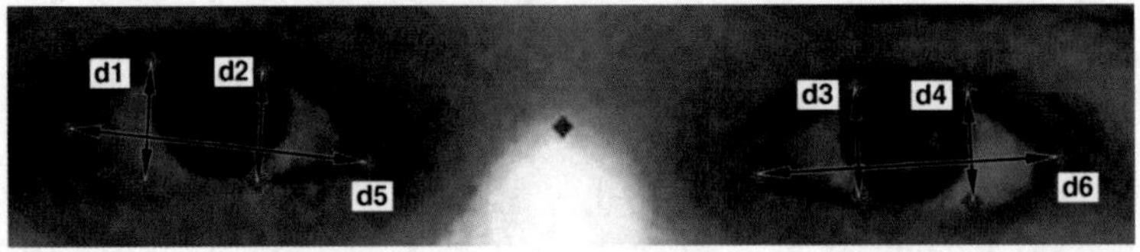

Initially, the mean of the distances is calculated as follows:

$$m_1 = (d\text{-}1+d2+d3+d4)/4 \quad (1)$$

$$m_2 = (d5+d6)/2 \quad (2)$$

These means are used to calculate the judging metric. It can be written as:

$$judge = m_1/m_2 \quad (3)$$

The flag is set to 1 if the judging metric is above the threshold and 0 if it is below or equal to the threshold. The threshold used in this paper is 0.25. It would be inefficient to make decision, which is based on the flag at every step because it can detect the blinking of driver as unsafe and produce a warning. To overcome this issue, a queue is maintained that keeps the track of previous 29 values of the flag (queue size is 30). The size of queue can be tuned on the captured frames per second of the video stream (Deng *et al.* 2009).

Finally, if the mean of the queue is greater than 0.5, a warning is displayed on the monitor. The working of this subsystem is demonstrated in Fig. 3. This metric is commonly known as Eye Aspect Ratio or EAR.

Driver Activity Detection System

The proposed driver activity detection system using ensemble learning model. Ensemble learning model refers to the method of combining the predictive power of two or more models. Ensemble model usually outperforms its constituent models. For this particular case, the top 4 performing models are combined by first concatenating their outputs and then adding a few dense neural layers. The architecture of the proposed ensemble model is shown in Fig. 4.

During the training of the ensemble model, the Efficient Nets are frozen so that only newly added layer learns. The ensemble model outperforms the top 4 models by achieving an accuracy of 86.3%.

EXPERIMENTAL RESULTS AND DISCUSSION

In this section, the performance of the proposed drier fatigue detection system is evaluated.

Figure 3. Working of driver fatigue system: (a) safe situation, (b) safe situation, (c) warning situation, and (d) warning situation

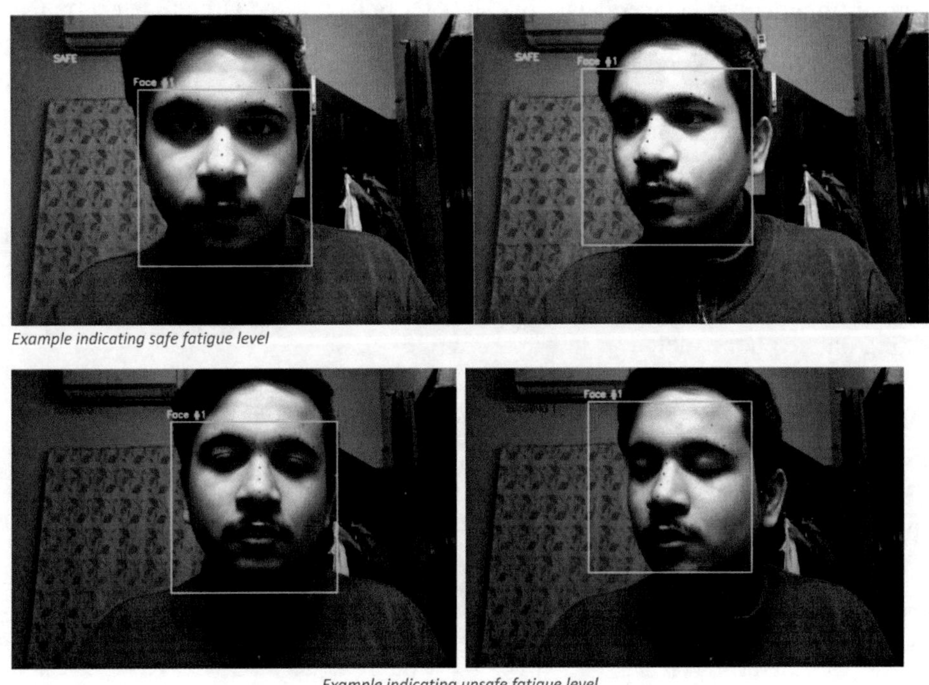

Example indicating safe fatigue level
Example indicating unsafe fatigue level

Figure 4. Architecture of the proposed ensemble model

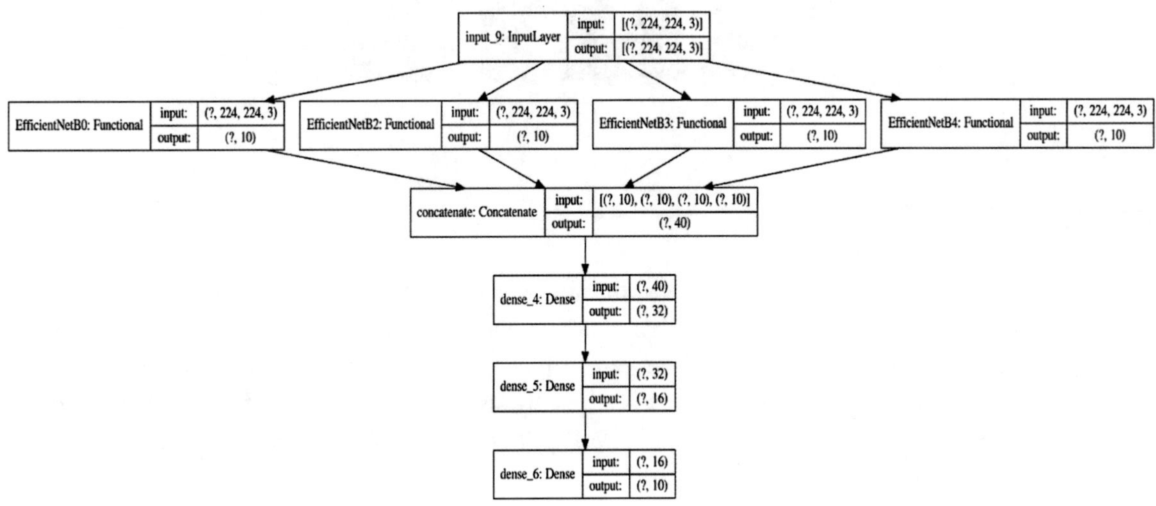

Dataset Used

The data used for training the CNN models is the State Farm Distracted Driver Detection Dataset (State-Farm's dataset 2020). This dataset consists of drivers' images, which were taken in a car with the driver engaging in a particular activity (i.e., talking, eating, makeup, texting, etc.). The proposed model predicts the current action the driver is performing. There are 10 classes in this dataset and these are given below:

- c0: safe driving
- c1: texting - right
- c2: talking on the phone - right
- c3: texting - left
- c4: talking on the phone - left
- c5: operating the radio
- c6: drinking
- c7: reaching behind
- c8: hair and makeup
- c9: talking to the passenger

There are 22,424 images, which makes it sufficiently large for generalization. Some images, which are taken from the dataset, are shown in Fig. 5

Figure 5. Some images taken form State Farm Distracted Driver Detection dataset

Dataset Split

For evaluating the CNN models, the data is split into two parts, i.e., training and validation. Since the dataset contains multiple images from a particular driver. There is a chance of data spillage. Data spillage in this case means that a different image of the same driver exists in both the splits. The data spillage may lead to false results. To avoid this, the dataset is carefully split through the driver id rather than number of images using a simple algorithm. The validation split contains about 19.3% of the total images and the rest of the images are used in training split.

Data Pre-Processing

The models require the images of a particular dimensions as input. All the chosen image classification, the state-of-the-art (SOTA) models require the image to be of 224x224 pixels with 3 channels. Hence, the images are resized to 224x224 pixels and normalized. The normalization helps the models to be converged faster. The output of these models is a ten neuron layer corresponding to the ten classes present in the dataset.

SOTA Models

About twenty one SOTA models are trained on the dataset that is described in Subsection 3.1. The training split is used for training and the validation split is used for finding which SOTA model performs better than the other models. The well-known SOTA models are

1. ResNets (and its variations)
2. DenseNets (and its variations)
3. InceptionNets (and its variations)
4. MobileNets (and its variations)
5. EfficientNets (and its variations)
6. VGG nets (and its variations)

Setting of Training Dataset

SOTA models are trained under similar conditions for fair comparison. The learning algorithm is Adam that helps in faster conversion as compared with the other learning algorithms. This is a multiple class classification problem. Therefore, the categorical cross entropy is used as the loss function. SOTA models are chosen for training by using their corresponding transfer weights from the ImageNet dataset. This process decreases the training time as compared to the randomly initialized weights. Finally, the accuracy is chosen as the evaluation metric. The performance comparison between the models is done by using the evaluation metric.

Brief About the SOTA Models

In the presented work, computer vision SOTA models are used. In this section, a brief about their architecture is discussed.

- **ResNet:** The core idea of ResNet is introducing a so-called “identity shortcut connection” that skips one or more layers. The authors of [2] argue that stacking layers shouldn’t degrade the network performance, because we could simply stack identity mappings (layer that doesn’t do anything) upon the current network, and the resulting architecture would perform the same. This indicates that the deeper model should not produce a training error higher than its shallower counterparts. They hypothesize that letting the stacked layers fit a residual mapping is easier than letting them directly fit the desired underlaying mapping. And the residual block above explicitly allows it to do precisely that. (Wu *et al.* 2009).
- **DenseNet:** It is similar to ResNet in architecture but with a few variations. In DenseNet, each layer obtains additional inputs from all preceding layers and passes on its own feature-maps to all subsequent layers. Concatenation is used. Each layer is receiving a “collective knowledge” from all

preceding layers. The layers are combined using concatenation rather than using addition, which is used in ResNet. (Huang *et al.* 2009)

- **InceptionNet:** The most straightforward way of improving the performance of deep neural networks is by increasing their size. The inceptionNet consists of Inception module. Inception Layer is a combination of 1×1 Convolutional layer, 3×3 Convolutional layer, 5×5 Convolutional layer with their output filter banks concatenated into a single output vector forming the input of the next stage, Now as we can see in image of naive version of inception module direct 3×3,5×5 convolutions are used which is too expensive to compute and so in the second image of inception module we used 1×1 convolution to reduce the dimension and which lead us to less expensive computation. (Tan *et al.* 2009).
- **MobileNet:** As the name applied, the MobileNet model is designed to be used in mobile applications. MobileNet uses depthwise separable convolutions. It significantly reduces the number of parameters when compared to the network with regular convolutions with the same depth in the nets. This results in lightweight deep neural networks. A depthwise separable convolution is made from two operations, Depthwise convolution and Pointwise convolution. (Szegedy *et al.* 2009).
- **EfficientNet:** EfficientNet is a convolutional neural network architecture and scaling method that uniformly scales all dimensions of depth/width/resolution using a compound coefficient. Unlike conventional practice that arbitrary scales these factors, the EfficientNet scaling method uniformly scales network width, depth, and resolution with a set of fixed scaling coefficients. The compound scaling method is justified by the intuition that if the input image is bigger, then the network needs more layers to increase the receptive field and more channels to capture more fine-grained patterns on the bigger image.
- **VGG Net:** VGGNet is invented by Visual Geometry Group (by Oxford University). To reduce the number of parameters, authors propose to use a small respective field to replace large one. They incorporate multiple non-linear rectification layers instead of a single rectification layer are more discriminative. It helps to decrease the number of parameters while keeping performance. For example, using 2 layers of 3×3 filter is equal to 1 layer of 5×5 filter but using fewer parameters. (Simonyan *et al.* 2009).

Transfer Learning

Transfer learning is a research problem in machine learning that focuses on storing knowledge gained while solving one problem and applying it to a different but related problem. The models converge faster if they are trained using transfer learning techniques than randomly initialized weights. Moreover, they perform better as well. The SOTA models that are used in this work are all trained using their existing transfer weights from ImageNet challenge. (West *et al.* 2009).

Ensemble Learning Method

Ensemble methods are techniques that create multiple models and then combine them to produce improved results. Ensemble methods usually produces more accurate solutions than a single model would. This has been the case in a number of machine learning competitions, where the winning solutions used ensemble methods. In this work, we consider simple average ensemble. In simple averaging method, for every instance of test dataset, the average predictions are calculated. This method often reduces overfit and improves accuracy (Dietterich *et al.* 2009). Ensemble method helps overcome shortcomings of individual models by combining their predictive powers. Some features that might be missed by one model could be caught by another one. Combining them results in more generalized and accurate result.

Results and Discussion

Among the twenty-one models trained, EfficientB0, Efficient-B2, Efficient-B3 and Efficient-B4 performed the best with 81.6%, 82.5%, 83.8% and 84.1% accuracies, respectively. Therefore, these models are combined together using ensemble learning to further increase their overall accuracy. Fig. 6 shows the training graph for first 30 epochs.

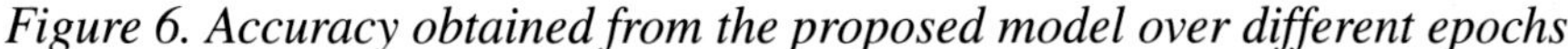

Figure 6. Accuracy obtained from the proposed model over different epochs

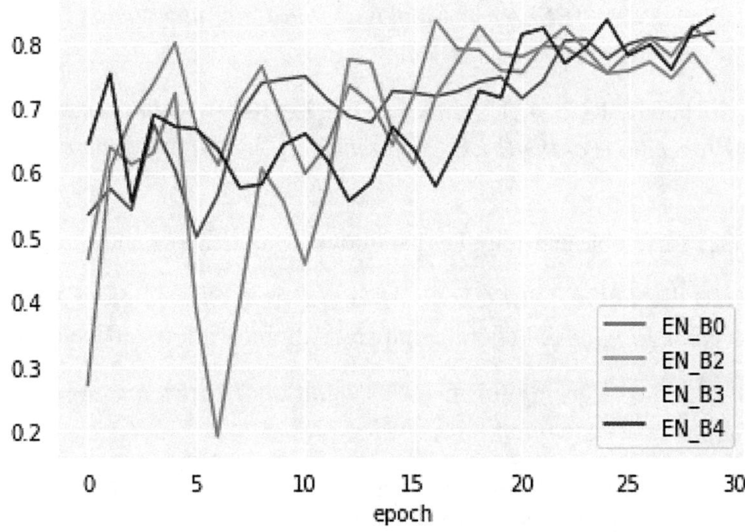

The ensemble model will be used to determine the current activity of the driver through a camera installed in the car. This will help in monitoring activity and provides the suggestions to the driver for a better and safe driving experience. Although the dataset is large enough and accuracy is decent, there is one limitation of this system. If the driver is tired and facing the wheel of the car, the system will classify the activity as safe driving but the driver might be drowsy which the system cannot detect. To overcome this problem, Driver Fatigue Detection System is introduced. This sub-system monitors fatigue, which is missing in the driver activity detection system.

CONCLUSION

This paper proposes an approach to detect distracted behaviour using an activity detector and fatigue detector. These detectors combine to provide a more robust framework. The activity detection system provides an accuracy of 86.3%, which can be further increased using a larger dataset and larger driver pool. The fatigue detection system incorporates the multiple facial statistics. In totality, these models' output is to be combined and can be integrated with a simple in-car alarm circuit that could alert the driver when it appears that she/he is distracted. The dashboard cameras do not have enough hardware to support sizeable deep learning models and internet of things could be utilized here. The trained model can be hosted on a cloud service that can be accessed by the car's camera. The research presented in this paper aims at ameliorating the alarming accident statistics by alerting drivers before any mishap can occur.

REFERENCES

Abouelnaga, Y., Eraqi, H. M., & Moustafa, M. N. (2018). *Real-time Distracted Driver Posture Classification.* arXiv:1706.09498.

Baheti, B., Gajre, S., & Talbar, S. (2018). Detection of Distracted Driver Using Convolutional Neural Network. In *Proceedings of the IEEE/CVF Conference on Computer Vision and Pattern Recognition Workshops*. IEEE. 10.1109/CVPRW.2018.00150

Deng, J., Dong, W., Socher, R., Li, L.-J., Li, K., & Fei-Fei, L. (2009). ImageNet: A large-scale hierarchical image database. In *Proceedings of the IEEE Conference on Computer Vision and Pattern Recognition.* IEEE.

Dietterich, T. G. (2002). Ensemble learning. The handbook of brain theory and neural networks, 2, 110-125.

Dinges, D. F., & Grace, R. (1998). *PERCLOS: A Valid Psychophysiological Measure of Alertness As Assessed by Psychomotor Vigilance*. Federal Highway Administration, Office of Motor Carriers.

He, K. (2016). Deep residual learning for image recognition. *Proceedings of the IEEE conference on computer vision and pattern recognition.*

Horng, W.-B., Chen, C.-Y., Chang, Y., & Fan, C.-H. (2004). Driver fatigue detection based on eye tracking and dynamic template matching. In *Proceedings of the IEEE International Conference on Networking, Sensing and Control.* IEEE. 10.1109/ICNSC.2004.1297400

Huang, G., Liu, Z., Maaten, L. V. D., & Weinberger, K. Q. (2017). Densely Connected Convolutional Networks. In *Proceedings of the IEEE Conference on Computer Vision and Pattern Recognition.* IEEE.

Jiangwei, C., Lisheng, J., Bingliang, T., Shuming, S., & Rongben, W. (2004). A monitoring method of driver mouth behavior based on machine vision. *Proceedings of IEEE Intelligent Vehicles Symposium.*

Palani, S., & Kothandaraman, S. (2013). *A Low Cost Drivers Drowsiness Detection System.* Academic Press.

Sagonas, C., Tzimiropoulos, G., Zafeiriou, S., & Pantic, M. (2013). A semi-automatic methodology for facial landmark annotation. *Proceedings of IEEE Int'l Conf. Computer Vision and Pattern Recognition (CVPR-W), 5th Workshop on Analysis and Modeling of Faces and Gestures (AMFG 2013).* 10.1109/CVPRW.2013.132

Simonyan, K., & Zisserman, A. (2014). *Very deep convolutional networks for large-scale image recognition.* arXiv preprint arXiv:1409.1556.

State Farm's Dataset. (n.d.). https://www.kaggle.com/c/state-farmdistracted-driver-detection/data

Suganya, G., Premalatha, M., Bharathiraja, S., & Agrawal, R. (2017). A low cost design to detect drowsiness of driver. *International Journal of Civil Engineering and Technology*, *8*, 1138–1149.

Szegedy, C., Vanhoucke, V., Ioffe, S., Shlens, J., & Wojna, Z. (2015). *Rethinking the Inception Architecture for Computer Vision.* arXiv:1512.00567.

Tan, M., & Le, Q. V. (2020). *EfficientNet: Rethinking Model Scaling for Convolutional Neural Networks* arXiv:1905.11946.

Wang, L., Wu, X., & Yu, M. (2007). Review of driver fatigue/drowsiness detection methods. *Journal of Biomedical Engineering*, *24*, 245–248.

West, J., Ventura, D., & Warnick, S. (2007). *Spring Research Presentation: A Theoretical Foundation for Inductive Transfer*. Brigham Young University, College of Physical and Mathematical Sciences.

Wu, Z., Shen, C., & Hengel, A. V. D. (2019). Wider or Deeper: Revisiting the ResNet Model for Visual Recognition. *Pattern Recognition*, *90*, 119–133.

Chapter 7
Application of Deep Learning Model Convolution Neural Network for Effective Web Information Retrieval

Suruchi Chawla
Shaheed Rajguru College, Delhi University, India

ABSTRACT

Convolution neural network (CNN) is the most popular deep learning method that has been used for various applications like image recognition, computer vision, and natural language processing. In this chapter, application of CNN in web query session mining for effective information retrieval is explained. CNN has been used for document analysis to capture the rich contextual structure in a search query or document content. The document content represented in matrix form using Word2Vec is applied to CNN for convolution as well as maxpooling operations to generate the fixed length document feature vector. This fixed length document feature vector is input to fully connected neural network (FNN) and generates the semantic document vector. These semantic document vectors are clustered to group similar document for effective web information retrieval. An experiment was performed on the data set of web query sessions, and results confirm the effectiveness of CNN in web query session mining for effective information retrieval.

INTRODUCTION

Convolution Neural Network(CNN) is the most popular deep learning method used for various applications like image recognition(Xiao et al.,2015,Zheng et al.,2017), computer vision and natural language processing(Collobert et al.,2011), face recognition(He et al.,2015), scene labeling(Shi, Bai, & Yao, 2016), action recognition, human pose estimation (Jain et al.,2014) (Donahue et al,2017)and document analysis(Kalchbrenner, Grefenstette, & Blunsom,2014). CNN is scalable for large data set and convert the data to a form that is easy to process without loss of features that are important for getting a good

DOI: 10.4018/978-1-7998-3299-7.ch007

prediction. Shared weights and local connectivity are some of the features of CNN thus produce accurate results. CNN performed significantly in the domain of computer vision and natural language processing. CNN uses filters of weights in convolution operations and Max pooling operations for feature learning at different level of abstraction using multilayer CNN starting with low level features to the high level feature vector that can be understood and classified. The feature vector is flattened and fed to Fully connected Neural Network(FNN) for classification at the output layer.(Deng, Abdel-Hamid, & Yu,2013;Long, Shelhamer, & Darrell, 2017;Lu, Javidi, & Lazebnik, 2016; Conneau et al.,2016)

Most tradition information retrieval models are based on the bag -of-words that assume the occurrences of terms to be completely independent but contextual information is necessary for identifying the search intent of a query term. Various translation model-based approach are been used to extract phrase-to-phrase relationships based on clickthrough data for bridging the gap between queries and documents. The experiments did not show clear indication of the retrieval effectiveness. The phrase-based translation model can only score phrase pairs found in the training data, and cannot generalize to new phrases (Gao, He, & Nie, 2010;Gao, Toutanova, & Yih., 2011).

CNN has been used primarily due to its learning ability because of the use of multiple feature extraction stages that extracts the representation from the data. The use of activation function on the output of CNN introduces non linearity. The non –linearity helps in learning of semantic differences in input data. The use of multiple linear and non linear processing units learns the complex representations of data at different level of abstraction.

In this chapter a novel application of CNN in web query session mining is proposed and used for effective information retrieval. The advantage of using CNN for document analysis is to extract the semantics of web documents by replacing the traditional bag of word TF.IDF document representation by word embedding Word2Vec where each word is represented as a vector to capture the rich contextual structure in a search query or document content. The matrix representation of document vector based on Word2Vec embedding is used for convolution operations and multiple filters are applied to capture the multiple features of document at different level of abstraction. Thus multiple feature maps are generated as a result of convolution operations and thereafter Max pooling operation is applied to each feature map to extract the feature of maximum weight that reduces the dimensionality of feature vector without loss of information. Thus the pooling operation decrease the computational power required to process the data through dimensionality reduction. The fixed length feature vector generated using Max pooling operation is transformed using non linear function at the hidden layer of the FNN and generates the abstract document semantic vector capturing features at the highest level of abstraction. Thus an application of CNN model in mining of clicked web document generates semantic document vectors. These semantic document vectors are clustered to group together documents that are semantically similar for effective information retrieval. Thus the use of CNN in web query session mining capture the semantics of documents in the form of vectors for clustering in contrast to TF.IDF keyword based document vectors/ontology based vectors. Thus the clusters of document semantic vectors based on CNN will contain more relevant documents for effective information retrieval. Experimental study was conducted to evaluate the effectiveness of CNN in web query session mining and results proved promising as well as confirmed the improvement in the average precision of search results based on the recommendation of documents in semantic clusters of documents. The performance of CNN in web query session mining for information retrieval was compared with TF.IDF document representation and ontology based document representation based on average precision of recommended search results. The results confirmed the effectiveness of CNN in web query session mining for effective information retrieval. The flowchart of the method based on using CNN in web search query session mining for effective Information Retrieval is shown below in Figure 1.(Chawla,Accepted 2020,in press)

Figure 1. Flowchart of using CNN in web query session mining for effective Information Retrieval

Offline processing

Data set of web query sessions is preprocessed and clicked documents are represented using word2vec in matrix form

The n clicked documents/ search query matrix of order n *k where k is the size of embedding.

The application of multiple convolution filters of a given region size and maxpooling operations on document matrix generates the fixed length vector.

This fixed length vector is input to FNN and generates the semantic vector at the output layer optimized using back propapgation.

K-means clustering of document semantic vectors and clusters are represented by cluster means.

Has training of CNN and generation of semantic vector of document/query completed

no

yes

Online Processing

Generation of query concept vector based on trained CNN

Use query/user profile concept vector for the selection of most similar cluster.

Use the selected cluster for the recommendation of clicked URLs.

User clicks to recommended urls are captured in user profile.

Generation of user concept profile based on trained CNN

Has user request for next webpage

yes

no

Stop

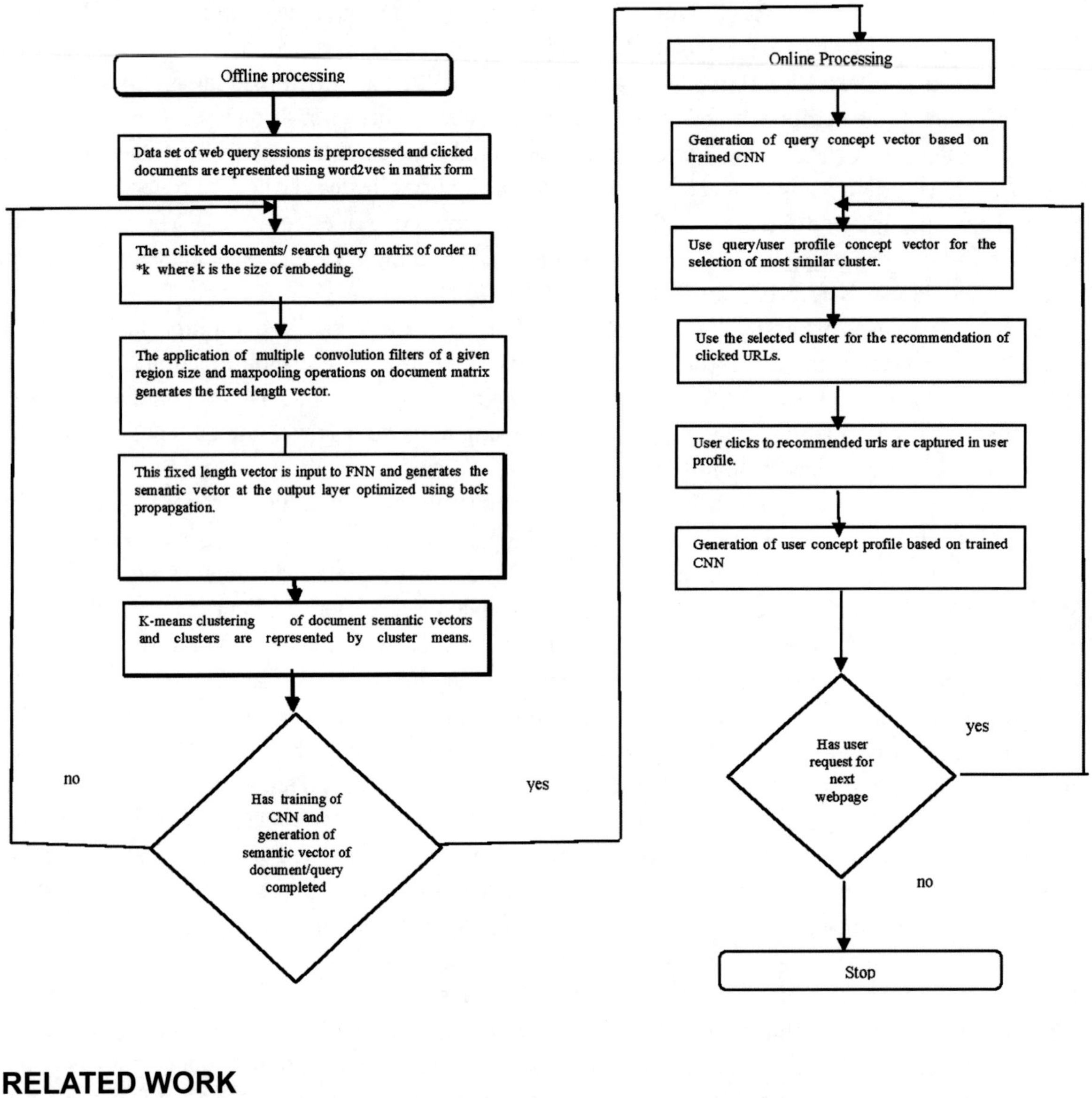

RELATED WORK

In (Lawrence et al.,1997) convolution neural networks were employed to identify the conceptual structure of an image. Faces represents a complex, multidimensional visual stimulus that was presented using a hybrid neural network combining local image sampling,self organizing map neural network and convolution neural network. In scene labelling each pixel is labelled with the category of the object it belongs to. A method was proposed using a convolution neural network and obtained accuracies on the sift flow dataset and Barcelona data set.(Farabet et al.,2012) CNN was used for semantic segmentation where each pixel was labelled with the class. Deep Convolutional Neural Networks (DCNN) had shown the improvement in the performance for image classification problem. (Krizhevsky et al., 2012; Sermanet et al., 2013; Simonyan & Zisserman, 2014; Szegedy et al., 2014; Chen et al., 2014).

Hierarchical Deep Convolution Neural Network was based on the assumption that some classes in image classification are more confusing than other classes. HD-CNN with CIFAR100-NN had shown the higher testing accuracy in comparison to other standard Deep Models.(Yan et al.,2019) The use of shared weights in CNN reduces the number of parameters in the action recognition system.(Kim, Lee, & Yang, 2007)

DNN used the multi hidden layer that performs the non linear transformation on input and generates the semantic of input data at various levels of abstraction required for various tasks. (Deerwester et al.,1990 ;Blei et al.,2003 ; Hofmann, 2017 ;Salakhutdinov and Hinton, 2009 ; Hinton and Salakhutdinov,2011 ; Tur et al.,2012; Socher et al.,2012). In (Huang et al.,2013) DSSM used hashing layer and feedforward neural network to map the input term vector to semantic vector. In (Shen et al., 2014b) word n gram where context window of size n=3 around a given word was used to generate the word trigram representation based on letter trigram representation.

CNN had been successfully applied in various domains like speech, image and natural language processing, (Collobert et al,2011 ; Yang and Li,2017) Semantic parsing (Yih et al.,2014),sentence modeling (Kalchbrenner et al.,2014), FaceRecognition (Lawrence et al.,1997), Scene labelling (Farabet et al.,2012).In (Bengio et al.,1994) CNN was used to develop model to recognize handwriting based on low resolution images using CNN.

In (Kim,2014) CNN was trained on pretrained Word2Vec for sentence classification tasks. In (Wang et al.,2015) semantic clustering based on CNN model was proposed and the effectiveness was confirmed based on the results of the experiments.

In (Johnson and Zhang, 2015) the model learns embeddings of text regions using an additional unsupervised learning and the results were significant. In (Gao et al.,2014) deep neural network CNN was used for text analysis of documents and relevant documents were recommended. In (Volkovs,2015) search logs were used to extract features for training neural network and regression model was used to personalize top-N document rankings for users. The results achieved an NDCG@10 of 0.80476.

In (Weston et al.,2014) CNN architecture was used to predict the hashtag for facebook post and embedding of words as well as sentences were generated for further use in document recommendations. In (Santos and Zadrozny, 2014) CNN was used for Part of Speech tagging. In (Kim et al.,2016 ; Zhang et al.,2015) CNN deep network was used for text categorization and sentiment analysis. In (Tang and Wang, 2018) convolution sequence embedding recommendation model was used for personalized top -n sequential recommendation and the model outperformed other related methods for top -N sequential recommendations.

In (Zhu, Zuo, & Ren,2020) modified region based fully convolution neural network was proposed to distinguish the similar objects in complex scenes with high accuracy. In (Pan et al.,2020) a novel DCNN architecture was proposed for automatic classification of food ingredients using feature fusion. In (Zhang et al.,2020) deep neural network was proposed for sentence semantic matching based on the sentence interactions and loss function. In (Ahmed, & Pathan,2020) deep learning algorithms were used for collective anomaly detection popular for denial of service(DoS) attack detection. In (Roshan et al.,2020) pretrained network was fine tuned based on preprocessed Kaggle data set and the parameters were optimised for automatic screening of diabetic retinopathy. In (Too et al.,2020) an empirical analysis of nonlinear activation function used in deep learning for image classification was done on Cifar-10,

SVHN, and PlantVillage data sets. The selection of the activation function is crucial in the training of deep learning networks because it has an impact on the training and performance of a network model.

In (Lu,2020) optimization of CNN convolution layer was proposed using quantum evolutionary algorithm. The network performance degradation due to many hidden convolutional layers was improved and the use of the network's computing resources was reduced. In (Wu et al.,2019) fully convolution neural network was used for the semantic segmentation of high resolution remote sensing images. In (Wang, Xing, & Liu,2020) efficient deep convolution neural network was proposed with an active stepwise pruning approach and can be deployed with restricted memory and computing power without any accuracy loss. In (Kiranyaz et al.,2021) the architecture of 1D CNN was reviewed along with its applications. In(Sarvamangala & Kulkarni, 2021) CNN application in comprehending the images of brain, breast, lung and other organs had been surveyed . The review of the application of CNN in text analysis is given in Table 1.

Table 1. Review of contribution of CNN in text analysis

Main Contribution	Reference
CNN was used for sentence classification tasks	Kim,2014
Deep neural network CNN was used for text analysis of documents and relevant documents were recommended	Gao et al.,2014
CNN deep network was used for text categorization and sentiment analysis	Kim et al.,2016 ; Zhang et al.,2015
Deep neural network was proposed for sentence semantic matching based on the sentence interactions and loss function	Zhang et al.,2020

BASIC CONCEPTS

CNN Architecture

CNN architecture has three main features like Local Receptive Fields, Shared weights and Spatial temporal subsampling that makes it different from multilayer perceptrons . CNN consists of multiple convolution layer followed by Max pooling layers. Convolution layer apply multiple filters that are meant to capture the features at different level of abstractions. Maxpooling reduces the dimensionality of feature vector without loss of information. The fixed length feature vector is generated after the application of multi convolution layer and maxpooling layer. This fixed length feature vector is fed to FNN to generate the abstract vector of the highest level for classification at the output layer. The architecture of CNN for document semantic vector generation is shown below in Figure 2.

Convolution Layer

In convolution layer multiple filters were applied to perform convolution operation on the input. Filters are the weight matrices that are learnable during the training of CNN. These filters extend through the full depth of input based on the stride size. Feature maps are generated after the convolution of filters with the input to capture the features at different level of abstraction. Application of multiple filters on input generates the multiple feature maps. (Nair & Hinton,2010)

Max Pooling Layer

The Max pooling layer performs its operation after the convolution layer. Max-Pooling operation reduces the dimensionality of data without the loss of information. Various Pooling functions are used like Max pooling, average pooling or L2-norm pooling. Max pooling is the most commonly used pooling function. It uses the small block of order m*n and extract the maximum value from feature maps based on the block of selected size. Thus the pooling operation decrease the computational complexity required to process the data through the dimensionality reduction.

Fully Connected Neural Network

Fully connected neural network consists of the input layer, hidden layer and output layer. The neurons in the input layer are connected to every neuron in the hidden layer and neuron in the hidden layer is connected to every neuron in the output layer. The input is transformed using non linear transformation function at the hidden layer and the output is generated at the output layer.

Figure 2. CNN architecture that uses Document Matrix as input and generates semantic document vector as output

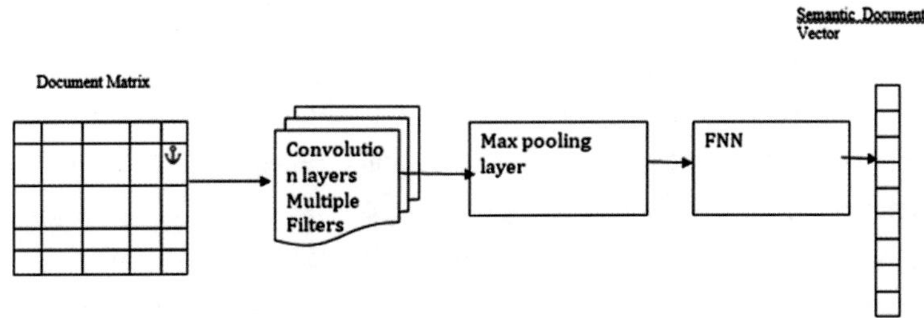

Text Preprocessing: Search Query and Document Representation Using Word2Vec

One -hot encoded vector representation of document vocabulary generates the sparse vector even for the related words as it does not consider the context of word and dependence of one word on the other word.

Word embedding is the most commonly used method to represent the document vocabulary based on the Natural Language Processing. The aim is to generate the representation of the words such that words with similar context have similar vector representation. The cosine similarity between vectors of words with similar context should be close to 1.The advantage of word embedding is that context of a word in a document is captured including semantic and syntactic similarity relation with other words.

Word2Vec (Mikolov et al.,2013) and Glove(Pennington et al.,2014) are the commonly used Word embedding techniques. Word embedding identifies the context of a word in a document as well as it also determines the semantic, syntactic similarity and relations with other words. These pre-trained vectors have been used for various classification tasks. The clicked documents of web query sessions are processed and represented as a matrix where each row represents a pre-trained Word2Vec vectors for each distinct word of vocabulary present in document.

In this chapter the document of length n is represented by n*k1 matrix based on Word2Vec word embedding where k1 is the size of word vector embedding. A simple CNN model with one hidden layer is trained on pretrained word vectors. The model showed excellent performance by tuning of its hyperparameters.

Training of the CNN for the Generation of Semantic Document/Query Vector

Convolution neural network is applied in web search query session mining to extract the semantic document vector. These semantic document vectors captures the features at the highest level of abstraction without loss of information.

The clickthrough web search query session log consists of search query and its associated clicked URLs. Data set of web search logs is preprocessed to get the collection of web search query sessions. It is based on assumption that search query is atleast partially relevant to clicked document associated with it.Word2Vec embedding is used to capture the context of word where each word is represented by vector.Word2Vec is used to map the document word vector to matrix representation. The document vector of n words is represented in the matrix form of order n*k1 using the concatenation of k1 dimensional pretrained Word2Vec for every word in the document vector.

CNN uses filters of weights that perform convolution operation on input based on stride size sliding through the input and generates the variable length feature map depending on the size of input.Thus the application of multiple filters on input generates multiple feature maps of variable length and capturing the features at various level of abstraction. The Max-pooling operation is applied to each feature map and extract the maximum feature value from each feature map therefore generates the fixed length feature vector. This fixed length vector is applied to the FNN for non linear transformation and generates the document/query semantic feature vector at the output layer.

The training of CNN is done by adjusting convolution matrix Filter weights W_c, FNN weights as well as bias based on backpropagation through stochastic gradient descent with the objective of maximizing the probability of relevant document given search query. The objective of training optimization is to minimize the loss function using equation(1), equation(2) & equation (3) as given below.

$$L(\Lambda) = -\log \prod_{(Q,D^+)} P(D^+ \mid Q) \tag{1}$$

$$P(D^+ \mid Q) = \frac{\exp(\gamma R(Q, D^+))}{\sum_{D' \in D} \exp(\gamma R(Q, D'))} \tag{2}$$

$$R(Q, D) = \cos\text{ine}(y_Q, y_D) = \frac{y_Q^T y_D}{\|y_Q\| \|y_D\|} \tag{3}$$

Where D^+ is the clicked document and approximate D by including D^+ and J randomly selected unclicked documents $\{^- D^-_j ;j=1..J\}$

y_Q and y_D are the semantic concept vector of query and document. The cosine similarity measures relevancy score between the query and document semantic vectors.

^ denotes the parameter set of Convolution latent semantic model(CLSM) to learn that include W_c (convolution matrix) and FNN weights as well as bias .

Thus multiple filters with a given height and width generate multiple feature maps and form the output of the convolution operation. The output of the convolution layer is a variable length multiple feature maps depending on the length of the input word sequence. The activation function such as tanh are used for nonlinear transformation in multi-layer networks.

Max pooling operation is applied to each feature vector to extract the feature of maximum weight that reduces the dimensionality of feature vector without loss of information. Thus pooling operation decrease the computational complexity required to process the data through dimensionality reduction. Thus the resulting fixed length feature vector obtained after convolution operation and Max pooling operation undergoes non linear transformation at the hidden layer of the network and generates the abstract document semantic vector capturing features at highest level of abstraction that can be classified.

The fully connected layer maps the query/document to semantic vector in the lower dimensional vector space at the output layer. (Kim,2014 ;Shen et al., 2014b) Thus the application of CNN model in mining of clicked web document generates semantic document vectors for clustering.

CLUSTERING OF SEMANTIC CLICKED WEB DOCUMENTS VECTORS FOR EFFECTIVE INFORMATION RETRIEVAL

CNN uses convolution operation and Max pooling operation on input and generates the abstract representation of document vector that represent its semantics. These semantic document vectors are clustered using K-means algorithm.

K-means algorithm is used for clustering because it is simple and efficient for the wide variety of data types. K-means has been used because of low computational requirements and has low memory requirements. These clusters of document concept vectors group relevant clicked documents in a given domain for effective Information Retrieval. The stepwise execution of the offline processing is given in Algorithm 1.

Algorithm 1. Clustering of preprocessed document semantic vector

Offline Processing

1. Data set of clicked URLs is preprocessed and generate the query sessions along with its clicked URLs.
2. The TF.IDF word vector of documents is represented in matrix form using Word2Vec word embedding.
3. The n length document/query keyword vector is represented as n*k1 based on pre-trained vectors Word2Vec
4. A convolution layer applies filter $W_c \in R^{h1k1}$, which is applied to a window of h1 words (h1 =3) and embedding size(k1=28) to produce a new feature.
5. These multiple filters are applied to entire input document matrix using window size of h1 words at a time and is moved through the input matrix with stride size =1 to produce multiple variable length feature maps.
6. These multiple feature maps are used by Max- pooling operation to extract the maximum value feature $\hat{c}1$ = maximum{c1} for every feature map. Thus model uses 300 filter of size 3*28(h1*k1) followed by maxpooling to obtain fixed size feature vector of size 300.
7. This fixed size feature vector is transformed nonlinearly through FNN layer and high-level semantic concept vector of documents/query is generated at the output layer.
8. The query and all the associated clicked documents semantic concept vector are used to compute their cosine similarity.
9. The model is trained by adjusting W_c, FNN weights and biases using stochastic gradient descent back propagation with learning rate= 0.01 using equations (1)(2)(3).
10. The hyperparameters of trained CNN are optimized based on the validation dataset.
11. Use the trained CNN for the generation for document/query concept vectors.
12. K-means is used for clustering document concept vectors based on semantics and clusters are represented by cluster means.
13. The cluster analysis was done based on WCSS to access the quality of clusters of web documents.

The computational time required for offline processing is separate and is not included in the time required for online processing. The stepwise execution of the online processing is given in Algorithm 2.

Algorithm 2. Online processing

1. The user search query issued for web search is input to trained CNN for generating the query concept vector.
2. The search query semantic vector select the most similar j^{th} cluster based on cosine similarity measure with cluster centroids.
3. The List of document OR_j in the cluster j is selected for recommendation.
4. The clicked documents in list OR_j are recommended in order of their cosine similarity score with search query semantic vector as per equation (3).
5. On user request for the next search web page
    a. The current user semantic profile vector is generated based on clicked document semantic vector and is represented as $current\_usersessionvector_t$.
    b. The most similar j thcluster is selected based on cosine similarity of the $current_usersessionvector_t$concept vector and clusters centroids.
    c. Goto step 3.

else

current user search session is ended.

EXPERIMENTAL EVALUATION

The experiment was performed on the data set of web query sessions containing search query and clicked URLs. The steps used for implementing the experiment is given as follows

1. Data set of web query sessions is collected in the selected domains Academics, Entertainment and Sports.

2. Web query session data set is preprocessed and matrix representation of document content is generated using Word2Vec.
3. Data set is partitioned into training and Validation data set.
4. Training of CNN is done using training data set for the generation of optimal semantic document vector where optimization is done based on minimizing the loss function.
5. Use the trained CNN on validation data set to evaluate the CNN model performance in generating the semantic document vector effectively.
6. K-means is used for clustering document semantic vectors generated using trained CNN.
7. The performance of semantic clusters of documents is evaluated based on average precision of recommended search results using clusters.
8. Domainwise comparison of average precision of personalized search results using CNN with other related work.

An architecture was designed for capturing the data set of web query sessions. The GUI interface of the architecture displaying search results retrieved for a given search query is shown in Figure 3 below. The architecture is used for the generation of data set, the users were required to issue search queries to GUI to retrieve the google search results along with check boxes. The user's clicks to Google search results were captured through check boxes and were stored as search query session with unique user id in database. (Chawla,(Accepted.2020), in press)

Figure 3. GUI displaying the google search results with check boxes

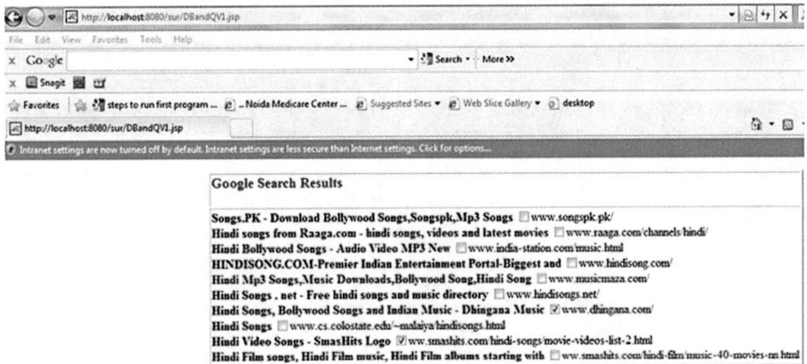

The data set was collected for the duration of two months and was preprocessed to obtain the collection of web query sessions in the format as follows.

Web Query session=(search query,{clicked documents}+)

The clicked document content is represented in the matrix form using word2Vec. The entire web query session data set is partitioned to training and validation data set. The sample of 15,192 and 10,000 queries sessions were used as training and validation data set. The training data set was used for learning of parameters of CNN based on clickthrough data and hyperparameters were fine tuned based on validation data set. The statistics of data set of web query sessions used for training as well as testing is given as follows in Table 2.(Chawla,(Accepted.2020), in press)

Table 2. Description of DataSet of web query sessions

Duration of data set collections	2 months from Jan 2019 to Feb 2019
Number of users	Around 60 users with expertise in selected domains
Total number of distinct query sessions	25,192
Total number of selected domains	3
Total number of distinct clicked URLs	1,76,344
Total number of distinct terms in vocabulary	22,169
Average number of terms per query	3.4
Word embedding vector size	28

Table 3. CNN configuration showing the parameters and their values used during training

Parameter	Values
Filter W_c height h1	Range 3-5
Number of Filters	Range 300-600
Pooling method	Max pooling
Activation Function	Tanh
Maxpooling layer output(Fixed Length feature vector)	300
Stride size	1
Input size for FNN	300
Number of hidden layer	1
Number of neuron in output layer FNN	128
CNN Learning parameters	W_c, FNN weights, biases
CNN parameter optimization	Backpropagation based on stochastic gradient descent.

During the training of CNN, various parameters of CNN such as the number of filters was varied in the range of 300 to 600 and size of filter h1 was varied in the range of 3 to 5. Thus as the region size is increased, learning model parameters also increases and the complexity of parameter learning is increased. A simple CNN shows significant results on various benchmarks using hyperparameter tuning and pre-trained word vectors. (Mitra,2015) . It is found that as the number of filters varies from 100 to 600, the running time is increased and more than 600 filters are not recommended as it involves the extra effort that is not worth it. So considering the trade- off between performance and computational time. It is recommended to use the values on the border of the range instead of using larger values (Bengio,2012). The activation function tanh has been suggested to use in one-layer CNNs for fixed number of filter and region size as the baseline. 1-max pooling is found to perform well even better than k-max pooling which extracts k max values from feature vector maintaining the relative order of values (Boureau et al.,2011).

In this experiment the best results were obtained for the 300 filters of size h1*k1, filter region size h1 =3 and k1=28 with stride size=1 applied to document matrix. Max pooling was used to extract the fixed-length global feature vector. Therefore 300 is the dimensionality of both convolution layer as well as max pooling layer. tanh is used as the activation function. The output layer of fully connected neural network has 128 neurons. Two CNN were used for mapping query/document to concept vector. The configuration of CNN that was used for experimental study is given as follows in Table 3. (Chawla,(Accepted.2020), in press)

The model uses 300 filters/feature transformation matrix of specific window size to obtain multiple feature maps. The application of maxpooling on 300 variable length feature maps generates the fixed length feature vector of size 300(maximum value from each feature map). The output layer of CNN generates semantic document vector of size 128.

The snapshot of execution of CNN for 100 iterations on data set of clicked documents/search query using pretrained Word2Vec in tensorflow is given below in Figure 4.(Chawla,(Accepted.2020), in press)

Figure 4. Implementation of the CNN algorithm in tensorflow on data set of web query session

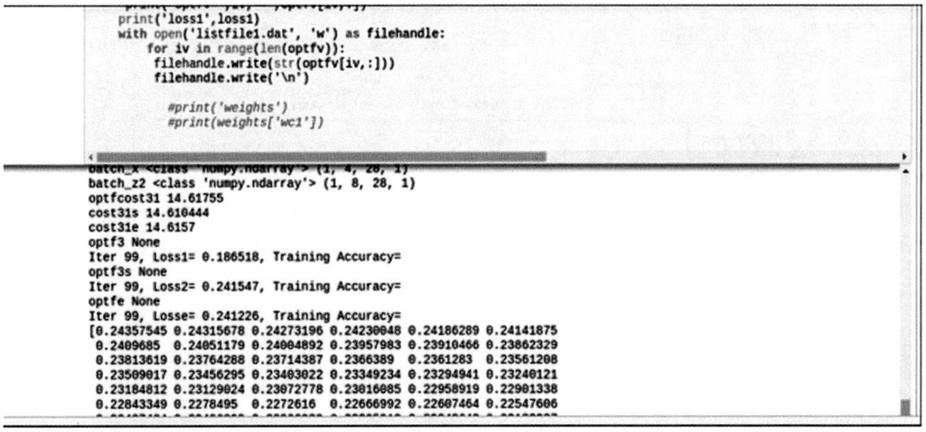

```
print('loss1',loss1)
with open('listfile1.dat', 'w') as filehandle:
    for iv in range(len(optfv)):
     filehandle.write(str(optfv[iv,:]))
     filehandle.write('\n')

       #print('weights')
       #print(weights['wc1'])
```

```
batch_z2 <class 'numpy.ndarray'> (1, 8, 28, 1)
optfcost31 14.61755
cost31s 14.610444
cost31e 14.6157
optf3 None
Iter 99, Loss1= 0.186518, Training Accuracy=
optf3s None
Iter 99, Loss2= 0.241547, Training Accuracy=
optfe None
Iter 99, Losse= 0.241226, Training Accuracy=
[0.24357545 0.24315678 0.24273196 0.24230048 0.24186289 0.24141875
 0.2409685  0.24051179 0.24004892 0.23957983 0.23910466 0.23862329
 0.23813619 0.23764288 0.23714387 0.2366389  0.2361283  0.23561208
 0.23509017 0.23456295 0.23403022 0.23349234 0.23294941 0.23240121
 0.23184812 0.23129024 0.23072778 0.23016085 0.22958919 0.22901338
 0.22843349 0.2278495  0.2272616  0.22666992 0.22607464 0.22547606
```

During the training of CNN based on clickthroughdata, the optimization is done based on minimization of loss function as per equations (1)(2)(3). The document concept vector was generated using trained CNN.

K-means clustering was used for clustering clicked document concept vector generated using CNN. WCSS is good measure of cluster quality based on sum of squared distances of samples to their closest cluster center. WCSS is the output of K-Means clustering class of sklearn.cluster module in python. WCSS was computed in reference to clusters of document vectors using (CNN/TF.IDF) obtained using K-Means. The results in Figure 5 & Figure 6. compare the clusters quality based on WCSS using CNN based semantic document vector/ Simple TF.IDF keyword based vector. The x shows the number of clusters k that varies from 1 to 4. The y axis shows WCSS that is measure of dissimilarity of data points from within clusters to their respective cluster centers for different value of x.

The graph in Figure 6. shows that for CNN based document semantic vector, the WCSS decreases more rapidly in comparison to TF.DF document vector. The low value of WCSS signifies that within cluster dissimilarity of data points to their cluster centers decreases due to effective document clustering using CNN based document semantic vector representation.(Chawla,(Accepted.2020), in press)

Figure 5. Clusters quality WCSS versus number of clusters using TF.IDF based Simple Clustering

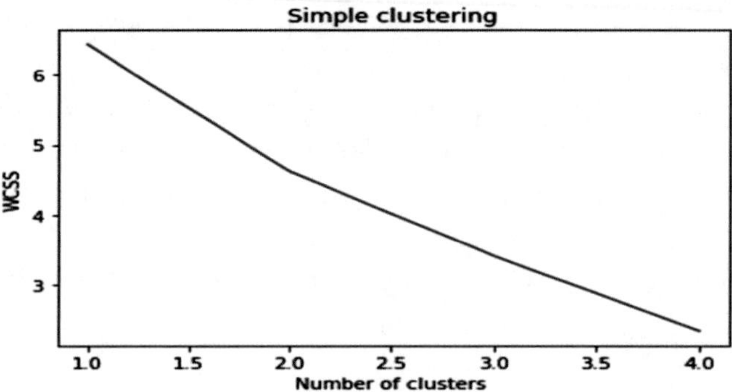

Figure 6. Clusters quality WCSS versus number of clusters using CNN based Semantic clustering

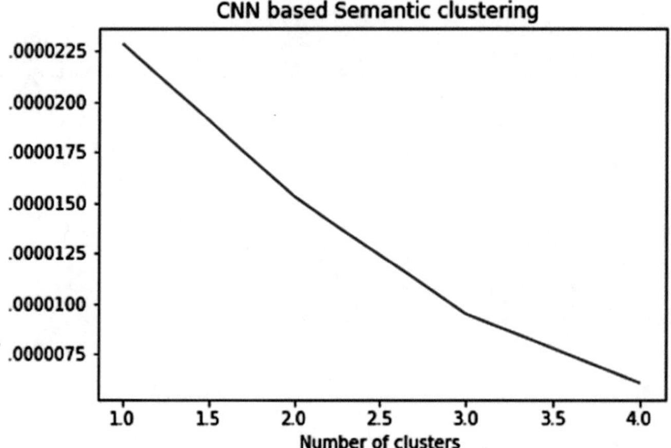

The sum of squared distances of document vectors to their most similar cluster centroids(WCSS) was plotted for different value of K as shown in Figure 5 & Figure 6 . The low value of WCSS signifies that within cluster similarity of data points increases. Thus using elbow method, K=3 was selected as optimal number of semantic clusters fit for the selected data set. This shows that CNN proves to be effective in generating the semantic representation of document vectors in comparison to TF.IDF vector for improving the quality of clusters. These clusters are further used for information retrieval during web search.

Table 4. Average precision of various PWS Techniques in selected domains based on recommended web search documents

Search Queries Used for Information Retrieval	Average Precision@10 Based on Recommended Search Results Retrieved Using PWS Techniques								
	TF.IDF Based PWS			Ontology Based PWS			CNN Based PWS		
	Academics	Sports	Entertainment	Academics	Sports	Entertainment	Academics	Sports	Entertainment
Q1	0.48	0.63	0.49	0.83	0.49	0.63	0.94	**0.82**	**0.73**
Q2	0.63	0.74	0.73	0.89	0.63	0.738	0.89	**0.89**	**0.74**
Q3	0.49	0.738	0.49	0.94	0.82	0.82	0.89	**0.96**	**0.89**
Q4	0.62	0.74	0.63	0.88	0.82	0.74	0.94	**0.93**	**0.82**
Q5	0.63	0.74	0.74	0.82	0.88	0.89	0.82	**0.94**	**0.93**
Q6	0.63	0.63	0.628	0.73	0.89	0.88	0.83	**0.935**	**0.94**
Q7	0.49	0.628	0.29	0.73	0.94	0.74	0.94	**0.89**	**0.93**
Q8	0.73	0.738	0.74	0.82	0.82	0.64	0.89	**0.82**	**0.73**
Q9	0.63	0.485	0.63	0.73	0.89	0.82	0.94	**0.82**	**0.82**
Q10	0.62	0.628	0.63	0.82	0.82	0.887	0.74	**0.887**	**0.825**
Q11	0.29	0.485	0.29	0.74	0.94	0.89	0.88	**0.82**	**0.94**
Q12	0.63	0.738	0.74	0.73	0.97	0.94	0.89	**0.89**	**0.94**
Q13	0.62	0.63	0.63	0.83	0.82	0.968	0.94	**0.94**	**0.97**
Q14	0.3	0.74	0.49	0.89	0.89	0.97	0.89	**0.89**	**0.96**
Q15	0.63	0.63	0.29	0.94	0.82	0.82	0.82	**0.935**	**0.89**
Q16	0.49	0.49	0.63	0.89	0.89	0.82	0.89	**0.885**	**0.88**
Q17	0.62	0.485	0.625	0.88	0.82	0.88	0.94	**0.89**	**0.89**
Q18	0.63	0.63	0.63	0.83	0.738	0.89	0.89	**0.94**	**0.94**
Q19	0.63	0.628	0.63	0.74	0.74	0.94	0.94	**0.89**	**0.887**
Q20	0.63	0.485	0.63	0.94	0.82	0.97	0.89	**0.94**	**0.88**
Q21	0.63	0.628	0.73	0.94	0.89	0.82	0.74	**0.89**	**0.94**
Q22	0.63	0.74	0.628	0.83	0.887	0.82	0.89	**0.887**	**0.96**
Q23	0.48	0.63	0.48	0.83	0.94	0.88	0.94	**0.82**	**0.94**
Q24	0.28	0.49	0.49	0.73	0.97	0.89	0.89	**0.887**	**0.96**
Q25	0.63	0.74	0.63	0.83	0.94	0.93	0.97	**0.822**	**0.94**
Average precision	0.5628	0.63464	0.58164	0.8304	0.843	0.84852	0.8888	**0.88872**	**0.89088**

(Chawla,(Accepted.2020), in press)

Thus Information Retrieval with CNN for Personalized Web Search(PWS) was compared with PWS based on TF.IDF(Chawla, and Bedi,2007),PWS based on ontologies(Chawla,2018), classic IR based on average precision of recommended search results using 25 test queries based on semantic clusters of web documents in selected domains as shown in Table 4 . Assuming majority of users does not search beyond the first web page containing 10 search results therefore average precision @ 10 is computed that measure the precision of recommended 10 search results thus giving weightage to top ranked relevant documents as given in equation (4).

$$Precision = \frac{numberofrelevantdocuments}{numberofretrieveddocuments} \quad (4)$$

The average precision of recommended search results using PWS with CNN shows the significant percentage improvement in comparison to other PWS techniques over classicIR as given below in Table 5.

Table 5. Percentage improvement in average precision of various PWS Techniques over ClassicIR

Domains	Average Precision of PWS Techniques				% Improvement Over Classic IR		
	Classic IR	PWS (TF.IDF)	PWS (Ontology)	PWS (CNN)	PWS (TF.IDF)	PWS (Ontology)	PWS (CNN)
Academics	0.4536	0.5628	0.8304	0.88	24.07	83.06	94
Entertainment	0.47088	0.58164	0.84852	0.89088	23.52	80.19	89.19
Sports	0.46436	0.63464	0.843	0.88872	36.69	81.5	91.3

(Chawla,(Accepted.2020), in press)

The domainwise average precision of search results using PWS with CNN/PWS/ PWS(ontologies)/ classicIR is given below in Figure 7.

Figure 7. Comparison of average precision of search results- ClassicIR, PWS with TFIDF, PWS with ontologies and PWS with CNN

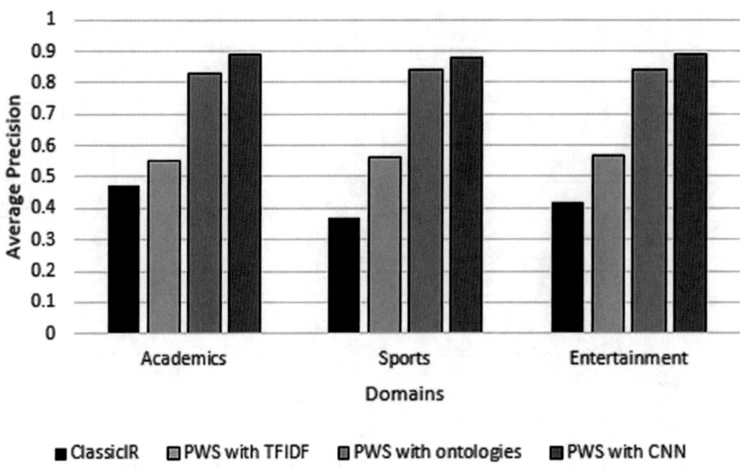

The experiment results shows the improvement in the average precision of recommended search result based on semantic clusters of web documents using PWS with CNN. Thus the results confirm the effectiveness of CNN in extracting high-level semantic document/query vector. Due to effective clustering of document concept vector based on using CNN in mining document content, there is an increase in the number of relevant documents selected for recommendation and therefore there is significant improvement in the precision of search results.

CONCLUSION

In this chapter, application of deep learning model CNN in web search query session mining for effective information retrieval is explained. Web clicked documents are represented in matrix form using Word2Vec. The CNN uses multiple filters to apply convolution operation on documents and generates the multiple variable length feature map. Thereafter Max pooling is applied on the feature maps to extract the maximum value and generates the fixed length feature vector. This fixed length feature vector is input to FNN and non linear transformation is applied to feature vector and generates the semantic document vector. These document vector are clustered using K-means and generates the semantic clusters of documents. These semantic clusters of web documents are used for information retrieval for web search. Experiment was performed using CNN on the data set of web search query sessions for web page recommendations based on clusters and results were compared with PWS(TF.IDF) and PWS(ontology). The results confirms the effectiveness of CNN based document representation in comparison to TF.IDF and ontology based document representation and therefore the cluster quality is improved for effective Information Retrieval.

REFERENCES

Ahmed, M., & Pathan, A. S. K. (2020). Deep learning for collective anomaly detection. *International Journal on Computer Science and Engineering*, *21*(1), 137–145.

Bengio, Y. (2012). Practical rec-ommendations for gradient-based training of deep architectures. In *Neural Networks: Tricks of the Trade* (pp. 437–478). Springer. doi:10.1007/978-3-642-35289-8_26

Bengio, Y., LeCun, Y., & Henderson, D. (1994). Globally trained handwritten word recognizer using spatial representation, convolutional neural networks, and hidden Markov models. In Advances in neural information processing systems (pp. 937-944). Academic Press.

Blei, D. M., Ng, A. Y., & Jordan, M. I. (2003). Latent dirichlet allocation. *Journal of Machine Learning Research*, *3*(Jan), 993–1022.

Chawla, S. (2018). Ontology-Based Semantic Learning of Genetic-Algorithm Optimised Back Propagation Artificial Neural Network for personalized web search. *International Journal of Applied Research on Information Technology and Computing*, *9*(1), 21–38. doi:10.5958/0975-8089.2018.00003.9

Chawla, S. (in press). Application of Convolution Neural Network in web query session mining for Personalized Web Search. *International Journal on Computer Science and Engineering*.

Chawla, S., & Bedi, P. (2007). Personalized Web Search using Information Scent. In *International Joint Conferences on Computer, Information and Systems Sciences, and Engineering*. Springer.

Chen, L. C., Papandreou, G., Kokkinos, I., Murphy, K., & Yuille, A. L. (2014). *Semantic image segmentation with deep convolutional nets and fully connected crfs.* arXiv preprint arXiv:1412.7062.

. Collobert, R., Weston, J., Bottou, L., Karlen, M., Kavukcuoglu, K., & Kuksa, P. (2011). Natural language processing (almost) from scratch. *Journal of Machine Learning Research, 12*, 2493-2537.

Conneau, A., Schwenk, H., Barrault, L., & Lecun, Y. (2016). *Very deep convolutional networks for text classification.* arXiv preprint arXiv:1606.01781.

Deerwester, S., Dumais, S. T., Furnas, G. W., Landauer, T. K., & Harshman, R. (1990). Indexing by latent semantic analysis. *Journal of the American Society for Information Science*, *41*(6), 391–407. doi:10.1002/(SICI)1097-4571(199009)41:6<391::AID-ASI1>3.0.CO;2-9

Deng, L., Abdel-Hamid, O., & Yu, D. (2013, May). *A deep convolutional neural network using heterogeneous pooling for trading acoustic invariance with phonetic confusion. In 2013 IEEE international conference on acoustics, speech and signal processing*. IEEE.

Donahue, J., Anne Hendricks, L., Guadarrama, S., Rohrbach, M., Venugopalan, S., Saenko, K., & Darrell, T. (2017). Long-term recurrent convolutional networks for visual recognition and description. *IEEE Transactions on Pattern Analysis and Machine Intelligence*, *39*(4), 677–691. doi:10.1109/TPAMI.2016.2599174 PMID:27608449

Farabet, C., Couprie, C., Najman, L., & LeCun, Y. (2012). Learning hierarchical features for scene labeling. *IEEE Transactions on Pattern Analysis and Machine Intelligence*, *35*(8), 1915–1929. doi:10.1109/TPAMI.2012.231 PMID:23787344

Gao, J., He, X., & Nie, J.-Y. (2010). Clickthrough-based translation models for web search: from word models to phrase models. CIKM, 1139-1148. doi:10.1145/1871437.1871582

Gao, J., Pantel, P., Gamon, M., He, X., & Deng, L. (2014). Modeling interestingness with deep neural networks. In *Proceedings of the 2014 Conference on Empirical Methods in Natural Language Processing (EMNLP)* (pp. 2-13). 10.3115/v1/D14-1002

Gao, J., Toutanova, K., & Yih, W.-T. (2011). Clickthrough-based latent semantic models for web search. SIGIR, 675-684. doi:10.1145/2009916.2010007

He, K., Zhang, X., Ren, S., & Sun, J. (2015). Spatial pyramid pooling in deep convolutional networks for visual recognition. *IEEE Transactions on Pattern Analysis and Machine Intelligence*, *37*(9), 1904–1916. doi:10.1109/TPAMI.2015.2389824 PMID:26353135

Hinton, G., & Salakhutdinov, R. (2011). Discovering binary codes for documents by learning deep generative models. *Topics in Cognitive Science*, *3*(1), 74–91. doi:10.1111/j.1756-8765.2010.01109.x PMID:25164175

Hofmann, T. (2017, August). Probabilistic latent semantic indexing. In *ACM SIGIR Forum* (Vol. 51, No. 2, pp. 50-57). ACM.

Huang, P. S., He, X., Gao, J., Deng, L., Acero, A., & Heck, L. (2013, October). Learning deep structured semantic models for web search using clickthrough data. In *Proceedings of the 22nd ACM international conference on Information & Knowledge Management* (pp. 2333-2338). ACM. 10.1145/2505515.2505665

Jain, A., Tompson, J., LeCun, Y., & Bregler, C. (2014, November). Modeep: A deep learning framework using motion features for human pose estimation. In *Asian conference on computer vision* (pp. 302-315). Springer.

Johnson, R., & Zhang, T. (2015). Semi-supervised convolutional neural networks for text categorization via region embedding. In Advances in neural information processing systems (pp. 919-927). Academic Press.

Kalchbrenner, N., Grefenstette, E., & Blunsom, P. (2014). A convolutional neural network for modelling sentences. *Proceedings of the Association for Computational Linguistics (ACL)*, 655–665. 10.3115/v1/P14-1062

Kim, H. J., Lee, J. S., & Yang, H. S. (2007, June). Human action recognition using a modified convolutional neural network. In *International Symposium on Neural Networks* (pp. 715-723). Springer. 10.1007/978-3-540-72393-6_85

Kim, Y. (2014). *Convolutional neural networks for sentence classification*. doi:10.3115/v1/D14-1181

Kim, Y., Jernite, Y., Sontag, D., & Rush, A. M. (2016, March). Character-aware neural language models. *Thirtieth AAAI Conference on Artificial Intelligence*.

Kiranyaz, S., Avci, O., Abdeljaber, O., Ince, T., Gabbouj, M., & Inman, D. J. (2021). 1D convolutional neural networks and applications: A survey. *Mechanical Systems and Signal Processing*, *151*, 107398. doi:10.1016/j.ymssp.2020.107398

Krizhevsky, A., Sutskever, I., & Hinton, G. E. (2012). Imagenet classification with deep convolutional neural networks. *Advances in Neural Information Processing Systems*.

Lan, Le Roux, Bach, Ponce, & LeCun. (2011). Ask the locals: multi-way local pooling for im- age recognition. In *Computer Vision (ICCV), 2011 IEEE International Conference on*, (pp. 2651–2658). IEEE.

Lawrence, S., Giles, C. L., Tsoi, A. C., & Back, A. D. (1997). Face recognition: A convolutional neural-network approach. *IEEE Transactions on Neural Networks*, *8*(1), 98–113. doi:10.1109/72.554195 PMID:18255614

Long, J., Shelhamer, E., & Darrell, T. (2017). Fully convolutional networks for semantic segmentation [PAMI]. *IEEE Transactions on Pattern Analysis and Machine Intelligence*, *39*(4), 640–651. doi:10.1109/TPAMI.2016.2572683 PMID:27244717

Lu, T. C. (2020). CNN Convolutional layer optimisation based on quantum evolutionary algorithm. *Connection Science*, 1–13. doi:10.1080/09540091.2020.1841111

Lu, Y., Javidi, T., & Lazebnik, S. (2016). Adaptive object detection using adjacency and zoom prediction. In *Proceedings of the IEEE Conference on Computer Vision and Pattern Recognition* (pp. 2351-2359). 10.1109/CVPR.2016.258

Mikolov, T., Chen, K., Corrado, G., & Dean, J. (2013). *Efficient estimation of word representations in vector space*. arXiv preprint arXiv:1301.3781.

Mitra, B. (2015, August). Exploring session context using distributed representations of queries and reformulations. In *Proceedings of the 38th international ACM SIGIR conference on research and development in information retrieval* (pp. 3-12). ACM. 10.1145/2766462.2767702

Nair, V., & Hinton, G. E. (2010, January). Rectified linear units improve restricted boltzmann machines. *Proceedings of the 27th International Conference on Machine Learning (ICML-10).*

Pan, L., Li, C., Zhou, Y., Chen, R., & Xiong, B. (2020). A combinational convolutional neural network of double subnets for food-ingredient recognition. *International Journal of Embedded Systems, 13*(4), 439–448. doi:10.1504/IJES.2020.110658

Pennington, J., Socher, R., & Manning, C. (2014). Glove: Global vectors for word representation. In *Proceedings of the 2014 conference on empirical methods in natural language processing (EMNLP)* (pp. 1532-1543). 10.3115/v1/D14-1162

Roshan, S. M., Karsaz, A., Vejdani, A. H., & Roshan, Y. M. (2020). Fine-tuning of pre- trained convolutional neural networks for diabetic retinopathy screening: A clinical study. *International Journal on Computer Science and Engineering, 21*(4), 564–573.

Salakhutdinov, R., & Hinton, G. (2009). Semantic hashing. *International Journal of Approximate Reasoning, 50*(7), 969–978. doi:10.1016/j.ijar.2008.11.006

Santos, C. D., & Zadrozny, B. (2014). Learning character-level representations for part- of-speech tagging. In *Proceedings of the 31st International Conference on Machine Learning (ICML-14)* (pp. 1818-1826). Academic Press.

Sarvamangala, D. R., & Kulkarni, R. V. (2021). Convolutional neural networks in medical image understanding: A survey. *Evolutionary Intelligence*, 1–22. PMID:33425040

Sermanet, P., Eigen, D., Zhang, X., Mathieu, M., Fergus, R., & LeCun, Y. (2013). *Overfeat: Integrated recognition, localization and detection using convolutional networks.* arXiv preprint arXiv:1312.6229.

Shen, Y., He, X., Gao, J., Deng, L., & Mesnil, G. (2014b). Learning Semantic Representations Using Convolutional Neural Networks for Web Search. *Proceedings of WWW 2014.* 10.1145/2567948.2577348

Shi, B., Bai, X., & Yao, C. (2016). An end-to-end trainable neural network for image-based sequence recognition and its application to scene text recognition. *IEEE Transactions on Pattern Analysis and Machine Intelligence, 39*(11), 2298–2304. doi:10.1109/TPAMI.2016.2646371 PMID:28055850

Simonyan, K., & Zisserman, A. (2014). *Very deep convolutional networks for large-scale image recognition.* arXiv preprint arXiv:1409.1556.

Socher, R., Huval, B., Manning, C. D., & Ng, A. Y. (2012, July). Semantic compositionality through recursive matrix-vector spaces. In *Proceedings of the 2012 joint conference on empirical methods in natural language processing and computational natural language learning* (pp. 1201-1211). Association for Computational Linguistics.

Szegedy, C., Reed, S., Erhan, D., Anguelov, D., & Ioffe, S. (2014). *Scalable, high-quality object detection.* arXiv preprint arXiv:1412.1441.

Tang, J., & Wang, K. (2018, February). Personalized top-n sequential recommendation via convolutional sequence embedding. In *Proceedings of the Eleventh ACM International Conference on Web Search and Data Mining* (pp. 565-573). ACM. 10.1145/3159652.3159656

Too, E. C., Yujian, L., Gadosey, P. K., Njuki, S., & Essaf, F. (2020). Performance analysis of nonlinear activation function in convolution neural network for image classification. *International Journal on Computer Science and Engineering*, *21*(4), 522–535.

Tur, G., Deng, L., Hakkani-Tür, D., & He, X. (2012, March). Towards deeper understanding: Deep convex networks for semantic utterance classification. In *2012 IEEE international conference on acoustics, speech and signal processing (ICASSP)* (pp. 5045- 5048). IEEE.

Volkovs, M. (2015). *Context models for web search personalization*. arXiv preprint arXiv:1502.00527.

Wang, P., Xu, J., Xu, B., Liu, C., Zhang, H., Wang, F., & Hao, H. (2015). Semantic clustering and convolutional neural network for short text categorization. In *Proceedings of the 53rd Annual Meeting of the Association for Computational Linguistics and the 7th International Joint Conference on Natural Language Processing* (Vol. 2, pp. 352-357). 10.3115/v1/P15-2058

Wang, S., Xing, C., & Liu, D. (2020). Efficient deep convolutional model compression with an active stepwise pruning approach. *International Journal on Computer Science and Engineering*, *22*(4), 420–430.

Weston, J., Chopra, S., & Adams, K. (2014). #tagspace: Semantic embeddings from hashtags. In *Proceedings of the 2014 conference on empirical methods in natural language processing (EMNLP)* (pp. 1822-1827). 10.3115/v1/D14-1194

Wu, Z., Gao, Y., Li, L., Xue, J., & Li, Y. (2019). Semantic segmentation of high- resolution remote sensing images using fully convolutional network with adaptive threshold. *Connection Science*, *31*(2), 169–184. doi:10.1080/09540091.2018.1510902

Xiao, T., Xu, Y., Yang, K., Zhang, J., Peng, Y., & Zhang, Z. (2015). The application of two-level attention models in deep convolutional neural network for fine-grained image classification. In *Proceedings of the IEEE conference on computer vision and pattern recognition* (pp. 842-850).

Yan, Z., Piramuthu, R., Jagadeesh, V., Di, W., & Decoste, D. (2019). *Hierarchical deep convolutional neural network for image classification*. U.S. Patent 10,387,773.

Yang, J., & Li, J. 2017. Application of deep convolution neural network. *Proceedings of 14th International Computer Conference on Wavelet Active Media Technology and Information Processing (ICCWAMTIP)*, 229-232.

Yih, W. T., He, X., & Meek, C. (2014). Semantic parsing for single-relation question answering. In *Proceedings of the 52nd Annual Meeting of the Association for Computational Linguistics* (*Vol. 2*, pp. 643-648). Academic Press.

Zhang, X., Lu, W., Li, F., Zhang, R., & Cheng, J. (2020). A deep neural architecture for sentence semantic matching. *International Journal on Computer Science and Engineering*, *21*(4), 574–582.

Zhang, X., Zhao, J., & LeCun, Y. (2015). Character-level convolutional networks for text classification. In Advances in neural information processing systems (pp. 649-657). Academic Press.

Zheng, H., Fu, J., Mei, T., & Luo, J. (2017). Learning multi-attention convolutional neural network for fine-grained image recognition. In *Proceedings of the IEEE international conference on computer vision* (pp. 5209-5217). 10.1109/ICCV.2017.557

Zhu, X., Zuo, J., & Ren, H. (2020). A modified deep neural network enables identification of foliage under complex background. *Connection Science*, *32*(1), 1–15. doi:10.1080/09540091.2019.1609420

Chapter 8
Cosine Transformed Chaos Function and Block Scrambling-Based Image Encryption

Shelza Dua
National Institute of Technology, Kurukshetra, India

Bharath Nancharla
National Institute of Technology, Kurukshetra, India

Maanak Gupta
Tennessee Technological University, USA

ABSTRACT

The authors propose an image encryption process based on chaos that uses block scrambling to reduce the correlation among the neighboring pixels and random order substitution for slightly changing the value of the pixel. The chaotic sequence for encrypting the image is generated by using two 3D logistic maps called enhanced logistic map and intertwining logistic map; the cos function helps in reducing linearity. The entire encryption process is composed of scrambling, image rotation, and random order substitution. Scrambling is used for permuting the pixels in the image so that we can reduce the correlation among the neighboring pixels, and this is followed by image rotation which can ensure that shuffling of pixels is done to the remaining pixels in the image, and at last the authors use random order substitution where they bring the small change in the pixel value. The proposed method has the capability of encrypting digital colored images into cipher form with high security, which allows only authorized ones who hold the correct secret key to decrypt the images back to original form.

DOI: 10.4018/978-1-7998-3299-7.ch008

INTRODUCTION

As a result of fast growth in computer network technologies, transmission of digital data over the network channels has rapidly increased, and it has become a convenient way to communicate in daily life. Most of the communication over the networks has been carried out in the form of images, as it conveys the information in a pictorial form to understand easily. However, it also gives a chance for the intruders to attack the communication channels and steal the information. The methods in digital image processing always focus on the advancement of visualizing the information and processing of bulky image information for storage and transmission. In a case where image has to be sent over the network, security is the primary issue which needs to be addressed.

Among various techniques like data hiding, watermarking, image encryption, steganography etc., which ensure image security when transmitted over the internet, image encryption is the most popular one. Image encryption encrypts the original image into unrecognized one (M. Yang et al., 2004), where original image is known as plaintext image and the encrypted image is called as cipher text image (Stinson, 2006).

One of the old traditional ways of encrypting the digital image is using a block cipher or stream cipher, which extracts the bulky plaintext image's data as a stream of one dimensional binary bit and then encrypting these bits. The well-known algorithms of this type of encrypting standards are Digital Encryption Standard (PUB, 1977), Advanced Encryption Standard (Rijmen & Daemen, 2001), Twofish Cipher (Schneier et al., 1999) and Blowfish Cipher (Schneier, 1993). However, using the above mentioned one dimensional algorithms are not efficient for encrypting the two dimensional image data, due to high correlation among the image pixels. Following sections gives a brief discussion about image encryption and chaos based image encryption.

Image Encryption

Encryption is basically changing the original data called as plaintext into an unreadable format called cipher text such that only authorized people can decrypt that back to plaintext and access the original data. Generally, the encryption standard uses the encryption key which is produced by the algorithm for encrypting the data or the information. In some cases, it is viable to decrypt the information without having the key by the intruders. However, for a well-organized encryption standard that uses a standard algorithm to generate the key, it is not possible to decrypt the same easily. Earlier encryption standards were often used to encrypt military information. However, the usage and exchange of information has changed from heavy or bulky devices systems to handheld devices in the last few decades. Hence, in this modern era, with the availability of internet in every part of the world, many new encryptions algorithms have developed. The modern encryption standards use the concepts of public key and symmetric key. Figure 1 shows the basic encryption approach.

Figure 1. Basic Encryption
(M. Yang et al., 2004)

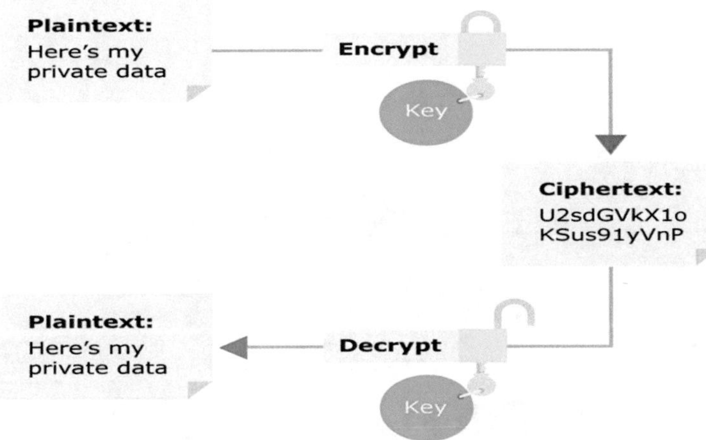

Basically, the entire encryption process is based on the keys that are used while encrypting the information. The most important and commonly used keys in cryptography are symmetric key and public key (which is also known as asymmetric key). In the symmetric key encryption process the key should be the same for both encryption as well as decryption side. Since the originator of the communication will share the key with the other party, it ensures that the communication between two parties is secured. Figure 2 shows the symmetric key encryption mechanism.

Figure 2. Symmetric Key Encryption
(Stinson, 2006)

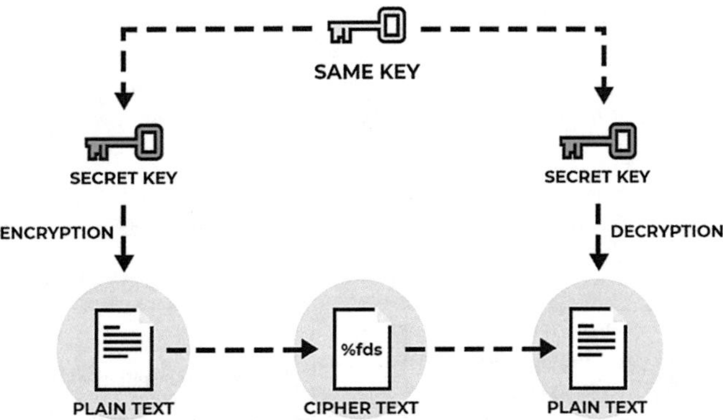

In the asymmetric key encryption process, the key is published so that it can be used by anyone to encrypt the information. On the other hand, only the receiver will have the access only to the decryption key, which allows him to read the sent information after decryption. Hence, in this way it ensures that the communication between two parties is secured. The most popular public key encryption schemes are Diffe-Hellman key exchange and RSA(Rivest-Shamir-Adleman). Figure 3 shows the asymmetric key encryption approach.

Figure 3. Asymmetric Key Encryption
(Stinson, 2006)

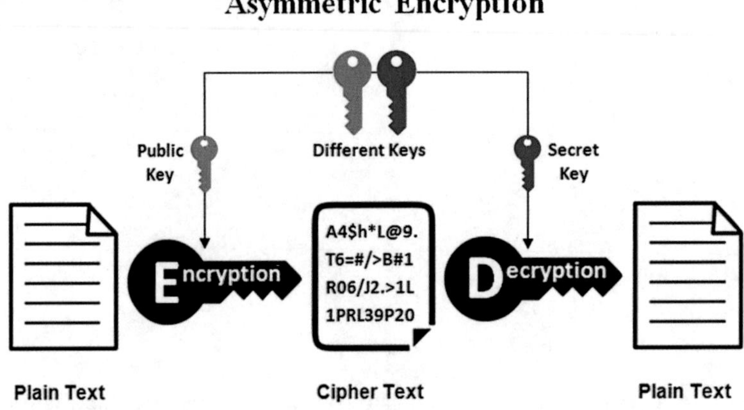

Chaos Based Image Encryption

From the past few decades, information technology is evolving rapidly and lot of information is transmitted over the communication channels in day to day basis. This content may be of text format or image format. Thus, image encryption comes into the picture to provide security. The old encryption algorithms like AES, RSA and DES etc. are good to encrypt the textual information. However, these fail to encrypt the image data with low computational cost as images possess huge information, and have high correlation among the pixels.

Figure 4. Chaos based image encryption
(Mao & Chen, 2005)

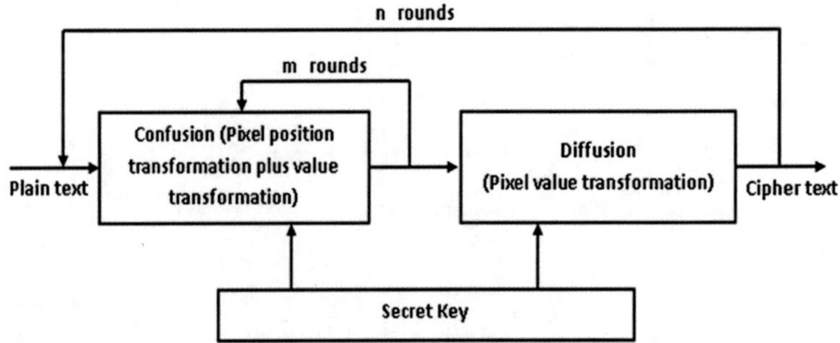

Among all the methods or algorithms available for digital image encryption, the chaos based image encryption are found to be good, because a chaotic system possesses randomness, sensitivity to initial conditions and high unpredictability properties (Mao & Chen, 2005). In the year 1997, Fridrich was the one, who first applied chaos for the image encryption purpose (Fridrich, 1997). After that many researches had worked in this area and proposed various extensions and improvements in chaos theory over the years (Behnia et al., 2008; Chen et al., 2004; Gao et al., 2006; Huang & Nien, 2009; Zhu et al., 2011). However, many proposed techniques consider the pixel data in the form of bit stream, which is inefficient. Another limitation is use of weak key or limited key space that makes easy for the intruders to know the information (Lian et al., 2005; Skrobek, 2007; T. Yang et al., 1998; Zhu et al., 2011). Chaos based image encryption standards use the concept of confusion-diffusion method. Permuting the pixels or changing the position of the pixels in the original image is known as confusion. Confusion is used to reduce the correlation among the adjacent pixels. Changing the pixel value in the original image is known as diffusion. Figure 4 shows the general architecture of a chaos based image encryption scheme.

A good image encryption standard basically depends on the initial conditions that are used while encrypting the image. It also shows the impact on the speed of and security of the encryption technique. The architecture of chaos gives scope to work in the area of development of secure and efficient image encryption in three dimensions. The researchers in recent years have worked on development of more complex chaos function, generation of more efficient scrambling technique and development of more secure diffusion technique. All together a good image encryption algorithm should try to exploit all these parameters to secure images from attacks. Next section discusses some of the recently proposed works by the researchers.

LITERATURE REVIEW

To develop a secure image encryption approach, the researchers have given many proposals such as use of multidimensional chaos maps, use of hybrid chaos maps, and use of techniques like DNA encoding, cellular automata, genetic algorithms etc. This section discusses some such recently proposed works.

Suri and Vijay (Suri & Vijay, 2019a), optimized two objectives entropy and CC, simultaneously by combining their chaos-DNA based image encryption approach with bi-objective genetic algorithm approach. The authors claimed their approach gives values for the two objectives. Suri and Vijay (Suri & Vijay, 2020) used two dimensional chaos map Coupled Map Lattice (CML) with DNA and bi-objective genetic algorithm to extend their earlier work and proposed a more secure image encryption approach. Also, Suri and Vijay (Suri & Vijay, 2019b) use multi-objective genetic algorithm to optimize the CML-DNA based image encryption approach.

Bisht et al. (Bisht et al., 2018) encrypted multiple images using combination of two-dimensional Cat Map and multiple one-dimensional chaotic maps. In their work, multiple images are encrypted based on the bit-level permutation, followed by confusion and diffusion process. Expand and shrink strategy is being employed for the bit-level permutation and Arnold cap map is used for the purpose of image encryption followed by diffusion. Initially, all the selected images are divided into corresponding bit-planes (even or odd) with the help of expansion technique and using this divided bit-planes a bigger image is developed. As part of permutation process, the chaotic functions Logistic-Sine, Logistic-Tent maps and Arnold Cat map are used for the generation of chaotic sequences. Tent-Sine map is used in diffusion phase which helps in changing the pixel value.

Dua ct al. (Dua et al., 2019) went one step ahead and used weighted bi-objective genetic algorithm with synchronous CML-DNA approach to encrypt color images. Also, Dua et al. (Dua et al., 2020) proved that Differential Evolution(DE) algorithm optimizes the ILM–DNA based approach for image encryption faster than genetic algorithm. In their work, used Secure Hash Function-2(SHA-2) the with one of the most powerful and faster evolutionary algorithms called Differential evolution (DE). ILM has been used for the purpose of permutation, and diffusion is done with the help of DNA encoding, and finally, DE is used for optimization. The following figure shows the proposed approach.

Figure 5. Bifurcation Diagram of 1D Logistic Map
(Fournier-Prunaret & Lopez-Ruiz, 2003)

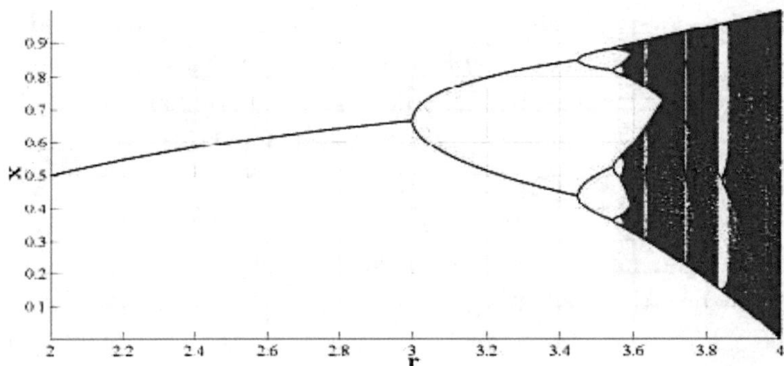

Jaroli et al. (Jaroli et al., 2018) used Arnold chaotic map and four dimensional differential equations to encrypt color images in their work. In this work, the authors proposed a new way of encrypting the color images by using four dimensional differential equations along with Arnold cat map. The entire image encryption process is divided into 3 steps. In the first step, key is produced by using the four dimensional equations, which in turn increases the chaotic random values range. In the second step, diffusion has been carried out to modify the pixel value and in the last step permutation of pixel are done.

In cryptography, chaotic maps are used to generate the chaotic sequence from the original image or input image and this chaotic sequence is used to scramble the image. The one dimensional chaotic maps are not widely popular because of its limitations like simple design with only one variable and restricted with few parameters. Moreover, the data distribution is non uniform which makes this chaotic map insecure (Agarwal, 2018). Hence, researchers tend to use multi-dimensional chaotic maps for generating the chaotic sequence which overcome the limitations of one dimensional chaotic maps. Also, transform function such as cosine and sine combination with chaos map help to improve the properties of the chaos function.

Recently, Dua et al. (Agarwal, 2018) used cosine transformation over ILM chaos map to proposed a more secure and efficient approach for image encryption. The authors claimed that cosine transformed ILM has uniform bifurcation diagram and more positive Lyupnov Exponent.

Motivated by the above literature review, we developed a chaotic structure which uses two three dimensional Logistic maps. One is used for the purpose of decreasing the correlation among the neighboring pixels, and the other is used to change the pixel value which in turn increases the confusion. The proposed work in this chapter for encrypting the image uses two 3D chaotic maps for the generation of chaotic sequence, which are holding the properties like complex dynamic behaviour with more non-linearity. The two 3D chaotic maps are ILM and enhanced Logistic map. The produced chaotic sequence is given as an input to the cosine function which intern produces new sequence. The proposed work is an extension of our work discussed in (Nancharla & Dua, 2020).

Rest of the chapter is organized as: Section 3 covers the details of the chaos maps used to develop the proposed scheme, Section 4 discusses the proposed system architecture, Section 5 describes the results and discusses the analysis part, and Section 6 concludes and discusses the future scope of the paper.

Table 1. Complexities of 1D Logistic Map and 2D Logistic Map

Parameter measurements		**1D Logistic Map (r)**		**2D Logistic Map (r)**	
		3.57 4.00 Start of Chaos End of Chaos		1.11 1.19 Start of Chaos End of Chaos	
Information Entropy	256	4.8115	7.6895	6.2605 6.5547	7.8944 7.8938
	512	5.2735	8.6773	7.1858 7.4551	8.8906 8.8900
Lyapunov Exponent		λ1	λ2	**λ*1* λ2**	**λ*1* λ2**
		0.0012	0.0693	0.3646 -0.1166	0.5654 -0.2108
Lyapunov Dimension		N/a	N/a	4.1287	3.6824

FUNDAMENTALS

ELM and ILM

The mathematical equation of the simplest and the most commonly use one dimensional Logistic map(LM) is given as:

$$1D\ Logistic\ Map = x_{i+1} = rx_i\left(1 - x_i\right) \tag{1}$$

where, r is control parameter x_0 and y_0 are considered as initial conditions. However, the one dimensional LM has serious shortcomings such as stable windows, blank windows and smaller key space.

Figure 5 gives the bifurcation diagram for the same. Hence, the one-dimensional LM is no longer used for the generation of chaotic sequence. Many authors proposed and identified that using a two-dimensional LM (Fournier-Prunaret & Lopez-Ruiz, 2003) for the chaotic sequence generation is far better than the one-dimensional LM because of complex chaotic behavior. The two-dimensional LM can be represented as:

$$2D\ Logistic\ Map = \begin{cases} x_{i+1} = r\left(3y_i + 1\right)x_i\left(1 - x_i\right) \\ y_{i+1} = r\left(3x_{i+1} + 1\right)y_i\left(1 - y_i\right) \end{cases} \tag{2}$$

Many researchers have analyzed and compared the two maps by considering non-identical initial value, and by using parameters Entropy (Shannon, 1948), Lyapunov Exponent (Kantz, 1994; Wolf et al., 1985), and Lyapunov Dimension (Chlouverakis & Sprott, 2005; Young, 1982). Table 1 shows the parameters Entropy and Lyapunov Exponent of a two- dimensional LM are completely dominating the one-dimensional LM, which shows how random and dynamic the 2D logistic map is.

Figure 6. Bifurcation diagram of Enhanced Logistic Map
(Ramasamy et al., 2019)

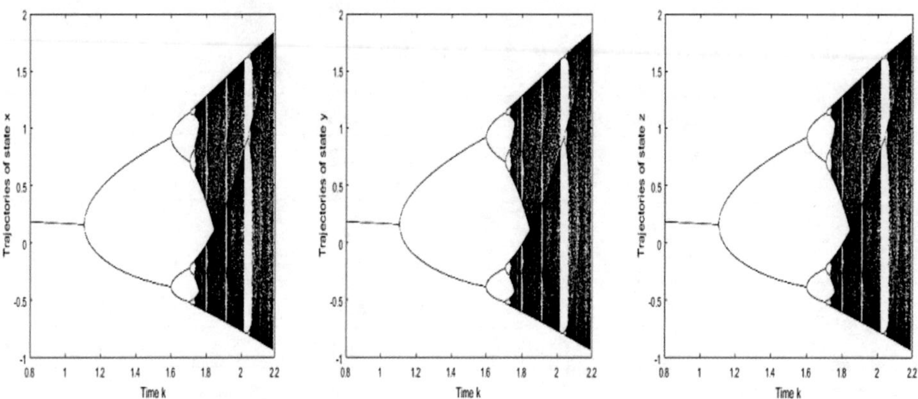

The next extension of two dimensional logistic map is 3-Dimensional Logistic map. This map is used to produce chaotic sequences for digital images same as the 2D logistic map, but the number of control parameters, variables and key space are increased. With this modification the security increases. The 3D logistic map is mathematically expressed as:

$$x_{i+1} = \alpha x_i \left(1 - x_i\right) + \beta {y_i}^2 x_i + \gamma {z_i}^3 \quad (3)$$

$$y_{i+1} = \alpha y_i \left(1 - y_i\right) + \beta {z_i}^2 y_i + \gamma {x_i}^3 \quad (4)$$

$$z_{i+1} = \alpha z_i \left(1 - z_i\right) + \beta {x_i}^2 z_i + \gamma {y_i}^3 \quad (5)$$

The three constant factors will increase the security of 3D Logistic maps. One of the recent version of 3D logistic maps is Enhanced Logistic Map (ELM) (Ramasamy et al., 2019), which deals with the Red, Green and Blue components of an image individually. This chaotic map increases the security of the image encryption by introducing chaotic diffusion method. It is mathematically defined as:

$$x_{i+1} = -\lambda x_i \left(1 - x_i\right) + \beta {y_i}^2 x_i + \alpha {z_i}^3 \quad (6)$$

$$y_{i+1} = -\lambda y_i \left(1 - y_i\right) + \beta {z_i}^2 y_i + \alpha {x_i}^3 \quad (7)$$

$$z_{i+1} = -\lambda z_i (1 - z_i) + \beta x_i^2 z_i + \alpha y_i^3 \tag{8}$$

The ranges of all the parameters of this chaotic map are slightly greater than the existing three-dimensional logistic map and thus is ensure that the security is higher than 3D Logistic map. Figure 6 and Figure 7 show the bifurcation diagram and Lyapunov Exponent of ELM, respectively.

Figure 7. Lyapunov Exponent of Enhanced Logistic Map
(Ramasamy et al., 2019)

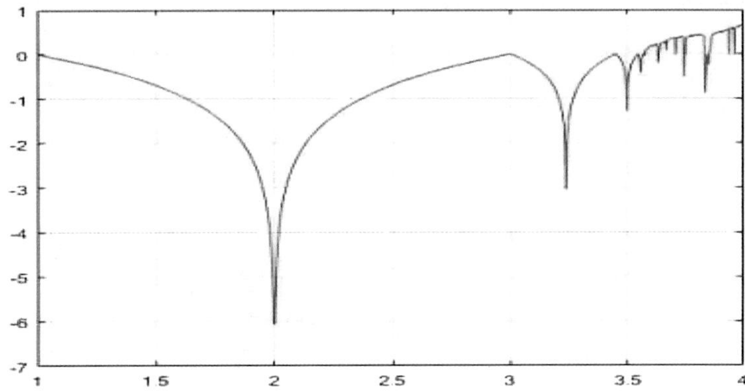

The other three dimensional Map used in the implementation of the proposed system is ILM, that is mathematically defined as:

$$x_{k+1} = \left[\lambda * l * y_k * (1 - x_k) + z_k\right] \bmod 1 \tag{9}$$

$$y_{k+1} = \left[\lambda * \beta * y_k + z_k * \left(1 + x_{k+1}^2\right)\right] \bmod 1 \tag{10}$$

$$z_{k+1} = \left[\lambda * \left(y_{k+1} + x_{k+1} + \gamma\right) * \sin\left(z_k\right)\right] \bmod 1 \tag{11}$$

where, λ, l, β, and γ have been defined using the results of work proposed in (Dua et al., 2020). Like ELM, ILM also handles all the shortcomings of LM.

Cosine Function

The cosine function or transformation is used to achieve more non-linearity among the pixels of the image. Equation 9 shows the cosine function used for the implementation of the proposed approach.

$$X_{i+1} = \cos\left(\pi\left(K\left(c, X_i\right) + J\left(d, X_i\right) + \beta\right)\right) \quad (12)$$

where, $K(c,X_i)$ and $J(d,X_i)$ denote the chaotic maps. c, d are the control parameter β *is a* constant. The used chaotic maps in this proposed approach are ILM and ELM. As mentioned in the above equation, this cosine function is applied after coupling the results of both the chaotic maps along with the constant β to produces the output.

PROPOSED SYSTEM

This section discusses the steps performed to implement the proposed image encryption scheme. We proposed a three level image encryption, which first constructs the tables, does block scrambling, and at last performs random order substitution. Figure 8 gives the block diagram of the proposed system.

Figure 8. Proposed system

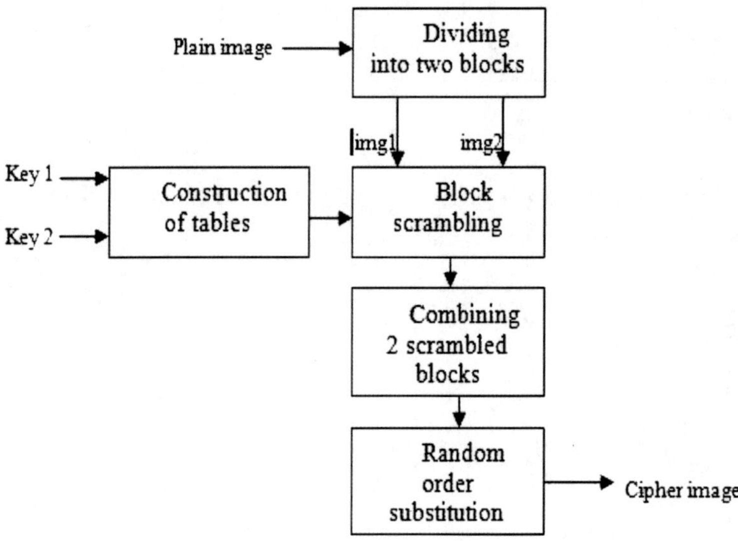

Initially, an original given input image is separated into two blocks equally and vertically. For example, if the original image is of size A × B, and A is even, then we get two images img_1 and img_2 after dividing the plain image as two separated blocks which have the size $A' \times B'$ where $A' = \frac{A}{2}$ and $B' = B$.

Tables Construction

Step 1: Produce chaotic matrix K_1 with the help of secret key (x_0, $\mu 1_)$ and ILM such that the range of elements will be from 1 to A'. Now by equation (12), iterate the chaotic system $W_0 + M'$ times (here M' is the size of img_1 and img_2 and $M' = A'B'$) to produce sequence k and then use equation (13) to quantify b and at last use equation 11 to this into K_1 of size $A' \times B'$.

$$x_{h+1} = \mu x_h \left(1 - x_h\right) \mu \in \left(0,4\right), x_h \in \left(0,1\right) \tag{13}$$

$$k_1 = \mathrm{mod}\left(floor\left(k \times 10^{14}\right), A'\right) + 1 \tag{14}$$

$$K_1 = reshape\left(k_1 A', B'\right) \tag{15}$$

Step 2: Similarly, produce the matrix K_2 by using the secret key (y_0, $\mu 2$) which ranges from 1 to B'.

Step 3: With respect to the generated chaotic matrices K_1 and K_2, build X coordinate table XT, swapping control table CT and Y coordinate table YT using the following three equations.

$$CT\left(p,q\right) = \begin{cases} 1 & abs\left(K_1\left(p,q\right) - p\right) < \frac{A'}{4} \; or \; abs\left(K_2\left(p,q\right) - p\right) < \frac{B'}{4} \\ 0 & others \end{cases} \tag{16}$$

$$XT\left(p,q\right) = \begin{cases} \mathrm{mod}\left(K_1\left(p,q\right) + \frac{A'}{4}, A'\right) + 1 & abs\left(K_1\left(p,q\right) - p\right) < \frac{A'}{4} \\ K_1\left(p,q\right) & others \end{cases} \tag{17}$$

$$YT\left(p,q\right) = \begin{cases} \mathrm{mod}\left(K_2\left(p,q\right) + \frac{B'}{4}, B'\right) + 1 & abs\left(K_2\left(p,q\right) - p\right) < \frac{B'}{4} \\ K_2\left(p,q\right) & others \end{cases} \tag{18}$$

Block Scrambling

With respect to the above three tables XT, CT and YT, we perform following three steps to swap the pixels in the two images.

Step 1: Considering the pixels in img_1.

if CT(*p,q*)= 0, exchange $img_1(p,q)$ with $img_1(XT(p,q), YT(p,q))$
else exchange $img_1(p,q)$ with $img_2(XT(p,q), YT(p,q))$

Figure 9. Plain Images

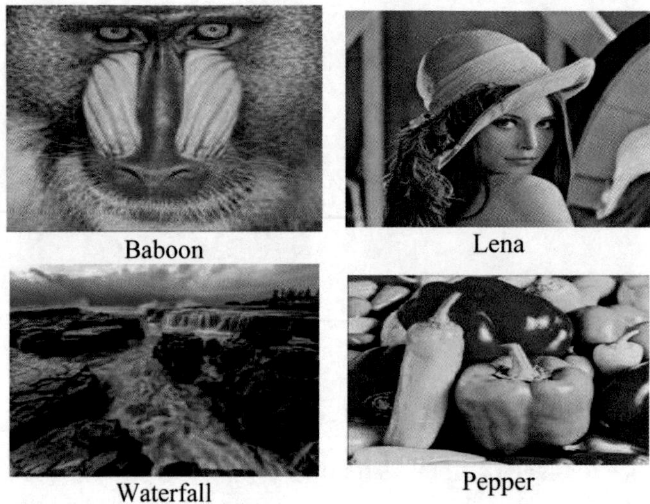

Step 2: Considering the pixels in img_1.

if CT(*p,q*)= 0, exchange $img_2(p,q)$ with $img_2(XT(p,q), YT(p,q))$
else exchange $img_2(p,q)$ with $img_1(XT(p,q), YT(p,q))$

Step 3: Now couple the both images img_1 and img_2 to form a image C of size A × B.

Random Order Substitution

This is the diffusion phase of the proposed approach, where we will change or modify the pixel value. To do that many algorithms exist already, which follow certain standard rules and because of these attackers finds easy to attack. To overcome this limitation, we use random order substitution which will substitute the values at given pixel position. To do this we generate the index matrix with the help of chaotic sequence for the substitution. Following are the required equations for performing random order substitution.

$$E_{I_{r,c},c} = \begin{cases} \left(P_{I_{r,c},c} + P_{I_{M,N},N} + \left\lfloor 2^{32} * A_{I_{r,c},c} \right\rfloor\right) \bmod M for r = 1, c = 1 \\ \left(P_{I_{r,c},c} + E_{I_{r-1,N},N} + \left\lfloor 2^{32} * A_{I_{r,c},c} \right\rfloor\right) \bmod M for r = 2 \sim N, c = 1 \\ \left(P_{I_{r,c},c} + E_{I_{r,c-1},c-1} + \left\lfloor 2^{32} * A_{I_{r,c},c} \right\rfloor\right) \bmod M for r = 1 \sim N, c = 2 \sim N \end{cases} \quad (19)$$

In the above equations, P is the result of block scrambling, and A is the generated chaotic matrix. and index matrix is named as I which is obtained by columns after sorting of A. M is taken as 256 (considering pixels are represented by 8 bits).

Table 2. Correlation among neighboring pixels

Images	Horizontal		Vertical		Diagonal	
	Plain	Cipher...	Plain	Cipher...	Plain	Cipher...
Baboon	0.925	-0.027	0.914	-0.045	0.964	-0.027
Plane	0.934	-0.031	0.967	-0.038	0.956	-0.033
Lena	0.956	-0.024	0.936	-0.031	0.948	-0.026
Pepper	0.915	-0.042	0.949	-0.043	0.962	-0.037

ANALYSIS AND RESULTS

The implementation of the proposed method is done in python on a computer which is having a windows 10 operating system with Intel i5 processor and 8GB RAM. We considered USC-SIPI "Aerials" dataset for choosing color images and examined the performance of the proposed approach on the following images. Figure 9 gives the images used for the same.

Key Space Analysis

The systems security increases if one uses the key with large space. To achieve high security, the proposed image encryption technique uses SHA-2 (Secure Hash Algorithm) to obtain a key with 256 bits of size which makes it difficult for the attackers to guess the key and retrieve the original information (Alvarez & Li, 2006).

Correlation Coefficient Analysis

Generally colored original images possess high correlation among the neighboring pixels. To build a better encryption system we need to have low correlation among these neighboring pixels in the cipher image as much as possible. One can analyze the correlation coefficient of the proposed method by choosing a pair of side by side pixels both from plain image and cipher image. The CC (Chen et al., 2004) is given as:

$$CC = \frac{\operatorname{cov}(I,J)}{\sqrt{Variance(X)}\sqrt{Variance(Y)}} \tag{20}$$

$$\operatorname{cov}(I,J) = E\left[(I_i - E(I))(J_i - E(J))\right] \tag{21}$$

The proposed system results shown in Table 2 describe that CC values are very low that indicates the relation among adjacent pixels is low.

NPCR and UACI Analysis

Differential attack is also equally important as statistical attack. In differential attack, the attackers will closely observe the behavior of the cipher image with the change done to pixels in the plain image, which are chosen randomly. In this comparison attackers may get some relationship between original image and encrypted image. The mathematical equations for calculating the UACI and NPCR are as follows:

$$NPCR = \frac{\sum_{i,j} D(i,j)}{M \times N} \times 100\% \tag{22}$$

$$UACI = \frac{1}{I \times J}\left[\sum_{i,j} \frac{\left|C_1(i,j) - C_2(i,j)\right|}{255}\right] \times 100\% \tag{23}$$

$$D(i,j) = \begin{cases} 0\, if\, C_1(i,j) = C_2(i,j); \\ 1\, if\, C_1(i,j) \neq C_2(i,j); \end{cases} \tag{24}$$

UACI and NPCR are the parameters to check whether the proposed encryption method can counter all the brute force attacks or not. Table 3 gives the NPCR and UACI values obtained for the image Baboon.

Table 3. Entropy, UACI and NPCR for Baboon Image

Measure	Proposed Method
Entropy	7.9836
UACI	26.870
NPCR	99.784

Entropy

Randomness of the image is estimated by using entropy given a position of pixel and following is the equation to calculate entropy (Ahmad & Hwang, 2016):

$$E = \sum_{1}^{256} P(i) \log\left(\frac{1}{P(i)}\right). \tag{27}$$

Entropy close to 8 indicates and it is very safe from the intruders. Table 3 gives the Entropy value obtained for the image Baboon.

PSNR Analysis

Peak signal-to-noise ratio is one of the parameters to check the quality of the encryption method. Typically, PSNR value is high for encryption systems which are said good which means the error is less. Error will be estimated by Mean square error. Mathematically, it is represented as:

$$PSNR = 10\log_{10}\frac{255.255}{\sqrt{MSE}} \tag{28}$$

$$MSE = \sum_{i=1}^{N}\sum_{j=1}^{M}\frac{\left[A\left(i,j\right)-B\left(i,j\right)\right]^{2}}{NM} \tag{29}$$

$A(i,j)$ represents the plain image pixel and $B(i,j)$ represent cipher image pixel. Table 4 gives the MSE and PSNR values.

Table 4. Result after Decryption

Images	MSE	PSNR
Baboon	12.7459	35.1048
Plane	12.0845	33.8170
Lena	14.6219	38.6148
Pepper	13.8031	32.9540

CONCLUSION

The main intension of this chapter is to protect the image data from the attackers, when transmitted over the network. To satisfy this requirement a new image encryption technique based on chaotic maps have been proposed. The proposed method uses 3D ILM with ELM to generate chaotic sequences. Then cosine function has been applied, which will produce more non uniformity in the image. This approach permutes the pixels and modify pixel value within the image by using block scrambling and random order substitution The proposed method ensures top level security for the images, which are being transmitted over the networks because of its secret key that is generated by SHA-2 function. The obtained experimental results show that the proposed method has very low correlation among the neighboring pixels, and its entropy values are almost equal to 8 which tells the effectiveness of proposed image encryption. The proposed approach exhibit better results than the encryption algorithms in recent times in terms of speed and computation. Hence, this approach can be used for efficient way of encrypting the image.

REFERENCES

Agarwal, S. (2018). A review of image scrambling technique using chaotic maps. *International Journal of Engineering and Technology Innovation*, *8*(2), 77.

Ahmad, J., & Hwang, S. O. (2016). A secure image encryption scheme based on chaotic maps and affine transformation. *Multimedia Tools and Applications*, *75*(21), 13951–13976. doi:10.100711042-015-2973-y

Alvarez, G., & Li, S. (2006). Some basic cryptographic requirements for chaos-based cryptosystems. *International Journal of Bifurcation and Chaos in Applied Sciences and Engineering*, *16*(08), 2129–2151. doi:10.1142/S0218127406015970

Behnia, S., Akhshani, A., Mahmodi, H., & Akhavan, A. (2008). A novel algorithm for image encryption based on mixture of chaotic maps. *Chaos, Solitons, and Fractals*, *35*(2), 408–419. doi:10.1016/j.chaos.2006.05.011

Bisht, A., Jaroli, P., Dua, M., & Dua, S. (2018). Symmetric Multiple Image Encryption Using Multiple New One-Dimensional Chaotic Functions and Two-Dimensional Cat Man. *Proceedings of the International Conference on Inventive Research in Computing Applications, ICIRCA 2018*, 676–682. 10.1109/ICIRCA.2018.8597245

Chen, G., Mao, Y., & Chui, C. K. (2004). A symmetric image encryption scheme based on 3D chaotic cat maps. *Chaos, Solitons, and Fractals*, *21*(3), 749–761. doi:10.1016/j.chaos.2003.12.022

Chlouverakis, K. E., & Sprott, J. C. (2005). A comparison of correlation and Lyapunov dimensions. *Physica D. Nonlinear Phenomena*, *200*(1–2), 156–164. doi:10.1016/j.physd.2004.10.006

Dua, M., Suthar, A., Garg, A., & Garg, V. (2020). An ILM-cosine transform-based improved approach to image encryption. *Complex & Intelligent Systems*, 1–17. doi:10.100740747-020-00201-z

Dua, M., Wesanekar, A., Gupta, V., Bhola, M., & Dua, S. (2019). Color image encryption using synchronous CML-DNA and weighted bi-objective genetic algorithm. *ACM International Conference Proceeding Series*, 121–125. 10.1145/3361758.3361780

Fournier-Prunaret, D., & Lopez-Ruiz, R. (2003). *Basin bifurcations in a two-dimensional logistic map.* ArXiv Preprint Nlin/0304059.

Fridrich, J. (1997). Image encryption based on chaotic maps. *1997 IEEE International Conference on Systems, Man, and Cybernetics. Computational Cybernetics and Simulation, 2*, 1105–1110. 10.1109/ICSMC.1997.638097

Gao, H., Zhang, Y., Liang, S., & Li, D. (2006). A new chaotic algorithm for image encryption. *Chaos, Solitons, and Fractals*, *29*(2), 393–399. doi:10.1016/j.chaos.2005.08.110

Huang, C. K., & Nien, H.-H. (2009). Multi chaotic systems based pixel shuffle for image encryption. *Optics Communications*, *282*(11), 2123–2127. doi:10.1016/j.optcom.2009.02.044

Jaroli, P., Bisht, A., Dua, M., & Dua, S. (2018). A Color Image Encryption Using Four Dimensional Differential Equations and Arnold Chaotic Map. *Proceedings of the International Conference on Inventive Research in Computing Applications, ICIRCA 2018*, 869–876. 10.1109/ICIRCA.2018.8597310

Kantz, H. (1994). A robust method to estimate the maximal Lyapunov exponent of a time series. *Physics Letters. [Part A]*, *185*(1), 77–87. doi:10.1016/0375-9601(94)90991-1

Lian, S., Sun, J., & Wang, Z. (2005). Security analysis of a chaos-based image encryption algorithm. *Physica A*, *351*(2–4), 645–661. doi:10.1016/j.physa.2005.01.001

Mao, Y., & Chen, G. (2005). Chaos-based image encryption. In *Handbook of geometric computing* (pp. 231–265). Springer. doi:10.1007/3-540-28247-5_8

Nancharla, B. K., & Dua, M. (2020). An image encryption using intertwining logistic map and enhanced logistic map. *Proceedings of the 5th International Conference on Communication and Electronics Systems, ICCES 2020*, 1309–1314. 10.1109/ICCES48766.2020.09138102

PUB. (1977). 46-3. data encryption standard. Federal Information Processing Standards, National Bureau of Standards, US Department of Commerce.

Ramasamy, P., Ranganathan, V., Kadry, S., Damaševičius, R., & Blažauskas, T. (2019). An image encryption scheme based on block scrambling, modified zigzag transformation and key generation using enhanced logistic—Tent map. *Entropy (Basel, Switzerland)*, *21*(7), 656. doi:10.3390/e21070656 PMID:33267370

Rijmen, V., & Daemen, J. (2001). Advanced encryption standard. Proceedings of Federal Information Processing Standards Publications, 19–22.

Schneier, B. (1993). Description of a new variable-length key, 64-bit block cipher (Blowfish). *International Workshop on Fast Software Encryption*, 191–204.

Schneier, B., Kelsey, J., Whiting, D., Wagner, D., Hall, C., & Ferguson, N. (1999). *The Twofish encryption algorithm: a 128-bit block cipher*. John Wiley & Sons, Inc.

Shannon, C. E. (1948). A mathematical theory of communication. *The Bell System Technical Journal*, *27*(3), 379–423. doi:10.1002/j.1538-7305.1948.tb01338.x

Skrobek, A. (2007). Cryptanalysis of chaotic stream cipher. *Physics Letters. [Part A]*, *363*(1–2), 84–90. doi:10.1016/j.physleta.2006.10.081

Stinson, D. R. (2006). *The RSA Cryptosystem and Factoring Integers in Cryptography Theory and Practice*. Chapman & Hall/CRC.

Suri, S., & Vijay, R. (2019a). A bi-objective genetic algorithm optimization of chaos-DNA based hybrid approach. *Journal of Intelligent Systems*, *28*(2), 333–346. doi:10.1515/jisys-2017-0069

Suri, S., & Vijay, R. (2019b). A Pareto-optimal evolutionary approach of image encryption using coupled map lattice and DNA. *Neural Computing & Applications*, 1–15.

Suri, S., & Vijay, R. (2020). A coupled map lattice-based image encryption approach using DNA and bi-objective genetic algorithm. *International Journal of Information and Computer Security*, *12*(2–3), 199–216. doi:10.1504/IJICS.2020.105156

Wolf, A., Swift, J. B., Swinney, H. L., & Vastano, J. A. (1985). Determining Lyapunov exponents from a time series. *Physica D. Nonlinear Phenomena*, *16*(3), 285–317. doi:10.1016/0167-2789(85)90011-9

Yang, M., Bourbakis, N., & Li, S. (2004). Data-image-video encryption. *IEEE Potentials*, *23*(3), 28–34. doi:10.1109/MP.2004.1341784

Yang, T., Yang, L.-B., & Yang, C.-M. (1998). Cryptanalyzing chaotic secure communications using return maps. *Physics Letters. [Part A]*, *245*(6), 495–510. doi:10.1016/S0375-9601(98)00425-3

Young, L.-S. (1982). Dimension, entropy and Lyapunov exponents. *Ergodic Theory and Dynamical Systems*, *2*(1), 109–124. doi:10.1017/S0143385700009615

Zhu, Z., Zhang, W., Wong, K., & Yu, H. (2011). A chaos-based symmetric image encryption scheme using a bit-level permutation. *Information Sciences*, *181*(6), 1171–1186. doi:10.1016/j.ins.2010.11.009

Chapter 9
An Improved Approach for Multiple Image Encryption Using Alternate Multidimensional Chaos and Lorenz Attractor

Mohit Dua
https://orcid.org/0000-0001-7071-8323
National Institute of Technology, Kurukshetra, India

Shelza Dua
National Institute of Technology, Kurukshetra, India

Priyanka Jaroli
Banasthali Vidyapith, India

Ankita Bisht
Banasthali Vidyapith, India

ABSTRACT

This chapter proposes a multiple image encryption method based on multi-dimensional chaotic equations. Four-dimensional differential chaotic equations of Lorenz attractor have been used to generate the initial security key, and alternate logistic maps have been used for encryption. Initially, three input images are used in a matrix form, where size of each image is M×N, and a composite image is derived by combining the one dimensional matrix of the input images, where size of the composite image matrix is 3×(M×N). Secondly, Lorenz attractor (LA) generates the security key using the composite matrix, and then alternate logistic map is applied with one-dimensional and two-dimensional logistic maps to confuse the matrix. In every iteration of logistic maps, XOR operation is used to encrypt the composite image, and at last, transformation is applied to diffuse the matrix. Finally, the encrypted composite image is obtained in the form of a confused matrix. The proposed algorithm reduces the correlation, increases entropy, and enhances performance of encryption.

DOI: 10.4018/978-1-7998-3299-7.ch009

INTRODUCTION

Nowadays, data security is a significant problem in computer networks and mobile device technology (Sankpal & Vijaya, 2014). The rapid advancement and evolution in transmission technologies have increased the security concerns about multimedia data as lots of data is being stored and transmitted in various patterns over the network. Thus the security of the digital data against eavesdropping and attackers is an important concern. Hence, the security algorithms have emerged as a vital research issues (KN, 2011)(Patel & Parikh, 2018). The digital data is of many types like audio, video, text and image. The digital image data has specific instinctive trait such as huge data size, high correlation between neighbouring pixels and strong redundancy etc. (Mohammad et al., 2017). The image data requires the high real-time tract in conversation. Hence, an encryption algorithm with high security is required (Bakhshandeh & Eslami, 2013). Due to these characteristics, the classic encryption algorithms such as Advanced Encryption Standard (AES)(Çavuşoğlu et al., 2017), Data Encryption Standard (DES) (Qian et al., 2009), Two Fish cipher (Agath et al., 2018), IDEA (Xu et al., 2016)etc. These algorithms are not effective and intact for real time digital image encryption.

Since last three decades, many researchers are using chaos based techniques for encrypting an image. The chaos and cryptography share many common characteristics that make chaos theory suitable for cryptography (Guan et al., 2005). The chaotic maps are an imperative part of the chaos theory and play a valuable role in image encryption (Özkaynak, 2018). The cryptography algorithms use the encryption key, rounds of chaotic maps for permutation and diffusion process for encryption. Moreover, phase space in such algorithms consists of finite set of integer numbers [9]. However, in chaotic maps, phase space consists of set of real number and these use iteration for encryption. The specialties of chaotic maps have encouraged researcher to invent many new and secure encryption algorithms (Suri & Vijay, n.d.a). The chaotic maps have many peculiarities such as sensitive to initial conditions, nonlinear dynamic behaviour, ergodicity, high speed and good computational power. The chaotic system works into two steps, generating security key and encryption is done by using this security key. These can be divided into two categories: one dimensional chaotic map and multi dimensional chaotic map (Li et al., 2018; Pak & Huang, 2017; Wang et al., 2018).

Recently, many image encryption algorithms have been proposed using the one dimensional chaotic map, two dimensional chaotic map, three dimensional chaotic map, four dimensional chaotic map and modified one dimensional chaotic map (Marotto, 1978). The one dimensional chaotic maps have simple structure, low computation cost and easy implementation. One dimensional chaotic map provides the limited range of dynamic chaotic behaviour and also uses less parameter for encryption (Pareek et al., 2005). However, one dimensional chaotic maps are easily cracked by using many methods like phase regression or nonlinear prediction methods (Baldovin & Robledo, 2002). Therefore, the multi dimensional technologies have been proposed.Multi dimensional chaotic map enhance the security in image encryption because of its complicated structure. Multi dimensional maps are more secure and effective than the low dimensional chaotic maps. These maps provide the large range of dynamic chaotic behaviour and good performance compared to one dimensional chaotic map (Murillo-Escobar et al., 2017). The proposed algorithm use non linear four dimensional differential equations and these equations are used the traditional three dimensional differential equation. These equations enumerate large range of dynamic chaotic state. Four dimensional differential equations generate pseudo random bit sequences (PRBS) and this method increases the speed and randomness of the key generation and an effect on the security of the image encryption (Murillo-Escobar et al., 2017; Tong et al., 2015).

This chapter proposes a novel multiple image encryption procedure based on multi-dimensional chaotic equations and chaotic maps. Four-dimensional differential chaotic equations generate the security key using Lorenz Attractor (LA). One-dimensional and two-dimensional logistic map equations are used alternatively to encrypt the multiple images. Initially, three images are use as a matrix form and size of each image is (M×N), each image is converted into one dimensional matrix and composite image is derived by combining the one dimensional matrix of each image and get a matrix with the size of (3×(M× N)).Secondly, Lorenz Attractor (LA) generates the security key using composite matrix and then applied the alternate logistic map with one dimensional and two dimensional logistic maps to permute the matrix. Every iteration of alternate logistic map, XOR operation is used to encrypt the composite image and at last applied transformation to diffuse the matrix. Finally, the encrypted composite image is obtained in the form of a confused matrix. The proposed encryption algorithm reduces the correlation, increase security and performance of encryption.

The remaining chapter describes as follows: Section 2 describes the chaotic maps (one dimensional logistic map (ODLM) and two dimensional logistic maps (TDLM)) and Lorenz Attractor (LA). Section 3 shows the proposed method, the experimental and simulation results are represents in section 4 and section 5 finally, concludes the proposal.

PRELIMINARIES

Chaos theory is extensively used for expanding the cryptography systems due to its exclusive properties. This portion of the chapter describes the chaotic maps used to implement the proposed multiple image encryption algorithm.

One Dimensional Logistic Map (ODLM)

A number of chaotic maps have been introduced in recent years and many are still under consultations which are used in multiple image encryption. However, a very simple, easy and broadly accepted chaotic map is logistic map which is used for concealing the data (Hua & Zhou, 2018). This map is simple to develop, has low computation power, gives stable states and intricate dynamic behavior. It is treated as one of the exceeding one dimensional chaotic map (Tavazoei & Haeri, 2007). This chaotic map produces the dynamic sequences and it is used in the confusion diffusion stage of the multiple image encryption algorithms. One dimensional logistic map (ODLM) is expressed by using the equation (1) (Zhou et al., 2014).

$$z_{l+1} = wz_l\left(1 - z_l\right) \quad (1)$$

Here, w and z_l are two function parameters that are used to control the dynamic sequences, which are generated by ODLM. z_l Lies in the interval of [0,1]. The function parameter w shows the dynamic behavior in the range of $3.5666 < w \leq 4$. In the proposed work the seed value w has been assigned the value 3.99889 (Politi et al., 2017; Tavazoei & Haeri, 2007; Zhou et al., 2014).

Two Dimensional Logistic Map (TDLM)

Dynamic image encryption systems prefer the multi dimensional chaotic system due to large range of the secret key space. A multi dimensional chaotic system generates more random sequences and it can be used in different forms. This system has unique characteristics that are used to develop new nonlinear and dynamic systems (Wu, Noonan, Yang et al, 2012).

In this chapter, the two dimensional logistic map (TDLM) that is expansion of the ODLM system has been used. TDLM generates larger key space and implements better control function as compared to ODLM (Jain & Rajpal, 2016). It has high Lyapunov exponent value that represents more dynamic behaviour. Hence, it is problematic for the attacker to predict the hidden information. It has dense periodic orbit and small periodic window, thus it is more safe and efficient for encryption algorithm. Two dimensional (TDLM) nonlinear chaotic function is defined as (Wu, Yang, Jin et al, 2012):

$$\begin{cases} x_{l+1} = x_l w_1 \left(1 - x_l\right) + U_1 y^2{}_l \\ y_{l+1} = y_l w_2 \left(1 - y_l\right) + U_2 \left(x^2{}_l + x_l y_l\right) \end{cases} \tag{2}$$

Here, $2.75 < w_1 \leq 3.4$, $2.75 < w_2 \leq 3.45$, $0.15 < U_1 \leq 0.21$ and $0.13 < U_2 \leq 0.15$. The values of *x, y* and *z* lies in the range of [0,1]. The coefficient w_1, w_2, U_1, U_2 and initial values of the x_0,y_0 are pre-assigned by the user for encryption algorithm (Jain & Rajpal, 2016; Wu, Yang, Jin et al, 2012).

Lorenz Attractor

Due to the exclusive characteristics of multi-dimensional chaotic systems, researchers are constantly researching the new differential chaotic equations by enhancing the existing differential chaotic equations. Four dimensional differential chaotic equation of Lorenz Attractor (LA) are based on the traditional three dimensional differential equations. A new four dimensional differential equation system of Lorenz Attractor (LA). It can be mathematically discussed by using equation (3).

$$\begin{cases} \frac{dz_1}{dt} = a\left(z_2 - z_1\right) \\ \frac{dz_2}{dt} = bz_4 + cz_2 + dz_1 - z_1 z_3 - z_3 z_4 \\ \frac{dz_3}{dt} = fz_3 + z_2 z_4 + z_1 z_2 \\ \frac{dz_4}{dt} = gz - ez_4 - 0.05 z_1 z_3 \end{cases} \tag{3}$$

Here z_1, z_2, z_3, z_4 are the system states and *a, b, c, d, e, f, g* are the constant system parameters. When the initial conditions of the system are(1,1,1,1) for z_1, z_2, z_3, z_4, things become easy for real-time applications. The step size is 0.000001 and constant function parameters are a=16, b=45, c=-2, d=45, e=16, f=-4, g=16. The four dimensional differential equation enumerates two Lorenz Attractor that uses four

Lyapunov exponents and the initial values are 2.11, 0, -15.19, and-24.73. The developed system provides a set of dynamic solution (Tong et al., 2015)(Akgul & Pehlivan, 2016; Gao & Chen, 2008).

PROPOSED ALGORITHM

This section illustrates the flow of the proposed method for multiple image encryption. The implemented algorithm uses three images that are represented in a matrix form and size of each image is (M×N). Initially, A composite image is derived by combining the one dimensional matrices of the three images and a matrix of size (3×(M×N)) is obtained. Secondly, Lorenz Attractor (LA) generates the security key using composite matrix and then the alternate logistic map with one dimensional and two dimensional logistic maps are applied to confuse the matrix. The final encrypted composite image is in the form of a confused matrix. Figure 1 gives the architecture of the proposed multiple image encryption algorithm.

Figure 1. Proposed Architecture for Image Encryption

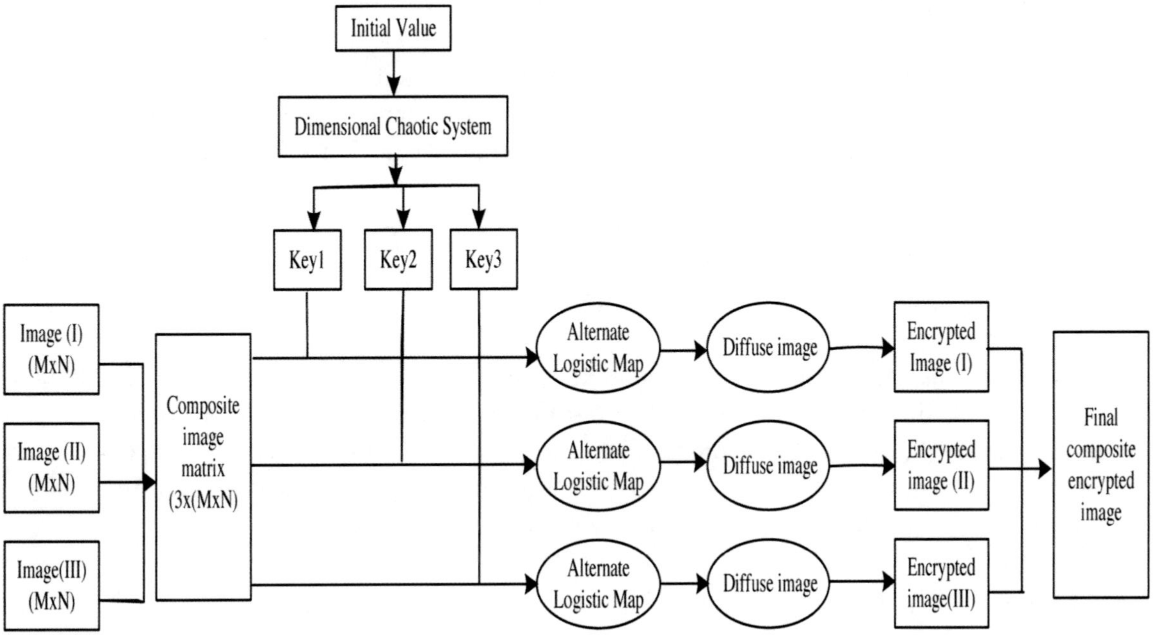

Design of Pseudo Random Bits Generator

In a multiple image encryption algorithm size of the key depends on the input images. For the proposed multiple image encryption algorithm, the size of the each image has been taken $M \times N$. The pseudo random bits generator generates the binary key streamsfor the composite image that has size $(3\times(M\times N))$. Four dimensional differential equations generate the key stream and this method reduces the time of encryption. The random bit sequences key1, key2 and key3 are obtained and used to encrypt the composite image. It uses the Runge-Kutta method to generate the multi dimensional sequence value. A good bit generator efficiently decreases the length of multi-dimensional chaotic sequence, thus largely decrease the time for the algorithm. The architecture diagram of random bits generator is shown in Figure 2 and algorithm 1 describes the steps used to generate deterministic random bit generator.

Encryption Procedure

The encryption process uses the three images(im1, im2, im3) and denoted as g^{im1},g^{im2},$g^{im3}$the size of the each image is (M×N)matrix and range of the matrix are 0 to255 and*h*th pixel value denotes the pixel value of im1, im2 and im3 matrix as

$$g_h^{im1}, g_h^{im2} \; and \; g_h^{im3} \left(h \in \left[0, M \times N - 1\right]\right),$$

correspondingly.

SIMULATION RESULT AND PERFORMANCE MEASUREMENTS

This section discusses the implementation results of the proposed image encryption technique. For implementation, MATLAB version 8.1 (R2013a), operating system window 7, and processor i-3 are used. The performance measure of multidimensional differential equation with alternate logistic chaotic map is done by using the parameters with the initial values $w = 3.99889$, $w_1 = 3.39$, $w_2 = 3.4489$, $L_1 = 0.21$, $U_2 = 0.15$, $x_0 = 0.345$, $y_0 = 0.365$, and $z_0 = 0.537$.

Input Image Data and Encrypted Image

Three gray scale images a “Lena”, “coins” and “Rice” are used for testing the proposed algorithm and the size of the each image is 256×256. Figure 3 (a-c) shows the input images for encryption.

Figure 4 shows the output of the proposed schema. Figure 4(a) shows the diffuse image of the Lena image; Figure 4(b) shows the diffuse image of the coins image; Figure 4(c) shows the diffuse image of the Rice image. Figure 4(d) shows the final encrypted composite image.

Key Space Analysis

In the multidimensional differential chaotic equation, the key space is dependent on the technique used for the chaotic system. In the proposed chaotic system, a four dimensional chaotic system has been used to provide four seed values. Hence, the key space of the system is $10^{14\times4}$ that it is more than 2^{186} and is capable to resist brute-force attack.

Algorithm 1. Generation of pseudo random bits sequence

Step1: Generate the multidimensional sequence by taking the initial value ($z10$, $z20$, $z30$, $z40$)of the differential chaotic system to iterate the equation (4) $(M\times N)/3+100$ times. This initial order increase the sensitivity of the initial conditions and remove the transient effect. Eliminate the initial 100 group values and then obtain the random sequences value z_1, z_2, z_3, z_4.

Step2: Discretize the multi dimensional sequence by taking the value of z_{j_k}. Here j=1,2,3,4 and k=1,2,3,...., $M\times N\div 3$ and then get the decimal value of the sequence by using equation (4) and this sequence is quantize and obtain the integer value z_1, z_2, z_3, z_4. It gets by using equation (5).

$$\varphi z_{jk} = z_{j_k} - floor\left(z_{j_k}\right) \quad (4)$$

$$z_{j_k} = \mathrm{mod}\left(floor\left(\varphi z_{jk} \times 10^{14}\right), 65536\right) \quad (5)$$

Step3: Select distinct bits of each multi dimensional sequence to generate the key. This key is in a integer form and mathematically it is show by equation (6).

$$z_{j_k} = v_{jk_{15}} * 2^{15} + v_{jk_{14}} * 2^{14} + v_{jk_{13}} * 2^{13} + \ldots\ldots + v_{jk_1} * 2^1 + v_{jk_0} \quad (6)$$

This bit selection procedure is decrease the correlation between the three pseudo random sequences and also increase the ratio of reusing. This procedure use crosswise bits of the each sequence.

Key1 show from 1st to 8th bit of $z_{1_k}, z_{2_k}, z_{3_k}$ and its mathematically represent as equation (7).

$$\begin{cases} key1\left(q\right) = v_{1k_7} * 2^7 + v_{1k_6} * 2^6 + v_{1k_5} * 2^5 + v_{1k_4} * 2^4 + v_{1k_3} * 2^3 + v_{1k_2} * 2^2 + v_{1k_1} * 2^1 + v_{1k_0} \\ \left\{key1\left(q+1\right) = v_{2k_7} * 2^7 + v_{2k_6} * 2^6 + v_{2k_5} * 2^5 + v_{2k_4} * 2^4 + v_{2k_3} * 2^3 + v_{2k_2} * 2^2 + v_{2k_1} * 2^1 + v_{2k_0} \right. \\ \left\{key1\left(q+2\right) = v_{3k_7} * 2^7 + v_{3k_6} * 2^6 + v_{3k_5} * 2^5 + v_{3k_4} * 2^4 + v_{3k_3} * 2^3 + v_{3k_2} * 2^2 + v_{3k_1} * 2^1 + v_{3k_0} \right. \end{cases}$$

(7)

Key2 show from 5th to 12th bit $z_{3_k}, z_{4_k}, z_{1_k}$ and its mathematically represent as equation (8).

$$\begin{cases} key2\left(q\right) = v_{1k_{11}} * 2^7 + v_{1k_{10}} * 2^6 + v_{1k_9} * 2^5 + v_{1k_8} * 2^4 + v_{1k_7} * 2^3 + v_{1k_6} * 2^2 + v_{1k_5} * 2^1 + v_{1k_4} \\ \left\{key2\left(q+1\right) = v_{3k_{11}} * 2^7 + v_{3k_{10}} * 2^6 + v_{3k_9} * 2^5 + v_{3k_8} * 2^4 + v_{3k_7} * 2^3 + v_{3k_6} * 2^2 + v_{3k_5} * 2^1 + v_{3k_4} \right. \\ \left\{key2\left(q+2\right) = v_{4k_{11}} * 2^7 + v_{4k_{10}} * 2^6 + v_{4k_9} * 2^5 + v_{4k_8} * 2^4 + v_{4k_7} * 2^3 + v_{4k_6} * 2^2 + v_{4k_5} * 2^1 + v_{4k_4} \right. \end{cases}$$

(8)

Key3 show from 9th to 16th bit $z_{3_k}, z_{4_k}, z_{2_k}$ and its mathematically represent as equation (9).

$$\begin{cases} key3\left(q\right) = v_{2k_{11}} * 2^7 + v_{2k_{10}} * 2^6 + v_{2k_9} * 2^5 + v_{2k_8} * 2^4 + v_{2k_7} * 2^3 + v_{2k_6} * 2^2 + v_{2k_5} * 2^1 + v_{2k_4} \\ \left\{key3\left(q+1\right) = v_{3k_{15}} * 2^7 + v_{3k_{14}} * 2^6 + v_{3k_{13}} * 2^5 + v_{3k_{12}} * 2^4 + v_{3k_{11}} * 2^3 + v_{3k_{10}} * 2^2 + v_{3k_9} * 2^1 + v_{3k_8} \right. \\ \left\{key3\left(q+2\right) = v_{4k_{15}} * 2^7 + v_{4k_{14}} * 2^6 + v_{4k_{13}} * 2^5 + v_{4k_{12}} * 2^4 + v_{4k_{11}} * 2^3 + v_{4k_{10}} * 2^2 + v_{4k_9} * 2^1 + v_{4k_8} \right. \end{cases}$$

Histogram Analysis

The histogram analysis of any image emphasizes its pixel distribution. An encryption algorithm should result in an encrypted image with a uniform distribution of pixels such that it becomes difficult to identify (Enayatifar et al., 2017; Mollaeefar et al., 2017; Sathyanarayana et al., 2011). The histogram of original images and obtained diffused images are shown in Figure 5. Figures 5(a), 5(e) and 5(i) are original input images and Figures 5(b), 5(f) and 5(j) show the histogram of the original input images, respectively. Figures 5(c), 5(g) and 5(k) are the diffused images and Figures 5(d), 5(h) and 5(l) show the histogram for diffused images, respectively. Figure 5(m) is the encrypted composite image and Figure 5(n) shows the histogram of the encrypted composite image.

Figure 2. Proposed pseudo random bits generator

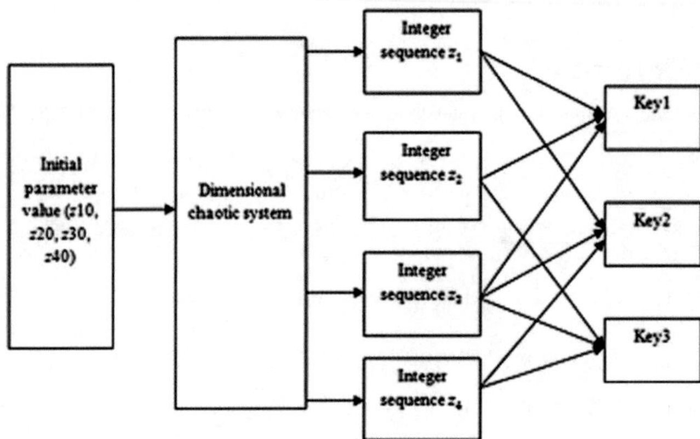

Correlation Distribution

In the encrypted image, the drawback of the high correlation between pixels should be removed. Correlation is stronger in original plaintext image and in the encrypted image the correlation must be weaker. It is evaluated between two vertical, horizontal and diagonal adjacent pixels in an image. In plaintext image and encrypted image many pairs of adjacent pixels are selected to analyze the correlation distribution (CD) (Bisht et al., 2019; Dua et al., 2019a; Tong et al., 2016). It is calculated by using the following equations

$$M_{x,z} = \frac{\operatorname{cov}(x,z)}{\sqrt{D(x)}\sqrt{D(z)}} \tag{35}$$

Here

$$\operatorname{cov}(x,z) = \frac{1}{N}\sum_{i=1}^{n}\left(x_i - E(x)\left(z_i - E(z)\right)\right) \tag{36}$$

$$D(x) = \frac{1}{N}\sum_{i=1}^{n}\left(x_i\right) \tag{37}$$

Algorithm 2. Encryption procedure steps

Step1: use the im1, im2 and im3 image matrices g^{im1}, g^{im2}, g^{im3} and convert each image into one dimensional matrix and get the composite matrix A with the size of the (3×(*M*×*N*)).

Step2: F_1, F_2, F_3 are determined by the image im1, im2 and im3 using the equation (10) to (12) and then transform the values of F_1, F_2, F_3. The transformation repels attack effectively using the equation (13) to (15).

$$F_1 = \sum_{l\in[0, M\times N-1]} g_l^{im1} / \left(M \times N \times 255\right) \quad (10)$$

$$F_2 = \sum_{l\in[0, M\times N-1]} g_l^{im2} / (M \times N \times 255) \quad (11)$$

$$F_3 = \sum_{l\in[0, M\times N-1]} g_l^{im3} / (M \times N \times 255) \quad (12)$$

$$\Delta = floor\left(\mathrm{mod}((F_1 + F_2 + F_3) \times 10^{12}, 256)\right) \quad (13)$$

$$\Delta 1 = floor\left(\mathrm{mod}\left(\frac{F_1 + F_2 + F_3}{2} \times 10^{12}, 256\right)\right) \quad (14)$$

$$\Delta 2 = floor\left(\mathrm{mod}\left(\frac{F_1 + F_2 + F_3}{3} \times 10^{12}, 256\right)\right) \quad (15)$$

Step3: Two dimensional logistic map equation and one dimensional logistic map are iterate by using w_1, w_2, U_1, U_2, x_0, y_0, z_0. Initial values are used in iteration and new x_l, y_l, z_l values are got in each iteration.

$p_1=(x_h\times10^{15})\mathrm{mod}256$ (16)

$p_2=(y_h\times10^{15})\mathrm{mod}256$ (17)

$p_3=(z_h\times10^{15})\mathrm{mod}256$ (18)

$$s_h = \begin{cases} \Delta - p_1, p_1 < \Delta \\ p_1 - \Delta, p_1 > \Delta \\ \Delta, p_1 = \Delta \end{cases}, x_h = \begin{cases} \Delta - p_1 / 256, p_1 < \Delta \\ p_1 - \Delta / 256, p_1 > \Delta \\ \Delta / 256, p_1 = \Delta \end{cases} \quad (19)$$

$$s_{h+MXN} = \begin{cases} \Delta 1 - p_2, p_2 < \Delta 1 \\ p_2 - \Delta 1, p_2 > \Delta 1 \\ \Delta 1, p_2 = \Delta 1 \end{cases}, y_h = \begin{cases} \Delta 1 - p_2 / 256, p_2 < \Delta 1 \\ p_2 - \Delta 1 / 256, p_2 > \Delta 1 \\ \Delta 1 / 256, p_2 = \Delta 1 \end{cases} \quad (20)$$

$$s_{h+MXNX2} = \begin{cases} \Delta 2 - p_3, p_3 < \Delta 2 \\ p_3 - \Delta 2, p_3 > \Delta 2 \\ \Delta 2, p_3 = \Delta 2 \end{cases}, z_h = \begin{cases} \Delta 2 - p_3 / 256, p_3 < \Delta 2 \\ n_3 - p_3 / 256, p_3 > \Delta 2 \\ \Delta 2 / 256, p_3 = \Delta 2 \end{cases} \quad (21)$$

continued on following page

Algorithm 2. Continued

Here, s_h is the hth number of random matrix and s ((3×(M×N)) is the size of the matrix). **Step4:**Continuous iterate the equation (2) and equation (1) and it is iterate alternatively using the following equation .Initially iterate equation (2) obtain the value of w_1, w_2, U_1, U_2, x_0, y_0. In every new iteration the value of x_l, y_l is obtain in as equation(22) to equation (26). $c_1 = \mathrm{mod}(z_i \times 10^{15}, M \times N)$ (22) $c_2 = \mathrm{mod}(1 - z_i) \times 10^{15}, M \times N)$ (23) $c_3 = floor(c_1 + c_2 + \Delta 2 / 2)$ (24) $x_0 = \mathrm{mod}(z_l + y_{l-1}, 1)$ (25) $y_0 = \mathrm{mod}(z_l + x_{l-1} + y_{l-1}, 1)$ (26)
When the equation (1) is continuous iteration using w, z_0 and obtain the new value of z_l in each iteration using equation (27) to equation(30). $c_1 = \mathrm{mod}(x_l \times 10^{15}, M \times N)$ (27) $c_2 = \mathrm{mod}(y_l \times 10^{15}, M \times N)$ (28) $c_3 = \mathrm{mod}((x_l + y_l - floor(x_l + y_l) \times 10^{15}, M \times N)$ (29) $z_0 = \mathrm{mod}(x_l + y_l, 1)$ (30) Transform the matrix and perform the XOR operation equation (31) to equation (33). *m(1,:)=cirshift(m(1,:),* c_1*)* (31) *m(2,:)=cirshift(m(2,:),* c_2*)* (32) *m(3,:)=cirshift(m(3,:),* c_3*)* (33) **Step5:** diffuse the value of all the images and obtain the finalcomposite encrypted image using the equation (34). *B(x,z)=(E(x,z)+B(x,z-1))mod256* (34) Here, *B(x,z-1)* is represent previous diffuse value after transformation and *(E(x, z))* is current value which is being carried out.

$$E(x) = \frac{1}{N}\sum_{i=1}^{n}\left(x_i - E\left(x\right)\right)^2 \quad (38)$$

Figure 6 and Figure 7 show that the correlation distribution (CD)for original plaintext images are not uniform and in the diffused image and final encrypted image are uniform (Dua et al., 2019b; Suneja et al., 2019).

Entropy Analysis

The entropy is procedure to measure the uncertainty present in the image. It also, measures the gray scale value is random or not. For a secure image, the entropy should be high and maximum value of entropy is 8 and minimum value is 0 (Bisht et al., 2018; Jaroli et al., 2018). The formula is used for calculate the entropy is expressed as:

Figure 3. Input data set (a-c)

$$H(p) = -\sum_{i=1}^{2^N-1} Q(p_i)\log_2 Q(p_i) \tag{39}$$

Here $Q(p_j)$ shows the probability (Sathyanarayana et al., 2011). Table 1 gives the entropy value of the input image and proposed encryption approaches.

Differential Evaluation

In differential analysis, the intruder normally does a small change in the original image. NPCR (number of pixels change rate) and UACI (unified average changing intensity) are the two measures used to evaluation of the performance an encryption algorithm against attackers. NPCR stands for the number of pixel change while changing a one pixel of the plain image changed. UACI represents the intensity difference between the original image and the ciphered image (Suri & Vijay, 2019; Suri & Vijay, n.d.b). The NPCR and UACI are mathematically represented as:

$$NPCR = \frac{\sum_{k,l} A(k,l)}{B \times C} \tag{40}$$

Where $A(k,l)$ is a two dimensional array which has been same size as cipher image and $B \times C$ shows total number of pixels in the plain image.

Figure 4. Output result of the proposed algorithm

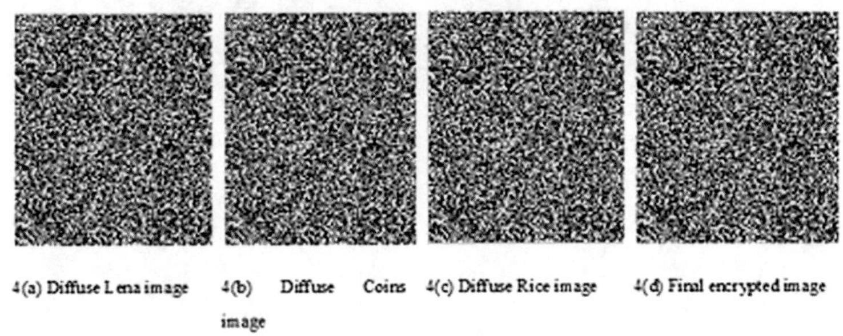

4(a) Diffuse Lena image
4(b) Diffuse Coins image
4(c) Diffuse Rice image
4(d) Final encrypted image

Figure 5. Histogram analysis of the original, diffuse and final encrypted image

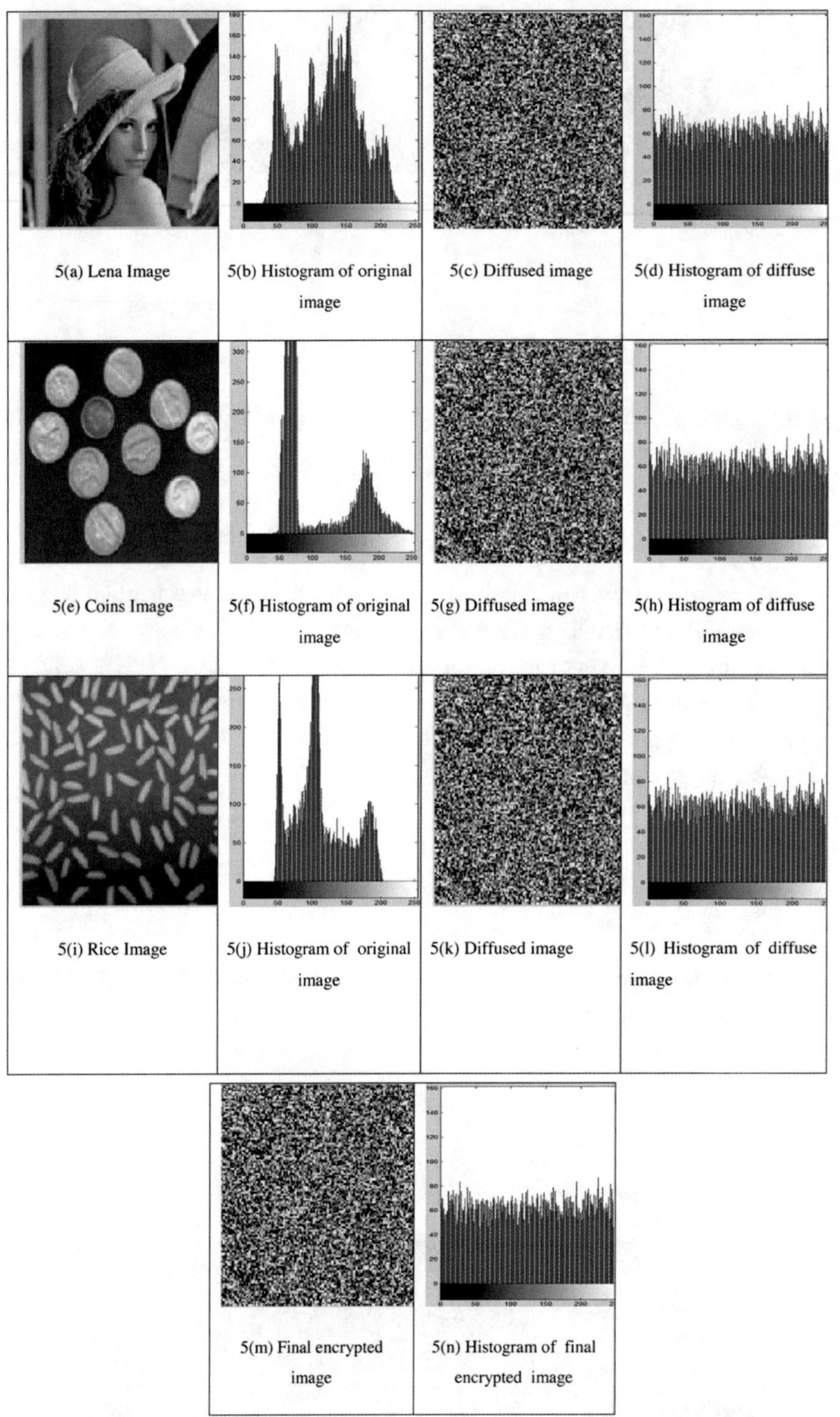

Figure 6. Correlation distribution of the original images

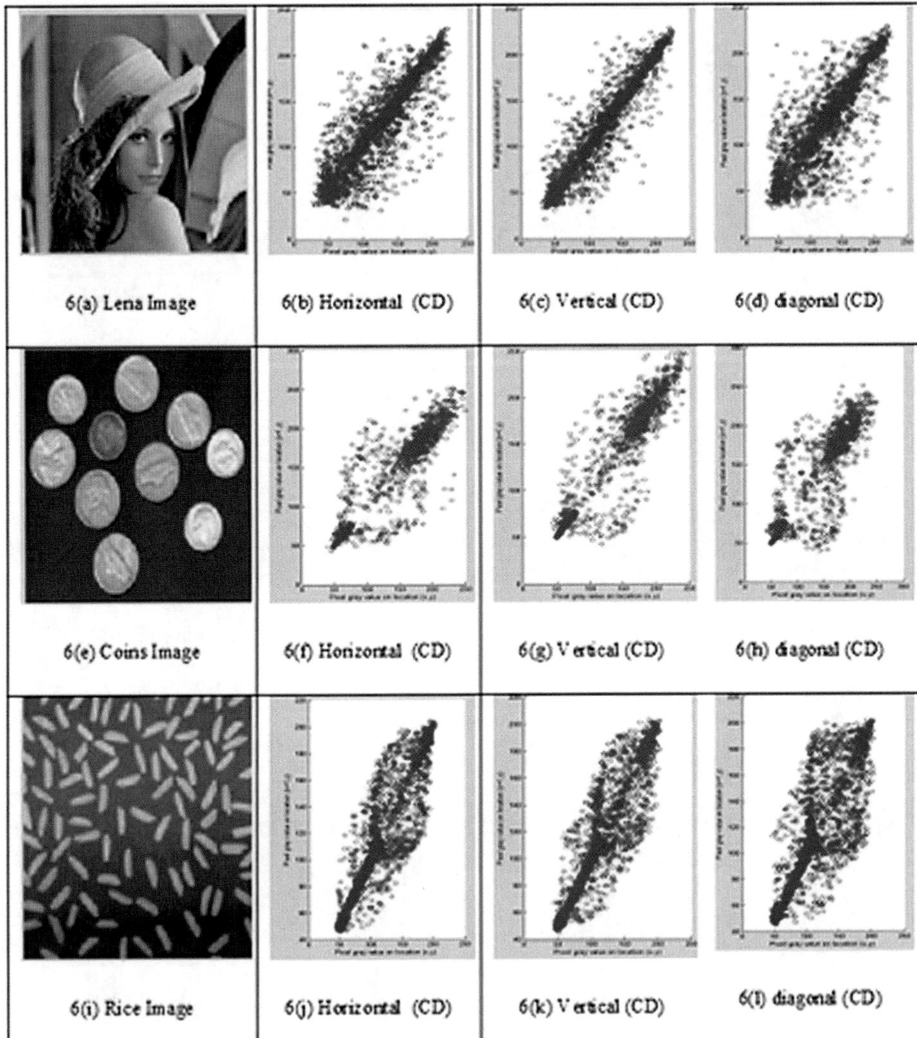

$$UACI = \frac{1}{B \times C}\left[\sum_{k,l}\frac{\left|H_1\left(k,l\right) - H\left(k,l\right)\right|}{255}\right] \times 100\% \quad (41)$$

where, B and C represent the width and height of the image and H_1 and H_2 are the cipher image before and after one pixel plain image change. Table 2 gives the NPCR and UACI value obtained after application of the proposed image encryption technique.

Figure 7. Correlation distribution of the encrypted images

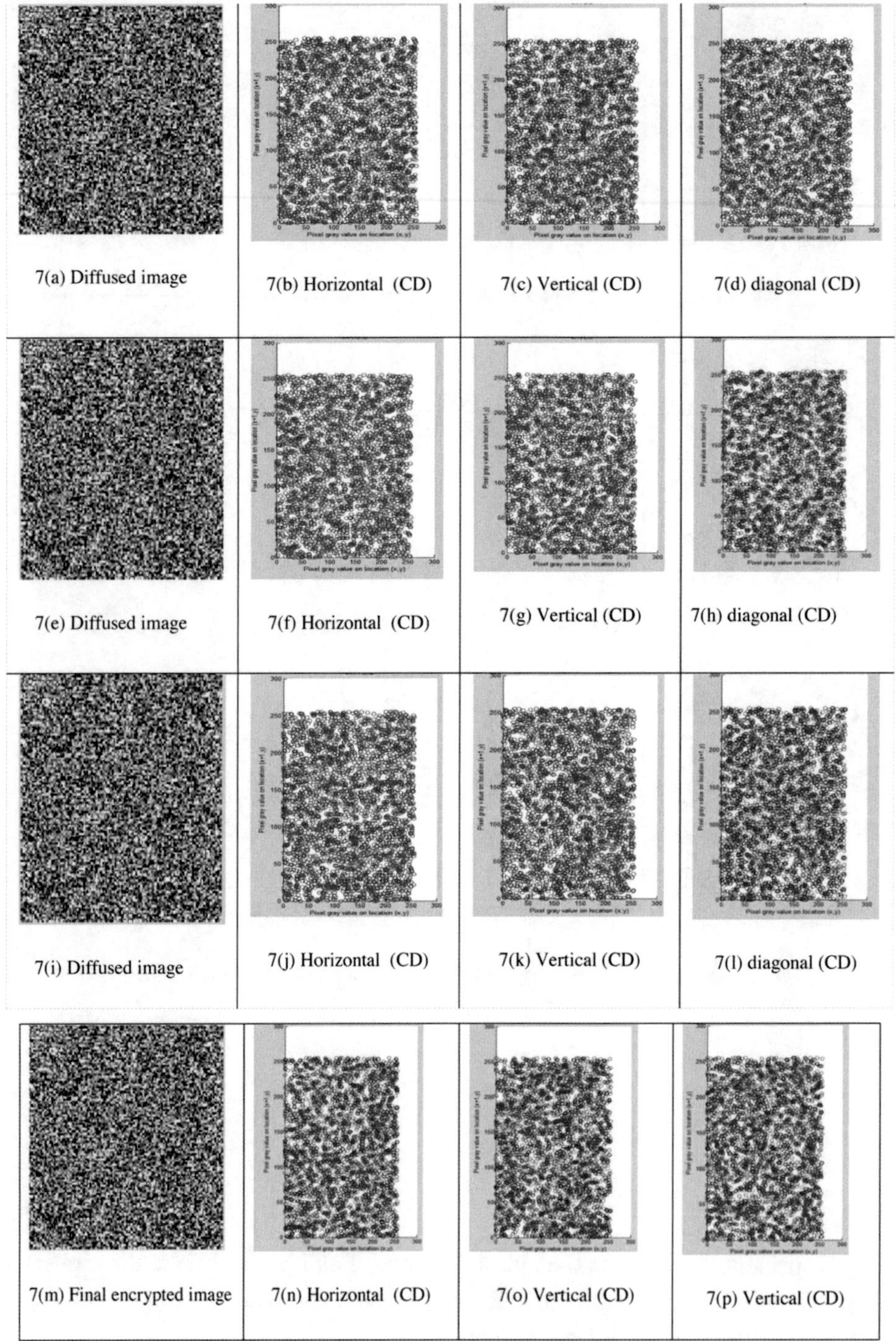

Table 1. Entropy of the encrypted and original image

Image	Plain Image Entropy	Encrypted Image Entropy
Lena	7.4023	7.9994
Coins	6.2818	7.9993
Rice	6.9108	7.9994

Table 2. NPCR and UACI values of the encrypted image

Image	NPCR	UACI
Lena	99. 7009	28.4404
Coins	99.7681	30.7298
Rice	99.5789	30.0209

CONCLUSION

The chapter has used alternate logistic function with four-dimensional differential equations to implement a secure multiple image encryption technique. Three images have been used to form a composite image by combining the one dimensional matrix representation of the three images. Lorenz Attractor (LA) has been used to generate the security key and the alternate logistic maps have been applied for encryption. In each iteration of alternate logistic map, XOR operation has been used to encrypt the composite image and transformation has been applied to diffuse the matrix. The encrypted composite image has been obtained in the form of a confused matrix. The results show that the multi-dimensional differential equation system results in better results in case of multiple image encryption. The work can be further extended by using more powerful encryption algorithms with the different high dimensional methods.

REFERENCES

Agath, A., Sidpara, C., & Upadhyay, D. (2018). *Critical Analysis of Cryptography and Steganography*. Academic Press.

Akgul, A., & Pehlivan, I. (2016). A new three-dimensional chaotic system without equilibrium points, its dynamical analyses and electronic circuit application. *Technical Gazette*, *23*(1), 209–214.

Bakhshandeh, A., & Eslami, Z. (2013). An authenticated image encryption scheme based on chaotic maps and memory cellular automata. *Optics and Lasers in Engineering*, *51*(6), 665–673. doi:10.1016/j.optlaseng.2013.01.001

Baldovin, F., & Robledo, A. (2002). Sensitivity to initial conditions at bifurcations in one-dimensional nonlinear maps: Rigorous nonextensive solutions. *EPL*, *60*(4), 518–524. doi:10.1209/epl/i2002-00249-7

Bisht, A., Dua, M., & Dua, S. (2019). A novel approach to encrypt multiple images using multiple chaotic maps and chaotic discrete fractional random transform. *Journal of Ambient Intelligence and Humanized Computing*, *10*(9), 3519–3531. doi:10.100712652-018-1072-0

Bisht, A., Jaroli, P., Dua, M., & Dua, S. (2018, July). Symmetric Multiple Image Encryption Using Multiple New One-Dimensional Chaotic Functions and Two-Dimensional Cat Man. In *2018 International Conference on Inventive Research in Computing Applications (ICIRCA)* (pp. 676-682). IEEE. 10.1109/ICIRCA.2018.8597245

Çavuşoğlu, Ü., Kaçar, S., Pehlivan, I., & Zengin, A. (2017). Secure image encryption algorithm design using a novel chaos based S-Box. *Chaos, Solitons, and Fractals*, *95*, 92–101. doi:10.1016/j.chaos.2016.12.018

Dua, M., Wesanekar, A., Gupta, V., Bhola, M., & Dua, S. (2019a). Differential evolution optimization of intertwining logistic map-DNA based image encryption technique. *Journal of Ambient Intelligence and Humanized Computing*, 1–16.

Dua, M., Wesanekar, A., Gupta, V., Bhola, M., & Dua, S. (2019b, August). Color Image Encryption using Synchronous CML-DNA and Weighted Bi-objective Genetic Algorithm. In *Proceedings of the 3rd International Conference on Big Data and Internet of Things* (pp. 121-125). 10.1145/3361758.3361780

Enayatifar, R., Abdullah, A. H., Isnin, I. F., Altameem, A., & Lee, M. (2017). Image encryption using a synchronous permutation-diffusion technique. *Optics and Lasers in Engineering*, *90*, 146–154. doi:10.1016/j.optlaseng.2016.10.006

Gao, T., & Chen, Z. (2008). A new image encryption algorithm based on hyper-chaos. *Physics Letters. [Part A]*, *372*(4), 394–400. doi:10.1016/j.physleta.2007.07.040

Guan, Z. H., Huang, F., & Guan, W. (2005). Chaos-based image encryption algorithm. *Physics Letters. [Part A]*, *346*(1-3), 153–157. doi:10.1016/j.physleta.2005.08.006

Hua, Z., & Zhou, Y. (2018). One-dimensional nonlinear model for producing chaos. *IEEE Transactions on Circuits and Systems. I, Regular Papers*, *65*(1), 235–246. doi:10.1109/TCSI.2017.2717943

Jain, A., & Rajpal, N. (2016). A robust image encryption algorithm resistant to attacks using DNA and chaotic logistic maps. *Multimedia Tools and Applications*, *75*(10), 5455–5472. doi:10.100711042-015-2515-7

Jaroli, P., Bisht, A., Dua, M., & Dua, S. (2018, July). A Color Image Encryption Using Four Dimensional Differential Equations and Arnold Chaotic Map. In *2018 International Conference on Inventive Research in Computing Applications (ICIRCA)* (pp. 869-876). IEEE. 10.1109/ICIRCA.2018.8597310

KN, S. (2011). *Image Encryption Techniques* (Doctoral dissertation). PES Institute of Technology.

Li, X., Zhou, C., & Xu, N. (2018). A Secure and Efficient Image Encryption Algorithm Based on DNA Coding and Spatiotemporal Chaos. *International Journal of Network Security*, *20*(1), 110–120.

Marotto, F. R. (1978). Snap-back repellers imply chaos in Rn. *Journal of Mathematical Analysis and Applications*, *63*(1), 199–223. doi:10.1016/0022-247X(78)90115-4

Mohammad, O. F., Rahim, M. S. M., Zeebaree, S. R. M., & Ahmed, F. Y. (2017). A Survey and Analysis of the Image Encryption Methods. *International Journal of Applied Engineering Research: IJAER, 12*(23), 13265–13280.

Mollaeefar, M., Sharif, A., & Nazari, M. (2017). A novel encryption scheme for colored image based on high level chaotic maps. *Multimedia Tools and Applications, 76*(1), 607–629. doi:10.100711042-015-3064-9

Murillo-Escobar, M. A., Cruz-Hernández, C., Cardoza-Avendaño, L., & Méndez-Ramírez, R. (2017). A novel pseudorandom number generator based on pseudorandomly enhanced logistic map. *Nonlinear Dynamics, 87*(1), 407–425. doi:10.100711071-016-3051-3

Özkaynak, F. (2018). Brief review on application of nonlinear dynamics in image encryption. *Nonlinear Dynamics, 92*(2), 1–9. doi:10.100711071-018-4056-x

Pak, C., & Huang, L. (2017). A new color image encryption using combination of the 1D chaotic map. *Signal Processing, 138*, 129–137. doi:10.1016/j.sigpro.2017.03.011

Pareek, N. K., Patidar, V., & Sud, K. K. (2005). Cryptography using multiple one-dimensional chaotic maps. *Communications in Nonlinear Science and Numerical Simulation, 10*(7), 715–723. doi:10.1016/j.cnsns.2004.03.006

Patel, A., & Parikh, M. (2018). *A Survey on Multiple Image Encryption Using Chaos Based algorithms And DNA Computing*. Academic Press.

Politi, A., Pikovsky, A., & Ullner, E. (2017). Chaotic macroscopic phases in one-dimensional oscillators. *The European Physical Journal. Special Topics, 226*(9), 1791–1810. doi:10.1140/epjst/e2017-70056-4

Qian, Jiang, & Qiu. (2009). A New Image Encryption Scheme Based on DES Algorithm and Chua's Circuit. *International Workshop on Imaging Systems and Techniques Shenzhen, China, IST 2009.*

Sankpal, & Vijaya. (2014). Image Encryption Using Chaotic Maps: A Survey. In *Fifth International Conference on Signals and Image Processing*. IEEE.

Sathyanarayana, S. V., Kumar, M. A., & Bhat, K. H. (2011). Symmetric Key Image Encryption Scheme with Key Sequences Derived from Random Sequence of Cyclic Elliptic Curve Points. *International Journal of Network Security, 12*(3), 137–150.

Suneja, K., Dua, S., & Dua, M. (2019, March). A review of chaos based image encryption. In *2019 3rd International Conference on Computing Methodologies and Communication (ICCMC)* (pp. 693-698). IEEE. 10.1109/ICCMC.2019.8819860

Suri, S., & Vijay, R. (2019). A synchronous intertwining logistic map-DNA approach for color image encryption. *Journal of Ambient Intelligence and Humanized Computing, 10*(6), 2277–2290. doi:10.100712652-018-0825-0

Suri, S., & Vijay, R. (n.d.a). A Bi-objective Genetic Algorithm Optimization of Chaos-DNA Based Hybrid Approach. *Journal of Intelligent Systems.*

Suri, S., & Vijay, R. (n.d.b). A Pareto-optimal evolutionary approach of image encryption using coupled map lattice and DNA. *Neural Computing and Applications*, 1-15.

Tavazoei, M. S., & Haeri, M. (2007). Comparison of different one-dimensional maps as chaotic search pattern in chaos optimization algorithms. *Applied Mathematics and Computation*, *187*(2), 1076–1085. doi:10.1016/j.amc.2006.09.087

Tong, X. J., Zhang, M., Wang, Z., Liu, Y., Xu, H., & Ma, J. (2015). A fast encryption algorithm of color image based on four-dimensional chaotic system. *Journal of Visual Communication and Image Representation*, *33*, 219–234. doi:10.1016/j.jvcir.2015.09.014

Tong, X. J., Zhang, M., Wang, Z., & Ma, J. (2016). A joint color image encryption and compression scheme based on hyper-chaotic system. *Nonlinear Dynamics*, *84*(4), 2333–2356. doi:10.100711071-016-2648-x

Wang, H., Xiao, D., Chen, X., & Huang, H. (2018). Cryptanalysis and enhancements of image encryption using combination of the 1D chaotic map. *Signal Processing*, *144*, 444–452. doi:10.1016/j.sigpro.2017.11.005

Wu, Y., Noonan, J. P., Yang, G., & Jin, H. (2012). Image encryption using the two-dimensional logistic chaotic map. *Journal of Electronic Imaging*, *21*(1), 013014. doi:10.1117/1.JEI.21.1.013014

Wu, Y., Yang, G., Jin, H., & Noonan, J. P. (2012). Image encryption using the two-dimensional logistic chaotic map. *Journal of Electronic Imaging*, *21*(1), 013014–1. doi:10.1117/1.JEI.21.1.013014

Xu, L., Li, Z., Li, J., & Hua, W. (2016). A novel bit-level image encryption algorithm based on chaotic maps. *Optics and Lasers in Engineering*, *78*, 17–25. doi:10.1016/j.optlaseng.2015.09.007

Zhou, Y., Bao, L., & Chen, C. P. (2014). A new 1D chaotic system for image encryption. *Signal Processing*, *97*, 172–182. doi:10.1016/j.sigpro.2013.10.034

Chapter 10
Simple Linear Iterative Clustering (SLIC) and Graph Theory-Based Image Segmentation

Chiranji Lal Chowdhary
https://orcid.org/0000-0002-5476-1468
Vellore Institute of Technology, Vellore, India

ABSTRACT

With the extensive application of deep acquisition devices, it has become more feasible to access deep data. The accuracy of image segmentation can be improved by depth data as an additional feature. The current research interests in simple linear iterative clustering (SLIC) are because it is a simple and efficient superpixel segmentation method, and it is initially applied for optical images. This mainly comprises three operation steps (i.e., initialization, local k-means clustering, and postprocessing). A scheme to develop the image over-segmentation task is introduced in this chapter. It considers the pixels of an image with simple linear iterative clustering and graph theory-based algorithm. In this regard, the main contribution is to provide a method for extracting superpixels with greater adherence to the edges of the regions. The experimental tests will consider biomedical grayscales. The robustness and effectiveness will be verified by quantitative and qualitative results.

INTRODUCTION

Image segmentation is one of the most important concepts in image processing and computer vision (Chowdhary & Acharjya, 2020; Chowdhary, 2011). In the image processing approaches, regions with high-frequency texture will be estimated by stipples, whereas regions with lower-frequency texture will be estimated by closed shapes (Chowdhary, Goyal & Vasnani, 2019). Creation of the closed shapes and taking a decision about the separation of an image into regions depend on covering pixels with similar properties. Therefore, there is a requirement for a proper image segmentation algorithm. Simple Linear

DOI: 10.4018/978-1-7998-3299-7.ch010

Iterative Clustering (SLIC) is one such segmentation algorithm which is suitable for splitting the image into proper regions. SLIC is efficient and this produces regions that adhere well to edges in the image. The pixels in SLIC clusters are combined in five-dimensional colour and they are plane spaced to efficiently generate compact and uniform superpixels (Stutz, Hermans & Leibe, 2018). The computer vision applications rely increasingly on superpixels but constitution of a successful superpixel algorithm does not always straightforward (Achanta et al., 2012). It is possible to treat a superpixel as a group of pixels that are identical in location, color, texture, etc. Superpixels can engage image redundancy and they transform computation at the pixel level into an operation at the region level, which can greatly reduce the complexity of subsequent tasks of image processing. In different image processing applications, such as image segmentation, saliency detection and classification, superpixel segmentation has become a significant pre-processing stage (Wang, Peng, Xiao & Liu, 2017).

It is important to describe current superpixel segmentation methods into three major categories: the spectral-graph-based method, the gradient-ascent-based method and the optimization-theory-based method. The most commonly used superpixel form is SLIC. Generally, it is a technique of local k-means clustering (Wang, Peng, Xiao & Liu, 2017; Chowdhary & Acharjya, 2016; Das & Chowdhary, 2017; Chowdhary & Mouli, 2012; Chowdhary & Mouli, 2013; Chowdhary et al., 2020). Galasso, Cipolla and Schiele (2012) show that frame-based superpixel segmentation combined with a few motion and appearance-based affinities are sufficient to obtain good video segmentation performance. This improves the performance for video sequences due to motion-clues. An image segmentation benchmark to videos allows coarse-to-fine video segmentations and multiple human annotations (Galasso, Cipolla & Schiele; 2012). The requirements for superpixels are mentioned in Table 1.

Table 1. Requirements of superpixels

Type	Descriptions
Partition	The superpixels are disorganized and each pixel should be assigned a label.
Connectivity	This is predicted that superpixels would represent connected sets of pixels.
Boundary Adherence	Superpixels should preserve image boundaries.
Compactness, Regularity and Smoothness	Superpixels must be compact, positioned frequently and should show smooth borders in the absence of image boundaries.
Efficiency	Superpixels must be efficiently produced.
Controllable Number of Superpixels	The total of produced superpixels must be controllable.

The superpixels are faster and have state-of-the-art boundary adherence that is more memory efficient. This increases the efficiency of algorithms for segmentation (Zitnick & Kang, 2007; Li, Wu & Chang, 2012; Achanta, Shaji, Smith, Lucchi, Fua & Süsstrunk, 2012). Simple linear iterative clustering (SLIC) is a superpixel generation adaptation of k-means, with two essential distinctions:

1. By restricting the search space to a region proportional to the superpixel scale, the number of distance calculations in the optimization is significantly reduced. In the number of pixels N- and regardless of the number of superpixels k, this decreases the complexity to be linear.

2. A weighted measure of distance blends color and spatial proximity, thus providing control over the scale and compactness of the superpixels at the same time.

SLIC is close to the method used in the sense of superpixel generation as a preprocessing phase for depth estimation, which was not thoroughly explored (Achanta, Shaji, Smith, Lucchi, Fua & Süsstrunk, 2012). Various techniques of superpixel segmentation are generated based on clustering (Chowdhary, Das, Gurani & Ranjan, 2018; Chowdhary, 2016; Shynu, Shayan & Chowdhary, 2020) techniques. These algorithms gradually refine the initial pixel clustering until the requirement specified has been met. During clustering, it only visits most pixels once while still achieving state-of-the-art efficiency among the clustering methods (Ren & Malik, 2003; Chowdhary & Shynu, 2011; Chowdhary, Sai & Acharjya, 2016; Tu et al., 2018).

An image is known as planar graph by graph-based algorithms, where pixels are vertices and pixel affinities are computed for connected pixels. By partitioning the graph, these algorithms compute superpixels. While the above methods vary in the techniques of graph merging or splitting, they both use hand-crafted superpixel calculation features (Van den Bergh et al., 2015; Tu et al., 2018). Graph-based techniques consider each pixel in a graph as a node. Resemblances are classified as edge weights between neighbouring pixels. By minimizing a cost function specified over the graph, superpixels are formed (Wang et al., 2017; Chowdhary, Darwish & Hassanien, 2019; Chowdhary, Ranjan & Jat, 2016; Yang et al., 2020). They are tabulated in Table 2.

Table 2. Graph-based method

Ref.	Categories	Descriptions
Shi & Malik, 2000; Wang et al., 2017	Normalized cuts (N-cuts) Algorithm	This recursively uses contour and texture signals to partition the graph of all pixels in the image. The cost function is defined by computing all the nodes in the graph with a fraction of the total edge connections. Standard superpixels are made. This is producing regular superpixels.
Felzenszwalb & Huttenlocher, 2004; Wang et al., 2017	Felzenszwalb and Huttenlocher (FH)	This precipitates pixels on the graph by using graph-based features of the data to determine a projected measurement of evidence for a boundary between the two regions. Through finding the optimal spanning tree of the constituent pixels, the superpixels are produced.
Perbet & Maki, 2011; Wang et al., 2017	Homogeneous Superpixels (HS)	Using Markov clustering, which is a graph-based algorithm using stochastic flow circulation, the HS calculates superpixels. The graph nodes in the input image correspond to the pixels. In order to define the edge weight, an adjacency matrix is initialized using a simple similarity measure.
Zhang et al., 2011; Wang et al., 2017	Superpixels via Pseudo-Boolean (PB) Optimization	As a multi-label assigning problem, the PB optimization formats superpixel segmentation. Initially, half-overlapping horizontal strips cover the input image. Each pixel has the ability to be assigned to one of two latent alternate strips.
Tang, Fu & Cao, 2012; Wang et al., 2017	Topology Preserved Regular Superpixel (TPS)	For achieving superpixel segmentation, TPS utilizes three phases. Next, it brings the initial seeds into a standard grid. Second, following maximum edge magnitude constraints, each seed is moved to the required boundary.
Shen et al., 2014; Wang et al., 2017	Lazy Random Walks (LRW) Superpixel	The representation of the input is transformed into a graph. The vertex of the graph is the pixel of the image and the edge of the Gaussian weighting function is defined.
Liu etal., 2011; Chowdhary et al., 2020; Wang et al., 2017	Entropy Rate Superpixels (ERS)	ERS has solution approach of superpixel segmentation on a graph as a problem of maximization and proposes a new objective function on the topology of the graph. The picture is mapped to a graph with vertices denoting the pixels and the weights of the edges denoting the similarities between pairs.

Kalinin & Sirota (2015) listed requirements to superpixel algorithms in Table 3. Consider I as the image vector, and P as the corresponding vector of pixel labels. The image is signified by a graph G=(V,E), with vertices V indicating the pixels and the edge weights denoting their pairwise similarity. The graph describes a global energy function, which is minimized with respect to the labels P:

$$E\left(P\right)=\lambda\sum_{v_i\in V}\phi(p_i\mid v_i)+\sum_{\left(v_i,v_j\right)\in E}\varphi\left(p_i,p_j\mid v_i,v_j\right),$$

where λ is a constant, and φ and ϕ can be defined as probability that pixels.

Table 3. Requirements to superpixel algorithms

Performance	As a preprocessing technique, superpixel segmentation is mostly used. For more processing, it should take less time than is needed.
Consistency	The limits of superpixels should be compatible with the limits of image objects.
Compactness and regularity	Superpixels should be identical in size and more or less convex in form for many applications. Such superpixels allow better local descriptors to be extracted and have fewer neighbors.

In our study, we hybridized two intelligent techniques such as Simple Linear Iterative Clustering (SLIC) and Graph Theory based Image Segmentation. The rest of the paper is organized as follows. Foundation of image segmentation and SLIC are briefly discussed in section 2. In Section 3, proposed works with preliminaries are discussed. The evaluation and result analysis are deliberated in Section 4. Further research directions are discussed in Section 5 followed by conclusion in Section 6.

BACKGROUND

Image segmentation is the process by which an image is divided into multiple segments which can then be used to simplify the process of analyzing the image. One of the ways to achieve this is by using superpixels and graph cuts. An effective segmentation relies on the tessellation of an image into superpixels, which is an image area that is better aligned with intensity edges as compared to a rectangular area.

The efficiency of segmentation depends on how many superpixels can be Extracted using different algorithms. Superpixels provide computational efficiency as they allow us to process the image using a lesser number of separate areas. They also are better at finding important boundaries in the image as compared to regular pixels. Most importantly, they increase the efficiency of graph construction. Suppose we have to make a graph of 20000×20000 pixels. It will be a very large representation. But by using superpixels, we can bring this down considerably. One such algorithm for image segmentation is the Simple Linear Iterative Clustering (SLIC). An optimal image segmentation method was introduced including single surface, single object; multi-surface and multi-object models. The segmentation in the medical field categorized in two folds:

1. **Single-object Segmentation:** Medical fields often require specific organs or tissues for a proper diagnosis. This can be done in polynomial time efficiently. In scans, organs often do not have a proper boundary. So, it is necessary to provide Haar restraints on the image to segment the organ properly. The initial work was done using the Boykov algorithm.
2. **Multi-object Segmentation:** This method is required in 2 cases: When the doctor needs different part of the same organ or tissue or when the doctor requires part of different organs or tissues. The first problem is similar to single-object segmentation and can be solved in a similar fashion. But in the second case, the minimization of energy function becomes an NP-hard problem. This means Boykov which were that the time taken to solve it is indeterministic polynomial. Some algorithm for this was suggested by not exact optimal but could find an approximate optimum solution.

Some studies discussed various other segmentation methods with their pros and cons and how they were improved. In work by Long et al. (2018), the use and importance of image segmentation in the medical field are discussed. Medical image processing has many steps: Noise removal, Segmentation, Classification, Reconstruction, Analysis using different techniques with different parameters and then visualizing the results. The paper discussed 5 algorithms that are commonly used in this field with their result analysis. One of the algorithms performs the segmentation and then compares it with previous results to help doctors reach a diagnosis. Brain tumour MRIs are often difficult to reach a conclusion with due to their high complexity and few linear features (Chowdhary, Shynu & Gurani, 2020; Das & Chowdhary, 2017; Tripathy, Das & Chowdhary, 2020). This problem is solved by using techniques that employ a classifier and can be trained to differentiate one class from another. For this, Local Independent Transformation-based classification is used. The researchers found that this method is highly reliable for the segmentation of medical images (Shi et al., 2017).

In work of (Chen & Pan, 2018), an unsupervised image segmentation method is proposed that works on the principle of optimum cuts in graphs. The algorithm can be used and modified for different applications. The algorithm makes use of the Minimum spanning tree, which is the smallest fully connected part of a tree. According to the authors, this method is more efficient than previous research as it needs a lesser number of image partitions while giving superior segmentation results. The algorithm generates a hierarchical segmentation after performing multiple binary divisions (OIFT algorithm), each iteration is having linear arithmetic complexity. This leads to the image being segmented into the required number of regions. A CNN variant for image segmentation called FCN is used. It improved upon the initial research by gathering high-level information using basic methods and then the low-level cues like boundary information and relationship among pixels, for more accurate results (Gupta, Dhanda & Kumar, 2018). They used FCN to extract pixel features, then SLIC to generate the superpixels. Then they merged the obtained results to get the boundary-optimized segmentation result. Finally, they use conditional random fields to optimize the result. It was found to have excellent feature extraction results while also adhering to the boundary of the image. So, the first step generated 2 results: a superpixel image and another one that has the features of the input image. These 2 results are then combined to optimize the boundary of the segmentation. Then CRF is used to recover the boundaries accurately. This method was shown to provide better results in boundary segmentation than previous works. Many studies on some object recognition and security were proposed during the last decade (Chowdhary & Mouli, 2012; Chowdhary, Muatjitjeja & Jat, 2015; Chowdhary, 2018; Chowdhary & Acharjya, 2018; Chowdhary, 2019).

A new feature representation for superpixel segmentation was proposed that uses better local characteristics of images and designed a content-adaptive superpixel segmentation algorithm (Bejar, Mansilla &

Miranda, 2018). In this algorithm, first, the colour, spatial, contour and texture features of each pixel are extracted from the input image. It uses an image gradient to compute WLD and contours. The different features have discriminability that is calculated and their weights are adjusted based on the partition of pixels (Zhao et al., 2018; Xiao, Zhou & Gong, 2018; Xu & Uberbacher, 1997; Todorovic & Nechyba, 2005). This series of operations is performed multiple times with the weights being updated every iteration. The number of iterations is decided beforehand. They used a post-processing method specified in another research paper to guarantee the connectivity inside superpixels. The datasets used were: Berkeley Segmentation Dataset, PASCAL Visual Object classes, PASCAL S and Weizmann Segmentation dataset.

Research works represented in the background review are summarized with the methods used and key findings are addressed in the Table 4.

Table 4. Summary of the background research works

Papers Cited	Methods Used	Key Findings
Yin et al. (2021)	SLIC superpixel segmentation method	The proposed method improved the segmentation results by using polarimetric SAR data sets. This provided better boundary adherence with compact and uniform superpixels.
Cong et al. (2018).	Superpixel clustering	Effectively improve the performance in image segmentation. Also, the substantial improvement was made with respect to computational complexity, processing time and the overall segmentation effect.
Liu & Duan (2020)	Color and depth image (RGB-D) image segmentation method based on superpixels and multi-feature fusion graph theory	This method overcomes the difficulty of segmenting adjacent objects with similar colors, and the results have good segmentation accuracy. The results of the graph-based segmentation experiment show that method has better semantically consistent segmentation than the existing methods, especially in regions with low-contrast RGB image edges.
Yang et al. (2021)	local stereo matching method based on SLIC space	The dense disparity map was obtained by a winner-takes-all approach and disparity refinement.

PROPOSED WORK

We create a graph that has the pixels in the image as its nodes and find the min-cut to separate the two parts. This method has one problem: Huge computational power requirement. Suppose we have a very large image with millions of pixels. That means there are millions of nodes in the graph which require a lot of energy to process. This can considerably reduce the efficiency of the system and can lead to wrong results.

To counter this problem, we used Superpixels. Superpixels are image patches that are better aligned with intensity edges than rectangular patches. So, the segmented image converted into these superpixels to reduce the number of nodes in the final graph. Then, the edge weights of the graph are calculated and using the max-flow/min-cut algorithm, the foreground and background are separated. This method makes use of the fact that there is often a sharp change in intensity at the object edges in an image. So, most of the superpixels generated will be part of a particular object in the image, making it easier to segment the image as superpixels are created according to the intensities of the pixels around a particular pixel. This method has applications in the medical industry. The scans in the medical field often contain other parts of the body which the doctor may need to check separately. Using this technique, they can separate the required organ from the other parts and check if there are any problems in the organ. It also can be used in segmenting videos where the user may need to separate a particular object from the other parts.

Our work is to separate an image's foreground from its background efficiently by minimizing the total number of nodes that are part of the graph used in the graph-cut approach. It is a very basic example of segmenting an image based on boundaries and regions. The user controls what part of the image the foreground and what part is the background is using special markers overcoming the inherent problems faced by automatic image segmentation.

Preliminaries

The python language has used to implement this work with support from of image processing libraries. Our Chapter consists of a lot of components that perform different function.

UI

To output the image and input the user marker scribbles, we have used the OpenCV library. When the app is run, the user is presented with an image and then can use his/her mouse to make marks on the image where they want. Background scribbles are blue and foreground scribbles are red. The user can change the scribble type by pressing \f" for foreground and \b" for background on the keyboard. The \r" key resets the scribbles. OpenCV provides functions to record mouse down and mouse up events which we then used as reference points to draw a line between.

Function to Divide an Image Into Superpixels

We have a function that takes the image as a parameter and creates superpixels. The scikit-image library has a function called slic() which is used to create the superpixels. Then we calculate the centres of the superpixels as they'll be used as a representation of the superpixel. This function returns an array of superpixel segments, H-S histograms for each superpixel and the neighbours of each superpixel.

Function to Find the Superpixels Under the Scribbles

This function returns the array of superpixels that are present under the foreground and background markers.

Function to Get Bool Mask

For a specific set of superpixel IDs, this function returns a mask for the selection.

Function for Graph-cutting

Using max ow library, we create a graph from the nodes generated as superpixels. Then according to the histograms of the nodes, we define 2 edges between them (forward and backwards). The weights of these edges depend on the similarity between the histograms of the nodes in question. If the histograms are not closely related, we add a low edge weight, else, high. So, when the min-cut algorithm is executed, the edges with the least weights and the least similarities are cut. This way, the segmentation of boundaries is ensured.

Main Proposed System

It is difficult, in many cases, for the system to properly distinguish between foreground and background in an image. In our work (Figure 1), the user will draw some lines of different colors which signify the object (foreground) and the background. First, we divide the image into superpixels taking into consideration the color and spatial proximity of pixels. Every superpixel forms one node of the graph. There will be 2 extra vertices: the source vertex (corresponding to the foreground) and the sink vertex (corresponding to the background). These 2 vertices are called terminal vertices. The source vertex will be connected to the non-terminal vertices by a directed edge and every non-terminal vertex to the sink vertex by a directed edge. The edge weights will be calculated according to the probability distribution functions of the superpixels which contain the user lines. Now, the image can be segmented by computing the min-cut in the graph. The superpixels with high probability near the source node will be part of the foreground and the others will be part of the background.

Figure 1. SLIC and Graph Theory based Image Segmentation System

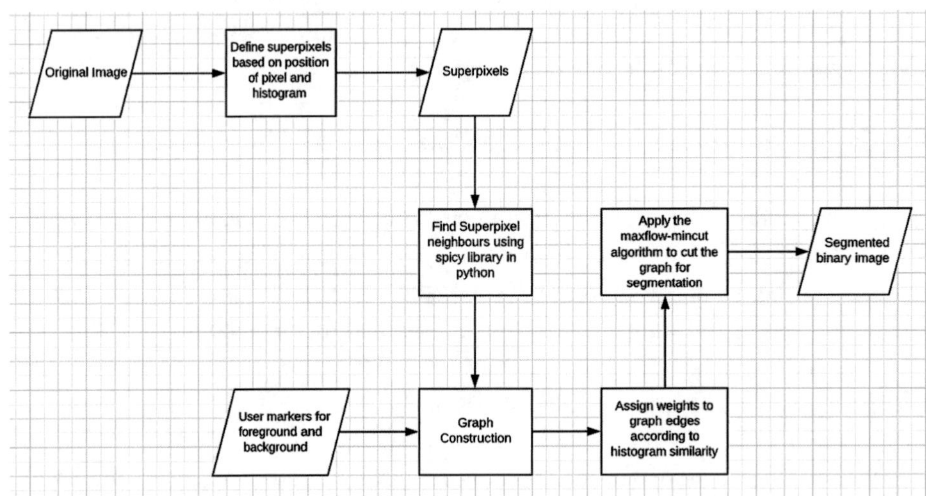

Using superpixels has many advantages over using single pixels as a representation of the given image:

1. Even though it is a little computationally expensive to generate superpixel groupings, it is still very efficient at reducing the complexity of the image from hundreds of thousands of single pixels to a few hundred to a thousand superpixels.
2. A single pixel is not usually a good representation of an image as on its own, it doesn't contain a lot of information relevant to the image. Superpixels are meaningful parts of the image.

3. Superpixels allow over-segmentation which, in turn, allows the application to find more important boundaries which would have been overlooked in case of single pixels. This ensures accurate segmentation.

EVALUATION AND RESULT ANALYSIS

The objective of this work was to efficiently separate the foreground of an image from its background. To get the most accurate information about the performance metrics, we changed the values of some variables in the code to see how it affected the final result.

From the above tables, we can see that:

1. As we increase the number of superpixel segments, the amount of markings needed to select the same zone increases as the segments are smaller and a greater number of markings are needed to select a greater number of smaller segments. But at the same time, a greater number of segments mean that the resolution for segment selection is more. This leads to more accurate selection as the user can mark exactly where he wants and only that spot will be selected. We found that an ideal number of segments for a generic image is around 300-500.
2. Compactness is the measure of how close the segments are to each other. This again determines how many lines the user would have to draw to select a region. If the compactness is increased, it would mean that there is more space in the superpixels and hence a lesser number of lines would have to be drawn to select the same number of superpixels. Also, the resolution of the image superpixels would be less. That means there is a high probability of the boundary between the foreground and background will be broken and we won't get an accurate result. In the images above, we note that as we increase the compactness of the superpixels, the segmentation becomes more accurate. The compactness balances color and space proximity. With higher values, spatial proximity is prioritized and the superpixels are square-shaped. They become more circular as this value is decreased.

Evaluation of image segmentation with precision performance is measured. This precision measure is calculated by dividing true positive measurement by summation of true positive and false positive.

$$Precision = \frac{True\,Positive}{True\,Positive + False\,Positive}$$

Table 5 is a tabular representation among three segmentation algorithms on the basis of precision and segmenting time (in seconds). In evaluation stage, the main significant performance is precision performance measurement. We are achieving a precision value of 93.02 for SLIC + Graph theory based image segmentation algorithm which is better over fuzzy c-mean and SLIC based image segmentation algorithms. The results of the segmentation show that the algorithm can better maintain the target's boundary and achieve more accurate segmentation.

Table 5. Comparison of evaluation index on few segmentation algorithms

Segmentation Algorithm	Precision	Segmentation Time in Seconds
FCM	84.67	6.83
SLIC	91.46	9.47
SLIC + Graph Theory	93.02	9.83

DISCUSSION

Image segmentation is one of the most important topics in computer vision. Its applications are endless and very important for a lot of things that are used in many fields in day-to-day work. This is the reason why this topic interested us and why we chose it as our project. We went through some really good research articles and papers which helped us get an insight into this topic. The method we employed in our project is a promising study of the field. The use of superpixels and graph-cut algorithms can pave the way to more advanced techniques for image segmentation with high accuracy and speed. The results of our project show that superpixels are a valid and efficient way to segment images into foreground and background using a lot less computational resources than traditional approaches. Our approach drastically decreased the number of nodes required to process the image as a graph. The main problem with our approach was that it is only able to segment the image into 2 parts.

CONCLUSION

Foreground-background image segmentation is an important application that can be used in the medical field to diagnose otherwise hidden problems. This implementation was tested with different values of parameters that may affect how it performs in real-time scenarios. It is built keeping that in mind and will successfully separate the object from the background with considerable accuracy. In this Chapter, we focus on segmenting the foreground and the background. There are two ways to achieve this: automatic and interactive (manual). In the automatic mode, the algorithm automatically detects what it thinks are the edges in the image and tries to separate the object from the background. This has its own set of problems, the major one being that sometimes it's difficult for it to detect what the foreground and background are. The interactive mode takes a different route and allows the user to paint different color markers on the image signifying the foreground and background. More number of markers means more accurate segmentation. This technique usually provides better results. These markers, depending on the colors assigned, cover the pixels that have to be a part of the signified part of the image no matter what. The user has complete control over what part of the image they want as the foreground and background. Finally we are achieving better segmentation by our proposed SLIC+Graph theory based segmentation. Our better claimed results are having precision percentage is 93.02.

REFERENCES

Achanta, R., Shaji, A., Smith, K., Lucchi, A., Fua, P., & Süsstrunk, S. (2012). SLIC superpixels compared to state-of-the-art superpixel methods. *IEEE Transactions on Pattern Analysis and Machine Intelligence*, *34*(11), 2274–2282. doi:10.1109/TPAMI.2012.120 PMID:22641706

Acharjya, D. P., & Chowdhary, C. L. (2018). Breast cancer detection using hybrid computational intelligence techniques. In *Handbook of Research on Emerging Perspectives on Healthcare Information Systems and Informatics* (pp. 251–280). IGI Global. doi:10.4018/978-1-5225-5460-8.ch011

Bejar, H. H., Mansilla, L. A., & Miranda, P. A. (2018, November). Efficient unsupervised image segmentation by optimum cuts in graphs. In *Iberoamerican Congress on Pattern Recognition* (pp. 359–367). Springer.

Chen, X., & Pan, L. (2018). A survey of graph cuts/graph search based medical image segmentation. *IEEE Reviews in Biomedical Engineering*, *11*, 112–124. doi:10.1109/RBME.2018.2798701 PMID:29994356

Chowdhary, C. L. (2011). Linear feature extraction techniques for object recognition: Study of PCA and ICA. *Journal of the Serbian Society for Computational Mechanics*, *5*(1), 19–26.

Chowdhary, C. L. (2016). A review of feature extraction application areas in medical imaging. *International Journal of Pharmacy and Technology*, *8*(3), 4501–4509.

Chowdhary, C. L. (2018). Application of Object Recognition With Shape-Index Identification and 2D Scale Invariant Feature Transform for Key-Point Detection. In *Feature Dimension Reduction for Content-Based Image Identification* (pp. 218–231). IGI Global. doi:10.4018/978-1-5225-5775-3.ch012

Chowdhary, C. L. (2019). 3D object recognition system based on local shape descriptors and depth data analysis. *Recent Patents on Computer Science*, *12*(1), 18–24. doi:10.2174/2213275911666180821092033

Chowdhary, C. L., & Acharjya, D. P. (2018). Singular Value Decomposition–Principal Component Analysis-Based Object Recognition Approach. *Bio-Inspired Computing for Image and Video Processing, 323*.

Chowdhary, C. L., Darwish, A., & Hassanien, A. E. (2021). Cognitive Deep Learning: Future Direction in Intelligent Retrieval. In Research Anthology on Artificial Intelligence Applications in Security (pp. 2152-2163). IGI Global.

Chowdhary, C. L., Das, T. K., Gurani, V., & Ranjan, A. (2018). An Improved Tumour Identification with Gabor Wavelet Segmentation. *Research Journal of Pharmacy and Technology*, *11*(8), 3451–3456. doi:10.5958/0974-360X.2018.00637.6

Chowdhary, C. L., Goyal, A., & Vasnani, B. K. (2019). Experimental Assessment of Beam Search Algorithm for Improvement in Image Caption Generation. *Journal of Applied Science and Engineering*, *22*(4), 691–698.

Chowdhary, C. L., & Mouli, P. C. (2012, March). Design and implementation of secure, platform-free, and network-based remote controlling and monitoring system. In *International Conference on Pattern Recognition, Informatics and Medical Engineering (PRIME-2012)* (pp. 195-198). IEEE. 10.1109/ICPRIME.2012.6208342

Chowdhary, C. L., & Mouli, P. C. (2013). Image Registration with New System for Ensemble of Images of Multi-Sensor Registration. *World Applied Sciences Journal*, *26*(1), 45–50.

Chowdhary, C. L., Muatjitjeja, K., & Jat, D. S. (2015, May). Three-dimensional object recognition based intelligence system for identification. In *2015 International Conference on Emerging Trends in Networks and Computer Communications (ETNCC)* (pp. 162-166). IEEE. 10.1109/ETNCC.2015.7184827

Chowdhary, C. L., Ranjan, A., & Jat, D. S. (2016). Categorical Database Information-Theoretic Approach of Outlier Detection Model. Annals. *Computer Science Series, 14*(2).

Chowdhary, C. L., Sai, G. V. K., & Acharjya, D. P. (2016). Decreasing false assumption for improved breast cancer detection. *Journal of Science and Arts*, *35*(2), 157–176.

Chowdhary, C. L., & Shynu, P. G. (2011). Applications of Extendable Embedded Web Servers in Medical Diagnosing. *International Journal of Computers and Applications*, *38*(6), 34–38. doi:10.5120/4615-6838

Chowdhary, C. L., Shynu, P. G., & Gurani, V. K. (2020). Exploring breast cancer classification of histopathology images from computer vision and image processing algorithms to deep learning. *Int. J. Adv. Sci. Technol*, *29*, 43–48.

Cong, L., Ding, S., Wang, L., Zhang, A., & Jia, W. (2018). Image segmentation algorithm based on superpixel clustering. *IET Image Processing*, *12*(11), 2030–2035. doi:10.1049/iet-ipr.2018.5439

Das, T. K., & Chowdhary, C. L. (2017). Implementation of Morphological Image Processing Algorithm using Mammograms. *Journal of Chemical and Pharmaceutical Sciences*, *10*(1), 439–441.

Felzenszwalb, P. F., & Huttenlocher, D. P. (2004). Efficient graph-based image segmentation. *International Journal of Computer Vision*, *59*(2), 167–181. doi:10.1023/B:VISI.0000022288.19776.77

Galasso, F., Cipolla, R., & Schiele, B. (2012, November). Video segmentation with superpixels. In *Asian conference on computer vision* (pp. 760-774). Springer.

Gupta, K. K., Dhanda, N., & Kumar, U. (2018, December). A comparative study of medical image segmentation techniques for brain tumor detection. In *2018 4th International Conference on Computing Communication and Automation (ICCCA)* (pp. 1-4). IEEE. 10.1109/CCAA.2018.8777561

Kalinin, P., & Sirota, A. (2015). A graph based approach to hierarchical image over-segmentation. *Computer Vision and Image Understanding*, *130*, 80–86. doi:10.1016/j.cviu.2014.09.007

Li, Z., Wu, X. M., & Chang, S. F. (2012, June). Segmentation using superpixels: A bipartite graph partitioning approach. In *2012 IEEE Conference on Computer Vision and Pattern Recognition* (pp. 789-796). IEEE.

Liu, G., & Duan, J. (2020). RGB-D image segmentation using superpixel and multi-feature fusion graph theory. *Signal, Image and Video Processing*, *14*(6), 1–9. doi:10.100711760-020-01647-x

Liu, M. Y., Tuzel, O., Ramalingam, S., & Chellappa, R. (2011, June). Entropy rate superpixel segmentation. In *CVPR 2011* (pp. 2097–2104). IEEE. doi:10.1109/CVPR.2011.5995323

Long, J., Feng, X., Zhu, X., Zhang, J., & Gou, G. (2018). Efficient superpixel-guided interactive image segmentation based on graph theory. *Symmetry*, *10*(5), 169. doi:10.3390ym10050169

Perbet, F., & Maki, A. (2011, June). Homogeneous Superpixels from Random Walks. In MVA (pp. 26-30). Academic Press.

Ren, X., & Malik, J. (2003, October). *Learning a classification model for segmentation*. IEEE. doi:10.1109/ICCV.2003.1238308

Shen, J., Du, Y., Wang, W., & Li, X. (2014). Lazy random walks for superpixel segmentation. *IEEE Transactions on Image Processing*, *23*(4), 1451–1462. doi:10.1109/TIP.2014.2302892 PMID:24565788

Shi, C., Wang, Y., Wang, C., & Xiao, B. (2017). Ground-based cloud detection using graph model built upon superpixels. *IEEE Geoscience and Remote Sensing Letters*, *14*(5), 719–723. doi:10.1109/LGRS.2017.2676007

Shi, J., & Malik, J. (2000). Normalized cuts and image segmentation. *IEEE Transactions on Pattern Analysis and Machine Intelligence*, *22*(8), 888–905. doi:10.1109/34.868688

Stutz, D., Hermans, A., & Leibe, B. (2018). Superpixels: An evaluation of the state-of-the-art. *Computer Vision and Image Understanding*, *166*, 1–27. doi:10.1016/j.cviu.2017.03.007

Tang, D., Fu, H., & Cao, X. (2012, July). Topology preserved regular superpixel. In *2012 IEEE International Conference on Multimedia and Expo* (pp. 765-768). IEEE. 10.1109/ICME.2012.184

Todorovic, S., & Nechyba, M. C. (2005). Dynamic trees for unsupervised segmentation and matching of image regions. *IEEE Transactions on Pattern Analysis and Machine Intelligence*, *27*(11), 1762–1777. doi:10.1109/TPAMI.2005.219 PMID:16285375

Tripathy, A. K., Das, T. K., & Chowdhary, C. L. (2020). Monitoring quality of tap water in cities using IoT. In *Emerging Technologies for Agriculture and Environment* (pp. 107–113). Springer. doi:10.1007/978-981-13-7968-0_8

Tu, W. C., Liu, M. Y., Jampani, V., Sun, D., Chien, S. Y., Yang, M. H., & Kautz, J. (2018). Learning superpixels with segmentation-aware affinity loss. In *Proceedings of the IEEE Conference on Computer Vision and Pattern Recognition* (pp. 568-576). IEEE.

Van den Bergh, M., Boix, X., Roig, G., & Van Gool, L. (2015). Seeds: Superpixels extracted via energy-driven sampling. *International Journal of Computer Vision*, *111*(3), 298–314. doi:10.100711263-014-0744-2

Wang, H., Peng, X., Xiao, X., & Liu, Y. (2017). BSLIC: Slic superpixels based on boundary term. *Symmetry*, *9*(3), 31. doi:10.3390ym9030031

Wang, M., Liu, X., Gao, Y., Ma, X., & Soomro, N. Q. (2017). Superpixel segmentation: A benchmark. *Signal Processing Image Communication*, *56*, 28–39. doi:10.1016/j.image.2017.04.007

Xiao, X., Zhou, Y., & Gong, Y. J. (2018). Content-adaptive superpixel segmentation. *IEEE Transactions on Image Processing*, *27*(6), 2883–2896. doi:10.1109/TIP.2018.2810541 PMID:29570089

Xu, Y., & Uberbacher, E. C. (1997). 2D image segmentation using minimum spanning trees. *Image and Vision Computing*, *15*(1), 47–57. doi:10.1016/S0262-8856(96)01105-5

Yang, F., Sun, Q., Jin, H., & Zhou, Z. (2020). Superpixel Segmentation with Fully Convolutional Networks. In *Proceedings of the IEEE/CVF Conference on Computer Vision and Pattern Recognition* (pp. 13964-13973). IEEE.

Yang, S., Lei, X., Liu, Z., & Sui, G. (2021). An efficient local stereo matching method based on an adaptive exponentially weighted moving average filter in SLIC space. *IET Image Processing*, ipr2.12140. doi:10.1049/ipr2.12140

Yin, J., Wang, T., Du, Y., Liu, X., Zhou, L., & Yang, J. (2021). SLIC Superpixel Segmentation for Polarimetric SAR Images. *IEEE Transactions on Geoscience and Remote Sensing*, 1–17. doi:10.1109/TGRS.2020.3047126

Zhang, Y., Hartley, R., Mashford, J., & Burn, S. (2011, November). Superpixels via pseudo-boolean optimization. In *2011 International Conference on Computer Vision* (pp. 1387-1394). IEEE. 10.1109/ICCV.2011.6126393

Zhao, W., Fu, Y., Wei, X., & Wang, H. (2018). An improved image semantic segmentation method based on superpixels and conditional random fields. *Applied Sciences (Basel, Switzerland)*, *8*(5), 837. doi:10.3390/app8050837

Zitnick, C. L., & Kang, S. B. (2007). Stereo for image-based rendering using image over-segmentation. *International Journal of Computer Vision*, *75*(1), 49–65. doi:10.100711263-006-0018-8

Chapter 11
COVID-19 Detection Using Chest X-Ray and Transfer Learning

Aditya Sharma
Jaypee University of Information Technology, India

Arshdeep Singh Chudey
Jaypee University of Information Technology, India

Mrityunjay Singh
https://orcid.org/0000-0001-8672-4250
Jaypee University of Information Technology, India

ABSTRACT

The novel coronavirus (COVID-19), which started in the Wuhan province of China, prompted a major outbreak that culminated in a worldwide pandemic. Several cases are being recorded across the globe, with deaths being close to 2.5 million. The increased number of cases and the newness of such a pandemic has resulted in the hospitals being under-equipped leading to problems in diagnosis of the disease. From previous studies, radiography has proved to be the fastest testing method. A screening test using the x-ray scan of the chest region has proved to be effective. For this method, a trained radiologist is needed to detect the disease. Automating this process using deep learning models can prove to be effective. Due to the lack of large dataset, pre-trained CNN models are used in this study. Several models have been employed like VGG-16, Resnet-50, InceptionV3, and InceptionResnetV2. Resnet-50 provided the best accuracy of 98.3%. The performance evaluation has been done using metrics like receiver operating curve and confusion matrix.

DOI: 10.4018/978-1-7998-3299-7.ch011

INTRODUCTION

Covid-19 originated in Wuhan, China in late 2019 with symptoms ranging from mild illness to pneumonia. The virus can spread through contact, droplets, and fomites. The virus has mild to no symptoms in over 80% of the cases that cause the rapid spreading of the virus (Beluz, J., 2020). This caused the disease to spread in a major part of the population because some carriers didn't develop any symptoms and hence didn't take any precautions. The virus has affected over 113 million people worldwide and over 2.5 million deaths have been reported (World Health Organisation, 2021). Symptoms commence 2-14 days after its exposure to the virus. These include chills, fever, sore throat, vomiting, cough diarrhea, etc. This virus mainly affects the respiratory organs and shows its symptoms in the lungs (McKeever, A., 2020). The hospitals are getting filled up at a high rate causing lack of services for the people who are in dire need of medical attention; these people include those who are suffering from fracture, cancer, heart diseases and some other urgent issues. Due to a large number of cases, the hospitals also run short of detection units for Covid-19. Detection of Covid-19 is of utmost importance until the vaccine is available in bulk. This requires a test that is fast and accurate enough to help in curbing the spread. The government of China has approved a reverse transcription-polymerase chain reaction (RT-PCR) which makes use of respiratory and blood samples and applies gene sequencing to it; this procedure has been introduced as the main screening test for the detection of the disease (Ai et al., 2020). The sensitivity of the RT-PCR test is highly variable and findings in China show a poor sensitivity relatively (Huang et al, 2017). In most of the cases, we are not able to detect the COVID-19 that results in a failure to prevent the disease from spreading (Wang et al., 2020). As the proper vaccination is also not available, therefore, it becomes a serious issue for prior detection of the disease and maintaining the protocols.

Covid-19 has symptoms that are similar to other respiratory diseases; therefore, having such symptoms is not a sure sign of having it. Deep learning techniques have made great leaps in the field of image processing, and are helpful to detect complex patterns from the images. These techniques require extensive training with great accuracy. A screening test using the X-Ray scan of the chest region has proved to be effective. For this method, a trained radiologist is needed to detect the patterns which indicate the disease in an X-Ray scan. Automating this process using deep learning models can prove to be effective. It will make the process fast and also help in cases where a trained radiologist isn't present. A screening method consisting of Chest radiography (CT) imaging has been employed in the detection of chest diseases like pneumonia as well. When employed in detection to diagnose of COVID-19 it has a high sensitivity for it (Fang et al., 2020). The Chest CT shows some ground-glass opacities which can be accessed by a trained radiologist (Minaee et al., 2020). This process can be done using a CNN architecture that provides efficient and accurate results. In this study, we use the variant of the existing convolutional neural network (CNN) models that are InceptionV3, InceptionResnetV2, Resnet-50, and VGG-16. This chapter explores the effectiveness of the different CNN models in separating the COVID positive patients from NON-COVID patients. We choose the CNN based models that have high accuracy and effectiveness in the field of image recognition. Due to lack of an appropriate dataset, we pose several problems and try to resolve them by using transfer learning to achieve the high accuracy; this also provides the benefit of less training time. We use the pre-trained CNN models and make use of transfer learning to provide accurate results. We have conducted this study on a publicly available dataset which consists of 142 chest X-ray images of covid positive patients and 142 chest X-ray images of non-covid patients. We have splitted the data set into 80%-20% of training and test sets, then fed it to various pre-trained CNN models to train them. Several models have been employed to diagnose the disease making the process fast and reliable. After the completion of training of the selected models, we have tested our modern on unseen data (i.e., testing data set) and report their accuracy. We achieve the testing accuracy for different CNN models as for VGG -16 96.7%, for Inception-V3 96%, for InceptionResnetV2 76.7% and for Resnet-50 98.3%. The Resnet-50 model has achieved great accuracy of 98.3%.

The organization of this paper is as follows: Section 2 describes the related work used for this study, and section 3 presents the dataset used. Section 4 and section 5 discusses our proposed approach; the results and discussion is discussed in Section 5. Finally, we conclude our work in Section 7 with possible future extension.

RELATED WORK

This section describes the different techniques and approaches used by various researchers for the detection of Covid-19. In literature, the researchers have done a lot of work for the early detection of COVID-19, and used CXR images, CT scans images, MRI scans images and even ultrasound images of the covid patient for Covid detection. Narin et. al. has proposed deep transfer learning methods for the detection of Covid-19, and achieved the highest accuracy of 98% using the Resnet-50 pre-trained model (Narin et al.,2020). Wang et. al. used a modified version of InceptionResnetV2 to predict Covid patients using CT scans, and achieved the highest accuracy of 89.5% (Wang, D. et al.,2020b). Horry et. al. performed covid-19 detection using images from three most commonly used modes X-Ray, Ultrasound and CT-Scan, and used optimized VGG-19 models for image modalities to show how models can be used for challenging and highly scarce covid-19 datasets (Horry, M.J. et al.,2020). They achieved a precision upto 86% for X-ray, 100% for Ultrasound and 84% for CT-scans.

Several researchers used CNN for feature extraction and then used ELM-based classifiers for predicting their architecture's performance. Das et. al. proposed automatic the Covid-19 detection using Ensemble Learning and Convolutional Neural Network of CXR images (Das et al.,2020). They have used three pre-trained models DenseNet201, Resnet50V2, and InceptionV3 and achieved the highest accuracy of 95.7% and sensitivity of 98%. Rajpal et. al. used an Extreme learning machine model called COV-ELM on CXR images (Rajpal et al.,2020). They extract the features on the basis of frequency and texture on the imaged and achieve an overall accuracy of 94.40%. Turkoglu et. al. proposed a Multiple Kernel ELM-based Deep Neural Network for detection of Covid-19, and made the use of CNN-based pre-trained DenseNet201 architecture for feature extraction and an ELM-based classifier on a different architecture to calculate the performance, they achieved an accuracy of 98.36% (Turkoglu, M. et al, 2021). Jain et. al. have used deep learning based CNN and compared their performance (Jain, R. et al,2021). They have made a comparison of different models like InceptionV3, Xception and ResNeXt, and achieved the highest accuracy of 97.97% for the Xception model.

On the other hand, a lot of work is focused on the use of CNN based pre-trained models for feature extraction, and different machine learning models like SVM, Decision trees, etc., for covid-19 detection. Sethy et al. present an approach based on the support vector machine (SVM) for classification instead of deep learning classifier (Sethy et al.,2020). Their proposed approach uses a ResNet50 model along with an SVM and achieves an accuracy of 95%. Enireddy et. al. (Enireddy, V. et al, 2020) have used the Hybrid Resnet and SVM for Covid-19 detection. The features are extracted using Resnet and classification was done using an SVM classifier, and obtained an accuracy of 94% when tested on a dataset consisting of Normal, Pneumonia, and Covid Patients. Narin et. al. also adopted the use of Resnet-50 for feature extraction and SVM model for classification (A. Narin,2020), and achieved the highest sensitivity value of 96.35% in a 5 fold cross-validation method. Hilal Arslan has proposed a new covid detection method from human Genome sequences using KNN classifier and CpG island features and they have an achieved an accuracy of 98.4%, precision of 98.4%, recall of 99.2%, and F1-Score of 98.8% (Arslan, H. et al.,2021). Yoo et. al. proposed a deep learning-based Decision Tree classifier which consisted of three binary trees. The first decision tree classified if the images were normal or normal. The second decision tree classified if the abnormal patients contained any sign of tuberculosis. Third, did the same for Covid-19. The average accuracy of the first and second decision tree was 98% and 80% respectively and the average accuracy for the third decision tree was 95% (Yoo, S. H. et al.,2020).

Table 1. Summarization of the existing works on COVID-19 Detection

S. No.	References	Techniques Used	Dataset Type Used	Achieved Accuracy
1	Wang et al.	InceptionResnetV2,a pretrained model	Covid patients CT scan	89.5%
2	Horrey et al.	Optimised VGG-19	X- ray,ultrasound and CT images	86%
3	Narin et al.	Resnet-50, a pretrained model	Chest X-ray images	98%
4	Das et al.	Densenet 201,Resnet50V2 and InceptionV3	CXR images	95.7%
5	Rajpal et al.	Cov-ELM, Extreme learning model	Chest X-ray images	94.40%
6	Turkoglu et. al.	ELM-based Deep Neural Network for detection of Covid-19	Chest CT scan images of Covid patients.	98.36%
7	Jain et al.	InceptionV3,Xception,ResneXtand SVM	Chest X-ray scan images of Covid patients.	97.97%
8	Sethy et al.	SVM	X-ray image of Covid patients	95%
9	Enireddy et al.	Resnet and SVM	Chest X-ray of pneumonia, normal and Covid patients	94%
10	Narin et al.	Resnet-50 and SVM	Chest X-ray images	96.35%
11	Hilal Arslan	KNN classifier and CpG island features	Human Genome Sequence	98.4%
12	Yoo et al.	Decision Tree	Chest X-ray	95%
13	Khanday et al.	Logistic Regression, Naive Bayes and feature engineering	Clinical text data	96.2%
14	Hussain et al.	AI imaging analysis	CXR images	97.66%
15	Xu et al.	Location Based classifier	X-ray of Covid-19 and influenza A pneumonia patients	86.7%
16	Waheed et al.	Covid GAN	CXR images	95%
17	Mohamed Loey	CGAN and ResNet50	Chest-CT radiography digital images	82.91%
18	Fei et al.	VB- Net, Neural network	CT scan images	91.6%
19	Arpan Mangal	CovidAid and ChextNet architecture	X-ray of normal,bacterial and viral patients	90.5%
20	Mohammad Rahimzadeh	Inception and Resnet50V2	X-ray images	91.4%

The other machine learning models or location-based classifiers were used for the detection of Covid-19 on both textual data and image data. Khanday et. al.(Khanday, A. et al,2020) decided to use various AI tools to control current havoc. They classified textual clinical reports into 4 classes and applied various machine learning algorithms. They performed feature engineering using terms like Bag of Words, Report Length and Team Frequency. The best results were achieved by Logistic Regression and Naive Bayes and that was a testing accuracy of 96.2%. Hussain et. al. developed an AI imaging analysis tool for the classification of covid-19 based on CXR images, and achieved the highest accuracy, sensitivity, and specificity of 97.56%, 97.44%, and 97.66% respectively for detection of Covid-19 vs. non-Covid-19 viral pneumonia (Hussain, L., Nguyen, T., Li, H. et al.,2020). Xu et. al. used a location-based classifier to separate out COVID-19 patients from healthy cases and Influenza-A viral pneumonia. The model used by them was employed on CT images and gave an accuracy of 86.7% (Xu, X. et al.,2020).

The researchers had faced a problem of the unavailability of a dataset consisting of lung X-ray images of covid positive patients. Waheed et. al. proposed a method for the detection of synthetic CXR images by developing an Auxiliary Classifier Generative Adversarial Network-based model known as CovidGan (Waheed, A.et al, 2020). By adding synthetic images they achieved the best accuracy of up to 95%. Mohamed Loey used classical data augmentation along with CGAN to generate more images for the detection of covid-19 (Loey, M. et al., 2020). They came to the conclusion that Resnet50 was the most suitable option providing the highest test accuracy of 82.91%. Various other architectures were used based on modified pre-trained CNNs. Shan et. al. proposed a "VB-Net" Neural Network to detect covid-19 virus from CT Scan (Shan, F. et al,2003). They evaluated the performance by comparing automatically segmented infection regions with manually-delineated ones. They obtained a dice similarity coefficient of 91.6% and a mean estimation error of 0.3% for the whole lung. Mangal e. al. proposed a method called CovidAID in which he used a DenseNet based ChextNet architecture to separate normal, bacterial, and viral pneumonia patients (Mangal, A. et al., 2020). They achieved the highest accuracy of 90.5% with a sensitivity of 100% for covid-19 infection. Rahimzadeh et. al. proposed a modified convolutional Neural Network for detection of Covid-19 which was based on concatenation of Inception and Resnet50V2 (Rahimzadeh, M.,2020). The overall average accuracy obtained by all the models was 91.4%. Table 1 exhibits a summary of the existing work in the area of COVID-19 detection.

COVID-XRAY DATASET

The dataset used consists of Chest X-Ray images which are fed to the CNN models to test their efficiency. The dataset used for Covid positive patients is a Github repository which was shared by Dr. Joseph Cohen(*ieee8023/covid-chestxray- dataset*. (2020)).This dataset is approved by the University of Montreal's Ethics committee. The data is obtained from sources available publicly as well as from collections from hospitals and doctors. The diagnosis in all the images has been confirmed using polymerase chain reaction (PCR).This dataset was used to obtain data for COVID positive patients for training and testing purposes.

The dataset for the normal patients was obtained from a Kaggle repository named "Chest X-Ray Images (Pneumonia)" (Mooney, P., 2020).There are 5863 images in this dataset that are divided into two categories Pneumonia and Normal, which were collected from pediatric patients of 1 to 5 years old from Guangzhou Women and Children Medical center. After removing low-quality scans, the diagnosis of the images was graded by two expert physicians before being allowed for training in AI purposes. The data consists of 1583 normal images.

In this study, a subset of these normal images was obtained to train the models.

Figure 1. Normal patient's Chest X-ray Image

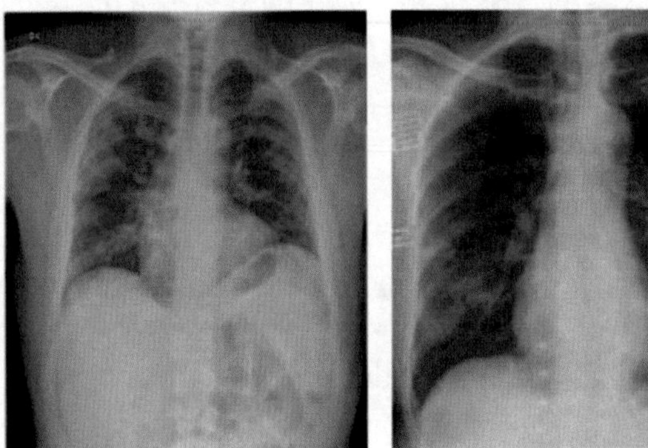

Data Pre-Processing

To create a balance between chest x-ray images of Covid patients and normal patients, we selected 142 images of the normal patient's dataset from Kaggle(Mooney, P., 2020). So the dataset we used finally consisted of 142 images of COVID positive patients and 142 images of Non-COVID patients. These are further split into training and test sets to be fed to the CNN models. The training set consists of 112 images for both Covid patients and normal patients and the test set consists of 30 images for each class. These images were resized to 224X224 pixel sizes. Figure 1 and Figure 2 exhibits the Chest X-rays of Normal patients and Covid patients respectively.

Figure 2. Covid patient's chest X-ray image

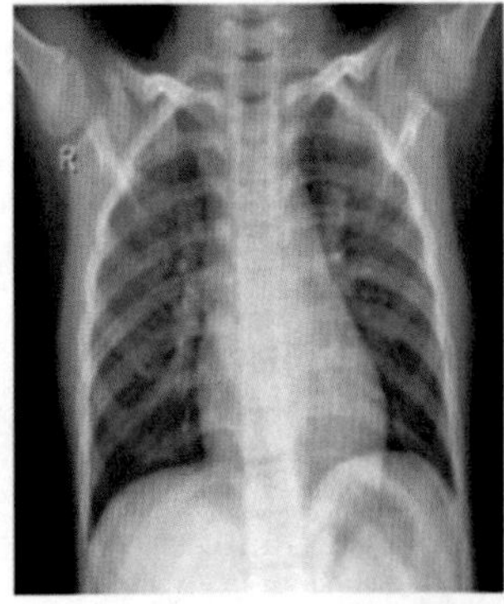

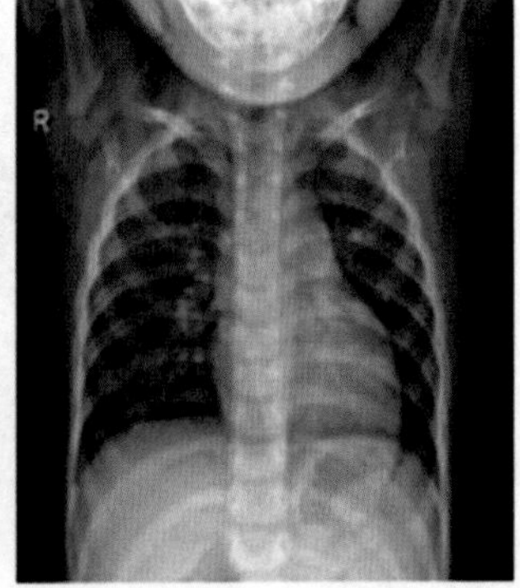

TRANSFER LEARNING

Machine Learning has become a crucial part of a technology-driven society. It is used for recommendation systems in e-commerce, to filter content for specific users, to predict various diseases, to make recommendations for professional car racing, and for many more applications. It has countless applications in the modern world and is way more accurate than humans in certain applications.

Earlier the use of conventional machine-learning was not efficient in extracting features from raw data. It was difficult for engineers to extract data in case the complexity of data was high. This problem was solved by the introduction of deep learning. Deep learning is a part of machine learning, this branch of machine learning which focuses on detecting objects and recognizing speech. It is inspired by the human brain and works in a similar fashion. Recently various deep learning techniques have shown astonishing results in terms of medical image processing (LeCun, Y.,1998; Ren, S. et al.2016). By applying these techniques to medical data, we expect to get significant insights from the images (He, K., Zhang, X., Ren, S., Sun, J., 2016). In the recent era, computer vision models are doing far better than humans in medical images like cancer identification in MRI scans, diabetes mellitus, skin cancer [4], and breast cancer. It consists of networks called neural networks. These networks consist of multiple layers which become more abstract as one goes deeper into the network. The raw data is fed to the network and it automatically learns complex patterns from the data. The various layers used in this network make use of a backpropagation algorithm to change the network to improve its performance (LeCun, Y. et al, 2015). In the process, the network is introduced to a desirable output which is known as the training stage. The layers consist of adjustable parameters called weights. They are changed during the back propagation algorithm. Then we make use of a function named cost function which measures the difference between the output and input. This difference is then reduced by the network by changing its weights. This is generally done by using stochastic gradient descent. This method is carried out by showing the inputs and outputs and then computing the average gradient then changing the weights. This process is done in small steps until the difference between input and output is eliminated. The network obtained after this procedure is then used to make predictions on unseen data which is known as the test stage. This stage tells us how well the model is performing by using performance metrics like accuracy, F1-score, etc. It is because of the improvement in artificial neural networks which consists of a lot of hidden layers which allow higher accuracy for image analysis. It has become a widely used technique because of its unmatched result for numerous purposes which include speech recognition, detecting objects, face recognition and natural language processing, etc.(Celik, Y. et al,2020).

While performing analysis on medical data the biggest problem faced is the lack of sufficient datasets which is a necessity of Deep learning. In the process, the data collected is then labeled for training which is very time consuming and costly. Although deep learning provides an effective way to extract complex features with ease when the data is used from some other distribution or some other task the model needs to be trained from scratch. In a real-world scenario, some tasks have a lot of labeled data on the other hand other tasks don't have enough. In this case transfer learning provides a solution by using the patterns learned from some other task that is similar. In the case of computer vision, the change in spatial orientation or using a different distribution of data results in the failure of regular machine learning techniques (S. J. Pan and Q. Yang,2010). Transfer learning can help in this regard. It is in a way inspired by human vision wherein the previous training on thousands of images can help one to learn new objects with ease. In the case of transfer learning replication, this type of system can help to reduce the training time by a large factor. This technique, therefore, helps in cases where labeled data is scarce. This can also be used to leverage the state-of-the-art models with very high performance which are specific and need to be trained from scratch for a new application, by making them generalized for similar applications. It provides a very proven approach to obtain precious data which is then transferred to the model to be trained(Narin, A et al.,2020).

OUR PROPOSED APPROACH

In this chapter, we study four different transfer learning models; each model poses variable depth and has a different number of hidden layers. All of the models though have been tested on the ImageNet Database. The structure of each adopted transfer learning method is given below:

VGG16

It is a widely popular pre-trained transfer learning method that has attained a top-5 accuracy of 92.7% on the Image Net dataset. VGG-16 came second in the Image Net competition of 2014 and the model achieved a top-5 error of 7.3% and the model has around 138 million parameters. The Visual Geometry Group (VGG) invented the VGG-16 model. The model contains 13 convolution layers and 3 fully connected layers: with the first two having 4096 channels and the third having 1000 channels. VGG's hidden layers use ReLU in place of Local Response Normalization (LRN) as LRN takes a lot of memory and training time and does not contribute anything significant in terms of accuracy. The network is around 2 times deeper than Alex Net and had smaller sized filters of (2X2 and 3X3) and the deeper model was achieved by stacking uniform convolutions. It is now still one of the most used image-recognition models. Figure 3 exhibits the architecture of our trained VGG-16 model.

Inception V3

It is a widely recognized pre-trained transfer learning method which is an extended version of Google Net and has attained an accuracy of 78.1% in about 170 epochs on the Image Net dataset. It is a 48 layer deep model. The model has been trained on 1.3 million images and 1000 classes on very powerful machines. The model is a successor of Inception V1 which had 24 million training parameters. It is very similar to Inception V2. The model has used factorized 7x7 convolutions and auxiliary classifiers to disseminate information lower down the network. The main benefit of Inception v3 was it helped to reduce input dimensions of the next layer to result in more efficient computations by the factorization method. Using Batch Normalization was one of the major achievements of the model.

Resnet50

It is also a very commonly used famous pre-trained model which has attained an accuracy of 80.67% on the Image Net dataset. Residual nets are 8 times deeper than VGG models but still less complex. An ensemble of all these residual nets achieves an error of 3.57% on the Image Net dataset. The model consists of 48 convolutional layers along with 1 average pooling and 1 max pooling. The model consists of 5 stages which each contains convolutional blocks and identity blocks. Both convolutional blocks and identity blocks consist of 3 convolutional layers. The model has around 23.521 million parameters. The model uses skip connection to add output from earlier layer to later layer; this can help in alleviating the problem of gradient vanishing.

InceptionResnetV2

A very popular state-of-the-art pre-trained transfer learning method that has achieved a `Top-5 accuracy of 95.3 on the 2012 ILSVRC Image Classification benchmark. It is a 164 layers deep model. It is a variation of the earlier InceptionV3 model. In the same paper of Inception V4, the same author introduced Inception ResNets. In this model Inception blocks were simplified, containing fewer parallel towers than Inception V3. The model was built on Inception architecture but assimilated architecture of Residual Nets after replacing filter concatenation stages of Inception architecture. By using residual connections we can avoid degradation problems caused by deep structures as well as reduce training time.

In all the model's weights are loaded from pre-trained Image Net and are not changed at all during the course of training of these CNNs. Like other parameters, include_top was set to be false as we didn't include the final pooling and fully connected layer, instead of in all the models we added Global average pooling and a dense output layer. These training processes help to extract features from input images.

Figure 3. The architecture of our trained VGG-16 Model

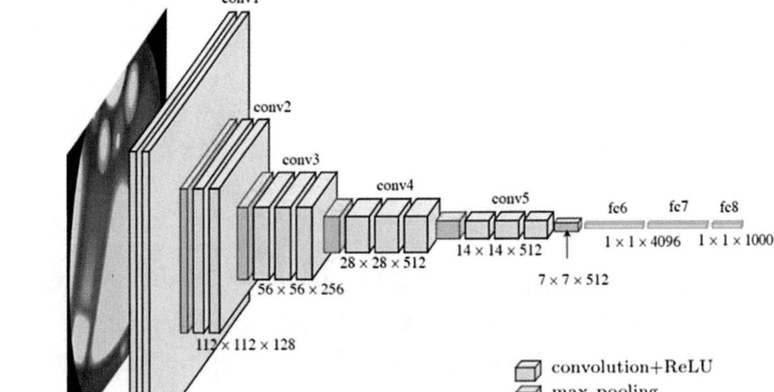

RESULTS AND DISCUSSION

This section presents the results obtained in this study for the detection of COVID-19 from the X-ray images of the chest. Now, we describe the experimental setup, performance metrics, and experimental results in detail.

Experimental Setup

We have used Python Programming language to train the model and all the experiments were performed on a Google Colaboratory. CNN models (Resnet-50, Inception v3, VGG-16, and Inception-ResNet V2) were pre-trained using the Adam Optimizer and the batch size was set to be 2 with a learning rate of 0.00001 in which all weights were randomly initialized. The number of epochs was experimentally set to be 25 for all the experiments. Then we did a random split of 80% and 20% on the dataset for training and testing purposes.

Performance Metrics

We have measured the performance of our deep learning model in terms of the five performance parameters that are: *accuracy, precision, recall, specificity, and F1-score.* The description of each parameter is given as:

$$\text{Accuracy} = (TN + TP)/ (TN + TP + FN + FP) \quad (1)$$

$$\text{Recall} = TP/ (TP + FN) \quad (2)$$

$$\text{Precision} = TP/ (TP + FP) \quad (3)$$

$$\text{Specificity} = TN/ (TN + FP) \quad (4)$$

$$\text{F1-Score} = 2*((\text{Precision}*\text{Recall})/ (\text{Precision} + \text{Recall})) \quad (5)$$

where, TP = true positives, TN = true negatives, FP = false Positives, and FN = false negatives.

True positive - Represents the patients that are correctly identified as covid-19 positive by the model
True negative -Represents the patients that are correctly identified as Normal.
False-positive - Represents the patients who are normal but misidentified as covid-19 positive
False-negative - Represents the patients that are covid-19 positive but misidentified as Normal by the model

Besides these criteria, we draw the confusion matrix and receiver operator characteristic (ROC) curve with respect to each model that we have adopted. The *confusion matrix* is a tool that can be used to evaluate the classification model to estimate whether an object is either correct or false. It is a matrix prediction that contains comparison of actual and predicted information. A ROC curve is a performance measurement tool which is used for classification problems at various threshold levels. ROC curve is used to measure the degree of spreadability meaning. It means it tells you how much the model is correctly able to distinguish between the classes. By analogy, higher the ROC-Score more accurate the model is in predicting Covid positive patients and Normal patients. The ROC curve is plotted against True Positive Rate (TPR) and False Positive Rate (FPR).

Experimental Results

Our model makes use of chest x-ray images to predict whether a patient is Covid positive or not. Famous CNN models like ResNet50, Inception V3, InceptionResNetV2, and VGG16 were trained as well as tested on the image dataset. Resnet50, InceptionV3, and VGG16 showed the highest training accuracy followed by Inception ResNet v2. The model was trained up to 25 epochs to avoid overfitting. However, it was seen that the Resnet50 model trained the fastest and when training loss values of Inception V3, Inception Resnet50, VGG16, and Inception V3 was compared it was seen that the loss value decreased in all these models during the training stage. It is worth considering so far that the numbers of reliably classified Covid positive X-ray images are still very limited and we have only 142 images so these performance metrics may not be very reliable.

Figures 4, 5, 6 and 7 exhibit the confusion matrix and the ROC curve derived for our adopted pre-trained models. From the confusion matrix, we observed that the Inception V3 model labeled 30 of its images as true positive and 28 of its images were labeled as true negative, the Resnet50 model labeled 30 of its images as true positive and 29 of the images were labeled as true negative, the VGG16 model labeled 28 of its images as true positive, and 30 of its images were labeled as true negative, and the Inception ResnetV2, on the other hand, labeled 16 of its images as true positive, and 28 of its images were labeled as true negative. From the ROC curve, we observe that the curve of Resnet-50 appeared to be the highest thus showing the best accuracy followed by VGG-16 and Inception V3. On the other hand, Table 2 exhibits the performance comparison of adopted models on the test dataset. From Table 2, we can observe that the Resnet50 model has obtained the best results with accuracy of 98%, specificity of 100%, and recall of 97%. The training speed was much higher in Resnet50 as compared to other pre-trained models. InceptionV3 gave us the second-best performance with the accuracy of 97%, recall of 94%, and specificity of 100%. The VGG-16 model has achieved pretty good results with accuracy of 97%, recall of 100%, and specificity of 94%. The lowest performance obtained was by InceptionResnetV2 with 77% accuracy, 0% recall, and 70% specificity. As a result, we can conclude that Resnet50 outperformed the other three models. In addition to these results, the main outcomes of our study are as follows:

1. Four detailed pre-trained models have been used i.e. InceptionV3, Resnet50, VGG16, Inception Resnet V2.
2. The data available at hand is limited because of the modernity of the subject, but as compared to previous studies the dataset of covid patients have increased showing more promising results,
3. We have used Chest X-ray images to detect covid patients, which can easily be obtained from the hospital quickly and without much hassle.
4. The proposed method does not contain any feature extraction or selection which makes it a complete end-to-end system.

Figure 4. Roc curve and confusion matrix for InceptionV3

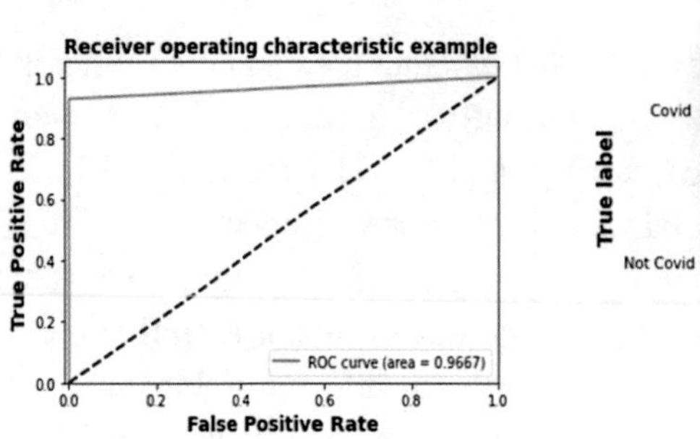

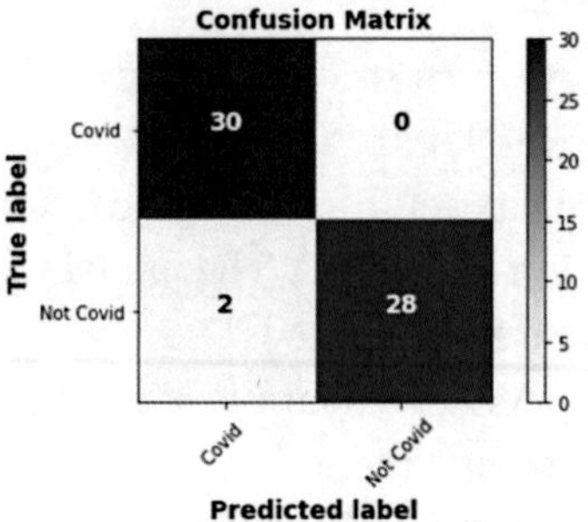

Figure 5. Roc curve and confusion matrix for Resnet-50

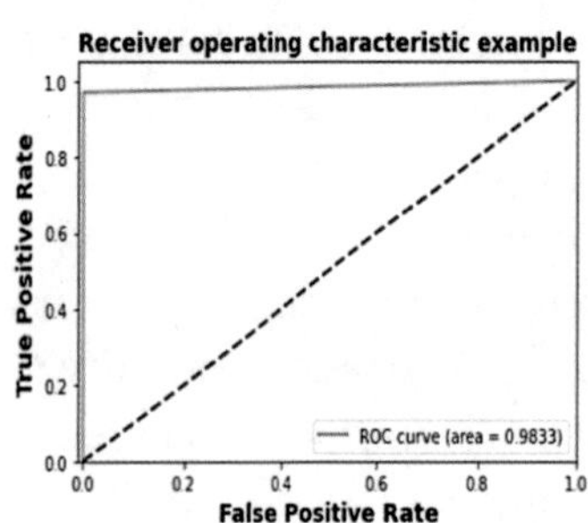

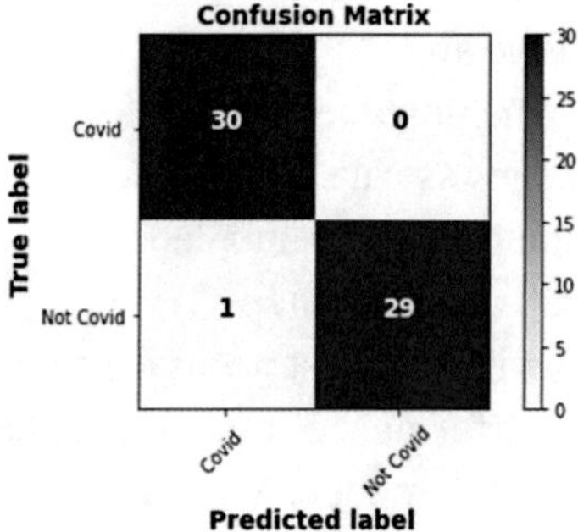

Figure 6. Roc curve and confusion matrix for VGG-16

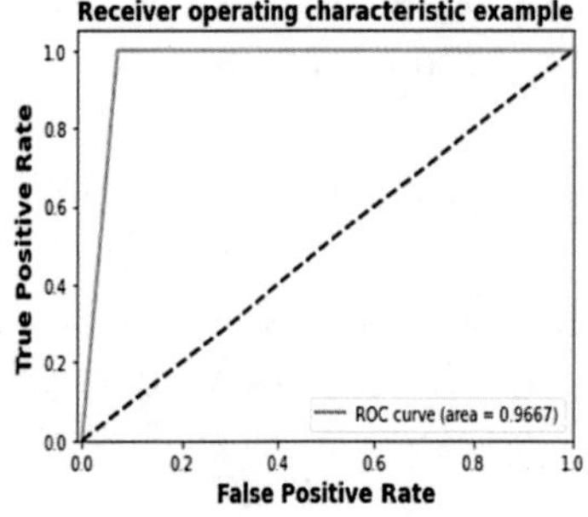

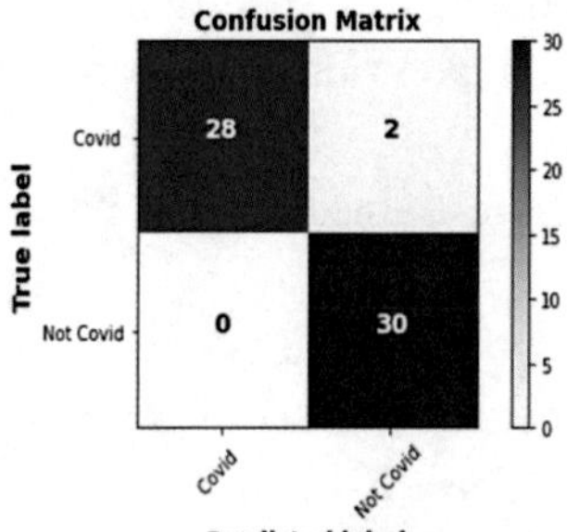

Figure 7. Roc curve and confusion matrix for InceptionResnetV2

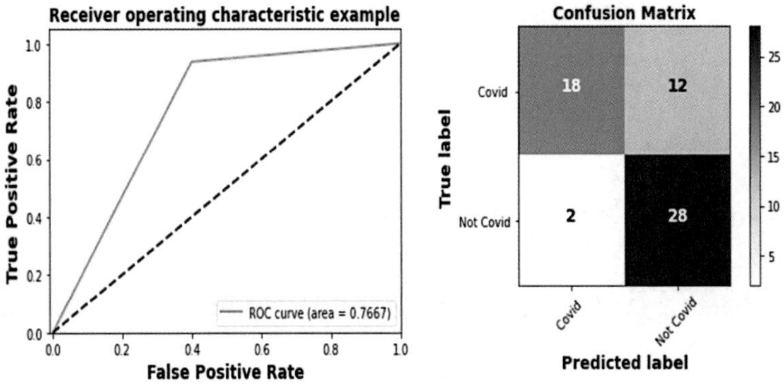

Table 2. Accuracy, Precision, Recall, Specificity and F1-Score of our adopted models used

Model	Accuracy	Precision	Recall	Specificity	F1-Score
InceptionV3	0.967	1.0000	0.9375	1.000	0.9677
Resnet50	0.983	1.0000	0.9677	1.000	0.9914
VGG-16	0.967	0.9334	1.0000	0.9375	0.9655
Inception Resnetv2	0.767	0.6000	0.9000	0.7000	0.7200

CONCLUSION AND FUTURE WORK

In the recent past, the Covid-19 pandemic has taken the world by surprise and affected many lives. In the present scenario, fighting with Covid-19 is the main aim of every nation in the world. The most important step is the detection of the disease. In this study, we used various CNN models (Resnet50, VGG16, InceptionV3, and InceptionResnetV2) to separate the Covid-19 infected patients from non-infected and then employed some measuring metrics like confusion matrix and ROC curves. The training and testing process results in the Resnet 50 model giving the best efficiency with an accuracy of 98%, and making it better for the detecting of Covid-19 using Chest X-ray images. In further studies classification performance of all the models can be increased with an increase of chest X-ray images of Covid positive patients in Dataset. It will be interesting to see when various other CNN architectures will be applied to this dataset. We can make a desktop application tool for the detection of Covid positive patients from normal patients who can be used by Hospitals and Clinics.

REFERENCES

Ai, T., Yang, Z., Hou, H., Zhan, C., Chen, C., Lv, W., Tao, Q., Sun, Z., & Xia, L. (2020). Correlation of chest CT and RT-PCR testing for coronavirus disease 2019 (COVID-19) in China: A report of 1014 cases. *Radiology*, *296*(2), E32–E40. doi:10.1148/radiol.2020200642 PMID:32101510

Arslan, H., & Arslan, H. (2021). A new COVID-19 detection method from human genome sequences using CpG island features and KNN classifier. *Engineering Science and Technology, an International Journal.*

Beluz, J., (2020). *How does the new coronavirus spread?* vox.com/2020/2/ 20/21143785/coronavirus-covid-19-spreadtransmission-how.

Bengio, Y., & LeCun, Y. (2007). Scaling learning algorithms towards AI. *Large-Scale Kernel Machines, 34*(5), 1-41.

Celik, Y., Talo, M., Yildirim, O., Karabatak, M., & Acharya, U. R. (2020). Automated invasive ductal carcinoma detection based using deep transfer learning with whole-slide images. *Pattern Recognition Letters, 133*, 232–239. doi:10.1016/j.patrec.2020.03.011

Colin, B. (2020). *Image Recognition with TransferLearning (98.5%).* https://thedatafrog.com/en/articles/image-recognition-transfer-learning/

Das, A. K., Ghosh, S., Thunder, S., Dutta, R., Agarwal, S., & Chakrabarti, A. (2021). Automatic COVID-19 detection from X-ray images using ensemble learning with convolutional neural network. *Pattern Analysis & Applications*, 1–14.

Dorj, U. O., Lee, K. K., Choi, J. Y., & Lee, M. (2018). The skin cancer classification using deep convolutional neural network. *Multimedia Tools and Applications, 77*(8), 9909–9924. doi:10.100711042-018-5714-1

Enireddy, V., Kumar, M. J. K., Donepudi, B., & Karthikeyan, C. (2020, December). Detection of COVID-19 using Hybrid ResNet and SVM. *IOP Conference Series. Materials Science and Engineering, 993*(1), 012046. doi:10.1088/1757-899X/993/1/012046

Fang, Y., Zhang, H., Xie, J., Lin, M., Ying, L., Pang, P., & Ji, W. (2020). Sensitivity of chest CT for COVID-19: Comparison to RT-PCR. *Radiology, 296*(2), E115–E117. doi:10.1148/radiol.2020200432 PMID:32073353

He, K., Zhang, X., Ren, S., & Sun, J. (2016). Deep residual learning for image recognition. In *Proceedings of the IEEE conference on computer vision and pattern recognition* (pp. 770-778). IEEE.

Hinton, G. E., & Salakhutdinov, R. R. (2006). Reducing the dimensionality of data with neural networks. *Science, 313*(5786), 504-507.

Horry, M. J., Chakraborty, S., Paul, M., Ulhaq, A., Pradhan, B., Saha, M., & Shukla, N. (2020). COVID-19 detection through transfer learning using multimodal imaging data. *IEEE Access: Practical Innovations, Open Solutions, 8*, 149808–149824. doi:10.1109/ACCESS.2020.3016780

Huang, G., Liu, Z., Van Der Maaten, L., & Weinberger, K. Q. (2017). Densely connected convolutional networks. In *Proceedings of the IEEE conference on computer vision and pattern recognition* (pp. 4700-4708). IEEE.

Hussain, L., Nguyen, T., Li, H., Abbasi, A. A., Lone, K. J., Zhao, Z., Zaib, M., Chen, A., & Duong, T. Q. (2020). Machine-learning classification of texture features of portable chest X-ray accurately classifies COVID-19 lung infection. *Biomedical Engineering Online*, *19*(1), 1–18. doi:10.118612938-020-00831-x PMID:33239006

Jain, R., Gupta, M., Taneja, S., & Hemanth, D. J. (2021). Deep learning based detection and analysis of COVID-19 on chest X-ray images. *Applied Intelligence*, *51*(3), 1690–1700. doi:10.100710489-020-01902-1

Khanday, A. M. U. D., Rabani, S. T., Khan, Q. R., Rouf, N., & Din, M. M. U. (2020). Machine learning based approaches for detecting COVID-19 using clinical text data. *International Journal of Information Technology*, *12*(3), 731–739. doi:10.100741870-020-00495-9 PMID:32838125

LeCun, Y., Bottou, L., Bengio, Y., & Haffner, P. (1998). Gradient-based learning applied to document recognition. *Proceedings of the IEEE*, *86*(11), 2278–2324. doi:10.1109/5.726791

Loey, M., Manogaran, G., & Khalifa, N. E. M. (2020). A deep transfer learning model with classical data augmentation and cgan to detect covid-19 from chest ct radiography digital images. *Neural Computing & Applications*, 1–13. PMID:33132536

Mangal, A., Kalia, S., Rajgopal, H., Rangarajan, K., Namboodiri, V., Banerjee, S., & Arora, C. (2020). *CovidAID: COVID-19 detection using chest X-ray.* arXiv preprint arXiv:2004.09803.

McKeever, A. (2020). Here's what coronavirus does to the body. *National Geographic*.

Minaee, S., Kafieh, R., Sonka, M., Yazdani, S., & Soufi, G. J. (2020). Deep-covid: Predicting covid-19 from chest x-ray images using deep transfer learning. *Medical Image Analysis*, *65*, 101794. doi:10.1016/j.media.2020.101794 PMID:32781377

Mooney, P. (2020). *Chest X-ray images (Pneumonia).* https://www. kaggle. com/paultimothymooney/chest-xray-pneumonia

Narin, A. (2020). *Detection of Covid-19 Patients with Convolutional Neural Network Based Features on Multi-class X-ray Chest Images. In 2020 Medical Technologies Congress*. TIPTEKNO. doi:10.1109/TIPTEKNO50054.2020.9299289

Narin, A., Kaya, C., & Pamuk, Z. (2020). *Automatic detection of coronavirus disease (covid-19) using x-ray images and deep convolutional neural networks.* arXiv preprint arXiv:2003.10849.

Pan, S. J., & Yang, Q. (2009). A survey on transfer learning. *IEEE Transactions on Knowledge and Data Engineering*, *22*(10), 1345–1359. doi:10.1109/TKDE.2009.191

Rahimzadeh, M., & Attar, A. (2020). *A new modified deep convolutional neural network for detecting COVID-19 from X-ray images.* arXiv preprint arXiv:2004.08052.

Rajpal, S., Kumar, N., & Rajpal, A. (2020). *Cov-elm classifier: An extreme learning machine based identification of covid-19 using chest-ray images.* arXiv preprint arXiv:2007.08637.

Ren, S., He, K., Girshick, R., & Sun, J. (2015). *Faster r-cnn: Towards real-time object detection with region proposal networks.* arXiv preprint arXiv:1506.01497.

Sethy, P. K., Behera, S. K., Ratha, P. K., & Biswas, P. (2020). *Detection of coronavirus disease (COVID-19) based on deep features and support vector machine*. Academic Press.

Turkoglu, M. (2021). COVID-19 Detection System Using Chest CT Images and Multiple Kernels-Extreme Learning Machine Based on Deep Neural Network. *IRBM*.

Waheed, A., Goyal, M., Gupta, D., Khanna, A., Al-Turjman, F., & Pinheiro, P. R. (2020). CovidGAN: Data augmentation using auxiliary classifier gan for improved covid-19 detection. *IEEE Access: Practical Innovations, Open Solutions*, *8*, 91916–91923. doi:10.1109/ACCESS.2020.2994762

Wang, D., Hu, B., Hu, C., Zhu, F., Liu, X., Zhang, J., Wang, B., Xiang, H., Cheng, Z., Xiong, Y., Zhao, Y., Li, Y., Wang, X., & Peng, Z. (2020). Clinical characteristics of 138 hospitalized patients with 2019 novel coronavirus–infected pneumonia in Wuhan, China. *Journal of the American Medical Association*, *323*(11), 1061–1069. doi:10.1001/jama.2020.1585 PMID:32031570

World Health Organisation. (2021). *WHO coronavirus disease (covid-19) dashboard*. Author.

Xu, B., & Meng, X. (n.d.). *A deep learning algorithm using CT images to screen for Corona Virus Disease (COVID-19)*. Preprint.

Xu, X., Jiang, X., Ma, C., Du, P., Li, X., Lv, S., Yu, L., Ni, Q., Chen, Y., Su, J., Lang, G., Li, Y., Zhao, H., Liu, J., Xu, K., Ruan, L., Sheng, J., Qiu, Y., Wu, W., ... Li, L. (2020). A deep learning system to screen novel coronavirus disease 2019 pneumonia. *Engineering*, *6*(10), 1122–1129. doi:10.1016/j.eng.2020.04.010 PMID:32837749

Yoo, S. H., Geng, H., Chiu, T. L., Yu, S. K., Cho, D. C., Heo, J., . . . Lee, H. (2020). Deep learning-based decision-tree classifier for COVID-19 diagnosis from chest X-ray imaging. *Frontiers in Medicine, 7*, 427.

Chapter 12
COVID-19-Related Predictions Using NER on News Headlines

Bidyut B. Hazarika
Western Michigan University, USA

Urvish Trivedi
University of South Florida, USA

Harshita Dahiya
National Institute of Technology, Kurukshetra, India

Nishtha Nandwani
National Institute of Technology, Kurukshetra, India

Aakriti Gupta
National Institute of Technology, Kurukshetra, India

ABSTRACT

Today, all the newspapers and online news content are flooded with the news of coronavirus (i.e., COVID-19). The virus has spread across the globe at an alarming rate. Thus, people need to remain updated about news regarding the ongoing pandemic which has taken whole world by storm. Therefore, named entity recognition (NER) is applied to extract important information from these news headlines and articles and further used for more applications related to COVID-19 in India. This chapter uses the SpaCy module to categorize the tokens extracted from the news headlines database into various pre-defined tags. Further, four different machine learning models, namely CRF Model, LSTM Model, LightGBM Model, and AdaBoost Model, are applied for performing tagging. After that, these tags are used to predict different information regarding COVID-19. Some of these applications include finding nearby hospitals and pharmacies, predicting future potential hotspots in India, worst affected states of India, gender-based comparisons, age group-based comparisons, and area-based spreading of the virus.

DOI: 10.4018/978-1-7998-3299-7.ch012

Table 1. Spread of coronavirus in India based on lockdown period

Lockdown Start Date	Total Cases	Deaths	Growth Rate (%)
Part 1 (Mar 24)	562	11	21.5
Part 2 (Apr 14)	11,393	392	11.4
Part 3 (May 3)	42,456	1,390	6.2
Part 4 (May 17)	95,679	3,023	5.2

INTRODUCTION

Today the world has become so technically advanced that the Internet has become the central point for all activities occurring around the globe. The Internet has a very important role to play in the lives of the people (Papacharissi & Rubin, 2000). The Internet itself contains very enormous data which maybe html pages, images, texts, audios, videos, etc. This information available on the Internet is also growing each day. Therefore, it becomes a very humongous task to maintain, update and store all this data on the Internet. There are many technologies that are available today for carrying out these processes (Chang, Kayed, Girgis & Shaalan, 2006). We can retrieve important information, prepare summary of whole information, identify the topic of the information and do a whole lot of other operations on the data available on the Internet (Soderland, 1997).

Thus, we can use various technologies of Machine Learning and Natural Language Processing (NLP) to manipulate the data accordingly as per the requirement. One of the main applications of NLP is NER i.e., Named Entity Recognition (Marrero, Urbano, Sanchez-Cuadrado, Morato & Gomez-Berbis, 2013; Mayfield, McNamee & Piatko, 2013; Lin & Hung, 2007). Any real-world object which has a particular meaning attached to it is known as an entity. The entities which tend to be more important, informative, and useful as compared to others are known as named entities.

Therefore, NER is basically the process of identifying important and useful entities and recognizing them so that they can be further used for many applications ("Named Entity Recognition: Applications and Use Cases", 2021). These entities can be anything ranging from names of persons, organizations, locations, cities, states, numeric values, languages, etc. The newer NER systems can classify these named entities into a wide range of categories and tags. This process of classifying the entities into specific categories is known as tagging (Tkachenko & Simanovsky, 2012).

The ongoing pandemic i.e., COVID-19 is an infectious respiratory disease, which originated from the city of Wuhan in China in December 2019 has now spread its roots to almost all countries of the world (Singhal, 2020). Various guidelines and preventive measures are being regularly issued by the WHO (World Health Organization) which has declared the outbreak of this virus as a pandemic. This virus has mild symptoms and generally spreads through air and contact. This virus has spread at a very fast rate which has brought the lives of people around the globe at a standstill.

The cases in India have crossed the 2-lakh mark while more than 6.4 million cases have been discovered worldwide ("India Coronavirus: 11,727,733 Cases and 160,437 Deaths - Worldometer", 2021). As a result, a nationwide lockdown had been imposed in India which prevented the spread of coronavirus to some extent as compared to other countries. Table 1 presents the information regarding the spread in India during lockdown periods.

The newspapers and the online news available on the Internet, is nowadays flooded with news & articles related to the coronavirus. Therefore, it becomes necessary to use NER tools to filter out important and relevant information about the coronavirus so that suitable and required actions can be taken well in time to curb its spread. We apply the NER technology to a database consisting of news headlines related to the ongoing pandemic i.e., COVID-19. We have found out the top 5 cities and top 5 states which have been worst affected the virus. Also, we find out nearby hospitals and pharmacies to these locations. Moreover, we also find out the neighboring cities which can become hotspots in near future. We also further extend the applications on the tokens and tags classified by the NER to show comparison based on various factors related to COVID-19, like which age group is the most affected, which gender is most affected, which area is most likely to be affected and so on. By using these predictions, we can take preventive measures in time so that the spreading of the virus can be curbed to a large extent.

The remainder of this paper is organized as follows. Section 2 covers related work and objectives of this study. Section 3 presents the overview of the proposed approach. Section 4 presents the various machine learning models with their algorithms. Section 5 includes the use cases of NER which are applied on COVID-19 database. Section 6 shows the observations and results. Section 7 evaluates the proposed approach. Section 8 discusses the advantages of the approach. Section 9 discusses the conclusions and future work.

RELATED WORK

This section presents the overview of various approaches related to named entity recognition on a news dataset for COVID-19 as present in the literature.

NER Tools

There are various open source NER tools already available which have been used and tested. Three most widely used and popular NER tools are: -

1. Stanford NER: - It is the java-based implementation of NER.
2. NLTK: - It is the python-based tool for classifying the entities.
3. Polygot: - It is the tool for NER where entities are formed of elements from various languages.

A study (Labs, 2021) was conducted to compare and analyze these three NER tools based on precision and recall. From the results it is very clear that the NER systems are quite efficient tools for extracting and classifying the tokens. Figure 1 presents the results which clearly indicate that Stanford NER performs the best as compared to other two NER tools.

Figure 1. Performance Matrix of various NER tools
("Named Entity Recognition: Applications and Use Cases", 2021)

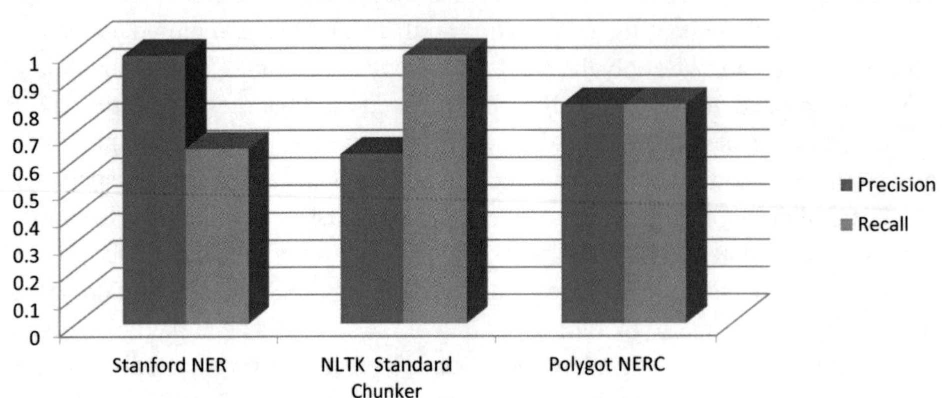

Approaches for Extracting Entities

There are various approaches for extracting and categorizing entities by the method of named entity recognition (Mansouri, Affendey & Mamat, 2008).

- **Lexicon based approach: -** In this approach a knowledge base is created which contains all the words or terms related to a topic which is categorized into various categories. Then for extracting entities we can perform searching in this knowledge base (Jonnalagadda, Cohen, Wu, Liu & Gonzalez, 2013).
- **Rule based approach: -** In this approach the grammatical rules are made on how to extract a particular type of entities and then these rules are followed accordingly (Eftimov, Koroušić & Korošec, 2017).
- **Machine Learning based systems: -** Various Machine Learning algorithms are applied on a hospital's database related to discharge summary of patients by extracting relevant features. Then this feature vector helps in extracting the entities and their tags (Jiang, Chen, Liu, Rosenbloom, Mani, Denny & Xu (2011).
- **Hybrid approach: -** The combination of one or more above discussed approach leads to a hybrid approach. A hybrid system is made up of rule-based system in combination with the clustering or lexicon-based approach by using a knowledge base (Thomas & Sangeetha, 2019).

In lexicon-based approach we need a knowledge base beforehand of all the entities that we are going to extract so this approach does not suit in a real time application like COVID-19. In rule-based approach we can extract certain entities which have a pre-defined rule like phone numbers, name etc. but not all types of entities. So, this approach is not suitable for COVID-19 related research. Machine learning based systems uses feature engineering which can extract any types of entities using the feature vector obtained. Hybrid approach also requires the use of rule-based approach inside it so this also doesn't prove to be useful for this study. Therefore, among all these approaches, machine learning systems prove to bc most appropriate in our research on COVID-19 based news headlines.

Machine Learning Models

Previously various approaches related to machine learning have been applied in the field of named entity recognition. A survey was conducted to review various NLP based approaches for code-switched i.e., multilingual text which a person utters in a general conversation (Sitaram, Chandu, Rallabandi & Black (2019). Further the hybrid combination of bidirectional LSTM and CNN is used for extracting features for identifying the tokens to categorize them into tags (Chiu & Nichols, 2016). According to survey neural network models perform better than the models that use feature engineering (Yadav & Bethard, 2019). The decision tree-based models like a combination of LSTM Model and CRF Model which captures long term dependencies prove to be very effective in case of capturing the named entities in different kinds of datasets (Jie & Lu, 2019). All the boosting algorithms of machine learning which are based on decision trees models have been evaluated based on their performance (Kadiyala & Kumar, 2018). The AdaBoost algorithm combines various weak classifiers into one strong classifier. The method by which AdaBoost algorithm boosts the performance of the weak classifiers, error that occurs in training the AdaBoost model and its applications are also described and known well (Cao, Miao, Liu & Gao, 2013). The AdaBoost algorithm generally performs boosting by downsizing the multi-classification problem to a two-class classification but it can be carried out without doing so as well having exponential loss function (Hastie, Rosset, Zhu & Zou, 2009). The two approaches for using the LightGBM model are namely, GOSS (Gradient based one-side sampling) and EFB (Exclusive Feature Bundling) (Ke, Meng, Finley, Wang, Chen, Ma, Ye & Liu, 2017).

Literature Work Related to COVID-19

A web-based automatic system allows a user to query the system to get evidence related to activities in the field of COVID-19 literature (Wang, Liu, Chauhan, Guan & Han, 2020). But author included only bio-medical entities such as gene, chemical, and disease in their research. A regression model of machine learning was used to predict the number of cases in India in next two weeks starting from 30th March 2020. The results showed that the cases would rise by an amount of 5000-6000 in upcoming two weeks (Pandey, Chaudhary, Gupta & Pal, 2020). But their whole research was based on only a single parameter i.e., number of cases. Another research applied statistical machine learning models to predict cases in future and predict the reproduction number at state and national level which helps in comparing the progression of the COVID-19 disease (Das, 2020). A CORD-19 open research dataset challenge for COVID-19 based dataset has been made and its quality is predicted to be 10% more than the SpaCy (Wang, Song, Guan, Li & Han, 2020). A natural language toolkit related to symptoms, virus, disease, gene etc. has been prepared using synonyms in English dictionary (Rashed, Frid, Guan, Li & Han, 2020). This toolkit is freely available on the Internet ("Aitslab/corona", 2021). Most of the researchers used number of cases as a sole parameter to predict the number of COVID-19 cases. Meanwhile some other researchers used a combination of 3 or 4 bio-medical entities. The following **objectives** have been identified using various parameters like Geo-Political entities, Location names, etc.: -

1. To compare the corona news headlines based on age, area and gender.
2. To identify the worst affected cities and states of India.
3. To predict the potential future hotspots of India.
4. To identify the hospitals and pharmacies near to the hotspot areas.

PROPOSED APPROACH

The main objective of this paper is to classify the named entities of the news headlines dataset into some pre-defined categories of tags like name of locations, organizations, persons, percentage, cardinals, ordinals, etc. By tagging the news headlines related to the corona virus, using the approach of Natural Language Processing (NLP), it becomes easy to get answers to various questions like:

- Which are the worst affected cities or states due to the corona virus?
- What are the neighboring or adjacent cities which might get affected due to the spreading of the virus?
- Which famous personalities got caught by the virus?

The answer to these questions can help to some extent by giving insight into the latest corona news updates, so that adequate precautionary measures can be taken well in time before the corona virus spreads to a larger area.

System Architecture

Figure 2 presents the system architecture of the proposed approach. This approach classifies the named entities from the corona related news headlines and uses it further to derive some useful applications. The project dataset comprises of news headlines related to COVID-19 which were collected from 15 March 2020 to 25 May 2020. These news headlines were collected from the verified sources like ("COVID-19 Corona Tracker", 2021) and 'Times of India' newspaper ("Times of India", 2021) and stored as a database in the .csv file. Then, perform tokenization on all the news headlines from the dataset to split them into tokens. After tokenization, tag the tokens through SpaCy module of python which includes POS tagging, parsing and IOB tagging. Feature generation and feature selection plays a major contribution in this paper. Features generated are described in detail in the subsection of the paper. After extraction of the features, a unique feature vector is created for every token. Total proposed features count is 44, which are used to improve the detection accuracy of the named entities. Different machine learning algorithms are used for predictions and measuring accuracy. CRF model is used which is most used for NER and best known for its accuracy. After performing NER, various applications like predicting the worst affected cities and states by COVID-19 are derived. Also, comparisons based on gender, age and area are done.

Figure 2. Workflow of the proposed approach

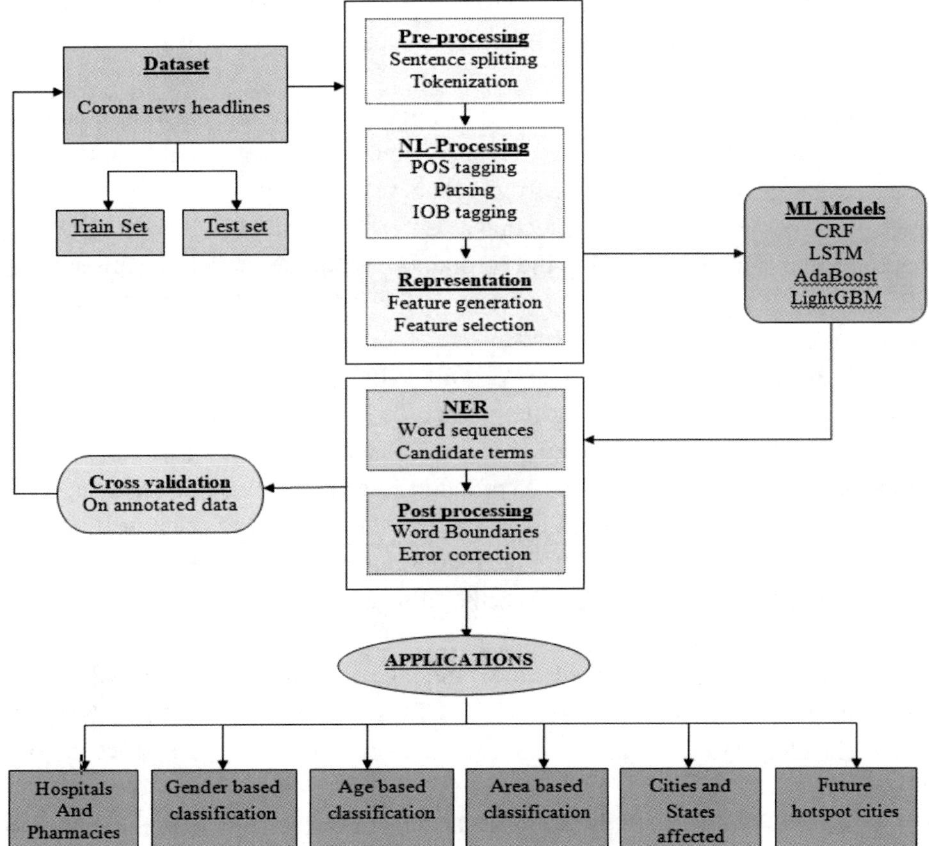

Selection of Features

Various features were extracted from the news headlines so that machine learning models could learn from them and use them to predict the entities for the news headlines in the testing set. In our work, we have used the following feature extraction methods for training our model: -

1. **Word N-Grams: -** By using the N-Grams feature we use the previous word and the next word as a feature vector for training our model. These are also known as contextual features. Thus, feature number 1 gives the next token, 15 gives the previous token and 30 gives the current token in enumerated form.28 represents the bias value.
2. **Uppercase and lowercase: -** If the whole word or token is found to be in capitals then it may suggest that the token is a name of organization or is used to give stress at some particular word. Thus, feature number 10, 24 and 37 identifies uppercase words for next, previous, and current token respectively. Similarly, feature number 11, 25 and 38 identifies lowercase words for next, previous and current token respectively.
3. **Capitalization:** - If in the middle of the news headline we find some word which is capitalized, that means the first letter is capital followed by small letters, then it may indicate entities describ-

ing a person's name, some location, city, state, etc. Thus, feature number 2, 16 and 31 identifies this for next, previous, and current token respectively. Whether a word is a title or not is detected by the feature number 9, 23 and 36 of the feature vectors set respectively for next, previous, and next token.

4. **Presence of Digits:** - If the word extracted is a digit then it may suggest a cardinal value, which in our case may tell number of corona cases in a particular area. Thus, feature number 8, 22 and 33 identifies this for next, previous, and current token, respectively.
5. **Presence of Percentage sign:** - By detecting a percentage symbol (%) in a word, we may come to know about some statistics regarding the corona virus. So, the model may predict the B-Percent and I-Percent tag easily. Thus, feature number 12, 26 and 39 identifies this for next, previous and current token respectively.
6. **Monetary Values:** - Presence of monetary symbols like $, etc., may be used to detect words that are money tags. So, the model can easily predict the B-Money and I-Money tags. Thus, feature number 13, 27 and 40 identifies this for next, previous, and current token, respectively.
7. **Date Values:** - By detecting the presence of date values, we may detect date tags efficiently. So, the B-Date, I-Date, etc. tags can be easily detected by the model. Thus, feature number 5, 18 and 41 identifies whether a token is a month for next, previous, and current token, respectively. Similarly feature number 6, 19 and 42 identifies whether a token is a date for next, previous, and current token, respectively.
8. **Previous Word Tag:** - As mentioned above, the tag of the previous word will help in detecting the tag of the current word. Therefore, all the I-Tags would occur after the B-Tags without any exception. Therefore, we check the previous word in feature number 43 and second previous word in feature number 44.
9. **Special Symbols:** - Some symbols like backslash (/) or dot (.) may help the model in predicting date values which contain backslash in them, and dot may help in predicting person name tags like Mr. X so tags like B-Date, B-Person, I-person are easy to detect by the model. Thus, feature number 4, 17 and 34 detects the presence of dot in next, previous and current token respectively. Similarly, feature number 7, 20 and 35 detects the presence of slash in next, previous and current token respectively.
10. **Common Symbols:** -Some common symbols like brackets - (, {, [, etc. are generally followed by some common words which do not fall under a particular entity type. Therefore, these types of words can come under the Others Tag.
11. **Presence of alphanumeric characters: -** The presence of alphanumeric characters in a word is detected by the feature number 3, 21 and 32 for next, previous, and next token, respectively.
12. **Beginning or end of sentence: -** Whether the current token is BOS (Beginning Of Sentence) is detected by the feature number 14 while the EOS (End Of Sentence) is detected by the feature number 28.

Machine Learning Models

Following machine learning models are used in our work.

LSTM (Long Short-Term Memory)

LSTM is the special kind of RNN used for processing data sequence. LSTM networks are efficient in learning dependencies which are long term. In RNN there is a repeating module with a simple structure like of tan h layer whereas in LSTM the module which is repeating is not simple but has a chain like structure. Thus, in place of single layer, LSTM have four layers which interact with each other. LSTMs are widely used in applications such as handwriting recognition, language modeling and translation, speech synthesis and acoustic modeling of speech etc. In LSTM, 3 gates are used- Input gate, Forget gate and Output gate. These gates manage the amount of input to give it to the memory cell and the amount from the previous state to forget.

$$i_t = \delta\left(w_i\left[h_{t-1}, x_t\right] + b_i\right) \tag{1}$$

$$f_t = \delta\left(w_f\left[h_{t-1}, x_t\right] + b_f\right) \tag{2}$$

$$o_t = \delta\left(w_o\left[h_{t-1}, x_t\right] + b_o\right) \tag{3}$$

CRFs (Conditional Random Fields)

CRF is the combination of statistical and discriminative models. CRF is best suited for predicting tasks in which current prediction is affected by its neighbors' state. It is built upon the abstraction Markov Random Fields. CRF is often applied for NER, noise reduction, pattern recognition and gene prediction. CRF is a supervised learning algorithm which is proved better than the tree-based models for NER. Probability density function of CRF is: -

$$p(y \mid X, \in) = \frac{1}{Z\left(X\right)} \exp \sum_{i=1}^{n} \sum_{j} \in_j f_i\left(X, i, y_{i-1}, y_i\right) \tag{4}$$

Adaptive Boosting

Adaptive boosting or AdaBoost is an ensemble boosting type classifier. It is combination of various weak or poor performing classifiers. The model was used to achieve high accuracy and get a strong classifier.

$$F_T\left(x\right) = \sum_{t=1}^{T} f_t\left(x\right) \tag{5}$$

Working steps for the algorithm: -

1. Initially, training subset was selected randomly.
2. The AdaBoost model was trained iteratively by selection of the training set which was based on the last training's accurate prediction.
3. Higher weights were assigned to the observations which were classified wrong. This was done so that these observations get high probability in next observation for classification.
4. In all iterations, weights were also assigned to trained classifier based on their accuracy. More accurate classifier had higher weight.
5. The iteration of the process was continued till the whole training data was fitted.
6. The final prediction was done by majority 'vote' across all learning algorithms.

LightGBM

This is a framework for gradient boosting. LightGBM uses learning algorithms that are tree based. It has advantages of fast training speed, low memory usage, high accuracy and efficiency and large-scale data handling capacity. LightGBM supports various applications like regression, binary and multi classification, cross-entropy etc.

Working steps for the algorithm: -

For N boosting rounds and L as differentiable loss function-

Let (initial fit of dataset) $F_0\left(x\right) = \arg_\gamma \min \sum_{i=1}^{n} L(y_i, \gamma)$

For j=1 to N:

1. The pseudo residuals r_{ij} were calculated.
2. Decision tree $h_j\left(x\right)$ was fitted to r_{ij}.
3. The step multiplier γ_j was computed for every leaf of $h_j\left(x\right)$.
4. Let $F_j\left(x\right) = F_{j-1}\left(x\right) + \Lambda_j \gamma_j h_j\left(x\right)$. Here Λ_j represents the rate of learning for iteration j.

USE-CASES OF NER APPLIED

The named entities recognized by the machine learning models can be used to make various estimations regarding spread of Covid-19 in India. In this paper, the extracted entities were used to find out the following: -

Top Cities and States Affected

Corona virus has adversely affected the whole India. There are some cities and states which have become the major hotspots and have maximum number of cases. These hotspots are mentioned more frequently in news headlines than areas with a smaller number of cases. The 'GPE' tag was used to extract the locations mentioned frequently in the news. From the top hotspots estimated, the areas which require more focus and preventive measures by the government were found. Figure 3 presents the working algorithm that is to be followed for finding the top 5 cities and states which are affected by Covid-19 by using the predicted entities using NER.

Figure 3. Algorithm for finding top cities and states affected by COVID-19

Algorithm: Finding top cities and states affected by COVID-19
Input: Predicted entities using NER **Output:** List of top 5 cities and states affected

Start
Step 1. For each predicted entity
    If the value of tag is GPE, #(B-GPE and I-GPE tags) **then** append in list
Step 2. For each value in list
    If city database contain value, **then** append in top cities list **else** ignore
Step 3. For each value in list
    If state database contain value, **then** append in top states list **else** ignore
Step 4. Print top cities list and top states list
End

Neighboring Cities of Hotspots

The top 5 cities which are hotspots of corona India were predicted. The cities neighboring to these hotspots are also in danger and can become future hotspots. These cities were detected so that preventive measures can be taken in time. Geographically nearest cities to each hotspot city were found. Figure 4 presents the working algorithm that is to be followed for finding the neighboring cities to the worst affected cities affected by Covid-19 by using the top 5 cities extracted from section 5.1.

Figure 4. Algorithm for finding neighboring cities of hotpots

Algorithm: Finding neighbouring cities of hotspot
Input: Top 5 cities affected by COVID-19 from section 5.1 **Output:** List of neighbouring 5 cities of hotspots which can become future hotspots

Start
For each city in top cities list
    Step 1. Calculate the distance of this city from other cities in city database
    Step 2. Sort the distances in increasing order and append in a list
    Step 3. Print first 5 values from the list
End

Figure 5. Algorithm for finding nearby hospitals and Pharmacies to the most affected cities

Algorithm: Finding nearby hospitals and Pharmacies near most affected cities
Input: Top 5 cities affected by COVID-19 from section 5.1 **Output:** List of nearby hospitals and pharmacies to the most affected cities
Start **Step 1. Create** Google Maps API Key **Step 2. Initialize** object of google_places class with API key **Step 3. Call** nearby search function of google_places class with following parameters: - a) Latitude and longitude b) Radius c) Type of place (hospitals and pharmacies) **Step 4.** Required results are obtained from the output of the function. **Print** the results **End**

Hospitals and Pharmacies Near Most Affected Cities

Hospitals and Pharmacies are playing important role in this corona virus pandemic. They are source of much relevant information for controlling the disease. So hospitals and pharmacies in and near to hotspot cities were found with the help of Goggle Maps API. Figure 5 presents the working algorithm that is to be followed for finding the nearby hospitals and pharmacies to the most affected cities by using the top 5 cities extracted from section 5.1.

Gender Based Comparison of Affected People

The entities recognized by NER from the dataset can also be used to predict the effect of COVID-19 on gender basis. Under the O- tag there are various words such as man, woman, lady etc. that describe different genders. Count of all such words was calculated and used to predict the number of males and females affected. Figure 6 presents the working algorithm that is to be followed for doing gender-based comparison of people affected by Covid-19 by using the predicted entities using NER.

Figure 6. Algorithm for gender-based comparison of affected people

Algorithm: Doing gender-based comparison of affected people
Input: Predicted entities using NER **Output:** Gender based comparison results
Start **Step 1. Get** O- tags entities from all predicted entities **Step 2. Search** for specific words indicating towards male group #(man, boy, father etc) and maintain occurrence count **Step 3. Search** for specific words indicating towards female group #(woman, girl, lady, Mother etc) and maintain occurrence count **Step 4.** Plot resultant graph #(bar, pie) to make analysis of the results obtained **End**

Age Based Comparison of Affected People

Corona virus has affected people from all age groups. To study the amount of people infected in each age group, age searching regular expression was applied on the tokens extracted from dataset of news. After that the count of people affected in each age group on the basis of the news was calculated. Figure 7 presents the working algorithm that is to be followed for doing age-based comparison of people affected by Covid-19 by using the predicted entities using NER.

Figure 7. Algorithm for age-based comparison of affected people

Algorithm: Doing age-based comparison of affected people
Input: Predicted entities using NER **Output:** Age based comparison results
Start **Step 1. Get** O- tags entities from all predicted entities **Step 2. Do** regular expression matching on O-tag entities for extracting age **Step 3. Classify** the age values obtained into different age groups #(0-20, 20-40, 40-60, 60 Above) **Step 4. Plot** resultant graph #(pie) to make analysis of the results obtained **End**

Figure 8. Algorithm for area-based comparison of affected people

Algorithm: Doing area-based comparison of affected people
Input: Predicted entities using NER **Output:** Area based comparison results

Start
Step 1.. For each predicted entity
    If the value of tag is GPE, #(B-GPE and I-GPE tags) **then** append in list
Step 2. For each value in list
    If city database contain value **then** append in urban count list **else** ignore
Step 3. For each value in list
    If village database contain value **then** append in rural count list **else** ignore
Step 4. Get O- tags entities from all predicted entities
Step 2. Search for specific words indicating towards urban group #(city, district etc) and add the occurrences count to urban count list
Step 3. Search for specific words indicating towards rural group #(rural, village, taluk etc) and add the occurrences count to rural count list
Step 4. Plot resultant graph #(bar, pie) to make analysis of the results obtained
End

Area Based Comparison of Affected People

From big cities to villages, corona virus has spread across whole nation. To do the comparative study of the effects on urban and rural areas, the occurrences of cities and villages in the news dataset were counted. Figure 8 presents the working algorithm that is to be followed for doing area-based comparison of people affected by Covid-19 by using the predicted entities using NER.

Figure 9. Binary_logloss vs. number of iterations

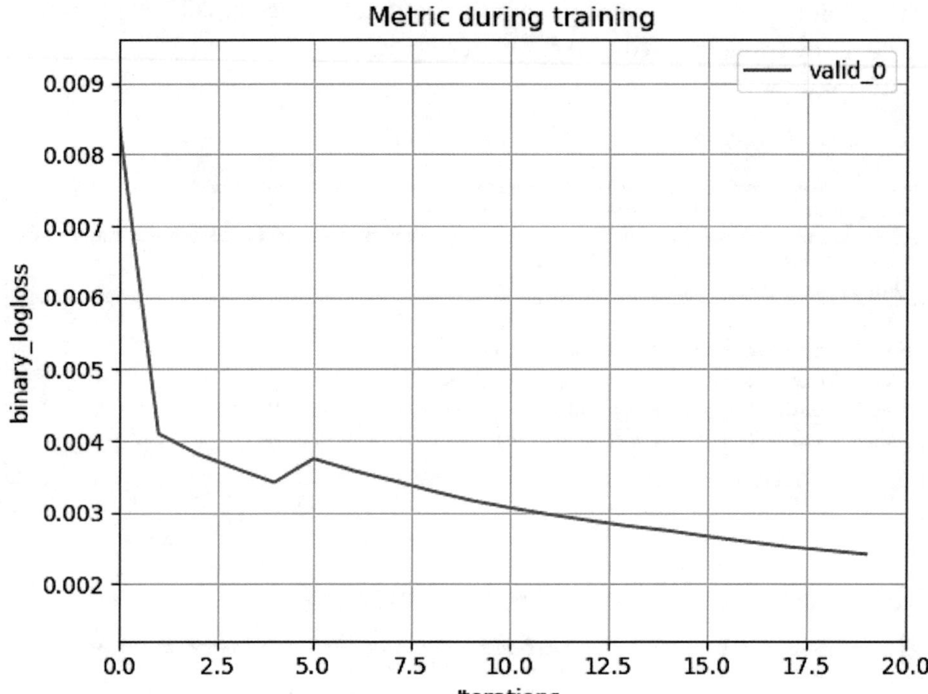

RESULTS AND OBSERVATIONS

Dataset

The news dataset consists of 2000 news headlines related to the Corona virus in India. The news was collected from 1st March 2020 to 25th May 2020 from the verified sources like www.coronatracker.com and 'Times of India' newspaper and stored as a database in the .csv file. After performing tokenization, a total of 41,169 tokens categorized into 35 different tags were extracted from the news dataset. The extracted tokens and tags were further used to make feature vector dataset for training the Machine Learning Models.

Experimental Results

The spaCy model recognized 35 different tags. The count of how many times each of the 35 tags occurred in the 2000 news headlines database was also made. Total 41,169 tokens were extracted out of which maximum tokens belonged to O-Tag i.e., 32391 tokens accounting nearly 78.67% of the total tokens in the database. The second most frequent tag was the GPE tag counting to 2381 tokens which is approximately 5.78% of the total tokens of the database. It was observed that several tags only occurred in very small number in the entire database like B-Law, B-Event, B-Language, etc.

CRF gave the best results among the 4 algorithms with accuracy of 97%. O-tag was in majority i.e., 78% of the total tags. F1-score of 95%, recall of 97% and precision of 95% were calculated through CRF. Thus, it proved efficient both in F1-score and precision.

In AdaBoost implementation, boosting algorithm SAMME was used, as it is specific method to deal with multi classification problems. Decision Tree was used as the base classifier. Accuracy obtained was around 82%. Recall of 82% and F1-score of 76% were obtained. CRF performed better than AdaBoost in both recall and F1-score.

Figure 10. LSTM Model Accuracy

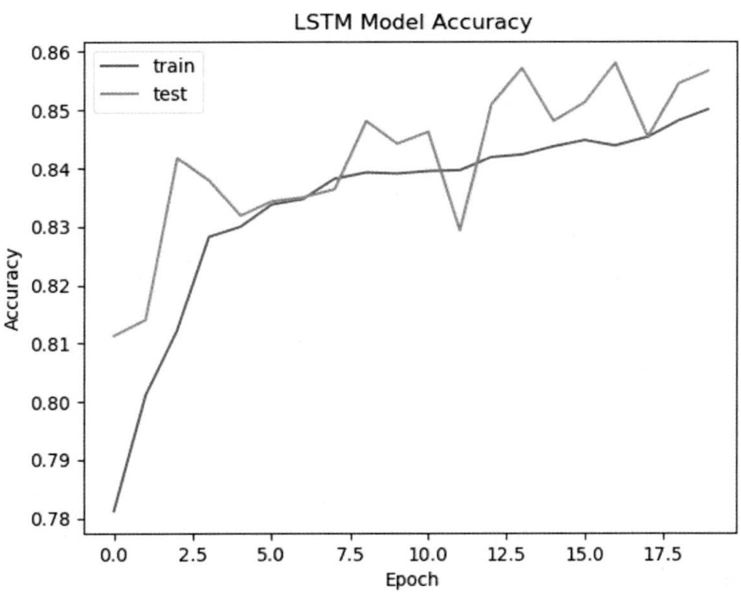

Another boosting algorithm lightGBM was used with boosting type gbdt (gradient boosting decision tree). Accuracy obtained was 90.5%, better than AdaBoost. Root mean square error of prediction was 8.75. Figure 9 presents the binary_logloss graph plotted against the number of iterations. On x-axis there is no. of iterations and on y-axis binary_logloss is plotted. From the graph it can be inferred that, binary_logloss decreased rapidly from 0.008 to 0.0035 as the number of iterations increased to 3. After that there was slight increase in loss between 3rd and 5th iteration. Further there was gentle slope of decrease of loss with increase in iterations.

Sequential **LSTM** model with 2 layers gave accuracy of **85%** using sparse categorical cross entropy loss function and rmsprop optimizer. Softmax was used as activation function. Model's validation accuracy obtained was 85.6%. Figure 10 presents the LSTM model accuracy graph plotted against number of epochs. On x-axis, there is number of epochs and on y-axis accuracy is plotted. For the training dataset, initially accuracy increased rapidly to 83% up to 4th epoch, after that there was gradual increase in accuracy up to 20th epoch. For test dataset, at some instances there were sudden increase and decrease but overall, the graph was increasing with num of epochs.

Figure 11 presents the LSTM model loss graph plotted against number of epochs. On y-axis, there is loss and on x–axis number of epochs. For train set, loss decreased rapidly from 1.1 to 0.7 up to 3rd epoch. After that there was gradual decrease in loss up to 20th epoch. For test set, the graph was overall decreasing with some exceptions.

Figure 11. LSTM Model Loss

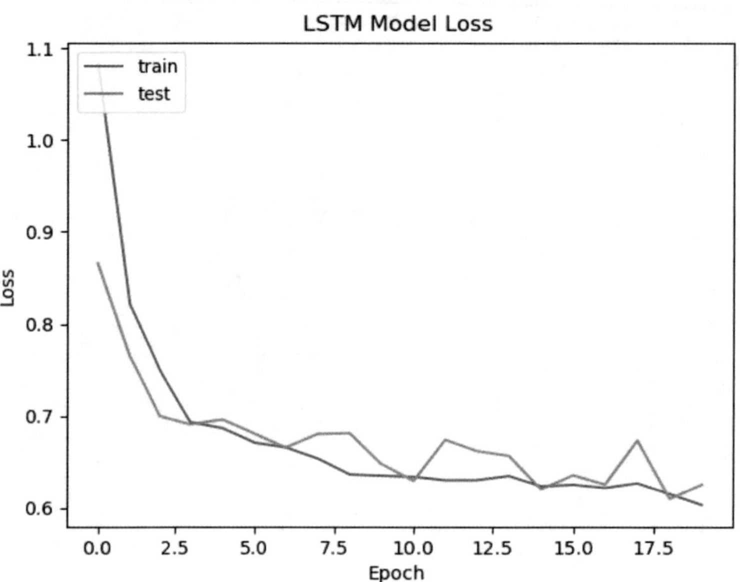

Table 2 presents the results obtained through various algorithms used. It is observed that CRF gave the best accuracy of 97% followed by LigthGBM 90.5%. LSTM gave satisfactory accuracy of 85%. The least accuracy was given by AdaBoost.

Table 2. Results of various algorithms used

S. No.	Algorithm	Accuracy (%)
1.	LSTM	85
2.	CRF	97
3.	AdaBoost	82
4.	LightGBM	90.5

Corona Related Prediction Results

The entities recognized by the machine learning algorithms from the news headlines of Coronavirus have lot of important information in them that can be extracted. With the help of most mentioned tokens of GPE and other tags following predictions are made: -

Figure 12. Gender based comparison of affected people

Corona news based on gender

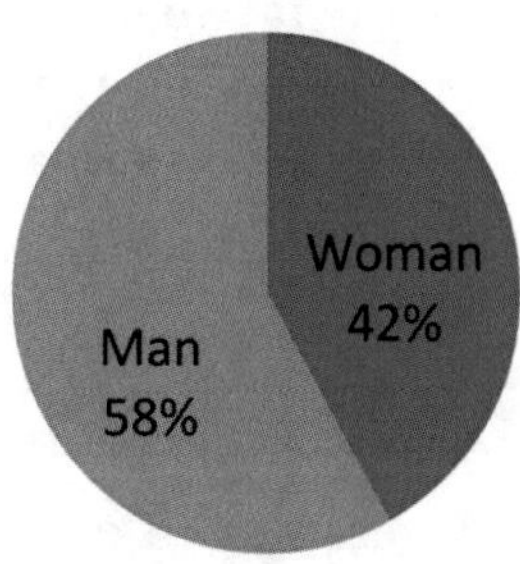

- **5 Cities most mentioned in news**: -

Most mentioned cities in news have high probability to be worst affected by the virus. The top 5 hotspots according to prediction are:

Delhi, Pune, Mumbai, Chennai, and Ahmedabad

- **5 states most mentioned in news:** -

From the most mentioned states in Corona news, it is concluded that the following states are most affected by the virus:

Rajasthan, Maharashtra, Gujarat, Uttar Pradesh, and Madhya Pradesh.

Figure 13. Area based comparison of affected people

Corona news based on area

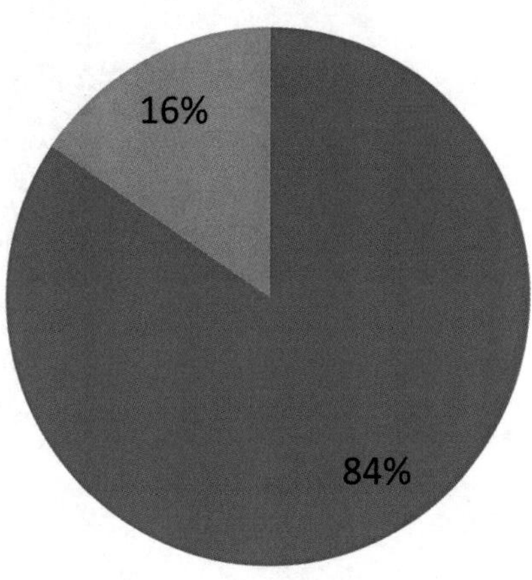

- **Gender-based comparison:** -

The effect of virus on different genders was studied with the help of count of words like man, woman, girl, boy etc. in the tokens of 'others' tag. From the count, it is inferred that male population is more affected as compared to females. Figure 12 presents the pie chart of affected man and woman. The chart shows that man population accounts 58% of total and woman population have share of 42%. Conclusion drawn is men are affected more than women.

- **Area-based comparison**: -

The spread of virus in urban and rural areas was observed, with the help of tokens having 'GPE' tags and 'others' tag. From the total urban and rural count, it is inferred that urban areas and people are affected far more than rural areas. Figure 13 presents that urban areas have 84% contribution and rural areas account 16% of total affected people. Conclusion drawn is urban areas are affected far more than rural areas.

- **Age-based comparison**

Corona virus has affected people from all age-groups. With the help age values mentioned in the news, the percentage of affected people in each category was calculated. Figure 14 presents that age-based comparison done. It is observed that most affected age groups are 20-40 and 40-60. Age group 20-40 accounts for 33% and 40-60 have 33% contribution. People above 60 and less than 20 contribute for 29% and 5% respectively.

Figure 14. Age based comparison of affected people

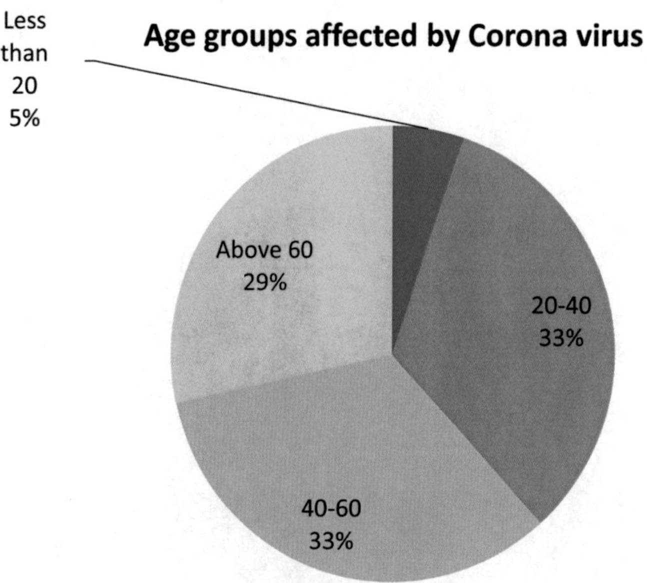

Evaluation of Our Approach

LightGBM was the fastest among the four algorithms that are implemented as it uses histogram-based algorithms which speeds up the training process and reduces the memory usage. In each iteration, model fit the negative gradient and learns about the decision trees. LightGBM model aim is to reduce the complexity of building the histogram (O (Data * Feature)) by down sampling the data and the features using GOSS (gradient based one side sampling) and EFB (exclusive feature bundling). This reduces the complexity to (O (DataNew * Bundle)) where DataNew < Data and Bundle << Feature. Performance of Adaboost depends on the data and weak learners. Complexity of Adaboost is trivially O(TF), where T is the number of weak learners and F is the runtime of the weak learners in use. It runs in acceptable real time but proved less accurate for multiclass classification. These boosting algorithms implemented proved to be efficient in runtime. On the other hand, CRF which proved to be best in terms of accuracy but required high computational time compared to the boosting algorithms. CRF require an iterative process to adjust the weights for the features. As there are large no. of features and many classes, CRF classifier need a lot of memory for training process which makes it difficult to retrain it for new samples. Thus, to decrease the memory usage limited memory quasi-Newton (L-BFGS) optimizer is used. This optimizer maintains several past guesses. This improved its runtime performance to some extent. LSTM model required largest runtime and proved very slow as they are very difficult to be trained because they require very high memory bandwidth. LSTM requires 4 linear layers per cell to run and that too for each sequence time step. Thus, generally LSTM ensemble is used for obtaining faster runtime performance.

ADVANTAGES OF OUR APPROACH

Named Entity Recognition is an excellent technique for processing natural language. NER helps to extract the important and informative part in the large text. This technique is very helpful for recognizing the main entities of the data. NER has been effectively used in various fields. Using this approach for the news headlines has come out be very useful and efficient. As range of our dataset was wide, NER worked decently well on it. The token extraction and tagging by spaCy model was very accurate and helped in training the ML models effectively.

The Machine Learning models used for multi-class classification also worked efficiently on our dataset. CRF (Conditional Random Fields) is the combination of statistical and discriminative models and is best suited for predicting tasks in which current prediction is affected by its neighbor's state. CRF gave the excellent accuracy of 97% and F1-score of 95%. So CRF proved to be the best among other algorithms. LSTM is deep learning model used for processing data sequence. LSTM networks are efficient in learning dependencies which are long term. The model gave accuracy of 85%. Adaptive Boosting or Ada-boost is an ensemble boosting type classifier. It is combination of various weak classifiers that are combined to achieve high accuracy and get a strong classifier. The boosting algorithm SAMME is specific to deal with multi classification problems. The model gave decent accuracy of 82%, which can be improved further. LigthGBM is a framework for gradient boosting. LightGBM uses learning algorithms that are tree based. It has advantages of fast training speed, low memory usage, high accuracy and efficiency and large-scale data handling capacity. LightGBM was very fast as its complexity is low because of its technique of down sampling data and features. Model gave good accuracy of 90.5% and root mean square error of prediction was 8.75. So, the different neural network models, ensemble algorithms and discriminative model applied on our dataset worked really well and helped effectively in making accurate predictions.

CONCLUSION AND FUTURE WORK

COVID-19 news headlines were taken from verified sources and dataset was prepared consisting of 2000 headlines for recognizing named entities. Further the SpaCy module was used to classify the tokens extracted from these news headlines into various tags that were pre-defined. Then, various machine learning classification models such as LSTM, CRF and boosting algorithms such as AdaBoost and LightGBM were used to predict the accuracy.

Further comparison of different machine learning approaches was done to achieve good results and high precision. Highest accuracy was obtained through CRF i.e., 97% and lowest was obtained through AdaBoost i.e., 82%.

Further the output from these models was applied to get various types of relevant and necessary information related to COVID-19. Various kinds of comparisons like which gender has been more affected by the virus, which age groups have been infected with corona virus more, whether urban or rural areas have seen more spread of the virus, etc. were performed. Further based on the news in the dataset, the worst affected cities and states were found out. Also, the nearby cities that could become future hotspots and nearby hospitals and pharmacies to these hotspots were also predicted. Thus, enough information was gathered from the news headlines dataset.

In our approach, news headlines dataset of 2000 news was collected from various sources. However, observing the scale of the spread of coronavirus across the globe, the news related to the virus has not seized to stop yet. Till the time this virus keeps on affecting lives of the people around the globe, this news dataset can be expanded to get more news regarding the virus and hence, more relevant information can be extracted from the news data.

For future study, the approach can be improved by designing more optimized deep neural network structure or hybrid network structure. Thus, more specialized deep neural networks could be developed.

More specialized type of data can be taken for deriving useful applications related to the disease for making important predictions like in our approach we tried age based, gender based, location-based classification. Thus, NER could be useful in more such domains. Also, the application can be improvised for Bio-NER instead of simple NER where biomedical entities could be extracted which could have rich functionalities to be beneficial for studies on biomedical side or social side.

REFERENCES

Aitslab/corona. (2021). Retrieved 23 March 2021, from https://github.com/Aitslab/corona

Cao, Y., Miao, Q., Liu, J., & Gao, L. (2013). Advance and Prospects of AdaBoost Algorithm. *Acta Automatica Sinica*, *39*(6), 745–758. doi:10.1016/S1874-1029(13)60052-X

Chang, C.-H., Kayed, M., Girgis, M., & Shaalan, K. (2006). A Survey of Web Information Extraction Systems. *IEEE Transactions on Knowledge and Data Engineering*, *18*(10), 1411–1428. doi:10.1109/TKDE.2006.152

Chiu, J., & Nichols, E. (2016). Named Entity Recognition with Bidirectional LSTM-CNNs. *Transactions of the Association for Computational Linguistics*, *4*, 357–370. doi:10.1162/tacl_a_00104

Coronavirus, I. (2021). *11,727,733 Cases and 160,437 Deaths - Worldometer*. Retrieved 23 March 2021, from https://www.worldometers.info/coronavirus/country/india/

COVID-19 Corona Tracker. (2021). Retrieved 23 March 2021, from https://www.coronatracker.com/

Das, S. (2020). *Prediction of COVID-19 disease progression in India: Under the effect of national lockdown.* arXiv preprint arXiv:2004.03147.

Eftimov, T., Koroušić Seljak, B., & Korošec, P. (2017). A rule-based named-entity recognition method for knowledge extraction of evidence-based dietary recommendations. *PLoS One*, *12*(6), e0179488. doi:10.1371/journal.pone.0179488

Hastie, T., Rosset, S., Zhu, J., & Zou, H. (2009). Multi-class AdaBoost. *Statistics and Its Interface*, *2*(3), 349–360. doi:10.4310ii.2009.v2.n3.a8

Jiang, M., Chen, Y., Liu, M., Rosenbloom, S., Mani, S., Denny, J., & Xu, H. (2011). A study of machine-learning-based approaches to extract clinical entities and their assertions from discharge summaries. *Journal of the American Medical Informatics Association*, *18*(5), 601–606. doi:10.1136/amiajnl-2011-000163

Jie, Z., & Lu, W. (2019). *Dependency-guided LSTM-CRF for named entity recognition.* arXiv preprint arXiv:1909.10148.

Jonnalagadda, S., Cohen, T., Wu, S., Liu, H., & Gonzalez, G. (2013). Using Empirically Constructed Lexical Resources for Named Entity Recognition. *Biomedical Informatics Insights*. Advance online publication. doi:10.4137/bii.s11664

Kadiyala, A., & Kumar, A. (2018). Applications of python to evaluate the performance of decision tree-based boosting algorithms. *Environmental Progress & Sustainable Energy*, *37*(2), 618–623. doi:10.1002/ep.12888

Ke, G., Meng, Q., Finley, T., Wang, T., Chen, W., Ma, W., ... Liu, T. Y. (2017). Lightgbm: A highly efficient gradient boosting decision tree. *Advances in Neural Information Processing Systems*, *30*, 3146–3154.

Labs, D. (2021). *District Data Labs - Named Entity Recognition and Classification for Entity Extraction.* Retrieved 23 March 2021, from https://districtdatalabs.silvrback.com/named-entity-recognition-and-classification-for-entity-extraction

Lin, Y. C., & Hung, P. H. (2007). *U.S. Patent No. 7,171,350*. Washington, DC: U.S. Patent and Trademark Office.

Mansouri, A., Affendey, L. S., & Mamat, A. (2008). Named entity recognition approaches. *International Journal of Computer Science and Network Security*, *8*(2), 339–344.

Marrero, M., Urbano, J., Sánchez-Cuadrado, S., Morato, J., & Gómez-Berbís, J. (2013). Named Entity Recognition: Fallacies, challenges and opportunities. *Computer Standards & Interfaces*, *35*(5), 482–489. doi:10.1016/j.csi.2012.09.004

Mayfield, J., McNamee, P., & Piatko, C. (2003). Named entity recognition using hundreds of thousands of features. In *Proceedings of the seventh conference on Natural language learning at HLT-NAACL 2003* (pp. 184-187). Academic Press.

Pandey, G., Chaudhary, P., Gupta, R., & Pal, S. (2020). *SEIR and Regression Model based COVID-19 outbreak predictions in India.* arXiv preprint arXiv:2004.00958.

Papacharissi, Z., & Rubin, A. (2000). Predictors of Internet Use. *Journal of Broadcasting & Electronic Media*, *44*(2), 175–196. doi:10.120715506878jobem4402_2

Rashed, S. K., Frid, J., & Aits, S. (2020). *English dictionaries, gold and silver standard corpora for biomedical natural language processing related to SARS-CoV-2 and COVID-19.* arXiv preprint arXiv:2003.09865.

Recognition, N. E. (2021). *Applications and Use Cases.* Retrieved 23 March 2021, from https://towardsdatascience.com/named-entity-recognition-applications-and-use-cases-acdbf57d595e

Singhal, T. (2020). A Review of Coronavirus Disease-2019 (COVID-19). *Indian Journal of Pediatrics*, *87*(4), 281–286. doi:10.100712098-020-03263-6

Sitaram, S., Chandu, K. R., Rallabandi, S. K., & Black, A. W. (2019). *A survey of code-switched speech and language processing.* arXiv preprint arXiv:1904.00784.

Soderland, S. (1997, August). Learning to Extract Text-Based Information from the World Wide Web. *KDD: Proceedings / International Conference on Knowledge Discovery & Data Mining. International Conference on Knowledge Discovery & Data Mining*, *97*, 251–254.

Thomas, A., & Sangeetha, S. (2019). An innovative hybrid approach for extracting named entities from unstructured text data. *Computational Intelligence*, *35*(4), 799–826. doi:10.1111/coin.12214

Times Of India. (2021). Retrieved 23 March 2021, from https://epaper.timesgroup.com/TOI/TimesOfIndia/index.html?a=c

Tkachenko, M., & Simanovsky, A. (2012, September). Named entity recognition: Exploring features. In KONVENS (pp. 118-127). Academic Press.

Wang, X., Liu, W., Chauhan, A., Guan, Y., & Han, J. (2020). *Automatic textual evidence mining in covid-19 literature.* arXiv preprint arXiv:2004.12563.

Wang, X., Song, X., Guan, Y., Li, B., & Han, J. (2020). *Comprehensive named entity recognition on cord-19 with distant or weak supervision.* arXiv preprint arXiv:2003.12218.

Yadav, V., & Bethard, S. (2019). *A survey on recent advances in named entity recognition from deep learning models.* arXiv preprint arXiv:1910.11470.

Chapter 13
Security Issues in Fog Computing and ML-Based Solutions

Himanshu Sahu
https://orcid.org/0000-0003-1202-6286
University of Petroleum and Energy Studies, India

Gaytri
University of Petroleum and Energy Studies, India

ABSTRACT

IoT requires data processing, which is provided by the cloud and fog computing. Fog computing shifts centralized data processing from the cloud data center to the edge, thereby supporting faster response due to reduced communication latencies. Its distributed architecture raises security and privacy issues; some are inherited from the cloud, IoT, and network whereas others are unique. Securing fog computing is equally important as securing cloud computing and IoT infrastructure. Security solutions used for cloud computing and IoT are similar but are not directly applicable in fog scenarios. Machine learning techniques are useful in security such as anomaly detection, intrusion detection, etc. So, to provide a systematic study, the chapter will cover fog computing architecture, parallel technologies, security requirements attacks, and security solutions with a special focus on machine learning techniques.

INTRODUCTION

Cybersecurity has become the highest priority and focus for any industry, organization, or government agency that adapted automation or smart infrastructure. With increased internet connectivity (including human to human as well as machine to machine) and dependency on the machine.), the risk has been increased manifold. Internet of things(IoT)(Tan and Wang 2010)-based smart infrastructure has changed the way of living, manufacturing, or the service industry. IoT is not only about micro-controllers, sensors, actuators, and other circuitry but also related to data processing. The data center processes the sensor

DOI: 10.4018/978-1-7998-3299-7.ch013

and device-generated data, to get insights from it so that it can be used for control or automation tasks, performance enhancement, management, and monitoring of the system.

Data transmitted to the cloud data center for processing usually consists of sensitive data that should be protected from unauthorized access. IoT as a business enabler, backbone of smart cities, industry 4.0 and smart home creates ease but in turn, exposes infrastructure (such as home, manufacturing unit, or power plant) control to the internet. Therefore, IoT security has become a very crucial component of cybersecurity, which includes the protection of data and control to unauthorized access.

The Number of IoT devices is growing exponentially which generates a large amount of data that is following the 3V's (Volume, Velocity, and Variety) can be classified as big data (Soia, Konnikova, and Konnikov 2019). Fog computing(Cisco White Paper: Fog Computing and the Internet of Things: Extend the Cloud to Where the Things Are What You Will Learn 2015) (Vaquero and Rodero-Merino 2014) came into the picture to make more efficient IoT infrastructure by reducing the dependency on a data center for data processing. Fog Computing provides midway data processing thus thwarts unnecessary data movement to the cloud. So Fog computing provides faster response and more secure IoT infrastructure to support localized processing of data. However, the distributed architecture makes it vulnerable to new types of attacks since maintaining trust and authentication is a challenging task. So, along with providing more secure IoT infrastructure, Fog computing adds new challenges related to security which consists of a mixed bag of old and new security threats. Therefore, it is obligatory to secure the fog nodes and data processed on the fog nodes from the adversary.

The traditional methods will not be sufficient for securing the Fog computing environment due to the dynamic nature, a large number of nodes, dependencies on the 3rd party vendors, distributed control, and a huge amount of generated data. The Fog computing threats can be classified as security and privacy threats. The requirements of a secure Fog computing environment are trust, authentication, protected data storage, reliable communication, data privacy, and confidentiality. To satisfy these requirements techniques such as trust management, encryption, and authentication are required along with intrusion detection.

Machine learning-based security solutions are very efficient in the scenario where a huge amount of data is present to process as well as attack patterns may be unknown (Xin et al. 2018). Since in Fog environment, the data is large so Machine learning techniques can be used to identify the anomaly, traffic classification, or nodes authenticity. Both supervised and unsupervised techniques are capable to provide security solutions. Along with machine learning, deep learning-based solutions such as LSTM are used to create intrusion detection systems.

So to provide the holistic view of fog computing security issues and solutions the chapter organization is as follows: first Fog computing is discussed, then security threats related to fog computing will be discussed and finally, the solutions will be discussed including machine learning solutions. The chapter organization is as follows in section 2 fog computing is discussed with its characteristics, in section 3 parallel technology are discussed, in section 4 3 types of fog architecture in detail, in section 5 security issues and solutions are discussed, and in section 6 machine learning-based solutions and finally conclusion is provided.

FOG COMPUTING

Fog Computing (Iorga et al. 2018) (Vaquero and Rodero-Merino 2014) is a new computing model to support the Internet of Things (IoT)(Li, Xu, and Zhao 2015)(Tan and Wang 2010) and Cloud Computing(Bohn et al. 2011) in order to improve the quality of service (QoS) of IoT infrastructure. It attempts to amend the centralized processing of data generated from IoT devices in the data center. It passes the data processing towards the edge of the network. Fog computing thus reduces the communication latency, which is the bottleneck of centralized processing and thereby providing support for real-time interactive applications as well as decreasing the load from a cloud data center. It facilitates computing at the edge devices (i.e. devices located near the edge of the network). Due to low communication, latencies and location awareness fog computing helps in creating time and location-dependent services that provide better user experience and customizable applications. Fog computing provides cloud services models (Bohn et al. 2011) such as Infrastructure as a service(IaaS), Platform as a service (PaaS), and Storage as a service (SaaS) at the edge devices and thereby provide the facility of running the data processing applications on the end devices such as access points, switches, and smart devices.

Fog computing provides compute, storage, control, communication services (in the same way as provided by cloud computing) which can run on the edge network devices (Bonomi 2011) (Kai, Cong, and Tao 2016) (Atlam, Walters, and Wills 2018). Fog computing tries to process the data in the proximity where it is generated. It reduces the communication overhead by size and frequency at the cost of increased computing requirements at the network edge. The data is processed locally with the proper support of intelligent devices.

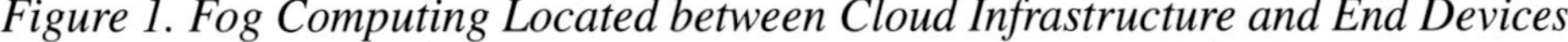

Figure 1. Fog Computing Located between Cloud Infrastructure and End Devices

Fog computing is different from cloud computing in terms of its proximity to the end-user, the dense and geographically distributed nodes, and the facility of mobility (Flavio Bonomi, Rodolfo Milito, Jiang Zhu 2012). On one hand, fog nodes are geographically distributed and located near to users and can be mobile whereas cloud computing is centrally and remotely located from the end-user. Figure 1 shows the location of fog in between the end devices and the cloud data center. The location of the fog node is near to the end devices, so it receives and collects the data from the end devices. The fog node can process the data by itself or forward the processing request to the data center.

Need for Fog Computing

- ***Evolution of IoT:*** IoT starts emerging from the last decade as a technology for automation in smart homes, industries, and smart cities. IoT devices (such as sensor nodes) generate data that is processed for automation and analytics. The number of devices was 15.41 billion in 2015, has reached 20.35 billion in 2017, and is expected to be 30.73 billion in 2020 and 75.44 billion worldwide by 2025 (Statista Research Department 2019). These colossal number of devices are generating large among of data with high velocity, variety, and variability are also known as big data (NIST Big Data Public Working Group 2015). In the Cloud computing model, centralized processing is used so it requires movement of the input data to the data center and results back from the data center. Thus, centralized processing is becoming inefficient for IoT, due to the frequent bidirectional communication causing transmission delay, communication overhead, and server overloading. Therefore, a need to process a large portion of the data locally is created which can improve the efficiency of the IoT infrastructure.
- ***Limitation of Current Computing Paradigm:*** In the current Cloud computing paradigm, the problem arises due to the single point of processing of data at the data center and the physical distance between the user and data center. This causes increased communication costs as well as latency. Cloud data centers employ virtualization techniques (such as VMware(VMware n.d.) and Docker(Docker n.d.)) to serves as many clients as requested but located at some specific places with all the required resources. The efficiency of these data centers is not questionable, but the data generated from the IoT devices is having high volume and velocity, which is causing the data center to choke resulting in a poor quality of service (QoS) and response time. As provided by (Kim and Schulzrinne 2013) it's evident that the latency of the result increases with the distance since it depends on network speed and distance. QoS and response time are directly related to the user experience so a new solution that can improve QoS is required and resolve the issue of centralized processing.

Fog computing can solve these problems by providing computing at the edge devices and thereby offload the data center and better QoS to the end-user.

Fog Computing vs. Edge Computing

The terms fog computing and edge computing are being interchangeably used but they are not the same having some similarities and some differences. Both Edge and Fog computing try to localize the computation services at the end devices, which are provided by the cloud data center. The Difference is that edge computing is focused on localizing the cloud services whereas fog computing is an extension or decision node where fog node decides whether the processing can be done at the local i.e. the fog node or the centralized cloud data center. Therefore, edge computing tries to localize the cloud services whereas fog computing extends the cloud services at the user end. Apart from this Fog computing supports dynamic configuration and intelligent logic whereas edge computing has fixed and simple logic associated with them.

Characteristics of Fog Computing

Fog computing (Gupta et al. 2017)(Vaquero and Rodero-Merino 2014) is a computing paradigm with numerous nodes mostly wireless, sometimes autonomous, and distribute (geographically distant). These cooperating nodes communicate and synchronize among them to carry out storage/processing tasks or provide a platform for the IoT devices. The Fog node can transfer the data to the cloud or process itself. Fog computing can offload security services (authentication, encryption, etc.) from the cloud. Thus, Fog computing located in the proximity of the edge network (and between cloud and things) offloads the data center and provides context and location-aware, real-time application development for high QoS and secure IoT architecture. Based on the above discussion, the fog computing characteristics are described below in details. These characteristics in contrast with cloud computing:

1. **Low Latency and location Awareness:** Fog computing provides the services at the edge of the network, so the communication latency is lessened, and the results are received in reduced time i.e. Response time is improved. The location is known with the fog node, so the applications are running on a fog node are aware of the client location. The location-aware feature helps in providing better user-oriented services.
2. **Widespread Geographical Distribution:** In contrast with centrally located data centers of cloud computing the Fog nodes are widespread and geographically distributed. These geographically distributed nodes can work together to process a large volume of data locally. This geographical distribution also covers the underlying distributed IoT infrastructure.
3. **Mobility:** Fog nodes consist of IoT devices that can be fixed or mobile but are mostly mobile thus supports mobility with the end device associated with the node.
4. **Heterogeneity:** Fog computing includes various heterogeneous data generation and processing nodes. Different types of sensors, embedded systems, actuators, storage, and compute services nodes together create a Fog computing environment.

Figure 2. Characteristics of Fog Computing

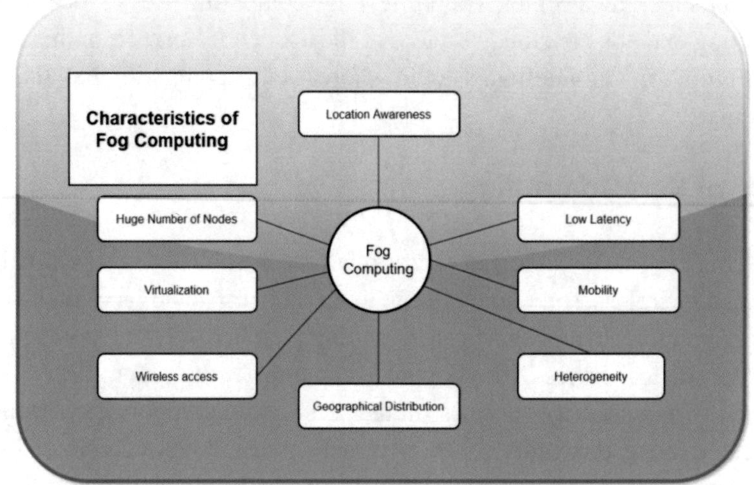

5. **A huge number of nodes:** The Fog computing environment generally consists of many nodes comprising sensors, actuators, embedded systems, communication, and cluster nodes. This large number of nodes can process a large amount of data locally in the coordination of each other.
6. **Virtualization:** It uses excessive virtualization to provide different services with the help of technologies such as Software-defined network (SDN), Software-defined radio, and Network function virtualization (NFV) (Sahu and Hungyo 2018).
7. **Role of wireless access:** Fog computing mostly uses wireless access in its communication and protocols, which provides support to mobility and ease of scalability.
8. **Real-time Applications:** Fog computing is best suited for real-time applications because it reduces the communication delay of a network so the results of data processing will not be delayed. So real-time applications will be easily supported by fog computing.

Following the above characteristics of fog computing is defined as (Flavio Bonomi, Rodolfo Milito, Jiang Zhu 2012) (Gupta et al. 2017) (Vaquero and Rodero-Merino 2014)

Def. "Fog Computing is a highly virtualized computing paradigm having huge numbers of heterogeneous nodes (consisting of IoT devices, compute, storage and IoT) ubiquitous and distributed communicating with each other to provide cloud services near to edge devices to offload cloud data center which is used to run real-time applications with low latency and location awareness."

FOG COMPUTING AND PARALLEL TECHNOLOGIES

Cloud Computing, Mist Computing(Uehara 2018), IOT are parallel technologies with fog computing. Cloud computing provides centralized processing of data whereas fog computing provides distributed computing at the edge of the network. Mist Computing is the extreme edge of a network having sensors and embedded systems and they collect and feed the data into the fog. Fog computing and all the parallel technologies have been discussed in detail below:

Fog Computing and IoT

IoT devices are generating a huge volume of data with variety as well as velocity. Not only that the number of devices is growing exponentially each year.

The number of devices was 15.41 billion in 2015, has reached 20.35 billion in 2017 and is expected to be 30.73 billion in 2020 and 75.44 billion worldwide by 2025. (Statista Research Department 2019)

Due to this ever-increasing data generated by IoT devices, cloud servers are not able to cater to the increasing requirement of cloud servers. The communication delay, limitation of bandwidth, and processing latency; cause the reduction of QoS in terms of response time. The IoT devices cluster node can also become a fog node for processing the data near the point at which data is generated.

Fog Computing and Cloud Computing

Fog computing is providing cloud services at the end devices. Cloud Computing provides infrastructure, platform, and storage using service models like IaaS, PaaS, and SaaS. The same way fog provides support for all three services but with the proximity to the edge devices where the data is being generated. The fog nodes reduce the communication burden to the cloud by significantly reducing the amount of data required to send to the cloud. Fog nodes decide whether to process the data locally or send it to the data center for processing.

Fog Computing and Software Defined Network

Software-Defined Network (SDN) (Sahu and Hungyo 2018) and Software-defined Storage (SDS) (Sahu and Singh 2018) is an evolving network paradigm that provides an adaptable, dynamic, and programmable network and storage. The SDN decouples the control and data plane of the networking devices and keeps the control plane at a centralized server. The SDN can help in optimizing the Fog network by providing an adaptable and dynamic network layer. There is also an architectural correspondence between both nodes both use two layers of architecture with distinct data and control planes. Thus, employing the SDN concepts in fog computing can improve the performance provided by fog computing. SDN can also help support security services by providing real-time traffic monitoring and blocking (Khan, Parkinson, and Qin 2017). SDS can be used to efficiently store and process the data generated at edge devices.

Fog Computing and Network Function Virtualization

Network Function Virtualization (NFV) (Sahu and Hungyo 2018) is an emerging trend in networking that virtualizes the network devices and functions by software technologies. Fog computing can exploit NFV to make the edge computing functionality to be virtualized. (Pushpa and Raj 2018) With the help of the NFV virtualization technique (such as hypervisor), virtual fog nodes can be created which can provide better resource sharing and utilization. Virtual fog nodes provide and scalable and high-performance system resulting in better real-time performance.

Fog Computing and Mobile Communication Network

Fog computing and Edge computing show a promising role in future mobile communication technologies such as 5G networks. The QoS promised by the 5G networks can't be delivered due to the limitation of current cloud data centers. If data generated from all IoT nodes are submitted to the cloud data center, the network will become congested and network performance will be decreased. To avoid bandwidth wastage and performance degradation scenario, it is crucial to hosting a data processing node near to the data generating nodes, So that high bandwidth of 5G can be efficiently used and only a limited amount of data will be reaching, the cloud to reduce the data center load (Gupta et al. 2017).

Fog Computing and Mist Computing

Mist computing (Iorga et al. 2018)(Uehara 2018) has been conceptualized as a lightweight fog computing environment consisting of a microcontroller that can feed data to the fog nodes. The mist computing nodes are the part of the network topology, which helps in bringing fog computing nearer to the edge devices. As compared to the fog node, mist nodes are nearer to the devices and have lesser computation power as compared to fog computing.

THE ARCHITECTURE OF FOG COMPUTING

Based on the reviewed literature there are two possible types of fog computing architecture, which will be discussed, are 3-tier architecture, 2-layer architecture, and 6-layer architecture. The 3-tier architecture deals with fog computing sandwiched between the cloud and things whereas the two-layer architecture deals with the internals of fog computing. The 6-layer fog architecture provides the functionality-wise layered architecture for the fog. Each architecture is described in detail below.

Three-Tier Architecture

The 3-tier architecture of fog computing (Hu et al. 2017) consists of the following 3 layers as a terminal layer, fog layer, and cloud layer as shown in figure 3. This architecture directly maps with the location of the fog computing between the cloud and end devices. Each layer is described as follows:

1. **Device Layer:** The device layer is the lowest layer of the hierarchy at which IoT devices (such as sensors, embedded systems, smart devices, smart vehicles, mobile devices, etc.) are present. This layer is closest to the real environment where actuators are also placed. This layer is the point where data is generated, and it is also closed to the end-user. This layer can also be termed as a sensing layer since all the sensors are placed in a geo-distributed location. The role of this layer is to collect the data and forward it to the upper layers.

Figure 3. Three-tier architecture of Fog Computing

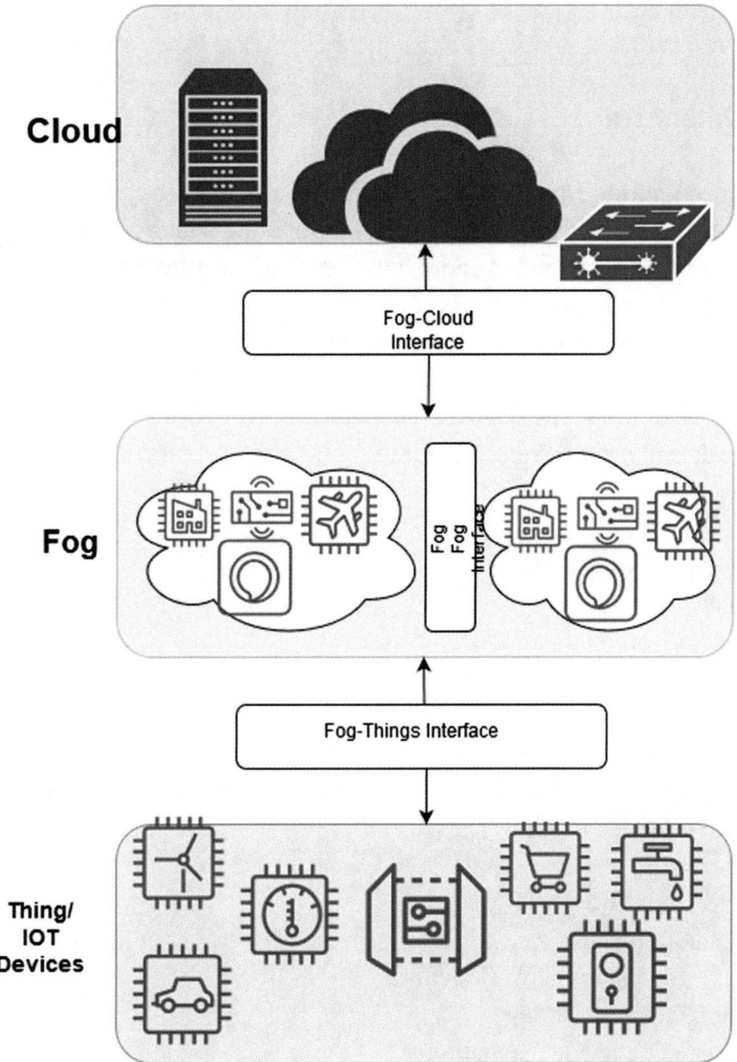

2. **Fog Layer:** The fog layer is the layer sandwiched between the Device layer and Cloud layer. In the fog layer, Fog nodes are present including communication devices and fog serves. Its location is such that it receives the data from the device/sensing layer. After receiving the data from the device layer, it can process it locally on a fog node or if required forwards it to the cloud layer. This layer is having communication as well as compute and store facilities. The fog nodes are geo disseminated in vast numbers and end devices can easily connect to these fog nodes to become part of the fog computing. These fog nodes are also directly connected to the cloud data center that is used to send and receive data from the cloud data center.
3. **Cloud Layer:** The top layer of the hierarchy consists of a cloud layer having high-performance servers for data processing and large storage for storing enormous data. This layer also provides

API for different fog applications. The cloud layer receives the data from the fog nodes and returns results to the fog node.

Two-Layer Architecture

Fog computing is a computing framework for storage, computing as well as networking. The 3-layer architecture is the most simplified architecture for fog computing which ideally depicts fog computing as an intermediate between IoT and cloud. A more functional architecture can be described by the two-layer architecture with well-defined responsibilities of each layer. Inspired by the SDN paradigm (Pushpa and Raj 2018) the two-layer architecture decouples the Data Plane and the Control Plane which bifurcates the functionality into two parts.

Data Plane and the Control plane (Chiang and Zhang 2016)

Data plane: The data plane is responsible for the collection and processing of data. The responsibilities are listed below.

1. Local content and bandwidth management
2. Cache at the network edge
3. Direct client-client communications
4. Support of Cloudlets and micro datacenters

Control plane: Control plane in fog computing is responsible for the management and control tasks such as content management, resource allocation, network configuration, and management, etc. Some examples of tasks are provided below:

1. Content Management Over the Top
2. Fog-RAN or radiofrequency access
3. Client-based heterogeneous network control
4. Customer-controlled cloud storage
5. Session management and edge signaling
6. Data analytics of Edge data collected.
7. Session management

Six Layer Architecture (Atlam, Walters, and Wills 2018)

The six-layer architecture shown in Figure 4 consist of the following six layers:

1. **Transport Layer:** The transport layer is the top layer of the fog computing architecture, which is used to send and receive data from the cloud. The data that is required to be processed in the cloud data center usually goes through a pre-processing phase and for a higher level of services that are not provided by fog computing. The transport layer consists of smart gateways, which send the data collected from the IoT sensor and transfers only a minimal amount of data to the cloud.
2. **Security Layer:** The security layer provides encryption-decryption service and integrity check service for the data. The security layer is one of the most important layers for ensuring secure fog

computing. Security layer services such as homomorphic encryption, authentication, and hash value calculation are available on this layer.

3. **Temporary Storage Layer:** The function of the temporary storage layer is used to store the preprocessed data before forwarding it to the transport layer. The security layer may encrypt the data before sending it to the transport layer.
4. **Preprocessing layer:** The preprocessing layer is used to perform the basic data processing task so that the data be normalized, trimmed, and filtered before sending it to the data center. By filtering, only the relevant data is sent to the data center and reducing the communication cost by removing the clutter data.
5. **Monitoring Layer:** The monitoring layer is a management layer that monitors the resource usage, services, activities, and responses. This layer is having an important role in the management of fog devices. All tasks and services are monitored along with the power consumption and resource usage.
6. **Physical and Virtualization Layer:** The physical and virtualization layer contains actual devices such as sensor nodes and IoT devices, virtual sensor networks, and wireless sensor networks. This layer is the lowest layer where the data is being generated. These devices and sensors are managed based on the services provided by them.

SECURITY AND PRIVACY CHALLENGES FOR FOG COMPUTING

Fog computing is a computing standard to provide the cloud services at the edge of the network to offload the data centers and reduce delays at the user end. Fog computing is suitable for the time and location-sensitive applications. Fog computing runs over IoT devices to provide processing of large, heterogeneous, and dynamic data in a time-bounded manner.

Fog computing helps in providing user-oriented services also known as client objectiveness. Client objectiveness includes low operational expenditure (OpEx), optimal resource usage, and privacy and data security. The plethora of functionality-based fog applications creates a variety of security and privacy issues. Out of these securities issues; some issues are inherited from cloud computing while some are unique to fog computing. As compared to cloud computing fog computing is assumed to be more secure. In Fog computing data is stored temporarily and forwarded to the data center in a non-real-time manner. The temporary storage and transient communication hinder the attacker to get access to the real-time data and do not provide sufficient time for an attack. Local data processing also prevents the outside attack using the internet since it is very complicated to make inbound connections. Even after having such advantages in fog scenarios, many security challenges persist. The direct applicability of the existing cloud computing method is infeasible due to the mobility, heterogeneity, and distributed environment.

The fog security and privacy issues are related to data, virtualization, segregation, network, malware, and monitoring (Stojmenovic and Wen 2014) which can be categorized into two types:

1. **Inherited from cloud computing:** The Privacy of user data and secure communication requirements is similar to cloud computing as in fog computing (Aljumah and Ahanger 2018) (Zissis and Lekkas 2012).

2. **Unique to fog computing:** Due to distributed processing of data in fog computing the requirement of trust and authentication and secure communication is one of the major challenges of fog computing (Aljumah and Ahanger 2018) (Khan, Parkinson, and Qin 2017).

Figure 4. Six-layer Architecture of Fog Computing

Fog Computing Architecture (Atlam, Walters, and Wills 2018)	
Transport Layer	The role of this layer is to upload the data to the cloud data center
Security Layer	The role of this layer is to data privacy and encryption-decryption etc.
Temporary Storage Layer	The role of this layer is to data distribution, replication and de duplication
Pre-Processing Layer	The role of this layer is to data analysis, filtering and trimming
Monitoring Layer	The role of this layer is to monitor resources, activity, service and responses
Physical and Virtualization Layer	Consist of virtual sensor network Consist of physical devices and wireless sensor network

Security Threats in Fog Computing

The Security and Privacy threats are shown in Figure 5 which provides a list of attacks hampering security as well as privacy.

Figure 5. Security Threats in Fog Computing

Security Threats in Fog Computing

SecurityAttack

- Dos Attack
- DDos Attack
- Collusion Attack
- Forgery Attack
- Jamming
- Spam Attack
- Impersonating Attack
- Tempering Attack
- Man in the Attack
- Eaves Dropping Attack

Privacy Attack

- Data Privacy Leak
- Location Privacy Leak
- Identification Privacy Leak
- Usage Privacy Leak

The following security threats are derived from (Aljumah and Ahanger 2018; Ni et al. 2018; Stojmenovic and Wen 2014) and grouped into 2 categories Security attack and privacy attack, which are discussed below in detail.

1. **Security Attack:** Security attack consists of those attacks, which are related to service blockage, forgery, tampering, or attack on the infrastructure. These security attacks are discussed in the scenario of fog computing.
   a. **Dos/DDoS attack:** Denial of Service (DoS) and Distributed Denial of Service (DDoS) attack are the traditional attack, which is applicable in any computing paradigm where there are online services present at the networked node. The DoS/ DDoS attack tries to choke the server/network by generating a large number of fake request packets to overwhelm the serv-

ing node which keeps the server busy in fulfilling the fake request and consequently denying legitimate requests to the server. Apart from the regular DDoS attack on a cloud data center, the fog node can also be targeted as the fog node is power bounded and computation limited so DDoS/Dos attack leads to the stall of services easily. (Paharia and Bhushan 2019) Provided different categories of DDoS attacks in fog environment as Application bug level DDoS, Infrastructural level DDoS, and Network Level DDoS attack.

b. **Collusion attack:** The collusion attack is inherited from the WSN. The Collusion attack refers to two groups of illegitimate nodes deceiving the set of IoT or Fog nodes to gain sensitive information. They work in collusion so a set of nodes can be participated to increase the strength of the attack. Fog computing environment consists of a large number of 3rd party unreliable servers. The problem of collusion attack is high due to the 3rd party server and the mobility of the IoT nodes(Yaseen et al. 2017). (X. Wang et al. 2020)(Zhang et al. 2019) have provided solutions to mitigate the collusion attack in a fog environment.
c. **Forgery attack:** In a forgery attack(Khan, Parkinson, and Qin 2017) an IOT device, edge device, or fog node tries to forge its identity to become part of the network as a legitimate node and then perform a malicious activity like false information injection, etc. Fog networks are an easy target of forgery attacks due to the inevitable requirement of the untrusted 3rd party service provides. Such an attack can be used to compromise the whole network if a malicious node becomes part of the network it can broadcast fake information which can cause the collapse of the entire system.
d. **Jamming attack:** The Origin of jamming attack is coming from the communication where the attacker tries the consume the whole bandwidth of the network by flooding the network. This is similar to the Dos attack but instead of the server, the network is chocked to block the network and so the services. Fog to cloud interface and fog to things interfaces are the target of such attacks in which the whole network bandwidth is consumed by the flooding of unnecessary packets.
e. **Spam attack:** Spam is the presence of false information like fake identity, false sensor data, redundant value, and information in the network. The collection and flooding of such information are known as spam attacks. In fog computing, the cluster nodes can be flooded with spam i.e. misleading information, which might be forwarded into the processing node causing malfunctioning and erroneous results.
f. **Man in the middle attack:** An attacker can block the communication between the Fog to cloud interface and Fog to things interface using the man in the middle attack. The attacker can block, replay and modify the communication between these interfaces (Stojmenovic and Wen 2014).

2. **Privacy Attack:** The fog computing and the IoT infrastructure constitutes the component of smart home, smart grid, smart traffic management, plant monitoring, and so on; where the end-user data is vital and preserving the privacy of the user information plays a key role in fog computing security. Privacy attack includes data, location, usage and identification data leak, which are described below.
   a. **Data Privacy Leak:** The user data collected from the sensor nodes or IoT devices, which may contain sensitive information. The collected user data is either processed at the fog node or forwarded to the data center. The data privacy needs to be maintained since the attack can

reveal vital user information like address, preferences, and views, which can be used against the user. Authentication and encryption techniques can be used to prevent data privacy leaks.

b. **Location Privacy Leak:** Fog applications are location-aware so these locations information is transmitted to the compute node of fog and cloud. If the user location is revealed by appending this information with other information fetched can be used to hamper the physical security of the user. As an example, in the case of the smart grid if the attacker gets the user information appended with the usage pattern it can be easily guessed that the user is present in his home at a particular time or not.
c. **Usage Privacy Leak:** Usage patterns can reveal user behavior and interactions with the system, which can be used to predict and analyze user behavior. For example, the smart meter reading can provide a sleeping time or the time when they are not home, thus violating the privacy of the user.
d. **Identification Privacy Leak:** The identification information contains user information like name mobile number and other information, which should be protected from an adversary. The fog node or IoT device may reveal such information, which should be protected.

Secure Fog Computing Techniques

After discussing the security and privacy issues the solutions towards a secure fog computing environment are discussed in this section, which can be used to mitigate the above-discussed problems.

Trust and Authentication

Fog computing services provided by different service providers consisting 3rd party vendor which are not always trustworthy, so trust and authentication are crucial to maintaining the security in the fog computing environment which indirectly affects the security of underlying IoT infrastructure. Authentication is necessary to validate the node to initiate to become the part of the network but it alone is not enough to ensure secure participation of the nodes since authentication can be achieved by replaying. So, trust is used to maintain security along with authentication.

Trust: Trust can be understood as an agreement to follow and maintain the predefined set of rules between two parties so that they can rely on each other that their actions are in accord and non-malicious. Trust is a crucial part of any cyber-physical system to create a sustainable environment where different resources and services are depending on each other in some computing environment (Kochovski et al. 2019).

In a Fog environment, trust must be maintained among devices participating in computation and communication. Trust is also required to be maintained between fog-cloud and fog-devices communication. Trust is an important aspect of security in fog computing due to the diversity and heterogeneity of the fog nodes. Trust maintenance is necessary to block the internal attack due to untrusted nodes. As a standard network security technique trust can be maintained in two ways as 1. Direct trust and 2. 3rd party trust management. The same trust management techniques in used fog computing to maintain trust in Fog environment:

1. Direct trust management: Direct trust management requires the two parties to trust each other. As in our case, two fog nodes can create trust among themselves but it is required that both devices should be properly authenticated.
2. 3rd party trust management: In 3rd party trust management two individuals implicitly trust each other because both share a relationship with a common third party, and that third party vouches for the trustworthiness of the two people. It requires a 3rd party authentication knows as a certification authority.
3. Reputation Based Trust model: The reputation-based trust model is successfully employed in Peer to Peer computing and e-commerce sites. For creating a reputation-based trust model for Fog computing it is required to ensure how to provide a unique identity to nodes and revoking the trust in case of malicious behavior. The fog node can join and leave a system at any time so maintaining trust is challenging in a fog environment.
4. Blockchain-based Trust Model: (Kochovski et al. 2019) presented a blockchain-based trust model for a fog-based video processing environment based on smart contracts. Blockchain technology works based on the ledger which can be used to maintain trust by using the immutable property of a blockchain ledger.

Authentication: Authentication is an important aspect of the fog computing paradigm since services are offered at massive scale end-users by fog nodes. To join a fog network IoT devices authentication is required. The PKI-based public key encryption trust methods are not applicable in fog networks. The PKI-based system is not scalable in case of a huge number of fog nodes and, they show poor performance due to the encryption-decryption process computational the fog nodes can't fulfill the requirement. Due to proximity available in the case of IoT devices alternate ways of authentication can also be employed like biometric, RFID, and NFC-based authentication. A device can authenticate itself by its unique RFID code or NFC code. In these types of authentication, proximity is also ensured during authentication.

(Ibrahim 2016) Provided a mutual authentication scheme for edge and fog computing. In the proposed methodology, they have used a master key for the roaming client, which can authenticate itself with other fog nodes. The method requires less computation so it can be implemented cost-effectively on the fog nodes.

End-User Data Privacy

The fog nodes contain data from the sensor that many times contain sensitive information. This sensitive information can be used to identify user behavior to use for malicious activity. Protection of such user data like smart meter data, health band data can be to identify patterns using pattern analysis techniques. These results can be used to launch an attack. User data privacy can be divided into 3 types of fog computing scenarios:

User data Privacy: Fog nodes at the edges collect the user data. The data that is generated from the sensors are collected by node either processed on the fog node or forwarded to the cloud for further processing. The user data that is generated and collected mostly contains sensitive information, which can be mined for finding the insights. These data follow a certain pattern that can be used for user behavior analysis or some pattern about the usage of devices. The smart home contains data generated and processed at the cloud. The commands and configuration of the smart home can be used to track user activity.

Location Privacy: The fog application is user location-aware so the user locations are exposed to the applications and these locations can reveal the user location data as well as the user migration and navigation pattern.

Secure Communication

The data in fog computing traverses through 2 interfaces fog cloud interfaces and fog things interfaces. The secure communication in fog computing needs to ensure the protection of sensors and devices to be intercepted during the transmission. Most of the communication in the case of fog networks takes place wirelessly so it becomes a security issue since wireless communication is more susceptible to attacks. The sniffing attack and jamming attacks are some attacks that can affect the communication adversely affected the services as well as the data leak, but these can be handled by securing wireless communication. Wireless communication has various security mechanisms like WEP and WPA, to ensure secure communication still the breaches can't be avoided. The configuration management communication should be out of bounds to provide more security to the network.

Role of SDN: SDN can be employed in fog networks to provide a dynamically configurable, scalable, and more secure network. The SDN-based fog networks will provide ease of management and a cost-effective solution that is more secure. The intelligence can also be easily incorporated due to the programmability provided by the SDN and Open Flow. The intelligent intrusion detection system for fog networks can be easily installed. The SDN network can easily be used in resource usage monitoring and traffic isolation.

Secure Data Storage

The user data after delivery to the fog node is either stored in the fog node storage or cloud data center storage. The security of these data stores needs to be maintained to preserve user data. Data integrity and prevention of unauthorized access are required for user data to be preserved. The data stores should be auditable so that data security can be ensured. Homomorphic encryption (Rivest, Dertouzos, and Adleman 1978) is very useful to safely store sensitive user data over the 3rd party server by using encryption that follows homomorphism on some set of operations.

Homomorphic Encryption (HE) is a kind of encryption scheme that allows a third party (e.g., cloud, service provider) to perform certain computable functions on the encrypted data while preserving the features of the function and format of the encrypted data (Acar et al. 2018).

These techniques used in cloud computing data can be used for fog computing but with an assurance of low latency, dynamic nature, and fog cloud interface. The use of homomorphic encryption is shown in Figure 6 where a user is sending the data to the cloud data center for processing after encryption using homomorphic encryption. Homomorphic encryption follows the property by which the data center can perform computation on the stored data without decryption. Homomorphic encryption uses lattice-based encryption such as Brakerski/Fan-Vercauteren (BFV) (Brakerski 2012) (Fan and Vercauteren 2012) and the Cheon-Kim-Kim-Song (CKKS) (Cheon et al. 2017) which are additively and multiplicatively homomorphic.

Figure 6. Homomorphic Encryption

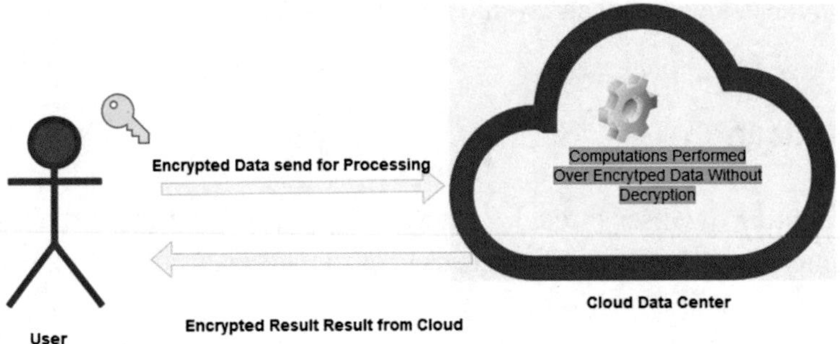

An implementation of HE is presented in (H. Wang, Wang, and Domingo-Ferrer 2018) where homomorphic encryption is used to preserve the node identity as well as the data. In the present work, authors have shown an ASAS as a data aggregator fog node, which collects data from other fog nodes and sends the data to the Cloud data center after applying homomorphic encryption, which provides privacy and bandwidth requirement.

Security and Privacy-Preserving Data Computation

Privacy-preserving computation is a crucial way to secure user data from stealing over cloud and fog nodes. The user data reaching the server for processing is encrypted by the private key of the user and stored in the data center. The privacy-preserving computation directly operates on the data without decryption of the data maintaining the data private but computable.

Verifiable Computing is a technique in which a cloud or fog computing node offloads its computing task to a non-trusted 3rd party server but still, the computation is verifiable. In fog computing, the users can offload computation to the fog node and can verify its computation.

Searchable Encryption helps to store the data in the data center and fog nodes with affecting data privacy. The data is stored in encrypted form but still, the search algorithm can work on the data without the need for decryption of the data. So, the user data can be securely stored on the 3rd party server.

MACHINE LEARNING SOLUTION FOR FOG COMPUTING

In cybersecurity, the pattern lies in the cyber-attacks are changing day by day. So machine learning/deep learning can be used to automatically detect a pattern in the network data to find the anomaly as well as the attacker node. Machine learning is one of the used techniques for anomaly detection by pattern analysis present in the data, which is used for securing the system (Xin et al. 2018). Fog computing is developed as a companion of cloud computing to process the huge data generated by IoT devices. The emergence of deep learning has shifted the focus of the researchers to use deep learning to get a more robust solution for security using pattern analysis. The intelligent system of fog computing helps in the prevention, detection, and mitigation of attacks in fog computing nodes.

(Sari 2018) Discusses the context-aware intelligence system for fog computing security. Incident detection and response are one of the major aspects of security for any computing environment.

Intrusion Detection Using Machine Learning

There are two ways to detect intrusion 1. Misuse/signature-based, 2. Anomaly detection and 3. Hybrid. Misuse/Signature-based detection is used in are predetermined pattern known as signature against which the logs or codes have been tested. Anomaly detection is finding irregular patterns in the data. These systems can be very useful in a case of unknown or new attacks on the system but it also suffers from false detection since it will categories all unseen behavior as an attack. Hybrid IDS which includes signature-based detection as well as anomaly-based detection is more useful. The following machine learning algorithm can be used in intrusion detection:

1. **Support Vector Machine (SVM):** SVM is a supervised ML technique useful for classification as well as regression. It uses the concept of hyperplanes for classification. It can be used pattern-based IDS in which it has been trained with the existing dataset and then it can be used to classify the attacks. The SVM-based classifier can be binary as well as multiclass classifier.
2. **Logistic Regression:** Logistic regression is a statistical model which uses sigmoid function to map the input with the probabilities to the class fitting. The sigmoid function is defined by equation (1):

$$F\left(x\right)=\frac{1}{1-e^{-x}} \tag{1}$$

Where f(x) is the probability output and x is the input.

3. **Linear Discriminant Analysis (LDA):** LDA is based on the Bayes theorem and it is used for classification. LDA calculates the probability using the following expression given by (2):

$$P\left(X,Y\mid x,y\right)=\frac{(P\mid f\left(C\left(x\right)\right)*C)}{\Sigma P\mid\mid *f\left(x\right)} \tag{2}$$

Where P(X,Y|x,y) is the probability of at (x,y), x is the input class, f(x) is the estimated probability and p|k is the prior probability.

4. **Random forest:** RF is based on the creation of multiple decision trees. These decision trees are used for training and at the end, each prediction from different trees is compiled to make a final prediction.(Zhou et al. 2020) have the RF-based approach to create an intrusion detection system.
5. **Ensemble method:** Ensemble learning is a way to utilize different ML methods cooperatively. The approach is made to improve the overall efficiency of the system by incorporation of the poor performing technique to provide a good result in collaboration. Bagging, Boosting, and stacking are some methods for ensemble learning. (Alrashdi et al. 2019)(Kumar Singh Gautam and Doegar 2018) have used ensemble learning to create the intrusion detection system.

Table 1. Significant recent work in the direction of secure fog computing

S. No.	Authors	Fog Security Issue	Technique	Relevance of the Work
1	(Sohal et al. 2018)	Device Security	Markov model, virtual honeypot	Provided an IDS for malicious edge device detection. They have used a 2 state markov model to classify the devices and virtual honey pot to store the data. They have shown the performance by using real attacks on virtual environments and achieved 92% best accuracy.
2	(Yaseen et al. 2018)	Collusion attack, IoT security	Customized iterative filtering algorithm, SDN,	Real-time tracking of collusion attack using the fog computing layer for the IoT infrastructure. Also added the SDN layer for flexibility. The contribution of the paper is significant in the terms of algorithms and mathematical proofs for the same. The model proves the applicability of the proposed model with limited resource as well as in can keep track the mobile node successfully.
3	(A. Diro and Chilamkurti 2018)	Network intrusion detection	LSTM, Distributed architecture	A Novel LSTM network for distributed cyber-attack detection by exploiting the fog nodes. Explored various attacks related to wireless communications.
4	(A. A. Diro, Chilamkurti, and Kumar 2017)	Data Privacy, Cryptographic technique	ECC based encryption for the publish-subscribe protocol	Proposed a novel lightweight encryption technique for IoT protocols that uses the publish-subscribe model. Two approaches provided one for encryption and the other for the key exchange. From the results, they have shown better efficiency as compared to RSA-based algorithms.
5	(Priyadarshini and Barik 2019)	Availability, DDoS Attack	SDN and LSTM	Proposed a Novel Source-based Distributed denial of service attack detection mechanism for Fog Computing. Used the SDN controller for the placement of the detection module. Shown very good accuracy for attack detection.
6	(Khater et al. 2019)	Intrusion detection system	Multi-Layer Perceptron	Proposed IDS based on MLP. They have a vector space representation of attacks using MLP. They also considered the computation power limitation of the fog node to provide a lightweight IDS system. Tested the performance on raspberry pi (as a fog node) and achieved 94% accuracy on ADFA-LD.
7	(Aliyu, Sheltami, and Shakshuki 2018)	Man in the middle attack	Lightweight encryption.	Proposed a fog node-friendly IDS along with an Intrusion prevention system. It can work on low resource systems such as fog nodes for the MITM attack. The used model followed a network design with one-hop distance between the fog node and the IDS node. Also reduces the packet encapsulation to improve efficiency.
8	(Hosseinpour et al. 2016)	Intrusion detection	Artificial immune system (AIS), smart data	Distributed AIS-based IDS inspired by the human immune system. It uses 3 layers of security at which fog nodes are used as the first line of defense at which anomaly detection is done, edge nodes are 2nd line of defense at which the analyzer unit is running, and cloud as 3rd line of defense at which training is done. Detection is done in the distributed way when more than the threshold node agrees at anomaly only then anomaly is considered.
9.	(Pacheco et al. 2020)	Availability, Adaptive IDS	ANN	Attempted to detect the compromised fog nodes and makes the communication system available in case of attack. The anomaly detection is adaptive so that it provides high accuracy and a low false rate.

6. **K mean clustering:** These algorithms are used for mapping data to a cluster out of the k clusters using means to find the membership to a particular cluster. (Jaber and Rehman 2020) Proposed a novel IDS for cloud computing by the incorporation of fuzzy c means clustering and SVM. The proposed algorithm first applies the fuzzy c mean clustering using the membership function of NSL-KDD dataset. In the second step, it applies the Genetic Algorithm and SVM for training the dataset. The fuzzy aggregation model is used to generate the output. The hybrid system (FCM-SVM) provided an accuracy of 97.37% for U2R attack on the NSL-KDD dataset. Similar to Dos attack it attained an accuracy of 99.10% and for probe 98.80% surpassing all the existing methods.

Relevant Work in Fog Security Based on ML

The ML-based learning methods are primarily used for the development of anomaly-based intrusion detection systems along with such DDoS detection. Artificial Neural Network(ANN), RF, Ensemble learning techniques have been used to create an IDS system for Fog computing. Deep learning-based solutions are available using RNN and LSTM. Table 1 will provide the summary of relevant work done in fog security using ML.

Deep Learning Security Solution

Machine learning has been used in intrusion detection with the help of pattern recognition but has limited applicability due to handcrafted features. In computer security, the new attacks always take a new shape, so handcrafted features seem to be least effective in protection against new attacks. Machine learning also suffers from scalability and accuracy when applied in the current network paradigm due to heterogeneity and a massive amount of data to be processed for security applications.

Deep Learning has already proved its significance in various applications like computer vision, recommendation systems, natural language processing, and speech processing. In contrast to machine learning deep learning mitigates the requirement of hand-crafted features since deep learning architecture is based on a deep neural network that automatically learns features from the training data. Deep learning has shown its potential application in security since it is more accurate in network intrusion detection systems (NIDS) (Shone et al. 2018).

(Priyadarshini and Barik 2019) provided an LSTM deep learning framework for mitigating DDoS attacks in a fog network. They implemented an SDN network to provide centralized control of the fog nodes. An LSTM network with 2 hidden layers with 128 neurons where the sigmoid function is used as an activation function and hyperbolic tangent function at the output layer. The model showed the best performance with an accuracy of 98.34 with 3 hidden layer LSTM and 20% dropouts.

LSTM based NIDS: Long short-term memory (LSTM) is a type of recurrent neural network, which can be used in the intrusion detection system. LSTM can learn features and patterns by analyzing the network traffic log data or real-time network traffic and classify them as an attack or normal traffic. LSTM network is resilient against adversaries. This is due to the complex learning mechanism and feedback present in the LSTM network, which makes complex for the adversary to adapt according to the LSTM algorithm. The feedback also facilitates an understanding of complex patterns with variable size windows. The work presented in the article (A. Diro and Chilamkurti 2018)employed an LSTM based attack detection architecture that works on distributed decision control by fog nodes. They proposed a deep learning-based method for cyber-attack detection which exploits the distributed nature of fog computing. They have proposed a stacked auto-encoder for creating an intrusion detection system in which the centralized node i.e. master provides the initial network configuration and the worker node will iterate to find the new weights for training. At each fog node, the training and detection task is performed separately, and then the best results are shared among all nodes. The trained network was then used to detect the attack which shown 99.20% accuracy.

Figure 7. LSTM network-based attack detection system
(A. Diro and Chilamkurti 2018)

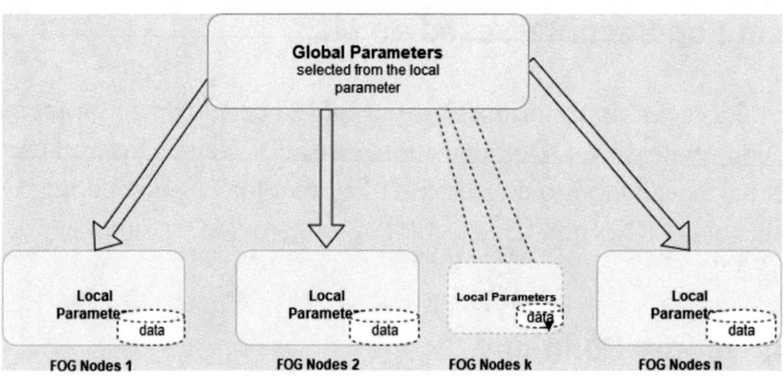

CONCLUSION

Fog computing provides cloud features near the edge of the network. Thus, Fog computing helps to offload the cloud data center. Apart from the platform, storage and compute services due to its location between and cloud, it can offload the security aspect from cloud and IoT devices to provide a real-time and fast response with low bandwidth. Fog computing being part of the network is susceptible to almost all types of network attacks. Fog node carries and stores sensitive user data, so it also needs to maintain the privacy of user data. Secure fog computing relies on authenticated fog nodes, secure communication (between fog to things and fog to the cloud), and protected user data. The 3rd party authentication is mostly in a fog environment due to the limited computation capability of fog nodes to run the encryption algorithms. The homomorphic algorithms are used for privacy-preserving data storage and processing. Machine learning and deep learning has shown its performance in the cybersecurity where it can provide some better solutions as compared to traditional methods. Due to the learning capability of ANN and Deep learning models, they are useful in providing solutions in the scenario of new types of attacks. NIDS and IPS are successfully designed using ML and DL. So, we have seen Fog computing and its importance to the IoT infrastructure and the inherited and new challenges. Along with this existing solutions have been potentially successful following the challenges. The solutions related to fog computing can be improved in the terms of robustness, resource efficiency (lightweight), and accuracy.

REFERENCES

Acar, A., Aksu, H., Uluagac, A. S., & Conti, M. (2018). A Survey on Homomorphic Encryption Schemes: Theory and Implementation. *ACM Computing Surveys*, *51*(4), 1–35. doi:10.1145/3214303

Aliyu, F., Sheltami, T., & Shakshuki, E. M. (2018). A Detection and Prevention Technique for Man in the Middle Attack in Fog Computing. Procedia Computer Science. doi:10.1016/j.procs.2018.10.125

Aljumah, A., & Ahanger, T. A. (2018). Fog Computing and Security Issues: A Review. *2018 7th International Conference on Computers Communications and Control, ICCCC 2018 – Proceedings*, 237–39. 10.1109/ICCCC.2018.8390464

Alrashdi, I. (2019). FBAD: Fog-Based Attack Detection for IoT Healthcare in Smart Cities. *2019 IEEE 10th Annual Ubiquitous Computing, Electronics and Mobile Communication Conference, UEMCON 2019.* 10.1109/UEMCON47517.2019.8992963

Atlam, H., Walters, R., & Wills, G. (2018). Fog Computing and the Internet of Things: A Review. *Big Data and Cognitive Computing*, *2*(2), 10. doi:10.3390/bdcc2020010

Bohn, R. B. (2011). NIST Cloud Computing Reference Architecture. *Proceedings - 2011 IEEE World Congress on Services, SERVICES 2011.* 10.1109/SERVICES.2011.105

Bonomi, F. (2011). Connected Vehicles, the Internet of Things, and Fog Computing. *The Eighth ACM International Workshop on Vehicular Inter-Networking (VANET).*

Bonomi, F., Milito, R., Zhu, J., & Addepalli, S. (2012). Fog Computing and Its Role in the Internet of Things. *Proceedings of the first edition of the MCC workshop on Mobile cloud computing,* (1), 13–16.

Brakerski, Z. (2012). Fully Homomorphic Encryption without Modulus Switching from Classical GapSVP. Lecture Notes in Computer Science (Including Subseries Lecture Notes in Artificial Intelligence and Lecture Notes in Bioinformatics). doi:10.1007/978-3-642-32009-5_50

Cheon, J. H., Kim, A., Kim, M., & Song, Y. (2017). Homomorphic Encryption for Arithmetic of Approximate Numbers. Lecture Notes in Computer Science (Including Subseries Lecture Notes in Artificial Intelligence and Lecture Notes in Bioinformatics). doi:10.1007/978-3-319-70694-8_15

Chiang, M., & Zhang, T. (2016). Fog and IoT: An Overview of Research Opportunities. *IEEE Internet of Things Journal*, *3*(6), 854–864. doi:10.1109/JIOT.2016.2584538

Cisco White Paper: Fog Computing and the Internet of Things: Extend the Cloud to Where the Things Are What You Will Learn. (2015). https://www.cisco.com/c/dam/en_us/solutions/trends/iot/docs/computing-overview.pdf

Diro, A., & Chilamkurti, N. (2018). Leveraging LSTM Networks for Attack Detection in Fog-to-Things Communications. *IEEE Communications Magazine*, *56*(9), 124–130. doi:10.1109/MCOM.2018.1701270

Diro, A. A., Chilamkurti, N., & Kumar, N. (2017). Lightweight Cybersecurity Schemes Using Elliptic Curve Cryptography in Publish-Subscribe Fog Computing. *Mobile Networks and Applications*, *22*(5), 848–858. doi:10.100711036-017-0851-8

Docker. (2021). https://www.docker.com/

Fan, J., & Vercauteren, F. (2012). Somewhat Practical Fully Homomorphic Encryption. *Proceedings of the 15th international conference on Practice and Theory in Public Key Cryptography.*

Gupta, Chakraborty, Ghosh, & Buyya. (2017). Fog Computing in 5G Networks: An Application Perspective. *Cloud and Fog Computing in 5G Mobile Networks: Emerging advances and applications*, 23–56.

Hosseinpour. (2016). An Intrusion Detection System for Fog Computing and IoT Based Logistic Systems Using a Smart Data Approach. *International Journal of Digital Content Technology and its Applications*.

Hu, P., Dhelim, S., Ning, H., & Qiu, T. (2017). Survey on Fog Computing: Architecture, Key Technologies, Applications and Open Issues. *Journal of Network and Computer Applications*.

Ibrahim, M. H. (2016). Octopus: An Edge-Fog Mutual Authentication Scheme. *International Journal of Network Security*, *18*(6), 1089–1101.

Iorga, M. (2018). *NIST Special Publication*. Fog Computing Conceptual Model.

Jaber, A. N., & Rehman, S. U. (2020). FCM–SVM Based Intrusion Detection System for Cloud Computing Environment. *Cluster Computing*.

Kai, Cong, & Tao. (2016). Fog Computing for Vehicular Ad-Hoc Networks: Paradigms, Scenarios, and Issues. *Journal of China Universities of Posts and Telecommunications, 23*(2), 56-65, 96. doi:10.1016/S1005-8885(16)60021-3

Khan, Parkinson, & Qin. (2017). Fog Computing Security: A Review of Current Applications and Security Solutions. *Journal of Cloud Computing*.

Khater, B. S. (2019). *A Lightweight Perceptron-Based Intrusion Detection System for Fog Computing*. Applied Sciences.

Kim, J. Y., & Schulzrinne, H. (2013). Cloud Support for Latency-Sensitive Telephony Applications. *Proceedings of the International Conference on Cloud Computing Technology and Science, CloudCom*.

Kochovski, P. (2019). Trust Management in a Blockchain Based Fog Computing Platform with Trustless Smart Oracles. *Future Generation Computer Systems*, *101*, 747–759. https://doi.org/10.1016/j.future.2019.07.030

Kumar Singh Gautam, R., & Amit Doegar, E. (2018). An Ensemble Approach for Intrusion Detection System Using Machine Learning Algorithms. *Proceedings of the 8th International Conference Confluence 2018 on Cloud Computing, Data Science and Engineering, Confluence 2018.*

Li, S., Da Xu, L., & Zhao, S. (2015). The Internet of Things: A Survey. *Information Systems Frontiers*.

Ni, J., Zhang, K., Lin, X., & Shen, X. S. (2018). Securing Fog Computing for Internet of Things Applications: Challenges and Solutions. *IEEE Communications Surveys and Tutorials*.

NIST Big Data Public Working Group. (2015). *NIST Special Publication 1500-1 - NIST Big Data Interoperability Framework: Volume 1, Definitions*. Author.

Pacheco, J., Benitez, V. H., Felix-Herran, L. C., & Satam, P. (2020). Artificial Neural Networks-Based Intrusion Detection System for Internet of Things Fog Nodes. *IEEE Access: Practical Innovations, Open Solutions*.

Paharia, B., & Bhushan, K. (2019). A Comprehensive Review of Distributed Denial of Service (DDoS) Attacks in Fog Computing Environment. Handbook of Computer Networks and Cyber Security: Principles and Paradigms.

Priyadarshini & Barik. (2019). A Deep Learning Based Intelligent Framework to Mitigate DDoS Attack in Fog Environment. *Journal of King Saud University - Computer and Information Sciences.*

Pushpa & Raj. (2018). Performance Enhancement of Fog Computing Using SDN and NFV Technologies. *Fog Computing: Concepts, Frameworks and Technologies.*

Rivest, Dertouzos, & Adleman. (1978). On Data Banks and Privacy Homomorphisms. *Foundations of Secure Computation.*

Sahu, H., & Hungyo, M. (2018). Introduction to SDN and NFV. In *Innovations in Software-Defined Networking and Network Functions Virtualization* (pp. 1–25). IGI Global.

Sahu, H., & Singh, N. (2018). Software-Defined Storage. In *Innovations in Software-Defined Networking and Network Functions Virtualization* (pp. 268–290). IGI Global.

Sari, A. (2018). Context-Aware Intelligent Systems for Fog Computing Environments for Cyber-Threat Intelligence. In Fog Computing: Concepts, Frameworks and Technologies. Academic Press.

Shone, N., Ngoc, T. N., Phai, V. D., & Shi, Q. (2018). A Deep Learning Approach to Network Intrusion Detection. *IEEE Transactions on Emerging Topics in Computational Intelligence*, *2*(1), 41–50.

Sohal, A. S., Sandhu, R., Sood, S. K., & Chang, V. (2018). A Cybersecurity Framework to Identify Malicious Edge Device in Fog Computing and Cloud-of-Things Environments. *Computers & Security.*

Soia, A., Konnikova, O., & Konnikov, E. (2019). The Internet of Things. *Proceedings of the 33rd International Business Information Management Association Conference, IBIMA 2019: Education Excellence and Innovation Management through Vision 2020.*

Statista Research Department. (2019). *Internet of Things (IoT) Connected Devices Installed Base Worldwide from 2015 to 2025.* https://www.statista.com/statistics/471264/iot-number-of-connected-devices-worldwide/

Stojmenovic, I., & Wen, S. (2014). The Fog Computing Paradigm: Scenarios and Security Issues. *2014 Federated Conference on Computer Science and Information Systems, FedCSIS 2014, 2*, 1–8.

Tan, L., & Wang, N. (2010). Future Internet: The Internet of Things. *ICACTE 2010 - 2010 3rd International Conference on Advanced Computer Theory and Engineering, Proceedings.*

Uehara, M. (2018). *Mist Computing: Linking Cloudlet to Fogs.* Studies in Computational Intelligence.

Vaquero, L. M., & Rodero-Merino, L. (2014). Finding Your Way in the Fog: Towards a Comprehensive Definition of Fog Computing. *Computer Communication Review*, *44*(5), 27–32.

VMware. (2021). https://www.vmware.com/

Wang, H., Wang, Z., & Domingo-Ferrer, J. (2018). Anonymous and Secure Aggregation Scheme in Fog-Based Public Cloud Computing. *Future Generation Computer Systems*, *78*, 712–719.

Wang, X. (2020). Reliable Customized Privacy-Preserving in Fog Computing. *IEEE International Conference on Communications.*

Xin, Y. (2018). Machine Learning and Deep Learning Methods for Cybersecurity. *IEEE Access: Practical Innovations, Open Solutions.*

Yaseen, Q. (2018). Collusion Attacks Mitigation in Internet of Things: A Fog Based Model. *Multimedia Tools and Applications*, *77*(14), 18249–18268.

Yaseen, Q., Jararweh, Y., Al-Ayyoub, M., & Al Dwairi, M. (2017). Collusion Attacks in Internet of Things: Detection and Mitigation Using a Fog Based Model. *SAS 2017 - 2017 IEEE Sensors Applications Symposium, Proceedings.*

Zhang, Y. (2019). APDP: Attack-Proof Personalized Differential Privacy Model for a Smart Home. *IEEE Access: Practical Innovations, Open Solutions.*

Zhou, Y., Cheng, G., Jiang, S., & Dai, M. (2020). Building an Efficient Intrusion Detection System Based on Feature Selection and Ensemble Classifier. *Computer Networks*, 174.

Zissis, D., & Lekkas, D. (2012). Addressing Cloud Computing Security Issues. *Future Generation Computer Systems.*

Chapter 14
Intrusion Detection Systems:
Current Trends and Future Challenges

Riya Bilaiya
National Institute of Technology, Kurukshetra, India

Priyanka Ahlawat
National Institute of Technology, Kurukshetra, India

Rohit Bathla
National Institute of Technology, Kurukshetra, India

ABSTRACT

The community is moving towards the cloud, and its security is important. An old vulnerability known by the attacker can be easily exploited. Security issues and intruders can be identified by the IDS (intrusion detection systems). Some of the solutions consist of network firewall, anti-malware. Malicious entities and fake traffic are detected through packet sniffing. This chapter surveys different approaches for IDS, compares them, and presents a comparative analysis based on their merits and demerits. The authors aim to present an exhaustive survey of current trends in IDS research along with some future challenges that are likely to be explored. They also discuss the implementation details of IDS with parameters used to evaluate their performance.

INTRODUCTION TO INTRUSION DETECTION SYSTEM

Now a day cyber-attacks are increasing rapidly in the network or internet which leads financial loss to the business. IDS is playing a significant role in today network to detect any malicious activities by internal or external intruders.

In today network IDS is play an important role in security architecture. Intrusion detection is a software or hardware that analyze the events which occurred in information systems or in network with sign of intrusions. IDS help to increase the Confidentiality, Integrity, and Availability of systems or network. Signature and patterns matching techniques for analysis the various files present in the network and

DOI: 10.4018/978-1-7998-3299-7.ch014

systems which analyze and detect by IDS. Cyber security plays an important role in today's technology. Some IDS are designed based on behavior on detection, audit source location and frequency of usage.

With rapid growth of cyber space for Information sharing also attract intruder to perform illegal activity over cyber space for capturing, tempering or other misuse of private and confidential information available over cyber space. Intruder can attack over the system whereas client based, or network-based firewall are not enough capable to resist these attacks over cyber space (Hatcher & Yu, 2018).

To establish a self-observe defense scheme in order to prevent the confidentially of modern organization, IDS systems play a vital role. IDS identify illegal movement over cyber space that compromises the truthfulness, privacy and accessibility of confidential information (Barbara et al., 2001; Hoque et al., 2012).

Traditional instruction deduction system (TIDS) collect the deep knowledge of intruder by constantly monitoring the intruder activity over cyberspace. TIDS system is grounded on pattern recognition of different source of auditing and intrusion by matching the rule offers the humanoid system expert. The model is done manually for a fresh style of intrusion ever discovered. The method of elementary restriction of this model is cannot be recognized by existing cyber space (Hosseinpour & Abu Bakar, 2010).

IDS is classified as per the method used and the basis of the detection. NIDS is used for the network monitor traffic and network analyze. It is used to protect the Local area network from the intrusion that has been caused by the host. HIDS are placed on the host in the network. It takes action and detects the malicious traffic. It collects the traffic which are incoming and outgoing in the network and identify attacks.

Component of IDS

1. **Information Collection blade**: This blade is responsible for collecting the events which will be used by next blade analysis engine to detect.
2. **Analysis Engine:** This is the core component of IDS called Sensor. Machine learning, Pattern matching, data mining can be used in intrusion detectors. This component is capable of the analyzer to detect an attack. Three type of detection: Misuse detection, Anomaly Detection, Hybrid Detection.
3. **Response Component**: This is responsible to control the reaction that how to respond if anything attacks detected by Analysis Engine. Response can be Active response and Passive Response.

Figure 1. Components of Intrusion Detection System

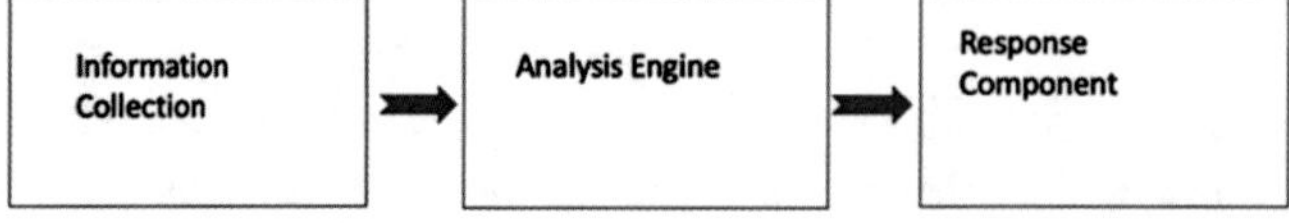

Procedure of IDS

IDS system has need of an appropriate combination of "bait and trap" for the front two surveys. Intrusion detection generated data is carefully checked for potential attacks (Hui & Liu, 2010; Malathi et al., 2018) Figure 1 shows the component of IDS. An intrusion detection approach sensor still has basic functions element- as a responsible analysis of intrusion detection engine. This sensor contains the mechanisms of decision making for the intrusion. Sensor collects the raw information from these sources: defense system, database, log files and inventory trajectories. The log file may embrace file system, user authorization information and etc. This information creates a benchmark to create decision support system (Bilaiya & Ahlawat, 2019; Barbara et al., 2001). The procedure is given by Figure 2.

Figure 2. IDS procedure in detail

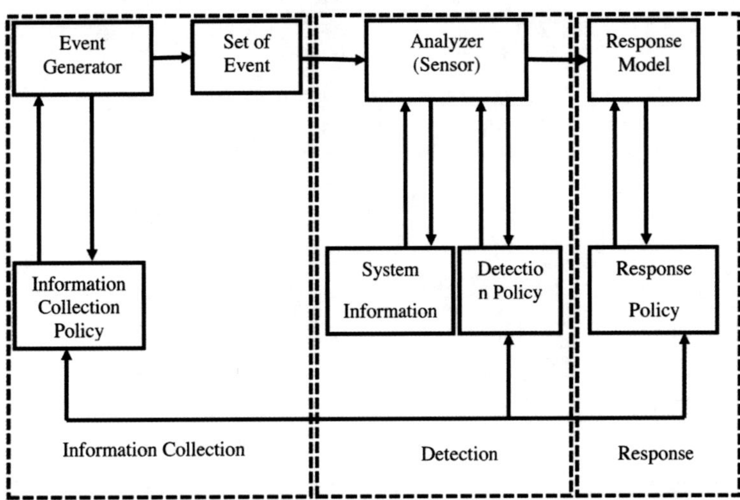

The main task of the sensor is to screen useful evidence and delete irrelevant data from all suspicious activities associated with the event. The sensor is combined with the Event Generator component data set. The sampling method is determined by the Event Builder rule that determines how to filter event notification information. The product of a generator coherent political events all events can be a system event log, or network packets. In some cases, the data storage is not used when the event is data streams directly to the analyzer. Once intrusion detection is detected, IDS alerts inform administrators. The next step is guaranteed, either by managers or by IDS itself, taking advantage of additional measures against (specific function of the block to terminate the session, system backup, interruption of system routing, legal infrastructure, etc.) (Barbara et al., 2001; Hatcher & Yu, 2018).

IDs is task in security policy. Among the different tasks that identify hackers, this is the most important. It may be useful to investigate criminal incidents and to install appropriate corrections to allow future attacks against specific persons or resources. Sometimes, an intrusion detection can result in erroneous warnings, example as a result of a network failure, attack description, email signatures (Hatcher & Yu, 2018).

Procedure of IDS is to control the illegal activity and events that happen over network or device system (Hatcher & Yu, 2018). The main purpose is to analyze traffic passing by and detect potential interventions in the system. IDS is an essential domain of our security strategies. IDS can change many tasks, but identifying hackers is one of the most basic. Contributes to obtaining evidence in cybercrime. It is also useful to find a forensic digital analysis to understand the attacker's activity.

Figure 3. Flow chart for activities performed by IDS

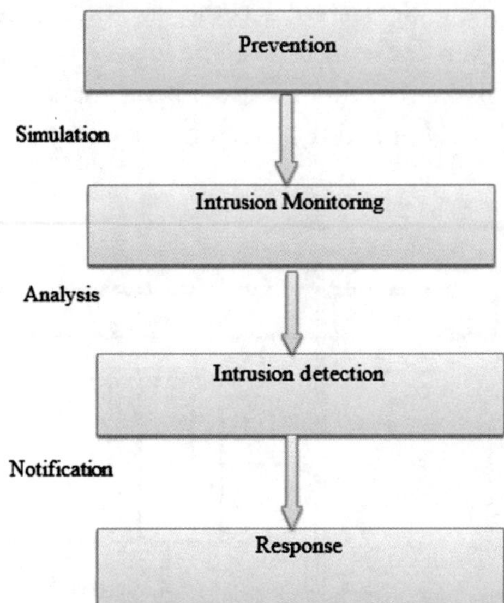

Requirements of IDSs

- If we expand an IDS into any system. That nevermore include extra difficulties into this current practice/ system.
- Each IDS would be designed toward such a means that this requires fewer method/system maintenance. This would perform fewer consideration including delivery charges.
- All performed IDS device well make thoroughly satisfactory.
- That never propose fresh vulnerability in the method
- Every condition of maintenance always be more concise including cost of the method will not be updated appearing in demote overall method performance.
- Worked continuously moreover transparent.
- Standards denote co-operating.
- Representatives are well imply clarity.
- This false-negative moreover false-positive flow always occur flat in the discovery stage.
- This always be effective.

Levels of IDSs Detection Methodologies

Signature Based or Rule-based IDS: These rules are of a predefined collection about commands identifying various safety attacks while that mode of sensor network behavior remains measured based upon one collection of laws.

Advantages

- Competent of Detects supplementary attacks.
- Energy dissipation is flat.

- Memory Utilization is more economical.

Disadvantages

- Drops well-known Attack.
- The detection frequency is weak.

Anomaly Based IDS: During here, anomaly based approach continuously utilized to analyze system projects and described as wicked or usual. Interruption remains classified as working with threshold value i.e., design beyond that value.

Advantages

- Discovers all these attacks having a signature.
- The energy consumption level is low.
- Memory Utilization is more trivial.

Disadvantages

- It cannot detect new attacks.
- The detection time is moderate.

Hybrid IDS: That is a unification of both the previous methodologies. It includes a couple of stages for detection; that is, one stage use signs to discover public attacks another subject to identifying extra attacks by mean of taking malicious and standard models including monitoring system behavior varying of regular.

Advantages

- It can identify both new and existing attacks.
- .Memory Utilization is average.
- The detection rate is high.

Disadvantages

- Demand more calculation.
- Require a number of resources.
- Energy consumption is low

Classification of IDS

- Host-based IDS: HIDS estimate evidence in one or more host systems, comprising the content of operational and executional files. This type of IDS collects events from host directly in the form of CPU utilization, OS log files, application logs, file system modification. HIDS are depend on OS type and effectively can detect the Buffer overflow in host systems. HIDS are capable to monitor the traffic which NIDS has failed to detect. Follow the Diagram:

- Network based IDS: NIDS estimate the seized information communication network, analyze the flow of information's moving around the communication system. NIDS basically a sniffer type which collects data directly from network in the form of Packets to detect the malicious activities like denial of service, Buffer overflow etc. NIDS monitor and analyze the inbound and outbound packet in the network.

Figure 4. HIDS and NIDS

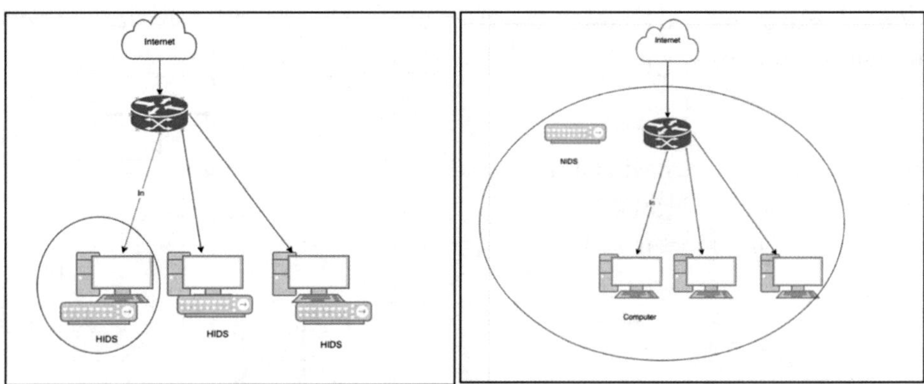

Some of the attacks like IP Based Denial of service (DoS) can be detected after only analyzing the headers of the packet. HIDS doesn't have capabilities to see Headers file of any packet, it can only be detected by NIDS.

IDS is also classified based on the action it takes:

1. Passive IDS
2. Reactive IPS

Difference between Passive IDS and Active IDS is same as a Security Guard and Security Camera. Camera can detect the activity while Guard can take action. In same way Passive IDS only can detect & record the malicious activity while active IDS can also take actions.

Snort is the best intrusion detection system is available freely for everyone and Lightweight HIDS is used for emerging detection. Snort is freely available for LINUX, UNIX and windows environment.

Various types of methods that are used to configure an IDS system. These anomalies detection method include statistical method, ambiguous logic method, rule-based technical errors, standards-based diffusion, and advanced technical transmission of neural network cells, data extraction techniques, and so forth. Based on statics and discovery rules.

Figure 5. IDS classification

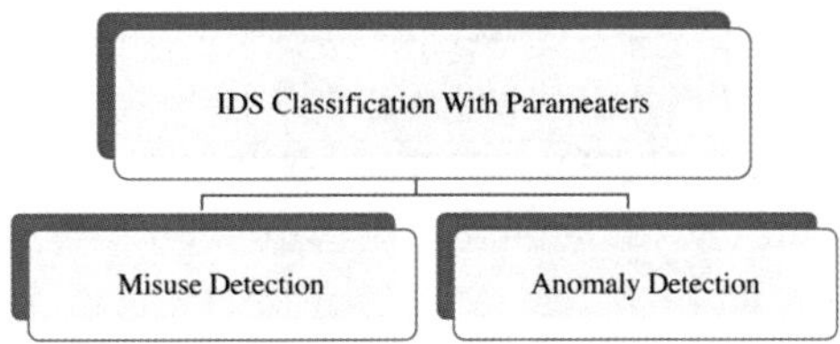

Misuse detection: Misuse results determine progress by linking their applicability to different domains. Use the misuse detectors to compare the model for analysis. These reagents search for events that correspond to a predefined template in the IDS. The equivalent forms of already existed attacks are entitled as signatures that are placed in the attack repository. If this match is detected, infiltration is detected. Sometimes the discovery of misuse is called "signature-based detection". Therefore, whenever it happens, the form is compiled and compared to the stored configuration. If no match is found, it means there is a trip. Misuse of detection easily fails with unidentified intrusions. Possible approach to solve this situation is to continuously apprise the attack repository on a regular or manual basis in a long and arduous process, or using automatically supervised learning algorithms. Unfortunately, the data sets used for this purpose are generally expensive and require that each instance of the game data be classified as ordinary or simple of information. Alternative approach to resolve that situation is to apply IDS model (Barbara et al., 2001; Hatcher & Yu, 2018).

Anomaly detection: Anomaly detection can detect newly created intrusions with help of repository of normal situation. However, the main trouble is to find the boundary among casual and suspicious behavior, because there are no abnormal samples at the learning stage. Anomaly detection is very inconvenient: it is extremely difficult to connect the alarm clock to the specific event that caused it. The scheme is actual difficult. There is no guarantee that the alarm will be activated if the activity is intrusively near "normal" activity or "abnormal activity".

Merits of IDS

There are many advantages of IDS in the network System s which are given below:

- IDS are used to identify the currently running application
- The system can identify the accomplishment of an attack
- IDS can also identify failure of attacks over the network
- It requires information about requirement of additional hardware.
- It also identifies whether the hosts performances is trouble or not.
- It also identifies invisible network attacks from single hosts

Demerits of Existing IDS

Most of the current IDS systems avoid such problems (Bilaiya & Ahlawat, 2019):

- The intervention detection system uses additional system resources that are constantly intercepted, even in the absence of any interference, because the internal stress detection system should work at any time. This is a problem with the use of resources.
- Replace the components of the internal detection system as a separate program. An attacker can disable or modify a program that runs on the system, detection system is unreliable or unnecessary. This is a problem of reliability.

Table explains the summary of dissimilarities among merits and demerits of the two approaches. The comparative analysis of different approaches of IDS is summarized and is given by Table 1.

Table 1. Comparison of different approaches of IDSs

S.N.	Misuse Based Detection	Anomaly Based Detection
1.	Require Continuous Updates	No Updates Required
2	No Initial Training	Training Is Required
3.	Needs Tuning As Per Environment	Tuning Is A Part Of Training Itself
4.	Cannot Detect Novel Attacks	Detect Any Novel Attacks
5.	Accurate Alerts	Vague Alerts
6.	Very Few False Positives	Huge Numbers Of False Positives
7.	Easy To Design	Difficult To Design

RELATED WORK

Wang *et al.* (Wang et al., 2008) introduced two exposure rules-based on some number of sensors applied to identify wicked nodes. Those are unique and duplicated node detection principles. Three system rules, i.e., range traveled by node, the possibility of recognizing the wicked node, and the typical range visited with the node meant practiced in both these WSN situations. The opportunity to identify this malicious link concerning distance covered with some wicked node in the system was calculated, applying the quantity of nodes disposed of in a selective area.

Wang *et al.* (Wang et al., 2011) proposed a way to combine the three different forms of IDS methods that are used at various points in the system. The initial one is on the sink level, named as the smart composite IDS. The next one is on the group administrator level, and the last one is on that node. IHIDS owned self-experienced section during extra special attacks as it primarily separated the unusual packets from the regular course and thus flowed those to the misuse discovery module for the protection of the system. Model was resource constrained, therefore they practiced that rule based model to understand the previous attack to succeed in those costs. Their system called'' misuse IDS.

Salehi *et al.* (Salehi et al., 2013) proposed an instruction detection system in which all identified the sink hole problem in a pair of stages. In the early stage they have divided a record of suspect connections by monitoring information variance within every nodes, and in every next stage, they recognized the sink hole attacker link of the record of suspect links by examining or monitoring the system traffic data movement.

Wazid *et al.* (Wazid et al., 2016) presented an IDS named different classes of sink-hole attack in a hierarchical sensor system. Discovery was proceed in two stages, in the very first phase it recognized the identity of the sink hole nodes with using various system production states, as an example, classification of various nodes, the completed track of a point between every node and others. Earlier, a link grew under the speculated class than that next stage method established some relationships as the sink hole attacker link, including the subsequent types (sink hole information delay link, sink hole information alteration node, and sink hole information dropping link).

Selvakumar *et al.* (Selvakumar et al., 2019) suggested an understanding Intrusion detection system, which, based on temporary argumentation, that worked on multi class analysis through a self-managed algorithm identified as fuzzy and rough based neighborhood algorithm'. The recommended structure held with eight stages. It was designed to overcome some complexity as it eliminated the unnecessary properties and practiced Allen's period's operatives.

Alaparthy and Morgera (Alaparthy & Morgera, 2018) proposed a multi-level IDS with WSN situation based about that protected method idea of the human physique. Factors before-mentioned essentially battery life, information or information volume, information transfer speed were used to complete that discovery. In the submitted work, some links were located near that sink node being a protected node, including any processing abilities, and when all developed a system between them to make molecular model review to detect the attack.

Sun *et al.* (Sun et al., 2018) introduced a multiple level Intrusion detection system with the help of an adverse model and an advanced indicator model to overcome the difficulties of resource restrained WSN. Primary element analysis was used to decrease the dimensions of discovering innovations that an additional decrease in the overall complexity of the network. That discovery can be specific, that changes as by the locations. The classified extended sensor connections package provides differentiated detections capabilities at different points. Hence, Wang *et al.* (Wang et al., 2013) presented an summary of the difficulty of IDS in a distributed wireless sensor network. That unique sensing detection and various detection situations was considered. This review of classified WSN was compared among the ability of classified WSN.

Wazid and Das (Wazid & Das, 2016) (Wazid & Das, 2017) introduced an intrusion detection system to some exposure of blackhole attacker links as strongly as to composite exception in WSN. That detection by source group head links in a WSN.

Jan *et al.* (Jan et al., 2019) executed a weight data IDS to reduce the various typical attack in IoT, with examining a system of source-nodes. All accepted the package transfer speed for the display from which some features were excerpted to overcome the timing absorbed to classify the traffic flow. However, the executed job not give the aspired outcome in the system, which had static traffic.

INTRUSION DETECTION SCHEMES

Specification-Based Intrusion Detection Design

That design is likewise recognized because of rule-based intrusion detection scheme. Next certain schemes, we have a collection of keys determining the attacks.

Advantages:

- Discovery happens quickly.
- Easy practices toward identifying attack
- More restricted complexity
- More important correctness during discovery.

Disadvantages:

- Abstraction
- cumulative voting.
- Hypotheses made.

Computational Intelligence and Information Mining Based Design

Smart IDS uses Information mining and Computational Intelligence procedures in machine interfaces because of unknown attacks exposure knowledge of this design. WSN covers difficulties because of insufficient support.

Advantages:

- Transmission expenses is more concise
- Generality
- Assured scalability.

Disadvantages:

- Discovery is Inactive
- Computational complexity is important Invalid signals are powerful.

The Game Theory Based Intrusion Detection Design

That system described accurately with a sport among members. The ID uses these different approaches means to defend the strategies that attackers regularly use.

Advantages:

- Do Not demand more information.
- Incompetent
- It depends on approachcs.

Disadvantages

- Desire to have experimented so time-consuming in the commencement
- The range is restricted.

Statistical Based Intrusion Detection Design

Mathematically based procedures are usually used for detection schemes invented for WSN. The probability method is used in these plans for regular, including irregular data as a case style.

Advantages:

- Mathematically proven.
- They are applied efficiently with an exact possibility relationships.

Disadvantages:

- Difficulties in understanding probability.
- No fit during multivariate information.

Motivation

Due to the high usage of the internet, risk are maximizing day by day. Provides step-by-step instructions for identifying various system attacks, including unexpected attacks, as a specific issue. An extensive data security investigation, an Intrusion Detection System (IDS), can isolate an attack that may have been internal or interrupted that has just happened. Interference is increasing the accuracy of laptops to effectively detect parasitic behaviors.(Hosseinpour & Abu Bakar, 2010)IDS is used for detecting the intruder present in the network and monitoring the system misuse activity and it is classification it as anomalous and normal.

Developing absolutely secure system is bit difficult most of the existing IDS system have the security flaws. They generate the false alarm. All kind of intrusion present in the network are not known.

Quickly identifying and detecting intruder can help to limit the damage from the infection. Past few years the most common attacks are Virus, Laptop t heft, Denial of Service and System Penetration, Unauthorized Access by Insiders and Insider Abuse of Net Access.

Research Gap

This analysis addresses the matter of reducing the quantity of options and properly distinctive relevant options from a collection of collected data for an anomaly-based intrusion detection system whereas maintaining integrity of the Data. Data nonheritable for an intrusion detection system oftentimes originates from multiple sources like system activity logs, content of knowledge packets and headers, system calls, memory and disk approach activities, and alternative information. Intrusion detection systems might also share these logs among other network devices for collaboration in a very distributed manner. Reducing the number of data that has relevancy needs categorizing the data from the logs into parameters, conjointly noted as dimensions. Data set of network traffic, attacks measure by the selection method represent explicit activities. This is implying that not all attacks measure found by a similar selection of options in all cases.

The intrusion detection system allows you to discover and divide activities on the network to get a breakpoint. Intrusion detection can be handled by detecting anomalies and signing (Bilaiya & Ahlawat, 2019; Malathi et al., 2018). Intrusion detection technology to analyze and monitor events on a computer or network of incidents of potential violations or the imminent threat of human rights violations.(Hui & Liu, 2010) William Stallings (Singh & Pandey, 2013) categorized IDS various parameters grounded on the detection, rule and numerical based anomaly detection. Stefano Zanero (Shargh, 2009) classified IDS mistreatment use or anomaly detection based detection concept.

In detecting anomalies, all abnormal cases are called intrusions and false alarms are expected when abnormal situations occur due to irregular behavior and not intrusion. Packet inhalation is the process of collecting network traffic by capturing data during transport and storing it for later analysis (Aljawarneh et al., 2018). In network security numerous techniques have projected to discover unauthorized use, misuse and abuse of laptop systems by each system internal and external intruders. Owing to the speedily increasing unauthorized activities, Intrusion Detection System (IDS) as element of defense-in-depth is extremely necessary as a result of ancient techniques cannot offer complete protection against intrusion for example:

1. The correlation of alarm isn't précised.
2. The detection and prediction of false positive and false negative rate is high.
3. The measure of abnormal behavior exploitation the pattern structure has restricted scope.

Implementation

The proposed IDS experiment may be performed in Matlab 7.8.0 software and well famous intrusion data set KDD cup99 provided by DARPA agency.

Consider KDD CUP 99 dataset used as experimental data, which is retrieved from DARPA 98 intrusion detection system evaluation. This data set is a collection of test set which is widely used in the detection of the instruction data. It includes about nearly 4.9 Million simulative attack record with 22 types of attack. It also provides a very large amount of data. The KDD Cup 99 data set of 10% alone are to be considered for Testing and Training with proposed research work. This training data set and Testing done with two types of attacks such as

1. DoS
2. U2R (user to Root)

KDD Cup99 is the data set which is involves for testing and training set. Data involves the major attack that are DoS and U2R (user to Root).

1. Denial-of-Service (DoS): A Denial-of-Service makes the services unavailable to legitimate user.
2. Remote-to-Local (R2L): A Remote-to-Local is the
3. A Attacker who had no privileges to access a private network from outside like Send mail, guess password, spy etc. over the internet.

Hybrid Probabilistic intrusion detection system that encapsulates extraction feature with pattern detection associated probabilistic classification model to spot an trespasser. during this framework at first, information square measure nonheritable then similarity and negative options square measure extracted. These negative and similarity options act as a key for pattern detection. Planned framework use passion distribution to explore negative feature and examine trespasser information in KDD9 Cup information set.

Hybrid IDS algorithm the genetic and whale algorithm in the first stage, all the data present in the NSL-KDD dataset is trained all the features. Output of the stages are classified. [AC = Actual class, PC = predicted class]

- Correctly classified record (AC == PC).
- Misclassified record (AC != PC)

Evaluation Parameters for IDS

Confusion matrix is a specialized table that determines the performance of an algorithm or classifiers. It is designed for binary as multi-classes of dataset. The term "confusion" is derived in that situation when the category/class of any data value is in dilemma situation i.e. it can be either of class I or class II. So, it creates confusion and that's why it is named as confusion matrix. The dimension of the matrix is represented as actual and predicted class of the classified data values. Below table illustrates the confusion matrix as well

Table 2. Confusion matrix

	Predicted-I	**Predicted-II**
Actual-1	(TP)	(FN)
Actual-0	(FP)	(TN)

TP = Detects condition when it is present
FN = Does not detect condition when it is present
FP = Detects condition when it is absent
TN = Does not detect condition when it is absent

1. **True Positive (TP) / Recall:** True Positive in this perspective is described as the amount of true positives separated through the entire amount of parts that actually apply to the positive category (i.e. the addition of true positives and false negatives, which are articles which weren't tagged as applying to the positive category but should have been).

It is the measure of positive events that were properly categorized as positive, as computed utilizing by the following equation:

$$Recall = \frac{TP}{TP + FN} \tag{1}$$

2. 2. **False Positive (FP):** It is the quantity of negative cases that were wrongly categorized as positive, as calculated utilizing by the following equation:

$$FP = \frac{FP}{TN + FP} \tag{2}$$

3. 3. **True Negative (TN):** It described as the quantity of negatives cases that were categorized appropriately, as computed utilizing by the following equation:

$$TN = \frac{TN}{TN + FP} \tag{3}$$

4. 4. **False Negative (FN):** The quantity with positive points which are mistakenly recognized as negative, as computed utilizing by the following equation:

$$FN = \frac{FN}{FN + TP} \tag{4}$$

Accuracy = (TP + TN) / (TP + TN +FP + FN)

Some Potential Applications IDS

Home Automation System

IDS implemented technology is cooperative among virtually every device. In our home instruments, proposes an intelligent automatic method. Users can compare home stuff based on the automation system everywhere in the system. Such a variety of schemes is extremely accommodating in these nations, which possess a higher quantity of old people. While the descendants of certain people can support their origins remotely with establishing that smart home instruments handling smartphones.

Air Contamination Monitoring System

Air contamination is a mainly general difficulty in certain eras. Contaminated air includes dangerous scraps before-mentioned as lead, carbon mono-oxide, sulfur di-oxide, and other heavy particles, which produce such a serious air contamination. This more diminishes the condition of the atmosphere, particularly in metro centers. Environment pollution is a main reason of the dangerous conditions such as asthmatic attacks, chronical obstruct pulmonary condition, waek lung capacity, destructive disease, and Pneumonitis. Hence, it enhances the importance of deploying some mechanisms to regulate air pollution in an area. Therefore, the researchers of WSN with IoT fields got up with amazing opinions to solve this difficulty. Recently produced IoT tools can control the degree of the atmosphere and transmit information to servers. So data can be more utilized to predict several defects linked to the quality of the air. Certain designs are essential to identify air contamination in a city. We can employ particle material indicator, gas sensor, cold, and condensation sensor to complete those procedures.

Automatic Health Monitoring System

Now a days the growth of the people growing extremely stressful, and people seem not to take burden of their health well. Typically, people do not operate for routine checkups. IoT designs, for instance, intelligent health monitor systems, can solve this difficulty. That seems to realize that health sensors in body of patient may sense the reading of pressure of blood, level of sugar, and heartbeat and automatically inform and if it is very important than the rest values In such a situation, smart sensor-based tools monitor the health of objects (i.e., patient) automatically and transmit data to the cloud server, which can be more accessed by doctors, nurses, and the relatives of that victim through the smartphones. Doctor can review the current health station of the victims at any time and everywhere from the world by offering that treatment of the before-mentioned sort of information conditions.

Modern Traffic Management System

Traffic difficulties remain beyond in around all metro capitals because of the growing plenty of transports in the area. Wireless sensor networks with IoT based projects like modern traffic manage method can defeat the problem. The intelligent traffic manage method consists of smart automobiles with the capability of Intelligent sensors, which can interact with each other. The information of certain transportations can be transferred into a cloud that can be utilized for additional procedures and forecasts. Since primary authorization may put an alert in fact of a huge movement in any distinct places. That directions be beneficial during the operators that exist in any emergencies. That can become their source toward specific support presented data on the event. That can further monitor traffic systems violators.

Advance Flood Detection With Avoidance

Flood remains a prevalent annual difficulty. Various lands were sustained with that regular hazard. It produces a lack of lives moreover damages the economics of a nation. That's why we require advance flood discovery to decrease the end of lives, including assets. Forward this operating with the area of wireless sensor networks with IoT developed an idea with the concept of an ancient food disclosure method. As a technique, detects flood situations applying a level of moisture, temperature, sea level, and profound level. Float sensors are employed for controlling the water level. Some flood sensor observes the stream of liquid. That has a liquid rotor, a hall sensor with a flexible device body. With all such monitored values may be reached with the help of a smartphone to prognosticate that flood like circumstances.

Intelligent Ant Theft System

Protection has displayed the main demands of modern society. All require to ensure house and business from each dynamic theft. Wireless sensor networks with IoT administrations can solve that difficulty. If any user operates out from their home, all become to shift on some antitheft method, which command control some levels, and any step toward that level tiles order sense warning over these dangerous operations. Within that case, if a thief opens some house, this extended operated sensor recognizes this because the exception carries identical information to every notification method which holds one micro-controller. The micro-controller later presents that a strong signal initiates that camera to catch a picture and posts that theft message to the owner concerning this house. When that user notices this image on their smartphone.

Safety System for Coke Mines

There regularly exists a lifetime uncertainty in coke mines. Coke deposits are particularly vulnerable areas wherever a mechanic can quickly lose a life. Accordingly, researchers operating in that field of Wireless sensor networks, including IoT, created a unique idea of a Safe System for coke mines. During the implementation design, require Arduino equipment to associated with an interface microcontroller, including the gasoline sensor and temperature sensor. An extended material was configured in such some means that ever the gasoline sensor identifies the level about gasoline following the aspired level, before a piece of alarm information was sent to each authorization concerning the toxic gasoline level. Toward such away, we can protect the individual lives of those people serving in the coke mines.

Smartly Agriculture

The population of the world is growing every day. Accordingly, to need a developing society, the agriculture industry needs a new smart structure as IoT. Agriculture bears by some difficulties, like an example, intense conditions of weather, growing change in weather, and different agents of environmental. Modern farming was based on IoT frameworks that support the to overcome wastage and improve fertility. The modern farming method is a high technology system that uses a little cost for producing the food clean and sustain for the amount. In a WSN with IoT smart farming, a method was formed to control the field with the sensors (like the factors, moisture, radiation, clay moisture, etc.) also to automate that propagation system. Adopting such each method, a producer can control the domain statuses practicing any smartphone from everywhere. This executes this a practical method as related over that traditional method. Intelligent agriculture can give many privileges before-mentioned as effective control of liquid (optimization about information and procedures) with fertilizers.

RESEARCH ISSUES AND CHALLENGES

Wireless sensors networks with IoT-based information situation gives a broad kind like utilization, before-mentioned as an intelligent house, intelligent transport, sensible health and care, and smart cities. That sort of information ecosystem requires different specifications so as real-time information processing, including passage like monitoring of a patient, environmental situation toward a manufacturing factory so on. The information gathered by these intelligent sensors is huge. Hence, we can use to significant information analytic system about that information to discover out a certain model from that like the future health-wise forecast of a victim. Such sort of information status is additionally a member of the Internet. Hence, it allows for conventional safety, isolation, and other difficulties. With all those difficulties, IDS in wireless sensors networks with IoT is one of the significant problems of these fields at which various researchers are directly operating. In the latter portion of the sector, we consider the modern difficulties for investigation. Then throughout public reviews, we present the features of later research ways of IDS in wireless sensor networks with IoT environment.

A. Security of Intrusion Detection Techniques

Largest of the intrusion detection techniques intended for WSN with IoT is nonsecure because they do not give full-proof security toward different kinds of attacks. Any of those recommended procedures in that discussion occur attack special and do not control for various attacks at the similar time. Hence, we require to produce such a variety of intrusion detection techniques that should be robust and safe toward various attacks at the corresponding time. Drafting of such a variety of methods can be a challenging difficulty due to the resource constraints of sensors with IoT methods.

B. Efficiency of Intrusion Detection Techniques

In Wireless sensor networks with IoT-based information environments, the WSN sensors and smart IoT sensors are resources constrained as they have less calculation capability and storehouse capability with short battery life. Therefore, such tools can not function calculation, transmission, and storage-intensive transactions that need more major strength in courses of such parameters — also recommended to use the small dimension of messages through the intrusion detection method. The reason behind that is, it may consume other resources of devices that cause quick battery waste of the sensors in transferring and collecting large information. Therefore, we require to create intrusion detection techniques in such a means that the proposed method should present fewer estimate costs, information costs, and warehouse costs externally, compromising the safety of the method.

C. Scalability of Intrusion Detection Techniques

Wireless sensor network with integrated IoT implies a sort of general system independent arrangement of different information models, including applications which possess their capacities and requirements. In that way, intrusion detection for such a kind of communication environment will be a challenging job. We can have Electronic Health Records of individual users, which are stored in an IoT-enabled cloud server for further processing. Many devices inside the Body Area Network create data and transfer it to the cloud. As a result, this creates a mixed network of different communicating devices. Hence, we require a particular type of intrusion detection technique which can protect all kinds of devices of such kind of communication environment. Henceforth, more extensive research is required in this area.

D. Isolation of Information Maintain Beyond Cloud Server

That division of information describes how we should handle the information across multiple designs. That WSN connected with IoT based knowledge is also applied as data-sensitive schemes, for example, smart health care. In such a demanding privacy situation, effective power sensors are embedded or connected everywhere the information of a victim to sense their energy knowledge and convey the data to the cloud for the warehouse, including processing. While we understand, such a sort of data ecosystem can be attacked by different kinds of intrusions. It suddenly enhances essentials to preserve the isolation of data, i.e., collected information and data in transition. Accordingly, we need extra profitable systems that maintain the privacy of the collected data and data in transition. So, privacy aware intrusion detection systems should designed for IoT ecosystem in which device user's isolation should preserved.

E. Heterogeneity of WSN and IoT Delivery Condition

Wireless sensor network with IoT based delivery conditions varies in characteristics as we possess various kinds of tools extending from full edged desktops, laptops, private digital accessories to low powered sensing tools, and low-end RFID chips. Besides, certain tools operate below those teachings of various models of information rules. Here is also essential to maintain that these methods are distinct in terms of their transmission area, warehouse volume, counting energy, and running method. Hence, we require to produce an efficient intrusion detection procedure in such a form that it defends every diverse type of designs and associated technologies.

F. Cross Platform Intrusion Detection

Heterogeneity regarding the WSN with the IoT situation makes a difficulty if we prepare to expand any intrusion discovery techniques. This heterogeneity supports each inter-connection about various utilization areas. Without related terms, it additionally builds objections while creating an efficient intrusion detection method. For instance, if an intelligent house application needs to obtain some data from a health-care sensing device, the intrusion detection needs to be reliable and cooperative so that the form should recover that information from each end system without difficulty. Still, it remains deserving of recording that most of the moment, information is stored above some cloud during which various intrusion devices are required. Hence, during such classes of applications, we require effective and robust intrusion detection systems to implement seamless connectivity beyond the multiple IoT stages.

CONCLUSION AND FUTURE SCOPE

Now a day, community is moving towards the cloud and its security is in more important and its really needed to research and think about it. Old vulnerability has been known by the attacker; it can be easily exploited. To deal with the security solution and intruder which is insider the network can be identified by the IDS. Some of the solution consist of network firewall, anti-malware, malicious entities and fake traffic are detected through packet sniffing. Signature and patterns matching techniques for analysis the various files present in the network and systems which analyze and detect by IDS. In future work should be done on accuracy and to reduce the false alarm. Patches should be provided so, that vulnerability should not exploit.

REFERENCES

Alaparthy & Morgera. (2018). A multi-level intrusion detection system for wireless sensor networks based on immune theory. *IEEE Access*, *6*, 47364-47373.

Aljawarneh, S., Aldwairi, M., & Yassein, M. B. (2018). Anomaly-based intrusion detection system through feature selection analysis and building hybrid efficient model. *Journal of Computational Science, 25*, 152–160. doi:10.1016/j.jocs.2017.03.006

Barbara, D., Wu, N., & Jajodia, S. (2001). Detecting novel network intrusions using bayes estimators. In *Proceedings of the 2001 SIAM International Conference on Data Mining*, (pp. 1-17). Society for Industrial and Applied Mathematics. 10.1137/1.9781611972719.28

Bilaiya, R., & Ahlawat, P. (2019). Hybrid Evolutionary Approach for IDS by Using Genetic and Poisson Distribution. In *International Conference on Inventive Computation Technologies*, (pp. 766-773). Springer.

Hatcher, W. G., & Yu, W. (2018). A survey of deep learning: Platforms, applications and emerging research trends. *IEEE Access: Practical Innovations, Open Solutions, 6*, 24411–24432. doi:10.1109/ACCESS.2018.2830661

Hoque, M. Bikas, & Naser. (2012). *An implementation of intrusion detection system using genetic algorithm.* arXiv preprint arXiv:1204.1336.

Hosseinpour, F., & Abu Bakar, K. (2010). Survey on artificial immune system as a bio-inspired technique for anomaly based intrusion detection systems. In *2010 International Conference on Intelligent Networking and Collaborative Systems*, (pp. 323-324). IEEE. 10.1109/INCOS.2010.40

Hui, Y., & Liu, J. (2010). Intrusion detection based on immune dynamical matching algorithm. In *2010 International Conference on E-Business and E-Government*, (pp. 1342-1345). IEEE. 10.1109/ICEE.2010.342

Jan, Ahmed, Shakhov, & Koo. (2019). Toward a lightweight intrusion detection system for the Internet of Things. *IEEE Access, 7*, 42450-42471.

Li, Tug, Meng, & Wang. (2019). Designing collaborative blockchained signature-based intrusion detection in IoT environments. *Future Gener. Comput. Syst., 96*, 481-489.

Malathi, Reddy, & Jayaseeli. (2018). A survey on anomaly based host intrusion detection system. Journal of Physics: Conference Series, 1000(1).

Salehi, S. A., Razzaque, M. A., Naraei, P., & Farrokhtala, A. (2013). Detection of sinkhole attack in wireless sensor networks. *Proc. IEEE Int. Conf. Space Sci. Commun. (IconSpace)*, 361-365. 10.1109/IconSpace.2013.6599496

Selvakumar, Karuppiah, Sairamesh, Islam, Hassan, Fortino, & Choo. (2019). Intelligent temporal classification and fuzzy rough set-based feature selection algorithm for intrusion detection system in WSNs. *Inf. Sci., 497*, 77-90.

Shargh. (2009). Using artificial immune system on implementation of intrusion detection systems. In *2009 Third UKSim European Symposium on Computer Modeling and Simulation*, (pp. 164-168). IEEE.

Singh, N., & Pandey, Y. (2013). Dendritic Cell Algorithm and Dempster Belief Theory Using Improved Intrusion Detection System. *International Journal of Advanced Research in Computer Science and Software Engineering, 3*(7).

Sun, Xu, Liang, & Zhou. (2018). An intrusion detection model for wireless sensor networks with an improved V-detector algorithm. *IEEE Sensors J.*, *18*(5), 1971-1984.

Wang, Fu, & Agrawal. (2013). Gaussian versus uniform distribution for intrusion detection in wireless sensor networks. *IEEE Trans. Parallel Distrib. Syst.*, *24*(2), 342-355.

Wang, Wang, Xie, Wang, & Agrawal. (2008). Intrusion detection in homogeneous and heterogeneous wireless sensor networks. *IEEE Trans. Mobile Comput.*, *7*(6), 698-711.

Wang, Yan, Wang, & Liu. (2011). An integrated intrusion detection system for cluster-based wireless sensor networks. *Expert Syst. Appl.*, *38*(12), 15234-15243.

Wazid & Das. (2016). An efficient hybrid anomaly detection scheme using k-means clustering for wireless sensor networks. *Wireless Pers. Commun.*, *90*(4), 1971-2000.

Wazid & Das. (2017). A secure group_based blackhole node detection scheme for hierarchical wireless sensor networks. *Wireless Pers. Commun.*, *94*(3), 1165-1191.

Wazid, Das, Kumari, & Khan. (2016). Design of sinkhole node detection mechanism for hierarchical wireless sensor networks. *Secur. Commun. Netw.*, *9*(17), 4596-4614.

KEY TERMS AND DEFINITIONS

Snort: These uses stateless string matching for detection of attacks and is most commonly used technique.

Web IDS: This system is based on pattern matching and thresholds for detection of attacks. It is complex than Snort because of the thresholds that requires expert domain knowledge about the difference between normal behavior and attack behavior.

Chapter 15
Vulnerability Assessment and Malware Analysis of Android Apps Using Machine Learning

Pallavi Khatri
ITM University, Gwalior, India

Animesh Kumar Agrawal
ITM University, Gwalior, India

Aman Sharma
Independent Researcher, India

Navpreet Pannu
Independent Researcher, India

Sumitra Ranjan Sinha
Independent Researcher, India

ABSTRACT

Mobile devices and their use are rapidly growing to the zenith in the market. Android devices are the most popular and handy when it comes to the mobile devices. With the rapid increase in the use of Android phones, more applications are available for users. Through these alluring multi-functional applications, cyber criminals are stealing personal information and tracking the activities of users. This chapter presents a two-way approach for finding malicious Android packages (APKs) by using different Android applications through static and dynamic analysis. Three cases are considered depending upon the severity level of APK, permission-based protection level, and dynamic analysis of APK for creating the dataset for further analysis. Subsequently, supervised machine learning techniques such as naive Bayes multinomial text, REPtree, voted perceptron, and SGD text are applied to the dataset to classify the selected APKs as malicious, benign, or suspicious.

DOI: 10.4018/978-1-7998-3299-7.ch015

INTRODUCTION

In recent years Android operating system has become popular in mobiles and has overtaken the other platforms available in the market. There are over 2.5 billion active users in the market. Popularity of Android as an open source, easy to implement platform to the developers has led to development of varied apps that can be downloaded from Google play store and 3rd party stores. Cybercriminals are finding an easy gateway to a device through these permission based apps. With the increased use of various apps on Android based devices, the probability of malware attacks is increasing every second. Attacks done through the apps are more difficult to detect using conventional methods. Numerous methods have been proposed and various new techniques have been researched to analyze the malware so that the source of compromise can be identified. But the issue remains relevant because innovative methods are being used to pilfer a device. In order to handle the increased malware proliferation, various researchers have worked extensively on Machine Learning based malware analysis and have been successful to a great extent in classifying a given sample as malicious or benign. However, the malware development is fast outpacing the identification and the containment process, thereby giving impetus to more quality research in this field. While increased security mechanism has been put in place to filter out malicious content from being downloaded, it has not been able to prevent spread of malicious apps among android users. Some of these applications are gathering large amount of sensitive information from the user as well as from the android device without taking prior permission of the user. In order to install an application in an android device, there is a need to grant certain permissions by the user so that the app has the exclusively consent of the user to access its private or sensitive data. Every Android app after development is deployed after assembling and compiling in to an APK file. APK file includes the code of the application (".dex" files), different dependencies (.jar) and resources, and the AndroidManifest.xml file. AndroidManifest.xml file is an important file that provides the information about the application features and configuration for the particular application. It also includes the information of the APIs regarding permissions, activities, services, contents. This file is important while doing malware analysis of a device. Android malware analysis can be done statically and dynamically. Static analysis detects the malicious behavior in the source code, data files, or the binary files without executing the application. However, this technique has a major drawback wherein it is impossible to detect any code obfuscation or dynamic code loading. Static analysis also supports signature based analysis using which signature of the malicious application (.APK) can be checked to maintain the integrity of a particular APK. Basic static analysis is straightforward and can be quick, but it's largely ineffective against sophisticated malware and does not do behavior analysis of the APK. Dynamic analysis is a malware detection technique that evaluates the malicious behavior of an app by executing the application in a real environment. The main advantage of this technique is that it detects dynamic code loading and records the application behavior during runtime. Any network activity like connecting with CNC server or any outbound connection and any sensitive data pilferage is reflected during the dynamic analysis. Malware analysis normally uses static analysis as it gives fair idea about the malicious behavior of an app. However, static analysis is incomplete without dynamic analysis as dynamic analysis helps in corroborating the findings of static analysis and also gives vital evidence to a forensic investigator. This work uses a comprehensive approach for malware analysis wherein both static and dynamic analysis along with Machine Learning (ML) based techniques is used. An android device with multiple apps installed on it is used to check the behaviour of an app and identify if it's depicting a malicious behaviour. Various analytical tools for static analysis are used to extract out the features from an app that includes Permissions and APIs and identify the maliciousness of the app. These features then form a training data 2 set which are used to train ML based algorithms. A very popular framework called WEKA (Waikato Enabled for Knowledge Analysis) is used to execute ML based algorithms for malware analysis of an app. Number of apps on play store is more than 2.1 million apps and is growing continuously. With these many apps it is practically not possible to analyse all the apps. The various apps can be classified into different broad categories like dating, antivirus, gaming, social media, etc. based on their functionality. Hence, the best approach is to analyse few apps from each of the popular categories and extract features from it so that they can be analyzed for its maliciousness. Here, the dating category has been chosen because of its popularity. The proposed solution utilizes this approach to apply four machine learning algorithms (Naïve Bayes multinomial text, REPtree, Voted Perceptron and SGD) and predict probability of it being malicious.

OTHER CONTRIBUTIONS

Lot of work has been done in malware classification problem field and few of the recent contributions are summarized in this section that will help to give new dimension to our research work and propose a unique approach with an aim to achieve higher accuracy.

Authors (Agrawal A.K. et al, 2018) have done a comparative study of mobile forensic tools that are used for artifacts extraction from large scale android devices irrespective of OS version. The authors have highlighted the pros and cons of the various tools with the help of experiments.

Authors (Agrawal, A. K. et al, 2018) have worked on an unrooted mobile device. The authors have demonstrated how data can be extracted from an android mobile device which is not rooted. This work incorporates TWRP mechanism to flash custom recovery and perform forensic analysis of android device.

The work presented by the authors (Raymond Choo, et al, 2018) talks about android malware analysis using Machine Learning techniques. Static analysis of the malware has been presented in the paper using two approaches one being app permission based and other being analysis of source code of the app using machine learning algorithms. The source code analysis approach had better accuracy (95%) in classifying a give sample as malware over permission based approach (89%). The concept of ensemble learning has been introduced by the authors to test various ML algorithms for malware classification. The advantage of the approach proposed by the authors over the existing signature based anti-malware solutions/classification is that it does not have to wait for the malware signature to be released. Also the experiments do not require the android phone to be rooted.

Work in (Shalaginov A, et al, 2017) describes in detail the various Machine Learning based static malware analysis techniques in order to classify the characteristics of malicious PE32 Windows files. The authors have given detailed analysis of various ML based malware classification techniques and have utilised them to identify whether a given sample is benign or malicious. With the help of experiments, the authors have shown improved accuracy in identifying the malicious sample by ML based algorithms as compared to conventional methods. The various ML techniques have also been explained for a researcher to comprehend and utilize the knowledge in applying in his research.

The research presented in (Sushma Verma, et al,. 2017) is based on analysis of permissions and intent of an android operating system to detect malware. The work is based on utilizing ML algorithms on WEKA tool kit. Two popular decision tree based classification algorithms namely ID3 and C4.5 (or J48) were used to classify 620 malicious and 850 benign applications. The intents and permissions were extracted as features and fed to ML algorithms and an accuracy of 94% was achieved by the authors.

In (Hongwei Zhao, et.al, 2018), the authors talks about application of ML algorithms for dynamic malware analysis. Samples which are both malicious and benign are taken and analysed in Cuckoo Sandbox, which is a virtualized isolated environment. The report generated from this analysis, which is in JSON format, features are extracted and analysed in WEKA framework. The WEKA framework offers large number of ML based methods. The extracted features in CSV format are fed to the WEKA algorithms and the results are analysed to find out the accuracy of identification of malware samples. The authors have concluded the widely accepted fact that ensemble based techniques have better capability in detecting malwares.

Work in (K Sethi, et al., 2017) presents a ML based framework to detect different types of file extensions and classify them as malicious or benign. Macro classifiers are used for detection of malware files and Micro for further subdividing them into different families of malware like Trojan, Spyware, etc. Cuckoo Sandbox is used to extract features of the files under test and WEKA is used to test ML models to check which model is able to give a better accuracy of classification of malicious file. As per the authors, decision tree model (J48) gives 100% accuracy, SMO 99% and Random Forest tree 97%. However, they have also brought the fact that the smaller sample size (220) could be the reason for 100% accuracy in case of J48 model test.

Extracting features from an android app and applying ML based algorithms on it for classification has been implemented in (Dimitris Geneiatakis, et al., 2018). Performance of two well-known ML algorithms i.e. K-Nearest Neighbour (K-NN) and the Support Vector Machine (SVM) has been evaluated using Variance and sum of API and permissions features. This approach relies on statistical properties of the features and claims to have better accuracy in malware classification.

Various supervised ML algorithms to classify an app as malicious or benign based on the various permissions it gives through AndroidManifest.xml file are used by work done in (Andrew H. Sung, et al,. 2018). Based on the results of the experiments carried out by various algorithms, it was deduced that KNN produces the most accurate results and is able to classify the malicious apps in a much better way.

The authors in (Rajni Jindal, et al,.2018) have proposed a tool called DroidMark in this paper to carry out malware analysis. The APK files are reverse engineered to find sources of sensitive data leakage without taking the consent of the user. Various features are extracted and fed to WEKA classifier. Bayesian Network classifier is used to classify the data set and an accuracy of 96.88% is claimed by the authors.

Permission based analysis of APK files by assigning a score to each permission which appears in the APK file and then using these permissions as features to analyse them in ML based algorithms is discussed in (A. Kumar, et al,. 2019). The authors have proposed called FAMOUS based on their research which can automate the process of feature extraction from apps and analyse the results. Based on their analysis, it is concluded that Random Forest algorithm classifies the samples most accurately. In order to better assimilate their findings, the APK files have been taken from four different android phones and compared with the training set already obtained from a set of malicious and benign samples.

The research in (NaserPeiravian. et al,. 2013)talks about extraction of android permissions and APIs from an app and using them as features to further analyse it using ML based techniques with the ultimate aim of finding out whether a given app is malicious or not. A total of 2510 apps in near equal proportion of benign and malicious are chosen to experiment upon and it was deduced through experiments that Bagging algorithm gave the best result in classification of data.

Work in (Hossain Shahriar, et al,. 2017) tries to detect malicious android applications based on the category of application and not by individually testing each app in a sandboxed environment. The app which is under test is first categorised into one of the categories like games, communication, etc. Then the dangerous permissions of that app are compared with its category to check if its permissions are different from the category permissions. A total of 1200 samples are taken and categorised into five different heads and Latent Semantic Indexing technique is applied to retrieve permissions from the app.

The authors (Sharma A, et al., 2018) have demonstrated data extraction from a virtual android phone and have brought out that the same concept can be applied to a real android device for forensic analysis. This concept can be applied for carrying out malware analysis using ML techniques in the current research.

The research work presented by the author in (Songhao Lou, et al,.2019) introduces a new technique TFDROID which further divides the malicious application based on their functions and using cluster algorithm applications categorize them as benign and suspicious depending upon their behaviour. This approach detected the malware with 93.7% accuracy through machine learning based method. The author has used clustering algorithm but had failed in carrying out dynamic analysis of applications. Also, the clustering algorithm needs to be improved.

For Windows as well as android application based on the security and detection of malware, various methods were used for identifying the signature, behaviour of applications for detection of malware (Syed Fakhar Bilal et al,.2019). The approach was only applicable to specific situation and requirement. DERBIN named solution has been proposed by the author in this paper which can identify the malwares in android during run time in the smartphones. This method includes static analysis combined with feature extraction of the application and further setting up these features in a joint vector space. The approach was only applicable to specific situation and requirement and 97% of accuracy was achieved but with some errors as some of the features were not included. Through this method author failed in detecting the new malwares. Even, ML generated result was not so efficient although 5 techniques were used by the author for detection of malware.

Static and dynamic analysis of an app is carried out in (Alessandro Bacci et al,. 2018). The work uses ML approach for malware detection. Detection of malwares through dynamic analysis performed quite well for obfuscated and non-obfuscated type of malware. The author failed to describe which approach of detection correctly classified applications in the learning phase when no samples were available. Two methods using ML technique was applied on the derived features from dynamic and static analysis. Correct classification of application based on new transformation techniques was not done during the experimentation. In addition to this, code obfuscation was evaluated in dynamic analysis whereas static analysis based detection worked quite well for non-obfuscated samples.

The research by the author in the paper (Michal Kedziora et al,. 2018) focused on the examination of ML algorithms by taking three attributes selection algorithms and to check the efficiency amongst these three for detecting the malware. Distinctive features were taken for classifying the malwares and by using static analysis method malwares were detected for the Android mobile system. Total of five algorithms were used for classification K-NN, SVM, Random Forest and Logistic Regression with selection of three attributes algorithms for the identification of the malwares. Feature extraction analysis was done by using class code of Java. Random forest, K-NN proved to be more efficient with 80.7% probability of correctly detecting the malware. However, three attributes taken during classification results did not justify the approach used as reverse engineering of java code used is not connecting to the ML based approach.

An anomaly based malware detection framework has been proposed by authors of (Mariam Al et al,. 2017). Two categories of application benign and malicious were installed in the Android device to check the behaviour pattern of those applications.ML approach in (Mariam Al et al,. 2017)uses with seven algorithms Decision Tree, K Nearest Neighbour, Logistic Regression, Multilayer Perceptron Neural Network, Naïve Bayes, Random Forest, and Support Vector Machine for the classification of apps.

On the basis of the performance of these algorithms identification of the malicious app was made. 10 fold cross validation approach was also used in the machine learning algorithms to clearly bring out the results. Parameters chosen were not enough to clarify which is the best algorithm for malware detection. Signature based approach for malware detection was missing during the analysis which is a major drawback in this paper.

Authors of (Andrew H. Sung et al., 2018) have evaluated different types of ML based algorithm in the paper. Static analysis was used for detecting the malware in the applications. 11120 total numbers of applications with malware as well as 5560 benign samples from dataset of DREBIN was taken. Accuracy achieved was 94% which brings out the effectiveness of ML approach in detecting malwares. A total of 8 features were used to analyse the parameters and accuracy of detection. However, how the features were selected was not justified and only static analysis of application was done, anomaly based detection was missing in the paper.

The approach used in (Zhuo Ma et al., 2019) combines ML learning algorithm with control flow graph for android malware detection. Control flow graph was constructed for obtaining information of API and dataset was created accordingly. Multiclass classification based model was constructed to find the family of malicious application. Based on the dataset ensemble model was constructed for the confirmation of the approach. The experimentation was conducted on 10010 benign APK's and 10683 malicious applications. Accuracy obtained by using ML based approach was 98.98% by choosing three parameters in classification of algorithms. Only three parameters were used for the detecting the malware which is a limited approach. Authors did not address what is the API position in malicious code. The exact reason for the malicious behaviour of the application was not justified.

A malware detection system SIGPID that can identify the most important and relevant information for classifying an app as malicious or benign is implemented by (Jin Li et al., 2018). The approach used is scalable and efficient for detecting the malwares. Instead of only analysing and permission extraction of Android phones a three level approach of permission data mining was identified which was most effective for determining malicious as well as benign applications. SVM was used as a classifier in classification method of machine learning. Through this method of classification, 90% accuracy was achieved and only 22 permissions were used against the approach. This method appeared to be efficient for permission analysis of APK and was applicable for small number of application dataset. Only one algorithm was used to determine the malware type.

PROPOSED METHODOLOGY

Feature extraction is the most important aspect to analyse any problem using Machine Learning based algorithms. Hence there is a need to extract the features correctly from the apps under test so that they can be accordingly classified as malicious or benign. To classify an app this work first does the vulnerability analysis of the apps and the results are tabulated based on the severity of the vulnerability found i.e. High and Medium. and Permission Based. Secondly, the permissions are extracted from the androidmanifest. xml file for each of the apps and categorized as Dangerous, Normal and Signature based on how they can impact the user data privacy. And finally a dynamic analysis is done to check whether the app is leaking user's sensitive information by communicating with a Command and Control (C&C) Server. The novelty of approach is that three different aspects have been investigated, which to the knowledge of the authors has not been done earlier, and then fed to supervised Machine Learning based algorithms to check their efficacy.

The derived advantage of this approach is that it not only does a Vulnerability Analysis of an App but it also checks if its benign or malicious without the need to execute it, thereby preventing any sort of infection to the individual machine or network.

A total of 150 dating apps are randomly picked and analyzed and results are tabulated. The reason behind choosing the dating category apps is that they are more popular among the individuals these days. As per the survey of online dating 49% of the users are using dating apps more than any other category of the applications which are available in the market. These apps collect lot of personal and user sensitive information in addition to financial details of the user thereby making them prone to cyber-attacks. The attack is carried out by embedding malware into the mobile device of the user though different means. Hence, in order to trace the origin of these attacks and catch the cyber criminals it is imperative that a through malware analysis of the device is done as part of the mobile forensics. One of the most common methodologies used for carrying out an attack is to place malicious apps on the app store or 3rd party stores and tempt the user to download and install them. The novel method presented in this work can help in white listing those apps which are non-malicious and educating the people about the malicious apps so that infection of their devices can be reduced if not prevented completely.

The complete malware analysis process is as shown in Figure1. This study uses static and dynamic malware analysis techniques. Two frameworks for this study have been proposed i.e. Static analysis framework and Dynamic analysis framework and the complete experiment has been split in to three different case studies.

Static Analysis Framework

Static analysis comprises of different phases i.e. Application Gathering, APK Extraction, Report Generation, Logic Implementation, Dataset Creation and Implementation of ML based Algorithms which are as described below: -

- **Application Gathering:** A total of 150 APK samples were collected from Google play store or third-party website (APKpure.com) for analysis.
- **APK Extraction**: After collection, the app was installed on the android device (physical/virtual). After installing the application, the .APK file of that running application was extracted through an open source tool 'APK extractor'. The .APK file was then analyzed for finding the potential vulnerabilities based on the severity (High, Medium and Low).
- **Report Generation**: In this step, a report was generated in .csv format by using the results obtained from the static analysis.
- **Logic Implementation**: From the .csv reports obtained, the data was extracted and the algorithm which is described later in this research was implemented.
- **Dataset Creation**: The dataset created from the results obtained after implementing the algorithms on 150 apps was split into two sets namely Training and Test Dataset.
- **Implementation of ML based Algorithm**: Finally ML based algorithms were used for proper classification of the apps as malicious, benign or malicious and determining the performance of the implemented logic.

Figure 1. Proposed Analysis Framework

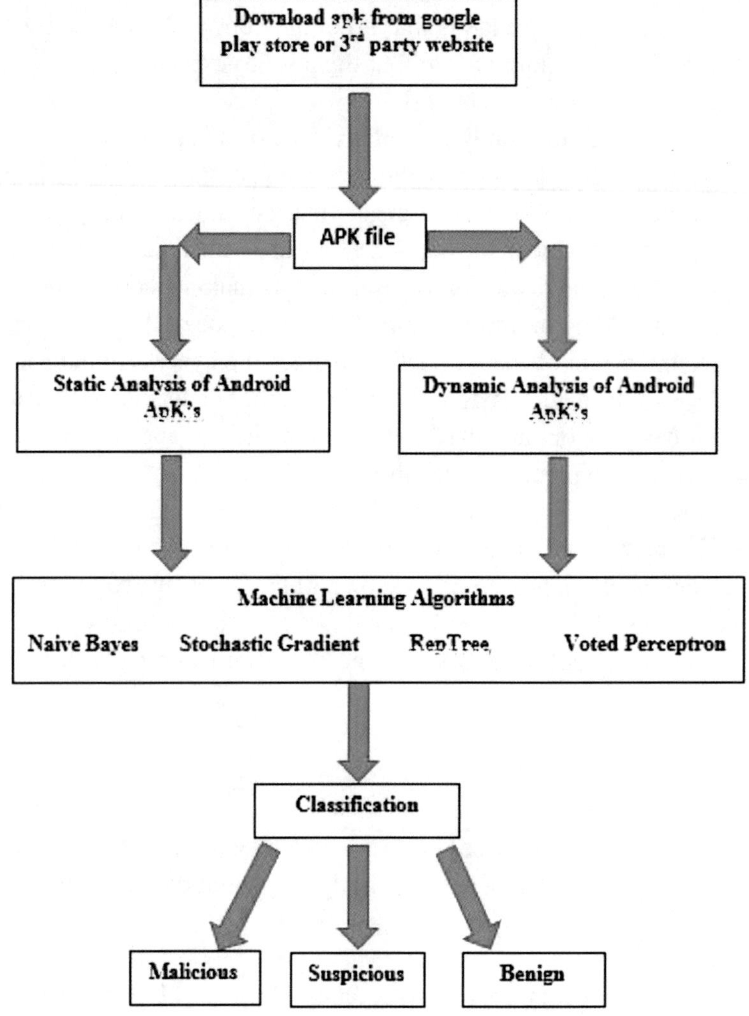

Dynamic Analysis Framework

Dynamic analysis was done by executing the android applications and monitoring its live behavior. During the dynamic analysis it's important to analyze behavior of the app. Our main focus was to determine the category of APK i.e. whether it's malicious or not with the help of four ML techniques.

From a pool of 150 applications, 20 applications were randomly chosen for the dynamic analysis. First, randomly chosen applications were tested using a Web based Dynamic analysis tool Hi-tech Bridge. A similar analysis was done by submitting the APK on VirusTotal. The report generated by the tool clearly revealed the IP addresses, Hosts, Suspect URLs to which the APK's were communicating. Suspected URLs and their corresponding IP addresses were noted down as per report generated by Hi-tech Bridge and VirusTotal. IP reputation check was then used to check the maliciousness of the obtained IP address and URL.

The results obtained from the Static and Dynamic Analysis of the APK's above were converted into a dataset of .csv format and fed to Machine Learning algorithms for the proper classification of the dataset. In order to apply ML algorithm on the results obtained from the static and dynamic analysis, there is a need to convert this data set into features. Each of the tested apps has different features to which a numeric weightage is assigned. Based on the logic, each of the app can be classified as malicious, benign or suspicious.

Using ML Algorithms

Supervised learning algorithm with feature selection have been employed including classification as well as clustering algorithms. By using supervised learning, we have observed that it was able to detect and identify the malicious, benign and suspicious APKs with its best rate of detection. The algorithms being used in the paper are chosen on the basis of their effectiveness and their identification rate of detection of APKs. The various supervised learning algorithm used for the research are as explained.

- **Naive Bayes multinomial text**: It refers to an instance of specific type of a Naive Bayes classifier using the multinomial distribution for each of the feature. Naive Bayes algorithm operates on the string attributes specifically. It has the capability to only work on strings rather than other input attributes.
- **REPtree:** REPtree uses the logic tree regression, giving rise to multiple trees in unique iterations. By this approach it is able to find the best suited one from all the trees generated. REP Tree is a best and quick learner tree building decision tree by using all the information obtained during the split criteria reducing further the error during pruning. REPtree builds decision tree using information gain/variance and prunes it using reduced error pruning. It sorts values for numeric attributes once missing values are dealt with by splitting the corresponding instances into pieces.
- **Voted Perceptron:** Voted Perceptron is an algorithm categorised as supervised learning Perceptron based which is taking the benefit from the data which is linearly separable. It is easy to implement and is quite efficient for computation as compared to other algorithms in the Perceptron category in Machine Learning. Perceptron - Perceptron learning rule, only supports binary data, provides a binary output and uses the Sign transfer function. Voted Perceptron algorithm replaces and transforms missing values and further transforms nominal attributes into binary ones.
- **SGD text:** Stochastic Gradient Descent (SGD) is an easy way out approach and even too efficient for learning the discriminative linear classifiers under the functions like Support Vector Machines and Logistic Regression. This algorithm is efficient for large scale learning mechanism especially for text learning and processing language naturally.

The performance is calculated on the basis of following indicators: Accuracy, Correctly classified instances, Incorrectly classified instances, Precision, Recall, True Positive as defined below: -

- **Correctly identified instances**: These are those instances which help in the correct identification of a classifier by making assumptions.

$$Correctly\ Identified\ Instances = \frac{Number\ of\ correct\ predictions\ made}{Total\ number\ of\ predictions\ made}$$

- **Incorrectly identified instances**: They pinpoint those instances which are not precise by classifiers.

$$Incorrectly\ Identified\ Instances = \frac{Number\ of\ incorrect\ predictions\ made}{Total\ number\ of\ predictions\ made}$$

- **Recall**: It is defined as the ratio between the actual instances that are acquired after classification to the total number of relevant instances.

$$Recall = \frac{True\ Positive\left(TP\right)}{True\ Positive\left(TP\right) + False\ Negative\left(FN\right)}$$

- **Precision**: It is the ratio of the true positive and total of true positive and false positive. It depicts the relevant results.

$$Precision = \frac{True\ Positive\left(TP\right)}{True\ Positive\left(TP\right) + False\ Positive\left(FP\right)}$$

Classification Phase

The final outcome of the proposed algorithm is the classification of the APK's in one of the three categories i.e. Malicious, Suspicious or Benign. This classification is based on the features which have been extracted in the static analysis and then fed to the ML algorithms. The most important parameter on which this classification depends is the Threshold Value (TV) and its comparison with the Threat Score (TS) and Combined Threat Score (CTS). Based on the generated score CTS, a comparison is made with the TV and accordingly the APK is classified in one of the three categories as shown in Table 1.

Table 1. APK Classification (Where X1=CTS)

S.No	Class Type	Condition
1	Malicious	**X1>0.5 or 0.6**
2	Benign	**X1<0.5 or 0.6**
3	Suspicious	**X1=0.5 or 0.6**

EXPERIMENTAL SETUP

For the purpose of obtaining results using ML, two datasets were taken for identification of APK's. Dataset 1 (TD1) is used as a Training Dataset and Dataset 2 (TD2) is used as Test Dataset. On these two datasets, four different ML algorithms were applied namely Naive Bayes Multinomial text, REPtree, Voted Perceptron, SGD text and each of them was analyzed. A dataset of 50 apps was taken as Training Dataset and a set of 100 apps was taken as test dataset to check the efficacy of the algorithms applied.

Firstly, the behavior of APK's was estimated by the vulnerabilities found in the APK (High, Medium, Permissions related). Low category vulnerabilities were left out to prevent any skewness in the experiment results. A sample listing of TD1 is shown in Figure 2.

Figure 2. Training Dataset (TD1)

Application name	High Severity Threats:	Medium Severity T	permission related
FaceApp	Improper Export of your	ADB Backup allowe	android.permission.ACC
okdone	Improper Export of your	WebView addJavas	co.hinge.app.permission
Aisle	Unsafe files deletion,M	Missing protection	android.permission.REC
WeDate	Unsafe files deletion,Im	WebView addJavas	android.permission.WRI
MeetYa	Improper Export of your	WebView addJavas	android.permission.WRI
Arena Chat	Unsafe files deletion,Im	WebView addJavas	android.permission.CAM
SMS Sherlar	Unsafe files deletion,Im	WebView addJavas	android.permission.ACC
Ringoid: Dating	Improper Export of your	WebView addJavas	android.permission.REA
50more: Meet singles over 50	Using Activities/Improp	Logging Sensitive,V	android.permission.REA
Meet usa: Chat & Meet friend	Using Activities/Improp	Logging Sensitive,V	android.permission.REA

To classify the APK's as Malicious, Suspicious and Benign on the basis of the results which are obtained in Figure 2, a new method has been proposed in this work. This method basically uses three major values to classify the APK's viz Threshold, Threat Score and Cumulative Threat Score.

Setting Up the Threshold

In case of Machine Learning based algorithms, results obtained from multiple classifiers produces 100% accuracy in some cases which is practically not possible. This is why there is a need to test and validate our results with multiple classifiers like Naive Bayes Multinomial text, Reptree, Voted Perceptron and SGD text. Another important aspect is to finalize the threshold value for each application which is vital to classify them as Malicious, Suspicious and Benign. In this approach, 02 threshold values have been chosen based on hit and trial method so as to formulize the algorithm used in the research. The process starts with taking different threshold values and carrying out the experiments. Bases on the experimental results, two threshold values are finalized. If only one threshold is taken the ultimate classification or decision making gets inclined only to one corner which means all the APK's in the dataset will be either Malicious, Suspicious or Benign because the number of vulnerabilities varies from APK to APK. So for the same dataset two threshold values are taken to make decision making or classification more relevant and justified in case of large and scalable dataset of APK's.

Each vulnerability for a given APK has been assigned a specific weightage, which is also known as Threat Score (TS). Default threat score for multiple vulnerabilities are chosen arbitrarily.

Setting Up Threat Score (TS)

- Threat Score for critical vulnerability TS(c)== 0.3
- Threat Score for medium vulnerability TS(m)== 0.2
- Threat Score for permission related vulnerability TS(p)== 0.1

Calculating the Cumulative Threat Score (CTS)

The sum of the TS for different vulnerabilities will decide the Cumulative Threat Score (CTS) for every APK. The value of CTS is compared with the threat value to determine the maliciousness of the APK's. To increase the efficiency of the classifier or the decision-making approach, multiple APK were tested through their dataset with two different threshold values. This made the overall approach more authentic and unique with the changing value of CTS according to the corresponding number of vulnerabilities and Threat Score.

Algorithm: To Calculate Threat Score of APK

```
   Where threshold  = 0.5
Set c*=
SSL Implementation Check - SSL Certificate
Using Activities/Improper Export of Android score Application Activities
File unsafe Delete Check
Missing Certificate Pinning

Set m*=
Protection of text fields from copying the text and pasting outside your app
score
Logging Sensitive information score
Protection of capturing screenshots & sharing screens outside your app score
Usage of Adb Backup score

Set p*=
android.permission.READ_CONTACTS
android.permission.UPDATE_DEVICE_STATS
```

```
android.permission.WRITE_CONTACTS
android.permission.CAMERA
android.permission.ACCESS_FINE_LOCATION

Set value: Threat score
TS(c)== 0.3
TS(m)== 0.2
TS(p)== 0.1

Set threshold value = (z)

Set value: Cumulative Threat Score
CTS(X) == TS(c)*number of critical vulnerabilities present in APK+ TS
(m)*number of medium vulnerabilities present in APK+ TS(p)*number of permis-
sion related vulnerabilities present in APK
Decision-making or verdict choosing algorithm
CTS (X) > threshold (z)==Malicious
CTS (X) < threshold (z)==Benign
CTS (X)= threshold (z)==Suspicious
(*Vulnerability categorized as [Critical (c), Medium (m), Permission related
(p)])
```

Classification Based on Training Dataset (TD1)

In this, a dataset of APK's was prepared with a threshold as 0.5 and the APK's remained the same as given in Figure 3. A dataset TD1 with the changed threshold is marked as a Training Dataset.

Figure 3. Training Dataset of 10 APKs (TD1)

No.	1: Application name Nominal	2: High Severity Threats: Nominal	3: Medium Severity Threats: Nominal	4: permission related Nominal
1	Joyride	Improper Export of your Android Servic...	ADB Backup allowed,We...	android.permissio...
2	Hinge	Improper Export of your Android Activiti...	WebView addJavascriptI...	co.hinge.app.perm...
3	YoCutie	Unsafe files deletion,Missing Certifica...	Missing protection again...	android.permissio...
4	Galaxy	Unsafe files deletion,Improper Export ...	WebView addJavascriptI...	android.permissio...
5	YouLove	Improper Export of your Android Servic...	WebView addJavascriptI...	android.permissio...
6	Coffee Meets Bagel	Unsafe files deletion,Improper Export ...	WebView addJavascriptI...	android.permissio...
7	Match	Unsafe files deletion,Improper Export ...	WebView addJavascriptI...	android.permissio...
8	RandoChat	Improper Export of your Android Broad...	WebView addJavascriptI...	android.permissio...
9	FaceApp	Using Activities/Improper Export of An...	Logging Sensitive,WebVi...	android.permissio...
10	okdone	Using Activities/Improper Export of An...	Logging Sensitive,WebVi...	android.permissio...

Algorithm has been used to find CTS of the APK and results of the same is given in Figure 3. In order to classify the dataset, the threshold value was taken to be 0.5. Applications having more value than 0.5 were categorized as Malicious, less than 0.5 as Benign and equal to 0.5 as Suspicious. A .csv file was then created using this test dataset and was given as input to the four ML algorithms which is tabulated below in Figure 5 and the verdict graph for the same has also been created in Figure 6. Results generated using Algorithm for classifying the APK's is discussed in result section.

Classification Based on Test Dataset (TD2)

In this, out of 150 APK's a test dataset of another 10 APK's was prepared with a threshold value of 0.6 as given in Figure 4. The main reason for creating a test dataset is to validate the classifier algorithm and the approach that has been used in this research. The classifiers which were applied on Training Dataset were applied on Test Dataset also.

Figure 4. Test Dataset (TD2)

No.	1: Application name	2: High Severity Threats: Nominal	3: Medium Severity Threats: Nominal	4: permission related Nominal
1	e-Harmony	Unsafe TrustManager implementat...	ADB Backup allowed,WebView addJavascriptInterface Remot...	android.permission.ACCESS_COARSE_LOCATIO...
2	Elite Single...	Missing Certificate Pinning,Improp...	WebView addJavascriptInterface Remote Code Execution,Mis...	co.hinge.app.permission.C2D_MESSAGE android....
3	Chat Video	Missing Certificate Pinning,Unsafe ...	Missing protection against screenshots & screensharing	android.permission.RECORD_AUDIO,
4	Blendr	Unsafe files deletion,Improper Exp...	WebView addJavascriptInterface Remote Code Execution,Mis...	android.permission.WRITE_EXTERNAL_STORAG...
5	Chispa	Improper Export of your Android Se...	WebView addJavascriptInterface Remote Code Execution,Mis...	android.permission.WRITE_EXTERNAL_STORAG...
6	Curvy Singl...	Improper Export of your Android Act...	WebView addJavascriptInterface Remote Code Execution,Co...	android.permission.CAMERA android.permission....
7	Meetic	Unsafe files deletion,Improper Exp...	WebView addJavascriptInterface Remote Code Execution,Mis...	android.permission.ACCESS_COARSE_LOCATIO...
8	Muzmatch	Unsafe TrustManager implementat...	WebView addJavascriptInterface Remote Code Execution,Mis...	android.permission.READ_EXTERNAL_STORAGE ...
9	buzz Arab	Unsafe files deletion,Unsafe Trust...	Logging Sensitive,WebView addJavascriptInterface Remote ...	android.permission.READ_EXTERNAL_STORAGE ...
10	You Love	Unsafe TrustManager implementat...	Logging Sensitive,WebView addJavascriptInterface Remote ...	android.permission.READ_EXTERNAL_STORAGE ...

Algorithm has been used to find CTS of the APK's and results of the same are given in Figure 7. In order to classify the dataset, the threshold value was taken to be 0.6. Applications having more value than 0.6 were categorized as Malicious, less than 0.6 as Benign and equal to 0.6 as Suspicious. A .csv file was then created using this test dataset and was given as input to the four ML algorithms which was tabulated and the verdict graph for the same is as shown in Figure 8. Results generated using Algorithm for classifying the APK's is discussed in Result section.

Figure 5. Classification of APK's, Threshold=0.5

Application name	Critical Severity Threats:TS(c)	Medium Severity Threats:TS(m	Permission related:TS(p)	threat score (CTS)	Threasold (z)	verdict
Joyride	Improper Export of your Android Services,I	ADB Backup allowed,WebView	android.perm	0.7	0.5	malicious
Hinge	Improper Export of your Android Activities	WebView addJavascriptInterfa	co.hinge.app.	0.46	0.5	benign
YoCutie	Unsafe files deletion,Missing Certificate Pi	Missing protection against scre	android.perm	0.36	0.5	benign
Galaxy	Unsafe files deletion,Improper Export of y	WebView addJavascriptInterfa	android.perm	0.6	0.5	malicious
YouLove	Improper Export of your Android Services,I	WebView addJavascriptInterfa	android.perm	0.9	0.5	malicious
Coffee Meets Bagel	Unsafe files deletion,Improper Export of y	WebView addJavascriptInterfa	android.perm	0.68	0.5	malicious
Match	Unsafe files deletion,Improper Export of y	WebView addJavascriptInterfa	android.perm	0.7	0.5	malicious
RandoChat	Improper Export of your Android Broadcast	WebView addJavascriptInterfa	android.perm	0.34	0.5	benign
FaceApp	Using Activities/Improper Export of Androi	Logging Sensitive,WebView ad	android.perm	0.6	0.5	malicious
okdone	Using Activities/Improper Export of Androi	Logging Sensitive,WebView ad	android.perm	0.6	0.5	malicious

Figure 6. Verdict graph against 10 APK using Algorithm 1 threshold 0.5

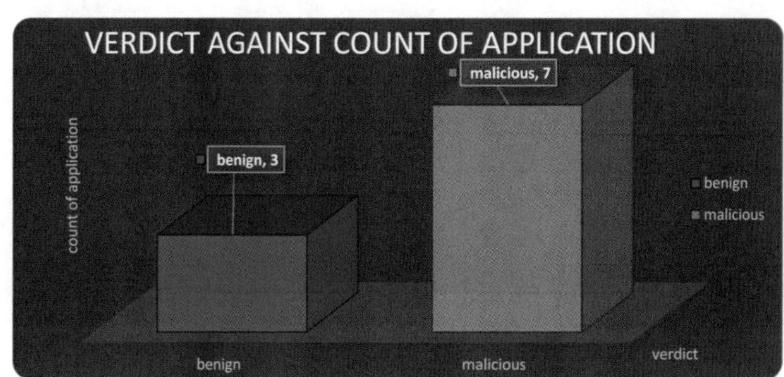

Table 2. Performance table of classifiers for training dataset TD1

S.No.	Classifiers	Correctly Identified Instances (%)	Incorrect Classified Instances (%)	True Positive	Precision	Recall
1	Naive Bayes Multinominal text	70	30	1.0	0.70	1.0
2	SGD text	70	30	1.0	0.70	1.0
3	REPtree	70	30	1.0	0.70	1.0
4	Voted Perceptron	80	20	1.0	0.77	1.0

DYNAMIC ANALYSIS

Dynamic analysis of the randomly chosen 20 applications was done by executing the applications. After executing the applications live or running the applications in sandbox environment, it was observed that suspicious communication was being made by few applications. If an APK was making a network communication, the reputation of the URL and the IP that were communicating were checked and the application was categorized according to the IP reputation checker. According to IP reputation checker, applications are categorised as suspicious, safe and malicious. We also checked the domain reputation of the IPs with which the APKs are making any communication. The result obtained from dynamic analysis of APK's are showcased and discussed subsequently.

Figure 7. Classification of APK's, threshold=0.6

Application name	Critical Severity Threats: CTS(C)	Medium Severity Threats:	permission related	score	threasold	remark
e-Harmony	Unsafe TrustManager implementation,Improper Export	ADB Backup allowed,WebView addJavascrip	android.permission.ACCESS_COARSE_LOCATION	0.7	0.6	malicious
Elite Singles	Missing Certificate Pinning,Improper Export of your An	WebView addJavascriptInterface Remote Co	co.hinge.app.permission.C2D_MESSAGE android.	0.5	0.6	benign
Chat Video	Missing Certificate Pinning,Unsafe files deletion	Missing protection against screenshots & scr	android.permission.RECORD_AUDIO,	0.4	0.6	benign
Blendr	Unsafe files deletion,Improper Export of your Android	WebView addJavascriptInterface Remote Co	android.permission.WRITE_EXTERNAL_STORAGE,	0.6	0.6	suspecious
Chispa	Improper Export of your Android Services,Improper Exp	WebView addJavascriptInterface Remote Co	android.permission.WRITE_EXTERNAL_STORAGE,	0.9	0.6	malicious
Curvy Singles	Improper Export of your Android Activities,Unsafe files	WebView addJavascriptInterface Remote Co	android.permission.CAMERA android.permission	0.7	0.6	malicious
Meetic	Unsafe files deletion,Improper Export of your Android	WebView addJavascriptInterface Remote Co	android.permission.ACCESS_COARSE_LOCATION	0.7	0.6	malicious
Muzmatch	Unsafe TrustManager implementation,Improper Export	WebView addJavascriptInterface Remote Co	android.permission.READ_EXTERNAL_STORAGE a	0.3	0.6	benign
buzz Arab	Unsafe files deletion,Unsafe TrustManager implementa	Logging Sensitive,WebView addJavascriptInt	android.permission.READ_EXTERNAL_STORAGE a	0.6	0.6	suspecious
You Love	Unsafe TrustManager implementation,Using Activities/	Logging Sensitive,WebView addJavascriptInt	android.permission.READ_EXTERNAL_STORAGE a	0.6	0.6	suspecious

Figure 8. Verdict graph against 10 APK using algorithm 1 threshold 0.6

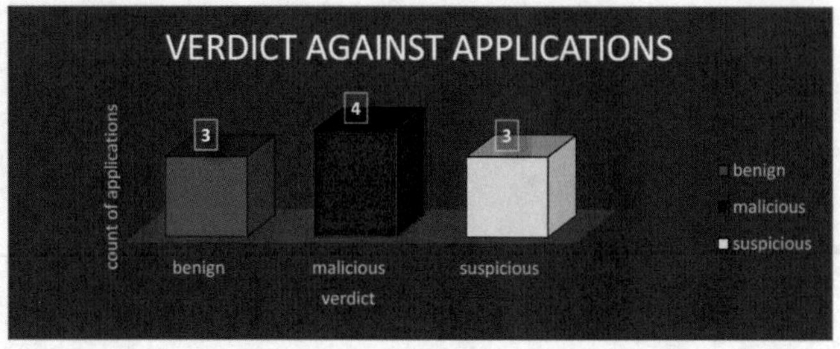

Table 3. Performance table of classifiers for Test dataset TD2.

S.No.	Classifiers	Correctly Identified Instances (%)	Incorrect Classified Instances (%)	True Positive	Precision	Recall
1	Naive Bayes Multi nominal text	57.1	42.8	1.00	0.57	1.00
2	SGD text	57.1	42.8	1.00	0.57	1.00
3	REP tree	57.1	42.8	1.00	0.57	1.00
4	Voted Perceptron	71.4	28.5	1.00	0.66	1.00

RESULTS AND DISCUSSION

As per the APK Classification Logic when applied to the dataset (TD1) of 10 APK's 03 came out to be benign and 07 malicious as shown in Figure 5. The verdict graph for the classification was also created to demonstrate the results with more clarity as shown in the Figure 6.

Table 4. Performance table of classifiers for training dataset TD1 (150 APK's)

S.No.	Classifiers	Correctly Identified Instances (%)	Incorrect Classified Instances(%)	True Positive	Precision	Recall
1	Naive Bayes Multinominal text	52	48	1.0	0.52	1.0
2	SGD text	74	25	1.0	0.67	1.0
3	REPtree	70	30	1.0	0.70	1.0
4	Voted Perceptron	52	48	1.0	0.52	1.0

Figure 9. Verdict graph against 150 APKs using algorithm 1 threshold 0.5

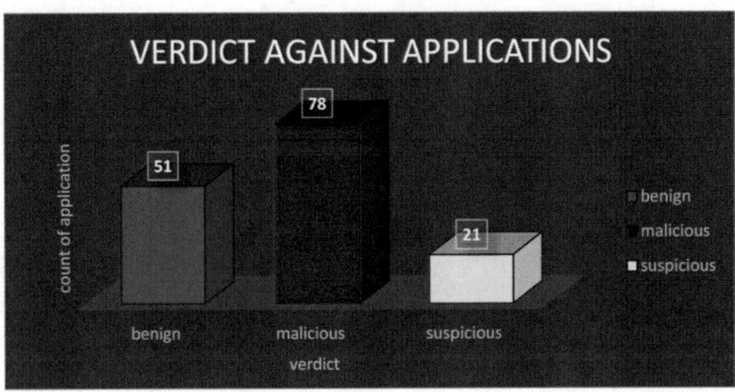

Table 5. Performance table of classifiers for Test dataset TD2 (150 APK's)

S.No.	Classifiers	Correctly Identified Instances (%)	Incorrect Classified Instances (%)	True Positive	Precision	Recall
1	Naive Bayes Multinominal text	37	63	1.0	0.37	1.0
2	SGD text	71	29	1.0	0.82	1.0
3	REPtree	37	63	1.0	0.37	1.0
4	Voted Perceptron	52	48	1.0	0.52	1.0

To check the efficacy of the results that we obtained from the classification logic and also to check which ML classifier classifies the dataset correctly and more efficiently, dataset (TD1) was fed as an input to the classifiers and it was then properly trained to achieve non-partisan output. Finally, It was observed that Voted Perceptron classifier performed with 80% accuracy with realistic performance indicators True positive, Precision and Recall, whereas SGD text, Naive Bayes multi nominal text, REPtree classifiers performance was 70%, the lowest in classifying the instances correctly as shown in Table 2.

Figure 10. Verdict graph against 150 APKs using algorithm 2 threshold 0.6

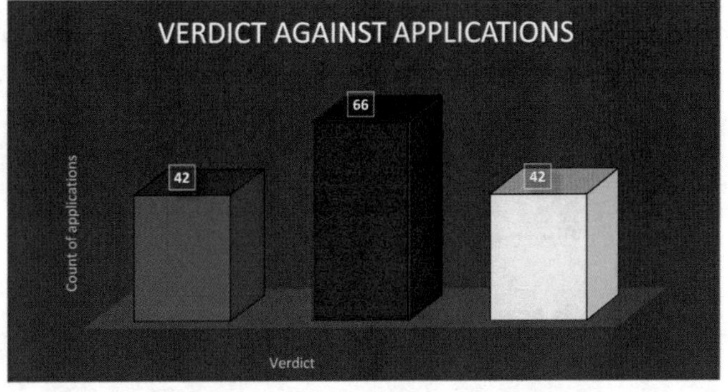

Figure 11. APK communicating with External IPs

Mobile App External Communications

Static mobile application security test revealed the following remote hosts where the mobile application may send or receive data:

Hostname	IP:Port	SSL Encryption	Web Server Security	Phishing Susceptibility
www.jivesoftware.com	35.238.7.255:80	N	N/A	14 malicious websites found
www.inkscape.org	140.211.9.79:80	N	N/A	38 malicious websites found
prosody.im	46.43.15.35:443	A+	A+	4 malicious websites found
igniterealtime.org	52.58.216.59:443	A-	B+	3 malicious websites found
api.foursquare.com	151.101.126.202:443	A	C+	2 malicious websites found
www.whatsapp.com	31.13.80.53:443	A	A	1007 malicious websites found

Figure 12. IP Reputation of connecting IPs as per Dynamic Analysis

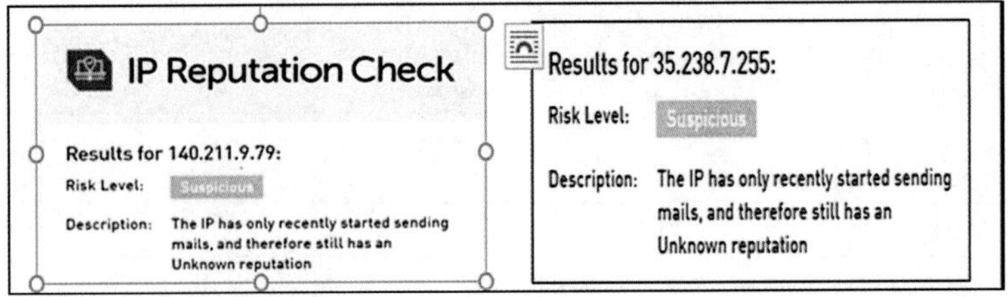

Similarly the approach was applied on the test dataset (TD2) of 10 APK's as discussed in section 4., 03 came out to be benign and 04 as malicious and 03 are comes under suspicious verdict as shown in Figure 7. The verdict graph for the classification was also created to demonstrate the results with more clarity as shown in the Figure 8.

The test dataset (TD2) is then analyzed and proper classification is done by using the same classifiers that was used in training dataset TD1. According to the classification done by ML classifiers, performance of Voted Perceptron classifier is 71.4% for correctly identifying the instances. Moreover, this classifier is able to categorize the instances properly whereas other classifier achieves the lowest 57.1% for categorizing the instances.

The experiment once completed for 10 APK's was now then repeated for 150 APK's to check the scalability of the proposed methodology and the results generated are tabulated below in table 3 & table 4 and the verdict graph for the same is shown in Figure 9 & Figure 10 for TD1 and TD2 respectively.

As discussed in Section 5, dynamic analysis of the APKs was carried out which helped us in determining the behavior of the APKs used in the research. The results obtained are given in Figure 11.

Table 6. Classification based on Dynamic Analysis (150 APKs)

S.No	Class Type	Condition
1	Malicious	**IP Reputation malicious**
2	Benign	**IP Reputation safe**
3	Suspicious	**IP Reputation suspicious**

Figure 13. Pool of 20 APKs out of 150 extracted for Dynamic Analysis

Application Name	Condition	Verdict
Joyride	IP Reputation malicious	Malicious
Hinge	IP Reputation safe	Benign
YoCutie	IP Reputation suspicious	Suspicious
Galaxy	IP Reputation safe	Benign
YouLove	IP Reputation malicious	Malicious
Coffee Meets Bagel	IP Reputation suspicious	Suspicious
Match	IP Reputation malicious	Malicious
RandoChat	IP Reputation suspicious	Suspicious
FaceApp	IP Reputation malicious	Malicious
Okdone	IP Reputation safe	Benign
Chat With Girls	IP Reputation suspicious	Suspicious
Random Chat App With Girls	IP Reputation suspicious	Suspicious
QueContactos Dating	IP Reputation safe	Benign
Fotka find and meet people around You	IP Reputation suspicious	Suspicious
dating app for adults	IP Reputation safe	Benign
Indian Girls Video Chat	IP Reputation malicious	Malicious
buzz Arab	IP Reputation safe	Benign
Datedating	IP Reputation malicious	Malicious
Chat Roulette	IP Reputation safe	Benign
LuvFree	IP Reputation safe	Benign

Figure 11 shows the IP addresses to which the APKs are communicating and it also gives the information about the phishing susceptibility of the IPs that are making connections. IP reputation check was then carried out as given in Figure 12 for the IP addresses to verify the behavior and to classify the APKs i.e. malicious, suspicious or benign. APK's having reputation as malicious were classified as malicious, safe as benign and suspicious as suspicious as shown in Table 5.

Based on the classification discussed above out of 20 APK's that were chosen for dynamic analysis 08 were benign, 06 were malicious and 06 were suspicious. The results of the classification are shown in Figure 13 and the verdict graph for the same is shown in Figure 14.

The experiment once completed for 20 APK's was now then repeated for 150 APK's to check the scalability of the proposed methodology and the results generated are tabulated below in Figure 15.

Figure 14. Verdict graph against 20 APK's for Dynamic Analysis

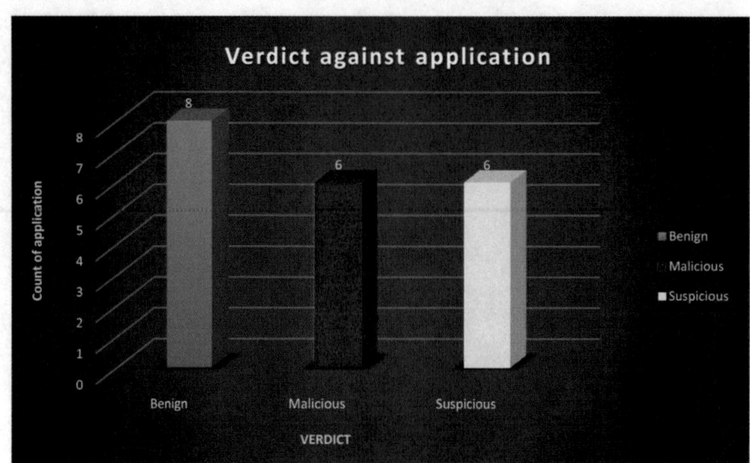

Figure 15. Verdict graph against 150 APK's for Dynamic Analysis

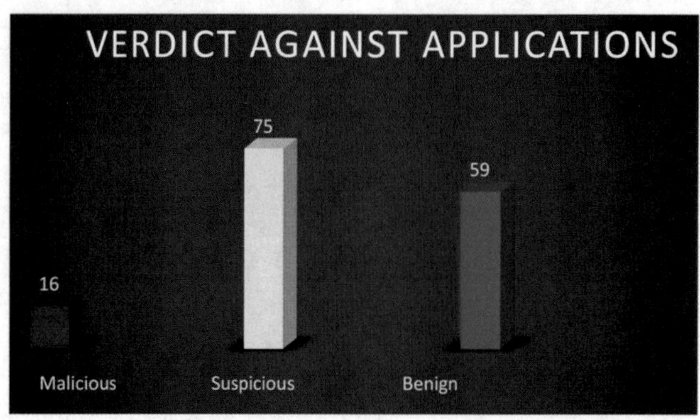

CONCLUSION AND FUTURE WORK

Malware analysis is an important facet of mobile forensics because of increased attacks on mobiles to steal personal data. One of the most common methodology used is to place malicious apps on the app store or 3rd party stores and lure the user to download and install them. The method presented in this research helps in identifying the malicious apps through machine learning based techniques and also helps in categorization of different applications. In this paper, we have considered five most popular categories of the apps for the Static and Dynamic analysis. The results obtained for finding the performance of a classifier helps in classifying the class type of malicious APK's. The experimentation showed different types of features extraction from the APK's with their evaluation that was done using machine learning classifiers (Naive Bayes Multinominal text, REPtree, Voted Perceptron, SGD Text). Overall, the performance achieved by Voted Perceptron classifier was considered the best for determining the accuracy and precision with 80% in case of classification of APK's based on severity in TD1 whereas all the other three algorithms turns out to be the lowest However, the machine learning approach followed resulted in better performance of the classifiers. From the analysis it was retrieved that mostly dating applications were under malicious category and gaming applications were under suspicious category. The findings can be extended to other apps also.

In our future work we intend to automate the complete process so that more number of apps can be successfully analyzed and more precise result can be achieved by using machine learning techniques. Moreover, this experiment can be done for other platforms like iOS and Windows.

ACKNOWLEDGMENT

The authors would like to express sincere gratitude to ITM University Gwalior for providing the platform to work in machine learning as well as mobile forensics.

REFERENCES

Agrawal, A. K., Khatri, P., & Sinha, S. R. (2018). Comparative Study of Mobile Forensic Tools. In *Advances in Data and Information Sciences* (pp. 39–47). Springer. doi:10.1007/978-981-10-8360-0_4

Agrawal, A. K., Sharma, A., Sinha, S. R., & Khatri, P. (n.d.). Forensic of An Unrooted Mobile Device. *International Journal of Electronic Security and Digital Forensics*.

Al Ali, M., Svetinovic, D., Aung, Z., & Lukman, S. (2017, December). Malware detection in android mobile platform using machine learning algorithms. In *2017 International Conference on Infocom Technologies and Unmanned Systems (Trends and Future Directions) (ICTUS)* (pp. 763-768). IEEE. 10.1109/ICTUS.2017.8286109

Bacci, A., Bartoli, A., Martinelli, F., Medvet, E., Mercaldo, F., & Visaggio, C. A. (2018). Impact of Code Obfuscation on Android Malware Detection based on Static and Dynamic Analysis. In ICISSP (pp. 379-385). doi:10.5220/0006642503790385

Bilal, S. F., Bashir, S., Khan, F. H., & Rasheed, H. (2018, October). Malwares Detection for Android and Windows System by Using Machine Learning and Data Mining. In *International Conference on Intelligent Technologies and Applications* (pp. 485-495). Springer.

Cyren IP Reputation Check. (n.d.). https://www.cyren.com/security-center/cyren-ip-reputation-check

Geneiatakis, D., Baldini, G., Fovino, I. N., & Vakalis, I. (2018, February). Towards a mobile malware detection framework with the support of machine learning. In *International ISCIS Security Workshop* (pp. 119-129). Springer. 10.1007/978-3-319-95189-8_11

Gordon, K. (n.d.). *Topic: Online dating in the United States*. Retrieved from https://www.statista.com/topics/2158/online-dating/

Kedziora, M., Gawin, P., Szczepanik, M., & Jozwiak, I. (2018). *Android Malware Detection Using Machine Learning And Reverse Engineering*. doi:10.5121/csit.2018.81709

Kumar, A., Kuppusamy, K. S., & Aghila, G. (2018). FAMOUS: Forensic Analysis of MObile devices Using Scoring of application permissions. *Future Generation Computer Systems*, *83*, 158–172. doi:10.1016/j.future.2018.02.001

Li, J., Sun, L., Yan, Q., Li, Z., Srisa-an, W., & Ye, H. (2018). Significant permission identification for machine-learning-based android malware detection. *IEEE Transactions on Industrial Informatics*, *14*(7), 3216–3225. doi:10.1109/TII.2017.2789219

Lou, S., Cheng, S., Huang, J., & Jiang, F. (2019, March). TFDroid: Android Malware Detection by Topics and Sensitive Data Flows Using Machine Learning Techniques. In *2019 IEEE 2nd International Conference on Information and Computer Technologies (ICICT)* (pp. 30-36). IEEE.

Ma, Z., Ge, H., Liu, Y., Zhao, M., & Ma, J. (2019). A Combination Method for Android Malware Detection Based on Control Flow Graphs and Machine Learning Algorithms. *IEEE Access: Practical Innovations, Open Solutions*, *7*, 21235–21245. doi:10.1109/ACCESS.2019.2896003

Milosevic, N., Dehghantanha, A., & Choo, K. K. R. (2017). Machine learning aided Android malware classification. *Computers & Electrical Engineering*, *61*, 266–274. doi:10.1016/j.compeleceng.2017.02.013

Mobile App Security Test by ImmuniWeb. (n.d.). Retrieved from https://www.htbridge.com/mobile/

Peiravian, N., & Zhu, X. (2013, November). Machine learning for android malware detection using permission and api calls. In *2013 IEEE 25th international conference on tools with artificial intelligence* (pp. 300-305). IEEE. 10.1109/ICTAI.2013.53

Rana, M. S., Gudla, C., & Sung, A. H. (2018). Evaluating Machine Learning Models for Android Malware Detection: A Comparison Study. In *Proceedings of the 2018 VII International Conference on Network, Communication and Computing* (pp. 17-21). ACM.

Rana, M. S., & Sung, A. H. (2018). Malware Analysis on Android using Supervised Machine Learning Techniques. *International Journal of Computer and Communication Engineering*, *7*(4), 178–188. doi:10.17706/IJCCE.2018.7.4.178-188

Rathi, D., & Jindal, R. (2018). *DroidMark: A Tool for Android Malware Detection using Taint Analysis and Bayesian Network.* arXiv preprint arXiv:1805.06620.

Sethi, K., Chaudhary, S. K., Tripathy, B. K., & Bera, P. (2018, January). A Novel Malware Analysis Framework for Malware Detection and Classification using Machine Learning Approach. In *Proceedings of the 19th International Conference on Distributed Computing and Networking* (p. 49). ACM. 10.1145/3154273.3154326

Shahriar, H., Islam, M., & Clincy, V. (2017, March). Android malware detection using permission analysis. In *SoutheastCon 2017* (pp. 1–6). IEEE. doi:10.1109/SECON.2017.7925347

Shalaginov, A., Banin, S., Dehghantanha, A., & Franke, K. (2018). Machine learning aided static malware analysis: A survey and tutorial. In *Cyber Threat Intelligence* (pp. 7–45). Springer. doi:10.1007/978-3-319-73951-9_2

Sharma, A., Agrawal, A. K., Kumar, B., & Khatri, P. 2018, March. Forensic Analysis of a Virtual Android Phone. In *International Conference on Communication, Networks and Computing* (pp. 286-297). Springer.

Statistics, M., & Report, T. AV-TEST. (2019, April 25). Retrieved from https://www.av-test.org/en/statistics/malware/

Verma, S., & Muttoo, S. K. (2016). An Android Malware Detection Framework-based on Permissions and Intents. *Defence Science Journal*, *66*(6), 618–623.

Zhao, H., Li, M., Wu, T., & Yang, F. (2018). Evaluation of Supervised Machine Learning Techniques for Dynamic Malware Detection. *International Journal of Computational Intelligence Systems*, *11*(1), 1153–1169.

Chapter 16
Locally-Adaptive Naïve Bayes Framework Design via Density-Based Clustering for Large Scale Datasets

Faruk Bulut
https://orcid.org/0000-0003-2960-8725
Istanbul Rumeli University, Turkey

ABSTRACT

In this chapter, local conditional probabilities of a query point are used in classification rather than consulting a generalized framework containing a conditional probability. In the proposed locally adaptive naïve Bayes (LANB) learning style, a certain amount of local instances, which are close the test point, construct an adaptive probability estimation. In the empirical studies of over the 53 benchmark UCI datasets, more accurate classification performance has been obtained. A total 8.2% increase in classification accuracy has been gained with LANB when compared to the conventional naïve Bayes model. The presented LANB method has outperformed according to the statistical paired t-test comparisons: 31 wins, 14 ties, and 8 losses of all UCI sets.

INTRODUCTION

As a probability-based classifier, Naïve Bayes has a worldly wide fame in supervised learning area due to its velocity, simplicity, effectiveness, high accuracy rates, and white-box structure. On the other hand, it always creates a general conditional probability assumption for the whole dataset. Creating a general hypothesis for a huge dataset is usually inconvenient for overall performance. Hence, this situation might be violated in practical applications. Some sub-regions of the same dataset might be handled differently from others. Rather than a generalized probability rule for the entire dataset, it will be better to handle the local density based regions separately.

DOI: 10.4018/978-1-7998-3299-7.ch016

In supervised learning, Naive Bayes classifier (NB) is a member of probabilistic classifier family based on Bayesian theorem. This classifier depends on the strong (naive) independence assumptions between features. Naive Bayes is a simple and common technique for constructing a classifier. As an eager learner, NB method is easy to implement, fast in prediction, quick in constructing a generalized rule. It also performs well in multi-class prediction. With the less training data points, NB technique in most cases might outperform other models such as logistic regression and Multi-Layer Perceptrons (MLP). In other words, NB classifier gives high bias and low variance especially when the dataset is sparse. Additionally, NB gives more accurate predictions in case of categorical input variables compared to real variables. For numerical variables, normal distribution is assumed such as the bell curve as a strong assumption. Furthermore, NB is accepted as quite robust to both irrelevant and noisy data.

However, NB method has some weaknesses in some cases. If a categorical variable is not observed in predefined training dataset, the system will produce a 0 (zero) probability. In this circumstance, prediction becomes impossible due to the "Zero Frequency". Zero probabilities are generally painful for the NB Classifier. Therefore, this makes a barrier to predict classes of new records. The "Zero Frequency" problem is to be solved by some smoothing methods such as Laplace (Additive) and Lidstone methods (Kikuchi et al., 2015).

Another constraint of NB is the assumption of independent estimators. In real life applications, it is nearly impossible to set prediction algorithms which are completely independent from each other. Also, if some pairs of attributes in a dataset have strong positive or negative correlations, apparently NB gives worse predictions (Par et al., 2019).

The main problem for the classical NB method is the constructed general and globalized hypothesis for the entire dataset. A global approximation is used throughout the classification phase. The local regions and the location of the query point are not important in this case. However, some parts in the same dataset can be statistically different from others in numerous aspects. A collection of points in a dataset might have some inner complex parts. Hence, this type of a dataset needs to be decomposed into less complex sub-regions. Datasets containing complex sub-regions are not always applicable in creating a unique global approach. That is why there might exist a combination of local models for a dataset containing complex structures.

When the dataset is very huge to learn, it will be better to divide the set into local regions due to the benefits of divide and conquer approach. For this purpose, each sub-region which has some individual, local, and different specifications from others should be accepted as a unique and a discrete dataset.

In the literature, several key measures which provide independent characterization have been proposed in order to analyze datasets in classification complexity (Ho et al., 2002). These key measures are regarded as meta-features that describe the related feature spaces. For example, number of samples, number of attributes, and number of class labels are the basic statistical meta-features. These types of insufficient specifications display solely the denseness or sparseness of a dataset. There are, of course, some other extended theoretical features such as complex geometrical metrics which are defined in the literature (Basu & Ho., 2006a): geometrical characteristics of the class distribution, labeled classes which are separated or interleaved in a dataset, linearly separable data distribution, overlapped regions, attribute efficiencies, fraction of class boundaries, Leave-One-Out error rate of the 1-Nearest-Neighbor classifier, nonlinearity of a linear classifier, and fraction of maximum covering spheres are some of the meta-features. Each of the calculated results taken from the metrics indicate the requirement of decomposing a dataset into sub-regions. It is also confirmed that these kinds of measures have great influence on the classification performance.

In these mentioned cases, local approximations might give more accurate predictions than globalizations. Normally NB focuses on independent attributes, it makes a general approach to the work space. In this study, we have aimed to analyze elaborately the characteristics of a local region in a dataset by proposing a novel mechanism called as LANB (Locally Adaptive Naïve Bayes). The LANB classifier handles the regions of the dataset separately so that the overall learning performance is expected to boost. The hypothesis of this proposed study stands on the fact that discretization of complex parts and localized classification model are curtail for better prediction rather than a globalized classification model.

The rest of the study contains four more additional sections. In Section 2, there are some related studies published in this area. Section 3 describes both the current methodology and proposed model. Section 4 gives the experimental results and some related discussions. Finally, there is the conclusion of the study in Section 5.

RELATED STUDIES

In the literature, there are plenty of NB learner variations and forms. From its birth, many enhanced types and combinations have been proposed to boost the performance. It has also been applied to many scientific fields and experimented in most of engineering problems. NB is also the basis of some proposed new methods such as Averaged one-dependence estimators (AODE) as a probabilistic classification method, Bayesian Belief Network, Perceptron classifier, Random Naive Bayes, NBTree, logistic regression and data mining (Lu et al., 2012), (Zhang et al., 2021). Additionally, NB Method has been examined in many decision support systems such as spam filtering, speech and hand writing recognition, intrusion detection, document categorization, text classification, fraud detection, credit scoring, bioinformatics engineering and so on (Qin et al., 2012).

In order to enhance the performance of NB classifier, various types of NB methods have been developed. In a survey manuscript (Bache & Lichman, 2013), there is a detailed research of the improved NB classifier types. It is stressed that there are four types of improved approaches. These categorized types are feature selection, structure extension, local learning, and finally data expansion. The selected enhanced NB methods against classic NB classifier are experimentally tested on a collection of UCI datasets that is a machine learning benchmark repository. The success and the effectiveness of these methods are therefore evaluated in this study (Jiang et al., 2007).

In a text classification study, NB method is improved with various smoothing methods. They have acquired significant enhancement in classification performance of NB by using smoothing methods (Narayanan et al., 2013). Additionally, most of these methods have been applied so as to detect the spam messages in another research paper (Peng et al., 2018).

Another research paper recently presents a novel study called Differential Evolution-Naive Bayes (DE-NB). This method takes advantage of integrating differential evolution with NB for feature selection in order to enhance NB classifier. In this approach, DE is firstly applied to search out an optimal subset of dimensional reduction in the original feature space, and then it constructs a NB classifier on the subset of the attributes reduction. Some experimental results over UCI datasets are presented where distinctly show the comparisons with NB, Cfs-BS (Correlation Feature Selection - Best First), Decision Tree (C4.5), k-NN (k Nearest Neighbors), SVM (Support Vector Machine) algorithms. The recommended DE-NB method has acquired higher accuracy in classification (Li et al., 2015).

A systematic study has been proposed in order to increase the ranking performance of k-NN by using NB in another study. In the combination of k-NN and NB, they have presented a critical problem in assigning a real value to a test instance, which is the lack of training data when the k parameter is small. In this regression problem, they have proposed a solution to deal with this problem by cloning so as to expand the training data. Each of the *k* closest neighbors is duplicated and the duplicates are added to the training dataset. k-NN, NB, NBTree, and the Instance Cloning Local Naive Bayes model have been tested on the UCI datasets. In the AUC (Area Under Receiver Operating Characteristics Curve) performance comparisons of algorithms, their suggested model has significantly outperformed well (Jiang et al., 2005), (Jiang & Guo, 2005).

In another study, convolutional NB, NB ensemble, and NB-Tree (Naïve Bayes and decision tree) are used in Ensemble classification. As it is known, ensemble learning is used to enhance the classification phase where the training phase needs more executional time than normal. Usually collection of different forms of certain classifiers are used on the same dataset and the majority voting is accepted as an aggregation model. Also, they have presented applicability of NB classifier ensemble for traffic incident detection. The experimental results have shown that the performances of five rules of NB classifier in ensemble learning are apparently better than the traditional NB and also slightly better than the NB-Tree in some indicators. More importantly, the performance of NB classifier ensemble has remained very stable throughout the experiments (Liu et al., 2014).

Karlos et al. (2017) proposed a locally weighted naïve Bayes classifier to encompass the power of both NB and k-NN algorithms. They have implemented a self-labeled weighted variant of local learner using the Naive Bayes Classifier as the base learner of self-training scheme. Similarly, Frank et al. (2012) has proposed a locally weighted Naive Bayes classifier which produces some improvement in performance. These types of local approaches have been implemented in text classifications (Jiang et al., 2013), in image processing (McCann & Lowe, 2012), and in wireless sensor networks (Zwartjes, 2017). Lately, in this area, an attribute and instance weighted naive Bayes learner (AIWNB) containing a combination of both lazy and eager learning approaches has been presented (Zhang et al., 2021). Additionally, recent developments related with this specific supervised and unsupervised area are examined and placed broadly into the survey study (Sen et al., 2020).

Different from these mentioned studies above, the presented approach in this chapter assigns a best fitted framework for the whole dataset by aggregating the local decisions to acquire a better performance.

PROPOSED METHODOLOGY

Before examining the proposed methodology, it will be better to remind the current basics of the Bayes Rule and Bayesian Classifier. Naive Bayes Classifier, also known as Bayesian Classification, is one of the most classification techniques based on the Bayes Rule of conditional probability. In this technique, each attribute of a dataset has an effect on calculation. The definition of Bayes Method is defined in the following section.

Conventional Bayes Rule (Bayes Theorem)

Determining the best hypothesis, which is namely the most probable hypothesis from some space *H*, is crucial for classification problems over a training data *D*. This Rule enables a way to compute the probability of a hypothesis by the Equation 1.

$$P\left(h \mid D\right) = \frac{P\left(h \mid D\right) \cdot P\left(h\right)}{P\left(D\right)} \tag{1}$$

To define and examine Bayes Theorem, it is necessary to introduce the notations. *P*(*h*) stands for the initial probability which hypothesis *h* holds, until observing the training dataset. *P*(*h*) is the prior probability of *h*, a correct hypothesis. If there is no such prior knowledge, then the same prior probability might be directly assigned to each of the candidate hypothesis. *P*(*D*) indicates the prior probability. The posterior probability of *h*, *P*(*h*|*D*) refers the probability of hypothesis *h* given the observing data *D*. As a confidence value, the posterior probability *P*(*h*|*D*) shows the influence of the training dataset *D*, contrary to the prior probability *P*(*h*), which is independent of *D* (Jones, 2015).

Conventional Bayesian Classifier

This method, also known as the Naïve Bayes Classifier, has a big connection to the conditional probability, the Bayes Rule. In this technique, all attributes of a dataset have equal weights on prediction. In other words, attributes are independent in contribution in classification. A conditional probability is determined at the first step via analyzing the contribution of each "independent" attribute. A classification of a test instance is done by combining the probabilities. This "Naive" approach assumes the independence among the various attribute values as seen in the Equation 2.

$$P\left(s_i \mid C_j\right) = \arg\max_{c_j \in C} P\left(c_j\right) \prod_{k=1}^{p} P\left(x_{ik} \mid C_j\right), \left(x \in X, c \in C\right) \tag{2}$$

where a given data value x_i the probability that a related data sample, s_i, is in class C_j is described by *P* (C_j | x_i). *C* is the set of class labels. Function argmax assigns most-probable class to the test data. Training dataset might be used to determine *P* (x_i), *P* (x_i | C_j), and *P*(C_j). For each of the attribute x_i, the amount of occurrences of each attribute value x_i can be counted in order to determine *P*(x_i). Likewise, the probability *P* (x_i | C_j) can be predicted by counting how often each value can be found in the training dataset. When classifying a new point, the prior and conditional probabilities generated from the training dataset are used to make classification. This is done by aggregating the values of the different attributes from the point. Sample s_i has *p* independent attribute values { $x_{i1}, x_{i2}, x_{i3}, \ldots . x_{ip}$ }. It is accepted that *P* (x_{ik} | C_j) will be calculated for each class C_j and attribute x_{ik}. Lastly it becomes easy to predict the P (t_i | C_j) result. To compute *P* (s_i), it is easy to find the likelihood that s_i is in each class group. The probability that s_i is in a class is the multiplication of the conditional probabilities for each of the attribute values. Thus, it becomes easy to classify the new upcoming instance as the highest probability of all (Chen et al., 2020).

Density-Based Spatial Clustering Method

DBSCAN (Density-based spatial clustering of applications with noise) is a very popular and efficient clustering algorithm for such datasets having density based distributions (Ester et al., 1996). Some nodes in a dataset may lie in a group by shaping a special and discrete pattern. Since these nested patterns are actually different from each other, they should be grouped in a separate cluster. In addition, the OPTICS algorithm, which is a density-based algorithm, works as an extended DBSCAN algorithm in this area as an alternative one.

On the other hand, distance based clustering methods such as k-means bisect directly the data distributions into some parts where the local points are very close to each other. This situation is clearly demonstrated in Figure 1. The same dataset containing a certain three types of data distribution style is divided into clusters by the most popular clustering techniques, DBSCAN and k-Means.

Figure 1. Difference between DBSCAN and k-means methods over the same dataset

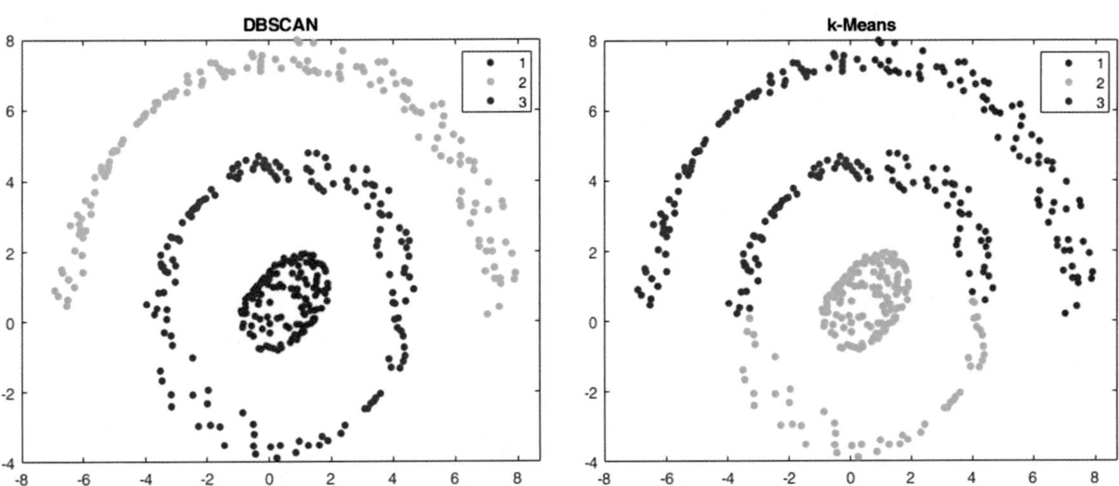

The main advantage of DBSCAN is that it has a parameter independent structure when compared each other. In the given illustration in Figure 1, the number of cluster is set to 3 manually for the k-means method.

*k*D-Tree Data Structure

The *k*D-Tree (*k* Dimensional tree) is a binary space partitioning (BSP) method in data structure. Basically the *k*D-Tree model is an improved form of Binary Search Tree (BST). BST is used only for the data laid on one dimensional space. Data points in *k* dimensional space are put into *k*D-Tree in order to searching, deleting, and insert an instance in $O(\log n)$ complexity (Gill & Hooda, 2021). It efficiently contains and organize the high dimensional datasets. Using this type of a data structure in this application has decreased the cumulative computational time. Similarly, checking the closest samples nearby the test point with the Exhaustive (Sequential) search technique might be regarded as a time consuming operation. This negative side is eliminated by the help of the kD-Tree data container. As it is known, the complexity of reaching an element in the kD-Tree structure is $O(\log n)$ where it is in $O(n)$ Exhaustive search. This type of a structure is used to store data samples in an efficient and fast container in order to enhance the overall execution performance in this study.

Locally Adaptive Naïve Bayes (LANB) Learning

As it is mentioned in this chapter, the main handicap for the NB learner is to create a general hypothesis for the whole dataset. In this model, the characteristical specifications of sub-regions in a dataset are not ignored. Namely, it is very important where a data point locates in the feature space. The prediction is not performed for a data point without probing its location. If the point is either in a certain class region or out of the class boundary, the classification is performed according to the generalized probabilities (Basu & Ho, 2006b).

In the present chapter, we would like to overcome the current obstacles of NB by suggesting a new adaptive approach. A fitted mechanism is developed by handling regions of the data point separately. The closest neighbors, which are distributed around the test point, create a general hypothesis for classification.

Figure 2. An illustration of data point distribution in two dimensional space

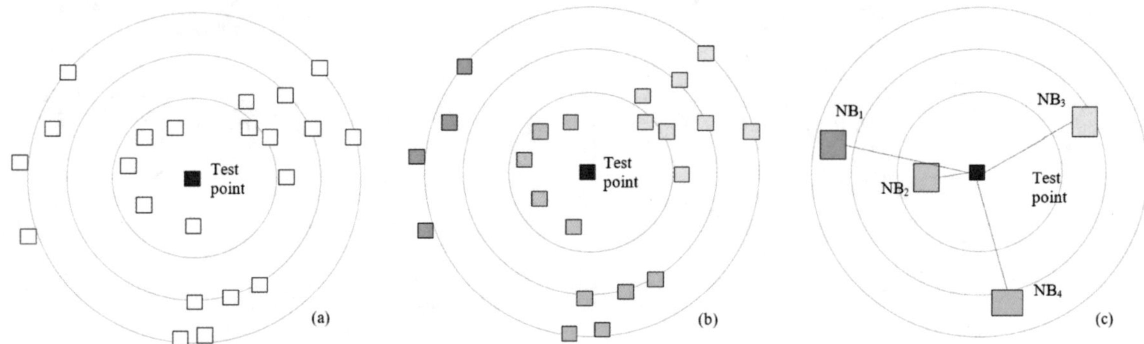

In Figure 2, there is an illustration of data distribution in two dimensional space. In the section a, the red query point is surrounded with some white points whose class labels are not known. There are also some virtual orbits where the data points are positioned. The red colored query point will be classified by the LNAB algorithm. In the second b, the points are grouped into four different clusters according to their layout style by implementing the DBSCAN method. For each cluster, a specific Naïve Bayes framework is computed. In the section c, each NB framework is virtually located in its corresponding cluster centroids. Therefore, local NB classifier is created at the learning phase before classifying a test point. The query point is finally separately asked to each of the NB classifiers in the space. Each computational result is aggregated for the query point x_q as in the given regression formula 3 as:

$$\hat{f}\left(x_q\right) \leftarrow \underset{c \in C}{\arg\max} \sum_{i=1}^{k} \delta\left(c, f_{NB}\left(x_i\right)\right) \tag{3}$$

where C is the finite set of class labels defined as $\{c_1, c_2, c_3, \ldots, c_s\}$. k is the number of NB clusters. $x_i \ldots x_k$ denotes the k closest NB decisions, and $\delta(a,b)=1$ if a=b and $\delta(a,b)=0$ otherwise. The f: R®*C function* makes a calculation for each class and assigns the maximum argument to xq $_a$s the class label.

If the query point has a numerical v*alue* rather than a class label, the classification formula for the query point is changed as follows in the Equation 4:

$$f\left(x_q\right) = \frac{1}{k}\sum_{i=1}^{k} f_{NB}\left(x_i\right) \tag{4}$$

The Euclidean distance can be normally used to calculate the distance between query point and local NB classifiers. The closest NB classifier will affect the classification result more than the others. Namely, the furthest NB classifier gives a meagre contribution to the calculation. How much the NB classifiers affect the query point is described by the following formula 5:

$$w_i = \frac{1}{dist^2\left(x_q, NB_i\right)} \tag{5}$$

where w_i is the weight of the ith NB Classifier. As a reference point, NB_i is the centroid which represents the corresponding cluster virtually. There are some various types of weight methods in the literature such as $1/d$, $1/d^2$, and $1/d^3$. In contrast to the $1/d$ style, the $1/d^2$ style gives more weights to the closer classifiers and vice versa. In the empirical studies, it has been observed that the $1/d^2$ style produces better performances than the others. The corporative function which aggregates the decisions of the NB classifiers might be written as in the Equation 6:

$$h_i = \frac{w_i}{\sum_{j=1}^{k} w_j} \tag{6}$$

where the h_i hypothesis is the weight of the ith NB method. The total weight of the NB classifiers should be obviously equal to 1 as in the Equation 7:

$$H = \sum_{i=1}^{k} h_i = 1 \tag{7}$$

where k denotes the number of the sub regions. The $LANB(x_q)$ function is used to find the final class label of the test point where $LANB$: R®C.

$$LANB\left(x_q\right) = \arg\max_{c \in C}\left(h_i \cdot NB_i^c\left(x_q\right)\right) \tag{8}$$

The function performs a separate calculation for each class and assigns the maximum argument as a class label where C indicates the set of class labels defined as $\{c_1,c_2,c_3,\ldots,c_s\}$. The $NB_i^c\left(x_q\right)$ function calculates the probability of each class. Consequently, the extended style of the $LANB(x_q)$ function to generate a global approach is as follows in the Equation 9 (Bulut & Amasyali, 2016):

$$LANB\left(x_q\right) = \underset{c\in C}{\arg\max}\left(\frac{\sum_i^k w_i \cdot NB_i^c\left(x_q\right)}{\sum_j^k w_j}\right) \tag{9}$$

The cooperative aggregation function assigns different weights to each of the local NB classifiers.

EXPERIMENTAL RESULTS AND DISCUSSIONS

Large Scale Dataset Preparation Procedure

Different types of 53 well-known UCI datasets have been chosen for the empirical studies. In the original form of UCI datasets, few of the instances have missing values and some attributes have categorical nominal values. Before experiments, some changes in the Weka software platform (Hall et al., 2009) have been performed over these datasets without damaging their originalities. Nominal values have been converted to numerical values, missing values have been replaced, and finally all the values are normalized using the Min-Max normalization method. In the columns of Table 1, there are basic statistics for the UCI datasets such as number of points, number of attributes, and number of class labels. This information gives a basic notion for the workspace.

In Machine Learning, the 0-Rule (Zero Rule) is the accuracy rate of random prediction for any dataset. The 0- Rule gives the ratio of most frequent class label of all. This accuracy rate gives a basic idea about the class distribution of the set. Moreover, any classifier is expected to give more accuracy rate than the 0-Rule.

Application of LANB

On the MATLAB environment, 5×2 Cross Validation method (Raschka, 2018) is used throughout the tests to investigate the performances of all the class probability prediction methods. Alternately, in the 5×2 Fold Cross Validation, the dataset is randomly divided into two equal parts. In the first fold, the first and the second part are retained as evaluation (test) and train parts respectively. At this step, performance of evaluation part is calculated over training part. In the same fold, the parts are then reversed. 5 folds are repeated and totally 10 performance measurements are obtained. The overall accuracy is statistically calculated by averaging the 10 results.

Table 1. Basic statistics of the 53 UCI datasets

Names	# of Points	# of Attrbt.	# of Clss.	0-R Acc.	Names	# of Points	# of Attrbt.	# of Clss.	0-R Acc.
Abalone	4153	10	19	16.59	Landform	300	6	15	6.67
Anneal	890	62	4	76.85	Letter	20000	16	26	4.07
Audiology	169	69	5	33.72	Lymph	142	37	2	57.05
Autos	202	71	5	33.17	Monk	122	6	2	50.77
Badges	294	10	2	71.45	movementLibras	360	90	15	5.56
balance-scale	625	4	3	45.76	Mushroom	8124	112	2	51.8
breast-cancer	286	38	2	70.3	Pageblocks	5473	10	5	89.77
breast-w	699	9	2	65.52	primary-tumor	302	23	11	27.81
Cmc	1473	9	3	42.7	Ringnorm	7400	20	2	50.49
Cnae	1080	855	9	11.11	Segment	2310	18	7	14.29
col10	2019	7	10	29.87	sensorDisc	2212	12	3	42.81
Colic	368	60	2	63.05	sensorRead	5456	24	4	40.41
column3C	310	6	3	48.39	Sick	3772	31	2	93.88
credit-a	690	42	2	55.51	Sonar	208	60	2	53.38
credit-g	1000	59	2	70	Soybean	675	83	18	13.63
d159	7182	32	2	51.78	Spambase	4601	57	2	60.6
Diabetes	768	8	2	65.11	Splice	3190	287	3	51.88
Ecoli	327	6	5	43.73	Titanic	2201	3	2	67.7
Glass	205	9	5	37.08	Transfusion	748	4	2	76.21
heart-statlog	270	13	2	55.56	Vehicle	846	18	4	25.51
Hepatitis	155	19	2	79.38	Vote	435	16	2	61.38
hillValley	606	100	2	50.33	Vowel	990	11	11	9.09
Hypothyroid	3770	31	3	92.33	Waveform	5000	40	3	33.84
Ionosphere	351	33	2	64.1	wineCultivars	153	13	3	39.89
Iris	150	4	3	33.33	Yeast	1479	8	9	31.3
kr-vs-kp	3196	39	2	52.22	Zoo	84	16	4	48.89
Labor	57	26	2	64.67					

Additionally, these 10 accuracy results in a vector are conducted into the Paired T-Test Comparison analysis. The Paired T-Test, which is statically a performance measuring tool, is used to compare two performance results. In other words, the Paired T-Test metric is used to compare statistically the overall performances of the two distinct classifiers (Hsu & Lachenbruch, 2009). This tool produces three types of outputs: if the first classifier is better than the other, it will be "*win*", if it is worse, it will be "*loss*", and if equal, it will be "*tie*".

In this stage, it should be emphasized that there is no need to use some other performance metrics such as the Precision, Recall, F1-Score, MCC (Matthews Correlation Coefficient) (Chicco & Jurman,

2020), and ROC (Receiver Operating Characteristic) (Narkhede, 2018) for this study (Bulut, 2016). The Paired T-Test results are definitely sufficient in evaluation of the algorithms.

Experimental Results

All the algorithms used in this study are implemented and tested on the MATLAB R2020b and Weka v3.8.5 environments by using a computer having standard specifications. In Table 2, 10NN refers to the *k*-NN method where the related parameter *k*=10, the closest points. *k*-NN method is added to this study in order to analyze the overall classification operations. This corresponding column can be used for comparison among the all other methods. In the second and third columns, there are the accuracy results of simple NB and LANB classifiers respectively. In the next column, "%Inc." indicates the percentage increase of performance from NB to LANB. In the last column, win-tie-loss T-Test results of NB-LANB comparisons are placed.

Totally T-Test comparisons have resulted in 31 *wins*, 14 *ties*, and 8 *loss*es as in Table 2. Outperforming in 31 datasets clearly shows that LANB is better than the convolutional NB method.

At the last row, arithmetic average results can be seen in the corresponding columns. It totally gives an 8.202 increase when compared to the simple NB method. It should be underlined that the proposed LANB method outperforms.

The experimental results prove that the LABN method gives more accurate results when compared with the others. The findings indicate that LANB outperforms significantly than the regular NB method in evaluations.

These experimental studies indicate that a modified model of Naïve Bayes learner enhances significantly the cumulative classification performance by dealing with the local characteristics of a given feature space. As a consequence, focusing local areas by creating locally adaptive experts in order to generate a global expert system gives a successful classification.

CONCLUSION

This chapter represents a combination of both supervised and unsupervised learning techniques for large scale datasets. A locally adaptive NB learner, which relaxes an independent assumption by learning local sub regions, is proposed. In the presented methodology of Locally Adaptive Naïve Bayes strategy, a local Naïve Bayes classifiers which is closer to the query point plays a greater role when compared with the other local classifiers. In the empirical studies, the proposed method has given more accurate classification results. In conclusion, it can be stated that the discriminative aspect of this study is to make a globalization by aggregating the localizations.

AVAILABILITY

The codes written in MATLAB, the experimental outputs in Microsoft Excel, the suit of test datasets, and the other relevant documents are publicly downloadable in the web site below for examinations and progressive studies: (https://sites.google.com/site/bulutfaruk/study-of-locally-adaptive-naive-bayes-learner).

Table 2. The overall accuracy results of 53 datasets

NB-LANB Comparison											
	10NN	**NB**	**LANB**	**% Inc.**	**T-Test**		**10NN**	**NB**	**LANB**	**% Inc.**	**T-Test**
abalone	0.246	0.255	0.259	1.9	*tie*	landform	0.915	0.985	0.951	-3.5	*loss*
anneal	0.943	0.769	0.798	3.8	*win*	letter	0.920	0.666	0.824	23.7	*win*
audiology	0.595	0.374	0.391	4.7	*win*	lymph	0.806	0.770	0.799	3.7	*win*
autos	0.520	0.556	0.623	12.0	*win*	monk	0.738	0.841	0.918	9.2	*win*
badges	0.999	0.781	0.814	4.2	*win*	movementLibras	0.519	0.631	0.709	12.4	*win*
balance-scale	0.878	0.895	0.929	3.7	*win*	mushroom	0.999	0.881	0.982	11.5	*win*
breast-cancer	0.729	0.703	0.676	-3.8	*loss*	pageblocks	0.947	0.939	0.960	2.2	*tie*
breast-w	0.965	0.965	0.952	-1.4	*tie*	primary-tumor	0.458	0.278	0.435	56.4	*win*
cmc	0.479	0.526	0.516	-1.8	*tie*	ringnorm	0.643	0.986	0.885	-10.2	*loss*
cnae	0.789	0.107	0.140	30.6	*win*	segment	0.938	0.895	0.945	5.6	*win*
col10	0.694	0.645	0.716	11.1	*win*	sensorDisc	0.984	0.887	0.963	8.5	*win*
colic	0.777	0.783	0.803	2.6	*tie*	sensorRead	0.814	0.825	0.891	8.0	*win*
column3C	0.761	0.797	0.793	-0.5	*tie*	sick	0.955	0.938	0.951	1.4	*tie*
credit-a	0.831	0.703	0.797	13.4	*win*	sonar	0.674	0.742	0.697	-6.2	*loss*
credit-g	0.719	0.701	0.689	-1.7	*loss*	soybean	0.859	0.393	0.760	93.0	*win*
d159	0.932	0.856	0.933	8.9	*win*	spambase	0.826	0.534	0.803	50.5	*win*
diabetes	0.738	0.735	0.717	-2.4	*tie*	splice	0.765	0.618	0.711	14.9	*win*
ecoli	0.857	0.851	0.860	1.0	*tie*	titanic	0.329	0.778	0.456	-41.4	*loss*
glass	0.636	0.627	0.657	4.7	*win*	transfusion	0.774	0.744	0.737	-0.9	*tie*
heart-statlog	0.817	0.796	0.792	-0.4	*tie*	vehicle	0.665	0.584	0.686	17.4	*win*
hepatitis	0.834	0.825	0.855	3.7	*win*	vote	0.924	0.898	0.925	3.0	*win*
hillValley	0.508	0.498	0.546	9.6	*win*	vowel	0.653	0.701	0.675	-3.6	*loss*
hypothyroid	0.930	0.938	0.976	4.0	*win*	waveform	0.806	0.796	0.798	0.2	*tie*
ionosphere	0.793	0.901	0.861	-4.4	*loss*	wineCultivars	0.962	0.974	0.967	-0.7	*tie*
iris	0.964	0.957	0.945	-1.3	*tie*	yeast	0.573	0.463	0.552	19.1	*win*
kr-vs-kp	0.882	0.652	0.859	31.8	*win*	zoo	0.988	0.907	0.986	8.7	*win*
labor	0.814	0.673	0.793	17.9	*win*	AVARAGE	0.775	0.727	0.767	8.202	

REFERENCES

Bache, K., & Lichman, M. (2013). *UCI Machine Learning Repository*. http://archive.ics.uci.edu/ml

Basu, M., & Ho, T. K. (Eds.). (2006a). *Data complexity in pattern recognition*. Springer Science & Business Media. doi:10.1007/978-1-84628-172-3

Basu, M., & Ho, T. K. (Eds.). (2006b). *Measures of Geometric Complexity Classification Problems, Book: Data Complexity in Pattern Recognition*. Springer Science & Business Media. doi:10.1007/978-1-84628-172-3

Bulut, F. (2016, April). Performance evaluations of supervised learners on imbalanced datasets. In 2016 Electric Electronics, Computer Science, Biomedical Engineerings' Meeting (EBBT) (pp. 1-4). IEEE. doi:10.1109/EBBT.2016.7483677

Bulut, F., & Amasyali, M. F. (2016). Katı kümeleme ve yeni bir geçiş fonksiyonuyla uzman karışımlarında sınıflandırma. *Gazi Üniversitesi Mühendislik Mimarlık Fakültesi Dergisi, 31*(4).

Chen, S., Webb, G. I., Liu, L., & Ma, X. (2020). A novel selective naïve Bayes algorithm. *Knowledge-Based Systems*, *192*, 105361. doi:10.1016/j.knosys.2019.105361

Chicco, D., & Jurman, G. (2020). The advantages of the Matthews correlation coefficient (MCC) over F1 score and accuracy in binary classification evaluation. *BMC Genomics*, *21*(1), 1–13. doi:10.118612864-019-6413-7 PMID:31898477

Ester, M., Kriegel, H. P., Sander, J., & Xu, X. (1996, August). Density-based spatial clustering of applications with noise. In Int. Conf. *Data Mining and Knowledge Discovery*, *240*, 6.

Frank, E., Hall, M., & Pfahringer, B. (2012). *Locally weighted naive bayes*. arXiv preprint arXiv:1212.2487.

Gill, S., & Hooda, M. (2021). The Design Perspective of the Structures Based on kd Tree. In *Rising Threats in Expert Applications and Solutions* (pp. 515–524). Springer. doi:10.1007/978-981-15-6014-9_61

Hall, M., Frank, E., Holmes, G., Pfahringer, P., Reutemann, P., & Witten, I.H. (2009The WEKA Data Mining Software: An Update. *SIGKDD Explorations*, *11*(1).

Ho, T. K., & Basu, M. (2002). Complexity measures of supervised classification problems. *Pattern Analysis and Machine Intelligence, IEEE Transactions on, 24*(3), 289-300.

Hsu, H., & Lachenbruch, P. A. (2008). *Paired T Test. Wiley Encyclopedia of Clinical Trials*. doi:10.1002/9780471462422.eoct969

Jiang, L., Cai, Z., Zhang, H., & Wang, D. (2013). Naive Bayes text classifiers: A locally weighted learning approach. *Journal of Experimental & Theoretical Artificial Intelligence*, *25*(2), 273–286. doi:10.1080/0952813X.2012.721010

Jiang, L., & Guo, Y. (2005, November). Learning lazy naive Bayesian classifiers for ranking. In *Tools with Artificial Intelligence, 2005. ICTAI 05. 17th IEEE International Conference on*. IEEE.

Jiang, L., Wang, D., Cai, Z., & Yan, X. (2007). Survey of improving naive Bayes for classification. In *Advanced Data Mining and Applications* (pp. 134–145). Springer Berlin Heidelberg. doi:10.1007/978-3-540-73871-8_14

Jiang, L., Zhang, H., & Su, J. (2005). Learning k-nearest neighbor naive bayes for ranking. In *Advanced Data Mining and Applications* (pp. 175–185). Springer Berlin Heidelberg. doi:10.1007/11527503_21

Jones, M. T. (2015). *Artificial Intelligence: A Systems Approach: A Systems Approach. Jones & Bartlett Publishing.*

Karlos, S., Fazakis, N., Panagopoulou, A.-P., Kotsiantis, S., & Sgarbas, K. (2017). Locally application of naive Bayes for self-training. *Springer Evolving Systems*, *8*(1), 3–18. doi:10.100712530-016-9159-3

Kikuchi, M., Yoshida, M., Okabe, M., & Umemura, K. (2015, August). Confidence interval of probability estimator of Laplace smoothing. In *Advanced Informatics: Concepts, Theory and Applications (ICAICTA), 2015 2nd International Conference on* (pp. 1-6). IEEE. 10.1109/ICAICTA.2015.7335387

Li, J., Fang, G., Li, B., & Wang, C. (2015). A Novel Naive Bayes Classifier Model Based on Differential Evolution. In *Intelligent Computing Theories and Methodologies* (pp. 558–566). Springer International Publishing. doi:10.1007/978-3-319-22180-9_55

Liu, Q., Lu, J., Zhao, K., & Chen, S. (2014). Naive Bayes classifier ensemble for traffic incident detection. In *Transportation Research Board 93rd Annual Meeting* (No. 14-1014). 10.1155/2014/383671

Lu, H., Lin, J., & Zeng, X. X. (2012). Research and Application of Improved Naive Bayesian Classification Algorithm. *Journal of Hunan University (Natural Sciences), 12*, 11.

McCann, S., & Lowe, D. G. (2012, June). Local naive bayes nearest neighbor for image classification. In *2012 IEEE Conference on Computer Vision and Pattern Recognition* (pp. 3650-3656). IEEE. 10.1109/CVPR.2012.6248111

Narayanan, V., Arora, I., & Bhatia, A. (2013). Fast and accurate sentiment classification using an enhanced Naive Bayes model. In *Intelligent Data Engineering and Automated Learning–IDEAL 2013* (pp. 194–201). Springer Berlin Heidelberg. doi:10.1007/978-3-642-41278-3_24

Narkhede, S. (2018). Understanding auc-roc curve. *Towards Data Science*, *26*, 220–227.

Par, Ö. E., Sezer, E. A., & Sever, H. (2019, April). Small and Unbalanced Data Set Problem in Classification. In *2019 27th Signal Processing and Communications Applications Conference (SIU)* (pp. 1-4). IEEE. 10.1109/SIU.2019.8806497

Peng, W., Huang, L., Jia, J., & Ingram, E. (2018, August). Enhancing the naive Bayes spam filter through intelligent text modification detection. In *2018 17th IEEE International Conference On Trust, Security And Privacy In Computing And Communications/12th IEEE International Conference On Big Data Science And Engineering (TrustCom/BigDataSE)* (pp. 849-854). IEEE. 10.1109/TrustCom/BigDataSE.2018.00122

Qin, F., Tang, X. J., & Cheng, Z. K. (2012, July). Application and research of multi-label Naïve Bayes Classifier. In *Intelligent Control and Automation (WCICA), 2012 10th World Congress on* (pp. 764-768). IEEE.

Raschka, S. (2018). *Model evaluation, model selection, and algorithm selection in machine learning.* arXiv preprint arXiv:1811.12808.

Sen, P. C., Hajra, M., & Ghosh, M. (2020). Supervised classification algorithms in machine learning: A survey and review. In *Emerging technology in modelling and graphics* (pp. 99–111). Springer. doi:10.1007/978-981-13-7403-6_11

Zhang, H., Jiang, L., & Yu, L. (2021). Attribute and instance weighted naive Bayes. *Pattern Recognition, 111*, 107674.

Zwartjes, G. J. (2017). *Adaptive Naive Bayes classification for wireless sensor networks.* University of Twente.

Chapter 17
RFID Security Issues, Defenses, and Security Schemes

Atul Kumar
National Institute of Technology, Kurukshetra, India

Ankit Kumar Jain
https://orcid.org/0000-0002-9482-6991
National Institute of Technology, Kurukshetra, India

ABSTRACT

Radio frequency identification (RFID) consists of a tag and reader. The RFID system is used in various places, such as finding the location of devices and toll payment. In computer security, CIA (confidentiality, integrity, authentication) is the primary concern for RFID security. In existing scenario, there are various threats present in the RFID system such as de-synchronization attack, disclosure attack, tracking attack and so on. There are various threats that RFID systems are vulnerable to such as a de-synchronization attack, disclosure attack, dos attack, and tracking attack. This chapter discusses various attacks on the RFID system in terms of confidentiality, integrity, and availability as these devices contain a limited amount of memory and low power battery. Therefore, these devices need a lightweight solution for the RFID system. Hence, this chapter additionally discusses various authentication schemes such as lightweight scheme and ultra-lightweight scheme for RFID systems.

INTRODUCTION

Internet of things (IoT) consists of various heterogeneous devices, i.e., sensor, tag, reader, barcode, smart card. These devices connect the network without human interaction. These devices contain an inadequate amount of memory and a smaller power battery. In 2017, 8.4 billion "things" are connected to the internet, and it will increase 20.4 billion in 2020. Thus, these huge devices create a large amount of power and communication data in the network. Hence, there are various lightweight protocols like low power personal area networks over IPv6 (6LowPAN), ZigBee. that are employed. IEEE 802.15.4

DOI: 10.4018/978-1-7998-3299-7.ch017

standard used by most of the sensors networks, which provide low power and low rate communication over the network.

Barcode labels can be used to identify the system. However, it contains low storage capacity and also not reprogrammable. RFID is used to identify an object in the network. In 2018, 76,644 million RFID tags sold in various industries like health care, retail. However, there are twenty-five billion NFC/HF RFID tags sold in 2018. The RFID system comprises two components tag and reader. The reader reads information from the tag and also processes this information. The reader stores various pieces of information like tag identification, security key. An RFID tag consists of two components, such as microchip and antenna. The RFID tags consist of four types of memory: reserved memory, electronic product code (EPC) memory, TID memory, and user memory.

There are three types of tags used in the RFID system, namely active tag, semi-passive tag, and passive tag. An active tag contains a battery that is used to communicate with the reader. These types of tags are costly than passive tags. Passive tags cannot contain a power battery. It receives power from the reader. Mainly, the passive tag can operate on three frequencies like low frequency, high frequency, and ultra-high frequency. The low frequency (LF) passive tag operates on 125 kHz to 134 kHz. It can operate from 1 cm to 10 cm and has a longer wavelength. High frequency (HF) passive tag can operate on 13.56 MHz frequency and sense up to 1 meter. Ultra-high frequency (UHF) tag can operate on 865 MHz to 960 MHz and also ranging from more than 1 meter. The passive tag use in the passport, electronic tolls, supply chains. Semi-passive tags contain a small power battery. When the semi-passive tags are not in the range of the reader, its usage its power. However, when the tags come in a range of the reader. Then, it receives power from the reader through an electric or magnetic field as similar to the passive tag (Finkenzeller, 2010). Fig. 1 describes various types of tags communicating to the RFID system.

There are various security issues in the IoT application, such as authentication, authorization, and privacy. There are various types of cryptography schemes uses in IoT security, such as public-key cryptography and symmetric-key cryptography. As, public-key cryptography schemes include RSA, Diffie-Hellman key exchange. However, these schemes require lots of bandwidth and power consumption. Due to this, the elliptic curve is introduced, which provides fewer communication steps than RSA, Diffie-Hellman. Symmetric key cryptographic schemes use simple bit-wise operation (XOR, OR, AND, Rotate), cyclic redundancy checksum, and symmetric encryption. Symmetric-key cryptography schemes require less power and communication steps than public-key cryptography.

This chapter consists of six sections. The first section describes the introduction of the RFID system. This section describes various types of RFID tags like active tags, passive tags, semi-passive tags. The second section presents analyses of various attacks possible on RFID systems such as eavesdropping, de-synchronization attack, disclosure attack, tracking attack, replay attack, denial of service attack. The fourth section presents an analysis of various security schemes like lightweight schemes (Liao et al., Zhao et al., Chen et al. etc.) and ultra-lightweight schemes (SASI, Gossamer, LMAP, SLAP, KMAP) for RFID system. These schemes provide mutual authentication and cryptographic algorithm for the RFID system. Section five contains the future scope for the RFID system. Section six presents the conclusion of the paper. The last section describes the overall conclusion of the entire paper.

Figure 1. Various types of RFID tag communicating on RFID system

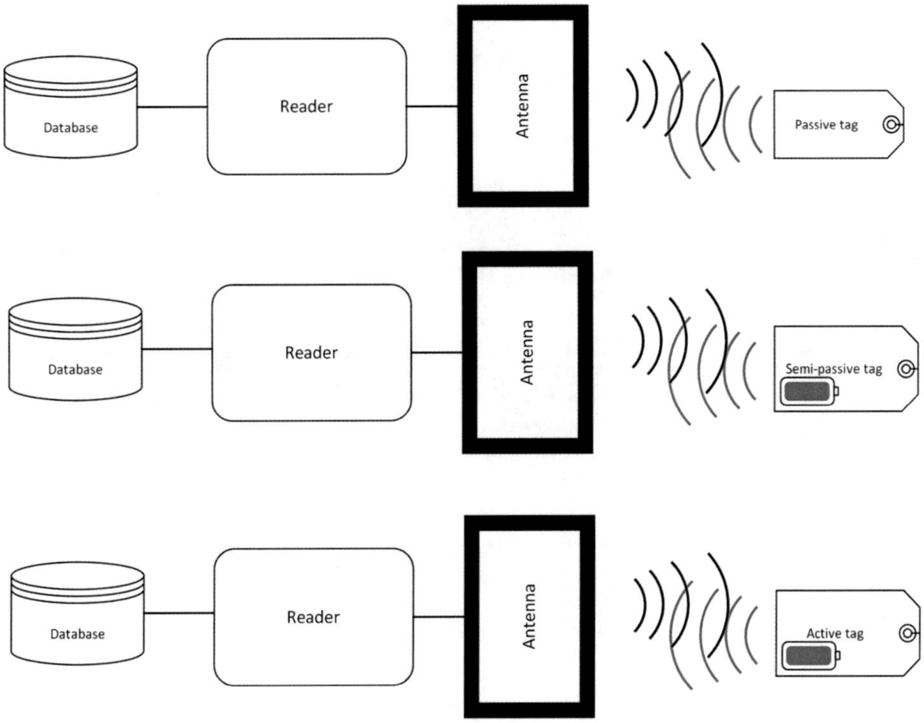

Attacks

The RFID system consists of various types of tags and a reader. These tags consist of a limited amount of memory and low power capacity. However, there are various other issues in terms of authentication, privacy, forward security. Due to these issues, there are various attacks possible on RFID systems such as eavesdropping, de-synchronization attack, disclosure attack, de-synchronization attack, cloning attack. Figure 1 shows various attacks possible on the RFID system in terms of confidentiality, Integrity, and Availability.

Figure 2. Various attacks on RFID system

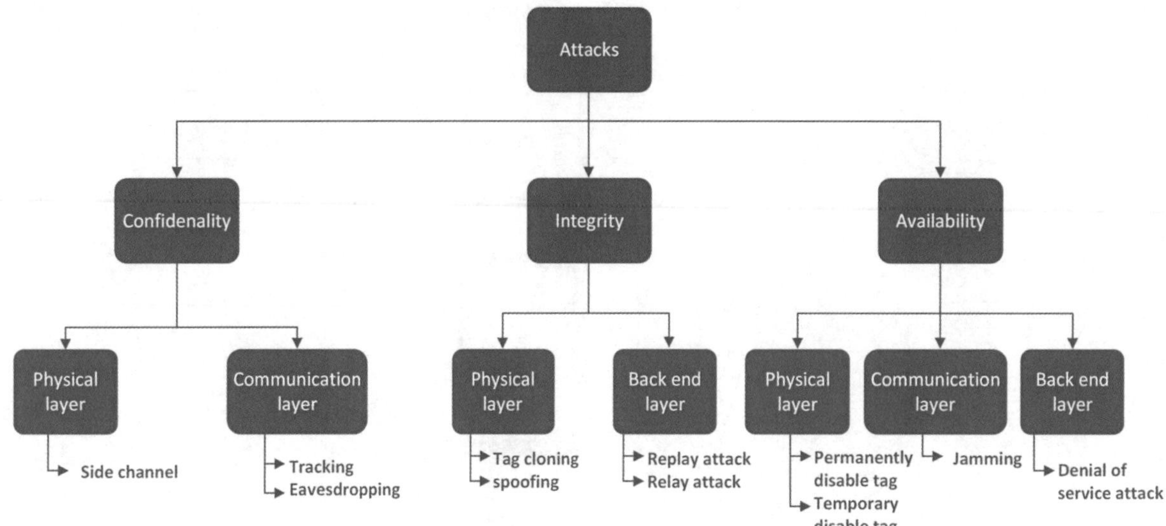

Confidentiality

In a computer network, confidentiality consists of accessing sensitive information and protected data by authorized users. In confidentiality, privacy is a primary concern for the legitimate user. There are various threats in the RFID system to defend confidentiality, such as side-channel, tracking, eavesdropping, key compromise, and privacy violation.

Side-Channel Attack

In this attack, the adversary can extract sensitive information using electromagnetic fields as well as timing information. This attack exploits the confidentiality of the system. This attack can be made using the power analysis method. The power analysis method consists of extracting information using a variety of power supply. Differential power analysis can also perform using a side-channel attack.

Eavesdropping

Eavesdrop attack is a passive attack. In this attack, the tag comes in a range of the reader. During the exchange of messages between tag and reader, the attacker steals secret information or message packets communicating between tags and a reader. Hence, this attack hides the confidentiality of data.

Tracking Attack

In tracking attacks (Phan, 2009), the adversary obtains the correct ID of the tag. The tracking attack compromises the privacy of the RFID system. Juel and Weis (Juels & Weis, 2007) proposed a un-traceability model. In this model, there are three phases to computes the identity of the tags, such as the learning phase, challenge phase, and guessing phase. The learning phase consists of eavesdrops whole message packets between communication networks. In the challenge phase, the challenger is given two tags ID1 and ID2 to the adversary. Then, the third phase consists of guessing tag identity by the adversary. If the adversary can find the exact identity of the tag, then the adversary wins the game.

Disclosure Attack

In a disclosure attack, the adversary could steal confidential information. There are two types of disclosure attacks: identity disclosure attack and full disclosure attack. Identity disclosure attack consists of stealing the identity of the tag. In fully disclosure attack consists of steal all information of the tag, i.e., shared key, an ID of the tag (Arco & Santis, 2011; Safkhani & Shariat, 2018). The adversary performs disclosure attacks in two ways: recursive linear cryptanalysis and differential cryptanalysis. Recursive linear cryptanalysis is a passive attack, and it requires only one authentication session to perform a disclosure attack. In this attack, the adversary first finds all the unknown parameters within the protocol. Then, it creates a linear equation for all its unknown variables. Recursive differential cryptanalysis (RDC) attack consists of a probabilistic attack and requires more than one authentication session to perform this attack (Ahmadian, Salmasizadeh, & Aref, 2013b). The disclosure attack can also perform using exploits of T-functionality (Klimov & Shamir, 2010) of the protocol.

Integrity

Integrity ensures consistency, trustworthiness of data during communication channels from any modification by unauthorized people. There are various threats to defend the integrity of RFID systems such as cloning, spoofing attack, replay attack, relay attack.

Cloning Attack

In the cloning attack, the adversary creates replica malicious nodes or clones of the tag. Then, the adversary places these malicious nodes in communication networks. After that, these malicious nodes interact with a genuine reader (Lehtonen, Ostojic, Ilic, & Michahelles, 2009). These nodes extract sensitive information about the entire network.

Spoofing Attack

This attack is an impersonation attack in which the adversary establishes malicious devices in the communication channel. The adversary impersonates a genuine tag node and gets all its privileges and information. Then, this information stores in a malicious node.

Replay Attack

In the replay attack (Liao & Hsiao, 2014a), the adversary eavesdrops packet between communication channels. After this, the adversary transmits these old genuine authenticate packets to the tag. The tag node authenticates these original packets. Hence, the attacker misuses these pieces of information or message packets to unauthorized access to the system.

Relay Attack

This attack is known as a man-in middle attack. This attack consists of the modification of eavesdrops message packets. Therefore, A relay attack is an active attack. In this attack, the adversary placed malicious devices in a communication channel between legitimate tags and a reader. Then, the adversary believes the tag/reader that this device is a legitimate reader/tag. Hence, genuine tags/readers interact with these malicious devices.

Availability

In a computer system, availability refers to access resources or information by the genuine user in a specified location. Data availability defines the data that must be available to a legitimate user. In the RFID system, there are various threats to availability in the RFID system, such as disabling tag, denial of service attack, de-synchronization attack.

Temporary Disabling Tag

The adversary can temporary disable tag using aluminum foil, which shields it from electromagnetic waves. The temporary disabling tag can be unintentional, such as tag covered with ice. Temporary disabling of tag can perform using two interferences: active interference as well as passive interference. In the case of passive interference consists of disabling tags due to collisions of radio interference, power switching supplies. In the active interference consists of disabling tag using jamming by the adversary.

Permanent Disabling Tag

A permanent disabling tag consists of possible threats that destructive of a tag from the RFID system. The adversary can permanent disabling tag using tag removal, tag destruction, and kill command. In tag removal, the adversary can easily be removed RFID tag from expensive product and place at another cheaper product. So, it cannot easily to tracking these RFID tags. In tag destruction, the adversary can destroy an RFID tag. Tag destruction can be done by chemical exposure or applying pressure. The adversary can also use the kill command to disable the tag permanently. This command consists of permanently erase all data stored in the tag.

Jamming Attack

In a jamming attack, the adversary stops communication between genuine tag and reader so that the tag node cannot interact with the reader. The adversary creates a signal as equivalent to the reader so that the tag cannot communicate with the reader.

Denial of Service Attack

In this attack, the adversary can block the RFID tag from the system. RFID devices contain limited storage capacity and having a low power battery. So, the adversary takes advantage of this, and it transmits many packets to the communication channel. Due to this, there will increase in bandwidth of the communication channel. Much power of the tag can use in receiving these large packets. Due to power constraints, RFID tags can remove from an RFID system.

De-Synchronization Attack

In an RFID system, the attacker would disturb communicating between tag and reader. In this attack, the adversary break synchronization between tag and reader (Safkhani & Bagheri, 2016). In the case of the ultra-lightweight scheme, the reader assigns IDS, shared key to tag. Both of the tag and reader update its shared key and IDS after authenticating each other. There are two ways to perform a de-synchronization attack.

Firstly, the adversary eavesdrops message packets between tag and reader. The adversary modifies these message packets. Then, it transmits these modified message packets to tag. After receiving these packets, the tag validates these message packets. The adversary succeeds if the tag sends an authenticate packet to the adversary. The tag updates its shared key and IDS. Hence, the adversary computes de-synchronization between tag and reader (Arco & Santis, 2011).

In a second way, the reader and tag contain old and new keys and ID as K1, IDS1 and K2, IDS2. The tag comes in the range of the reader, and it transmits IDS to the reader. The reader computes an authentication message packet and transmits these packets to the tag. The tag validates these packets and transmits message packets to the reader. After, the tag updates its key and IDS as K2, IDS2 and K3, IDS3. The adversary blocks these message packets between tag and reader. Hence, the genuine reader cannot receive message packets from a tag. Then, the reader computes from K2, IDS2, and transmits it to the tag. The tag authenticates message packet using K2, IDS2 and updates its key as K3, IDS3 and K4, IDS4. Hence, both the tag and the reader contain different shared keys and IDS. Thus, de-synchronization occurs between tags and a reader (Bilal, Masood, & Kausar, 2009).

SOLUTIONS AND RECOMMENDATIONS

To provide security in RFID tags, RFID tags categories into four types of class such as full-fledged class, simple class, lightweight class, and ultra-lightweight classes. Full fledge classes, RFID tags computes computation, such as asymmetric operation. The full-fledge tags require enormous power and computational capacity. In simple classes, RFID tags can compute the pseudo-random number and hash function. This class tag requires lesser battery power than a full-fledged class tag. In lightweight classes, RFID tags can compute check-sum, elliptic curves. These tags are lessor costly than full-fledged class tags and simple class tags. The lightweight tags consist of various security issues such as eavesdropping, mutual authentication, forward security, privacy. Privacy is an essential concern for the RFID system. In privacy, a tracking attack can be performing by the adversary to computes the identity of the tag. Juel & Weis proposed the cryptanalysis model for un-traceability. In mutual authentication, both genuine tags and a reader validate each other. However, the adversary can break mutual authentication between tag and reader through disclosure attack, replay attack.

The fourth class of tags are ultra-lightweight tags; these tags require much lessor cost than other class tags. These ultra-lightweight tags only compute simple operations such as XOR, Rotate, OR, AND. However, these tags consist of various security issues such as tracking attack, de-synchronization attack, disclosure attack. In ultra-lightweight class, tracking attacks performs through T-function (i.e., XOR, OR,

AND operation) (Barrero, Hernández-Castro, Peris-Lopez, Camacho, & R-Moreno, 2014). The mutual authentication for these tags is very weak and quickly computes by the adversary. Hence, it is essential to create a secure algorithm to defend against these attacks. However, a limited amount of memory and computational capacity causes difficult for the researcher to create an efficient and secure algorithm.

Authentication can be used to provide resistance from various attacks. However, in order to provide authentication, there contains an extra amount of communication and computational are required. However, RFID devices contain a limited amount of power and computational overhead. Hence, the researcher suggests various algorithms (i.e., lightweight or ultra-lightweight authentication) to provide unilateral authentication or mutual authentication. In unilateral authentication is a one-way authentication. The only server can validate genuine tags to compute authentication. Server spoofing attacks can perform in unilateral authentication. In the case of mutual authentication, a genuine reader can validate genuine tag and vice versa.

Public Key Cryptography

Asymmetric key cryptography or public-key cryptography consists of two different keys: a public key, and private key. In public key is used to encrypt data to form ciphertext while the private key is used to decrypt into original data. In cryptography, there are various public-key cryptography scheme: RSA, Diffie-Hellman key exchange. However, this scheme provides tremendous computational overhead. Due to this, the elliptic curve introduces that requires a lessor computational overhead.

Elliptic curve:

Let A, B is the point on the elliptic curve over a finite field P. Let (X_A, Y_A), (X_B, Y_B) represents points on this curve. Then, the equation represents the elliptic curve as:

$$Y^2 \equiv X^3 + aX + b$$

Where a, b is constant, then point (X_c, Y_c) as:

$$X_c = \lambda^2 - X_A - X_B \left(\bmod P\right)$$

$$Y_c = \lambda(X_A - X_c) - Y_B \left(\bmod P\right)$$

Where λ represents the slope of the lines and calculates as:

$$\lambda = \frac{y_B - y_A}{x_B - x_A} \bmod p, if\ A \neq B$$

$$\lambda = \frac{3X^2{}_A + a}{2Y_A} \bmod p, if\ A == B$$

Hash Function

A one-way hash function is defining as map arbitrary string length to fixed length. The hash function is define as h: A ® B, where A = {0, 1}* and B = {0, 1}^{n}, n bit of an output length. There are various hash functions available such as SHA, MD5. However, these hashes require much computational overhead. Hence, there is a various lightweight hash function for RFID system such as PRESENT, Quark (Aumasson, Henzen, Meier, & Naya-Plasencia, 2013), SQUASH, SPONGEMT (Bogdanov et al., 2011), MAC, HMAC. Quark is a lightweight Hash function developed by Aumasson in 2010. In this, there are three types of Quark, such as U-Quark, D-Quark, and T-Quark. In U-Quark consists of 64 bits security, and requires 1379 gate equivalents (GE). In D-Quark consists of 80 bits security. In T-Quark consists of 112 bits security, and it requires 2296 GE.

Authentication

Authentication is an essential concern for RFID devices. This section describes various types of lightweight authentication schemes as well as ultra-lightweight authentication scheme. In a lightweight authentication scheme consists of public-key cryptography like elliptic curve, hash function. In case of ultra-lightweight scheme consists of symmetric-key cryptography in which it uses simple operations such as OR, AND, XOR, ROT.

Lightweight Authentication Scheme

Lee et al. (Lee, Batina, & Verbauwhede, 2008) proposed a lightweight authentication scheme for the RFID system, which uses the elliptic curve. In this scheme, the server selected a random number and transmitted it to the tag. After receiving a random number, the tag generated a random number and computed T_1, T_2 and, V using the elliptic curve. Then, this message packets transmitted to the server. After receiving message packets, the server computed the inverse of an elliptic curve to authenticate tag. This scheme is a unilateral authentication scheme. In this scheme, the memory requirement by the system for storing the private key and public key are 652 bits, and communication overhead between networks is 82 bytes. This scheme provided confidentiality, scalability, forward secrecy, and availability. However, this scheme cannot withstand the impersonation attack and tracking attack (Bringer, Chabanne, & Icart, 2008).

Liao & Hsiao (Liao & Hsiao, 2014b) proposes a mutual authentication scheme for the RFID system. This scheme computes a random number to generate T_s. Then, the server transmits T_s to the tag. After receiving packets, the tag generates $Auth_t$, and R_t and transmits it to the server. The server computes X_1 using an elliptic curve and check it in its database. Then, successful authentication, it generates authentication message packets $Auth_s$ and transmits it to the tag. Then, the tag receives an authenticate message packet from the server. This scheme consists of 1280 bits of communication overhead and uses five multiplication during authentication. So, this scheme provides mutual authentication. This scheme provides anonymity, forward security, availability, impersonation attack. Figure 3 explains the Liao et al. mutual authentication scheme for the RFID system.

After that, Zhao et al. (Zhao, 2014) find an attack on Liao et al. scheme such as key management. Then, Zhao et al. (Zhao, 2014) proposed another mutually authenticate scheme for the RFID system. This scheme should be suitable for the health care environment. In this scheme, the total memory required for the private key, and a public key is 652 bits, and communication overhead between tag and server is

82 bytes. This scheme provides mutual authentication, Anonymity, Availability, forward security, impersonation attack. This scheme can not provide key comprise problems, replay attack, impersonation attack, server spoofing attack, DoS attack, location tracking attack, and cloning attack.

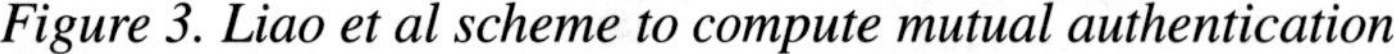

Figure 3. Liao et al scheme to compute mutual authentication

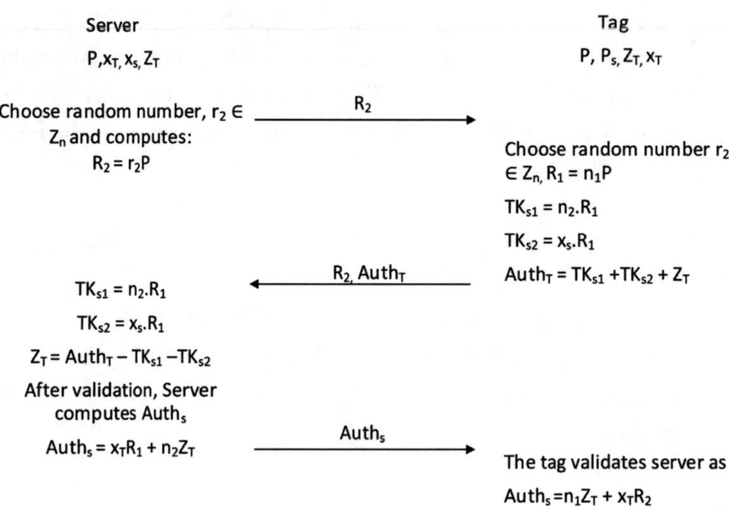

He et al. (He, Kumar, Chilamkurti, & Lee, 2014) proposed an authentication scheme for the RFID system with an ID verifier transfer protocol. This scheme consists of 1440 bits + 480w bits of storage capacity for the server, and tag required 1760 bits of storage capacity. Hence, the total storage requirements of an RFID system is 3200 and 480w bits. The running time of the elliptic curve for multiplication operation on 5 MHz tag is 0.064 second, and PIV 3 GHZ server is 0.83 ms (Cao, Kou, & Du, 2010; Gódor, Giczi, & Imre, 2010). Hence, running time for server and tag to compute elliptic multiplication is 2.49ms and 0.192 seconds. The communication cost of this scheme for server and tag is 640 bits and 640 bits, respectively. Hence, the total communication cost between tag and server is 1280 bits. This scheme consists of mutual authentication between tag and reader, confidentiality, anonymity, availability, forward security, and also provides resistance from various attacks like DoS attack, replay attack, tag masquerade attack, server spoofing attack, DoS attack, location tracking attack, cloning attack.

Ryu et al. (Ryu, Kim, & Yoo, 2015) propose another authentication scheme for the RFID system. In this scheme requires 2*TH and 2*TM where TH is the time required to compute hash function, and TM defines as the time required to compute elliptic multiplication. This scheme consists of 960 bits of communications cost for the RFID system. This scheme provides resistance from various attacks like traceability, forward security, server spoofing, and cloning attack. However, this scheme cannot provide mutual authentication between RFID devices.

Chien et al. (Chen & Chou, 2015) proposed a mutual authentication scheme for RFID devices. In this scheme, the server computes C_1, C_2, Sn using an elliptic curve and hash function. Then, it transmits it to tag. After receiving message packets, the tag verifies these message packets. After successful authentication, it generates a random number and computes C_3, c, and d. The tag transmits these packets to the server. After receiving message packets, the server validates these packets through a hash function.

This scheme provides 1440 bits of communication overhead and also uses three hash functions and four multiplication during mutual authentication. This scheme provides un-traceability, forward security, and resistance from a cloning attack. However, this scheme cannot present from a server spoof attack and a replay attack (Shen, Shen, Khan, & Lee, 2017).

Ultra-Lightweight Authentication Scheme

There is various ultra-lightweight mutual authentication protocol (UMAP) proposed to make RFID system secure and reliable. These protocols use simple bitwise operations such as XOR, OR, ROT, AND. These operations are simple and can apply to the passive tag. In 2006, the author (Peris-lopez, Hernandez-castro, Tapiador, & Ribagorda, 2002) proposed a lightweight scheme name as Lightweight mutual authentication scheme (LMAP). This scheme uses index-pseudonyms (IDS) number consists of storing of information of tag. This scheme contains a shared key that divides into four types of each 96 bits. This scheme uses EEPROM of 480 bits of memory. The tag ID stored in RAM of 96-bits. This scheme consists of only bitwise operations such as XOR, OR, ROT, AND. These operations easily implemented on the RFID tag. This scheme assumes that communication between tag and reader is insecure while communication takes place between the reader and the database through a secure channel. This scheme consists of three phases: tag identification phase, mutual authentication phase, and pseudo-random and key updating phase. The tag identification phase consists of identifying a genuine tag by the reader. After the tag identification phase, the mutual authentication phase takes place. This phase consists of authenticating both reader and tag. The reader generates two random numbers and computes messages A, and B. In the tag identification phase consists of validating messages A, and B by the tag. Then, tag computes message packets C and transmits it to the reader. The reader verifies message packets C. After, validating C, mutual authentication takes place between tag and reader. The third phase consists of pseudo-random and key updating phase. This phase consists of updating IDS and shared key after every successful authentication through a random number generated during mutual authentication. This scheme consists of a communication message generates by the tag that is 2L, and the total number of messages for mutual authentication is 4L. The memory requirement for a tag is 6L. The author suggests that this scheme provides tag anonymity, data integrity, confidentiality, and mutual authentication. However, this scheme cannot provide security against various attacks such as replay attacks, de-synchronization attacks.

Chien et al. (Chien, 2007) proposed an authentication scheme for the RFID system and named as Strong authentication and strong integrity (SASI). This scheme uses OR, Rotate, and XOR operations. This scheme uses two random numbers that are only generated by the reader. Hence, this scheme easily implemented on ultra-lightweight tags. This scheme uses two shared keys and updated after every successful authentication. This scheme consists of a memory requirement on the tag that is 7L. The communication messages generate by tag is 2L. The total number of messages for mutual authentication is 4L. This scheme provides mutual authentication, data integrity. The author suggests that this scheme provides resistance from various attacks such as replay attack, de-synchronization attack, disclosure attack, tracking attack. However, the author (Phan, 2009) proved that this scheme could not resist from de-synchronization attack, disclosure, and tracking attack. Figure 4 discusses about the SASI algorithm for the RFID system.

Peris-Lopez et al. (Peris-Lopez, Hernandez-Castro, Tapiador, & Ribagorda, 2008) proposed an authenticate scheme for the RFID system and named as Gossamer. This scheme address the limitation of the SASI scheme. This scheme uses XOR, +, AND, Rotate, and Mixbits operations to authenticate RFID devices. The MIXBITS operations consist of addition (+) and bitwise right shift operation. Hence, MIXBITS operation can smoothly perform on the passive device. This scheme uses two shared keys and two random numbers during mutual authentication. This scheme consists of storage cost is 7L, and the communication cost is 5L. Still, this scheme provides low throughput. This scheme provides security against various attacks such as a full-disclosure attack. However, this scheme cannot provide security against tracking and de-synchronization attacks.

Tian et al. (Tian, Chen, & Li, 2012) proposed an authentication scheme for the RFID system and named this scheme as RAPP. This scheme uses bitwise operation such as XOR, Rot(A, B), Per(A, B) where Per(A, B) is permutation operation. This scheme consists of total memory capacity for a tag is 5L. The communication messages generated by the tag are 2L, and the total number of messages generated for mutual authentication is 5L. However, this scheme consists of various security issues such as a de-synchronization attack, full disclosure attack, traceability attack, and formal security attack (Ahmadian, Salmasizadeh, & Aref, 2013a; Bagheri, Safkhani, Peris-Lopez, & Tapiador, 2012; Najam-ul-islam, 2017).

Yeh et al. (Yeh, Lo, & Winata, 2010) proposed an ultra-lightweight authentication scheme for the RFID system. This scheme consists of various operations such as NOT, XOR, OR, ROT. This scheme consists of memory requirements on these tags is 3L. The communication messages generated by the RFID tag are 2L. Similarly, the total number of messages for mutual authentication is 2L. However, this scheme consists of various security issues such as a de-synchronization attack, full disclosure attack, traceability attack, and formal security attack (Najam-ul-islam, 2017).

David et al. (David & Prasad, 2009) proposed an authentication scheme for the RFID system. This scheme consists of XOR, AND operations to mutual authentication between tag and reader. This scheme consists of memory requirements on these tags is 5L. The communication messages generated by the RFID tag are 3L. However, this scheme consists of various security issues such as a de-synchronization attack, full disclosure attack, traceability attack, and formal security attack (Najam-ul-islam, 2017).

In 2006, Peris et al. (Peris-lopez, Hernandez-castro, Estevez-tapiador, & Ribagorda, 2006) proposed a lightweight authentication scheme for RFID system and named as EMAP. This scheme uses various bitwise operations like OR, XOR, AND. This scheme requires 6L storage cost for authentication, and communication cost between tag and reader is 5L. This scheme provides data integrity, mutual authentication, forward security, user data confidentiality, and tag anonymity. This scheme also provides resistance from various attacks like a man-in-the-middle attack, replay attack. However, this scheme cannot provide resistance from various attacks such as a de-synchronization attack, disclosure attacks, and tracking attack.

In 2006, Peris et al. (Peris-Lopez, Hernandez-Castro, Estevez-Tapiador, & Ribagorda, 2006) proposed a lightweight authentication scheme for RFID system and named as M2AP. This scheme uses various operations like OR, AND, XOR, +. The storage requirements to compute authentication is 6L, and communications cost between tag and reader is 5L. This scheme provides user data confidentiality, tag anonymity, data integrity, mutual authentication, forward security, and also resistance from various attacks such as man-in-the-middle attack, replay attack. However, this scheme cannot provide resistance from various attacks such as de-synchronization attacks, disclosure attacks, tracking attacks.

Zhuang et al. (Zhuang, Zhu, & Chang, 2014) proposed an ultra-lightweight authentication scheme in 2014 and named this scheme as R2AP. This scheme uses a bitwise operation such as XOR, ROT, and Rec(A, B). In this scheme consists of total memory requirement on a tag to compute mutual authentication between tag and reader is 5L, and communication cost for transmitted messages and receiving messages is 7L. In this total messages, the communication messages generated by the tag is 2L. This scheme provides mutual authentication, forward security, and also resistance from a man-in-the-middle attack. However, this scheme cannot provide resistance from various attacks such as a de-synchronization attack, disclosure attacks, tracking attack, and security of diffusion function (Luo, Wen, Su, & Huang, 2018).

Mujahid et al. (Mujahid, Najam-ul-Islam, & Shami, 2015) proposed an ultra-lightweight authentication scheme named as RCIA for RFID system using a recursive hash function. In this scheme consists of total memory requirement on the tag to compute mutual authentication between tag and reader is 7L, and communication cost for transmitted messages and receiving messages is 6L. In this total messages, the communication messages generated by the tag is 2L. This scheme provides resistance from various attacks like de-synchronization attack, disclosure attacks, tracking attack, mutual authentication, and replay attack. However, this scheme cannot provide resistance from the diffusion function (Luo et al., 2018).

Tewari (Gupta, 2017) proposed another authentication scheme for a passive tag. This scheme uses rotate function and XOR operation during mutual authentication. However, this scheme consists of 2 shared keys between tag and reader. Tewari et al. use two random numbers during mutual authentication. In this scheme consists of storage cost is 7L, and communication cost between tag and reader is 3L. Tewari et al. proposed that this scheme resistance from various attacks such as de-synchronization, disclosure, tracking, replay attack, forward security. However, this scheme cannot resist from disclosure attack (Safkhani & Bagheri, 2017).

SLAP (Luo et al., 2018) scheme uses a bitwise operation such as XOR, left rotate, and conversion function, i.e., con(P, Q). In this scheme consists of memory requirement on the tag is 7L. The communication messages generated on the tag are 1.5L. Also, the total communication messages for authentication is 4L.

Con (P, Q) function manages to enhance the security of the authentication protocol. The con(P, Q) consists of three phases, such as grouping, arrange, and composition.

1. Grouping: In this phase consists of dividing P and Q into many substrings according to the hamming weights of P and Q. A threshold "T" is used to set the size of the substring.
2. Rearrange: This phase consists of an arrangement of P and Q to form P' and Q'. Then, the left rotates of each substring of A' and B' with their respective hamming weight to form P'' and Q''.
3. Composition: In this phase consists of XOR operation of P'' and Q'' to get con(P, Q).

The author suggests that this scheme provides security against various attacks such as a de-synchronization attack, disclosure attack, tracking attack, and diffusion attack.

KMAP (Najam-ul-islam, 2017) scheme uses two bitwise operation ROT, XOR operations. This scheme uses two shared key, and two random number to mutual authenticate RFID devices. This scheme also uses counter value, which is increasing by one after every unsuccessful authentication. The author also set the threshold value, i.e. 8. So, after eight unsuccessful authentications, the tag is sleep after some time and cannot interact with another node. The author uses pseudo-Kasami code (K_c) to mutual authenticate RFID devices. This scheme uses two bitwise operators XOR and left rotate (ROT). To compute $K_c(X)$ such as:

Figure 4. SASI authentication scheme

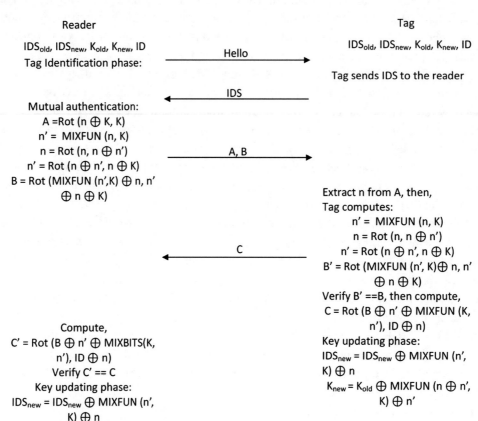

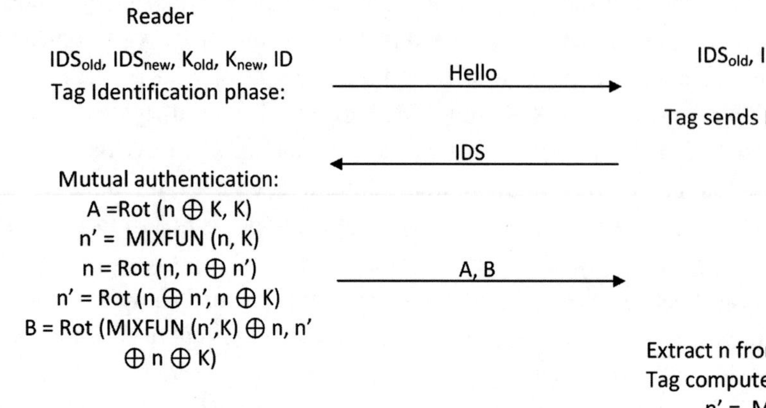

$$K_c(X) = X \text{ Å } Rot(X, HW(X))$$

Where HW(X) consists of the hamming weight of X and Rot (X, b) define as the left rotates of X with b digit. The hamming weight is defining as the number of bits counts of 1 in X. E.g. let us assume that X = 1010101011111110101, Then HW(X) = number of 1's in X = 13. The memory requirement on the tag is 7L, and also communication messages generated by tag is 2L. In this scheme, the total number of messages for mutual authentication is 4L. This scheme provides authentication, tag privacy, and integrity. The author suggests that this scheme provides resistance from various attacks such as de-synchronization attack, replay, tractability, probabilistic attacks.

FUTURE RESEARCH DIRECTIONS

An RFID system consists of various security schemes to provide authentication, but these schemes provide low-level authentication. The adversary can bypass these security schemes to unauthorized access to the system. Hence, it is crucial to develop an efficient security scheme for these small RFID devices. However, the RFID system consists of limited capacity power devices which does not support huge processing capacity. So, these schemes will be lightweight or ultra-lightweight.

1. **Ultra-lightweight Hash function**: In authentication schemes consists of an asymmetric scheme that uses lightweight hash function and elliptic curve. So, these authentication schemes directly depend upon these hash functions. Hence, it is essential to develop an ultra-lightweight hash function that provides unidirectional and also processing capacity is very low.
2. **Strong authentication scheme:** RFID devices consists of various authentication schemes. However, these schemes consist of various security issues. Hence, research should create an efficient authentication scheme for the RFID system.

CONCLUSION

RFID widely use in various applications such as healthcare applications, smart cards, animal detection systems, defense applications. In these applications, there are a large number of tags require for the RFID system. Due to its popularity in the RFID system, high security requires for RFID system. However, RFID devices contain low power battery and low computational power. Due to this, the traditional security scheme cannot directly apply to the RFID system. Therefore, many researchers proposed various security schemes for the RFID system. However, there are various possible attacks on these schemes which hide confidentiality, integrity, or availability of RFID systems. So, we analyze various threats in terms of confidentiality, integrity, and availability of the RFID system. We also analyze various types of security schemes such as lightweight or ultra-lightweight schemes available for the RFID systems.

REFERENCES

Ahmadian, Z., Salmasizadeh, M., & Aref, M. R. (2013a). Desynchronization attack on RAPP ultralightweight authentication protocol. *Information Processing Letters*, *113*(7), 205–209. doi:10.1016/j.ipl.2013.01.003

Ahmadian, Z., Salmasizadeh, M., & Aref, M. R. (2013b). Recursive linear and differential cryptanalysis of ultralightweight authentication protocols. *IEEE Transactions on Information Forensics and Security*, *8*(7), 1140–1151. doi:10.1109/TIFS.2013.2263499

Arco, P. D., & Santis, A. De. (2011). *On Ultralightweight RFID Authentication Protocols*. Academic Press.

Aumasson, J.-P., Henzen, L., Meier, W., & Naya-Plasencia, M. (2013). Quark: A lightweight hash. *Journal of Cryptology*, *26*(2), 313–339. doi:10.100700145-012-9125-6

Bagheri, N., Safkhani, M., Peris-Lopez, P., & Tapiador, J. E. (2012). Cryptanalysis of RAPP, an RFID Authentication Protocol. *IACR Cryptology EPrint Archive*, *2012*, 702.

Barrero, D. F., Hernández-Castro, J. C., Peris-Lopez, P., Camacho, D., & R-Moreno, M. D. (2014). A genetic tango attack against the David–Prasad RFID ultra-lightweight authentication protocol. *Expert Systems: International Journal of Knowledge Engineering and Neural Networks*, *31*(1), 9–19. doi:10.1111/j.1468-0394.2012.00652.x

Bilal, Z., Masood, A., & Kausar, F. (2009). Security analysis of ultra-lightweight cryptographic protocol for low-cost RFID tags: Gossamer protocol. In *2009 International Conference on Network-Based Information Systems* (pp. 260–267). IEEE. 10.1109/NBiS.2009.9

Bogdanov, A., Knežević, M., Leander, G., Toz, D., Varıcı, K., & Verbauwhede, I. (2011). SPONGENT: A lightweight hash function. In *International Workshop on Cryptographic Hardware and Embedded Systems* (pp. 312–325). Springer.

Bringer, J., Chabanne, H., & Icart, T. (2008). Cryptanalysis of EC-RAC, a RFID identification protocol. In *International Conference on Cryptology and Network Security* (pp. 149–161). Springer. 10.1007/978-3-540-89641-8_11

Cao, X., Kou, W., & Du, X. (2010). A pairing-free identity-based authenticated key agreement protocol with minimal message exchanges. *Information Sciences*, *180*(15), 2895–2903. doi:10.1016/j.ins.2010.04.002

Chen, Y., & Chou, J. S. (2015). ECC-based untraceable authentication for large-scale active-tag RFID systems. *Electronic Commerce Research*, *15*(1), 97–120. doi:10.100710660-014-9165-0

Chien, H.-Y. (2007). SASI: A new ultralightweight RFID authentication protocol providing strong authentication and strong integrity. *IEEE Transactions on Dependable and Secure Computing*, *4*(4), 337–340. doi:10.1109/TDSC.2007.70226

David, M., & Prasad, N. R. (2009). Providing strong security and high privacy in low-cost RFID networks. In *International conference on Security and privacy in mobile information and communication systems* (pp. 172–179). Springer. 10.1007/978-3-642-04434-2_15

Finkenzeller, K. (2010). *RFID handbook: fundamentals and applications in contactless smart cards, radio frequency identification and near-field communication*. John Wiley & Sons. doi:10.1002/9780470665121

Gódor, G., Giczi, N., & Imre, S. (2010). Elliptic curve cryptography based mutual authentication protocol for low computational capacity RFID systems-performance analysis by simulations. In *2010 IEEE International Conference on Wireless Communications, Networking and Information Security* (pp. 650–657). IEEE. 10.1109/WCINS.2010.5541860

Gupta, A. T. B. B. (2017). Cryptanalysis of a novel ultra-lightweight mutual authentication protocol for IoT devices using RFID tags. *The Journal of Supercomputing*, *73*(3), 1085–1102. doi:10.100711227-016-1849-x

He, D., Kumar, N., Chilamkurti, N., & Lee, J. H. (2014). Lightweight ECC Based RFID Authentication Integrated with an ID Verifier Transfer Protocol. *Journal of Medical Systems*, *38*(10), 116. Advance online publication. doi:10.100710916-014-0116-z PMID:25096968

Juels, A., & Weis, S. A. (2007). Defining strong privacy for RFID. *Proceedings - Fifth Annual IEEE International Conference on Pervasive Computing and Communications Workshops, PerCom Workshops 2007, 13*(1), 342–347. 10.1109/PERCOMW.2007.37

Klimov, A., & Shamir, A. (2010). *New Applications of T-Functions in Block Ciphers and Hash Functions*. doi:10.1007/11502760_2

Lee, Y. K., Batina, L., & Verbauwhede, I. (2008). EC-RAC (ECDLP based randomized access control): Provably secure RFID authentication protocol. In 2008 IEEE international conference on RFID (pp. 97–104). IEEE.

Lehtonen, M., Ostojic, D., Ilic, A., & Michahelles, F. (2009). Securing RFID systems by detecting tag cloning. In *International Conference on Pervasive Computing* (pp. 291–308). Springer. 10.1007/978-3-642-01516-8_20

Liao, Y. P., & Hsiao, C. M. (2014a). A secure ECC-based RFID authentication scheme integrated with ID-verifier transfer protocol. *Ad Hoc Networks, 18*, 133–146. doi:10.1016/j.adhoc.2013.02.004

Liao, Y. P., & Hsiao, C. M. (2014b). A secure ECC-based RFID authentication scheme integrated with ID-verifier transfer protocol. *Ad Hoc Networks, 18*, 133–146. doi:10.1016/j.adhoc.2013.02.004

Luo, H., Wen, G., Su, J., & Huang, Z. (2018). SLAP : Succinct and Lightweight Authentication Protocol for low-cost RFID system. *Wireless Networks, 24*(1), 69–78. doi:10.100711276-016-1323-y

Mujahid, U., Najam-ul-Islam, M., & Shami, M. A. (2015). Rcia: A new ultralightweight rfid authentication protocol using recursive hash. *International Journal of Distributed Sensor Networks, 11*(1), 642180. doi:10.1155/2015/642180

Najam-ul-islam, U. M. M. (2017). A New Ultralightweight RFID Authentication Protocol for Passive Low Cost Tags : KMAP. *Wireless Personal Communications, 94*(3), 725–744. doi:10.100711277-016-3647-4

Peris-lopez, P., Hernandez-castro, J. C., Estevez-tapiador, J. M., & Ribagorda, A. (2006). *EMAP : An Efficient Mutual-Authentication Protocol for Low-Cost RFID Tags*. Academic Press.

Peris-Lopez, P., Hernandez-Castro, J. C., Estevez-Tapiador, J. M., & Ribagorda, A. (2006). M 2 AP: a minimalist mutual-authentication protocol for low-cost RFID tags. In *International conference on ubiquitous intelligence and computing* (pp. 912–923). Springer. 10.1007/11833529_93

Peris-lopez, P., Hernandez-castro, J. C., Tapiador, J. M. E., & Ribagorda, A. (2002). *LMAP : A Real Lightweight Mutual Authentication Protocol for Low-cost RFID tags*. Academic Press.

Peris-Lopez, P., Hernandez-Castro, J. C., Tapiador, J. M. E., & Ribagorda, A. (2008). Advances in ultralightweight cryptography for low-cost RFID tags: Gossamer protocol. In *International Workshop on Information Security Applications* (pp. 56–68). Springer.

Phan, R. C. W. (2009). Cryptanalysis of a new ultralightweight RFID authentication protocolSASI. *IEEE Transactions on Dependable and Secure Computing, 6*(4), 316–320. doi:10.1109/TDSC.2008.33

Ryu, E.-K., Kim, D.-S., & Yoo, K.-Y. (2015). On elliptic curve based untraceable RFID authentication protocols. In *Proceedings of the 3rd ACM Workshop on Information Hiding and Multimedia Security* (pp. 147–153). ACM. 10.1145/2756601.2756610

Safkhani, M., & Bagheri, N. (2016). Generalized Desynchronization Attack on UMAP: Application to RCIA, KMAP, SLAP and SASI + protocols. International Association for Cryptologic Research, 905–912.

Safkhani, M., & Bagheri, N. (2017). Passive secret disclosure attack on an ultralightweight authentication protocol for Internet of Things. *The Journal of Supercomputing*, *73*(8), 3579–3585. doi:10.100711227-017-1959-0

Safkhani, M., & Shariat, M. (2018). Implementation of secret disclosure attack against two IoT lightweight authentication protocols. *The Journal of Supercomputing*, *74*(11), 6220–6235. Advance online publication. doi:10.100711227-018-2538-8

Shen, H., Shen, J., Khan, M. K., & Lee, J. H. (2017). Efficient RFID Authentication Using Elliptic Curve Cryptography for the Internet of Things. *Wireless Personal Communications*, *96*(4), 5253–5266. doi:10.100711277-016-3739-1

Tian, Y., Chen, G., & Li, J. (2012). A new ultralightweight RFID authentication protocol with permutation. *IEEE Communications Letters*, *16*(5), 702–705. doi:10.1109/LCOMM.2012.031212.120237

Yeh, K.-H., Lo, N. W., & Winata, E. (2010). An efficient ultralightweight authentication protocol for RFID systems. *Proc. of RFIDSec Asia*, *10*, 49–60.

Zhao, Z. (2014). A secure RFID authentication protocol for healthcare environments using elliptic curve cryptosystem. *Journal of Medical Systems*, *38*(5), 46. doi:10.100710916-014-0046-9 PMID:24756871

Zhuang, X., Zhu, Y., & Chang, C.-C. (2014). A New Ultralightweight RFID Protocol for Low-Cost Tags: R $$^{ } $$ AP. *Wireless Personal Communications*, *79*(3), 1787–1802. doi:10.100711277-014-1958-x

Compilation of References

. Collobert, R., Weston, J., Bottou, L., Karlen, M., Kavukcuoglu, K., & Kuksa, P. (2011). Natural language processing (almost) from scratch. *Journal of Machine Learning Research, 12*, 2493-2537.

Abdullah, S., Khalid, M., Yusof, R., & Omar, K. (2006). License Plate Recognition Using Multi-Cluster And Multilayer Neural Networks. *Information And Communication Technologies*, *1*(April), 1818–1823. doi:10.1109/ICTTA.2006.1684663

Abouelnaga, Y., Eraqi, H. M., & Moustafa, M. N. (2018). *Real-time Distracted Driver Posture Classification.* arXiv:1706.09498.

Acar, A., Aksu, H., Uluagac, A. S., & Conti, M. (2018). A Survey on Homomorphic Encryption Schemes: Theory and Implementation. *ACM Computing Surveys*, *51*(4), 1–35. doi:10.1145/3214303

Achanta, R., Shaji, A., Smith, K., Lucchi, A., Fua, P., & Süsstrunk, S. (2012). SLIC superpixels compared to state-of-the-art superpixel methods. *IEEE Transactions on Pattern Analysis and Machine Intelligence*, *34*(11), 2274–2282. doi:10.1109/TPAMI.2012.120 PMID:22641706

Acharjya, D. P., & Chowdhary, C. L. (2018). Breast cancer detection using hybrid computational intelligence techniques. In *Handbook of Research on Emerging Perspectives on Healthcare Information Systems and Informatics* (pp. 251–280). IGI Global. doi:10.4018/978-1-5225-5460-8.ch011

Agarwal, S. (2018). A review of image scrambling technique using chaotic maps. *International Journal of Engineering and Technology Innovation*, *8*(2), 77.

Agath, A., Sidpara, C., & Upadhyay, D. (2018). *Critical Analysis of Cryptography and Steganography*. Academic Press.

Agnihotri, Verma, & Tripathi. (2017). *Variable Global Feature Selection Scheme for Automatic Classification of Text Documents*. Elsevier. . doi:10.1016/j.eswa.2017.03.057

Agrawal, A. K., Sharma, A., Sinha, S. R., & Khatri, P. (n.d.). Forensic of An Unrooted Mobile Device. *International Journal of Electronic Security and Digital Forensics.*

Agrawal, A. K., Khatri, P., & Sinha, S. R. (2018). Comparative Study of Mobile Forensic Tools. In *Advances in Data and Information Sciences* (pp. 39–47). Springer. doi:10.1007/978-981-10-8360-0_4

Ahat & Bankert. (1996). *A Comparative Evaluation of Sequential Feature Selection Algorithms*. Academic Press.

Ahmadian, Z., Salmasizadeh, M., & Aref, M. R. (2013a). Desynchronization attack on RAPP ultralightweight authentication protocol. *Information Processing Letters*, *113*(7), 205–209. doi:10.1016/j.ipl.2013.01.003

Ahmadian, Z., Salmasizadeh, M., & Aref, M. R. (2013b). Recursive linear and differential cryptanalysis of ultralightweight authentication protocols. *IEEE Transactions on Information Forensics and Security*, *8*(7), 1140–1151. doi:10.1109/TIFS.2013.2263499

Ahmad, J., & Hwang, S. O. (2016). A secure image encryption scheme based on chaotic maps and affine transformation. *Multimedia Tools and Applications*, *75*(21), 13951–13976. doi:10.100711042-015-2973-y

Ahmed, M., & Pathan, A. S. K. (2020). Deep learning for collective anomaly detection. *International Journal on Computer Science and Engineering*, *21*(1), 137–145.

Ai, T., Yang, Z., Hou, H., Zhan, C., Chen, C., Lv, W., Tao, Q., Sun, Z., & Xia, L. (2020). Correlation of chest CT and RT-PCR testing for coronavirus disease 2019 (COVID-19) in China: A report of 1014 cases. *Radiology*, *296*(2), E32–E40. doi:10.1148/radiol.2020200642 PMID:32101510

Aitslab/corona. (2021). Retrieved 23 March 2021, from https://github.com/Aitslab/corona

Akgul, A., & Pehlivan, I. (2016). A new three-dimensional chaotic system without equilibrium points, its dynamical analyses and electronic circuit application. *Technical Gazette*, *23*(1), 209–214.

Akhtar, A., Khanum, A., Khan, S. A., & Shaukat, A. (2013). Automated plant disease analysis (APDA): performance comparison of machine learning techniques. *2013 11th International Conference on Frontiers of Information Technology*, 60–65.

Al Ali, M., Svetinovic, D., Aung, Z., & Lukman, S. (2017, December). Malware detection in android mobile platform using machine learning algorithms. In *2017 International Conference on Infocom Technologies and Unmanned Systems (Trends and Future Directions) (ICTUS)* (pp. 763-768). IEEE. 10.1109/ICTUS.2017.8286109

Alaparthy & Morgera. (2018). A multi-level intrusion detection system for wireless sensor networks based on immune theory. *IEEE Access : Practical Innovations, Open Solutions*, *6*, 47364–47373.

Alhaj, Siraj, Zainal, Elshoush, & Elha. (2016). *Feature Selection Using Information Gain for Improved Structural-Based Alert Correlation*. Academic Press.

Ali, H. M., & Alwan, Z. S. (2017). *Car accident detection and notification system using smartphone*. LAP LAMBERT Academic Publishing.

Aliyu, F., Sheltami, T., & Shakshuki, E. M. (2018). A Detection and Prevention Technique for Man in the Middle Attack in Fog Computing. Procedia Computer Science. doi:10.1016/j.procs.2018.10.125

Aljawarneh, S., Aldwairi, M., & Yassein, M. B. (2018). Anomaly-based intrusion detection system through feature selection analysis and building hybrid efficient model. *Journal of Computational Science*, *25*, 152–160. doi:10.1016/j.jocs.2017.03.006

Aljumah, A., & Ahanger, T. A. (2018). Fog Computing and Security Issues: A Review. *2018 7th International Conference on Computers Communications and Control, ICCCC 2018 – Proceedings*, 237–39. 10.1109/ICCCC.2018.8390464

Alqudah, A. M., Alquraan, H., Qasmieh, I. A., Alqudah, A., & Al-Sharu, W. (2020). *Brain Tumor Classification Using Deep Learning Technique—A Comparison between Cropped, Uncropped, and Segmented Lesion Images with Different Sizes.* ArXiv Preprint ArXiv:2001.08844.

Alrashdi, I. (2019). FBAD: Fog-Based Attack Detection for IoT Healthcare in Smart Cities. *2019 IEEE 10th Annual Ubiquitous Computing, Electronics and Mobile Communication Conference, UEMCON 2019.* 10.1109/UEMCON47517.2019.8992963

Al-Shamma, O., Fadhel, M. A., Hameed, R. A., Alzubaidi, L., & Zhang, J. (2018). Boosting convolutional neural networks performance based on FPGA accelerator. *International Conference on Intelligent Systems Design and Applications*, 509–517.

Alvarez, G., & Li, S. (2006). Some basic cryptographic requirements for chaos-based cryptosystems. *International Journal of Bifurcation and Chaos in Applied Sciences and Engineering*, *16*(08), 2129–2151. doi:10.1142/S0218127406015970

Amara, J., Bouaziz, B., Algergawy, A., & others. (2017). A Deep Learning-based Approach for Banana Leaf Diseases Classification. *BTW (Workshops)*, 79–88.

Anagnostopoulos, C. E. (2014). License Plate Recognition : A breif tutorial. *IEEE Transactions on Intelligent Transportation Systems Magazine*, *6*(1), 59–67. doi:10.1109/MITS.2013.2292652

Anagnostopoulos, C. N. E., Anagnostopoulos, I. E., Loumos, V., & Kayafas, E. (2006). A License Plate-Recognition Algorithm for Intelligent Transportation System Applications. *IEEE Transactions on Intelligent Transportation Systems*, *7*(3), 377–392. doi:10.1109/TITS.2006.880641

Anju, & Budhiraja, S. (2011). A Review of License Plate Detection and Recognition Techniques. *National Workshop Cum Conference on Recent Trends in Mathematics and Computing*.

Arco, P. D., & Santis, A. De. (2011). *On Ultralightweight RFID Authentication Protocols*. Academic Press.

Arsenovic, M., Karanovic, M., Sladojevic, S., Anderla, A., & Stefanovic, D. (2019). Solving current limitations of deep learning based approaches for plant disease detection. *Symmetry*, *11*(7), 939. doi:10.3390ym11070939

Arslan, H., & Arslan, H. (2021). A new COVID-19 detection method from human genome sequences using CpG island features and KNN classifier. *Engineering Science and Technology, an International Journal*.

Arth, C., Limberger, F., & Bischof, H. (2007). Real-Time License Plate Recognition on an Embedded DSP-Platform. In *IEEE Conference Computer Vision Pather Recognition* (pp. 1–8). 10.1109/CVPR.2007.383412

Atila, Ü., Uçar, M., Akyol, K., & Uçar, E. (2021). Plant leaf disease classification using EfficientNet deep learning model. *Ecological Informatics*, *61*, 101182. doi:10.1016/j.ecoinf.2020.101182

Atlam, H., Walters, R., & Wills, G. (2018). Fog Computing and the Internet of Things: A Review. *Big Data and Cognitive Computing*, *2*(2), 10. doi:10.3390/bdcc2020010

Aumasson, J.-P., Henzen, L., Meier, W., & Naya-Plasencia, M. (2013). Quark: A lightweight hash. *Journal of Cryptology*, *26*(2), 313–339. doi:10.100700145-012-9125-6

Babaee, M., Dinh, D. T., & Rigoll, G. (2017). *A deep convolutional neural network for background subtraction*. arXiv preprint arXiv:170201731.

Bacci, A., Bartoli, A., Martinelli, F., Medvet, E., Mercaldo, F., & Visaggio, C. A. (2018). Impact of Code Obfuscation on Android Malware Detection based on Static and Dynamic Analysis. In ICISSP (pp. 379-385). doi:10.5220/0006642503790385

Bache, K., & Lichman, M. (2013). *UCI Machine Learning Repository*. http://archive.ics.uci.edu/ml

Baeza-Yates, R., & Ribeiro-Neto, B. (1999). *Modern Information Retrieval*. ACM Press.

Bagheri, N., Safkhani, M., Peris-Lopez, P., & Tapiador, J. E. (2012). Cryptanalysis of RAPP, an RFID Authentication Protocol. *IACR Cryptology EPrint Archive*, *2012*, 702.

Baheti, B., Gajre, S., & Talbar, S. (2018). Detection of Distracted Driver Using Convolutional Neural Network. In *Proceedings of the IEEE/CVF Conference on Computer Vision and Pattern Recognition Workshops*. IEEE. 10.1109/CVPRW.2018.00150

Bakhshandeh, A., & Eslami, Z. (2013). An authenticated image encryption scheme based on chaotic maps and memory cellular automata. *Optics and Lasers in Engineering*, *51*(6), 665–673. doi:10.1016/j.optlaseng.2013.01.001

Baldovin, F., & Robledo, A. (2002). Sensitivity to initial conditions at bifurcations in one-dimensional nonlinear maps: Rigorous nonextensive solutions. *EPL, 60*(4), 518–524. doi:10.1209/epl/i2002-00249-7

Banks, J., Carson, J. S. II, Nelson, B. L., & Nicol, D. M. (2010). *Discrete-Event System Simulation* (5th ed.). Pearson Education.

Barbara, D., Wu, N., & Jajodia, S. (2001). Detecting novel network intrusions using bayes estimators. In *Proceedings of the 2001 SIAM International Conference on Data Mining*, (pp. 1-17). Society for Industrial and Applied Mathematics. doi:10.1137/1.9781611972719.28

Barbedo, J. G. A. (2018). Factors influencing the use of deep learning for plant disease recognition. *Biosystems Engineering, 172*, 84–91.

Barbedo, J. G. A. (2016). A review on the main challenges in automatic plant disease identification based on visible range images. *Biosystems Engineering, 144*, 52–60. doi:10.1016/j.biosystemseng.2016.01.017

Barbedo, J. G. A. (2019). Plant disease identification from individual lesions and spots using deep learning. *Biosystems Engineering, 180*, 96–107. doi:10.1016/j.biosystemseng.2019.02.002

Barnich, O., & Van Droogenbroeck, M. (2009). ViBe: a powerful random technique to estimate the background in video sequences. In *Acoustics, Speech and Signal Processing, 2009. ICASSP 2009. IEEE International Conference on, 2009.* IEEE. 10.1109/ICASSP.2009.4959741

Barrero, D. F., Hernández-Castro, J. C., Peris-Lopez, P., Camacho, D., & R-Moreno, M. D. (2014). A genetic tango attack against the David–Prasad RFID ultra-lightweight authentication protocol. *Expert Systems: International Journal of Knowledge Engineering and Neural Networks, 31*(1), 9–19. doi:10.1111/j.1468-0394.2012.00652.x

Basodi, S., Ji, C., Zhang, H., & Pan, Y. (2020). Gradient amplification: An efficient way to train deep neural networks. *Big Data Mining and Analytics, 3*(3), 196–207. doi:10.26599/BDMA.2020.9020004

Basu, M., & Ho, T. K. (Eds.). (2006a). *Data complexity in pattern recognition*. Springer Science & Business Media. doi:10.1007/978-1-84628-172-3

Behnia, S., Akhshani, A., Mahmodi, H., & Akhavan, A. (2008). A novel algorithm for image encryption based on mixture of chaotic maps. *Chaos, Solitons, and Fractals, 35*(2), 408–419. doi:10.1016/j.chaos.2006.05.011

Bejar, H. H., Mansilla, L. A., & Miranda, P. A. (2018, November). Efficient unsupervised image segmentation by optimum cuts in graphs. In *Iberoamerican Congress on Pattern Recognition* (pp. 359–367). Springer.

Beluz, J., (2020). *How does the new coronavirus spread?* vox.com/2020/2/ 20/21143785/coronavirus-covid-19-spreadtransmission-how.

Bengio, Y., & LeCun, Y. (2007). Scaling learning algorithms towards AI. *Large-Scale Kernel Machines, 34*(5), 1-41.

Bengio, Y., LeCun, Y., & Henderson, D. (1994). Globally trained handwritten word recognizer using spatial representation, convolutional neural networks, and hidden Markov models. In Advances in neural information processing systems (pp. 937-944). Academic Press.

Bengio, Y. (2012). Deep learning of representations for unsupervised and transfer learning. *Proceedings of ICML Workshop on Unsupervised and Transfer Learning*, 17–36.

Bengio, Y. (2012). Practical rec-ommendations for gradient-based training of deep architectures. In *Neural Networks: Tricks of the Trade* (pp. 437–478). Springer. doi:10.1007/978-3-642-35289-8_26

Beygelzimer, A., Dasgupta, S., & Langford, J. (2008). *Importance weighted active learning*. arXiv preprint arXiv:0812.4952.

Bhatti, F., Shah, M. A., Maple, C., & Islam, S. U. (2019). A novel internet of things-enabled accident detection and reporting system for smart city environments. *Sensors (Basel), 19*(9), 2071.

Bilaiya, R., & Ahlawat, P. (2019). Hybrid Evolutionary Approach for IDS by Using Genetic and Poisson Distribution. In *International Conference on Inventive Computation Technologies*, (pp. 766-773). Springer.

Bilal, S. F., Bashir, S., Khan, F. H., & Rasheed, H. (2018, October). Malwares Detection for Android and Windows System by Using Machine Learning and Data Mining. In *International Conference on Intelligent Technologies and Applications* (pp. 485-495). Springer.

Bilal, Z., Masood, A., & Kausar, F. (2009). Security analysis of ultra-lightweight cryptographic protocol for low-cost RFID tags: Gossamer protocol. In *2009 International Conference on Network-Based Information Systems* (pp. 260–267). IEEE. 10.1109/NBiS.2009.9

Bisht, A., Dua, M., & Dua, S. (2019). A novel approach to encrypt multiple images using multiple chaotic maps and chaotic discrete fractional random transform. *Journal of Ambient Intelligence and Humanized Computing, 10*(9), 3519–3531. doi:10.100712652-018-1072-0

Bisht, A., Jaroli, P., Dua, M., & Dua, S. (2018). Symmetric Multiple Image Encryption Using Multiple New One-Dimensional Chaotic Functions and Two-Dimensional Cat Man. *Proceedings of the International Conference on Inventive Research in Computing Applications, ICIRCA 2018*, 676–682. 10.1109/ICIRCA.2018.8597245

Blei, D. M., Ng, A. Y., & Jordan, M. I. (2003). Latent dirichlet allocation. *Journal of Machine Learning Research, 3*(Jan), 993–1022.

Bloisi, D., & Iocchi, L. (2012). Independent multimodal background subtraction. CompIMAGE, 39-44.

Bogdanov, A., Knežević, M., Leander, G., Toz, D., Varıcı, K., & Verbauwhede, I. (2011). SPONGENT: A lightweight hash function. In *International Workshop on Cryptographic Hardware and Embedded Systems* (pp. 312–325). Springer.

Bohn, R. B. (2011). NIST Cloud Computing Reference Architecture. *Proceedings - 2011 IEEE World Congress on Services, SERVICES 2011.* 10.1109/SERVICES.2011.105

Bonomi, F. (2011). Connected Vehicles, the Internet of Things, and Fog Computing. *The Eighth ACM International Workshop on Vehicular Inter-Networking (VANET).*

Bonomi, F., Milito, R., Zhu, J., & Addepalli, S. (2012). Fog Computing and Its Role in the Internet of Things. *Proceedings of the first edition of the MCC workshop on Mobile cloud computing,* (1), 13–16.

Braga & Weisburd. (2015). *Police innovation and crime pre- vention: Lessons learned from police research over the past 20 years.* Academic Press.

Brahimi, M., Boukhalfa, K., & Moussaoui, A. (2017). Deep learning for tomato diseases: Classification and symptoms visualization. *Applied Artificial Intelligence, 31*(4), 299–315. doi:10.1080/08839514.2017.1315516

Brakerski, Z. (2012). Fully Homomorphic Encryption without Modulus Switching from Classical GapSVP. Lecture Notes in Computer Science (Including Subseries Lecture Notes in Artificial Intelligence and Lecture Notes in Bioinformatics). doi:10.1007/978-3-642-32009-5_50

Brauer, F., Rieger, R., Mocan, A., & Barczynski, W. M. (2011, October). Enabling Information Extraction by Inference of Regular Expressions from Sample Entities. *Proceedings of the 20th ACM Conference on Information and Knowledge Management, CIKM 2011.* 10.1145/2063576.2063763

Bringer, J., Chabanne, H., & Icart, T. (2008). Cryptanalysis of EC-RAC, a RFID identification protocol. In *International Conference on Cryptology and Network Security* (pp. 149–161). Springer. 10.1007/978-3-540-89641-8_11

Bulut, F. (2016, April). Performance evaluations of supervised learners on imbalanced datasets. In 2016 Electric Electronics, Computer Science, Biomedical Engineerings' Meeting (EBBT) (pp. 1-4). IEEE. doi:10.1109/EBBT.2016.7483677

Bulut, F., & Amasyali, M. F. (2016). Katı kümeleme ve yeni bir geçiş fonksiyonuyla uzman karışımlarında sınıflandırma. *Gazi Üniversitesi Mühendislik Mimarlık Fakültesi Dergisi, 31*(4).

Busch, C., Domer, R., Freytag, C., & Ziegler, H. (1998). Feature based recognition of traffic video streams for online route tracing. In *IEEE Vehicular Technology Conference* (pp. 1790–1794). 10.1109/VETEC.1998.686064

Califf, M. E., & Mooney, R. J. (1999, July). Relational Learning of Pattern-Match Rules for Information Extraction. *Proceedings of the 16th National Conference on Artificial Intelligence (AAAI-99)*, 328-334.

Calvillo, Padilla, Muñoz, Ponce, & Fernandez. (2013). Searching Research Papers Using Clustering and Text Mining. IEEE.

Cao, X., Kou, W., & Du, X. (2010). A pairing-free identity-based authenticated key agreement protocol with minimal message exchanges. *Information Sciences*, *180*(15), 2895–2903. doi:10.1016/j.ins.2010.04.002

Cao, Y., Miao, Q., Liu, J., & Gao, L. (2013). Advance and Prospects of AdaBoost Algorithm. *Acta Automatica Sinica*, *39*(6), 745–758. doi:10.1016/S1874-1029(13)60052-X

Çavuşoğlu, Ü., Kaçar, S., Pehlivan, I., & Zengin, A. (2017). Secure image encryption algorithm design using a novel chaos based S-Box. *Chaos, Solitons, and Fractals*, *95*, 92–101. doi:10.1016/j.chaos.2016.12.018

Celik, Y., Talo, M., Yildirim, O., Karabatak, M., & Acharya, U. R. (2020). Automated invasive ductal carcinoma detection based using deep transfer learning with whole-slide images. *Pattern Recognition Letters*, *133*, 232–239. doi:10.1016/j.patrec.2020.03.011

Chai, Y., Ren, J., Zhao, H., Li, Y., Ren, J., & Murray, P. (2016). Hierarchical and multi-featured fusion for effective gait recognition under variable scenarios. *Pattern Analysis & Applications*, *19*(4), 905–917. doi:10.100710044-015-0471-5

Chang, C.-H., Kayed, M., Girgis, M., & Shaalan, K. (2006). A Survey of Web Information Extraction Systems. *IEEE Transactions on Knowledge and Data Engineering*, *18*(10), 1411–1428. doi:10.1109/TKDE.2006.152

Chang, S., Chen, L., Chung, Y., Chen, S., & Member, S. (2004). *Automatic License Plate Recognition*. Academic Press.

Chawla, S., & Bedi, P. (2007). Personalized Web Search using Information Scent. In *International Joint Conferences on Computer, Information and Systems Sciences, and Engineering*. Springer.

Chawla, S. (2018). Ontology-Based Semantic Learning of Genetic-Algorithm Optimised Back Propagation Artificial Neural Network for personalized web search. *International Journal of Applied Research on Information Technology and Computing*, *9*(1), 21–38. doi:10.5958/0975-8089.2018.00003.9

Chawla, S. (in press). Application of Convolution Neural Network in web query session mining for Personalized Web Search. *International Journal on Computer Science and Engineering*.

Chen, L. C., Papandreou, G., Kokkinos, I., Murphy, K., & Yuille, A. L. (2014). *Semantic image segmentation with deep convolutional nets and fully connected crfs.* arXiv preprint arXiv:1412.7062.

Chen, G., Mao, Y., & Chui, C. K. (2004). A symmetric image encryption scheme based on 3D chaotic cat maps. *Chaos, Solitons, and Fractals*, *21*(3), 749–761. doi:10.1016/j.chaos.2003.12.022

Chen, J., Chen, J., Zhang, D., Sun, Y., & Nanehkaran, Y. A. (2020). Using deep transfer learning for image-based plant disease identification. *Computers and Electronics in Agriculture*, *173*, 105393. doi:10.1016/j.compag.2020.105393

Chen, S., Webb, G. I., Liu, L., & Ma, X. (2020). A novel selective naïve Bayes algorithm. *Knowledge-Based Systems*, *192*, 105361. doi:10.1016/j.knosys.2019.105361

Chen, X., & Pan, L. (2018). A survey of graph cuts/graph search based medical image segmentation. *IEEE Reviews in Biomedical Engineering*, *11*, 112–124. doi:10.1109/RBME.2018.2798701 PMID:29994356

Chen, Y., & Chou, J. S. (2015). ECC-based untraceable authentication for large-scale active-tag RFID systems. *Electronic Commerce Research*, *15*(1), 97–120. doi:10.100710660-014-9165-0

Chen, Y., Jiang, H., Li, C., Jia, X., & Ghamisi, P. (2016). Deep feature extraction and classification of hyperspectral images based on convolutional neural networks. *IEEE Transactions on Geoscience and Remote Sensing*, *54*(10), 6232–6251. doi:10.1109/TGRS.2016.2584107

Chen, Z., Liu, C., & Chang, F. (2009). *Automatic License-Plate Location and Recognition Based on Feature Salience*. Academic Press.

Cheon, J. H., Kim, A., Kim, M., & Song, Y. (2017). Homomorphic Encryption for Arithmetic of Approximate Numbers. Lecture Notes in Computer Science (Including Subseries Lecture Notes in Artificial Intelligence and Lecture Notes in Bioinformatics). doi:10.1007/978-3-319-70694-8_15

Chiang, M., & Zhang, T. (2016). Fog and IoT: An Overview of Research Opportunities. *IEEE Internet of Things Journal*, *3*(6), 854–864. doi:10.1109/JIOT.2016.2584538

Chicco, D., & Jurman, G. (2020). The advantages of the Matthews correlation coefficient (MCC) over F1 score and accuracy in binary classification evaluation. *BMC Genomics*, *21*(1), 1–13. doi:10.118612864-019-6413-7 PMID:31898477

Chien, H.-Y. (2007). SASI: A new ultralightweight RFID authentication protocol providing strong authentication and strong integrity. *IEEE Transactions on Dependable and Secure Computing*, *4*(4), 337–340. doi:10.1109/TDSC.2007.70226

Chiu, J., & Nichols, E. (2016). Named Entity Recognition with Bidirectional LSTM-CNNs. *Transactions of the Association for Computational Linguistics*, *4*, 357–370. doi:10.1162/tacl_a_00104

Chlouverakis, K. E., & Sprott, J. C. (2005). A comparison of correlation and Lyapunov dimensions. *Physica D. Nonlinear Phenomena*, *200*(1–2), 156–164. doi:10.1016/j.physd.2004.10.006

Choubey, S., & Sinha, G. R. (2011). Pixel Distribution Density based character recognition For Vehicle License Plate. In *IEEE 3rd International Conference on Electronics Computer Technology* (Vol. 5, pp. 26–30). 10.1109/ICECTECH.2011.5941950

Chowdhary, C. L., & Acharjya, D. P. (2018). Singular Value Decomposition–Principal Component Analysis-Based Object Recognition Approach. *Bio-Inspired Computing for Image and Video Processing, 323.*

Chowdhary, C. L., Darwish, A., & Hassanien, A. E. (2021). Cognitive Deep Learning: Future Direction in Intelligent Retrieval. In Research Anthology on Artificial Intelligence Applications in Security (pp. 2152-2163). IGI Global.

Chowdhary, C. L., Ranjan, A., & Jat, D. S. (2016). Categorical Database Information-Theoretic Approach of Outlier Detection Model. Annals. *Computer Science Series, 14*(2).

Chowdhary, C. L. (2011). Linear feature extraction techniques for object recognition: Study of PCA and ICA. *Journal of the Serbian Society for Computational Mechanics*, *5*(1), 19–26.

Chowdhary, C. L. (2016). A review of feature extraction application areas in medical imaging. *International Journal of Pharmacy and Technology*, *8*(3), 4501–4509.

Chowdhary, C. L. (2018). Application of Object Recognition With Shape-Index Identification and 2D Scale Invariant Feature Transform for Key-Point Detection. In *Feature Dimension Reduction for Content-Based Image Identification* (pp. 218–231). IGI Global. doi:10.4018/978-1-5225-5775-3.ch012

Chowdhary, C. L. (2019). 3D object recognition system based on local shape descriptors and depth data analysis. *Recent Patents on Computer Science*, *12*(1), 18–24. doi:10.2174/2213275911666180821092033

Chowdhary, C. L., Das, T. K., Gurani, V., & Ranjan, A. (2018). An Improved Tumour Identification with Gabor Wavelet Segmentation. *Research Journal of Pharmacy and Technology*, *11*(8), 3451–3456. doi:10.5958/0974-360X.2018.00637.6

Chowdhary, C. L., Goyal, A., & Vasnani, B. K. (2019). Experimental Assessment of Beam Search Algorithm for Improvement in Image Caption Generation. *Journal of Applied Science and Engineering*, *22*(4), 691–698.

Chowdhary, C. L., & Mouli, P. C. (2012, March). Design and implementation of secure, platform-free, and network-based remote controlling and monitoring system. In *International Conference on Pattern Recognition, Informatics and Medical Engineering (PRIME-2012)* (pp. 195-198). IEEE. 10.1109/ICPRIME.2012.6208342

Chowdhary, C. L., & Mouli, P. C. (2013). Image Registration with New System for Ensemble of Images of Multi-Sensor Registration. *World Applied Sciences Journal*, *26*(1), 45–50.

Chowdhary, C. L., Muatjitjeja, K., & Jat, D. S. (2015, May). Three-dimensional object recognition based intelligence system for identification. In *2015 International Conference on Emerging Trends in Networks and Computer Communications (ETNCC)* (pp. 162-166). IEEE. 10.1109/ETNCC.2015.7184827

Chowdhary, C. L., Sai, G. V. K., & Acharjya, D. P. (2016). Decreasing false assumption for improved breast cancer detection. *Journal of Science and Arts*, *35*(2), 157–176.

Chowdhary, C. L., & Shynu, P. G. (2011). Applications of Extendable Embedded Web Servers in Medical Diagnosing. *International Journal of Computers and Applications*, *38*(6), 34–38. doi:10.5120/4615-6838

Chowdhary, C. L., Shynu, P. G., & Gurani, V. K. (2020). Exploring breast cancer classification of histopathology images from computer vision and image processing algorithms to deep learning. *Int. J. Adv. Sci. Technol*, *29*, 43–48.

Chunjing, Y., Yueyao, Z., Yaxuan, Z., & Liu, H. (2017). Application of convolutional neural network in classification of high resolution agricultural remote sensing images. *The International Archives of the Photogrammetry, Remote Sensing and Spatial Information Sciences*, 42.

Cisco White Paper: Fog Computing and the Internet of Things: Extend the Cloud to Where the Things Are What You Will Learn. (2015). https://www.cisco.com/c/dam/en_us/solutions/trends/iot/docs/computing-overview.pdf

Cleveland, W. S., Grosse, E., & Shyu, W. M. (2017). Local regression models. In *Statistical models in S* (pp. 309–376). Routledge.

Coates, A., Ng, A., & Lee, H. (2011). An analysis of single-layer networks in unsupervised feature learning. *Proceedings of the fourteenth international conference on artificial intelligence and statistics*, 215-223.

Colin, B. (2020). *Image Recognition with TransferLearning (98.5%).* https://thedatafrog.com/en/articles/image-recognition-transfer-learning/

Cong, L., Ding, S., Wang, L., Zhang, A., & Jia, W. (2018). Image segmentation algorithm based on superpixel clustering. *IET Image Processing*, *12*(11), 2030–2035. doi:10.1049/iet-ipr.2018.5439

Conneau, A., Schwenk, H., Barrault, L., & Lecun, Y. (2016). *Very deep convolutional networks for text classification.* arXiv preprint arXiv:1606.01781.

Coronavirus, I. (2021). *11,727,733 Cases and 160,437 Deaths - Worldometer*. Retrieved 23 March 2021, from https://www.worldometers.info/coronavirus/country/india/

Cortes, C., & Vapnik, V. (1995). Support-Vector Networks. *Machine Learning*, *20*(3), 273–297. doi:10.1007/BF00994018

COVID-19 Corona Tracker. (2021). Retrieved 23 March 2021, from https://www.coronatracker.com/

Cui, Y., Yang, G., Veit, A., Huang, X., & Belongie, S. (2018). Learning to evaluate image captioning. *Proceedings of the IEEE Conference on Computer Vision and Pattern Recognition*, 5804-5812.

Cyren IP Reputation Check. (n.d.). https://www.cyren.com/security-center/cyren-ip-reputation-check

Das, S. (2020). *Prediction of COVID-19 disease progression in India: Under the effect of national lockdown.* arXiv preprint arXiv:2004.03147.

Das, A. K., Ghosh, S., Thunder, S., Dutta, R., Agarwal, S., & Chakrabarti, A. (2021). Automatic COVID-19 detection from X-ray images using ensemble learning with convolutional neural network. *Pattern Analysis & Applications*, 1–14.

Das, T. K., & Chowdhary, C. L. (2017). Implementation of Morphological Image Processing Algorithm using Mammograms. *Journal of Chemical and Pharmaceutical Sciences*, *10*(1), 439–441.

David, M., & Prasad, N. R. (2009). Providing strong security and high privacy in low-cost RFID networks. In *International conference on Security and privacy in mobile information and communication systems* (pp. 172–179). Springer. 10.1007/978-3-642-04434-2_15

Davis, J. W., & Keck, M. A. (2005). A two-stage template approach to person detection in thermal imagery. IEEE. doi:10.1109/ACVMOT.2005.14

Deb, K., Chae, H.-U., & Jo, K.-H. (2009). Vehicle license plate detection method based on sliding concentric windows and histogram. *Journal of Computers*, *4*(8), 771–777. doi:10.4304/jcp.4.8.771-777

Deb, K., Vavilin, A., Kim, J.-W., Kim, T., & Jo, K.-H. (2010). Projection and least square fitting with perpendicular offsets based vehicle license plate tilt correction. *Proceedings of the SICE Annual Conference*, 3291–3298.

Deerwester, S., Dumais, S. T., Furnas, G. W., Landauer, T. K., & Harshman, R. (1990). Indexing by latent semantic analysis. *Journal of the American Society for Information Science*, *41*(6), 391–407. doi:10.1002/(SICI)1097-4571(199009)41:6<391::AID-ASI1>3.0.CO;2-9

Deng, J., Dong, W., Socher, R., Li, L.-J., Li, K., & Fei-Fei, L. (2009). ImageNet: A large-scale hierarchical image database. In *Proceedings of the IEEE Conference on Computer Vision and Pattern Recognition*. IEEE.

Deng, L., Abdel-Hamid, O., & Yu, D. (2013, May). *A deep convolutional neural network using heterogeneous pooling for trading acoustic invariance with phonetic confusion. In 2013 IEEE international conference on acoustics, speech and signal processing*. IEEE.

Dey, N., & Ashour, A. (Eds.). (2016). *Classification and clustering in biomedical signal processing*. IGI Global.

Dhaliwal, J., Puglisi, S. J., & Turpin, A. (2012, April). Practical Efficient String Mining. *IEEE Transactions on Knowledge and Data Engineering*, *24*(4), 735–744. doi:10.1109/TKDE.2010.242

Dietterich, T. G. (2002). Ensemble learning. The handbook of brain theory and neural networks, 2, 110-125.

Dinges, D. F., & Grace, R. (1998). *PERCLOS: A Valid Psychophysiological Measure of Alertness As Assessed by Psychomotor Vigilance*. Federal Highway Administration, Office of Motor Carriers.

Diro, A. A., Chilamkurti, N., & Kumar, N. (2017). Lightweight Cybersecurity Schemes Using Elliptic Curve Cryptography in Publish-Subscribe Fog Computing. *Mobile Networks and Applications*, *22*(5), 848–858. doi:10.100711036-017-0851-8

Diro, A., & Chilamkurti, N. (2018). Leveraging LSTM Networks for Attack Detection in Fog-to-Things Communications. *IEEE Communications Magazine*, *56*(9), 124–130. doi:10.1109/MCOM.2018.1701270

Dlagnekov, L., & Belongie, S. (2005). *Recognizing Cars.* Dept. Computer Science Engineering, University. California, San Diego, Tech. Rep. CS2005-0833.

Dlagnekov, L. (2004). *License Plate Detection Using AdaBoost.* Computer Science and Engineering Dept.

Docker. (2021). https://www.docker.com/

Dogru, N., & Subasi, A. (2018). Traffic accident detection using random forest classifier. *Proceedings of the 2018 15th Learning and Technology Conference (LT)*, 40-45.

Donahue, J., Anne Hendricks, L., Guadarrama, S., Rohrbach, M., Venugopalan, S., Saenko, K., & Darrell, T. (2017). Long-term recurrent convolutional networks for visual recognition and description. *IEEE Transactions on Pattern Analysis and Machine Intelligence*, *39*(4), 677–691. doi:10.1109/TPAMI.2016.2599174 PMID:27608449

Dorj, U. O., Lee, K. K., Choi, J. Y., & Lee, M. (2018). The skin cancer classification using deep convolutional neural network. *Multimedia Tools and Applications*, *77*(8), 9909–9924. doi:10.100711042-018-5714-1

Dua, M., Suthar, A., Garg, A., & Garg, V. (2020). An ILM-cosine transform-based improved approach to image encryption. *Complex & Intelligent Systems*, 1–17. doi:10.100740747-020-00201-z

Dua, M., Wesanekar, A., Gupta, V., Bhola, M., & Dua, S. (2019). Color image encryption using synchronous CML-DNA and weighted bi-objective genetic algorithm. *ACM International Conference Proceeding Series*, 121–125. 10.1145/3361758.3361780

Dua, M., Wesanekar, A., Gupta, V., Bhola, M., & Dua, S. (2019a). Differential evolution optimization of intertwining logistic map-DNA based image encryption technique. *Journal of Ambient Intelligence and Humanized Computing*, 1–16.

Duan, T. D., Duc, D. A., & Tran, L. H. D. (2004). Combining Hough Transform and Contour Algorithm for Detecting Vehicles' License-Plates. In *International Symposium on Intelligent Multimedia Video Speech Processing* (pp. 747–750). Academic Press.

Duan, T. D., Du, T. L. H., Phuoc, T. V., & Hoang, N. V. (2005). Building an Automatic Vehicle License-Plate Recognition System. *International Conference in Computer Science - RIVF'05,* 59–63.

Du, S., Ibrahim, M., Shehata, M., & Badaway, W. (2012). Automatic License Plate Recognition (ALPR): A State-of-the-Art Review. *IEEE Transactions on Circuits and Systems for Video Technology*, *23*(2), 311–325. doi:10.1109/TCSVT.2012.2203741

Eftimov, T., Koroušić Seljak, B., & Korošec, P. (2017). A rule-based named-entity recognition method for knowledge extraction of evidence-based dietary recommendations. *PLoS One*, *12*(6), e0179488. doi:10.1371/journal.pone.0179488

Enayatifar, R., Abdullah, A. H., Isnin, I. F., Altameem, A., & Lee, M. (2017). Image encryption using a synchronous permutation-diffusion technique. *Optics and Lasers in Engineering*, *90*, 146–154. doi:10.1016/j.optlaseng.2016.10.006

Enireddy, V., Kumar, M. J. K., Donepudi, B., & Karthikeyan, C. (2020, December). Detection of COVID-19 using Hybrid ResNet and SVM. *IOP Conference Series. Materials Science and Engineering*, *993*(1), 012046. doi:10.1088/1757-899X/993/1/012046

Erhan, D., Courville, A., Bengio, Y., & Vincent, P. (2010). Why does unsupervised pre-training help deep learning? *Proceedings of the Thirteenth International Conference on Artificial Intelligence and Statistics*, 201–208.

Ester, M., Kriegel, H. P., Sander, J., & Xu, X. (1996, August). Density-based spatial clustering of applications with noise. In Int. Conf. *Data Mining and Knowledge Discovery, 240*, 6.

F., A., & H., N. (2004). Automatic Licence Plate Recognition System. In *AFRICON Conference Africa* (p. Vol. 1, pp 45–50). Academic Press.

Faiz, A. B., Imteaj, A., & Chowdhury, M. (2015). Smart vehicle accident detection and alarming system using a smartphone. In *2015 International Conference on Computer and Information Engineering (ICCIE)*, (pp. 66-69). IEEE.

Fang, Y., Zhang, H., Xie, J., Lin, M., Ying, L., Pang, P., & Ji, W. (2020). Sensitivity of chest CT for COVID-19: Comparison to RT-PCR. *Radiology*, *296*(2), E115–E117. doi:10.1148/radiol.2020200432 PMID:32073353

Fan, J., & Vercauteren, F. (2012). Somewhat Practical Fully Homomorphic Encryption. *Proceedings of the 15th international conference on Practice and Theory in Public Key Cryptography.*

Farabet, C., Couprie, C., Najman, L., & LeCun, Y. (2012). Learning hierarchical features for scene labeling. *IEEE Transactions on Pattern Analysis and Machine Intelligence*, *35*(8), 1915–1929. doi:10.1109/TPAMI.2012.231 PMID:23787344

Felzenszwalb, P. F., & Huttenlocher, D. P. (2004). Efficient graph-based image segmentation. *International Journal of Computer Vision*, *59*(2), 167–181. doi:10.1023/B:VISI.0000022288.19776.77

Feng, G., Li, S., Sun, T., & Zhang, B. (2018). A probabilistic model derived term weighting scheme for text classification. *Pattern Recognition Letters*, *110*, 23–29. Advance online publication. doi:10.1016/j.patrec.2018.03.003

Ferentinos, K. P. (2018). Deep learning models for plant disease detection and diagnosis. *Computers and Electronics in Agriculture*, *145*, 311–318. doi:10.1016/j.compag.2018.01.009

Finkenzeller, K. (2010). *RFID handbook: fundamentals and applications in contactless smart cards, radio frequency identification and near-field communication.* John Wiley & Sons. doi:10.1002/9780470665121

Fogue, M., Garrido, P., Martinez, F. J., Cano, J.-C., Calafate, C. T., & Manzoni, P. (2013). A system for automatic notification and severity estimation of automotive accidents. *IEEE Transactions on Mobile Computing*, *13*(5), 948–963.

Fournier-Prunaret, D., & Lopez-Ruiz, R. (2003). *Basin bifurcations in a two-dimensional logistic map.* ArXiv Preprint Nlin/0304059.

Frank, E., Hall, M., & Pfahringer, B. (2012). *Locally weighted naive bayes.* arXiv preprint arXiv:1212.2487.

Freitag, D., & Kushmerick, N. (2000, July). Boosted Wrapper Induction. *Proceedings of the 17th National Conference on Artificial Intelligence (AAAI-2000)*, 577-583.

Fridell, L. A., & Wycoff, M. A. (Eds.). (2004). *Community policing: The past, present, and future.* Annie E. Casey Foundation and Police Executive Research Forum.

Fridrich, J. (1997). Image encryption based on chaotic maps. *1997 IEEE International Conference on Systems, Man, and Cybernetics. Computational Cybernetics and Simulation, 2*, 1105–1110. 10.1109/ICSMC.1997.638097

Galasso, F., Cipolla, R., & Schiele, B. (2012, November). Video segmentation with superpixels. In *Asian conference on computer vision* (pp. 760-774). Springer.

Gao, J., He, X., & Nie, J.-Y. (2010). Clickthrough-based translation models for web search: from word models to phrase models. CIKM, 1139-1148. doi:10.1145/1871437.1871582

Gao, J., Toutanova, K., & Yih, W.-T. (2011). Clickthrough-based latent semantic models for web search. SIGIR, 675-684. doi:10.1145/2009916.2010007

Gao, H., Zhang, Y., Liang, S., & Li, D. (2006). A new chaotic algorithm for image encryption. *Chaos, Solitons, and Fractals*, *29*(2), 393–399. doi:10.1016/j.chaos.2005.08.110

Gao, J., Pantel, P., Gamon, M., He, X., & Deng, L. (2014). Modeling interestingness with deep neural networks. In *Proceedings of the 2014 Conference on Empirical Methods in Natural Language Processing (EMNLP)* (pp. 2-13). 10.3115/v1/D14-1002

Gao, T., & Chen, Z. (2008). A new image encryption algorithm based on hyper-chaos. *Physics Letters. [Part A]*, *372*(4), 394–400. doi:10.1016/j.physleta.2007.07.040

Gao, Y., Liu, Y., Zhang, H., Li, Z., Zhu, Y., Lin, H., & Yang, M. (2020). Estimating gpu memory consumption of deep learning models. *Proceedings of the 28th ACM Joint Meeting on European Software Engineering Conference and Symposium on the Foundations of Software Engineering*, 1342–1352. 10.1145/3368089.3417050

Gebbers, R., & Adamchuk, V. I. (2010). Precision agriculture and food security. *Science*, *327*(5967), 828–831. doi:10.1126cience.1183899 PMID:20150492

Geneiatakis, D., Baldini, G., Fovino, I. N., & Vakalis, I. (2018, February). Towards a mobile malware detection framework with the support of machine learning. In *International ISCIS Security Workshop* (pp. 119-129). Springer. 10.1007/978-3-319-95189-8_11

Gill, M. (2006). *CCTV: Is it effective?* Academic Press.

Gill, S., & Hooda, M. (2021). The Design Perspective of the Structures Based on kd Tree. In *Rising Threats in Expert Applications and Solutions* (pp. 515–524). Springer. doi:10.1007/978-981-15-6014-9_61

Godbehere, A. B., Matsukawa, A., & Goldberg, K. (2012). Visual tracking of human visitors under variable-lighting conditions for a responsive audio art installation. *American Control Conference (ACC)*, 4305-4312. 10.1109/ACC.2012.6315174

Gódor, G., Giczi, N., & Imre, S. (2010). Elliptic curve cryptography based mutual authentication protocol for low computational capacity RFID systems-performance analysis by simulations. In *2010 IEEE International Conference on Wireless Communications, Networking and Information Security* (pp. 650–657). IEEE. 10.1109/WCINS.2010.5541860

Gordon, K. (n.d.). *Topic: Online dating in the United States*. Retrieved from https://www.statista.com/topics/2158/online-dating/

Guan, Z. H., Huang, F., & Guan, W. (2005). Chaos-based image encryption algorithm. *Physics Letters. [Part A]*, *346*(1-3), 153–157. doi:10.1016/j.physleta.2005.08.006

Guo, J. M., & Liu, Y. F. (2008). License plate localization and character segmentation with feedback self-learning and hybrid binarization techniques. *IEEE Transactions on Vehicular Technology*, *57*(3), 1417–1424. doi:10.1109/TVT.2007.909284

Guo, Q., Wang, F., Lei, J., Tu, D., & Li, G. (2016). Convolutional feature learning and Hybrid CNN-HMM for scene number recognition. *Neurocomputing*, *184*, 78–90.

Gupta, Chakraborty, Ghosh, & Buyya. (2017). Fog Computing in 5G Networks: An Application Perspective. *Cloud and Fog Computing in 5G Mobile Networks: Emerging advances and applications*, 23–56.

Gupta, K. K., Dhanda, N., & Kumar, U. (2018, December). A comparative study of medical image segmentation techniques for brain tumor detection. In *2018 4th International Conference on Computing Communication and Automation (ICCCA)* (pp. 1-4). IEEE. 10.1109/CCAA.2018.8777561

Gupta, A. T. B. B. (2017). Cryptanalysis of a novel ultra-lightweight mutual authentication protocol for IoT devices using RFID tags. *The Journal of Supercomputing*, *73*(3), 1085–1102. doi:10.100711227-016-1849-x

Gutiérrez, S., Hernández, I., Ceballos, S., Barrio, I., Díez-Navajas, A. M., & Tardaguila, J. (2021). Deep learning for the differentiation of downy mildew and spider mite in grapevine under field conditions. *Computers and Electronics in Agriculture*, *182*, 105991. Advance online publication. doi:10.1016/j.compag.2021.105991

Gu, X., Angelov, P. P., Zhang, C., & Atkinson, P. M. (2018). A massively parallel deep rule-based ensemble classifier for remote sensing scenes. *IEEE Geoscience and Remote Sensing Letters*, *15*(3), 345–349.

Habrard, A., Bernard, M., & Sebban, M. (2003). Improvement of the State Merging Rule on Noisy Data in Probabilistic Grammatical Inference. In N. Lavrač, D. Gamberger, H. Blockeel, & L. Todorovski (Eds.), *Machine Learning: ECML 2003*. doi:10.1007/978-3-540-39857-8_17

Hall, M., Frank, E., Holmes, G., Pfahringer, P., Reutemann, P., & Witten, I.H. (2009The WEKA Data Mining Software: An Update. *SIGKDD Explorations*, *11*(1).

Han, J., Zhang, D., Hu, X., Guo, L., Ren, J., & Wu, F. (2015). Background prior-based salient object detection via deep reconstruction residual. *IEEE Transactions on Circuits and Systems for Video Technology*, *25*(8), 1309–1321. doi:10.1109/TCSVT.2014.2381471

Hasan, R. I., Yusuf, S. M., & Alzubaidi, L. (2020). Review of the state of the art of deep learning for plant diseases: A broad analysis and discussion. *Plants*, *9*(10), 1302. doi:10.3390/plants9101302 PMID:33019765

Hastie, T., Rosset, S., Zhu, J., & Zou, H. (2009). Multi-class AdaBoost. *Statistics and Its Interface*, *2*(3), 349–360. doi:10.4310ii.2009.v2.n3.a8

Hatcher, W. G., & Yu, W. (2018). A survey of deep learning: Platforms, applications and emerging research trends. *IEEE Access : Practical Innovations, Open Solutions*, *6*, 24411–24432. doi:10.1109/ACCESS.2018.2830661

Hau, W., Wang, Z., Wang, H., Zheng, K., & Zhou, X. (2017, March). Understand Short Texts by Harvesting and Analyzing Semantic Knowledge. *IEEE Transactions on Knowledge and Data Engineering*, *29*(3), 499–512. doi:10.1109/TKDE.2016.2571687

He, D., Kumar, N., Chilamkurti, N., & Lee, J. H. (2014). Lightweight ECC Based RFID Authentication Integrated with an ID Verifier Transfer Protocol. *Journal of Medical Systems*, *38*(10), 116. Advance online publication. doi:10.100710916-014-0116-z PMID:25096968

He, K., Zhang, X., Ren, S., & Sun, J. (2015). Spatial pyramid pooling in deep convolutional networks for visual recognition. *IEEE Transactions on Pattern Analysis and Machine Intelligence*, *37*(9), 1904–1916. doi:10.1109/TPAMI.2015.2389824 PMID:26353135

He, K., Zhang, X., Ren, S., & Sun, J. (2016). Deep residual learning for image recognition. *Proceedings of the IEEE conference on computer vision and pattern recognition*, 770-778.

Hemanth, D. J., Anitha, J., Son, L. H., & Mittal, M. (2018). Diabetic Retinopathy Diagnosis from Retinal Images Using Modified Hopfield Neural Network. *Journal of Medical Systems*, *42*(12), 247. doi:10.100710916-018-1111-6 PMID:30382410

Hinton, G. E., & Salakhutdinov, R. R. (2006). Reducing the dimensionality of data with neural networks. *Science*, *313*(5786), 504-507.

Hinton, G., Deng, L., Yu, D., Dahl, G. E., Mohamed, A., Jaitly, N., Senior, A., Vanhoucke, V., Nguyen, P., Sainath, T. N., & Kingsbury, B. (2012). Deep neural networks for acoustic modeling in speech recognition: The shared views of four research groups. *IEEE Signal Processing Magazine*, *29*(6), 82–97. doi:10.1109/MSP.2012.2205597

Hinton, G., & Salakhutdinov, R. (2011). Discovering binary codes for documents by learning deep generative models. *Topics in Cognitive Science*, *3*(1), 74–91. doi:10.1111/j.1756-8765.2010.01109.x PMID:25164175

Ho, T. K., & Basu, M. (2002). Complexity measures of supervised classification problems. *Pattern Analysis and Machine Intelligence, IEEE Transactions on, 24*(3), 289-300.

Ho, W. T., Lim, H. W., & Tay, Y. H. (2009). Two-stage license plate detection using gentle adaboost and SIFT-SVM. In *Proceedings - 2009 1st Asian Conference on Intelligent Information and Database Systems, ACIIDS 2009* (pp. 109–114). 10.1109/ACIIDS.2009.25

Hofmann, M., Tiefenbacher, P., & Rigoll, G. (2012). Background segmentation with feedback: The pixel-based adaptive segmenter. In *Computer Vision and Pattern Recognition Workshops (CVPRW), 2012 IEEE Computer Society Conference on, 2012*. IEEE.

Hofmann, T. (2017, August). Probabilistic latent semantic indexing. In *ACM SIGIR Forum* (Vol. 51, No. 2, pp. 50-57). ACM.

Hong, S., & Kim, H. (2010). An integrated GPU power and performance model. *Proceedings of the 37th Annual International Symposium on Computer Architecture*, 280–289. 10.1145/1815961.1815998

Hoque, M. Bikas, & Naser. (2012). *An implementation of intrusion detection system using genetic algorithm.* arXiv preprint arXiv:1204.1336.

Horng, W.-B., Chen, C.-Y., Chang, Y., & Fan, C.-H. (2004). Driver fatigue detection based on eye tracking and dynamic template matching. In *Proceedings of the IEEE International Conference on Networking, Sensing and Control*. IEEE. 10.1109/ICNSC.2004.1297400

Horry, M. J., Chakraborty, S., Paul, M., Ulhaq, A., Pradhan, B., Saha, M., & Shukla, N. (2020). COVID-19 detection through transfer learning using multimodal imaging data. *IEEE Access: Practical Innovations, Open Solutions*, *8*, 149808–149824. doi:10.1109/ACCESS.2020.3016780

Hosseinpour. (2016). An Intrusion Detection System for Fog Computing and IoT Based Logistic Systems Using a Smart Data Approach. *International Journal of Digital Content Technology and its Applications*.

Hosseinpour, F., & Abu Bakar, K. (2010). Survey on artificial immune system as a bio-inspired technique for anomaly based intrusion detection systems. In *2010 International Conference on Intelligent Networking and Collaborative Systems*, (pp. 323-324). IEEE. doi:10.1109/INCOS.2010.40

Hsu, C. W., & Lin, C. J. (2002). A comparison of methods for multiclass support vector machines. *IEEE Transactions on Neural Networks*, *13*(2), 415–425. doi:10.1109/72.991427 PMID:18244442

Hsu, H., & Lachenbruch, P. A. (2008). *Paired T Test. Wiley Encyclopedia of Clinical Trials*. doi:10.1002/9780471462422.eoct969

Hu, P., Zhao, Y., Yang, Z., & Wang, J. (2002). Recognition of gray character using gabor filters. In *5th International Conference on Information Fusion, FUSION 2002* (*Vol. 1*, pp. 419–424). Academic Press.

Huang, P. S., He, X., Gao, J., Deng, L., Acero, A., & Heck, L. (2013, October). Learning deep structured semantic models for web search using clickthrough data. In *Proceedings of the 22nd ACM international conference on Information & Knowledge Management* (pp. 2333-2338). ACM. 10.1145/2505515.2505665

Huang, C. K., & Nien, H.-H. (2009). Multi chaotic systems based pixel shuffle for image encryption. *Optics Communications, 282*(11), 2123–2127. doi:10.1016/j.optcom.2009.02.044

Huang, G., Liu, Z., Maaten, L. V. D., & Weinberger, K. Q. (2017). Densely Connected Convolutional Networks. In *Proceedings of the IEEE Conference on Computer Vision and Pattern Recognition*. IEEE.

Huang, G., Liu, Z., Van Der Maaten, L., & Weinberger, K. Q. (2017). Densely connected convolutional networks. In *Proceedings of the IEEE conference on computer vision and pattern recognition* (pp. 4700-4708). IEEE.

Huang, Y. P., Chen, C. H., Chang, Y. T., & Sandnes, F. E. (2009). An intelligent strategy for checking the annual inspection status of motorcycles based on license plate recognition. *Expert Systems with Applications, 36*(5), 9260–9267. doi:10.1016/j.eswa.2008.12.006

Hua, Z., & Zhou, Y. (2018). One-dimensional nonlinear model for producing chaos. *IEEE Transactions on Circuits and Systems. I, Regular Papers, 65*(1), 235–246. doi:10.1109/TCSI.2017.2717943

Hui, Y., & Liu, J. (2010). Intrusion detection based on immune dynamical matching algorithm. In *2010 International Conference on E-Business and E-Government*, (pp. 1342-1345). IEEE. doi:10.1109/ICEE.2010.342

Hu, J., Lin, Y., Tang, J., & Zhao, J. (2020). A new wind power interval prediction approach based on reservoir computing and a quality-driven loss function. *Applied Soft Computing, 92*, 106327. doi:10.1016/j.asoc.2020.106327

Hung, K., & Hsieh, C. (2010). *A Real-Time Mobile Vehicle License Plate Detection and Recognition.* Academic Press.

Hu, P., Dhelim, S., Ning, H., & Qiu, T. (2017). Survey on Fog Computing: Architecture, Key Technologies, Applications and Open Issues. *Journal of Network and Computer Applications.*

Hussain, L., Nguyen, T., Li, H., Abbasi, A. A., Lone, K. J., Zhao, Z., Zaib, M., Chen, A., & Duong, T. Q. (2020). Machine-learning classification of texture features of portable chest X-ray accurately classifies COVID-19 lung infection. *Biomedical Engineering Online, 19*(1), 1–18. doi:10.118612938-020-00831-x PMID:33239006

Ibrahim, M. H. (2016). Octopus: An Edge-Fog Mutual Authentication Scheme. *International Journal of Network Security, 18*(6), 1089–1101.

Iorga, M. (2018). *NIST Special Publication.* Fog Computing Conceptual Model.

Jaber, A. N., & Rehman, S. U. (2020). FCM–SVM Based Intrusion Detection System for Cloud Computing Environment. *Cluster Computing.*

Jain, A., & Rajpal, N. (2016). A robust image encryption algorithm resistant to attacks using DNA and chaotic logistic maps. *Multimedia Tools and Applications, 75*(10), 5455–5472. doi:10.100711042-015-2515-7

Jain, A., Tompson, J., LeCun, Y., & Bregler, C. (2014, November). Modeep: A deep learning framework using motion features for human pose estimation. In *Asian conference on computer vision* (pp. 302-315). Springer.

Jain, R., Gupta, M., Taneja, S., & Hemanth, D. J. (2021). Deep learning based detection and analysis of COVID-19 on chest X-ray images. *Applied Intelligence, 51*(3), 1690–1700. doi:10.100710489-020-01902-1

Jan, Ahmed, Shakhov, & Koo. (2019). Toward a lightweight intrusion detection system for the Internet of Things. *IEEE Access : Practical Innovations, Open Solutions, 7*, 42450–42471.

Jaroli, P., Bisht, A., Dua, M., & Dua, S. (2018). A Color Image Encryption Using Four Dimensional Differential Equations and Arnold Chaotic Map. *Proceedings of the International Conference on Inventive Research in Computing Applications, ICIRCA 2018*, 869–876. 10.1109/ICIRCA.2018.8597310

Jeyabharathi, D. (2016). Vehicle tracking and speed measurement system (VTSM) based on novel feature descriptor: diagonal hexadecimal pattern (DHP). *J Visual Commun Image Rep, 40*(B), 816–830.

Jeyabharathi, D. (2017). Background subtraction and object tracking via key frame-based rotational symmetry dynamic texture. *Adv Image Process Tech Appl.* . ch013 doi:10.4018/978-1-5225-2053-5

Jeyabharathi, D., & Dejey, D. (2016). A novel rotational symmetry dynamic texture (RSDT) based sub space construction and SCD (similar-congruent-dissimilar) based scoring model for background subtraction in real time videos. *Multimedia Tools and Applications, 75*(24), 17617–17645. doi:10.100711042-016-3772-9

Jeyabharathi, D., & Dejey, D. (2018). *New feature descriptor: extended symmetrical-diagonal hexadecimal pattern for efficient background subtraction and object tracking*. Comput Elect Eng.

Jiang, L., & Guo, Y. (2005, November). Learning lazy naive Bayesian classifiers for ranking. In *Tools with Artificial Intelligence, 2005. ICTAI 05. 17th IEEE International Conference on*. IEEE.

Jiang, D., Mekonnen, T. M., Merkebu, T. E., & Gebrehiwot, A. (2012). Car Plate Recognition System. In *IEEE International Conference on Intelligent Networks and Intelligent Systems* (pp. 9–12). IEEE.

Jiang, L., Cai, Z., Zhang, H., & Wang, D. (2013). Naive Bayes text classifiers: A locally weighted learning approach. *Journal of Experimental & Theoretical Artificial Intelligence, 25*(2), 273–286. doi:10.1080/0952813X.2012.721010

Jiang, L., Wang, D., Cai, Z., & Yan, X. (2007). Survey of improving naive Bayes for classification. In *Advanced Data Mining and Applications* (pp. 134–145). Springer Berlin Heidelberg. doi:10.1007/978-3-540-73871-8_14

Jiang, L., Zhang, H., & Su, J. (2005). Learning k-nearest neighbor naive bayes for ranking. In *Advanced Data Mining and Applications* (pp. 175–185). Springer Berlin Heidelberg. doi:10.1007/11527503_21

Jiang, M., Chen, Y., Liu, M., Rosenbloom, S., Mani, S., Denny, J., & Xu, H. (2011). A study of machine-learning-based approaches to extract clinical entities and their assertions from discharge summaries. *Journal of the American Medical Informatics Association, 18*(5), 601–606. doi:10.1136/amiajnl-2011-000163

Jiangwei, C., Lisheng, J., Bingliang, T., Shuming, S., & Rongben, W. (2004). A monitoring method of driver mouth behavior based on machine vision. *Proceedings of IEEE Intelligent Vehicles Symposium.*

Jiao, J., Ye, Q., & Huang, Q. (2009). A configurable method for multi-style license plate recognition. *Pattern Recognition, 42*(3), 358–369. doi:10.1016/j.patcog.2008.08.016

Jie, Z., & Lu, W. (2019). *Dependency-guided LSTM-CRF for named entity recognition.* arXiv preprint arXiv:1909.10148.

Jin, X., Jie, L., Wang, S., Qi, H. J., & Li, S. W. (2018). Classifying wheat hyperspectral pixels of healthy heads and Fusarium head blight disease using a deep neural network in the wild field. *Remote Sensing, 10*(3), 395. doi:10.3390/rs10030395

Johnson, R., & Zhang, T. (2015). Semi-supervised convolutional neural networks for text categorization via region embedding. In Advances in neural information processing systems (pp. 919-927). Academic Press.

Jones, M. T. (2015). *Artificial Intelligence: A Systems Approach: A Systems Approach. Jones & Bartlett Publishing.*

Jonnalagadda, S., Cohen, T., Wu, S., Liu, H., & Gonzalez, G. (2013). Using Empirically Constructed Lexical Resources for Named Entity Recognition. *Biomedical Informatics Insights.* Advance online publication. doi:10.4137/bii.s11664

Joshi, R. C., Kaushik, M., Dutta, M. K., Srivastava, A., & Choudhary, N. (2021). VirLeafNet: Automatic analysis and viral disease diagnosis using deep-learning in Vigna mungo plant. *Ecological Informatics, 61*, 101197. doi:10.1016/j.ecoinf.2020.101197

Juels, A., & Weis, S. A. (2007). Defining strong privacy for RFID. *Proceedings - Fifth Annual IEEE International Conference on Pervasive Computing and Communications Workshops, PerCom Workshops 2007, 13*(1), 342–347. 10.1109/PERCOMW.2007.37

Kadiyala, A., & Kumar, A. (2018). Applications of python to evaluate the performance of decision tree-based boosting algorithms. *Environmental Progress & Sustainable Energy, 37*(2), 618–623. doi:10.1002/ep.12888

Kahraman, F., Kurt, B., & Gökmen, M. (2003). License Plate Character Segmentation Based on the Gabor Transform and Vector Quantization. In *International Symposium on Computer and Information Sciences.* (pp. 381–388). Springer. 10.1007/978-3-540-39737-3_48

Kai, Cong, & Tao. (2016). Fog Computing for Vehicular Ad-Hoc Networks: Paradigms, Scenarios, and Issues. *Journal of China Universities of Posts and Telecommunications, 23*(2), 56-65, 96. doi:10.1016/S1005-8885(16)60021-3

Kalchbrenner, N., Grefenstette, E., & Blunsom, P. (2014). A convolutional neural network for modelling sentences. *Proceedings of the Association for Computational Linguistics (ACL)*, 655–665. 10.3115/v1/P14-1062

Kalinin, P., & Sirota, A. (2015). A graph based approach to hierarchical image over-segmentation. *Computer Vision and Image Understanding, 130*, 80–86. doi:10.1016/j.cviu.2014.09.007

Kamat, V., & Ganesan, S. (2002). An efficient implementation of the Hough transform for detecting vehicle license plates using DSP'S. In *Real-Time Technology and Applications Symposium* (pp. 58–59). IEEE.

Kamilaris, A., & Prenafeta-Boldú, F. X. (2018). Deep learning in agriculture: A survey. *Computers and Electronics in Agriculture, 147*, 70–90. doi:10.1016/j.compag.2018.02.016

Kang, H., & Chen, C. (2020). Fast implementation of real-time fruit detection in apple orchards using deep learning. *Computers and Electronics in Agriculture, 168*, 105108. doi:10.1016/j.compag.2019.105108

Kang, X., Xiang, X., Li, S., & Benediktsson, J. A. (2017). PCA-based edge-preserving features for hyperspectral image classification. *IEEE Transactions on Geoscience and Remote Sensing, 55*(12), 7140–7151.

Kantz, H. (1994). A robust method to estimate the maximal Lyapunov exponent of a time series. *Physics Letters. [Part A], 185*(1), 77–87. doi:10.1016/0375-9601(94)90991-1

Karlos, S., Fazakis, N., Panagopoulou, A.-P., Kotsiantis, S., & Sgarbas, K. (2017). Locally application of naive Bayes for self-training. *Springer Evolving Systems, 8*(1), 3–18. doi:10.100712530-016-9159-3

Kaur, B., Sharma, M., Mittal, M., Verma, A., Goyal, L. M., & Hemanth, D. J. (2018). An improved salient object detection algorithm combining background and foreground connectivity for brain image analysis. *Computers & Electrical Engineering, 71*, 692–703. doi:10.1016/j.compeleceng.2018.08.018

Kedziora, M., Gawin, P., Szczepanik, M., & Jozwiak, I. (2018). *Android Malware Detection Using Machine Learning And Reverse Engineering*. doi:10.5121/csit.2018.81709

Ke, G., Meng, Q., Finley, T., Wang, T., Chen, W., Ma, W., ... Liu, T. Y. (2017). Lightgbm: A highly efficient gradient boosting decision tree. *Advances in Neural Information Processing Systems, 30*, 3146–3154.

Khaing. (2010, January). *Enhanced Features Ranking and Selection using Recursive Feature Elimination(RFE) and k-Nearest Neighbor Algorithms in Support Vector Machine for Intrusion Detection System*. Academic Press.

Khan, N. Y., & Ali, N. (2007). *Distance and Color Invariant Automatic License Plate Recognition System*. Academic Press.

Khan, Parkinson, & Qin. (2017). Fog Computing Security: A Review of Current Applications and Security Solutions. *Journal of Cloud Computing*.

Khanday, A. M. U. D., Rabani, S. T., Khan, Q. R., Rouf, N., & Din, M. M. U. (2020). Machine learning based approaches for detecting COVID-19 using clinical text data. *International Journal of Information Technology*, *12*(3), 731–739. doi:10.100741870-020-00495-9 PMID:32838125

Khater, B. S. (2019). *A Lightweight Perceptron-Based Intrusion Detection System for Fog Computing*. Applied Sciences.

Kikuchi, M., Yoshida, M., Okabe, M., & Umemura, K. (2015, August). Confidence interval of probability estimator of Laplace smoothing. In *Advanced Informatics: Concepts, Theory and Applications (ICAICTA), 2015 2nd International Conference on* (pp. 1-6). IEEE. 10.1109/ICAICTA.2015.7335387

Kim, D.-E., & Kwon, D.-S. (2015). Pedestrian detection and tracking in thermal images using shape features. In *Ubiquitous Robots and Ambient Intelligence (URAI), 2015 12th International Conference on, 2015*. IEEE. 10.1109/URAI.2015.7358920

Kim, Y. (2014). *Convolutional neural networks for sentence classification*. doi:10.3115/v1/D14-1181

Kim, H. J., Lee, J. S., & Yang, H. S. (2007, June). Human action recognition using a modified convolutional neural network. In *International Symposium on Neural Networks* (pp. 715-723). Springer. 10.1007/978-3-540-72393-6_85

Kim, J. Y., & Schulzrinne, H. (2013). Cloud Support for Latency-Sensitive Telephony Applications. *Proceedings of the International Conference on Cloud Computing Technology and Science, CloudCom.*

Kim, S. K., Kim, D. W., & Kim, H. J. (1996). A Recognition of Vehicle Licence Plate Using A Genetic Algorithm Based Segmentation. In *Proceedings of 3rd IEEE International Conference on Image Processing* (pp. 661–664). IEEE.

Kim, Y., Jernite, Y., Sontag, D., & Rush, A. M. (2016, March). Character-aware neural language models. *Thirtieth AAAI Conference on Artificial Intelligence.*

Kiranyaz, S., Avci, O., Abdeljaber, O., Ince, T., Gabbouj, M., & Inman, D. J. (2021). 1D convolutional neural networks and applications: A survey. *Mechanical Systems and Signal Processing*, *151*, 107398. doi:10.1016/j.ymssp.2020.107398

Klimov, A., & Shamir, A. (2010). *New Applications of T-Functions in Block Ciphers and Hash Functions*. doi:10.1007/11502760_2

KN, S. (2011). *Image Encryption Techniques* (Doctoral dissertation). PES Institute of Technology.

Kochovski, P. (2019). Trust Management in a Blockchain Based Fog Computing Platform with Trustless Smart Oracles. *Future Generation Computer Systems*, *101*, 747–759. https://doi.org/10.1016/j.future.2019.07.030

Kranthi, S., Pranathi, K., & Srisaila, A. (2011). Automatic Number Plate Recognition. *International Journal of Advance Technology*, *2*(3), 408–422.

Krizhevsky, A., Sutskever, I., & Hinton, G. E. (2012). Imagenet classification with deep convolutional neural networks. *Advances in Neural Information Processing Systems*, 1097–1105.

Krizhevsky, A., Sutskever, I., & Hinton, G. E. (2012). *Imagenet classification with deep convolutional neural networks*. Advances in Neural Information Processing Systems.

Kulkarni, P., Khatri, A. P. B., & Shah, K. (2009). Automatic Number Plate Recognition (ANPR). In *2009 19th International Conference Radioelektronika* (pp. 111–114). IEEE.

Kumar Singh Gautam, R., & Amit Doegar, E. (2018). An Ensemble Approach for Intrusion Detection System Using Machine Learning Algorithms. *Proceedings of the 8th International Conference Confluence 2018 on Cloud Computing, Data Science and Engineering, Confluence 2018.*

Kumar, A., Kuppusamy, K. S., & Aghila, G. (2018). FAMOUS: Forensic Analysis of MObile devices Using Scoring of application permissions. *Future Generation Computer Systems*, *83*, 158–172. doi:10.1016/j.future.2018.02.001

Kuznetsova, A., Maleva, T., & Soloviev, V. (2020). Using YOLOv3 algorithm with pre-and post-processing for apple detection in fruit-harvesting robot. *Agronomy (Basel)*, *10*(7), 1016. doi:10.3390/agronomy10071016

La Vigne, N. G., Lowry, S. S., Markman, J. A., & Dwyer, A. M. (2011). *Evaluating the use of public surveillance cameras for crime control and prevention.* US Department of Justice, Office of Community Oriented Policing Services. Urban Institute, Justice Policy Center.

Labs, D. (2021). *District Data Labs - Named Entity Recognition and Classification for Entity Extraction.* Retrieved 23 March 2021, from https://districtdatalabs.silvrback.com/named-entity-recognition-and-classification-for-entity-extraction

Lan, Le Roux, Bach, Ponce, & LeCun. (2011). Ask the locals: multi-way local pooling for im- age recognition. In *Computer Vision (ICCV), 2011 IEEE International Conference on*, (pp. 2651–2658). IEEE.

Lawrence, S., Giles, C. L., Tsoi, A. C., & Back, A. D. (1997). Face recognition: A convolutional neural-network approach. *IEEE Transactions on Neural Networks*, *8*(1), 98–113. doi:10.1109/72.554195 PMID:18255614

Le, W., & Li, S. (2006). A hybrid license plate extraction method for complex scenes. In *Proceedings - International Conference on Pattern Recognition* (Vol. 2, pp. 324–327). Academic Press.

LeCun, Jackel, Bottou, Brunot, Cortes, Denker, & Drucker. (1995). Comparison of learning algorithms for handwritten digit recognition. *International Conference on Artificial Neural Networks*, 60, 53-60.

LeCun, Y., Bengio, Y., & Hinton, G. (2015). Deep learning. *Nature*, *521*(7553), 436–444. doi:10.1038/nature14539 PMID:26017442

Lecun, Y., Bottou, L., Bengio, Y., & Haffner, P. (1998). Gradient based learning applied to document recognition. *Proceedings of the IEEE*, *86*(11), 2278–2324. doi:10.1109/5.726791

LeCun, Y., Kavukcuoglu, K., & Farabet, C. (2010). Convolutional networks and applications in vision. *Proceedings of 2010 IEEE International Symposium on Circuits and Systems*, 253-256.

Lee, H. J., Chen, S. Y., & Wang, S. Z. (2004). Extraction and recognition of license plates of motorcycles and vehicles on highways. *Proceedings - International Conference on Pattern Recognition*, *4*, 356–359.

Lee, Y. K., Batina, L., & Verbauwhede, I. (2008). EC-RAC (ECDLP based randomized access control): Provably secure RFID authentication protocol. In 2008 IEEE international conference on RFID (pp. 97–104). IEEE.

Lee, E. R., Kim, P. K., & Kim, H. J. (1994). Automatic Recognition of a Car Licence Plate using Colour Image Processing. In *1st International Conference on Image Processing* (Vol. 2, pp. 301–305). 10.1109/ICIP.1994.413580

Lee, H., & Kwon, H. (2017). Going deeper with contextual CNN for hyperspectral image classification. *IEEE Transactions on Image Processing*, *26*(10), 4843–4855. doi:10.1109/TIP.2017.2725580 PMID:28708555

Lehtonen, M., Ostojic, D., Ilic, A., & Michahelles, F. (2009). Securing RFID systems by detecting tag cloning. In *International Conference on Pervasive Computing* (pp. 291–308). Springer. 10.1007/978-3-642-01516-8_20

Lekhana, G. C., & Srikantaswamy, R. (2012). Real Time License Plate Recognition System. *International Journal of Advanced Technology & Engineering Research*, *2*(4), 5–9.

Liang. (2015). Automatic Traffic Accident Detection Based on the Internet of Things and Support Vector Machine. *International Journal of Smart Home*, *9*(4), 97–106.

Lian, S., Sun, J., & Wang, Z. (2005). Security analysis of a chaos-based image encryption algorithm. *Physica A*, *351*(2–4), 645–661. doi:10.1016/j.physa.2005.01.001

Liao, Y. P., & Hsiao, C. M. (2014a). A secure ECC-based RFID authentication scheme integrated with ID-verifier transfer protocol. *Ad Hoc Networks*, *18*, 133–146. doi:10.1016/j.adhoc.2013.02.004

Li, B., Zeng, Z., Zhou, J., & Dong, H. (2008). An Algorithm for License Plate Recognition Using Radial Basis Function Neural Network. In *International Symposium on Computer Science and Computational Technology* (pp. 569–572). 10.1109/ISCSCT.2008.272

Li, D., Wang, R., Xie, C., Liu, L., Zhang, J., Li, R., Wang, F., Zhou, M., & Liu, W. (2020). A recognition method for rice plant diseases and pests video detection based on deep convolutional neural network. *Sensors (Basel)*, *20*(3), 578. doi:10.339020030578 PMID:31973039

Li, J., Fang, G., Li, B., & Wang, C. (2015). A Novel Naive Bayes Classifier Model Based on Differential Evolution. In *Intelligent Computing Theories and Methodologies* (pp. 558–566). Springer International Publishing. doi:10.1007/978-3-319-22180-9_55

Li, J., Sun, L., Yan, Q., Li, Z., Srisa-an, W., & Ye, H. (2018). Significant permission identification for machine-learning-based android malware detection. *IEEE Transactions on Industrial Informatics*, *14*(7), 3216–3225. doi:10.1109/TII.2017.2789219

Lin, Y. C., & Hung, P. H. (2007). *U.S. Patent No. 7,171,350*. Washington, DC: U.S. Patent and Trademark Office.

Li, S., Da Xu, L., & Zhao, S. (2015). The Internet of Things: A Survey. *Information Systems Frontiers*.

Li, Tug, Meng, & Wang. (2019). Designing collaborative blockchained signature-based intrusion detection in IoT environments. *Future Generation Computer Systems*, *96*, 481–489.

Liu, Q., Lu, J., Zhao, K., & Chen, S. (2014). Naive Bayes classifier ensemble for traffic incident detection. In *Transportation Research Board 93rd Annual Meeting* (No. 14-1014). 10.1155/2014/383671

Liu, B., Zhang, Y., He, D., & Li, Y. (2018). Identification of apple leaf diseases based on deep convolutional neural networks. *Symmetry*, *10*(1), 11. doi:10.3390ym10010011

Liu, C., Li, H.-C., Liao, W., Philips, W., & Emery, W. J. (2019). Variational Textured Dirichlet Process Mixture Model with Pairwise Constraint for Unsupervised Classification of Polarimetric SAR Images. *IEEE Transactions on Image Processing*.

Liu, G., & Duan, J. (2020). RGB-D image segmentation using superpixel and multi-feature fusion graph theory. *Signal, Image and Video Processing*, *14*(6), 1–9. doi:10.100711760-020-01647-x

Liu, G., Nouaze, J. C., Touko Mbouembe, P. L., & Kim, J. H. (2020). YOLO-tomato: A robust algorithm for tomato detection based on YOLOv3. *Sensors (Basel)*, *20*(7), 2145. doi:10.339020072145 PMID:32290173

Liu, J., & Wang, X. (2020). Tomato diseases and pests detection based on improved Yolo V3 convolutional neural network. *Frontiers in Plant Science*, *11*, 898. doi:10.3389/fpls.2020.00898 PMID:32612632

Liu, M. Y., Tuzel, O., Ramalingam, S., & Chellappa, R. (2011, June). Entropy rate superpixel segmentation. In *CVPR 2011* (pp. 2097–2104). IEEE. doi:10.1109/CVPR.2011.5995323

Liu, P., Choo, K.-K. R., Wang, L., & Huang, F. (2017). SVM or deep learning? A comparative study on remote sensing image classification. *Soft Computing*, *21*(23), 7053–7065.

Liu, Z., Wu, J., Fu, L., Majeed, Y., Feng, Y., Li, R., & Cui, Y. (2019). Improved kiwifruit detection using pre-trained VGG16 with RGB and NIR information fusion. *IEEE Access: Practical Innovations, Open Solutions*, *8*, 2327–2336. doi:10.1109/ACCESS.2019.2962513

Li, X., Zhou, C., & Xu, N. (2018). A Secure and Efficient Image Encryption Algorithm Based on DNA Coding and Spatiotemporal Chaos. *International Journal of Network Security*, *20*(1), 110–120.

Li, Z., Wu, X. M., & Chang, S. F. (2012, June). Segmentation using superpixels: A bipartite graph partitioning approach. In *2012 IEEE Conference on Computer Vision and Pattern Recognition* (pp. 789-796). IEEE.

Loey, M., Manogaran, G., & Khalifa, N. E. M. (2020). A deep transfer learning model with classical data augmentation and cgan to detect covid-19 from chest ct radiography digital images. *Neural Computing & Applications*, 1–13. PMID:33132536

Long, J., Feng, X., Zhu, X., Zhang, J., & Gou, G. (2018). Efficient superpixel-guided interactive image segmentation based on graph theory. *Symmetry*, *10*(5), 169. doi:10.3390ym10050169

Long, J., Shelhamer, E., & Darrell, T. (2017). Fully convolutional networks for semantic segmentation [PAMI]. *IEEE Transactions on Pattern Analysis and Machine Intelligence*, *39*(4), 640–651. doi:10.1109/TPAMI.2016.2572683 PMID:27244717

Lou, S., Cheng, S., Huang, J., & Jiang, F. (2019, March). TFDroid: Android Malware Detection by Topics and Sensitive Data Flows Using Machine Learning Techniques. In *2019 IEEE 2nd International Conference on Information and Computer Technologies (ICICT)* (pp. 30-36). IEEE.

Lu, H., Lin, J., & Zeng, X. X. (2012). Research and Application of Improved Naive Bayesian Classification Algorithm. *Journal of Hunan University (Natural Sciences)*, *12*, 11.

Luo, H., Wen, G., Su, J., & Huang, Z. (2018). SLAP : Succinct and Lightweight Authentication Protocol for low-cost RFID system. *Wireless Networks*, *24*(1), 69–78. doi:10.100711276-016-1323-y

Lu, T. C. (2020). CNN Convolutional layer optimisation based on quantum evolutionary algorithm. *Connection Science*, 1–13. doi:10.1080/09540091.2020.1841111

Lu, Y., Javidi, T., & Lazebnik, S. (2016). Adaptive object detection using adjacency and zoom prediction. In *Proceedings of the IEEE Conference on Computer Vision and Pattern Recognition* (pp. 2351-2359). 10.1109/CVPR.2016.258

Maddalena, L., & Petrosino, A. (2010). A fuzzy spatial coherence-based approach to background/foreground separation for moving object detection. *Neural Computing & Applications*, *19*(2), 179–186. doi:10.100700521-009-0285-8

Mahini, H., Kasaei, S., Dorri, F., & Dorri, F. (2006). An efficient features-based license plate localization method. In *Proceedings - International Conference on Pattern Recognition* (Vol. 2, pp. 841–844). 10.1109/ICPR.2006.239

Majeed, A. (2019). Improving time complexity and accuracy of the machine learning algorithms through selection of highly weighted top k features from complex datasets. *Annals of Data Science*, *6*(4), 599–621. doi:10.100740745-019-00217-4

Malathi, Reddy, & Jayaseeli. (2018). A survey on anomaly based host intrusion detection system. *Journal of Physics: Conference Series*, *1000*(1).

Maldonado, A. D., Uusitalo, L., Tucker, A., & Thorsten Blenckner, P. A. (2019). Aguilera, and A. Salmerón. "Prediction of a complex system with few data: Evaluation of the effect of model structure and amount of data with dynamic bayesian network models. *Environmental Modelling & Software*, *118*, 281–297.

Mangal, A., Kalia, S., Rajgopal, H., Rangarajan, K., Namboodiri, V., Banerjee, S., & Arora, C. (2020). *CovidAID: COVID-19 detection using chest X-ray.* arXiv preprint arXiv:2004.09803.

Mansouri, A., Affendey, L. S., & Mamat, A. (2008). Named entity recognition approaches. *International Journal of Computer Science and Network Security*, *8*(2), 339–344.

Mao, S., Li, Y., Ma, Y., Zhang, B., Zhou, J., & Wang, K. (2020). Automatic cucumber recognition algorithm for harvesting robots in the natural environment using deep learning and multi-feature fusion. *Computers and Electronics in Agriculture*, *170*, 105254. doi:10.1016/j.compag.2020.105254

Mao, Y., & Chen, G. (2005). Chaos-based image encryption. In *Handbook of geometric computing* (pp. 231–265). Springer. doi:10.1007/3-540-28247-5_8

Marotto, F. R. (1978). Snap-back repellers imply chaos in Rn. *Journal of Mathematical Analysis and Applications*, *63*(1), 199–223. doi:10.1016/0022-247X(78)90115-4

Marrero, M., Urbano, J., Sánchez-Cuadrado, S., Morato, J., & Gómez-Berbís, J. (2013). Named Entity Recognition: Fallacies, challenges and opportunities. *Computer Standards & Interfaces*, *35*(5), 482–489. doi:10.1016/j.csi.2012.09.004

Matas, J., & Zimmermann, K. (2005). Unconstrained licence plate and text localization and recognition. In *IEEE Conference on Intelligent Transportation Systems, Proceedings, ITSC* (Vol. Sept., pp. 225–230). 10.1109/ITSC.2005.1520111

Mayfield, J., McNamee, P., & Piatko, C. (2003). Named entity recognition using hundreds of thousands of features. In *Proceedings of the seventh conference on Natural language learning at HLT-NAACL 2003* (pp. 184-187). Academic Press.

Ma, Z., Ge, H., Liu, Y., Zhao, M., & Ma, J. (2019). A Combination Method for Android Malware Detection Based on Control Flow Graphs and Machine Learning Algorithms. *IEEE Access: Practical Innovations, Open Solutions*, *7*, 21235–21245. doi:10.1109/ACCESS.2019.2896003

McCann, S., & Lowe, D. G. (2012, June). Local naive bayes nearest neighbor for image classification. In *2012 IEEE Conference on Computer Vision and Pattern Recognition* (pp. 3650-3656). IEEE. 10.1109/CVPR.2012.6248111

McKeever, A. (2020). Here's what coronavirus does to the body. *National Geographic*.

Megalingam, R. K., Krishna, P., Pillai, V. A., & Hakkim, R. V. I. (2010). Extraction of License Plate Region in Automatic License Plate Recognition. In *International Conference on Mechanical and Electrical Technology (ICMET 2010)* (pp. 496–501). 10.1109/ICMET.2010.5598409

Menotti, D., Chiachia, G., Falcão, A. X., & Oliveira Neto, V. J. (2014). Vehicle license plate recognition with random convolutional networks. In *Vehicle license plate recognition with random convolutional networks. In 2014 27th SIBGRAPI Conference on Graphics, Patterns and Images* (pp. 298–303). 10.1109/SIBGRAPI.2014.52

Mikolov, T., Chen, K., Corrado, G., & Dean, J. (2013). *Efficient estimation of word representations in vector space.* arXiv preprint arXiv:1301.3781.

Milosevic, N., Dehghantanha, A., & Choo, K. K. R. (2017). Machine learning aided Android malware classification. *Computers & Electrical Engineering*, *61*, 266–274. doi:10.1016/j.compeleceng.2017.02.013

Minaee, S., Kafieh, R., Sonka, M., Yazdani, S., & Soufi, G. J. (2020). Deep-covid: Predicting covid-19 from chest x-ray images using deep transfer learning. *Medical Image Analysis*, *65*, 101794. doi:10.1016/j.media.2020.101794 PMID:32781377

Mitra, B. (2015, August). Exploring session context using distributed representations of queries and reformulations. In *Proceedings of the 38th international ACM SIGIR conference on research and development in information retrieval* (pp. 3-12). ACM. 10.1145/2766462.2767702

Mobile App Security Test by ImmuniWeb. (n.d.). Retrieved from https://www.htbridge.com/mobile/

Mohammad, O. F., Rahim, M. S. M., Zeebaree, S. R. M., & Ahmed, F. Y. (2017). A Survey and Analysis of the Image Encryption Methods. *International Journal of Applied Engineering Research: IJAER*, *12*(23), 13265–13280.

Mohanty, S. P., Hughes, D. P., & Salathé, M. (2016). Using deep learning for image-based plant disease detection. *Frontiers in Plant Science*, *7*, 1419. doi:10.3389/fpls.2016.01419 PMID:27713752

Mollaeefar, M., Sharif, A., & Nazari, M. (2017). A novel encryption scheme for colored image based on high level chaotic maps. *Multimedia Tools and Applications*, *76*(1), 607–629. doi:10.100711042-015-3064-9

Mooney & Nahm. (2005). Text Mining with Information Extraction. *Proceedings of the 4th International MIDP Colloquium*, 141-160.

Mooney, P. (2020). *Chest X-ray images (Pneumonia)*. https://www. kaggle. com/paultimothymooney/chest-xray-pneumonia

Mujahid, U., Najam-ul-Islam, M., & Shami, M. A. (2015). Rcia: A new ultralightweight rfid authentication protocol using recursive hash. *International Journal of Distributed Sensor Networks*, *11*(1), 642180. doi:10.1155/2015/642180

Murillo-Escobar, M. A., Cruz-Hernández, C., Cardoza-Avendaño, L., & Méndez-Ramírez, R. (2017). A novel pseudorandom number generator based on pseudorandomly enhanced logistic map. *Nonlinear Dynamics*, *87*(1), 407–425. doi:10.100711071-016-3051-3

Nair, V., & Hinton, G. E. (2010, January). Rectified linear units improve restricted boltzmann machines. *Proceedings of the 27th International Conference on Machine Learning (ICML-10).*

Najam-ul-islam, U. M. M. (2017). A New Ultralightweight RFID Authentication Protocol for Passive Low Cost Tags : KMAP. *Wireless Personal Communications*, *94*(3), 725–744. doi:10.100711277-016-3647-4

Nancharla, B. K., & Dua, M. (2020). An image encryption using intertwining logistic map and enhanced logistic map. *Proceedings of the 5th International Conference on Communication and Electronics Systems, ICCES 2020*, 1309–1314. 10.1109/ICCES48766.2020.09138102

Nanni, L., Maguolo, G., & Pancino, F. (2020). Insect pest image detection and recognition based on bio-inspired methods. *Ecological Informatics*, *57*, 101089. doi:10.1016/j.ecoinf.2020.101089

Narayanan, V., Arora, I., & Bhatia, A. (2013). Fast and accurate sentiment classification using an enhanced Naive Bayes model. In *Intelligent Data Engineering and Automated Learning–IDEAL 2013* (pp. 194–201). Springer Berlin Heidelberg. doi:10.1007/978-3-642-41278-3_24

Narin, A., Kaya, C., & Pamuk, Z. (2020). *Automatic detection of coronavirus disease (covid-19) using x-ray images and deep convolutional neural networks.* arXiv preprint arXiv:2003.10849.

Narin, A. (2020). *Detection of Covid-19 Patients with Convolutional Neural Network Based Features on Multi-class X-ray Chest Images. In 2020 Medical Technologies Congress*. TIPTEKNO. doi:10.1109/TIPTEKNO50054.2020.9299289

Narkhede, S. (2018). Understanding auc-roc curve. *Towards Data Science*, *26*, 220–227.

Nathan, V. S. L., Ramkumar, J., & Priya, S. K. (2004). New Approaches for License Plate Recognition System. In *International Conference on Intelligent Sensing and Information Process* (pp. 149–152). Academic Press.

National Institute of Justice (NIJ), US Department of Justice, Office of Justice Programs, & United States of America. (2003). CCTV: Constant cameras track violators. *NIJ Journal*, *249*, 16–23.

Nguyen, T.P., Pham, C.C., Ha, S.V-U., & Jeon, J.W. (2018). Change Detection by Training a Triplet Network for Motion Feature Extraction. *IEEE Transactions on Circuits and Systems for Video Technology*.

Niculescu-Mizil, A., & Caruana, R. (2005). Predicting good probabilities with supervised learning. In *Proceedings of the 22nd international conference on Machine learning*, (pp. 625-632). ACM.

Nieto, M. (1997). *Public video surveillance: is it an effective crime prevention tool?* California Research Bureau, California State Library.

Ni, J., Zhang, K., Lin, X., & Shen, X. S. (2018). Securing Fog Computing for Internet of Things Applications: Challenges and Solutions. *IEEE Communications Surveys and Tutorials*.

Nijhuis, J. A. G., Ter Brugge, M. H., Helmholt, K. A., Pluim, J. P. W., Spaanenburg, L., Venema, R. S., & Westenberg, M. A. (1995). Car license plate recognition with neural networks and fuzzy logic. In *Proceedings of ICNN'95-International Conference on Neural Networks* (Vol. 5, pp. 2232–2236). IEEE. 10.1109/ICNN.1995.487708

NIST Big Data Public Working Group. (2015). *NIST Special Publication 1500-1 - NIST Big Data Interoperability Framework: Volume 1, Definitions*. Author.

Noh, S., & Jeon, M. (2012). A new framework for background subtraction using multiple cues. In *Asian Conference on Computer Vision*, 2012. Springer.

Özkaynak, F. (2018). Brief review on application of nonlinear dynamics in image encryption. *Nonlinear Dynamics*, *92*(2), 1–9. doi:10.100711071-018-4056-x

Pacheco, J., Benitez, V. H., Felix-Herran, L. C., & Satam, P. (2020). Artificial Neural Networks-Based Intrusion Detection System for Internet of Things Fog Nodes. *IEEE Access: Practical Innovations, Open Solutions*.

Paharia, B., & Bhushan, K. (2019). A Comprehensive Review of Distributed Denial of Service (DDoS) Attacks in Fog Computing Environment. Handbook of Computer Networks and Cyber Security: Principles and Paradigms.

Pak, C., & Huang, L. (2017). A new color image encryption using combination of the 1D chaotic map. *Signal Processing*, *138*, 129–137. doi:10.1016/j.sigpro.2017.03.011

Palani, S., & Kothandaraman, S. (2013). *A Low Cost Drivers Drowsiness Detection System*. Academic Press.

Pandey, G., Chaudhary, P., Gupta, R., & Pal, S. (2020). *SEIR and Regression Model based COVID-19 outbreak predictions in India.* arXiv preprint arXiv:2004.00958.

Pan, L., Li, C., Zhou, Y., Chen, R., & Xiong, B. (2020). A combinational convolutional neural network of double subnets for food-ingredient recognition. *International Journal of Embedded Systems*, *13*(4), 439–448. doi:10.1504/IJES.2020.110658

Pan, S. J., & Yang, Q. (2009). A survey on transfer learning. *IEEE Transactions on Knowledge and Data Engineering*, *22*(10), 1345–1359. doi:10.1109/TKDE.2009.191

Papacharissi, Z., & Rubin, A. (2000). Predictors of Internet Use. *Journal of Broadcasting & Electronic Media*, *44*(2), 175–196. doi:10.120715506878jobem4402_2

Par, Ö. E., Sezer, E. A., & Sever, H. (2019, April). Small and Unbalanced Data Set Problem in Classification. In *2019 27th Signal Processing and Communications Applications Conference (SIU)* (pp. 1-4). IEEE. 10.1109/SIU.2019.8806497

Pareek, N. K., Patidar, V., & Sud, K. K. (2005). Cryptography using multiple one-dimensional chaotic maps. *Communications in Nonlinear Science and Numerical Simulation, 10*(7), 715–723. doi:10.1016/j.cnsns.2004.03.006

Parisi, R., Di Claudio, E. D., Lucarelli, G., & Orlandi, G. (1998). Car plate recognition by neural networks and image processing. In *IEEE International Symposium on Circuits System* (Vol. 3, pp. 195–198). 10.1109/ISCAS.1998.703970

Patel, A., & Parikh, M. (2018). *A Survey on Multiple Image Encryption Using Chaos Based algorithms And DNA Computing*. Academic Press.

Patricio, D. I., & Rieder, R. (2018). Computer vision and artificial intelligence in precision agriculture for grain crops: A systematic review. *Computers and Electronics in Agriculture, 153*, 69–81.

Peiravian, N., & Zhu, X. (2013, November). Machine learning for android malware detection using permission and api calls. In *2013 IEEE 25th international conference on tools with artificial intelligence* (pp. 300-305). IEEE. 10.1109/ICTAI.2013.53

Peng, W., Huang, L., Jia, J., & Ingram, E. (2018, August). Enhancing the naive Bayes spam filter through intelligent text modification detection. In *2018 17th IEEE International Conference On Trust, Security And Privacy In Computing And Communications/12th IEEE International Conference On Big Data Science And Engineering (TrustCom/BigDataSE)* (pp. 849-854). IEEE. 10.1109/TrustCom/BigDataSE.2018.00122

Pennington, J., Socher, R., & Manning, C. (2014). Glove: Global vectors for word representation. In *Proceedings of the 2014 conference on empirical methods in natural language processing (EMNLP)* (pp. 1532-1543). 10.3115/v1/D14-1162

Perbet, F., & Maki, A. (2011, June). Homogeneous Superpixels from Random Walks. In MVA (pp. 26-30). Academic Press.

Peris-lopez, P., Hernandez-castro, J. C., Estevez-tapiador, J. M., & Ribagorda, A. (2006). *EMAP : An Efficient Mutual-Authentication Protocol for Low-Cost RFID Tags*. Academic Press.

Peris-lopez, P., Hernandez-castro, J. C., Tapiador, J. M. E., & Ribagorda, A. (2002). *LMAP : A Real Lightweight Mutual Authentication Protocol for Low-cost RFID tags*. Academic Press.

Peris-Lopez, P., Hernandez-Castro, J. C., Estevez-Tapiador, J. M., & Ribagorda, A. (2006). M 2 AP: a minimalist mutual-authentication protocol for low-cost RFID tags. In *International conference on ubiquitous intelligence and computing* (pp. 912–923). Springer. 10.1007/11833529_93

Peris-Lopez, P., Hernandez-Castro, J. C., Tapiador, J. M. E., & Ribagorda, A. (2008). Advances in ultralightweight cryptography for low-cost RFID tags: Gossamer protocol. In *International Workshop on Information Security Applications* (pp. 56–68). Springer.

Phan, R. C. W. (2009). Cryptanalysis of a new ultralightweight RFID authentication protocolSASI. *IEEE Transactions on Dependable and Secure Computing, 6*(4), 316–320. doi:10.1109/TDSC.2008.33

Politi, A., Pikovsky, A., & Ullner, E. (2017). Chaotic macroscopic phases in one-dimensional oscillators. *The European Physical Journal. Special Topics, 226*(9), 1791–1810. doi:10.1140/epjst/e2017-70056-4

Potharaju, S. P., & Sreedevi, M. (2018). Correlation Coefficient Based Feature Selection Framework Using Graph Construction. *Gazi University Journal of Science, 31*(3), 775–787.

Priyadarshini & Barik. (2019). A Deep Learning Based Intelligent Framework to Mitigate DDoS Attack in Fog Environment. *Journal of King Saud University - Computer and Information Sciences*.

PUB. (1977). 46-3. data encryption standard. Federal Information Processing Standards, National Bureau of Standards, US Department of Commerce.

Pushpa & Raj. (2018). Performance Enhancement of Fog Computing Using SDN and NFV Technologies. *Fog Computing: Concepts, Frameworks and Technologies.*

Qian, Jiang, & Qiu. (2009). A New Image Encryption Scheme Based on DES Algorithm and Chua's Circuit. *International Workshop on Imaging Systems and Techniques Shenzhen, China, IST 2009.*

Qin, F., Tang, X. J., & Cheng, Z. K. (2012, July). Application and research of multi-label Naïve Bayes Classifier. In *Intelligent Control and Automation (WCICA), 2012 10th World Congress on* (pp. 764-768). IEEE.

Rahimzadeh, M., & Attar, A. (2020). *A new modified deep convolutional neural network for detecting COVID-19 from X-ray images.* arXiv preprint arXiv:2004.08052.

Rahman, C. A., Badawy, W., Tn, C., Radmanesh, A., & Tp, C. (2003). *A Real Time Vehicle's License Plate Recognition System.* Academic Press.

Rahnemoonfar, M., & Sheppard, C. (2017). Deep count: Fruit counting based on deep simulated learning. *Sensors (Basel), 17*(4), 905.

Rajpal, S., Kumar, N., & Rajpal, A. (2020). *Cov-elm classifier: An extreme learning machine based identification of covid-19 using chest-ray images.* arXiv preprint arXiv:2007.08637.

Ramasamy, P., Ranganathan, V., Kadry, S., Damaševičius, R., & Blažauskas, T. (2019). An image encryption scheme based on block scrambling, modified zigzag transformation and key generation using enhanced logistic—Tent map. *Entropy (Basel, Switzerland), 21*(7), 656. doi:10.3390/e21070656 PMID:33267370

Rana, M. S., Gudla, C., & Sung, A. H. (2018). Evaluating Machine Learning Models for Android Malware Detection: A Comparison Study. In *Proceedings of the 2018 VII International Conference on Network, Communication and Computing* (pp. 17-21). ACM.

Rana, M. S., & Sung, A. H. (2018). Malware Analysis on Android using Supervised Machine Learning Techniques. *International Journal of Computer and Communication Engineering, 7*(4), 178–188. doi:10.17706/IJCCE.2018.7.4.178-188

Raschka, S. (2018). *Model evaluation, model selection, and algorithm selection in machine learning.* arXiv preprint arXiv:1811.12808.

Rashed, S. K., Frid, J., & Aits, S. (2020). *English dictionaries, gold and silver standard corpora for biomedical natural language processing related to SARS-CoV-2 and COVID-19.* arXiv preprint arXiv:2003.09865.

Rathi, D., & Jindal, R. (2018). *DroidMark: A Tool for Android Malware Detection using Taint Analysis and Bayesian Network.* arXiv preprint arXiv:1805.06620.

Recognition, N. E. (2021). *Applications and Use Cases.* Retrieved 23 March 2021, from https://towardsdatascience.com/named-entity-recognition-applications-and-use-cases-acdbf57d595e

Ren, S., He, K., Girshick, R., & Sun, J. (2015). *Faster r-cnn: Towards real-time object detection with region proposal networks.* arXiv preprint arXiv:1506.01497.

Ren, J., Han, J., & Dalla Mura, M. (2016). Special issue on multimodal data fusion for multidimensional signal processing. *Multidimensional Systems and Signal Processing, 27*(4), 801–805. doi:10.100711045-016-0441-0

Ren, J., Jiang, J., Wang, D., & Ipson, S. (2010). Fusion of intensity and inter-component chromatic difference for effective and robust colour edge detection. *IET Image Processing, 4*(4), 294–301. doi:10.1049/iet-ipr.2009.0071

Ren, X., & Malik, J. (2003, October). *Learning a classification model for segmentation.* IEEE. doi:10.1109/ICCV.2003.1238308

Reynolds, D. (2015). Gaussian mixture models. Encyclopedia of Biometrics, 827-832.

Rijmen, V., & Daemen, J. (2001). Advanced encryption standard. Proceedings of Federal Information Processing Standards Publications, 19–22.

Rivest, Dertouzos, & Adleman. (1978). On Data Banks and Privacy Homomorphisms. *Foundations of Secure Computation*.

Roshan, S. M., Karsaz, A., Vejdani, A. H., & Roshan, Y. M. (2020). Fine-tuning of pre- trained convolutional neural networks for diabetic retinopathy screening: A clinical study. *International Journal on Computer Science and Engineering*, *21*(4), 564–573.

Ryu, E.-K., Kim, D.-S., & Yoo, K.-Y. (2015). On elliptic curve based untraceable RFID authentication protocols. In *Proceedings of the 3rd ACM Workshop on Information Hiding and Multimedia Security* (pp. 147–153). ACM. 10.1145/2756601.2756610

Sadeghyan. (2018). *A New Robust Feature Selection Method using Variance-Based Sensitivity Analysis*. Academic Press.

Saedi, S. I., & Khosravi, H. (2020). A deep neural network approach towards real-time on-branch fruit recognition for precision horticulture. *Expert Systems with Applications*, *159*, 113594.

Saez, J. A., Derrac, J., Luengo, J., & Herrera, F. (2014). Statistical Computation of Feature Weighting Schemes through Data Estimation for Nearest Neighbor Classifiers. *Pattern Recognition*, *47*(12), 3941–3948. Advance online publication. doi:10.1016/j.patcog.2014.06.012

Safkhani, M., & Bagheri, N. (2016). Generalized Desynchronization Attack on UMAP: Application to RCIA, KMAP, SLAP and SASI + protocols. International Association for Cryptologic Research, 905–912.

Safkhani, M., & Bagheri, N. (2017). Passive secret disclosure attack on an ultralightweight authentication protocol for Internet of Things. *The Journal of Supercomputing*, *73*(8), 3579–3585. doi:10.100711227-017-1959-0

Safkhani, M., & Shariat, M. (2018). Implementation of secret disclosure attack against two IoT lightweight authentication protocols. *The Journal of Supercomputing*, *74*(11), 6220–6235. Advance online publication. doi:10.100711227-018-2538-8

Sagonas, C., Tzimiropoulos, G., Zafeiriou, S., & Pantic, M. (2013). A semi-automatic methodology for facial landmark annotation. *Proceedings of IEEE Int'l Conf. Computer Vision and Pattern Recognition (CVPR-W), 5th Workshop on Analysis and Modeling of Faces and Gestures (AMFG 2013)*. 10.1109/CVPRW.2013.132

Sahu, H., & Hungyo, M. (2018). Introduction to SDN and NFV. In *Innovations in Software-Defined Networking and Network Functions Virtualization* (pp. 1–25). IGI Global.

Sahu, H., & Singh, N. (2018). Software-Defined Storage. In *Innovations in Software-Defined Networking and Network Functions Virtualization* (pp. 268–290). IGI Global.

Sahu, P., Chug, A., Singh, A. P., Singh, D., & Singh, R. P. (2020). Implementation of CNNs for Crop Diseases Classification: A Comparison of Pre-trained Model and Training from Scratch. *IJCSNS*, *20*(10), 206.

Salakhutdinov, R., & Hinton, G. (2009). Semantic hashing. *International Journal of Approximate Reasoning*, *50*(7), 969–978. doi:10.1016/j.ijar.2008.11.006

Salehi, S. A., Razzaque, M. A., Naraei, P., & Farrokhtala, A. (2013). Detection of sinkhole attack in wireless sensor networks. *Proc. IEEE Int. Conf. Space Sci. Commun. (IconSpace)*, 361-365. doi:10.1109/IconSpace.2013.6599496

Sankpal, & Vijaya. (2014). Image Encryption Using Chaotic Maps: A Survey. In *Fifth International Conference on Signals and Image Processing*. IEEE.

Santos, C. D., & Zadrozny, B. (2014). Learning character-level representations for part- of-speech tagging. In *Proceedings of the 31st International Conference on Machine Learning (ICML-14)* (pp. 1818-1826). Academic Press.

Santos, T. T., de Souza, L. L., dos Santos, A. A., & Avila, S. (2020). Grape detection, segmentation, and tracking using deep neural networks and three-dimensional association. *Computers and Electronics in Agriculture*, *170*, 105247.

Sarfraz, M., Ahmed, M. J., & Ghazi, S. A. (2003). Saudi Arabian License Plate Recognition System. In *IEEE International Conference on Electronic Circuit system* (pp. 898–901). IEEE.

Sari, A. (2018). Context-Aware Intelligent Systems for Fog Computing Environments for Cyber-Threat Intelligence. In Fog Computing: Concepts, Frameworks and Technologies. Academic Press.

Sarvamangala, D. R., & Kulkarni, R. V. (2021). Convolutional neural networks in medical image understanding: A survey. *Evolutionary Intelligence*, 1–22. PMID:33425040

Sathyanarayana, S. V., Kumar, M. A., & Bhat, K. H. (2011). Symmetric Key Image Encryption Scheme with Key Sequences Derived from Random Sequence of Cyclic Elliptic Curve Points. *International Journal of Network Security*, *12*(3), 137–150.

Savary, S., Ficke, A., Aubertot, J.-N., & Hollier, C. (2012). *Crop losses due to diseases and their implications for global food production losses and food security*. Springer.

Schneier, B. (1993). Description of a new variable-length key, 64-bit block cipher (Blowfish). *International Workshop on Fast Software Encryption*, 191–204.

Schneier, B., Kelsey, J., Whiting, D., Wagner, D., Hall, C., & Ferguson, N. (1999). *The Twofish encryption algorithm: a 128-bit block cipher*. John Wiley & Sons, Inc.

Seetharaman, V., Sathyakhala, A., Vidhya, N. L. S., & Sunder, P. (2004). License plate recognition system using hybrid neural networks. In IEEE Annual Meetig Fuzzy Information (pp. 363–366). doi:10.1109/NAFIPS.2004.1336309

Selvakumar, Karuppiah, Sairamesh, Islam, & Hassan, Fortino, & Choo. (2019). Intelligent temporal classification and fuzzy rough set-based feature selection algorithm for intrusion detection system in WSNs. *Inf. Sci.*, *497*, 77–90.

Sen Pan, M., Xiong, Q., & Yan, J. B. (2009). A new method for correcting vehicle license plate tilt. *International Journal of Automation and Computing*, *6*(2), 210–216. doi:10.100711633-009-0210-8

Sen Pan, M., Yan, J. B., & Xiao, Z. H. (2008). Vehicle license plate character segmentation. *International Journal of Automation and Computing*, *5*(4), 425–432. doi:10.100711633-008-0425-0

Sen, P. C., Hajra, M., & Ghosh, M. (2020). Supervised classification algorithms in machine learning: A survey and review. In *Emerging technology in modelling and graphics* (pp. 99–111). Springer. doi:10.1007/978-981-13-7403-6_11

Sermanet, P., Eigen, D., Zhang, X., Mathieu, M., Fergus, R., & LeCun, Y. (2013). *Overfeat: Integrated recognition, localization and detection using convolutional networks*. arXiv preprint arXiv:1312.6229.

Sethi, K., Chaudhary, S. K., Tripathy, B. K., & Bera, P. (2018, January). A Novel Malware Analysis Framework for Malware Detection and Classification using Machine Learning Approach. In *Proceedings of the 19th International Conference on Distributed Computing and Networking* (p. 49). ACM. 10.1145/3154273.3154326

Sethy, P. K., Behera, S. K., Ratha, P. K., & Biswas, P. (2020). *Detection of coronavirus disease (COVID-19) based on deep features and support vector machine*. Academic Press.

Shahriar, H., Islam, M., & Clincy, V. (2017, March). Android malware detection using permission analysis. In *SouthEastCon 2017* (pp. 1–6). IEEE. doi:10.1109/SECON.2017.7925347

Shalaginov, A., Banin, S., Dehghantanha, A., & Franke, K. (2018). Machine learning aided static malware analysis: A survey and tutorial. In *Cyber Threat Intelligence* (pp. 7–45). Springer. doi:10.1007/978-3-319-73951-9_2

Shan, B. (2011). Vehicle License Plate Recognition Based on Text-line Construction and Multilevel RBF Neural Network. *Journal of Computers (Taiwan)*, *6*(2), 246–253. doi:10.4304/jcp.6.2.246-253

Shannon, C. E. (1948). A mathematical theory of communication. *The Bell System Technical Journal*, *27*(3), 379–423. doi:10.1002/j.1538-7305.1948.tb01338.x

Shapiro, V., & Gluhchev, G. (2004). Multinational license plate recognition system: Segmentation and classification. In *Proceedings - International Conference on Pattern Recognition* (Vol. 4, pp. 352–355). Academic Press.

Shargh. (2009). Using artificial immune system on implementation of intrusion detection systems. In *2009 Third UKSim European Symposium on Computer Modeling and Simulation*, (pp. 164-168). IEEE.

Sharif, M., Khan, M. A., Iqbal, Z., Azam, M. F., Lali, M. I. U., & Javed, M. Y. (2018). Detection and classification of citrus diseases in agriculture based on optimized weighted segmentation and feature selection. *Computers and Electronics in Agriculture*, *150*, 220–234.

Sharma, A., Agrawal, A. K., Kumar, B., & Khatri, P. 2018, March. Forensic Analysis of a Virtual Android Phone. In *International Conference on Communication, Networks and Computing* (pp. 286-297). Springer.

Shastri, M., Roy, S., & Mittal, M. (2019). *Stock Price Prediction using Artificial Neural Model: An Application of Big Data*. ICST Transactions on Scalable Information Systems.

Shen, H., Shen, J., Khan, M. K., & Lee, J. H. (2017). Efficient RFID Authentication Using Elliptic Curve Cryptography for the Internet of Things. *Wireless Personal Communications*, *96*(4), 5253–5266. doi:10.100711277-016-3739-1

Shen, J., Du, Y., Wang, W., & Li, X. (2014). Lazy random walks for superpixel segmentation. *IEEE Transactions on Image Processing*, *23*(4), 1451–1462. doi:10.1109/TIP.2014.2302892 PMID:24565788

Shen, Y., He, X., Gao, J., Deng, L., & Mesnil, G. (2014b). Learning Semantic Representations Using Convolutional Neural Networks for Web Search. *Proceedings of WWW 2014*. 10.1145/2567948.2577348

Shi, B., Bai, X., & Yao, C. (2016). An end-to-end trainable neural network for image-based sequence recognition and its application to scene text recognition. *IEEE Transactions on Pattern Analysis and Machine Intelligence*, *39*(11), 2298–2304. doi:10.1109/TPAMI.2016.2646371 PMID:28055850

Shi, C., Wang, Y., Wang, C., & Xiao, B. (2017). Ground-based cloud detection using graph model built upon superpixels. *IEEE Geoscience and Remote Sensing Letters*, *14*(5), 719–723. doi:10.1109/LGRS.2017.2676007

Shi, J., & Malik, J. (2000). Normalized cuts and image segmentation. *IEEE Transactions on Pattern Analysis and Machine Intelligence*, *22*(8), 888–905. doi:10.1109/34.868688

Shi, X., Zhao, W., & Shen, Y. (2005). Automatic License Plate Recognition System Based on Color Image Processing. In *International Conference on Computational Science and Its Applications* (pp. 1159–1168). 10.1007/11424925_121

Shone, N., Ngoc, T. N., Phai, V. D., & Shi, Q. (2018). A Deep Learning Approach to Network Intrusion Detection. *IEEE Transactions on Emerging Topics in Computational Intelligence*, *2*(1), 41–50.

Simonyan, K., & Zisserman, A. (2014). *Very deep convolutional networks for large-scale image recognition*. arXiv preprint arXiv:1409.1556.

Singhal, T. (2020). A Review of Coronavirus Disease-2019 (COVID-19). *Indian Journal of Pediatrics*, *87*(4), 281–286. doi:10.100712098-020-03263-6

Singh, N., & Pandey, Y. (2013). Dendritic Cell Algorithm and Dempster Belief Theory Using Improved Intrusion Detection System. *International Journal of Advanced Research in Computer Science and Software Engineering*, *3*(7).

Sitaram, S., Chandu, K. R., Rallabandi, S. K., & Black, A. W. (2019). *A survey of code-switched speech and language processing.* arXiv preprint arXiv:1904.00784.

Skogan, W. G. (2004). Community Policing: Common Impediments to Success: The Past, Present and Future. In *Community Policing: The Past, Present and Future*. The Annie E. Casey Foundation.

Skrobek, A. (2007). Cryptanalysis of chaotic stream cipher. *Physics Letters. [Part A]*, *363*(1–2), 84–90. doi:10.1016/j.physleta.2006.10.081

Socher, R., Huval, B., Manning, C. D., & Ng, A. Y. (2012, July). Semantic compositionality through recursive matrix-vector spaces. In *Proceedings of the 2012 joint conference on empirical methods in natural language processing and computational natural language learning* (pp. 1201-1211). Association for Computational Linguistics.

Soderland, S. (1997, August). Learning to Extract Text-Based Information from the World Wide Web. *KDD: Proceedings / International Conference on Knowledge Discovery & Data Mining. International Conference on Knowledge Discovery & Data Mining*, *97*, 251–254.

Sohal, A. S., Sandhu, R., Sood, S. K., & Chang, V. (2018). A Cybersecurity Framework to Identify Malicious Edge Device in Fog Computing and Cloud-of-Things Environments. *Computers & Security.*

Soia, A., Konnikova, O., & Konnikov, E. (2019). The Internet of Things. *Proceedings of the 33rd International Business Information Management Association Conference, IBIMA 2019: Education Excellence and Innovation Management through Vision 2020.*

Spampinato, G., & Curti, S. (2019). *Method for advanced and low cost cross traffic alert, related processing system, cross traffic alert system and vehicle.* U.S. Patent Application 10/242,272.

Spasic, I. (2018, February). Acronyms as an Integral Part of Multi-Word Term Recognition – A Token of Appreciation. *IEEE Access: Practical Innovations, Open Solutions*, *6*, 8351–8363. doi:10.1109/ACCESS.2018.2807122

Srivastava, Rajitha, & Agarwal. (2017). An efficient image classification using bag-of-words based on SURF and texture features. In *2017 14th IEEE India Council International Conference (INDICON)*, (pp. 1-6). IEEE.

State Farm's Dataset. (n.d.). https://www.kaggle.com/c/state-farmdistracted-driver-detection/data

Statista Research Department. (2019). *Internet of Things (IoT) Connected Devices Installed Base Worldwide from 2015 to 2025.* https://www.statista.com/statistics/471264/iot-number-of-connected-devices-worldwide/

Statistics, M., & Report, T. AV-TEST. (2019, April 25). Retrieved from https://www.av-test.org/en/statistics/malware/

St-Charles, P.-L., & Bilodeau, G.-A. (2014). Improving background subtraction using local binary similarity patterns. In *Applications of Computer Vision (WACV), 2014 IEEE Winter Conference on, 2014.* IEEE. 10.1109/WACV.2014.6836059

St-Charles, P.-L., Bilodeau, G.-A., & Bergevin, R. (2014). Flexible background subtraction with self-balanced local sensitivity. *Proceedings of the IEEE Conference on Computer Vision and Pattern Recognition Workshops*, 408-413. 10.1109/CVPRW.2014.67

Stinson, D. R. (2006). *The RSA Cryptosystem and Factoring Integers in Cryptography Theory and Practice.* Chapman & Hall/CRC.

Stojmenovic, I., & Wen, S. (2014). The Fog Computing Paradigm: Scenarios and Security Issues. *2014 Federated Conference on Computer Science and Information Systems, FedCSIS 2014, 2*, 1–8.

Stutz, D., Hermans, A., & Leibe, B. (2018). Superpixels: An evaluation of the state-of-the-art. *Computer Vision and Image Understanding*, *166*, 1–27. doi:10.1016/j.cviu.2017.03.007

Suganya, G., Premalatha, M., Bharathiraja, S., & Agrawal, R. (2017). A low cost design to detect drowsiness of driver. *International Journal of Civil Engineering and Technology*, *8*, 1138–1149.

Sujatha, R., Chatterjee, J. M., Jhanjhi, N. Z., & Brohi, S. N. (2021). Performance of deep learning vs machine learning in plant leaf disease detection. *Microprocessors and Microsystems*, *80*, 103615. doi:10.1016/j.micpro.2020.103615

Suneja, K., Dua, S., & Dua, M. (2019, March). A review of chaos based image encryption. In *2019 3rd International Conference on Computing Methodologies and Communication (ICCMC)* (pp. 693-698). IEEE. 10.1109/ICCMC.2019.8819860

Sun, Xu, Liang, & Zhou. (2018). An intrusion detection model for wireless sensor networks with an improved V-detector algorithm. *IEEE Sensors Journal*, *18*(5), 1971–1984.

Suri, S., & Vijay, R. (n.d.a). A Bi-objective Genetic Algorithm Optimization of Chaos-DNA Based Hybrid Approach. *Journal of Intelligent Systems.*

Suri, S., & Vijay, R. (n.d.b). A Pareto-optimal evolutionary approach of image encryption using coupled map lattice and DNA. *Neural Computing and Applications*, 1-15.

Suri, S., & Vijay, R. (2019). A synchronous intertwining logistic map-DNA approach for color image encryption. *Journal of Ambient Intelligence and Humanized Computing*, *10*(6), 2277–2290. doi:10.100712652-018-0825-0

Suri, S., & Vijay, R. (2019a). A bi-objective genetic algorithm optimization of chaos-DNA based hybrid approach. *Journal of Intelligent Systems*, *28*(2), 333–346. doi:10.1515/jisys-2017-0069

Suri, S., & Vijay, R. (2019b). A Pareto-optimal evolutionary approach of image encryption using coupled map lattice and DNA. *Neural Computing & Applications*, 1–15.

Suri, S., & Vijay, R. (2020). A coupled map lattice-based image encryption approach using DNA and bi-objective genetic algorithm. *International Journal of Information and Computer Security*, *12*(2–3), 199–216. doi:10.1504/IJICS.2020.105156

Szegedy, C., Reed, S., Erhan, D., Anguelov, D., & Ioffe, S. (2014). *Scalable, high-quality object detection.* arXiv preprint arXiv:1412.1441.

Szegedy, C., Vanhoucke, V., Ioffe, S., Shlens, J., & Wojna, Z. (2015). *Rethinking the Inception Architecture for Computer Vision.* arXiv:1512.00567.

Szegedy, C., Liu, W., Jia, Y., Sermanet, P., Reed, S., Anguelov, D., Erhan, D., Vanhoucke, V., & Rabinovich, A. (2015). Going deeper with convolutions. *Proceedings of the IEEE conference on computer vision and pattern recognition*, 1-9.

Szegedy, C., Liu, W., Jia, Y., Sermanet, P., Reed, S., Anguelov, D., ... Rabinovich, A. (2015). Going deeper with convolutions. *Proceedings of the IEEE Conference on Computer Vision and Pattern Recognition*, 1–9.

Talaviya, T., Shah, D., Patel, N., Yagnik, H., & Shah, M. (2020). Implementation of artificial intelligence in agriculture for optimisation of irrigation and application of pesticides and herbicides. *Artificial Intelligence in Agriculture*, *4*, 58–73. doi:10.1016/j.aiia.2020.04.002

Tan, L., & Wang, N. (2010). Future Internet: The Internet of Things. *ICACTE 2010 - 2010 3rd International Conference on Advanced Computer Theory and Engineering, Proceedings.*

Tan, M., & Le, Q. V. (2020). *EfficientNet: Rethinking Model Scaling for Convolutional Neural Networks* arXiv:1905.11946.

Tang, D., Fu, H., & Cao, X. (2012, July). Topology preserved regular superpixel. In *2012 IEEE International Conference on Multimedia and Expo* (pp. 765-768). IEEE. 10.1109/ICME.2012.184

Tang, J., & Wang, K. (2018, February). Personalized top-n sequential recommendation via convolutional sequence embedding. In *Proceedings of the Eleventh ACM International Conference on Web Search and Data Mining* (pp. 565-573). ACM. 10.1145/3159652.3159656

Tan, M., & Le, Q. (2019). Efficientnet: Rethinking model scaling for convolutional neural networks. *International Conference on Machine Learning*, 6105–6114.

Tavazoei, M. S., & Haeri, M. (2007). Comparison of different one-dimensional maps as chaotic search pattern in chaos optimization algorithms. *Applied Mathematics and Computation*, *187*(2), 1076–1085. doi:10.1016/j.amc.2006.09.087

Thomas, A., & Sangeetha, S. (2019). An innovative hybrid approach for extracting named entities from unstructured text data. *Computational Intelligence*, *35*(4), 799–826. doi:10.1111/coin.12214

Thome, N., Vacavant, A., Robinault, L., & Miguet, S. (2011). A cognitive and video-based approach for multinational License Plate Recognition. *Machine Vision and Applications*, *22*(2), 389–407. doi:10.100700138-010-0246-3

Tian, Y., Chen, G., & Li, J. (2012). A new ultralightweight RFID authentication protocol with permutation. *IEEE Communications Letters*, *16*(5), 702–705. doi:10.1109/LCOMM.2012.031212.120237

Times Of India. (2021). Retrieved 23 March 2021, from https://epaper.timesgroup.com/TOI/TimesOfIndia/index.html?a=c

Tkachenko, M., & Simanovsky, A. (2012, September). Named entity recognition: Exploring features. In KONVENS (pp. 118-127). Academic Press.

Todorovic, S., & Nechyba, M. C. (2005). Dynamic trees for unsupervised segmentation and matching of image regions. *IEEE Transactions on Pattern Analysis and Machine Intelligence*, *27*(11), 1762–1777. doi:10.1109/TPAMI.2005.219 PMID:16285375

Tong, X. J., Zhang, M., Wang, Z., Liu, Y., Xu, H., & Ma, J. (2015). A fast encryption algorithm of color image based on four-dimensional chaotic system. *Journal of Visual Communication and Image Representation*, *33*, 219–234. doi:10.1016/j.jvcir.2015.09.014

Tong, X. J., Zhang, M., Wang, Z., & Ma, J. (2016). A joint color image encryption and compression scheme based on hyper-chaotic system. *Nonlinear Dynamics*, *84*(4), 2333–2356. doi:10.100711071-016-2648-x

Too, E. C., Yujian, L., Gadosey, P. K., Njuki, S., & Essaf, F. (2020). Performance analysis of nonlinear activation function in convolution neural network for image classification. *International Journal on Computer Science and Engineering*, *21*(4), 522–535.

Tripathy, A. K., Das, T. K., & Chowdhary, C. L. (2020). Monitoring quality of tap water in cities using IoT. In *Emerging Technologies for Agriculture and Environment* (pp. 107–113). Springer. doi:10.1007/978-981-13-7968-0_8

Tur, G., Deng, L., Hakkani-Tür, D., & He, X. (2012, March). Towards deeper understanding: Deep convex networks for semantic utterance classification. In *2012 IEEE international conference on acoustics, speech and signal processing (ICASSP)* (pp. 5045- 5048). IEEE.

Turkoglu, M. (2021). COVID-19 Detection System Using Chest CT Images and Multiple Kernels-Extreme Learning Machine Based on Deep Neural Network. *IRBM*.

Tushara & Vardhini. (2016). Wireless vehicle alert and collision prevention system design using atmel microcontroller. In *2016 International 22 Conference on Electrical, Electronics, and Optimization Techniques (ICEEOT),* (pp. 2784-2787). IEEE.

Tu, W. C., Liu, M. Y., Jampani, V., Sun, D., Chien, S. Y., Yang, M. H., & Kautz, J. (2018). Learning superpixels with segmentation-aware affinity loss. In *Proceedings of the IEEE Conference on Computer Vision and Pattern Recognition* (pp. 568-576). IEEE.

Uehara, M. (2018). *Mist Computing: Linking Cloudlet to Fogs*. Studies in Computational Intelligence.

Vacavant, A., Chateau, T., Wilhelm, A., & Lequievre, L. (2012). A benchmark dataset for foreground/background extraction. ACCV 2012, Workshop: Background Models Challenge.

Vafaie & De Jong. (1997, November). *Genetic Algorithms as a Tool for Feature Selection in Machine Learning*. Academic Press.

Van den Bergh, M., Boix, X., Roig, G., & Van Gool, L. (2015). Seeds: Superpixels extracted via energy-driven sampling. *International Journal of Computer Vision, 111*(3), 298–314. doi:10.100711263-014-0744-2

Vaquero, L. M., & Rodero-Merino, L. (2014). Finding Your Way in the Fog: Towards a Comprehensive Definition of Fog Computing. *Computer Communication Review, 44*(5), 27–32.

Verma, S., & Muttoo, S. K. (2016). An Android Malware Detection Framework-based on Permissions and Intents. *Defence Science Journal, 66*(6), 618–623.

Vishwanath, N., Somasundaram, S., Baburajani, T. S., & Nallaperumal, N. K. (2012). A Hybrid Indian License Plate Character Segmentation Algorithm for Automatic License Plate Recognition System. In *IEEE International Conference on Computational Intelligence and Computing Research* (pp. 1–4). 10.1109/ICCIC.2012.6510322

VMware. (2021). https://www.vmware.com/

Volkovs, M. (2015). *Context models for web search personalization*. arXiv preprint arXiv:1502.00527.

Waheed, A., Goyal, M., Gupta, D., Khanna, A., Al-Turjman, F., & Pinheiro, P. R. (2020). CovidGAN: Data augmentation using auxiliary classifier gan for improved covid-19 detection. *IEEE Access: Practical Innovations, Open Solutions, 8*, 91916–91923. doi:10.1109/ACCESS.2020.2994762

Wan, C., Wang, Y., Liu, Y., Ji, J., & Feng, G. (2019). *Composite Feature Extraction and Selection for Text Classification*. IEEE. doi:10.1109/ACCESS.2019.2904602

Wang, X., Liu, W., Chauhan, A., Guan, Y., & Han, J. (2020). *Automatic textual evidence mining in covid-19 literature.* arXiv preprint arXiv:2004.12563.

Wang, X., Song, X., Guan, Y., Li, B., & Han, J. (2020). *Comprehensive named entity recognition on cord-19 with distant or weak supervision.* arXiv preprint arXiv:2003.12218.

Wang, Y., Jodoin, P.-M., Porikli, F., Konrad, J., & Benezeth, Y. (2014). CDnet2014: An expanded change detection benchmark dataset. In *Computer Vision and Pattern Recognition Workshops (CVPRW), 2014 IEEE Conference on, 2014*. IEEE.

Wang, D., Hu, B., Hu, C., Zhu, F., Liu, X., Zhang, J., Wang, B., Xiang, H., Cheng, Z., Xiong, Y., Zhao, Y., Li, Y., Wang, X., & Peng, Z. (2020). Clinical characteristics of 138 hospitalized patients with 2019 novel coronavirus–infected pneumonia in Wuhan, China. *Journal of the American Medical Association, 323*(11), 1061–1069. doi:10.1001/jama.2020.1585 PMID:32031570

Wang, F., Man, L., Wang, B., Xiao, Y., Pan, W., & Lu, X. (2008). Fuzzy-based algorithm for color recognition of license plates. *Pattern Recognition Letters*, *29*(7), 1007–1020. doi:10.1016/j.patrec.2008.01.026

Wang, Fu, & Agrawal. (2013). Gaussian versus uniform distribution for intrusion detection in wireless sensor networks. *IEEE Transactions on Parallel and Distributed Systems*, *24*(2), 342–355.

Wang, H., Peng, X., Xiao, X., & Liu, Y. (2017). BSLIC: Slic superpixels based on boundary term. *Symmetry*, *9*(3), 31. doi:10.3390ym9030031

Wang, H., Wang, Z., & Domingo-Ferrer, J. (2018). Anonymous and Secure Aggregation Scheme in Fog-Based Public Cloud Computing. *Future Generation Computer Systems*, *78*, 712–719.

Wang, H., Xiao, D., Chen, X., & Huang, H. (2018). Cryptanalysis and enhancements of image encryption using combination of the 1D chaotic map. *Signal Processing*, *144*, 444–452. doi:10.1016/j.sigpro.2017.11.005

Wang, L., Wu, X., & Yu, M. (2007). Review of driver fatigue/drowsiness detection methods. *Journal of Biomedical Engineering*, *24*, 245–248.

Wang, M., Liu, X., Gao, Y., Ma, X., & Soomro, N. Q. (2017). Superpixel segmentation: A benchmark. *Signal Processing Image Communication*, *56*, 28–39. doi:10.1016/j.image.2017.04.007

Wang, P., Xu, J., Xu, B., Liu, C., Zhang, H., Wang, F., & Hao, H. (2015). Semantic clustering and convolutional neural network for short text categorization. In *Proceedings of the 53rd Annual Meeting of the Association for Computational Linguistics and the 7th International Joint Conference on Natural Language Processing* (Vol. 2, pp. 352-357). 10.3115/v1/P15-2058

Wang, S., Xing, C., & Liu, D. (2020). Efficient deep convolutional model compression with an active stepwise pruning approach. *International Journal on Computer Science and Engineering*, *22*(4), 420–430.

Wang, Wang, & Xie, Wang, & Agrawal. (2008). Intrusion detection in homogeneous and heterogeneous wireless sensor networks. *IEEE Transactions on Mobile Computing*, *7*(6), 698–711.

Wang, X. (2020). Reliable Customized Privacy-Preserving in Fog Computing. *IEEE International Conference on Communications.*

Wang, Y. R., Lin, W. H., & Horng, S. J. (2011). A sliding window technique for efficient license plate localization based on discrete wavelet transform. *Expert Systems with Applications*, *38*(4), 3142–3146. doi:10.1016/j.eswa.2010.08.106

Wang, Yan, Wang, & Liu. (2011). An integrated intrusion detection system for cluster-based wireless sensor networks. *Expert Systems with Applications*, *38*(12), 15234–15243.

Wang, Z., Ren, J., Zhang, D., Sun, M., & Jiang, J. (2018). A deep-learning based feature hybrid framework for spatiotemporal saliency detection inside videos. *Neurocomputing*, *287*, 68–83. doi:10.1016/j.neucom.2018.01.076

Wanniarachchi, W. K. I. L., Sonnadara, D. U. J., & Jayananda, M. K. (2007). License Plate Identification Based on Image Processing Techniques. In *Second International Conference on Industrial and Information Systems, ICIIS 2007* (pp. 8–11). 10.1109/ICIINFS.2007.4579205

Wazid & Das. (2016). An efficient hybrid anomaly detection scheme using k-means clustering for wireless sensor networks. *Wireless Personal Communications*, *90*(4), 1971–2000.

Wazid & Das. (2017). A secure group_based blackhole node detection scheme for hierarchical wireless sensor networks. *Wireless Personal Communications*, *94*(3), 1165–1191.

Wazid, Das, Kumari, & Khan. (2016). Design of sinkhole node detection mechanism for hierarchical wireless sensor networks. *Secur. Commun. Netw., 9*(17), 4596-4614.

West, J., Ventura, D., & Warnick, S. (2007). *Spring Research Presentation: A Theoretical Foundation for Inductive Transfer*. Brigham Young University, College of Physical and Mathematical Sciences.

Weston, J., Chopra, S., & Adams, K. (2014). #tagspace: Semantic embeddings from hashtags. In *Proceedings of the 2014 conference on empirical methods in natural language processing (EMNLP)* (pp. 1822-1827). 10.3115/v1/D14-1194

Wolf, A., Swift, J. B., Swinney, H. L., & Vastano, J. A. (1985). Determining Lyapunov exponents from a time series. *Physica D. Nonlinear Phenomena, 16*(3), 285–317. doi:10.1016/0167-2789(85)90011-9

World Health Organisation. (2021). *WHO coronavirus disease (covid-19) dashboard*. Author.

Wu, H. H. P., Chen, H. H., Wu, R. J., & Shen, D. F. (2006). License plate extraction in low resolution video. In *Proceedings - International Conference on Pattern Recognition* (Vol. 1, pp. 824–827). Academic Press.

Wu, Y., Noonan, J. P., Yang, G., & Jin, H. (2012). Image encryption using the two-dimensional logistic chaotic map. *Journal of Electronic Imaging, 21*(1), 013014. doi:10.1117/1.JEI.21.1.013014

Wu, Z., Gao, Y., Li, L., Xue, J., & Li, Y. (2019). Semantic segmentation of high- resolution remote sensing images using fully convolutional network with adaptive threshold. *Connection Science, 31*(2), 169–184. doi:10.1080/09540091.2018.1510902

Wu, Z., Shen, C., & Hengel, A. V. D. (2019). Wider or Deeper: Revisiting the ResNet Model for Visual Recognition. *Pattern Recognition, 90*, 119–133.

Xiao, T., Xu, Y., Yang, K., Zhang, J., Peng, Y., & Zhang, Z. (2015). The application of two-level attention models in deep convolutional neural network for fine-grained image classification. In *Proceedings of the IEEE conference on computer vision and pattern recognition* (pp. 842-850).

Xiao, X., Zhou, Y., & Gong, Y. J. (2018). Content-adaptive superpixel segmentation. *IEEE Transactions on Image Processing, 27*(6), 2883–2896. doi:10.1109/TIP.2018.2810541 PMID:29570089

Xin, Y. (2018). Machine Learning and Deep Learning Methods for Cybersecurity. *IEEE Access: Practical Innovations, Open Solutions*.

Xiong, C., & Huang, W. (2009). License Plate Location Based on Compound Mathematical Morphology. In *2009 Third International Conference on Genetic and Evolutionary Computing* (pp. 701–704). IEEE. 10.1109/WGEC.2009.134

Xu, B., & Meng, X. (n.d.). *A deep learning algorithm using CT images to screen for Corona Virus Disease (COVID-19)*. Preprint.

Xu, L., Li, Z., Li, J., & Hua, W. (2016). A novel bit-level image encryption algorithm based on chaotic maps. *Optics and Lasers in Engineering, 78*, 17–25. doi:10.1016/j.optlaseng.2015.09.007

Xu, X., Jiang, X., Ma, C., Du, P., Li, X., Lv, S., Yu, L., Ni, Q., Chen, Y., Su, J., Lang, G., Li, Y., Zhao, H., Liu, J., Xu, K., Ruan, L., Sheng, J., Qiu, Y., Wu, W., ... Li, L. (2020). A deep learning system to screen novel coronavirus disease 2019 pneumonia. *Engineering, 6*(10), 1122–1129. doi:10.1016/j.eng.2020.04.010 PMID:32837749

Xu, Y., & Uberbacher, E. C. (1997). 2D image segmentation using minimum spanning trees. *Image and Vision Computing, 15*(1), 47–57. doi:10.1016/S0262-8856(96)01105-5

Yadav, V., & Bethard, S. (2019). *A survey on recent advances in named entity recognition from deep learning models*. arXiv preprint arXiv:1910.11470.

Yadav, M., Purwar, R. K., & Mittal, M. (2018). Handwritten Hindi character recognition: A review. *IET Image Processing, 12*(11), 1919–1933. doi:10.1049/iet-ipr.2017.0184

Yan, Y., Ren, J., Li, Y., Windmill, J., & Ijomah, W. (2015). Fusion of dominant colour and spatial layout features for effective image retrieval of coloured logos and trademarks. In *Multimedia Big Data (BigMM), 2015 IEEE International Conference on, 2015*. IEEE. 10.1109/BigMM.2015.43

Yan, Z., Piramuthu, R., Jagadeesh, V., Di, W., & Decoste, D. (2019). *Hierarchical deep convolutional neural network for image classification*. U.S. Patent 10,387,773.

Yan, D., Hongqing, M., Jilin, L., & Langang, L. (2001). A High Performance License Plate Recognition System Based On The Web Technique. In *IEEE International Conference on Intelligent* (pp. 325–329). IEEE.

Yang, F., Sun, Q., Jin, H., & Zhou, Z. (2020). Superpixel Segmentation with Fully Convolutional Networks. In *Proceedings of the IEEE/CVF Conference on Computer Vision and Pattern Recognition* (pp. 13964-13973). IEEE.

Yang, J., & Li, J. 2017.Application of deep convolution neural network. *Proceedings of 14th International Computer Conference on Wavelet Active Media Technology and Information Processing (ICCWAMTIP)*, 229-232.

Yang, M., Bourbakis, N., & Li, S. (2004). Data-image-video encryption. *IEEE Potentials, 23*(3), 28–34. doi:10.1109/MP.2004.1341784

Yang, S., Lei, X., Liu, Z., & Sui, G. (2021). An efficient local stereo matching method based on an adaptive exponentially weighted moving average filter in SLIC space. *IET Image Processing*, ipr2.12140. doi:10.1049/ipr2.12140

Yang, T., Yang, L.-B., & Yang, C.-M. (1998). Cryptanalyzing chaotic secure communications using return maps. *Physics Letters. [Part A], 245*(6), 495–510. doi:10.1016/S0375-9601(98)00425-3

Yan, Y., Ren, J., Li, Y., Windmill, J. F., Ijomah, W., & Chao, K.-M. (2016). Adaptive fusion of color and spatial features for noise-robust retrieval of colored logo and trademark images. *Multidimensional Systems and Signal Processing, 27*(4), 945–968. doi:10.100711045-016-0382-7

Yan, Y., Ren, J., Sun, G., Zhao, H., Han, J., Li, X., Marshall, S., & Zhan, J. (2018). Unsupervised image saliency detection with Gestalt-laws guided optimization and visual attention based refinement. *Pattern Recognition, 79*, 65–78. doi:10.1016/j.patcog.2018.02.004

Yan, Y., Ren, J., Zhao, H., Sun, G., Wang, Z., Zheng, J., Marshall, S., & Soraghan, J. (2018). Cognitive fusion of thermal and visible imagery for effective detection and tracking of pedestrians in videos. *Cognitive Computation, 10*(1), 94–104. doi:10.100712559-017-9529-6

Yaseen, Q., Jararweh, Y., Al-Ayyoub, M., & Al Dwairi, M. (2017). Collusion Attacks in Internet of Things: Detection and Mitigation Using a Fog Based Model. *SAS 2017 - 2017 IEEE Sensors Applications Symposium, Proceedings.*

Yaseen, Q. (2018). Collusion Attacks Mitigation in Internet of Things: A Fog Based Model. *Multimedia Tools and Applications, 77*(14), 18249–18268.

Yee, T. H., & Lau, P. Y. (2018). Mobile vehicle crash detection system. In *2018 International Workshop on Advanced Image Technology (IWAIT)*, (pp. 1-4). IEEE.

Yeh, K.-H., Lo, N. W., & Winata, E. (2010). An efficient ultralightweight authentication protocol for RFID systems. *Proc. of RFIDSec Asia, 10*, 49–60.

Yih, W. T., He, X., & Meek, C. (2014). Semantic parsing for single-relation question answering. In *Proceedings of the 52nd Annual Meeting of the Association for Computational Linguistics* (*Vol. 2*, pp. 643-648). Academic Press.

Yin, J., Wang, T., Du, Y., Liu, X., Zhou, L., & Yang, J. (2021). SLIC Superpixel Segmentation for Polarimetric SAR Images. *IEEE Transactions on Geoscience and Remote Sensing*, 1–17. doi:10.1109/TGRS.2020.3047126

Yoo, S. H., Geng, H., Chiu, T. L., Yu, S. K., Cho, D. C., Heo, J., . . . Lee, H. (2020). Deep learning-based decision-tree classifier for COVID-19 diagnosis from chest X-ray imaging. *Frontiers in Medicine, 7*, 427.

Young, L.-S. (1982). Dimension, entropy and Lyapunov exponents. *Ergodic Theory and Dynamical Systems*, *2*(1), 109–124. doi:10.1017/S0143385700009615

Zabalza, J., Ren, J., Zheng, J., Zhao, H., Qing, C., Yang, Z., Du, P., & Marshall, S. (2016). Novel segmented stacked autoencoder for effective dimensionality reduction and feature extraction in hyperspectral imaging. *Neurocomputing*, *185*, 1–10. doi:10.1016/j.neucom.2015.11.044

Zeiler, M. D., & Fergus, R. (2014). Visualizing and understanding convolutional networks. In *European conference on computer vision*, (pp. 818-833). Springer.

Zhang, X., Zhao, J., & LeCun, Y. (2015). Character-level convolutional networks for text classification. In Advances in neural information processing systems (pp. 649-657). Academic Press.

Zhang, C., Niu, Z., Jiang, P., & Fu, H. (2012). Domain-Specific Term Extraction from Free Texts. *Proceedings of 9th IEEE International Conference on Fuzzy System and Knowledge Discovery (FSKD 2012)*, 1290-1293. 10.1109/FSKD.2012.6234350

Zhang, H., Jiang, L., & Yu, L. (2021). Attribute and instance weighted naive Bayes. *Pattern Recognition*, *111*, 107674.

Zhang, H., Jia, W., He, X., & Wu, Q. (2006). Learning-Based License Plate Detection Using Global and Local Features. In *International Conference. Pattern Recognition*, *2*, 1102–1105.

Zhang, X., Lu, W., Li, F., Zhang, R., & Cheng, J. (2020). A deep neural architecture for sentence semantic matching. *International Journal on Computer Science and Engineering*, *21*(4), 574–582.

Zhang, Y. (2019). APDP: Attack-Proof Personalized Differential Privacy Model for a Smart Home. *IEEE Access: Practical Innovations, Open Solutions*.

Zhang, Y., Hartley, R., Mashford, J., & Burn, S. (2011, November). Superpixels via pseudo-boolean optimization. In *2011 International Conference on Computer Vision* (pp. 1387-1394). IEEE. 10.1109/ICCV.2011.6126393

Zhao, J., Ma, S., Han, W., Yang, Y., & Wang, X. (2012). Research and Implementation of License Plate Recognition Technology. In *2012 24th Chinese Control and Decision Conference (CCDC)* (pp. 3768–3773). Academic Press.

Zhao, H., Li, M., Wu, T., & Yang, F. (2018). Evaluation of Supervised Machine Learning Techniques for Dynamic Malware Detection. *International Journal of Computational Intelligence Systems*, *11*(1), 1153–1169.

Zhao, R., & Mao, K. (2018, April). Fuzzy Bag-of-Words Model for Document Representation. *IEEE Transactions on Fuzzy Systems*, *26*(2), 794–804. doi:10.1109/TFUZZ.2017.2690222

Zhao, W., Fu, Y., Wei, X., & Wang, H. (2018). An improved image semantic segmentation method based on superpixels and conditional random fields. *Applied Sciences (Basel, Switzerland)*, *8*(5), 837. doi:10.3390/app8050837

Zhao, Y. (2000). Mobile phone location determination and its impact on intelligent transportation systems. *IEEE Transactions on Intelligent Transportation Systems*, *1*(1), 55–64.

Zhao, Z. (2014). A secure RFID authentication protocol for healthcare environments using elliptic curve cryptosystem. *Journal of Medical Systems*, *38*(5), 46. doi:10.100710916-014-0046-9 PMID:24756871

Zhao, Z., Bouwmans, T., Zhang, X., & Fang, Y. (2012). A fuzzy background modeling approach for motion detection in dynamic backgrounds. In *Multimedia and signal processing* (pp. 177–185). Springer. doi:10.1007/978-3-642-35286-7_23

Zheng, H., Fu, J., Mei, T., & Luo, J. (2017). Learning multi-attention convolutional neural network for fine-grained image recognition. In *Proceedings of the IEEE international conference on computer vision* (pp. 5209-5217). 10.1109/ICCV.2017.557

Zheng, J., Liu, Y., Ren, J., Zhu, T., Yan, Y., & Yang, H. (2016). Fusion of block and keypoints based approaches for effective copy-move image forgery detection. *Multidimensional Systems and Signal Processing*, *27*(4), 989–1005. doi:10.100711045-016-0416-1

Zhong, N., Li, Y., & Grance, T. (2012, January). Effective Pattern Discovery for Text Mining. *IEEE Transactions on Knowledge and Data Engineering*, *24*(1).

Zhou, X., Yang, C., & Yu, W. (2013). Moving object detection by detecting contiguous outliers in the low-rank representation. *IEEE Transactions on Pattern Analysis and Machine Intelligence*, *35*(3), 597–610. doi:10.1109/TPAMI.2012.132 PMID:22689075

Zhou, Y., Bao, L., & Chen, C. P. (2014). A new 1D chaotic system for image encryption. *Signal Processing*, *97*, 172–182. doi:10.1016/j.sigpro.2013.10.034

Zhou, Y., Cheng, G., Jiang, S., & Dai, M. (2020). Building an Efficient Intrusion Detection System Based on Feature Selection and Ensemble Classifier. *Computer Networks*, 174.

Zhu & Goldberg. (2009). Introduction to semi-supervised learning. *Synthesis Lectures on Artificial Intelligence and Machine Learning, 3*(1), 1-130.

Zhuang, X., Zhu, Y., & Chang, C.-C. (2014). A New Ultralightweight RFID Protocol for Low-Cost Tags: R $$^{} $$ AP. *Wireless Personal Communications*, *79*(3), 1787–1802. doi:10.100711277-014-1958-x

Zhu, X., Zuo, J., & Ren, H. (2020). A modified deep neural network enables identification of foliage under complex background. *Connection Science*, *32*(1), 1–15. doi:10.1080/09540091.2019.1609420

Zhu, Z., Zhang, W., Wong, K., & Yu, H. (2011). A chaos-based symmetric image encryption scheme using a bit-level permutation. *Information Sciences*, *181*(6), 1171–1186. doi:10.1016/j.ins.2010.11.009

Zissis, D., & Lekkas, D. (2012). Addressing Cloud Computing Security Issues. *Future Generation Computer Systems*.

Zitnick, C. L., & Kang, S. B. (2007). Stereo for image-based rendering using image over-segmentation. *International Journal of Computer Vision*, *75*(1), 49–65. doi:10.100711263-006-0018-8

Zoph, B., & Le, Q. V. (2016). *Neural architecture search with reinforcement learning*. arXiv preprint arXiv:1611.01578.

Zunino, R., & Rovetta, S. (2000). Vector quantization for license-plate location and image coding. *IEEE Transactions on Industrial Electronics*, *47*(1), 159–167. doi:10.1109/41.824138

Zwartjes, G. J. (2017). *Adaptive Naive Bayes classification for wireless sensor networks*. University of Twente.

About the Contributors

Mohit Dua is a PhD in Computer Engineering from National Institute of Technology (An Institution of National Importance), Kurukshetra, India. He did his B.Tech. degree with Hons. in Computer Science and Engineering from Kurukshetra University, Kurukshetra, India in 2004 and M.Tech degree in Computer Engineering with distinction from National Institute of Technology(An Institution of National Importance), Kurukshetra, India in 2012. He is working as Assistant Professor in Department of Computer Engineering at NIT, Kurukshetra, India with more than 14 years of academic and research experience. He is a life member of Computer Society of India (CSI) and Indian Society for Technical Education (ISTE). His research interests include Pattern Recognition, Image and Speech processing, Theory of Formal languages and Statistical modeling. He has published more than 50 publications in various reputed international journals/conferences.

Ankit Kumar Jain is presently working as Assistant Professor in National Institute of Technology, Kurukshetra, India. He received Master of technology from Indian Institute of Information Technology Allahabad (IIIT) India and PhD degree from National Institute of Technology, Kurukshetra. His general research interest is in the area of Information and Cyber security, Phishing Website Detection, Web security, Mobile Security, Online Social Network and Machine Learning. He has published many papers in reputed journals and conferences.

* * *

Rajitha B. is working as Asst. Professor in Motilal Nehru National Institute of Technology Allahabad. She has completed Ph.D from MNNIT Allahabad, she received the B.Tech degree, in computer science and engineering from Kamala Institute of Technology Science, Karimnagar, Andhra Pradesh, after that She has completed master degree from Karunya University, Coimbatore, India in CSE. Her current research interest includes Digital image processing, Pattern Recognition, Computer Vision, Algorithms, Compression, Biometrics, Face recognition and Medical Image Processing. She has Published various SCI journals papers and multiple conferences papers.

Shamantha Rai B. is currently working as an Associate Professor and Head of the Information Science & Engineering department at Sahyadri College of Engineering & Management, Mangaluru. He is serving as a reviewer for various reputed journals of ScienceDirect, Springer, etc. His area of interest includes Wireless Networks, Data Analytics, and Blockchain.

Suruchi Chawla is an Assistant Professor, Department of Computer Science, Shaheed Rajguru College of Applied Sciences for Women, University of Delhi, INDIA. She received her PhD degree in 2011 from the Department of Computer Science, University of Delhi, INDIA. Her current research interests are Web Intelligence, Information Retrieval, Machine learning techniques and Deep Learning techniques.

Chiranji Lal Chowdhary is an Associate Professor in the School of Information Technology & Engineering at VIT University, where he has been since 2010. He received a B.E. (CSE) from MBM Engineering College at Jodhpur in 2001, and M. Tech. (CSE) from the M.S. Ramaiah Institute of Technology at Bangalore in 2008. He received his PhD in Information Technology and Engineering from the VIT University Vellore in 2017. From 2006 to 2010 he worked at M.S. Ramaiah Institute of Technology in Bangalore, eventually as a Lecturer. His research interests span both computer vision and image processing. Much of his work has been on images, mainly through the application of image processing, computer vision, pattern recognition, machine learning, biometric systems, deep learning, soft computing, and computational intelligence. He has given few invited talks on medical image processing. Professor Chowdhary is editor/co-editor of 3 books and is the author of over forty articles on computer science. He filed two patents deriving from his research. Google Scholar Link: https://scholar.google.com/citations?user=PpJt13oAAAAJ&hl=en.

Kesavaraja D. has completed his B.E (CSE) from Jayaraj Annapackiam CSI College of Engineering, Nazareth under Anna University Chennai in 2005, M.E (CSE) from Manonmaniam Sundaranar University, Tirunelveli in 2010 and Ph.D (I&CE) from Anna University, Chennai in April 2019. He is a co-author of a book titled "Fundamentals of Computing and Programming" and "Fundamentals of LaTeX Programming". He is currently working as an Assistant Professor, Department of CSE, Dr.Sivanthi Aditanar College of Engineering, Tiruchendur. He has 14 years and 1 month of Teaching Experience. He received SAP Award of Excellence from IIT Bombay and Outstanding Reviewer Award from Elsevier. He has published many National and International Journal and conference papers. He has served as a reviewer for scientific journals such as Springer, Elsevier, IET, T&F and Technical Programme Committee Member for International Conferences. He has guided a student R&D Project Sponsored by IE (I), Kolkatta and TNSCST. His research interests include Cloud Computing, Internet of Things and Blockchain. More information at www.k7cloud.in.

Sasireka D. has completed her B.E degree in the department of IT from Dr.Sivanthi Aditanar College of Engineering, Tiruchendur, India, under Anna University Chennai in 2008. She has completed her M.Tech degree in the department of computer science and Engineering from Manonmaniam Sundaranar University, Tirunelveli, in 2011. She is currently doing her doctorate from VV College of Engineering, Tisaiyanvilai, India. Her research interests include Image processing, Network security.

Harshita Dahiya is a 2020 B.Tech graduate in Computer Engineering from NIT Kurukshetra.

Pawan Kumar Dahiya received his B.E. (Electronics and Communication Engg.) degree (Hons.) from VCE, Rohtak, Haryana-India (affiliated to M.D. Univ., Rohtak) in 1999. He has received his Ph.D. degree in Electronics and Communication Engg. from M.D. University, Rohtak (India). He served as a Development Engineer in the Research and Development Dept. of Belgian American Radio Corporation (BARCO). He has worked as a lecturer ECE. Dept. in Hindu College of Engg., Sonipat and currently working as Associate Professor in ECE Dept. in Deenbandhu Chhotu Ram University of Science & Technology, Murthal, Sonipat, (India). He was Coordinator of TEQIP Cell of the University which has been selected for a grant of 12.5 crores from world-bank for Scaling-up Postgraduate Education & Demand-Driven Research & Development and Innovation. He is Coordinator of the Centre for Research, Innovation & Development (CRID) in the University. He is Coordinator of Research & Development Unit under CRID. He has published more than 30 research papers in journals & Proc. of National & International conferences. He is a life member of ISTE and Secy. of ISTE Chapter in the University which has won the Best Chapter Award in 2004. His interests include Evolutionary Computation applications to Digital System Design, Embedded System Design, Digital VLSI and ALPR System.

Shelza Dua is currently working as an Assistant Professor in the Department of Electronics and Communication Engineering in National Institute of Technology,Kurukshetra. She is having 10 year of teaching and research experience with research contribution in the area of image encryption, pattern recognition and image encryption.

Jeyabharathi Duraipandy has completed her B.E degree in the department of computer science and Engineering from Jayaraj Annapackiam CSI College of Engineering, Nazareth, India, under Anna University Chennai in 2009. She has completed her M.E degree in the department of computer science and Engineering from Manonmaniam Sundaranar University, Tirunelveli, in 2013. She is completed her doctorate from Anna Regional Campus – Tirunelveli, Tirunelveli in 2018, in the field of video processing. She is currently working as an Assistant Professor in department of Information Technology, Sri Krishna College of Technology, Coimbatore. Her research interests include Image processing, Network security.

Aakriti Gupta is a 2020 B.Tech graduate in Computer Engineering from NIT Kurukshetra.

Maanak Gupta is an Assistant Professor in Computer Science at Tennessee Technological University, Cookeville, USA. He received M.S. and Ph.D. in Computer Science from the University of Texas at San Antonio (UTSA) and has also worked as a postdoctoral fellow at the Institute for Cyber Security (ICS) at UTSA. His primary area of research includes security and privacy in cyber space focused in studying foundational aspects of access control and their application in technologies including cyber physical systems, cloud computing, IoT and Big Data. He has worked in developing novel security mechanisms, models and architectures for next generation smart cars, smart cities, intelligent transportation systems and smart farming. He is also interested in machine learning based malware analysis and AI assisted cyber security solutions. His research has been funded by the US National Science Foundation (NSF), NASA, US Department of Defense (DoD) and private industry. He holds a B.Tech degree in Computer Science and Engineering, India and an M.S. in Information Systems from Northeastern University, Boston, USA.

Pallavi Khatri is an Associate Professor, ITM University, Gwalior, India.

B. R. Marwah received his Bachelor degree in (B.Tech.) from Punjab Engineering College, Chandigarh, India, M. Tech. from University of Roorkee, Roorkee, Uttar Pradesh, India and Ph.D. Degree from IIT, Kanpur. He has a vast experience of 36 years in teaching at the Civil Engineering Department, IIT Kanpur, Uttar Pradesh, India. His research interests include Transportation System Engineering, Computer Simulation, etc.

Nishtha Nandwani is a Computer Engineer, graduated from NIT Kurukshetra in 2020.

Rithesh Pakkala P. is currently working as an Assistant Professor in the Department of Information Science & Engineering at Sahyadri College of Engineering & Management, Mangaluru. Mr. Pakkala currently pursuing his Ph.D. under Visvesvaraya Technological University, Belagavi, Karnataka, India in the area of data analytics and theory of computation. His area of interest includes Data Analytics, Machine Learning, and Theory of Computation.

Prakhyath Rai is currently working as an Assistant Professor in the Department of Information Science & Engineering at Sahyadri College of Engineering & Management, Mangaluru. Mr. Prakhyath Rai currently pursuing his Ph.D. under Visvesvaraya Technological University, Belagavi, Karnataka, India in the area of Text Mining. His research interest includes Knowledge Distillation, Data Analytics, Text De-Noising, Pattern Recognition, Machine Learning and Text Refinement.

Himanshu Sahu is currently working as an Assistant Professor (S.S) in Department of Cybernetics, School of Computer Science, University of Petroleum and Energy Studies, Dehradun. He has completed his B. Tech degree in computer science and engineering from J.K. Institute of Applied Physics and Technology from University of Allahabad. He has Completed his master's degree from Motilal Nehru National Institute of Technology in Computer Science with specialization in Information Security. His research areas are Machine Learning, Computer Vision, Computer Network and Cloud Computing. His publication includes book chapters, conference and journals from publisher like Springer and IGI global. He has completed training from various industry giants like Cisco, Xebia and IBM.

Aman Sharma is a research scholar who has completed his M.Tech from Gujarat Forensic Sciences University, Gandhinagar. His research interests include information security and mobile forensics. His paper have published in International Conference on Communication, Networks & Computing (CNC), Suscom and Indiacom.

Nitin Sharma received his B.E. (Electronics and Communication Engg.) degree (Hons.) from VCE, Rohtak, Haryana-India (affiliated to M.D. Univ., Rohtak) in 2001 and M.Tech. (Electronics and Communication Engineering) from GNDEC, Ludhiana, Punjab-India (affiliated to Punjab Technical University, Jalandhar, Punjab) in 2008. He is pursuing Ph.D. in Electronics and Communication Engineering from Deenbandhu Chhotu Ram University of Science and Technology, Murthal, Haryana-India. He is with the Electronics and Communication Department at Chandigarh University, Chandigarh-India. His research interests include Intelligent Transportation System, Image Processing, etc.

Amit Prakash Singh is working as Professor in University School of Information Communication & Technology, GGSIPU. He obtained Ph.D. in Information Technology from Guru Gobind Singh Indraprastha University, Delhi in 2011. He has worked in the area of Artificial Neural Networks. He has earlier worked as Lecturer in University of Hyderabad and Banasthali Vidyapith. His area of interest are Artificial Neural Network, Embedded System Design and Digital System Design. He is a member of IEEE, IETE & CSI. He has published more than 30 Research papers in International / National Journals and attended various National / International Workshops and Seminar. Dr. Singh visited UK, Portugal, Singapore and Thailand to present his research work in international conferences.

Index

A

B

C

D

E

T

V

W

Printed in the United States
by Baker & Taylor Publisher Services